THE
AMERICAN HOUR

*A Time of Reckoning
and the Once and Future
Role of Faith*

OS GUINNESS

THE FREE PRESS
A Division of Macmillan, Inc.
NEW YORK
Maxwell Macmillan Canada
TORONTO
Maxwell Macmillan International
NEW YORK OXFORD SINGAPORE SYDNEY

The Free Press
A Division of Macmillan, Inc.
866 Third Avenue, New York, N. Y. 10022

Maxwell Macmillan Canada, Inc.
1200 Eglinton Avenue East
Suite 200
Don Mills, Ontario M3C 3N1

Macmillan, Inc. is part of the Maxwell Communication Group of Companies.

First Free Press Paperback Edition 1994

Printed in the United States of America

printing number

1 2 3 4 5 6 7 8 9 10

Library of Congress Cataloging-in-Publication Data

Guinness, Os.
   The American hour : a time of reckoning and the once and future
role of faith / Os Guinness.
      p.   cm.
   Includes bibliographical references and index.
   ISBN 0–02–913173–1
      1. United States—Civilization—1970–   2. United States—Moral
conditions.   3. United States—Church history—20th century.
4. National characteristics, American.   I. Title.
E169.12.G845   1993
973.92—dc20   92–2406
                                                                 CIP

D.O.M
and to
CHRISTOPHER
with love, pride, and hope.

Contents

Part Three

THE COMING AMERICA

The Tourneying Hopes   281

A Crisis of the
Mandate of Heaven

There are times when history and human decisions appear to meet at a single point to cast the die of a nation's fortunes—for Rome, Caesar's crossing the Rubicon; for England, Sir Francis Drake's defeat of the Spanish Armanda; for the United States, the first shots fired at Lexington and Concord.

There are other times when the fateful hinge is a period and not a day, when the accumulated consequences of an era stamp history as sharply as any date or event. So it was with the Civil War era; thus it was also with the Depression years.

There are still other times when the sudden impact of events in one nation reveals like nothing else the consequences of a period-long buildup of forces in another. So it was with the Eastern European revolution of 1989–90 and the light it cast on the condition of America toward the close of the American Century.

The astonishing year of 1989 has been called the year of the century. Glowing comparisons were made to 1648, when the Peace of Westphalia ended the Thirty Years' War, and to 1815, when the second Treaty of Paris brought a century of relative peace after the Napoleonic wars. At the very least, 1989 joined 1917 and 1945 to form the three great pivotal years in the twentieth century and the three tidal turns of American involvement in the world. History could be heard. The pace of time quickened. Everyone living felt more alive than before. Suddenly and beyond all predictions, the democratic revolution in Central and Eastern Europe broke out in a firestorm arc of freedom. When it was over, Soviet totalitarianism lay beyond repair, Marxism was thoroughly discredited in Europe and beyond, the Berlin Wall had fallen, and democracy had replaced socialism as the revolutionary hope

1

of millions around the world. Never before had a world empire shed its colonies so completely and quickly—all in a single season.

The Communist czars—like Louis XIV, Napoleon Bonaparte, Kaiser Wilhelm, and Chancellor Adolf Hitler before them—had failed in their bid to dominate Europe and then the world. The twentieth century's first great totalitarian regime was going the way of the second, Nazism, and of the older premodern political orders before them. Exactly two hundred years after the French Revolution started, the Russian Revolution had shown itself spent, and violent revolution itself had become the ancien régime. Modernity and its standard bearer, democratic capitalism, had triumphed again.

It is true that in the first moments of Soviet crisis and American triumph there was a puzzling hollowness in the winner's camp. Everything had gone America's way, but the epicenter of change was found not in Washington but Moscow. Despite his far weaker hand, it was the Soviet leader who set the pace and sought to dictate the terms and interpret the events. American leaders appeared to be "waiting for Gorbachev." They seemed content to be bystanders to history rather than its agents this time. Western business pressed home the capitalist triumph by raising the Golden Arches in the heart of Moscow's Red Square. But the nation that had once acted so forcefully in the postwar reconstruction of Western Europe, and more recently in the miniwars of Grenada and Panama, seemed cautious to a fault in the face of its greatest opportunity for a generation. When it came to American imagination and initiatives in relation to the new world emerging, neither American will nor wallet were much in evidence at first. "Yes, you are the Superpower," London's *Economist* reminded Americans early in 1990.[1]

Twelve short months later, the picture seemed to be transformed. What the end of the Cold War whispered, the victory of the Persian Gulf War shouted. American leaders and commentators now proclaimed a dominance in world affairs stronger than at any time since the end of World War II. Operation Desert Storm had been a swift and stunning success: Kuwait was free; Iraq was pulverized; the former superpower rival—the Soviet Union— was sidelined; war critics and faint hearts were routed; the generation-old ghosts of military debacle and technological incompetence were exorcised; the American president was riding high with record polling popularity; and for the first time since Vietnam, American leaders talked openly about a New World Order and a Second American Century.

Iraqi president Saddam Hussein's "mother of all battles" had turned out to be America's second "splendid little war." Whereas Germany and Japan could compete with the United States when the yardstick was economic, the addition of raw military power and international determination left America unrivaled. Despite the tragic and messy aftermath, and the smugness of the therapeutic comfort ("the war that made us feel good about ourselves"), the American victory in the gulf bespoke undeniable accomplishments. What Secretary of State James Baker heralded at the outset as a defining moment was widely hailed at the end as a transforming moment.

The American caesar advanced at the head of his twenty-seven-nation alliance and with the might of his aerial legions. He drew a line in the desert sand and stayed to teach the first lesson about his vision of the New World Order. "No one—no one in the whole world," President Bush boasted, "doubts us anymore."[2] Following its failure in 1917 and mixed success in 1945, the United States was embarking on a third attempt to build a global order founded on international law, collective security, and American democratic ideals.

Thus the lights dimmed and the fanfare sounded for imperial America's third grand endeavor in history-shaping on the order of the *pax romana* and *pax britannica*. America's New World Order was to be unveiled, variously understood as her *pax moderna, pax kapital, pax democritica, pax occidentalis,* or simply the *pax americana: phase three.* All that was missing in America's triumphal procession, one observer noted, was the Roman slave whispering in the ear of the victorious commander in chief, "This too shall pass away."

This book is that whisper in the ear. It argues that triumphalism is the wrong lesson to be learned from 1989, that this is not, as at least one author has recently asserted, "the end of history," that there is an obstacle blocking the prospects of an American renaissance, and that even the international opportunities after 1991 cannot be seized unless a deeper challenge is faced at home first. But the challenge does not come from the slate of problems commonly cited—supremely America's degenerating inner cities, mounting social problems, ballooning deficit, sluggish economy, and lackluster leadership. It lies far deeper. America's political order, in the form of representative democracy, and America's economic order, in the form of free market capitalism, were given a historic vindication through the second Russian revolution. But there are three—not two—parts to the ordering of the American republic. Transformations and corruptions in America's third order—the moral and cultural order—are casting a shadow over her triumphs in the political and economic orders.

At the present time of writing, with everything to be done and too much of it at once, the outcome of the European revolution and the development of the New World Order have yet to unfold. Time alone will show, for example, whether a post-Communist generation can emulate a post-Fascist generation in building free, prosperous, and pluralistic societies in accord with the promise of liberal democracy. Or whether 1989 will emulate 1848 in seeing its intoxicating promises betrayed and the dead hand of authoritarianism reasserted. But if 1989 marks the start of a momentous new chapter in what was once the Old World but is now the new, it also throws light on a critical state of affairs within the nation that was always modernity's "first new nation" and the epitome of liberal democracy—the United States.

A Single, Common Crisis

The reason for this sober examination is that, despite its historic political and economic triumphs, the American republic is entering its own time of reckoning, an hour of truth that will not be delayed. It is nearing the climax of a generation-long cultural revolution, or crisis of cultural authority. Under the impact of modernity, the beliefs, ideals, and traditions that have been central to Americans and to American democracy—whether religious, such as Jewish and Christian beliefs, or civic, such as Americanism—are losing their compelling cultural power. This crisis is not a crisis of legitimacy, like that of the Soviet Union, but a crisis of vitality that goes to the heart of America's character and strength. It therefore threatens to pose questions not only for America's continuing success and world domination, but for the vitality of democracy in America itself.

Seen from one angle, America's crisis of cultural authority is thoroughly and distinctively American. The roots go back to the late nineteenth century and to movements early in this century. But the first open phase of the crisis began to build up in the fifties until it broke out in the cultural revolution of the sixties, which came to a climax and peaked in 1968. Then, after a period of transition, the second phase was centered on the conservative counterrevolution, which came to a climax and peaked in 1986.

Both movements were highly influential in ways their critics prefer to overlook, although neither was as successful as claimed by its advocates. But the appearance of a revenge of the moderates or of a simple return to normalcy in the Bush years is deceptive. Set in train by the crisis, cultural change in America has gone too far, and political change can do too little to resolve the problems. The United States is now entering the third phase of the crisis with the beginning of a sort of cultural showdown. At stake are the authorities and moral assumptions that will prove decisive in shaping the public and private lives of Americans, and thus in determining how America tackles its lengthening list of serious problems.

Seen from another angle, America's crisis of cultural authority is America's variation of a wider crisis. As such it is part of what Czechoslovakia's former president Václav Havel calls the "single, common crisis" facing humanity in both West and East.[3] This wider crisis has been created by the collision between the impersonal and irresponsible forces of modernity and the respective notions of humanness, morality, and the environment in different countries and cultures.

In Peter Berger's illuminating picture, the present world situation is like a global laboratory with three giant test tubes in the foreground and others behind. Each of the main three represents intense chemical reactions caused by the impact of modernization on different cultural and political systems. The first test tube demonstrates the reaction of liberal democracy, or Western industrialism, to modernity. This socio-political system has engaged with modernity the longest. It has done so from a generally Christian and Jewish vantage point, and its ideals are deeply committed to going with the flow of modernity in terms of such principles and processes as individualism, political pluralism, freedom, and so on.

The second test tube demonstrates the reaction of totalitarian socialism to modernity. This system began to engage with modernity more than a century later than liberal democracy did, doing so from a Marxist rather than a Christian viewpoint. And importantly, it is ambivalent toward modernity rather than fully committed to it. For while Marxism is partly modernizing, in the sense that it claims to be a scientific theory and is directly opposed to traditional society, it is also countermodernizing. In essence, its totalitarianism is the attempt to reconstitute the monolithic unity of traditional society in a modern form, with the help of modern technology, modern ideology, and so on. So Marxism has found itself going against the flow of modernity in crucial ways.

The third test tube demonstrates the reaction of East Asian industrialism to modernity—Japan and the so-called "four little dragons": Korea, Singapore, Taiwan, and Hong Kong. These systems have engaged with modernity most recently. They come from a largely Buddhist and Confucian standpoint, rather than a Christian or Marxist one. Yet, like the Western experiment, they are deeply committed to modernity.[4]

Obviously the impact of modernity on different societies is mediated by certain variable factors, such as the stage of modernity (early or late), the character of the society's beliefs (whether Christian, Confucian, or Islamic, for example), and the society's general attitude toward modernity (whether favorable or hostile). Seen this way, 1989 represents a critical stage in the global reactions to modernity. Put simply, modernity helped to undo totalitarian socialism. When the challenge came down to a choice between such Marxist commitments as equality and such allurements of modernity as efficiency and prosperity, Central and Eastern Europeans chose modernity over Marxist ideology. Thus what happened in Central and Eastern Europe was not simply a triumph of faith and democratic ideals, or of the steadfastness of Westerners manning the ramparts of freedom over the last generation. It was also partly due to the irresistible impact of modernization on totalitarian socialism.

America's crisis is, of course, quite different from the predicament facing the former Soviet Union. I am not resurrecting the fallacy of moral equivalence. Both the American and the Soviet crises are taking place in the same phase of modernity, but there the similarities end. Because the American experiment as a liberal democracy goes with the flow of modernity, the challenge of modernity is never central or lethal; and because American liberal democracy has both a strength of ideas and a flexibility of institutions, it has far greater resilience in responding to such challenges. This is why, to America, the challenges of modernity are not challenges to its legitimacy, as with the USSR, but challenges to its vitality. So when the United States experiences a crisis of cultural authority, what is at stake is America's vitality as a free republic that would remain free and strong.

But whether viewed from an American or a more global perspective, the significance of the crisis is plain. One of history's fundamental lessons for democracy concerns the difference between winning freedom (as in the revolutions of 1776, 1789, and 1989), ordering freedom (as in the constitutions in 1787 and 1791), and sustaining freedom. The first is typically achieved in days, weeks, or months, and the second—which is Russia's level of testing today—in years or decades. But the third—which is America's present level of testing—is always a matter of many decades and long centuries. The Constitution, Benjamin Franklin said, offers Americans "a republic—if you can keep it."

Thus the outcome of the present crisis of cultural authority represents more than a swing, a cycle, or even an end-of-the-century battle between the sixties and the eighties. It is far more of a defining moment than the Gulf War. It could prove as decisive for the nation as the Depression years— depending on the outcome—and even as decisive as the era of the Civil War. The present moment is therefore the American Century's American Hour. It is an authentic *kairos* moment, one of those great times of reckoning in which Americans judge themselves and for which America will always be judged. This book is about that crisis of cultural authority, about what has led up to it and what is likely to affect the outcome. It is a book about the United States at a pivotal moment in the late twentieth century, but to broaden the perspective it begins half a world away when the century was only a few months young.

Jeremiad in Bronze

As I write, a small, round bronze medallion a little over two inches in diameter sits on the desk in front of me. It was struck to commemorate the eight-nation International Relief Force, which in August 1900 fought its way to rescue the beleaguered "foreign devils" who were under desperate siege during the infamous fifty-five days at Beijing. This was the twentieth century's first forerunner of the Kuwaiti crisis and first harbinger of crises of cultural authority.

On May 24 of that year, the British Legation in Beijing celebrated Queen Victoria's eighty-first and last birthday in an atmosphere of general calm and serenity. But within less than a month the rebellion of the Boxers, or the "Society of the Righteous Fists," engulfed the capital and a spasm of bloody violence convulsed China. By the time it was over, two hundred and fifty missionaries and more than thirty-two thousand "secondary devils" (Chinese Christians) were slaughtered. Westerners were hacked to death, children were beheaded in front of their parents' eyes, and carts were driven backward and forward over the half-naked bodies of young Chinese women evangelists until they were dead. The century that would multiply such crises and compute the victims of its violence in the millions was off to a running start.

In 1900 the retaliation of the Western powers was even worse than the rampage of the Boxers. After entering Beijing and rescuing the legations, some of the foreign troops set off on an orgy of systematic slaughter and looting. Beijing was sacked, the imperial palace looted and stripped, and thousands of innocent Chinese were massacred in a cruel and bloody rampage. If xenophobia was intensified in China, popular stereotypes about the "yellow peril" were hardened and confirmed across Europe and the United States.

The little medallion conjures up all this and more for me. Made vividly contemporary by the brutal massacre in Tiananmen Square in June 1989 and the similarities and contrasts to the siege of Kuwait in 1991, it is a mute but eloquent witness of inglorious deeds done in a faraway place when our century was only a few months old.

But the little medallion also holds a deeper fascination for me. I myself was born in China later, but my grandfather was there during the Boxer uprising. For thirty days he survived the massacre hair-raisingly by the grace of God and the skin of his teeth. At the time there were foreigners in China, and foreigners—my grandfather, a doctor, was one who loved and served the Chinese and was loved and esteemed by the Chinese in return. Having given his life for those he sought to help in a later outbreak of typhus, he lies buried in Beijing.

Beyond these family associations, the little medallion is eloquent in another way. It shows the mirror-image of itself that the West saw—and still sees—in such crises. On one side it depicts *Chien Men*, the great central gate of Beijing that was opened only to allow the passage of the emperor. This priceless part of Chinese heritage was destroyed in a few hours by the Boxers who set it on fire deliberately. To many Chinese, this catastrophe was a heavenly portent presaging the downfall of the Manchu dynasty.

The smoke and fire belching from the roof of the gate on the medallion is therefore more than a matter of artistic realism. It represents what the West saw as history's verdict on the fate of the premodern Chinese Empire. On the other side of the medallion, the artist reinforced the crisis of legitimacy using Western and Chinese symbols. He circled it with the Hebrew word *Ichabod* ("the glory has departed") and the Chaldean writing on the wall that interrupted Belshazzar's feast, "*Mene mene tekel upharsin*" ("you are weighed in the balances and found wanting").

The little medallion is therefore one of the first examples of the twentieth-century passion for sending "messages" and "signals." It is a trilingual jeremiad in bronze, the Western counterpoint to the spreading Chinese conviction that the Manchu dynasty had forfeited the Mandate of Heaven. Under the impact of its first encounter with modernity, Imperial China, like Imperial Russia a few years later, was in the terminal stages of a massive crisis of cultural authority.

Needless to say, the Chinese saw the crisis in their own traditional terms rather than in the context of modernity. To the heirs of the world's oldest civilization, China had always been the Middle Kingdom, the realm between heaven and earth, and the emperor was the Son of Heaven who had authority under the Mandate of Heaven. But this mandate was not irrevocable. It could be forfeited by corruption, so when "signs preceding the fall of dynasties" became apparent, revolt was considered both legitimate and beneficial. Such a fate, it was believed, was about to befall the Manchus under the cruel and eccentric Empress Dowager. The Dragon Throne that ruled a civilization that predated the golden ages of Athens and Rome had lost the Mandate of Heaven and was in irreversible decline.

For Westerners, however, the Chinese crisis was part of the wider impact of modernity—though to see the writing on the wall for the Manchus took little foresight and to say it in such grandiloquent terms took considerable hypocrisy. The Imperial Throne had only lasted so long because of the backing of the foreign powers and much of the record of their involvement was one of invasion, partition, exploitation, greed, and violence. In short, it was a story of Chinese humiliation and degradation. The fiber of old China, it was said, was dissolving into the sweet smoke of opium pipes crammed into Chinese mouths by greedy Western traders.

Exactly as with the Western response to the Soviet and Gulf crises, the first and strongest Western response to the China crisis in 1900 was to emphasize the contrast between East and West and more particularly the contrast between China and the United States. Plainly, the West saw itself as the incarnation of modernity, on the winner's side of history. But for any who paused to reflect, there were more than contrasts to be read. There were definite resemblances between China's crisis and Europe's own crisis of the mandate of heaven (which Friedrich Nietzsche called "the death of God" crisis), whether issuing later in a crisis of legitimacy as in Imperial Russia or a crisis of vitality as in Imperial Britain. But those resemblances were still concealed from most. And surely—for all but the most farsighted at the time—they would never apply to America. The United States was modernity's Most Favored Nation before she, in turn, conferred that benefit on others.

No two nations in 1900 could have seemed further apart in regard to national fortunes than China and the United States. Younger, richer, and with cleaner hands than its European partners, the United States stood at the opposite pole from China on almost every count. The world's "first new nation" stood over against the world's oldest, continuous civilization—a dynamic, moral, and idealistic society against one that was ancient, corrupt, and moribund; a rich and technologically advanced country against one that was poor and backward.

Small wonder that in 1900, as in 1991, such contrasts were the dominant impression. To a young American growing up in China at that time, both the old civilization and the new century seemed to herald the claim that American distinctiveness meant American destiny. Significantly, this period was exactly the background of Henry Luce, son of missionary parents, legendary cofounder of the Time-Life empire, and originator of the term, the "American Century."

The American Century—Where Are We Now?

Henry Luce announced the American Century in his celebrated editorial in *Life* in February 1941, the year that was the low point of the entire twentieth century. He followed it up a year later by setting up a department of Time, Inc., called "Q" (after the Q ships of World War I). His goal was to formulate proposals on the shape of the postwar world that the United States was to lead. "As America enters dynamically upon the world scene," he wrote, "we need most of all to seek and to bring forth a vision of America as a world power which is authentically American." Only such a vision that apprehends the meaning of our time "will guide us to the authentic creation of the twentieth century—our Century."[5]

Luce did not consider the editorial anything out of the ordinary. It echoed a speech he had given as a student at Yale in 1920; its proposals were remarkably close in outline to later Cold War strategy and Luce's championing of NATO and the Marshall Plan; and there was far less triumphalism in it than many realize today. ("So far, this century of ours has been a profound and tragic disappointment.")[6] But Luce was surprised and disappointed by the response to the editorial. Conservatives, who might have backed his aggressive drive, were in an isolationist mood, fearing a "Roosevelt war," and most liberals attacked his formulation. Some critics, such as Reinhold Niebuhr, chided Luce gently for his egoistic nationalism. Others derided him mercilessly. Luce's American Century, they said, was capitalist and militarist, more concerned with good profits than good neighbors. Vice-President Henry Wallace countered it with a speech on "The Century of the Common Man" and Max Lerner with an essay on "The People's Century."

But remove some of the more controversial personal factors and ideological overtones and the idea of the American Century remains invaluable in at least two ways. At one level, it accurately reflects the fact that for the greater part of this century the United States—for better or worse—has been, and still is, what sociologist Talcott Parsons called the world's "lead society." Just as the nineteenth century was the British Century, Luce thought, so the twentieth is the American Century, because the United States is the radiating center from which modernity and development has spread. Neither delight nor disapproval could alter this fact.

At another level, the term is an appropriate representation of one of the oldest and strongest American themes—that American distinctiveness means American destiny. ("Character is destiny," as Henry Luce said.) This theme, even if rejected as mythical, has been real in its consequences for the world. From the very earliest days, the sense of American newness and representativeness, of the inseparable closeness of American identity and purpose, has been a key part of perceptions of America, and not only by Americans. "I confess," wrote Alexis de Tocqueville after his travels in the early 1830s, "that in America I saw more than America; I sought there the image of democracy itself."[7] Whether it was the American people as St. Jean de Crèvecoeur's "new man," American history as Thomas Jefferson's "new chapter" in the history of man, the Founders' "new order of the ages," the United States as Abraham Lincoln's "new nation," or simply as the New World itself, America has always stood for something.

To Walt Whitman, America and democracy were "convertible terms."[8] To Frederick Jackson Turner, America was "another name for opportunity."[9] In many such ways, to its own citizens and to a great many others in the world, America has been as much a promise, an ideal, a future, and a myth as a reality. Whatever the other overtones, that core reality and that mythic sense of representativeness were both at the heart of the American Century. The United States was not simply in the lead. It was the carrier of the quintessence of the times. The city set upon a hill had become the world beacon of democratic freedom, history's working model of modernity, humankind's trailblazer for economic, scientific, and technological progress. Riding the tides and currents of the twentieth century, America was Hegel's "Idea" whose time had come across the Atlantic. Manifest destiny was China's Mandate of Heaven with an American aura.

There is no doubt that, viewed in this restricted sense, the American Century was born (and its first phase launched under Woodrow Wilson) in the twentieth century's first great pivotal year, 1917. This was the great climactic year of blood, which in Europe proved so fateful to the exhausted empires of the Romanoffs, the Habsburgs, and the Hohenzollerns. In Eastern and Central Europe long-stifled masses had torn down the decaying edifices of the old regimes. Even the Western European nations that survived the shocks and the strains had been given a decisive push away from their aristocratic pasts toward a more fully democratic future. Further afield 1917 saw Jerusalem liberated by General Allenby and Palestine declared a homeland for the Jews. European history in the old sense had come to an end. World history had begun. If only briefly, the United States had taken its place at the center of events.

Nor is there much doubt when phase two of the American Century reached its zenith. In August 1945, the century's second great pivotal year, four and a half years after Luce's editorial and a week after President Truman ordered the dropping of the second atomic bomb, Winston Churchill told the House of Commons, "America stands at this moment at the summit of the world."[10] Rarely had Churchillian rhetoric been grounded on more prosaic truth. Moral vigor, national enterprise, economic power, scientific and technological prowess—all the strengths and qualities of American life seemed to come together in the hour of victory to create a dazzling prospect for the American spirit. Even though many may have disapproved of the consequences implied in Churchill's assessment, few would have quarreled with the facts on which it was based. The United States under President

Roosevelt had come center stage again and, judging from the unfolding design of the *pax americana,* showed every intention of staying there this time.

But where is the American Century now? If the dramatic events of 1989 and the century's third great pivotal year are taken as a benchmark, what stage in its course has it reached and what does that mean for Americans and for the rest of the world? Does the United States have the resolve and the resources to carry forward phase three of the American Century and make it succeed where the earlier phases failed? What if modernity allows no lead society to lead forever, and America's crisis is hastened by its blindness toward the nature of its problem?

Sunset, New Dawn, or What?

In today's vastly different circumstances it is worth remembering how remarkably few in 1945 disapproved of the United States. After the Allied liberation of Algiers in 1943, André Gide, previously a supporter of the Soviets, gave free rein to his enthusiasm: "The Americans, in our old world, are liked by everyone and everywhere. So quick with their generosity, so friendly and smiling, so natural, that one joyfully accepts being in debt to them."[11] It was easy for Truman and Eisenhower to please Europeans, wrote the Italian journalist Luigi Barzini. "In their days America was the mother hen of the Western world, the most prosperous, powerful, generous, and courageous country of all."[12]

Four decades, several wars, a spiraling national debt, and countless stockpiled warheads later, hardly a phrase of Gide's enthusiasm would find such resonance in certain parts of the world today. Even before the renaissance of 1989, the prospects of a reunified Germany, and a greatly expanded democratic electorate and market, America's European allies were stronger, more independent, and preoccupied with "1992" and their own future. Japan, with the Tokyo Stock Exchange now worth almost double that of New York, has become the world's financial, as well as a manufacturing, superpower. Third World nations have awakened and have reacted strongly to American influence. More to the point, a growing chorus of world leaders are openly touting alternative values such as Confucian capitalism as superior to American-style democratic capitalism. And in the rise of Islamic fundamentalism the United States faces an anti-Western ideology as explosive and hungry as communism elsewhere and fascism earlier. The newly emerging multipolar world is no longer America's oyster.

Perhaps America's postwar superiority was artificially high. Perhaps the manner of its unconditional victory over Germany and Japan put the United States in an impossible situation. Certainly the way in which Americans sought to comprehend and cope with their unmanageable destiny makes an epic of proud and courageous, if flawed, heroism. But the *pax americana* was said to be on the wane, and a parliamentary successor of Churchill's described America even before the end of Ronald Reagan's first term in very different terms: "Huge and powerful still, but purposeless and ineffectual, the United States lies wallowing, like some dismasted man-of-war, in the trough of world events."[13]

"The American Century," Daniel Bell wrote from Harvard in the same vein, "lasted scarcely thirty years. It foundered on the shoals of Vietnam."[14] Luce's "first great American Century" was perhaps also the last. "In just twenty-five years," wrote social critic Felix Rohatyn, "we have gone from the American century to the American crisis. That is an astonishing turnaround —perhaps the shortest parabola in history."[15]

Such pessimistic estimates appear to be backed by a swelling chorus of voices around the world—from scholars and "declinist" commentators, such as Paul Kennedy of Yale, national leaders, such as Prime Minister Lee Kuan Yew of Singapore, and nations, such as Japan. Tracing either America's social decadence or the trajectory of its collapsing almightiness from Vietnam to ballooning deficits, their conclusions are similar. "American dominance cannot be restored," says Lee, "There has been a fundamental change in competitive positions, a permanent change . . . I do not see the Americans regaining the old lead from the Japanese or the West Europeans."[16] "Nowadays," wrote a Japanese editor in the late eighties, "America is compared to a sick and ill-humored uncle who is suffering from financial and family problems, paying no attention to chastity or discipline."[17]

Yet in other parts of the world, and most notably in the United States itself, the assessment would be exactly the opposite. "It is springtime for America once again," declared a jaunty President Reagan at the end of his first term.[18] His own presidency, he claimed, was a new beginning for America. "Somehow America has never been newer, never been younger, never been more filled with hope. . . . There is nothing the United States cannot do if those doubting Thomases would just stand aside and get out of the way."[19]

There was no stopping the flights of presidential rhetoric. The United States, Reagan said in Tom Paine's words, once more had in its power "to begin the world over again." Expanding on the theme later to the U.S. Chamber of Commerce, he declared the period we are going through to be "the vernal equinox of the human spirit—that moment in history when the light finally exceeded the darkness."[20] Or as he put it in his farewell address, "Once you begin a great movement, there's no telling where it will end. We meant to change a nation, and instead, we changed a world."[21]

Time magazine, true to its Lucean calling as America's chronicler-cum-cheerleader, hailed Reagan in 1986 as "a Prospero of American memories" and the New Patriotism as a "rebirth of the American spirit."[22] Just as the end of the war in 1812 led to the contented patriotism of the Era of Good Feelings, so the mid-1980s found America recovering from a mood of dispirited and defensive malaise and entering a buoyant time of pride and patriotism. Newsweek, in the same tenor, had elevated Reagan to the pantheon of "presidents who have succeeded in their time," principally because of his great skill as "a morale builder and a renewer of the faith."[23] Not to be outdone, the editor of U.S. News and World Report gave his judgment that "at the opening of 1989, America may be entering the most promising moment of its history."[24]

Unquestionably the highest panegyric to this resurgent patriotism was Francis Fukuyama's provocative essay, "The End of History?" that was later expanded into The End of History and the Last Man. Posited against Paul Kennedy's weighty "declinist" analysis, it was a short, sharp bugle blast of "endism." Far more than Mikhail Gorbachev's opportunistic reforms were behind the events of 1989, he claimed. Far more than hard-nosed realpolitik was needed to understand them. "What we may be witnessing is not just the end of the Cold War, or the passing of a particular period of postwar history, but the end of history as such: that is, the end point of mankind's ideological evolution and the universalization of Western liberal democracy as the final form of human government."[25]

Fukuyama's argument was the intellectuals' equivalent of presidential claims. But though bold and brilliant, it too was flawed. It overlooks a double problem for Western liberal democracy—the way in which its very success becomes self-undermining and in which many world leaders—particularly in Asia—are developing capitalism but within a Confucian and sometimes neoauthoritarian framework. Thus they openly spurn democratic values and human rights as Western, abstract, self-serving, and decadent. In short, to proclaim the end of history on the slender evidence of recent events and by overlooking the internal contradictions within liberal democracy itself is a logical and historical fallacy of the first order. It is also a dangerous national conceit that America can ill afford if it turns Americans away from facing their real problems.

On the plane of current events alone, however, the evidence has appeared to see-saw and not everyone was so sure that the New Patriotism was solid. For many, signs of conservative mortality appeared even during the

Reagan years: for conservatives in the eighties 1986 had become a curious rerun of 1968 for liberals in the sixties; in each year the respective movements claimed victory, only to see its high point prove a turning point, after which the tide turned and flowed relentlessly against them.

The well-ordered images in red-white-and-blue of 1986—the Olympic torch, Lady Liberty, tall ships, heroes in the gallery at the State of the Union addresses—gave way to a darker cataract of impressions—the Challenger explosion, family farm bankruptcies in the Midwest, Wall Street millionaires in handcuffs, star athletes dead from cocaine, marine officers subverting democracy to save it, presidential friends found guilty of peddling influence, a conservative nominee for the Supreme Court withdrawn for having literally "gone to pot," a religious charlatan in disgrace for debasing PTL from "Praise the Lord" to "Pass the Loot" and "Pay that Lady," Black Monday on the New York Stock Exchange, Washington as the "murder capital" of the nation, and a president said to conduct international summitry on the basis of astrological charts.

So it went in the late 1980s. Whatever the state of the Soviets, something, apparently, was rotten in the state of Denmark, too, and even the American Prospero did not escape responsibility. In 1986 there had been talk of repealing the Twenty-second Amendment and allowing Reagan to run for a third term. But by the time of the superpower summit in December 1987 the "nuclear cowboy" Reagan of old liberal fears had become the "useful idiot" Reagan of new conservative nightmares. Earlier, as the Iran-contra affair began to unfold, some Republicans were saying openly, "Let someone else be Reagan," and "None of this would have happened if Ronald Reagan were alive."

To such people, Reagan's Morning in America had become the morning after. There was little to choose between the Ayatollah Khomeini's verdict on Reagan's claims ("such vain imaginings")[26] and the reassessment of Reagan by *Time:* The essence of the change was "a return from the long vacation of the Reagan years . . . to discover that the old problems are still there, only in some ways worse."[27] In fact, conservative analyst Kevin Phillips concluded, "Ronald Reagan could even be remembered as the American president who presided over a larger national comedown than Vietnam."[28] For Jules Feiffer, the problem could be summed up in one word: "Americagate."[29]

George Bush, on the other hand, was having none of it. When he picked up Luce's theme in his 1988 presidential campaign, he was deliberate and unapologetic. America's work was not done; her force was not spent. "The American Century has not drawn to a close. We are not in decline. America has set in motion the major changes under way in the world today—the growth of democracy, the spread of free enterprise, the creation of a world market in goods and ideas. For the foreseeable future, no other nation, or group of nations, will step forward to assume leadership."[30] Clearly, the New World Order, announced appropriately at the Aspen Institute in Colorado and drawn in the sands of Kuwait, was a vision lacking only an occasion.

Obvious questions are raised. Should the Reagan-Bush springtime be viewed as such or as an Indian summer, the American equivalent of England's Edwardian era? Will the baton of modernity pass on to Japan or back to Europe and eventually to China, or have the commentators spoken too soon? Is the *pax americana* in eclipse and the American economic supremacy no more than a memory, or will America's beliefs and institutions prove resilient once again? Have we seen the end of what Alexis de Tocqueville predicted of the dominance of the Russian knout and the American moneybags, or are Americans rid of dangerously expansive illusions born of an artificial supremacy and now freed to exercise modest but significant responsibilities in the newly emerging multipolar world? Such questions are not idle, and they cannot be answered unless an understanding of America's crisis of cultural authority is made the starting point.

America and the Mandate of Heaven

Like Henry Luce, my own first lessons about the world were learned in China, but I am English and my teacher was a very different age from Luce's. Back in Beijing in 1900, one voice was listened to less than it deserved. Sir Robert Hart, who had lived in China since 1854, warned that the Boxer uprisings were far more than primitive xenophobia and frustrated patriotism. "In fifty years time," he predicted, "there will be millions of Boxers in serried ranks and war's panoply at the call of the Chinese Government: there is not the slightest doubt of that." Such men, armed, drilled, and disciplined, "will take back from foreigners everything foreigners have taken from them."[31]

His guess proved accurate almost to the year, and I vividly remember watching as an eight-year-old the climax of the Chinese revolution as Mao Tse-tung's troops took over Nanking after Chiang Kai-shek's ignominious flight to Taiwan. (To the British, the Generalissimo had long been "General Cash My-check.") I also went to Chefoo School where Luce had gone, and where we were visited by Madame Chiang, star protégé of Luce's press.

But it was also in China that I was given my first premonitions of the fallibility and follies of the West. I was too young to understand the fall of British Singapore or the reasons behind the collapse of America's China policy. But long before revolutionaries such as Franz Fanon and Che Guevara incited their people to rise up against foreign domination, and well ahead of recent events in Saigon, Teheran, and Beirut, I could feel for myself the rising hatred of foreigners, the nervous haste of embassy packing, and many of the signs of Western weakness and withdrawal later to be replayed in different lands to larger, televised audiences.

For Henry Luce's generation, history itself seemed to conspire in favoring American distinctiveness and destiny. For too many people in my own generation, the temptation has been to turn from such "dangerous and costly illusions" to minimize all national distinctiveness and regard American purpose with profound suspicion.

Is there a way today to steer between the "boosters" and the "blamers," the Polyannas and the Cassandras, between the perils of triumphalism and the failure of national nerve? Is there no choice other than the "declinists" or the "endists"? The wisest course, I suggest, is to skirt the treacherous quicksands of changing international circumstances and national credibility and start by charting the source and strength of American distinctiveness in terms of its own character in relation to the challenge of modernity. In other words, what makes America America is not measured best in GNP comparisons with Japan, nuclear firepower ratios in relation to the Soviets, or the polling figures on anti-Americanism among Iranian students. Such measurements may rise or fall. The distinctiveness and strength of America lies elsewhere, in its ideals and ideas.

Yet the choice of this other path is not an escape, for America's deepest problems today do not come from abroad, but from home. Indeed, so deeply does the crisis of cultural authority grow from the impact of modernity on what is distinctively American that Walter Lippmann, no less, analyzing one aspect of the problem, warned that "at stake is the mandate of heaven."[32]

The United States is not China, of course. Nor is the presidency the Dragon Throne; thus an American style of Middle-Kingdom thinking is no help. America's very distinctiveness is precisely what creates the distinctive American dilemma. All types of government, it was once believed, had their own principles and pathologies, their own defining character, and their own distinctive way of corruption. Thus a corrupted monarchy would decline toward tyranny, a corrupted aristocracy toward oligarchy, and a corrupted republic toward anarchy. For the Founders had faced up to the mortality of all republics: Just as human beings were vulnerable because subject to sin, republics were vulnerable because subject to corruption.

The "new nation" of the American republic was not only larger than any that had gone before, it was different. By far the largest and most important experiment in republican government since the fall of Rome, the United States was consciously founded on the "new science of politics" designed to compensate for the corruption of republican character, which had been the ruin of previous republics.

The Founders therefore wanted to cultivate virtue, but also to curb vice. The American republic depended not only upon ideals believed to be true, but upon institutions seen to have teeth. Both competing interests and civic ideals were necessary if liberty was to endure. Since people were expected to be factious rather than virtuous, reliance was placed not on morality alone but on mechanisms. If this balance were to hold as the Founders planned, the passage of time could be channeled into a force for fertility rather than futility.

This brilliant blend of ideas and institutions, idealism and realism, confidence and skepticism has been the fruitful soil in which America's robust political liberty and dynamic social vitality have flourished. But the character of the republic also marks out the likely course of its corruption. Whereas the Manchu emperors, ruling a state-dominated society, depended critically on the Mandate of Heaven for their legitimacy, the American republic, being a state-limiting society, depends critically on its own version of the Mandate of Heaven for its vitality. Well-designed institutions will not cover for the loss of long-deprived ideals indefinitely.

Here then we approach the American dilemma today: After a great sea-change in American life over the past few decades, the republic is approaching the climax of a generation-long crisis of cultural authority. At stake in the thousand and one changes and controversies that comprise this period of turbulence are the principles and patterns of authority by which personal lives and public life will be ordered. The nation that is the product of early modernity is in the midst of a time of testing under the impact of high modernity. The outcome will decide the crucial place future generations of Americans will give to ideals in general and to faiths in particular.

Two questions, therefore—one bearing on American ideals and the other on American institutions—raise issues that are now critical for the republic. The first question is intensely personal, but has a public dimension because of the connection between beliefs and public virtue: By what faiths ought Americans to live? The American answer to this question is that the government is excluded from giving an answer. The second question is thoroughly public in character and a public answer is appropriate and necessary to the well-being of the nation: By what understanding should these faiths be related to public life?

Simple sounding perhaps, but those questions are vital. Converging developments in history, society, law, and philosophy reveal with ever sharper clarity the audacious gamble that underlies the American experiment. The American republic simultaneously relies on ultimate beliefs (for otherwise it has no right to the rights by which it thrives), yet rejects any fixed, final, or official formulation of them (for here the First Amendment is clearest, most original, and most constructive). The republic will therefore always remain the "undecided experiment" in freedom, a gravity-defying gamble that stands or falls on the dynamism and endurance of its "unofficial" faiths.

If this testing leads to a turning away from America's historic sense of transcendent ideals and from the living sense of its tradition, the gamble will be lost and the American republic will decline. Democratic liberty, after all, is neither self-derived nor self-sustaining. It depends on sources beyond itself. As G. K. Chesterton wrote with characteristic double-edged insight after his visit to the United States in 1921, "Freedom is an eagle, whose glory is gazing at the sun."[33]

So momentous still is America's world and historical role and so misunderstood yet vital to it is the theme of faith that, among questions at the climax of the American Century, this theme amounts to the wild card factor. Thus, foolish and unfashionable though it may be to raise this theme, one thing is far more foolish: not to treat it at all, to deal with it in the desultory way it has been treated of late.

Recent public discussion of faith in America has tended to be limited to the controversial aspects of "religion and politics," therefore missing the crux of the problem. Most importantly of all, this view overlooks the fact that alongside the obvious crises of religious beliefs is the less noticed crisis of Enlightenment liberalism and the emergence of an American nihilism. To misread these crises leads to treating religion either as a nonissue, a purely private matter with no bearing on the public sphere, or as a nuisance factor, the bedeviling special interest of certain troublesome sectarian groups. Long periods of silence born of indifference have therefore been punctuated by fitful spasms of attention, the latter marked by a great deal of partisanship, ignorance, and hostility on both sides, not least at the highest levels. The last three presidential elections have provided ample examples of the confusion on this question.

Such a state of affairs betrays a perilous misunderstanding. America, I will argue, is at a stage in her history when the importance of faiths and the understanding of how they relate to public life is far more than a "religious issue," far wider than of purely party political or domestic significance, and far weightier than a journalistic issue-of-the-week. ("That issue," said the Democratic campaign manager in 1984, "has been given a full week." "Within days," claimed a Republican source at the same time, "God will be dead as a political issue.")[34]

It is therefore time, and past time, to recognize that the United States today is passing through a period of reckoning, when the deepest national issues have a critical religious component and the deepest religious issues have critical national consequences. Few things are therefore more in the public interest now than to understand the present significance of faiths in America and to assess their social, national, and international consequences.

But my argument is not only with those who refuse to take the faith factor seriously. It is directed as much against two general tendencies that take it deeply seriously but in opposing directions—toward the "reimposers" who seek simply to turn the clock back and place on everyone else their vision of an earlier state of affairs and toward the "removers" who seek to cleanse faith from public life altogether. The logic of both these extremes, I will argue, is mistaken. A key part of what each calls for is neither in their own best interests nor in the interests of America or the rest of the world.

Out on the Table

This book is written principally for thoughtful Americans who love their country deeply, who appreciate America's unsung strengths and virtues as well as her recent successes but who realize that all is not as well with America as recent celebration may suggest. What the book offers are three things: an analysis from an international perspective of what is currently America's deepest problem (the crisis of cultural authority), a proposal setting out a constructive solution to a key part of that problem (the reforging of a public philosophy for a civil public square), and a discussion of the prospects for an American renaissance.

Let me declare openly that I make no pretense of Olympian neutrality. Philosophically that would be impossible. Politically it would be irresponsible. Four perspectives shape this book. I write as a European, but one who believes more deeply in American first things than many Americans I know. I write as a Christian, but one who is committed to justice for people of all faiths and none, and not just for ourselves. I write as a social scientist, but one for whom committed critical thinking is as appropriate as detached academic inquiry and for whom the study of society must never belittle the importance of individual ideas, will, and action. And I write as someone who was privileged to propose and lead a major commemoration of the bicentennial of the U.S. Constitution—the Williamsburg Charter, which celebrated the religious liberty clauses of the First Amendment. The latter was not purely ceremonial. The Williamsburg Charter project worked to create practical and constructive solutions to the controversies surrounding questions about religion in public life, including a public school curriculum, *Living with our Deepest Differences,* on religious liberty in a pluralistic society.[35] No project could have been a more admirable introduction to some of the best and worst of recent responses to the issues of American public life.

Let me also state clearly that this book deliberately cuts across many current American arguments—for example, political arguments between conservatives and liberals, public philosophy arguments between communitarians and liberals, activist arguments between populists and elitists, and psychologically based arguments displaying the differences between optimists and pessimists. Emphatically, it is not an exercise in pessimism, blaming, or doom-crying. Nor is it a form of either "liberal-bashing" or "fundy-bashing."

It is important to say that the argument favors neither the "blamers" nor the "boosters." People are lining up for and against the end-of-history thesis and the decline-of-America thesis, and in some quarters responses to these notions have become a litmus test of patriotism. In the first place, the critical analysis of this book is neither recent nor sparing, but the chief conclusion is hopeful—an American renaissance is possible—and its central proposal for a new vision of public life is constructive. But the hopes for a renaissance are not empty boosterism. They are based on an assessment of American ideals and institutions and on the insistence that the crisis must be recognized in domestic affairs no less urgently than in international affairs. And that the only confidence worth having and the only proposals worth recommending are those fired in the furnace of facts faced and problems tackled.

Further, there will be little comfort here for those who play to their own gallery by equating the defense of liberty with disparaging either fundamentalism or liberalism. As regards fundamentalism, it is important to see that our expanding modern pluralism is not just a matter of new statistics but of a new stage, a stage at which pluralism and particularism (not relativism) now go hand in hand. At such a stage people must respect and treat civilly the decided particularities of fundamentalism no less than those of Judaism and humanism. As regards liberalism, even a glance at American history shows that the current hostility to the "L" word is about as sensible as a person claiming he was conceived by only one parent. Doubtless, too many liberals are tone-deaf to religion, which is no more excusable than the sometimes parallel liberal disdain for ordinary people. But liberal neglect of religion is fateful for liberals themselves—for example, in its impact on their concern for movements of social justice. When all is said and done, there is no getting around the fact that America itself is a liberal project par excellence and therefore Americans are fundamentally liberals. Indeed, to much of the world Americanism at its best is modernity's liberal project at its brightest.

Insistence on the world perspective is important, because all the world may soon feel the ripples flowing from this American time of testing. At the point where America and the diverse faiths of Americans meet are some of the deepest, most urgent, and most significant questions facing the world today. Future world conflicts are likely to occur at the points of contradiction between our increasing economic and technological interdependence and our enduring religious and cultural differences.

Above all, there are two questions that we in the late twentieth century cannot escape: First, beyond obvious things, such as collective security, what will be the vision and ordering principles of the *pax moderna* that could emerge after the end of the Cold War? Second, concerning one of those essential ordering principles, how do we live with our deepest—that is, our religiously and ideologically intense—differences? The American experiment is entering a critical stage, because in the end, the issues raised by America's crisis of cultural authority are central to the challenge of making the world safe for diversity and, thus, to both the peril and promise of our time.

PART ONE
THE CULTURAL REVOLUTION

The Troubled Horizon

Just before he retired as secretary of state, Dean Acheson was speaking to a prominent European. "Looking back," he said, "the gravest problem I had to deal with was how to steer, in this atomic age, the foreign policy of a world power saddled with the constitution of a small, eighteenth-century farmers' republic."[1] Today this remark could apply equally well in many areas outside the field of international relations. It raises an issue for America that recurs in countless forms: How does the United States currently stand in relation to its origins? As the bicentennial celebration of the Constitution illustrates, few other Western nations are so proud of their origins. Yet the question of the present's relationship to the past has been particularly urgent in the past few decades, and the answers given by the present decade may be decisive for many years to come.

The most obvious expression of this concern is the flood of articles, books, and commentaries over the last generation that claim that the United States is experiencing a transformation or restructuring. America, they claim with a host of different reasons, is at a historic turning point, decisive for itself and perhaps also for the world. The claim was asserted in 1961 in the influential Rockefeller report, *Prospect for America*, but since then the trickle of books on this topic has become a torrent with the very titles of current sellers telling the story—*Decade of Decision, America in Search of Itself, New Rules, The Next America, The Turning Point, Beyond the Turning Point, Megatrends, America II, More Like Us: Making America Great Again, Megatrends 2000, The End of History and the Last Man*, and so on.

Certain of the most pressing claims about a turning point stand head and shoulders above the rest. Among these, three are unquestionably the most common—that the United States is experiencing massive social changes as it shifts from an industrial to an information society, massive political changes as it undergoes another of its regular cycle of party realignments, and massive national and international changes as it adjusts to world realities after Vietnam and after the demise of the bipolar, superpower world of the Cold War era.

Yet from a wide-angle perspective, none of the other shifts rivals the importance of the crisis of cultural authority, if only because it is bound to prove decisive in America's response to them all. At stake are the principles and patterns of authority by which both personal lives and the life of the republic are to be ordered. If America is indeed in a testing time for ideals in general and faiths in particular, then this shift is momentous to the very character and endurance of the republic.

Two Foundational Questions

I said earlier that America's crisis of cultural authority is America's variation on the worldwide collision between the impersonal and irresponsible forces of modernity and the respective notions of humanness, morality, and the natural environment in different countries and cultures. Two underlying questions in this claim need a deeper answer.

First, what is meant by the term modernity? Such concepts as modernization and modernity are still widely misunderstood. Some people turn them into a kind of "rich man's Marxism," a deterministic movement that will inevitably sweep the world with prosperity, progress, and democratic revolutions. Others use the word modernity as if it were a fancy word of "change" or simply a condition of being "up to date."

As used here, modernity is much more than that. It refers to the character and system of the world produced by the forces of modernization and development. The words modern, modernity, and modernization derive from the Latin *modernus,* meaning "just now" or "of today," but modernity itself is far from modern in this narrow sense. It represents a long and titanic revolution in human experience that can be traced in two main ways.

The more common way is through the history of ideas. It focuses on human individuals and their ideas and will, and traces the line from revolutionary changes in ideas to their impact on society. This mode of analysis goes back at least to the seventeenth-century scientific revolution and follows the story through the eighteenth-century Enlightenment, the nineteenth-century romantic movement to the modernist and postmodern-ist movements in the twentieth century. The rarer but even more important way is through the sociology of knowledge. This mode of analysis focuses on society and social change, and traces the line in reverse. It follows the story from revolutionary changes in social context to their impact on ideas, going back to major structural and institutional developments in society—supremely those resulting from the capitalist revolution in the fifteenth century, the technological and industrial revolution in the eighteenth century, and the communications revolution in the twentieth century.

There is an immediate consequence of this broader definition that insists on emphasizing the structural and global dimensions of modernity. It heavily qualifies the use of the notion "postmodern." Modernism as a set of ideas may well have collapsed and "postmodern" may therefore be legitimate to describe the set of ideas that succeeds it. But to be postmodern in the structural sense is as yet inconceivable. Thus to bandy the term "postmodern," as if by definition it takes us beyond modernity, is a theoretical error with grave practical consequences. Modernity, in the deeper sense, is now a global force. What Max Weber pictured as an iron cage, Peter Berger as a gigantic steel hammer, and Anthony Giddens as a careening juggernaut cannot be checked merely by wafting the term postmodern. The depersonalizing and demoralizing forces of modernity proceed relentlessly. Americans caught up with "the end of history" should realize that "the end of the person" (and the end of morality and nature too) are far more important.

Second, what is meant by a crisis of cultural authority? Again, the term is often misunderstood because it is used only in a moralistic sense, usually as a term of lament (as over "hedonism," the "breakdown of the family," and the "drug epidemic"). In such cases, the stress is on the specific and the irreparable, and the object is more to deplore than to describe. But as used here, the term is primarily descriptive and refers to something far stronger and more comprehensive than any single example of its consequences. A crisis of cultural authority is at once more intangible and more important than any isolated outbreak. As stated in the introduction, this is the core of America's crisis of cultural authority: Under the impact of modernity, the beliefs, ideals, and traditions that have been central to Americans and to the character of American democracy—whether religious, such as Jewish and Christian beliefs, or civic, such as Americanism—are losing their cultural compelling power.

A crisis of cultural authority does not mean simply that some people in the nation are skeptical or critical of the nation's beliefs, traditions, and ideals, nor that there are deep divisions over what should be believed. Both these things are true of many societies. A crisis of cultural authority goes deeper than that. In America's case, it concerns the fact that the nation is torn in a series of so-called "culture wars," between the forces of those who are culturally conservative and those who are culturally progressive. But deeper still, it also concerns the fact that even those who say they believe in

America's beliefs, traditions, and ideals no longer show that they do in ways that they once did or in ways that former generations did.

Such a state of affairs has special significance for the United States. A crisis of cultural authority is important for any nation, but especially for a liberal democracy or any free society that would remain free. Because the human spirit is the primary form of democratic capital, the notion of cultural authority is both critical and complementary to freedom. When the cultural authority of beliefs, ideals, and traditions is strong and operative, external laws and coercions are unnecessary. Such beliefs, traditions, and ideals have the power to inspire, discipline, and constrain in a manner that does not contradict personal freedom.

As political theorist Hannah Arendt and others have argued, authority is the strongest survivor of a trio of forces—authority, religion, and tradition—that have been vital to Western civilization since Roman times. An *auctor* in Latin was a trustworthy writer, and thus a responsible leader, teacher, guarantor, or model whose beliefs and judgments were worthy to be followed. Authority is therefore especially vital to democracy because it fosters a form of uncoercive obedience that reinforces individual freedom. Being stronger than advice but less strong than a command, authority operates at a level between coercion by force alone (which is too hierarchical and repressive for democracy) and persuasion by argument alone (which is too egalitarian and utopian if applied everywhere).

In America's case the cultural authority of the "habits of the heart" of America's faiths and traditions has helped to inspire, order, and restrain the private and public lives of Americans and of wider American society. Importantly, too, it has provided American society with what the Romans would have called *gravitas,* or the weight, ballast, and equipoise of the ongoing American experiment.

Behind this high assessment of the importance of cultural authority and the seriousness of a crisis of cultural authority lies a cluster of axioms. First is that the character and strength of a culture resides in the power of its beliefs, ideals, and traditions to exert a double influence in society—disciplining as well as inspiring and empowering renunciations as well as release. Second is that this cultural authority is strongest when it is unconscious, unquestioned, and covers the whole of social life—addressing ordinary citizens no less than leaders, the concerns of private life as much as public life, and the issues of organizing the self as well as those of ordering society. Third in the cluster is that the deepest source and agency of this cultural authority lies in its faiths, so that it can be truly said that there is no strong and vital culture without a *cultus,* or source of worship and ultimate faith commitment. Fourth is that a crisis of cultural authority occurs when a culture's faiths lose their inner compelling power, either because a rival faith challenges them, or because, in changed circumstances, they fail to command a continuing assent from their own adherents. Fifth is that such a crisis does not occur suddenly or through any single event but as a long and profound shift in the foundations of a culture, which in turn triggers an avalanche of consequences that appear unrelated but unstoppable. Sixth is that the eventual decline or death of a culture is a stage beyond the crisis of cultural authority, when cultural authority weakens to the point where it is neither sufficiently respected nor replaced. And seventh is that every generation must cultivate and guard the sources of its cultural authority because no free republic is more than two or three generations away from the possibility of such a decline.

Understood this way, the United States has become afflicted over the last generation with a crisis of cultural authority similar to that which the ancient Greeks spoke of as "the gods switching sides," the traditional Chinese as "the crisis of the Mandate of Heaven," and nineteenth-century Europeans as "the death of God." Metaphors such as fraying, eroding, unraveling, and decomposing have become popular, but the prosaic fact is this: Under the conditions of late twentieth-century modernity, the cultural authority of American beliefs, ideals, and traditions is dissolving. Tradition is softening into a selective nostalgia for the past and transcendent faiths are melting into a suburbanesque sentiment that is vulnerable to the changing fashions of the therapeutic revolution. Thus with the *gravitas* of their cultural authority collapsing inward like the critical mass of an exploding star, parts of American society are beginning to flare out with the dazzling but empty brilliance of a great culture in a critical phase. The result is a grand national loss of confidence and dynamism. As a result of much leveling, even more unraveling, and no little reveling in both, American beliefs, ideals, and traditions are fast becoming a lost continent to many Americans.

If one were forced to state the crisis of cultural authority in a single sentence, it might be this: "Just say No" has become America's most nationally urgent slogan at the very moment when "Why not?" has become America's most publicly unanswerable question.

In sum, America's crisis of cultural authority touches many different authoritative figures, positions, and institutions, but at its heart it is a consequence of the decisive weakening of faiths as shapers of American life, both in public and private. Indeed, with the decreased influence of faiths on culture reinforcing the increased influence of culture on faiths, the crisis of cultural authority is in large part a crisis of America's faiths. "Our cultural revolution," as Philip Rieff wrote in the sixties, "does not aim, like its predecessors, at victory for some rival commitment, but rather at a way of using all commitments, which amounts to loyalty toward none." The American question, then, is "no longer as Dostoevsky put it: 'Can civilized men believe?' Rather: Can unbelieving men be civilized?"[2]

One way to grasp the crisis of cultural authority, then, is to view it as the national consequence of a crisis of beliefs. It must be stressed, however, that the crisis in question covers civic beliefs as well as moral and religious, and that it affects almost all the communities of faith, not simply the Christian churches. The problems of Protestantism, whether ecumenical or evangelical, need no elaboration. But in 1990, for example, a distinguished commission on Jewish education in North America found that "large numbers of Jews have lost interest in Jewish values, ideals, and behavior, and there are many who no longer believe that Judaism has a role to play in their search for personal fulfillment and identity."[3]

Thus almost across the board, beliefs, ideals, and traditions, which once both inspired and restrained Americans, are losing their binding address. No longer self-evident in theory or culturally compelling in practice, they lack their former integrity and effectiveness in decisively linking belief to behavior, private life to public life. The statistical indicators of religion may still be up, but the social influence is down. As America's third century under the Constitution begins, the music of the framers' primal chords is losing its resonance. For when it comes to the crisis of cultural authority, America's real loss in competitiveness is not with her contemporaries, such as the Germans and the Japanese, but with her ancestors, such as Jefferson and Madison.

Another way to grasp the crisis is to view it as the national consequence of a crisis of definitions and categories. Definitions and categories are vital to any healthy society, especially to one as oriented to personal achievement and public debate as the United States. Without them there are no agreed-upon goals, no common bearings, no public milestones to measure progress or even to find where one is. Yet, the philosopher Leszek Kolakowski writes, "Sometimes it seems as if all the words and signs that make up our conceptual framework and provide us with our basic system of distinctions are dissolving before our eyes."[4] In much public debate in America there is no longer clear distinction between human and animal, male and female, word and image, war and peace, invasion and liberation, law and violence, reason and madness, civilized and primitive, knowledge and ignorance, doctor and patient, citizenship and tribalism, persuasion and propaganda, art and pornography, reporting and fiction, character and instincts. The double impact of modern technologies and postmodern theories has led to a breaking, blunting, blurring, and blending of categories without precedent in Western history.

The crisis of definitions does not lie simply in the fact that enormous changes in standards have taken place over the last generation—one person's setback would be another's advance. It stems from the fact that the very notion of a canon and the notion of classifications and oppositions are in question. Identifiable personhood, reason, truth, a knowable world, meaningful language, the intentionality of agents in their own actions, and the significance of authors' right to meaning in their own texts—all such notions, definitions, and categories are vital to humanness, as well as to science and democracy. Yet they are currently dismissed as fictions or attacked as evidence of another group's bad faith, the tools of their intended oppression. And once the wasting and wrecking has been done, it is clear that the American center is not holding.

The result, at best, is a confused and undiscriminating America that in area after area has exchanged excellence for eclecticism, serious questing for truth for an endless stockpiling of uncertain perspectives. At worst, it leads to the creation of a perpetually fractious society, to a series of culture wars and the threat of a devaluation of values, and the reduction of life to the cheerful nihilism of a carnival of games. For without a scale by which to assess, the very notion of "value" becomes valueless. Endless reordering is only another name for disordering; the perpetual search for new forms is a sure road to formlessness; the destruction of all form is not disorderly so much as demonic. As political scientist Glenn Tinder has noted, "A nation that does not dare to make moral judgments is surely living under the shadow of nihilism."[5]

Too Precise by Half

Two warnings should be added. The first is that in the attempt to be clear about the crisis of cultural authority we are discussing, it is easy to become too precise and forget the element of the intangible. The Austrian writer Robert Musil aptly described a similar crisis in Vienna before World War I as "a mysterious disease of the times." What was it, he mused, that had got lost?

> Something imponderable. . . . Like what happens when a magnet lets the iron filings go and they tumble together again. . . . Or when a ball of string comes undone. . . . Or when a tension has slackened. . . . Or when an orchestra begins to play out of tune. . . . No one could have established the existence of any details that might not just as well have existed in earlier times too; but all the relations between things had

shifted slightly. . . . Sharp borderlines everywhere became blurred, and some new, indescribable capacity for entering into hitherto unheard-of relationships threw up new people and new ideas. These people and ideas were not wicked. No, it was only that the good was adulterated with a little too much of the bad, the truth with error, and the meaning with a little too much of the spirit of accommodation.[6]

That moment is precisely when overprecision becomes a danger, for either an analyst or an accuser. "There is nothing," Musil concluded of the Austrian crisis, "that one can hold responsible for this. Nor can one say how it all came about. It is no use attacking persons or ideas or definite phenomena. . . . The fact is simply that there is as much lack of everything as of nothing."[7]

The intangible is equally important in America's case, though the trends are neither unprecedented nor so indefinite. The American crisis of cultural authority has already moved beyond its first stage—that of perplexity, irritation, and a rebellion against authority, as in the 1960s. It could soon be moving out of its second stage—that of nostalgia for authority and attempted restoration, as in the 1980s. At some future moment it will then draw near to the climax of its third and fateful stage—the moment of reckoning when effective cultural authority either revives or sinks into oblivion, with dire consequences for the nation.

What is certain is that by their very nature and pedigree, American ideals and American faiths raise issues that go the furthest back in American history and the deepest down in American society. When such potent issues are disregarded or misunderstood, the combination of their historical importance and contemporary misrepresentation makes them into the storm center of cultural controversy and, as we shall see, the wild card factor in the American future. Importantly, then, the crisis of cultural authority is far more than a crisis of tradition, or a crisis for traditionalists. The problem touches all Americans, liberals as well as conservatives, the younger generation no less than the older, because it is a crisis of what it takes to keep America strong and successful.

A second warning is also needed. It should be underscored again that America's crisis of cultural authority does not stem from either the political order or the economic order. While it influences them both in the end, it stems from the moral and cultural order. The latter includes the family, churches and synagogues, schools, the universities, the press and the media, the arts at large, the entertainment world, and the whole world of leisure. Many commentators see few problems on the horizon today because they neglect this third order and therefore overlook the crisis of cultural authority. Concentrating almost exclusively on the political and the economic realms, they have a blind spot when it comes to the sphere of the moral and cultural. Others minimize the cultural factor because they regard it purely as a reflection of the political and economic order—almost as Marx did. Only those who take the moral and cultural order seriously and who follow the interplay between the moral/cultural sphere and the political and economic spheres can recognize the full range of challenges that now face the American republic. A crisis in America's third order is of first-order importance.

American politics has been characterized by a succession of grand pivotal issues—between 1775 and 1824, essentially constitutional, dealing with the institutional arrangements of the new political community; between 1825 and 1892, essentially sectional, involving regional tensions between North and South and Old East and New West; and since then until the 1960s, essentially economic and social, centering on the problems of industrial growth and social welfare.[8] If this is so, the United States is now in the fourth great era, and the grand pivotal issue, around which debate and conflict are swirling, is cultural.

The revolution of 1989 therefore served to underscore what Richard John Neuhaus called "the recentering of the cultural."[9] The disordering of ideals, the unraveling of consensus, the shrinking of long-range perspective —these problems are cultural before they become political. Political and economic arguments remain after 1989, but more about means than ends. Representative democracy and the mainly free market have won the argument of ends for the time being. But in the aftermath of the ending of these old debates, even stronger and older cultural debates have become central. In terms of which faiths, how those faiths are to relate to each other, and what place they are to be given in the self-understanding of the republic, the United States is in the throes of a grand crisis of cultural authority.

A Pinch of Salt Is in Order

Of course, we are right to handle all such claims, including this one, with a deal of caution. Every age sees itself as falling away in morals. The landscape of American history is dotted with claims of "watersheds" and "great divides." All that trembles does not fall and many a "tidal wave of the future" has proved to be only a minor eddy. Most turning points, let alone headlines, barely register on the scales of history, and the pitfalls in "turning point talk" are legion. "Today more than ever," Daniel Boorstin cautions, "we need to sharpen our vocabulary and remind ourselves of the difference between history and current events, between 'revolution' and the kinds of 'turning points' that confuse our views of the latest bulletins."[10]

For one thing, we all see the world from our own perspective, whether as individuals or as generations. Nothing is more natural than to see all history as leading up to our own insight. Thus the more superhuman the perspective the grander the claims will tend to be. When Winston Churchill's first volume of war memoirs appeared, Arthur Balfour remarked: "Winston has written an enormous book about himself and called it *The World Crisis.*"

Further, as American history shows, the chances are great that what is taken as a historic turning point will prove to be only the presentation of one of America's "other faces" or another swing in America's celebrated "cycles." Far from being as simple and straightforward to understand as it first appears, the United States is a puzzling and contradictory country—deeply idealistic yet irredeemably pragmatic; strongly committed to change yet essentially conservative; mostly self-confident, even crusading, yet highly prone to bouts of self-castigation and public confessing. The darker and more troubled face of America is rarer than the sunny optimism and prosperous blandness of the well-known face the world has come to expect. But the former is no less American than the latter, and its reappearance from time to time should not be mistaken for a turning point.

Indeed, the great American tug-of-war is not simply between contrasting periods and moods—wilderness versus settlement, self-confidence versus self-castigation, public action versus private interest, obsession versus obliviousness, colonial-mansion mind versus skyscraper will, and so on. The struggle is continuous and internal because the two faces can usually be seen at once. Charles Dickens captured this contradiction in *Martin Chuzzlewit:* "Martin knew nothing about America, or he would have known perfectly well that if its individual citizens, to a man, are to be believed, it always *is* depressed, and always *is* stagnated, and always *is* at an alarming crisis, and never was otherwise; though as a body they are ready to make oath upon the Evangelists at any hour of the day or night, that it is the most thriving and prosperous of all countries on the habitable globe."[11]

Worst of all, current claims about a turning point appear suspect because part of the hullabaloo and hype merely shows how fashionable trend-spotting has become. At first glance this seems to reverse the more traditional human attitude that G. K. Chesterton described as a game of "Cheat the Prophet" or "Keeping the Future Dark." All the players listen carefully to what the clever people say will happen, wait till the clever people die, bury them, and then go and do something else.

But the actual difference from the traditional attitude is less than it appears, because fashionable in this case may largely mean profitable. Trend-spotting itself has become a trend and a highly profitable one. Trend-spotters are the fortune-tellers of the modern world. In telling our fortunes, they make theirs. But even beyond that: In the wind-up to the fateful fascination of the year 2000, an astute marriage of marketing and psychology has given birth to an irresistible new genre—a secular premillennialism whose megatrends offer a sure-fire guarantee of megabucks.

Yet for all that, only a fool would ignore the more solid analyses and dismiss them as trend-spotting, particularly when a startling fact is recognized: In many cases, what is truly sensational is not the noisy claims of the charlatan but the probing questions of the serious reporter and the quiet conclusions of the sober-minded historian.

It is unquestionably true that modernity has reduced "crisis" to cliché; that a sense of change can be counted on as an unchanging element in a changing world; that Americans have as much of a flair for overstatement as the English do for understatement; that national pulse-taking and watershed divining have become a permanent pastime for some American observers; that in certain professions, such as politics and advertising, nothing is older than the claim to be new; and that the lengthening list of recently failed academic predictions is a lesson in the snags of secular soothsaying.[12]

Yet that something of profound consequence is at stake is beyond question. Or as one of America's leading political scientists concluded recently, "If everything in history, ultimately, is transition from something to something else, the present moment seems more than usually so."[13]

But what is at stake? Is there really a turning point and, if so, toward what? Is it merely the latest in the list of trends, such as the "greening," "squaring," "greying," and "shrinking" of America? Or does it entail a epoch-marking boundary of momentous significance, possibly even closing off a period that goes back to the very founding of the American colonies themselves? In Part One we turn first to examine the troubled horizon within which the crisis has arisen.

1

The Testing of National Identity

"We have no part in America. America has no place for us," shouted a young black rapper interviewed on the radio after the Los Angeles riots in May 1992. "We blacks will be mown down before we are melted down in a white man's society." Like the acrid pall of smoke that hung over south central Los Angeles after the bloodiest violence in American urban history, a rhetoric of rage has clouded parts of America and Americanism in recent years. There were many factors behind the riots—hopelessness, crime, police brutality, degrading poverty, the pitiless neglect of the poor and people of color by conservative administrations in the 1980s, the cynical divisiveness of political campaigning, the social dislocation of families with more guns than grown-ups, and the ever-present reservoir of American violence and racism. But the riots were also the bitter fruit of a deliberate and sustained rejection of Americanism and the idea of a single people and a common culture—in short, of a key component of American identity.

The Los Angeles riots stunned and shocked the world. The nation that had read the riot act to others on human rights was forced by its own riots to act over its own injustices. The cities that burned in the sixties because of rising expectations were burning in the nineties because of falling expectations. In the world capital of myth-making a capital-sized myth had itself been destroyed, for the riots were the ultimate bonfire of the vanities of the 1980s. They burned up a veil of national illusions and revealed the pent-up problems of a generation of rampant social decay. But they were linked not only to earlier riots but to other cultural developments, such as bilingualism and radical multiculturalism. As such, the same trends evident in inner cities also emerged in bitter debates at elite universities and in melodramatic

37

emotional discussions on popular talk shows. To trace all these links is to follow a spreading series of challenges that form a gathering crisis of identity for Americans.

The profound developments, changes, and shocks of the last generation have created problems that run far deeper than the "Blame America Firsters" or malevolent perceptions of an Ayatollah Khomeini. Their roots are older and more tangled than can be covered by a facile mention of such grand earlier crises as Vietnam or Watergate. At certain levels the problem has eaten into the foundational sense of national identity and purpose even for the staunchest of patriots, even after a successful war.

The mounting crisis of American identity has been evident to foreign observers for several decades, though it has taken extreme multiculturalism for it to dawn on the minds of most Americans and become one of the key issues of the nineties. But there is a simple reason why a crisis of national identity affects Americans especially deeply. An individual's sense of identity is like a modern nation's self-image and beliefs about itself. And this is true of no modern nation more than the United States. America is not America because of a single culture and a common language. America is characteristically a nation by intention and by ideas, so it depends crucially on an ongoing commitment of heart and mind. F. Scott Fitzgerald expressed this succinctly: "France was a land, England a people, but America, having about it still that quality of an idea, was harder to utter."[1]

A century earlier, British journalist Alexander Mackay had observed the same thing. The people of most countries were like the Scots and the Swiss—deeply attached to a place and its soil. But the fiercest American pride was not in a place but in principles, and the deepest affections were not toward the soil but toward the society in which those principles were embodied. "Every American is thus, in his own estimation, the apostle of a particular political creed."[2] Henry Luce, though not an immigrant, was typical of the American experience in this sense. Like many a new arrival off the boat, he was foreign-born and, having no hometown in America, he made America itself his hometown, fiercely, wholeheartedly, and tenaciously.

This commitment to a nationality of beliefs rather than bloodlines is part and parcel of America as the early child of modernity. It is also one reason why interpreting the meaning of America is a national necessity. Through the white-hot heat of experience, imagination, and will, Americans have forged a combination of ideas, ideals, and interests into a grand myth of identity in which national self-justification and national celebration are one. No proposition is less dry than the "American proposition." But this is also why, like any bold idea, the American proposition naturally invites judgments on its progress, why the need to prove it again and again has at times had to be underwritten in fire and blood, why the national yearning for affirmation sometimes degenerates into a kind of cultural hypochondria, and why such an ideas-and-ideals-based identity is specially vulnerable to a crisis of cultural authority. America is a nation in ceaseless search of community. Nothing is more American than the restless need to define and redefine America.

Multicultural concerns are now worldwide and the dark harvest of extreme ethnicity, separationism, and fragmentation is being reaped on all five continents. So the outcome of America's testing of national identity is significant to other nations following the world's "first new nation" on the seas of modernity. Even the smallest and most subtle of shifts in the meaning of America to Americans is bound to be significant, and the present issues could point to shifts that are far from small. Making the world all over again is a foolish impossibility, but the drive to reaffirm the American proposition is a perpetual American necessity that is becoming a national dilemma.

As American as ___?

There are three parts to the crisis of national identity. The first, and by far the most important, concerns the challenge to the character of "Americanism"—that vague but vital cluster of beliefs, myths, and images that was once thought to be central to the character and continuity of the American experience. "We have some things in this country," wrote Henry Luce in his famous essay in 1941, "which are infinitely precious and especially American."[3]

Needless to say, the rich cluster of notions that comprise Americanism never needed to be fully explicit or articulated. After his visit to America, G. K. Chesterton wrote of the odd resemblance between the American Constitution and the Spanish Inquisition, in that "America is the only nation in the world that is founded on a creed."[4] "It is built like a church," Denis Brogan reiterated, "on a rock of dogmatic affirmations."[5] Few people would disagree with these observations. But justly celebrated though the Declaration of Independence, the Constitution, and the Bill of Rights are, Americanism has been viewed as far wider and more diffuse than these three great documents. Difficult to define, it is dangerous to ignore.

James Baldwin touched on these vaguer but more vital unspoken assumptions in an essay in 1959 entitled "The Discovery of What It Means To Be an American." He crossed the Atlantic to live in Paris, he wrote, because he thought he "hated America." But, to his surprise, the experience of living in France awakened him to his Americanness and to the hidden laws and unspoken but profound assumptions that are American. "I proved, to my astonishment, to be as American as any Texan G.I. And I found my experience was shared by every American writer I knew in Paris."[6]

If this unspoken Americanism was strong even in a disgruntled self-exile like Baldwin, how much stronger it has been in the average American. Try asking any hundred Americans what America and Americanism means to them, what they would miss most if exiled from the United States, or what to them is genuinely "as American as apple pie." At first, a hundred different views might emerge, and no doubt the list would range from things as down-to-earth as Cokes, hamburgers, and baseball up to heroic national myths such as the part-facts, part-fantasies that swirl around the frontier and the lone cowboy. Myths do not lack in power because they are vague.

But probe these vague and varied responses more deeply and certain core themes usually begin to emerge: such themes as the openness, dynamism, self-reliance, egalitarianism, toughness, risk-taking, and enterprise of Americans. Probe them more deeply still and it becomes apparent that this mix of themes itself grows out of the matrix of democratic experiences, and at its center are the convictions and ideals that surround faith, freedom, the flag, and the family. These shared assumptions, writes Richard Reeves, author of *American Journey,* are "the things that for all practical (political) purposes define American thinking about America."[7]

Needless to say, talk of national character and common identity is always comparative and in America's case essentially an ideal that is never fully realized. It is a portrait of the world shot with a wide-angle lens and of the nation shot through rose-tinted lens. So no one should expect to pick up shared national characteristics with a close-up lens and no one should expect perfection. Thus a John Smith from London and a Paddy O'Rourke from Dublin would never be mistaken for each other by their wives and friends. But each would be indistinguishable from the other to an observer on Mars. Similarly, there are enormous differences between a Dallas Baptist, a Chicago Catholic, and a New York Jew, but each is "recognizably American." In certain important ways they are closer to their fellow citizens than to their fellow believers elsewhere in the world. Today's focus of attention is not on national identity, but on diversity and multiculturalism, group separateness and group sensitivities. But if ever the rage for ethnicity is assuaged and a sense of the common and the comparative is restored, it will be seen that the national equivalent of American "family resemblances" is real—if elusive and far from fixed.

This swing back from a passion for diversity is unlikely to occur soon.

Radical multiculturalism may prevail. Americanism may come to be viewed as purely fictitious and the notion of an American character entirely imaginary. But what matters for the crisis of cultural authority is that Americanism and American character were once perceived to be real. That fact alone gave them enormous social potency. Thus an undeniable element of the crisis of national identity is demonstrated simply by the futility of trying to discuss the problem at all in certain circles. What was once taken to be real and important is now treated as bogus and is ruled out of court.

Talk of Americanism and an American character may be mythical or simply an editorialized reflection of American conditions. But it goes back to the earliest days, prompted above all by the dawn-fresh newness of American experience. Americanism has been vital to America, not least where it has been mostly mythical. Its core assumptions and common ideals not only undergird and overarch popular notions of the American way of life, the American Dream, and the American creed. They mark out the boundaries between legitimate and illegitimate, patriotic and unpatriotic, American and un-American. They turn past ideals into present imperatives, provide American explanations for American experiences, and bridge the gap between performance and principle.

No other democratic nation has a set of notions quite comparable to Americanism, and no other people have spent so much time and ink explaining their own national character. "The American national character," Thomas Hartshorne wrote correctly, "has become an American national obsession."[8] Few things have been more important to the founding and maintenance of a people who started out sharing no natural community yet who wanted to make a drastic break with the past.

No Left or Right, Only Up or Down

Why have Americans shown such a national self-consciousness? Explanations abound that range from the earliest sense of "Puritan errand," which required perpetual reassessment, to the modern setting where much of American life is psychology writ large and therefore demands endless self-analysis. But what is obvious to an outsider is that the apparent vagueness of these notions belies their strength. Understanding Americanism helps to explain a host of experiences in America, such as the popularity of the Real American and the "hundred percent American," the earlier unpopularity of the "hyphenated-American," and the unthinkability of "un-American." Gaining citizenship to an American is not a matter of naturalization papers but rather a national baptism into shared ideals. America may profess to be pluralistic and all-tolerant, but to most people

"American Nazi" and "American Communist" are contradictions in terms.

At a higher level still, Americanism helps to explain why the United States remains virtually the sole democratic country with no record of any socialist representation in its government. "As American as ____" may appear vague, but woe betide anyone who mistakes vagueness for weakness. Americanism has long been regarded by socialists as a rival precisely because it acts as a surrogate for socialism. Even Karl Marx's comrades from the German Workers Club, who came to the United States after the failure of the 1848 revolution, almost all abandoned their socialism. One more recent socialist observed, "When we examine the meaning of Americanism, we discover that Americanism is to the American not a tradition or a territory, not what France is to the Frenchman or England is to an Englishman, but a doctrine—what socialism is to a socialist. . . . Americanism has thus served as a substitute for socialism. Every concept of socialism has its substitutive counterconcept in Americanism, and that is why the socialist argument falls so fruitlessly on the American ear."[9] ("I suggest to you there is no left or right," said Ronald Reagan in his Long March period in the sixties, "only an up or down."[10])

Above all, these notions of Americanism throw light on two features of the American experience that are of enormous importance at a time of expanding multicultural diversity. On the one hand, Americanism has provided America with a shared commitment to shared ideals, and thus with a vital sense of national unity that has counterbalanced its natural diversity. In terms of languages, ethnic origins, religious allegiances, and geographical variety, American society is the most varied on earth; whereas in terms of social and political diversity, the range has been remarkably narrow and the extremes remarkably rare. In America "middle"—as in Middletown, middle class, and Middle America—is not a matter of mediocrity but centrality. Far from a question of being average (as in the verbal associations of middling, middle-brow, and middle-income to the British), it has everything to do with being American. Americanism is composite at its core. Americans are nothing if not children of a crucible.

On the other hand, Americanism has provided America with a powerful commitment to moral conservatism that has counterbalanced its equal commitment to social change. These core assumptions and the supporting consensus therefore help to explain the remarkable strength and continuity of American character, despite apparently overwhelming pressures to the contrary. Between the censuses of 1790 and 1970, for example, the territory of the United States increased four times, the population density increased thirteen times, the population total no less than fifty-two times, and the nation as a whole made the titanic modern shift from being predominantly rural to overwhelmingly urban. In two centuries of rapid worldwide change, no nation changed more rapidly. Yet all the evidence in this period reveals a surprising continuity in what was perceived as the American national character and ideals. Contrary, therefore, to popular belief even in America, "the society of the future" has more of the past in it than many people realize. America's social dynamism and moral conservatism are closely linked— which is one reason why the flag and other symbols of Americanism are so explosive in the culture-wars struggle to define America.

To speak of Americanism is not to make the mistake of suggesting national uniformity, exaggerating consensus, or minimizing dissent. The United States is a single nation, but it is not a single culture. *E pluribus unum*, many point out, is a mystery as much as a motto. "Typically American" is always a large-scale generalization to which each real American is a potential exception. But while there is a riotous blend of diversity in America, the strong primary colors are provided by the shared myths of Americanism. With the tragic exception of the Civil War years, what unites Americans has always been stronger than what divides them.

It is also a mistake to think that Americanism can be understood by taking a mirror reading of anti-Americanism, because if Americanism is partly myth to Americans, it is almost completely so for foreigners. Most anti-Americanism has little to do with understanding or misunderstanding America. It has more to do with a sense of national consciousness asserted against the world's greatest power. At the end of the eighties, anti-Americanism was said to be fading in France and rising in Britain, Spain, and West Germany, while in the Middle East it became a passionate ideology in itself. (In a British survey in 1986, one out of five rated the United States a bigger threat to peace than the Soviet Union, and one-third saw nothing to choose between the two.)[11] At times the United Nations organization has even become a sort of temple of anti-Americanism just as the Middle East acts as the seminary of its most militant priests. "America is the reason for all our catastrophes and the source of all malice," says the manifesto of Lebanon's Party of God. "I swear by God that everything which is American is a sin for us," says Colonel Qaddafi.[12] Or as a typical Sandinista slogan put it, "To learn from the USSR is to advance; to learn from the USA is to retreat."

But whether real or imaginary, this rich legacy of Americanism is profoundly significant—above all for its striking demonstration of unity despite diversity and continuity despite change. So there is a special urgency to the current challenge to Americanism from five main directions, detailed below.

Indefinable, Indefensible

One part of the challenge has been directed at the very concept of Americanism, or of any notion of a national character. Americanism, some have said, is indefinable and unverifiable. It is so elusive that it is virtually waiting to be abused. It is almost impossible to do without, admitted Thomas Hartshorne, but the concept of national character is the intellectual's substitute for the cruder practice of racial stereotyping. "Perhaps under the circumstances it would be more accurate in certain respects to substitute for the term 'national character' the term 'national caricature.'"[13]

A second challenge is deadlier and more direct. In certain intellectual circles today, Americanism is summarily dismissed in favor of a new and opposing vision of multiculturalism. Americanism is rejected as a mask for insensitivity and repression, a conspiracy in favor of the European background, the upper class, the white race, and the male sex.

In a speech at Harvard in May 1990, Richard Darman, director of the Office of Management and Budget, lamented the waning of the "American romance." "As the American romantic spirit expands in foreign lands, it is oddly quiescent here at home—especially among the intelligentsia."[14] But such talk of Americanism, many say more typically, exaggerates continuities and overlooks change. It drowns out recognition of American diversity and breeds disdain for minorities. Americanism is mainly myth and impossible to define anyway. It confirms national blind spots, such as the failure to acknowledge violence, class, and elitism. And at its worst, they say, it is only a code word for Klanmanship and nativism. It overcame the ancient curse of Babel or the modern curse of the Balkans, but for those prizing diversity above unity the victory was actually a defeat.

The debunking and destruction of American myths has been the deliberate goal of certain intellectuals since the 1920s, especially on the Left. Americanism, and therefore most Americans, by definition are guilty of racism, chauvinism, ultranationalism, and authoritarianism. This diseased view of America is well illustrated by Harold Stearns's 1922 symposium *Civilization in the United States* or by H. L. Mencken's celebrated dismissal of Middletown as a "city in Moronia."[15] At first a minority concern, it gathered fresh momentum after the sixties. (One of Luce's biographers refers to him dismissively as "the preacher of Amprop" as if Luce and not Lincoln was responsible for "the American proposition.") Any indiscriminate destruction of national myth, historian David Potter warned, can lead to a serious deterioration in a society. "But oblivious to such possible impairment, American intellectuals, during the 1920s and later, set busily about laying their axes to the mythic underpinnings of American identity."[16]

These earlier attacks on Americanism pale in scale and significance beside more recent assaults, such as the extremes of radical multiculturalism and the opposition to celebrating the five hundredth anniversary of Columbus's discovery of the New World. Dr. Leonard Jeffries of the City College of New York epitomized the former in his reverse-racist contrast between the cold, materialistic, and aggressive "ice people" from Europe and the warm, community-minded "sun people" from Africa. (The Washington Monument, he says, is "an African monument of resurrection that was refashioned for George Washington, the slave-master bastard founding father.")[17] The city of Berkeley epitomized the latter in declaring 1992, the five hundreth anniversary of Columbus's landing, "The Year of Indigenous People."

For many of those who worked from the approved canon of determinism —gender, race, and class—multiculturalism as an undeniable social reality tipped over easily into anti-Americanism. In the grand celebration of otherness, diversity was difference and difference was destiny. The "Authorized Version" Americanism, by contrast, was dismissed simply as the ideology of assimilation—a power ploy about dressing alike, talking alike, forgetting where people came from, and forgetting what happened to them on the way.

The confusion bred by anti-Americanism has spread much wider than its authors—for example, in the common diffidence in American leaders about the "vision thing." The wide field of candidates in the 1988 presidential campaign, for instance, could not have been further from Blame America Firsters, but they had difficulties articulating a compelling vision of America. Despite following Ronald Reagan directly, with his renewal of the national identity and his convincing demonstration of the political effectiveness of having such a vision, they displayed a revealing diffidence about national vision. As Edward Crane and David Boaz of the Cato Institute noted, Americans in general are more ideological than the majority of Europeans, yet American intellectuals are much less preoccupied with ideology than European intellectuals. Senator Robert Dole was therefore representative of the candidates' general reluctance about the "vision thing." "I've been advised by people I have a lot of respect for not to play the vision game. Not yet. As soon as you have your vision, the press is going to dismantle it for you. And then, 'Oh, this is the guy's vision.' So, then you say, 'Well, then I'm going to get another vision.'"[18]

The result is that Americanism is poorly articulated by American leaders today and widely ridiculed by critics as a pet liberal hobby of the forties and fifties. It is attacked as if it were undefendable now and fashionable then only for ulterior reasons—to celebrate the new supremacy of the United States, to bolster an artificial national consensus in the face of worldwide Communism, to provide employment for a new intellectual industry, or simply to bolster European-American hegemony, over people of color.

A third challenge to Americanism has been directed at its particular components. For example, the last generation has witnessed an explicit, although limited, repudiation of religion as a key contributor to Americanism. Addressing the American Legion in 1955, President Eisenhower declared that "recognition of the Supreme Being is the first, the most basic, expression of Americanism. Without God, there could be no American form of Government, nor an American way of life."[19] Little exception was taken to this claim at the time. Indeed, from George Washington to Abraham Lincoln, Eisenhower, and beyond, the sense of the sovereignty of God above history has been a recurring theme in American self-understanding, a genuine point of consensus despite obvious dissent.

But if made today outside the context of a prayer breakfast for national leaders, such a statement would be hotly contested by key members of those American elites who are considered to be culture shaping, opinion forming, and agenda setting. (George Bush's seconding of Eisenhower came in the safety of remarks to the National Religious Broadcasters Convention: I "believe more than ever that one cannot be America's president without trust in God.")[20] What was once a minority objection is now established opinion, and certain questions are inevitably raised by this rejection of public reference to religion.

If the Constitution stands for the political dimension of Americanism, free enterprise for its economic dimension, equal opportunity for its social dimension, and idealism and pragmatism for its two characteristic attitudes, is there no longer a place for faiths as the spiritual contribution to Americanism? Can America's diverse religious traditions no longer contribute anything publicly to the faith of the republic? Has some more acceptable source of faith taken their place or is no faith necessary now because Americanism has assumed a religious character of its own and become the unspoken religion of the American people? The beginnings of this problem were recognized by outside observers even in the mid-forties. Denis Brogan wrote that if God was to be replaced in American experience, "what was to replace Him? Could anything replace Him but 'Democracy' made into an object of worship, or business, or success? Nobody knew; nobody knows, yet."[21]

A fourth part of the challenge has been directed at the strength of Americanism even where it is believed in wholeheartedly. Despite the fervor of the new patriotism in the eighties and the widespread signs of a return to "traditional values," Americanism appears not to be as solidly based as it used to be, even among those most hostile to the Blame America Firsters and the extreme multiculturalists.

Until recently, rapid social change had not destroyed the social fabric in America. That is partly because American society is based on an ideological commitment to change as a principle. Even more important, traditional ideals have given America continuity despite change. But what then of Daniel Yankelovich's "new rules," David Riesman's new "egocentrism," and other recent shifts in values? Are they only short-term fluctuations? Or after the successive shocks of the last three decades are we witnessing fundamental, long-term changes, such as over the place of the family—even among champions of the traditional family?

For a start, many of the values championed in the eighties—acquisitive individualism and unlimited growth—were hardly traditional. In addition, many that were genuinely traditional were stronger in rhetoric than in reality. Many conservatives who were seeking to restore traditional values have resorted to blaming "liberalism" and "secular humanism" instead of facing the immensity of their task. U.S. Census data, for example, showed that by 1990 homes with two parents and their own biological children made up only a third of American families. With the marriage rate down, the divorce rate high, fewer divorced people remarrying, and people living longer, the talk has been of nontraditional "post-marital society." Or again, reports demonstrate that for all the hoopla about traditional family values the 1980s were a "terrible decade for children," with the United States falling behind on more and more indicators of children's well-being.[22] But the most poignant contradictions of tradition were within the ranks of traditionalism itself—for example, Terry Dolan, the influential founder of the National Conservative Political Action Committee who simultaneously opposed abortion, supported prayer in schools, advocated gay rights, and died in 1986 of AIDS.

Nowhere were the contradictions over tradition more obvious in the 1980s than in the First Family. There was an underlying rift in the Reagans themselves between their conservative ideology and the counterpull represented by the worlds of film and fashion. In the end, conservative activist Paul Weyrich lamented, conservatives were routed by "the beautiful people."[23] For example, despite the Reagans' rhetorical support for traditional values, Nancy Reagan deleted a passage on abortion from the State of the Union message in 1987, saying, "I don't give a damn about the right-to-lifers."[24] As one long-time friend of Reagan's observed of a situation more like a daytime *Dynasty* than the president's vision of the traditional American family, "He extols religious and family values while rarely going to church or seeing his grandchildren."[25]

Yet as Phillip Hammond points out, modernity has made such contradictions almost inevitable: "Everyone can 'affirm' family values, of course,
but divorces are not likely to decrease, birthrates are not likely to increase,
women's participation in more and more arenas outside of the house is not
likely to be reversed, and children are not likely to find home an adequate
substitute for the technical training required to live in this modern world.
Traditional family values can be affirmed, therefore, but they are doomed to
be elusive in reality."[26] Thus the Reagan era thrived on simultaneously
playing to the widespread desire for order and tradition and pursuing policies
and habits that undermined them.

A fifth part of the challenge to Americanism has been directed at its
necessity and importance. From one side, voices are raised against America's
need for such a set of notions. A young nation, particularly one so free and
diverse, had an initial need for some underlying consensus of beliefs and
ideals, some public philosophy and common morality. But such things, these
voices claim, acted merely as temporary reassurances—boosters to the
national spirit in a day when nationality was neither set nor secure. Today
they can be discarded as superfluous.

This argument has an element of truth, but not where its supporters
think. Americanism is often rejected as a covert form of middle class
dominance that represses ethnic diversity. But the real reason Americanism
may be needed less now is that America has become more uniform rather
than more diverse. As Daniel Bell comments, most of the United States is
now characterized by the cultural sameness of the mass market. A common,
nationwide commitment to consumption and hedonism has helped to iron
out true diversity and marks "a new crisis of consciousness, for we have
become, for the first time, a common people in the hallmarks of culture."[27]

The Canadian philosopher George Grant blamed America's problem of
growing cultural uniformity on the imperialism of technology, for all its
surface offer of diversity. "Some like pizza, some like steaks, some like girls,
some like boys, some like synagogue, some like the mass. But we all do it in
churches, motels, restaurants indistinguishable from the Atlantic to the
Pacific."[28]

From another side, other voices argue that America can no longer afford
a set of notions like Americanism. Indeed, they say, there is an inexorable
logic in the movement from America standing for an idea to American id al
to American interventionism. Far better, they say, to abandon such
dangerous posturing. Utilitarianism, not utopianism, is the only ethic worth
fostering. Interests, not ideals, must be the prime concern. Unilateralism,
not multilateralism, is the best policy. Nationalism, not internationalism,
should be the overriding consideration. The question is no longer, "Are we

worthy of America?" but "Is America working for us?" The idea of Americanism may have shaped American nationhood, but only Americanism as an interest will allow the nation to survive. This strand of thought has long been evident among believers in realpolitik, such as in the speeches and writings of George Kennan. The prime concern of foreign policy, the realists have argued, is the interests of the national society and not its moral impulses.

Put these five kinds of questions together and their force is unmistakable. Whether expressed in scorn or diffidence, American uncertainty about Americanism has consequences. To be sure, the dangers associated with Americanism are real and need to be watched with an eagle eye. The blind spots and injustices must not be repeated. To be sure, there is no such thing, strictly speaking, as an American character. Americanism is an ideal and an aspiration, not a once-for-all accomplishment. To be sure, a sense of consensus and cultural conformity was particularly strong in the forties and fifties, owing as much to liberalism as to tradition. Talk of Americanism did go out of fashion in the sixties when, first, tradition and, later, liberalism came under attack and shared national ideals were disregarded in the scramble to do justice to minorities and alternatives. Yet the complete refusal even to consider Americanism in some circles is an equal, if opposite, error that is itself part of the present crisis. It strikes a blow at one of America's supreme achievements—maintaining its strong identity and keeping the nation whole even while building a multifaith, multiethnic, and multicultural democracy.

Americanism, the American proposition, and the American way of life are concepts that are no strangers to controversy. In one form or another they have become a problem to the rest of the world, as Old World leaders from George III to Pius IX discovered to their cost. But the current situation is different. If there is a crisis at all, it is not primarily because Americanism represents a crisis to anyone else, but because profound changes are now taking place within Americanism itself.

America's problem is not the loss of an identity-defining enemy—ideological enemies like communism can always be replaced by one-person enemies, such as a "madman Qaddafi," a "strongman Noriega," or a "Butcher of Baghdad Saddam Hussein." America's problem is internal. Because of the crisis of cultural authority, America's deeper problem is a weakening of her own identity. America's real defining moment is a crisis of self-definition. Americans must again ask themselves, Who are we? At stake is the vision of America that will become America's vision.

2

Originality or Original Sin?

"This country is a success," claimed an American writer recently about the United States, "in the same way that a Broadway show is a success. People are lined up at the box office for tickets of admission."[1] But such a claim reveals more than a showy pragmatism—America is a success because America works. Its street-savvy bravado conceals a missing note. America is no longer America because of ideals and purpose; there is no longer a rhetoric of high historical purpose. Indeed, the same writer sharpens the point. "The confusion of America's interests with humanity's interests is our original sin."[2]

Should America be regarded as unique or as universal in some way? Is the United States inimitable or somehow the inevitable future for the rest of the world? At stake in such questions is another key dimension of American identity—the traditional American claim to exceptionalism. This is a claim made not only by Americans but by outsiders. In the years of abundance after the Second World War it was virtually elevated into a ruling national doctrine. Exceptionalism is the second part of the American identity to be called into question by the crisis of cultural authority. In my opinion, it is less important than Americanism. Because of its exaggerations and distortions, America may well be better off without it. But because of its previous significance and strength, there is no question that without it America will be different.

God's Own Cause

Exceptionalism is the core theme of America's sense of high historical purpose; its driving notion of "American destiny" has always complemented the more open and undecided notion of the "American experiment." The claim that America has somehow been set apart from other nations with a European origin because the openness of its ideals is its strongest modern expression. Its economic possibilities have given it immunity from the threat of class divisions, and therefore from the growth of political movements hostile to the prevailing order. America's abundance, said a German visitor in 1906, makes her so exceptional that "all socialist utopias have come to grief on roast beef and apple pie."[3] " 'Born free,' " as Daniel Bell expressed the view, "America would, in the trials of history, get off 'scot-free.' "[4] Exceptionalism is faith in history's free lunch.

This way of putting the claim is only a strong, recent, and economic version of a persistent notion that has taken many forms and goes back prior to the identity of the United States itself. So vast and rich a continent, the notion runs, unvisited for centuries and undeveloped by anyone, God must have kept in reserve—an exceptional land kept under wraps for exceptional people. "Everything," exclaimed Alexis de Tocqueville, "is extraordinary in America."[5]

The origins of the notion are often traced to the English Puritans, who saw their revolution as "God's own Cause" and their Commonwealth (in Andrew Marvell's later words) as "the darling of heaven."[6] Following this lead and despite the failure of "God's Cause" in the mother country, the New England Puritans interpreted their pilgrimage in directly biblical terms. They went from the Egypt of England to the Canaan of New England and they spoke of themselves, in Increase Mather's term, as "our Israel." They were "the Lord's first born," entrusted with a "pious errand into the wilderness."[7] Thus with America, destiny even preceded discovery.

To the early Puritans, the great American historian Perry Miller stated in 1952, this errand was not a mere scouting expedition. "It was an essential maneuver in the drama of Christendom. The Bay Company was not a battered remnant of suffering Separatists thrown up on a rocky shore; it was an organized task force of Christians, executing a flank attack on the corruptions of Christendom."[8]

Perry Miller was a hard-headed agnostic. Yet he had long been disgusted with liberal impotence in the face of fascism in the thirties, and he had just returned from a year-long experience of deep and pervasive anti-Americanism in postwar Europe when he first put these words in a lecture at Brown University. He later titled his memoir of the year, "What Drove Me

Crazy in Europe." So perhaps this experience sharpened his formulation of why the Puritans left England. Perhaps the full-blooded Puritan purposeful-ness is clearer in their reflections in the 1640s rather than their statements when they first sailed in 1630. But the essential point is undeniable. Fired in the white-hot furnace of the Puritan awakening, a sense of chosenness and destiny has remained at the core of the American character ever since.

Later on, special features of American geography and history contributed to this sense generously. America possessed vast, cheap land, insulating oceans, a small population, and the absence of any feudal period or aristocratic class. Each of these factors lent weight to the momentum of the myth, so that it became mercenary as well as messianic, with an explicitly spiritual gloss. World history was culminating in America. The history of America was the story of "the Hand of God in history." Predestined emigration, which had been the substitute for one revolution in the Old World, became the seedbed for another in the New.

Puritan clergy may have been the first to propagate the idea of an "American Israel." But it was Thomas Jefferson, leading deist and champion of the Enlightenment, who proposed in 1785 that the seal of the new nation should represent the children of Israel led by a pillar of light. Even Thomas Paine, who ridiculed traditional Christian beliefs and has been the patron saint of humanists and free thinkers ever since, wrote that God Almighty was "visibly on our side."[9]

The actual term *manifest destiny* was first used in 1845 by John L. O'Sullivan, editor of *Democratic Review*. He argued fittingly for the reception of Texas into the Union and justified the policy as "the fulfillment of our manifest destiny to overspread the continent allotted by Providence for the free development of our yearly multiplying millions."[10] But the sense of destiny had already been coursing in the young nation's veins for decades. John Adams wrote in his diary in 1765, "I always consider the settlement of America with reverence and wonder, as the opening of a grand scene and design in Providence for the illumination of the ignorant, and the emancipation of the slavish part of mankind all over the earth."[11]

Herman Melville gave classic expression to this potent sense of excep-tionalism in *White-Jacket* in 1849:

> We Americans are the peculiar, chosen people—the Israel of our time; we bear the ark of the liberties of the world. God has predestined, mankind expects, great things from our race; and great things we feel in our souls. The rest of the nations must soon be in our rear. We are pioneers of the world; the advance-guard, sent on through the wilderness of untried things, to break a new path in the New World that is ours.[12]

Exceptionalism may have raced differently in the hearts of discoverers, pioneers, missionaries, traders, political leaders, and generals, but it has always throbbed powerfully. It was the source of America's purpose and the secret of its promise. It transformed American tasks into missions, American opinions into messages, and American struggles into crusades. Leading to a continental messianism at first, it expanded to a global messianism by the time of the Spanish-American War.

At the turn of the century, Senator Albert J. Beveridge announced that the annexation of the Philippines was part of God's plan for America. "He has marked the American people as His chosen Nation to finally lead in the regeneration of the world. This is the divine mission of America, and it holds for us all the profit, all the glory, all the happiness possible to man. We are trustees of the world's progress, guardians of its righteous peace."[13]

But such brazen messianic nationalism must not be stretched to illustrate too much, for present discussion of exceptionalism falls easily into two fallacies. One fallacy is to think that Manifest Destiny grew directly out of the Puritan sense of calling and Christian millennialism. On the contrary, Christian millennialism and American nationalism were mostly distinct until the 1890s and the Spanish-American War, because the earliest millennialism was linked to Christian internationalism, not Christian nationalism. God's providential purpose was for all nations, including the United States. It was not for the United States alone. To fuse millennialism and nationalism at an earlier period than it happened can become a form of false hindsight that obscures the real roots of nationalism and its contribution to later problems, such as Vietnam.

The other fallacy is to think that this sense of exceptionalism was limited to conservatives, chauvinists, Yankees, and WASPs or that it has been issued only in messianic nationalism. Like the Puritans from whom it came, it has had its darker mood too—one that exuded self-consciousness rather than chosenness, nervousness rather than nationalism, apocalypticism rather than messianism. And in its more positive mood it has supported arguments for isolationism as well as globalism, American universality as well as American uniqueness, anti-imperialism as well as imperialism. As recently as the fifties, its fanfares were played proudly in a liberal key.

"America," wrote Hugh Miller in 1948, "was not created to be supreme among the 'great powers.' It was created to inaugurate the transition of human society to just government. It is a missionary institution propagating a gospel to all men."[14] Not much is more characteristic of Americans than their traditional sense of universal moral mission.

Exceptionalism has gone through a myriad of mutations. Many differences and a wide span of years lie between the various strands—theological, geographical, historical, and economic—that compose the overall claim. But today it appears that a claim that has always been close to the heart of the American sense of identity and purpose no longer carries conviction for the nation as a whole.

The sense of destiny still flourishes serenely, as in the oratory of President Reagan and the hearts of most Americans he addressed. But in other quarters it is the object of open doubt and relentless attack, and many observers have pronounced it in irreversible decline. "Today," Daniel Bell concludes, "the belief in American exceptionalism has vanished with the end of empire, the weakening of power, the loss of faith in the nation's future. . . . There is no longer a Manifest Destiny or mission. We have not been immune to the corruption of power. We have not been the exception."[15]

Questions from Three Directions

If Americanism in one word is *democracy*, then exceptionalism in a word is *destiny*. And it is precisely the historical importance of Americans' sense of destiny that gives weight to important questions from three directions. The first type of question concerns the character and foundation of the claim to exceptionalism. Theologically speaking, the reasoning behind the identification of Israel and the American nation is now generally acknowledged to be faulty even by Christians. But if this strong version of exceptionalism is no longer tenable, many of the derivative versions that rely on historical, geographical, or economic factors have also lost their foundations. Quite simply, the United States is no longer exceptional in these areas and the distinctiveness it once had has lost its significance today.

Of course, the United States need not be equated with Old Testament Israel to be viewed within God's purposes. But whether because of deaf ears or weak voices, even this more moderate claim is rarely heard in public today. And in relation to almost all the major trends, the United States is experiencing the same forces as the rest of the modern world. American exceptionalism, it is said, is all a matter of the past.

So can the claim still be advanced and, if it can, which of the previous grounds for asserting it still stand? Or has it been called into question by a succession of events in recent decades and, if so, what does the loss of destiny mean for the United States in its late-imperial hour? And looking back, how much did the claim rest on principles and ideals in the first place (a "city upon a hill")? Or was that often merely a genteel illusion, fostered by the privileged American conditions of natural abundance and prosperity (a city upon cornfields and oil wells), but no more true than the myth of Washington's cherry tree or the fictions surrounding the Liberty Bell? In short, has America's sense of exceptionalism owed more to God or the accidents of geography? And has it recently amounted to a form of secularized puritanism, a puritanism shorn of its sense of transcendence, its source of strength?

The second type of question concerns the consequences of the claim to exceptionalism, or the consequences of its collapse and attempted reassertion. On the one hand, if the claim is still advanced is it beneficial today or does it lead inevitably to either an expansive self-esteem that is crippling or a sense of immunity that is foolish? Kevin Phillips speaks for many Americans who believe the latter when he says flatly, "The dubious doctrine of 'American exceptionalism'—based on the idea that this country is uniquely blessed, or that God takes special care of babies, drunks, and the United States of America—is a misconception that may soon head us to our undoing."[16] Or as Clayton Fritchey, former press secretary to President Truman, said to me at a private dinner in Washington in January 1985, "Self-righteousness and hypocrisy are the abiding curse of the United States."

This dark theme is nothing new in American experience. Tracing it from radical abolitionist William Lloyd Garrison through Henry David Thoreau and Herman Melville to David Starr Jordan, president of Stanford, sociologist Robert Bellah concludes, "A conception of chosenness that slips away from the controlling obligations of the covenant is a signpost to hell."[17]

In a carefully stated form, disquiet over exceptionalism is currently a powerful theme in the so-called "solvency school"—those foreign policy specialists whose "realism" easily shades over into anti-interventionism and then isolationism. Accordingly they opposed the Reagan Doctrine and the neoconservative concept of global democracy and warned of the danger of America's domestic economy being undermined by imperial ambitions born of exceptionalism. Senator William Fulbright's pilgrimage from being a champion of the American Century in World War II to being a foe of American overextension in Vietnam precedes and illustrates Paul Kennedy's more scholarly analysis of imperial overstretch today.

On the other hand, another question arises: What will the abandonment of the former sense of national purpose mean to Americans and to American involvement in the world? Why, for much of the time since Vietnam, has there been such a marked hesitancy on all sides over articulating a purposeful international vision? Or, when the internationalist rhetoric remained strong—as over the championing of universal human rights in the 1970s—why has the professed multilateralism often led to inaction as much as action, and to failure (as in Iran and Nicaragua) as much as success? Why, after all the more recent rhetoric of a New World Order after the Gulf War, are American leaders more respected for wheeling and dealing than for strategic policy and ideals? How are Americans to take a proper pride in the distinctive features of their culture and yet avoid the go-at-it-alone unilateralism or the democratic crusading that has so often accompanied the claim to exceptionalism in the past?

In 1986, following the convergence of the restored sense of American power and the somewhat fortuitous American contribution to the overthrow of President Marcos in the Philippines and President Duvalier in Haiti, the debate about American ideals and American interests came to the boil again even before the European revolution in 1989. A new spirit of interventionism was abroad in America and the language of crusading for democracy could be heard among both liberals and conservatives. "Democracy," they said, "is more important to us than naval bases." Boosted further by the events of 1989, it came to a crescendo in a series of urgent calls that, when the Cold War ended, the central purpose of American foreign policy should be to help democracy spread around the world.

What was then dubbed the new "democracy gang" included Democrats as well as Republicans: organizers, columnists, scholars, and theologians as well as politicians. But before the Iraqi invasion of Kuwait in 1990, it found little response in presidential leadership and it was ringed at once by powerful intellectual and political forces, ranging from "America Firsters," such as columnist Patrick Buchanan, to libertarians, liberals, and left-wingers. This "Mission Democracy thing," Buchanan charged, is "messianic globaloney."[18] Talk of a new *pax americana* is the work of "high priests of policy monotheism."[19]

Other more scholarly conservatives also counseled caution against the renewal of exceptionalism. Robert W. Tucker of Johns Hopkins University warned that "the idea of leading a democratic crusade around the world was quite instrumental in leading us to Vietnam."[20] Jeane Kirkpatrick pointed specifically to the mythic element of historic exceptionalism: "We've always been attracted to the idea of not only making the world safe for democracy, but also making the world a democratic Garden of Eden . . . I think it's just not practical as an operational goal."[21] Henry Kissinger wrote of his "misgivings about the prevailing self-righteousness" and cautioned against the "false dreams" of George Bush's New World Order.[22]

The loss of the old, assured sense of exceptionalism was bound to be specially acute for the United States because of the tension between its global power and its anti-imperialistic ideals. At least empires had no problems justifying the defense of their own interests, just as believers in American exceptionalism had no problems justifying their respective missions. But now that the United States has helped bring down old and new empires while boasting that it is not an empire, it stands largely alone in facing a newly awakened world, without the certainty of its former sense of purpose. So how does America define its interests in the world? How, after Vietnam, does it justify its interventions to the rest of the world and to itself? How, after the Gulf War, does it put content into the rallying cry of the New World Order? Was Charles de Gaulle correct that the United States had "yielded in her turn to that taste for intervention in which the instinct for domination cloaked itself"?[23]

English journalist Henry Fairlie recalled that Dean Acheson stung the British in the fifties when he remarked that "Britain has lost an empire, and has not yet found a role." But the words, Fairlie noted, now apply equally well to the United States. "America has solitarily assumed the burdens of empire when neither the times in which we live nor its own political tradition will allow it to use the arguments of empire; and neither its politicians nor its intellectuals have gone nearly deep enough in trying to find alternative arguments for the proper uses of power."[24]

French theorist Raymond Aron agreed. "In the twentieth century," he observed, "the strength of a great power is diminished if it ceases to serve an idea."[25] The United States was once resolutely anti-imperialist, in line with its own revolution and the right of peoples to self-determination. But once Western empires disappeared, the United States became only "negatively ideological," in that it was only opposed to regimes that were presently or potentially Communist. As many in the rest of the world see it, all that America is for is all that America is against.

This realization was behind the expectancy of many in the early nineties as they waited for strong American leadership at the end of the Cold War and the Gulf War. What was the American vision and what were the American ordering principles of the new *pax moderna?* Why did the United States commit itself so generously to Cold War interventions over a generation, yet refuse to spare more than government small-change to ease countries across the bumpy transition from communism to democratic capitalism? How could America be so commanding in the execution of Operation Desert Storm yet so uncertain over the articulation of the New World Order? If a genuine American renaissance will occur in the 1990s, at the very least it must include a renewed sense of national identity, purpose, and goals—as stated, led, and carried forward by the president himself. There is, as Richard Darman urges, an underlying seriousness to "the importance of being firstest."[26]

The same realization was behind Henry Luce's editorial about the American Century in 1941. Other nations can survive simply because they have endured so long, he wrote. "But this nation conceived in adventure and dedicated to the progress of man—this nation cannot truly endure unless there courses strongly through its veins from Maine to California the blood of purposes and enterprise and high resolve."[27]

Such questions raise a third and even deeper issue about exceptionalism. Could America have become what it is without its original sense of spiritual destiny? And without it, or what is left of it, can America remain what it has become? This concern is stronger than it may appear. Not only has the American sense of purpose been powerful, but its loss would be powerfully missed. Like the companion themes of Americanism, exceptionalism is essentially an idea and therefore can never be successfully replaced merely by an interest, a program, or a policy.

Few European observers or would-be imitators from around the world appreciate that this spiritual sense of destiny was a central secret of America's success. As Luigi Barzini argues, the American secret did not lie in technology, know-how, the work ethic, the urge to succeed, or just plain greed. "It was a spiritual wind that drove the Americans irresistibly ahead from the beginning. What was behind their compulsion to improve a man's lot was an all-pervading religious sense of duty, the submission to a God-given imperative, to a God-given code of personal behavior, the willing acceptance of all the necessary sacrifices, including death in battle. Few foreigners understand this, even today."[28]

Do all Americans show a better understanding? Or is the "vision thing" too easily dismissed? In the discussion of exceptionalism, far more is at stake than the freedom or otherwise of American life-chances and the standards of American living. Evidence in recent years, such as the Los Angeles Olympics, the Statue of Liberty centennial, the victory celebrations after Operation Desert Storm, or any Super Bowl television extravaganza, is a passionate confirmation of what has been seen before: American identity, American distinctiveness, and American mission have been welded together for so long that America's celebration and America's self-justification are one. The Americans' sense of well-being as a "people of plenty" is therefore not only a matter of affluence and mobility, but of purpose. It is also a key factor in their optimism, their openness to change, their sense of trust in their system as well as their attitude to people of other countries.

In an article questioning the consequences of exceptionalism in 1901, Mark Twain raised the question, "Shall we go on conferring our Civilization upon the peoples that sit in darkness, or shall we give those poor things a rest?" The people who sit in darkness, he wrote, had "begun to show alarm."[29] Today, when it has become physically dangerous to be an American abroad and when showing alarm has escalated to taking up arms in parts of the world, foreigners are only the most obvious of those who take exception to American exceptionalism. Exceptionalism to American ears may carry overtones of anti-imperialism, but to many foreigners it has long smacked of expansionism. What imperialism did for more crowded states, continental and then global expansion did for America. But this suspicion has now entered the United States itself. Because of the crisis of cultural authority, the very character of the claim, and not only its consequences, has been called into question in the hearts and minds of many Americans.

Rejoining Their Roots?

When combined, these two parts of the national identity crisis lead on to a third. If the grounds for the American claim to exceptionalism have been weakened, and if there has been a significant erosion of certain aspects of traditional Americanism, are we witnessing what is in effect a new stage of "Europeanization" or, to be more accurate, the collapse of the "non-Europeanness" of America? Czeslaw Milosz, for example, writes as a Polish émigré living in California, "America was first Europeanized technologically and surpassed Europe at once. Now America is being Europeanized again."[30]

Why does this matter? Back in 1922, H. L. Mencken complained of an earlier Europeanizing trend. Americans, he said, were "the illegitimate children of the English."[31] What would become of the American scholar if he could not borrow wholesale from the European scholar? Who would show American politicians the dotted lines for their signatures if it were not for British Foreign Secretaries and Prime Ministers like the Balfours and the Lloyd-Georges? Even the office of the secretary of state, he jibed, was "little more than the antechamber of the British Foreign Office."[32]

Mencken was exaggerating, of course. Besides, his critique of mobocracy was itself based on Nietzsche's essentially European philosophy. And anyway, since then the shoe has truly shifted to the other foot. Today most people would think more naturally of the "Americanization" of Europe (a word first used in the 1830s as a term of abuse). If by this they mean the American penetration of Europe through such things as blue jeans, T-shirts, rock music, hamburger chains, television soap operas, and the annual invasions of summer tourists, not to speak of the impact of American jargon, interest rates, and the nuclear shield, then the trend is undeniable.

As long as the United States continues to be the world's "lead society," modernization is bound to be essentially Americanization or "Coca-Colanization." America will remain the world's principal source of popular culture and the badges of cultural serfdom will be worn universally. There are signs that even America's last empire—dominance over international mass culture—is on the wane ("Worldbeat," for example, is an internationalist pop music inspired by neither New York, Los Angeles, or Nashville). But on the whole the trends of the recent past still prevail. "The whole of Europe, including France," Raymond Aron acknowledged in 1959, "is indeed in the process of becoming Americanized."[33] Currently, the trend is epitomized by Europe's first Disneyland, the $4 billion theme park opened near Paris in 1992 that was attacked by critics as France's "cultural Chernobyl."

The "Europeanization" of America, however, refers to something else. Obviously, for most Americans, for most of their history, it is a prosaic fact that Europe is the fountainhead of their culture and the birthplace of their ancestors. Yet despite this fact and long before the recent hostility toward "Eurocentrism," most Americans have usually assumed that Europe and America were fundamentally separated. Though two branches from a common stock, Europe and America were set apart by differences that were finally extreme, if elusive. The society of the New World, for example, displayed neither the high conservatism of European classes who survived from the world before 1789 nor the deep radicalism of the waves of subversion set in motion after then.

"Non-Europeanness" in this sense has been an important counterpoint to Americanism in ways that have gone beyond genuine differences. Where Americanism was often vague, non-Europeanness could be precise and even crude because it was defined only negatively. Europeanness was the blank sheet on which everything inadmissible and undesirable could be posted and attacked (rather as anti-Americanism is used in the Third World today). The easily invoked polarity thus helped in various ways to aid the process of national defining. It not only pointed to real distinctions, but provided a foil for defining national character, a stick with which to attack national shortcomings, and a simple two-term category to identify the enemy. "Europe" and "America" were states of mind as much as places on a map.

For all the anti-Eurocentrism, the problem nowadays is that the real differences have lessened and the mythical ones have either outgrown their usefulness or become dangerous. Thus even if America was different and really did escape the European extremes through the balance of its unique consensus—so that its progressivism was rarely revolutionary and its moralism never hidebound or archaic—there are signs that the collapse of America's traditional consensus means that the differences between the two continents are declining, just as points of similarity are growing.

In 1830, Friedrich Hegel predicted that the United States would be comparable to Europe when its wide open territories were filled, class structures had emerged, and scarcity had raised the possibility of conflict over resources. The last generation has met these requirements handily. Indeed, the twentieth century as a whole seems to have called into question the old antithesis. Two world wars and a severe depression were more of a shared experience for *Homo Americanus* and *Homo Europaenus.* More recent evidence for this growing convergence might include the increasing secularity of parts of American life, the increasingly ideological character of American politics, similar demographic trends, the implicit imperialism of America's world role, and the impact of European ideas on the United States that are no longer filtered automatically by fundamental American beliefs. (The earlier impress of Nietzsche is one example; the more recent influence of Jacques Derrida on the theory of interpretation is another.) America, it has been said, is now the same as Europe only more so.

"Europeanization," in the sense of the collapse of America's "non-Europeanness," obviously does not need to be a contradiction of the so-called "Asianization" of America. ("As we celebrate the country's 212th birthday," wrote Joel Kotkin and Yoriko Kishimoto in 1986, "it is time we Americans finally declare our independence from Europe and end our two-century old fixation with western civilization.")[34] But far more is meant than can be found at the merely trivial level—such as Europe's leading the fashions in luxury clothes, cars, and chocolate. At the more serious level, observers of the "Europeanization" of America point above all to the sense of maturing and secularity in modern America. For all the rhetoric about the New World, the people on the cutting edge of history, the nation with its face to the future, America's eternal youth, and so on, what is striking in America today is the aging of both of its population and its institutions and the general conservatism of its far from young and revolutionary stance in the world.

At many points the United States now stands in relation to the rest of the world as Europe once did to America—to the poor, privileged; to the moralistic, decadent; to the revolutionary, repressive; and to the newly emerging, settled and conservative. More stunning still, the European revolution of 1989 created a revolution in American expectations. After three centuries of Europeans traveling to America and of Americans traveling ever westward, the direction changed. As David Broder reported on his return from the fastest-moving story in the world, "Looking eastward for change, or turning toward Europe to see the future, is a reversal of American history."[35]

All this sense of aging is relative, of course, and it is not completely new. More than a century ago Herman Melville expressed his fears about the "Dark Ages of Democracy" that were to come. When the New World suddenly shared "old age's pains" and felt "the arrest of hope's advance," then the lament would go around the world, "No New World to mankind remains."[36] "America," wrote Gertrude Stein, "having begun the creation of the twentieth century . . . is now the oldest country in the world."[37] Of the world's major countries, Henry Steele Commager has written, the United States is "the oldest republic, the oldest democracy, the oldest federal system; it has the oldest written constitution and boasts the oldest of genuine political parties."[38]

This fact raises important questions. If the trend toward Europeanization is occurring, even in part, is it to be deplored as a crisis or welcomed as an important coming of age? Where were the differences real and where were they mythical? Has the simple-minded antithesis disappeared or has the negative definition simply shifted from non-European to non-Communist? What will the trend mean for America's understanding of itself, and for its dealings with the rest of the world? Was America ever really new or was she merely young and is she now growing old? Will the United States play a role, in regard to Europe, similar to that of Rome in regard to Greece?

No Trivial Matter

Each of these three issues—Americanism, exceptionalism, and Europeanization—carries a subtlety and power that no brief statement can pretend to convey. Take the last one, for example. For most Americans throughout most of their history, to be American was to be ex-European. Europe has been the central source of their civilization—the cherished log cabin was an import from Sweden, "Hail to the Chief" was an old Scots' boating song before it graced presidential appearances, and baseball was the development of an English export. Yet in many ways the chief meaning of America has been liberation from Europe and a repudiation of the past. The Promised Land of the New World provided a refuge from the tyranny, luxury, decadence, and irreligion of the Egyptian fleshpots of the Old.

Equally, for an important minority of Americans this Europe-America antithesis was reversed. The chief meaning of Europe has been liberation from America and a repudiation of the future. Thus in recurring waves after 1914, Old World cities, such as Paris, Florence, and Oxford, provided a refuge from the religion, conformity, mediocrity, and philistinism of the New, whether for writers and artists in the twenties, draft resisters in the sixties, or academics on sabbatical in any period. Either in body or in spirit, the American artist was destined to be an exile.

Plainly, then, it is no light thing to raise the question of the Europeanization of America. If the crisis of Americanism goes down to the core theme of American democracy and the crisis of exceptionalism to that of American destiny, then the question of Europeanization bears down on the notion of America as a radical new departure in history. Thus if traditional contrasts between Europe and America are becoming obsolete today, and America is less a "new order for the ages" than imagined (leaving that burden unshouldered, with the "new order" of communism having proved even less convincing), then Americans are confronted with a tension between the rhetoric about their past and the realities and responsibilities of their present. Myths and rhetoric, at least, may have to change. So too must styles of involvement.

Not so distant illusions of invincible global superiority are as out of the question now as the innocence of an earlier isolation. But what is the course to be steered between isolationism and globalism? How should national interests and national ideals be balanced? The United States is no longer the American Alexander imposing its will on all who come, but neither can the world afford an American Achilles sulking in his tent after Vietnam and Iran. Are we likely, in contrast to both, to see an American Archimedes, playing balancer to the shifting balances of power? What should the balancer's vision be? Are American ideas and ideals no longer for export or even a part of the balancer's calculations?

Just as Vietnam has been the rudest single shock to American self-understanding, so foreign relations can be relied on to hold up a permanent mirror of the world's opinion of America. But much more than national vanity or credibility is at stake. Is it now claimed, for example, that America needs no ideals and that her secret is success? Then the need to sustain success becomes an impossible national burden just when the way to define success is lost. Without an ideal by which to judge success, America would find her pursuit of success as soulless, wearisome, and repelling as many outside observers already fear it is.

One thing is sure. There can be no simple going back to the condition of earlier days. Neither a sense of tradition nor transcendence can be restored in five minutes. So the combined challenge of these questions is profound. If the burden of modernity means that the United States is a nation by intention and by ideas, then the process of defining and redefining America is ceaseless and inescapable. American identity, American distinctiveness, and American purpose have assumed different accents in different periods, but have always spoken with the same basic voice. Will that remain true?

A nation that discovered its distinctiveness in the process of a search for nationality is now being challenged to face a new set of questions. In essence the inquiry represents a spur to American self-understanding that could be as invaluable as it is inescapable. The American Century is in the midst of a most decisive decade—for America.

Instead of standing aside to allow America to put her unchallenged stamp on history, the American Century has closed in to put a challenging stamp on America. The warning given by John Courtney Murray in 1960 is even more appropriate after the events of the last twenty-five years. "The complete loss of one's identity is, with all propriety of theological definition, hell. In diminished forms it is insanity. And it would not be well for the American giant to go lumbering about the world today, lost and mad."[39]

3

The Black Holes of Modernity

"You might as well try to write the history of a grand ball as of a battle." The Duke of Wellington's judgment on military history applies even more to the problems of unraveling America's crisis of cultural authority simply and accurately. The superlabyrinth of modernity is so vast and complex that a full account of its interconnections is beyond any single mind, let alone the scope of a single book.

Yet the acknowledgment of such complexities and of the need for such care should not lead to paralysis. For, of all the overall consequences of modernity, one is central to both modernity and the crisis of cultural authority—the development Max Weber called "disenchantment," or C. S. Lewis "re-enchantment." It has been variously described as secularization or the loss of the traditional religious gravity and center in modern society. "The world has never been more worldly," Nietzsche wrote. "What characterizes modernity, I think," Philip Rieff writes, "is just this idea that men need not submit to any power—higher or lower—other than their own."[1]

The force of this disenchantment was powerfully active in Europe's crisis of cultural authority in the nineteenth century. It is currently wreaking its devastation on the American sense of transcendence and tradition through its impact in three particular domains—intellectual, social, and economic. The outcome is not the disappearance of American faiths but rather the devaluation of their cultural authority and the cultural disorientation that follows. Each of these three developments therefore becomes a factor in the crisis of cultural authority with something of the effect of an eclipse of the sun, or—more aptly still—of a black hole. At a certain point, the

65

dissolution of faith's authority and the disappearance of any positive force for truth and goodness turns into a high-density, negative, and devouring force for evil—in short, nihilism.

The Intellectual Declaration of Independence

The first of the black holes grows out of an intellectual development and concerns the current consequences of a decisive shift in America's cultural life that has been called "the American intellectual revolution."[2] The Jewish-Christian picture of a lawgiving God ordering the world has been ousted from its role as one of the generally accepted organizing assumptions of intellectual life. A constellation of diverse movements has moved into its place, mainly linked together by their common secular or naturalistic assumptions. As these in turn have passed through the successive transformations of romanticism, modernism, and postmodernism, some of them have become radically destructive of the intellectual justifications on which the American republic is founded.

To educated Americans, such a statement about the ousting of the biblical worldview and the arrival of postmodernism is old hat. But the story is worth repeating because many who know it well have overlooked its consequences, whereas others who know the consequences have overlooked the story. Also, that it needs to be said carefully and said now is a pointer to a distinctive feature of American history. What in most European countries occurred some time ago and is now virtually taken for granted even among European religious believers has been completed in the United States comparatively recently and is still a storm center of controversy. Current conservative outcries against relativism and secular humanism have been criticized as simplistic, exaggerated, and myopic. But at least they are a response to the distinctiveness of American history, and not a rationalization of America's past on the basis of Europe's. They serve as an important jolt on the seismograph that registers subterranean shifts in the social order.

Needless to say, the antecedents of this intellectual and cultural revolution lie largely outside America (in European thought), and their points of entry into American culture are largely outside the brief period chosen for our sketch. At Cambridge in 1837, for example, Ralph Waldo Emerson delivered his famous oration, "The American Scholar," which was later hailed by Oliver Wendell Holmes as the intellectual declaration of independence of the American people. Yet two periods have been especially decisive in this intellectual revolution, and the second—the 1960s—is central to our period.

The first was the period between 1912 and 1917 when the so-called "rebellion of the intellectuals" took place. Speeded, but not started, by World War I, the cultural revolt spread spontaneously and simultaneously in such fields as philosophy, psychology, art, literature, and politics, feting such prophets as Henri-Louis Bergson, Sigmund Freud, and H. G. Wells. ("Won't they get a surprise," Freud exclaimed to Carl Gustav Jung on first sighting the New York skyline in 1909, "when they hear what we have to say to them!")[3] Until then traditional culture had been one of the triple pillars of the late Victorian consensus, along with a sense of the certainty of moral values and a sturdy belief in human progress. As the former broke away, the strength of the other two was undermined for good and a period of innocence was brought to an end.

No revolutionary movement ever has an official launching, but in this case the critical year was 1913. Among other things, J. B. Watson announced behaviorism, T. S. Eliot discovered French symbolist poetry, Igor Stravinsky's "Rite of Spring" was first performed, Greenwich Village radicalism was in its heyday, the income tax amendment was passed, and Walter Lippmann published his progressivist *A Preface to Politics* ("we live in a revolutionary period and nothing is so important as to be aware of it").[4] But the year's most celebrated event was in February at the Sixty-ninth Regiment Armory in New York. Americans were dramatically introduced to European cubism and expressionism and the ferment of thinking that lay behind the dazzling colors. Reactions were violent but the show was a wild success. The Armory Show, as Mabel Dodge told Gertrude Stein, was the most important event in America since 1776.

From such beginnings the rebellion burst like a firecracker into the decade of the twenties, setting off a series of explosions such as jazz, ragtime, evolution, prohibition, movies, short skirts, and the Ku Klux Klan. The wisdom of the elders and what George Santayana called "the genteel tradition" was under assault and his generation was "in full career toward disintegration."[5] "The old order changeth," said Woodrow Wilson.[6] "The rock of ages," wrote Walter Lippmann, "has been blasted for us."[7] The past, according to Carl Sandburg, was "a bucket of ashes."[8]

The parallels between the period 1912–17 and the 1960s are instructive. Each followed a period of benign complacency, each shows the result of the combined impact of technological revolution and war, each displays a similar double-effect on the high-brow and the more popular culture, each created a fundamentalist reaction in the wake of the powerful clash of values, and each witnessed greatly exaggerated claims about a dramatic renaissance. In the earlier period, for example, Virginia Woolf made her celebrated pronouncement, "In or about December 1910, human character changed" (the Post-Impressionist exhibit had been earlier in Europe), while Ezra Pound predicted rashly that the American *risorgimento* would "make the Italian Renaissance look like a tempest in a teapot."[9] Similarly, Timothy Leary claimed extravagantly in the sixties that, because of LSD, "human beings born after the year 1943 belong to a different species from their progenitors."[10]

But more important than their parallels is their overall relationship. If 1912–17 is the early revolutionary period, the 1960s is its completion. After the changes initiated between 1912 and 1917, traditional Western Christian truths may have been routed from the universities and among the intellectual elite of America (as witnessed in the flow of ministerial candidates to other vocations); Protestantism may have lost its culture-shaping power. But— from the Protestants' point of view—the damage was largely limited, quarantined within numerically small pockets of American culture, however culturally powerful.

After the sixties, however, even this meager comfort had gone. Due to the expansion of education (especially following the GI Bill in 1944), the wider dissemination of new ideas through the mass media, and the rising postwar status of academics as new mandarins of the mind, the intellectual revolution burst its dams and flooded into almost every sector of American life. What had begun in the nineteenth century with Europe's greatest minds grappling with the challenges of modernity in its early stages came to its climax in the 1960s as American thinkers grappled with both modernity and the heirs of the nineteenth-century thought simultaneously. The deepest concern among more perceptive religious believers was the extent of its inroads into the religious community itself. Those crying relativism and secular humanism were not only fifty years too late, but they showed telltale signs of being touched by the very revolution they claimed to attack.

In the twenties and thirties, Protestantism's faltering grip was illustrated dramatically in a series of setbacks and fiascoes, such as the Scopes trial, the repeal of Prohibition, the unfrocking of J. Greshem Machen, the decline of Sabbath-keeping, and the replacement of the Protestant ethic by instant credit and mass consumption. Protestantism, taunted H. L. Mencken, "is down with a wasting disease."[11] The period of the twenties, said Robert Handy, was the church's "second disestablishment"[12] and the spiritual depression started even before the crash of 1929. But at least these reversals appeared mainly to be outside the world of the local churches. When the sixties and seventies were over, the primary evidence for the demise of the Christian faith as a culture-shaping power in America was the state of the churches themselves.

The crisis of cultural authority in the churches has been obvious, but has the "liberation" the two periods ushered in created problems for the nation too? George Santayana thought so after the first period. In his analysis of "The Intellectual Temper of the Age" in 1913 he saw that the characteristic civilization of Christendom had not disappeared, yet another civilization was beginning to take its place. But in the eruption of irrationalism in art, philosophy, religion, and literature, sheer vitality was being mistaken for lasting ideals and the seeds of anarchy were being sown in the world. In the long run these developments would lead not to the liberation of individuals but to the subjection of the individual to the majority.

With the virtual completion of the intellectual revolution in the sixties that began half a century earlier, Santayana's judgment ties in with questions raised freshly in our own time. Far more than Christian or Jewish pride is at stake in the dethroning of the biblical worldview in intellectual circles. For this event has wider cultural significance for America: It signifies the drying up of America's oldest, strongest source of individual and cultural meaning; it widens an enormous chasm between America's generally secular intellectual elite and the overwhelming majority of Americans who still understand and conduct their lives in terms of religious beliefs; it puts an impossible weight on Enlightenment liberalism when this faith in turn is running dry; and it clears the way for new sources of ideas that are openly at odds with those from which the American republic had traditionally gained its intellectual justifications.

Many have pointed out that, after the collapse of the Christian and Jewish worldviews, Enlightenment liberalism has not managed to maintain its recently won dominance. Indeed, the rise of "postmodernism" marks the decisive repudiation of the Enlightenment project as a whole. In the humanities departments of leading American universities many of the best minds have long been committed to non-liberal ideologies, such as relativistic indifferentism, humanistic Marxism, structuralism, critical legal studies, radical postmodernism, deconstructionism, radical feminism, Afrocentrism, and their successor movements.

Some people do not take these developments seriously. Philosopher Richard Rorty's nihilism, for example, is excused with the quip that "cheerful nihilism" is only a matter of "the leisure of the theory class." But to anyone who investigates the current academic standing of reason, truth, knowledge, human individuality, and even the meaning of meaning itself, the thought is hard to avoid: If this is not a crisis, it is certainly not an intellectual position on which to sustain a great civilization or even a satisfactory university.

Intellectual developments are beginning to provide a spawning ground for a new American nihilism, for which relativism is often a current synonym, "life-style" a current euphemism, and the notion of "privileged insight" a current weapon. "Demythologizing," "decanonizing," and "dehegemonizing" are far advanced. As Philip Rieff says of American higher education, "The remissive elites of our universities are 'radicals' in their singular skill in pulling up roots in a manner that must kill them."[13] America is moving fast from the old idea that everything means something to the new idea that nothing means anything.

Of course, there are inconsistencies in this situation. European critical analysis is the weapon of choice for attacking "Eurocentrism." The claim to the right to African roots is rooted in non-African, Western rights. It is true, too, that to continue this line of thought would fuel quite unwarranted suspicions against academia as a whole. Most Americans live lives that are well quarantined from any direct "contamination" from the ravages of postmodernism. But intellectual and cultural immunity is impossible in the modern world. One has only to look at American popular culture to see the practical outworking of radical ideas in ways that combine artistic brilliance and technological innovation with crass vulgarity and social destructiveness.

Some of the worst developments are in fact intellectual in origin but decidedly nonacademic now and exceedingly popular. The triumph of the therapeutic, for example, has been variously linked to such powerfully destructive trends as "the repeal of reticence" exemplified in America's diarrhetic talk shows, "the golden era of exoneration" exemplified in the "don't-blame-me-blame-my-parents" dissolution of responsibility, and "the revenge of the failure" exemplified in the destructive leveling of all leaders and heroes through an egalitarianism turned sour.

The virus of these developments in thought may well prove to be the AIDS of America's mind and soul. Does it matter that modern America has no view of the world that will give a unified meaning, not only to the individual but to society, not only to art but to science, progress, and crisis as well? What will be the social consequences of the concept that truth and meaning are nothing but a function of power? Or of the conclusion that there are no commanding truths left, because nothing is true and everything is doubted and permitted? Victory for the forces of the Enlightenment took longer to complete in America than elsewhere in the West, but it could prove pyrrhic, especially if the price has to be paid here first. Alasdair MacIntyre's verdict already confronts us as an alarm: "The barbarians are not waiting beyond the frontiers; they have already been governing us for quite some time."[14]

A Grand Pincer Movement

The second of the black holes of modernity grows from a social development. This is in many ways the least obvious and most abstract of the three, because just as history to many people is remote, so trends in society (and the social sciences that describe them) are hopelessly abstract. Society, after all, is not something anyone can lay their hands on; it is an abstraction. Also, since there are a myriad of potentially relevant social trends, the need to be selective is greatest over this type of development. And most importantly of all, this development is by far the hardest to reverse.

America's history and society are the result of the interplay between America's geography, space, openness, cultural diversity, and political freedom. Against this backdrop, the outline of the sociological impact of modernity is well known: the movement from rural to urban life, and thus from the organic solidarity of the preindustrial community to modern association. But of all the various developments that have stemmed from this grand change, one is now having a special impact on America—the gigantic pincer movement on American society created by the clash between the centralizing and decentralizing trends of modernity. As elsewhere in the world, the impact of modernization on traditional society has been explosive, exerting enormous structural pressures in two opposite directions at once. At the top, it has unleashed a strong trend toward centralization in the large, powerful institutions of the public sphere, such as the giant government, corporate, educational, and military superstructures of the modern world. At the bottom it has unleashed an equally strong trend toward decentralization or diffusion in the private worlds of individuals.

As this forking of society grows more pronounced, it sets against each other two opposing worlds, each with its own structures and styles—the bureaucratic and the personal, the organizational and the individual, the regulated and the expressive. The world of the public "megastructures" appears more bureaucratic, impersonal, and unresponsive the more centralized it grows, just as the miniworlds of the individual appear to grow more free, intimate, and expressive the more decentralized they are. The first world, some say, is epitomized by the manager and his or her colleagues and the second by the therapist and his or her clients.

To many people, it appears that the second of these forked trends— toward social decentralization or diffusion—is independent of the other and brings the blessing of greater social space for greater individual freedom. Far from being die-stamped into mass-produced uniformity as was feared a generation ago, American society has become a teeming market of varied options and opportunities, especially of life-styles. But as various examples show, the situation is not as simple as it appears and the balance sheet of gains and losses comes out more evenly than seems likely.

A dramatically visible example of the decentralizing trend is the rise of the so-called New Politics. This term does not mean the transient sixties-style coalition of "campus, ghetto, and suburb," as Jack Newfield defined New Politics then, but rather a far more enduring shift over the last thirty-five years that has transformed the style, as opposed to the substance, of contemporary politics. In America, as in many other countries, political parties have traditionally been the main building blocks in the political structures of the democratic and pluralist society. But ever since the "democratic revolution" in the 1820s and 1830s, parties have assumed an even more critical role in America. They have fostered a sense of unity at the national level that has overcome the native secessionist spirit of Americans that is born of diversity. Yet they have done so without producing the heavy centralization that went hand in hand with the emergence of nationhood in Europe.

American political parties focused concerns and energies at local, regional, state, and national levels and harnessed them to build a politically unified nation. From the local party at the grassroots to the leaders of the party in the White House, a vast web of political connections grew stronger and stronger, binding national unity in the process. This political unifying drive that emphasized organization rather than ideology served to muzzle moralism, tame conflict, and train compromise. The federalizing effect could be seen graphically even in the old city machines. For all their celebrated corruption, the latter were a key part of the bargaining process through which conflicting interests were mediated. As it was put graphically, "No America without democracy, no democracy without politics, no politics without parties, no parties without compromise and moderation."[15] Whereas in Europe sharply defined parties often come together after an election to create a coalition government, in America the more loosely defined parties have served to create a governing coalition *before* the election is fought.

Today the disregard of compromise and the declining power of the city machines are only two symptoms along with others, such as falling voter identification, the splintering of the old political groupings, and the trend toward social diffusion. Those who describe the present situation as a "no-party system" have gone too far. But the New Politics in America has resulted in a temporary decline of the importance of the political party and of patronage, and in the rise of a politics that is centered on candidates and focused on single issues. The first of these new emphases represents a shift from the party to a personality, and the second from the party platform to a problem or issue.

The overall result is a decisive shift from a politics that was more solid, enduring, and predictable to a politics-without-parties that is fluid, volatile, and unpredictable. Candidate-centered electioneering, single-issue politics, image-making manipulation of the media, and the rising influence of political action committees (PAC) are all expressions of this shift. And it is no accident that the new structures, such as PACs, and new styles of communication, such as political advertising, first became effective and even necessary in California, a politically flexible state conspicuous for the weakness of its party system and the strength of its media.

Similar decentralizing trends of varying intensity and importance can be seen in other areas. In the media, for example, the dominant trend in the early 1960s was toward corporatism and concentration. At that time there were two wire services, two genuinely national magazines, two near-national newspapers, and three television networks. The effect was to nationalize public opinion, fuse the republic into one audience, and place a disproportionate power to influence the American mind into the hands of the then-dominant liberal elite. But this concentration had no sooner occurred than it was offset, though not replaced, by the impact of the microchip revolution, particularly through cable and satellite television, home videos, the shift to the concept of "narrowcasting," and the catering to diverse minority interests. The extent of the latter countervailing trends has often been exaggerated, and as a result fortunes have been lost as fast as facts, but the underlying decentralizing trend is undeniable.

The recent "down-home" turn in religion provides a further illustration of the decentralizing trend. The large-scale denominational concerns and ecumenical movements of the fifties and sixties are out of fashion. Clear denominational affiliations have become increasingly blurred and unimportant to many believers at the grassroots level. What matters instead is freedom and spontaneity rather than structure and history, intimacy and sincerity rather than dogma and orthodoxy. In the process there has been a movement away from older denominational identifications and from a concern with the ecclesiastical bureaucracy toward blockbuster local megachurches and toward home-based groups of every sort.

Naturally there have been different assessments of this decentralizing trend. What is meat to the direct-mailing fund-raiser, megachurch minipope, or local radio station owner is poison to the hard-pressed party official, denominational bureaucrat, or television-network executive. Often these differences of perspective are deep and critical. In the battle over the family, for example, advocates of the traditional family describe the process of social diffusion as "fragmentation" while their opponents dismiss them as supporters of the "nostalgic family" and celebrate the liberation of "creative divorce." What is wrong is what is right. One person's fragmentation is another person's freedom—and vice versa.

But beyond the pros and cons of these immediate issues, there are certain major consequences of this pincer movement and of the trend toward social diffusion in particular. At first sight, the most obvious consequence is that the trend provides structural reinforcement for the relativistic direction of the intellectual developments seen earlier. Sometimes the effect of the decentralizing trend is to reinforce the substance of beliefs, such as individualism. Sometimes it reinforces styles of behavior, such as the expressive revolution. The trend therefore serves as a social spawning ground for every species of exaggerated individualism and ghettoized separatism, and deepens the potential for dislocation and incoherence in the overall national situation.

In the sphere of religion, for example, the trend toward decentralization creates room for unprecedented richness, diversity, and experiment. But it also deepens even further America's well-known propensity for individualism, hedonism, schism, sectarianism, and shallow thinking. Any thought of widespread spiritual discipline is made remote, any hope of genuine religious coherence utopian, and any possibility of serious popular theology forlorn.

In the short run, the potent logic of the decentralizing trend is pulling American society toward contentiousness and incoherence. According to the traditional American way, "single-issue politics" is as much a contradiction in terms as "single-interest neighborhoods" or "theme communities." Which is why the new political style is excellent for articulating claims but hopeless at aggregating them. Yet what began as a campaigning style in the late 1970s has now spread and become the governing style of the early 1990s. The old world of civility and camaraderie is under assault from the new world of negative attacks, preoccupation with character, the use of ethics as a political weapon, emphasis on style over substance, and the omnipresent hothouse atmosphere of media attention.

With the collapse of a national consensus and the weakening of the old political parties, the short-term trend in America is toward a chaotic encounter of claims and counterclaims, and therefore for administrative channels to become choked and society to be convulsed—a condition that George Will describes as "governmental gridlock."[16] The United States is harder to govern well.

In the long run, however, giving free rein to individualism may not, as the individualist hopes, give rise to less government but to more. The trend toward individualism and anti-institutionalism, which increases sovereign freedom in the private sphere, will be matched by the trend toward bureaucracy, which increases sovereign control in the public sphere. The growth of rights will be more than countered by the growth of regulations. Costlier television, costlier technology, and costlier law will favor the return of the big parties in the long run. Corrupted by greater and greater infusions of money, members of Congress dance to the tune of their financiers, not their constituents, and Congress itself becomes a grand reelection machine. Thus, as in the sphere of the media, the end result of decentralization could be a stronger centralization than ever before. The "entitlement society" and the expanded state will go hand in hand, and the United States will be harder to govern freely.

The irony of this unintended consequence not only casts the purported increase of freedom in a different light, but it focuses attention on other less obvious, darker results of the overall forking in society. Two, in particular, show how the grand pincer movement becomes a nihilistic force in American society. First, the grand pincer movement that both centralizes and decentralizes creates a genuine menace for democratic freedom in America because it threatens to weaken or destroy a key stratum of society—those middle-level communities that used to come between the parts now so sharply divided. These are the human-sized institutions, such as the neighborhood, the local church or synagogue, the labor union, the local political organization, the national voluntary agency like Girl Scouts, YMCA, and Red Cross. They stand midway between the small, private, face-to-face world of the individual and the larger public institutions of society.

This apparently fragile web of middle-level communities—Edmund Burke's "small platoons," Thomas Jefferson's "small republics," Peter Berger and Richard Neuhaus's "mediating structures"—is deeply important in any society, because these communities provide the matrix of meaning and belonging that is so vital both to individuals and to a genuinely pluralistic society.[17] But in America these middle-level communities are more important still. Free association is one of the secrets of American democracy. It creates a community-based pluralism that avoids the extremes of both individualism and collectivism, statism and laissez faire, alienation and dependency. From the Puritan-based town meetings in New England and the ethnic communities to the Lions Club, the PTA and the Scouts, America's mediating structures have been a fruitful seedbed for American freedom. To Americans as individuals, the greatest danger in this loss is human impoverishment, just as the danger for American democracy is the loss of the moral and civic foundations on which its own stability and diversity depend.

Second, the grand pincer movement also threatens individual freedom because the public is likely to dominate over the private, the bureaucratic over the individual, and the regulated over the spontaneous in the end. In each case the latter is likely to prove not so much free as dependent. The result will only be one type of authority substituting for another. Traditional authority will have been replaced by rational bureaucratic authority. Kings, ministers, party bosses, and authoritarian fathers will be replaced by managers, therapists, experts, and technicians.

Once again, the consequences are ironic. American sex has been liberated from morality only to fall prey to technique and an avalanche of anxiety-inducing manuals. The American family has been rescued from repressive tradition by caring experts only to be made dependent on its rescuer-experts. American politics has been freed from party bosses only to fall into the clutches of the financiers and pollster-computer wizards. In area after area, the outcome has not been the enhancement of freedom but an encroachment of the subtle tyranny of expertise, or in Christopher Lasch's apt description, the spread of a "paternalism without a father."[18] Unless understood and resisted, the effects of the grand pincer moment are a further nihilistic force and a contribution to the crisis of cultural authority.

The Devouring Dream

The third of the black holes of modernity grows out of an economic development. Economic factors have such obvious importance in the United States that the temptation is to begin with them and go no farther. They have therefore been left to the last. For most of its history America's potent blend of natural abundance and messianic drive has lent substance and splendor to its mythic status as a land of plenty. From the Icelandic sagas of "Leif the Lucky" down to the competing promises of today's politicians, advertisers, and television evangelists, prosperity as providence has been a basic theme in America's understanding of itself. Opportunity as the dream of success is one of the strongest bonds between American individuals and American society.

It is true that "getting a fair share of the national swag," as H. L. Mencken put it, has generally been easier in America than in any other western land.[19] But far beyond that, the American Dream, which is all about superabundance and unlimited possibilities, has become the human dream within reach across the Atlantic or (now) the Pacific. Little wonder that it is still a myth with muscle. Few things are more typically American than the reported assertion of Franklin D. Roosevelt that, if he could place one American book in the hands of every Soviet citizen, he would choose a Sears Roebuck catalog. To understand America, Boris Yeltsin said on returning to

Russia from his visit in 1989, "at least 100 million Soviets must pass through the American school of supermarkets."[20]

Whether by luck, good management, skillful public relations, or borrowing against the future, one of President Reagan's major political successes was to restore the power of the American Dream, and to some extent revive the business prosperity of the Coolidge era and the military security of the Eisenhower years. The "monetary industrial complex" was delivering again.[21] Talk of limitlessness and possibility was back in vogue. To a people for whom prosperity is a social as much as an economic fact, GNP also stands for Grand National Psychology.

But for key periods in the last three decades, the most telling economic factor was the relatively poor performance of the American economy. Suddenly, after one of the most prosperous quarter centuries in American history, the 1970s showed the worst economic performance for any decade since the 1930s. The early 1990s was the same after the 1980s. Major problems, such as inflation, the energy crisis, and the inability or unwillingness of government to control its budget, came together and exploded. The word "relatively" should be underscored, of course. In many instances America's performance was poor only in relation to its own high standards, and not by comparison with others.

At the most basic level—one to which full moral weight must be given—the earlier economic realities, such as unemployment, stagflation, high interest rates, low productivity, and mounting deficits, created stark and unpleasant situations for many people. While these urgent human problems should not be minimized, in the United States the performance of the economy—whether strong or weak—always has had other, less direct consequences for the nation as a whole.

In the first place, economic performance is a very practical hinge factor that has a strong bearing on noneconomic trends. Student activism, for example, was as frustrated by the recession in the 1970s as it was freed by the boom in the 1960s. So-called youthful idealism was suddenly transformed into realism, or as one student expressed it, "When jobs are tight it's wiser to keep your ideals to yourself."

Also, the state of the economy has intimate, though subtle, connections with deep national myths and expectations. This is obviously so in the case of the American Dream and American exceptionalism, which black separatists have therefore derided as "Whitey's Rainbow." But it is also true of less tangible things, such as openness to change, confidence in the future, or public trust and cooperation. Behind American ideals, such as equality and opportunity, are American realities, such as prosperity and mobility. Behind the magic of the system is the hidden power of Horatio Alger's "rags to riches" and William James's "bitch-goddess" success.

But far beyond these points, the extraordinary recent success of the American economy has put a Midas touch on the character of the American republic itself, even turning the American Dream into a devouring force and a third source of nihilism. It has done this by its leading role in the hedonistic revolution and the complete dominance of the consumption ethic in our time. The origins of this revolution can be traced to the late colonial period, when Puritans became Yankees and when it was said of Pennsylvania Quakers that, having come to do good, they ended by doing well. But it was in the late nineteenth century and the 1920s when the effects of the consumer revolution were first experienced on a nationwide scale. Even then it took the superabundance of the late forties and fifties to break through the wish frontier and complete what Christopher Lasch has called "the moral rehabilitation of desire."[22] Instead of its negative repute because of the classical link between the insatiability of appetites and the instability of societies, the concept of desire was made positive because it was harnessed to the indefinite expansion of productive forces, and therefore to rising expectations of goods, desires, and satisfaction.

In 1947 a marketing analyst told a business group that the fundamental challenge facing corporate America was to convince the public that the "hedonistic approach to life was a moral, not an immoral one."[23] In saying this, he was echoing—with an American moral spin—John Maynard Keynes's 1928 prediction that "abundance would bring the work ethic into discredit."[24] Clearly, the prediction was proved true and the business challenge swiftly and successfully met, for within a few years a complete revolution had been effected.

The result has been that high consumption in America is far more than the expression of a high standard of living. As abundance became superabundance, high consumption was transformed from an excess into an ethos and an ethic. Ted Morgan wrote approvingly, "The Eastern bloc has Marxism, and Americans have shopping-center theory."[25] In America, to be mall-adjusted is the opposite of mal-adjusted—its central philosophy summed up in the bumper sticker "Veni, vidi, Visa."

The hedonistic revolution came to full bloom in the money years—the eighties—with profligate debt occupying the place that permissive sex had in the sixties, and "toys" being to the American rich what drugs were to the poor. The good life became the life with goods. Possession became consumption and consumption addiction—to things and style. Saving was eclipsed by spending, and discipline and deferment by permissiveness and gratification. Many things American were not so much expensive because valued as they were valued because expensive. Success was dollars and dollars were debt, tax gains, and acquisition. Concern over salvation shifted to concern over self-realization, especially via intense experience and exuberant health. Serious consideration of substance dissolved into self-consciousness about style, and the illusion even arose that people could change identity at will with the minimum financial and psychic cost. Self-invention became one of the inalienable rights and prime business of all Americans.

Such facts as Michael Milken's $500 million annual salary, President Reagan's $2 million honorarium to speak briefly in Japan, or events such as Malcolm Forbes's $2 million birthday bash in Morocco came to symbolize the greed, ostentation, and let-them-eat-cakery that made the 1980s the second gilded age. Less flashy but no less revealing was the simple statistic that, according to demographers, on average in the eighties Americans opened junk mail for eight months of their lifetime.

There is a comic side to the Midas touch of American consumerism—Leonardo, Michelangelo, and other great masters of the Renaissance, for example, being pressed into service to help *Teenage Mutant Ninja Turtles* change art into products. But conservatives who bewail the destructiveness of anticapitalist attacks on American business and anti-American attacks on Western culture should acknowledge the far more lethal and antitraditional impact of what Robert Bellah has called "market totalitarianism." Market forces are invading and colonizing more of human life, subjecting it to the constraints and criteria of money. The result is an encroaching "commodification" of everything, the reduction of the human to the economic, behavior to self-interest, wisdom to "cost-effectiveness," success to "productivity," society to "an arena for competitive individualism," and human beings to "consumers" and "maximizers."

The resulting crisis is both economic and ethical—a loss of value and of values. When the noneconomic is commercialized and everyone and everything becomes a commodity, the famous "creative destruction" of capitalism turns on itself. Managing people and producing something is no longer the point of American business. All that matters is to buy, sell, own, and figure out a leveraged buyout of the world. The market nihilism that begins by reducing everything to products ends in reducing itself to Nietzsche's bare will to power. "I don't do it for the money," wrote Donald Trump, the epitome of the eighties' New Dealer, "I've got enough, much more than I'll ever need. I do it to do it."[26]

Americans can no longer afford to view 1980s-style capitalism as a purely conservative force. Or to fail to recognize what John Maynard Keynes meant when he described ethically unbounded capitalism as "absolutely irreligious," "without much public spirit," a mere heap of "possessors and pursuers."[27]

Nietzsche himself could hardly have said it better than "doing it to do it." Without continuing habits of ethical responsibility and mutual trust, capitalism diminishes humanness, destroys the cohesion of society, and produces conditions in which even the market itself cannot thrive.

This development may well trigger a procapitalist critique of capitalism to join the earlier anticapitalist critiques. Whereas aristocrats attack capitalism for its leveling of tastes, socialists for its exploitation of workers, and civic republicans for its corrupting of virtue, capitalists need to warn against capitalism undermining the success of capitalism. David Potter used to argue that the true message of America is not of "democracy revolutionizing the world," but of "abundance revolutionizing the world."[28] Today its greatest impact is on America and is nihilistic as much as revolutionary. But regardless of that, one thing is clear. Not only political elections but the mood, life-style, character, and now even the health of the "people of plenty" pivots crucially on the state of the pocketbook and the soul behind the hand that reaches for it.

Developments in these three spheres—intellectual, social, and economic—are like the black holes of modernity in relation to the crisis of cultural authority. They are not universal developments and their effects are not uniform. But they do have undeniable consequences. The myriad combinations and effects of these trends create an infinitely varied kaleidoscopic pattern, but with an unmistakable nihilistic tendency. Holding in mind these three developments, we can now turn to examine the outbreak of the crisis of cultural authority in the last four decades. The aim is to see how the interplay of these developments in the last generation forms the setting for the crisis of transcendence and tradition that now confronts America.

4

The "Golden" Fifties

The 1950s might appear an unlikely place to begin the recent story of America's crisis of cultural authority. For a start, the decade lies too far off for reminiscence without nostalgia, yet is too close for research without bias. Perhaps it should be allowed to slip quietly into history without the indignity of being turned into fuel for current partisan debates. Besides, the decade of the fifties was surely anything but revolutionary. Worse still, the very term *fifties* seems to smack of the worst excesses of the current rage for "generationalism" and "decadology."

The perils of thinking in terms of successive generations and decades are real. Whether the method used is serious history or end-of-the-decade pop-punditry, it is easy to fall into such pitfalls as distorted generalizations, wishful thinking, and commercialized fashion. (*Life* magazine, it is said, is America's designer fashion vehicle for trends just as *Vogue* is for clothes.) Yet the realities behind the trend are undeniable. Old units of social measurement, such as class and income, have grown obsolete. New time-centered units, such as generation, have become natural because of the sense of dynamism that accelerating change has introduced. As historians point out, it is no accident that a quartet of themes—progress, nostalgia, decades, and generation wars—arose together in the twenties as the natural and increasingly commercialized response to the cataract of change that the first two decades of the century introduced. For better or worse, America's sense of urgent and accelerating time and the American crisis of cultural authority are linked.

Yet when due care has been taken to avoid the pitfalls, there is a solid reason why the fifties is a useful place to begin: Despite the critical changes in

81

the culture that had been going on in certain circles since 1912, the 1950s (properly beginning in 1945, the Year of Victory) appear to be the last period in which there was a comparatively widespread innocence and intactness about much that was considered traditionally American. In this sense, "the fifties" for Americans is what "the myth of the nineteenth century" was for an earlier generation of Europeans—one long, cloudless summer of ordered contentment. But that impression masks a deeper and more interesting story. In regard to the crisis of cultural authority, the significance of the fifties is straightforward: They were the build-up years—the vital preface to the cultural revolution of the sixties.

On the one hand, today's golden view of the fifties must be qualified because it is partly the result of nostalgia and partly of certain unrepeatable historical features. With the genie out of the nuclear bottle, for instance, the heady euphoria of America's brief unipolar moment from July 1945 until August 1949 went unmatched until the brief heady days after the European revolution in 1989. (Even Winston Churchill spoke positively of the United States that was fortified by a nuclear arsenal that "God has willed.")[1] On the other hand, as we shall see, the fifties were not as traditional as thought at the time or as viewed in nostalgia now. They were abnormal as much as normal, unprecedented and unrealistic as much as traditional.

Thus the golden view of the fifties was partly the result of the seeming simplicity and sureness of certain features of American society at that time. Just how unsolid and nontraditional these features were is something we can see today. But three things in particular were instrumental in creating that impression and maintaining the sense of transcendence and tradition.

Three Pillars of Stability

First, America in the 1950s exhibited a strong sense of social stability. America in 1940 was still a rural, small-town nation. Incredible though it seems today, fewer than 50 percent of all Americans then lived in cities with more than ten thousand inhabitants. But vast social changes were taking place in the forties and fifties. By the beginning of 1950, two out of three Americans had moved into one of the great metropolitan regions, and many of them into the thickening city waistline of "suburbia." But the word "ghetto" had not been applied to the inner city and the consequences of this and other developments, such as the explosion of the television industry, were still to be felt. In the 1950s, American institutions from families up through public schools, law courts, and the military to the presidency itself appeared strong, inspiring both confidence and pride.

In the university world, mushrooming enrollments, expanding endowments, and an increasing integration into national life ushered in an expansive era for education and research. The new social confidence was so marked in the case of the family that the decade was hailed as witnessing a renaissance of the family. The divorce rate peaked in 1946 and declined steadily throughout the fifties while the marriage rate rose, the birthrate soared, and family life was celebrated almost universally as essential to "the American way" and "the American style."

Second, America possessed a strong sense of moral legitimacy in the 1950s. If asked why they believed in families, public schools, law courts, and the government, the great majority of people answered in terms of traditional verities that were mostly sympathetic to, if not rooted in, the Christian worldview. One could still speak accurately of *either* sex. "God's country" could still be said without self-consciousness. American institutions were not only strong; they were felt to be right and good, and assuredly so.

A good part of the strength of this impression is myth today. The 1950s was a fabled time and place, a journalist wrote later, when "pot" meant a useful cooking utensil, when "crack" was simply the sound of a baseball hitting a bat, when "grass" was something mowed rather than smoked, and when "corn" grew on stalks in the Midwest rather than in speeches during elections.[2] More importantly, much of the consensus that underlay the feeling of the moral rightness of things was vague and wide rather than deep. Equally, the consensus had a wide variety of impulses. But along with the need for patriotism inspired by the Cold War, the strongest contributor to the sense of moral legitimacy came from the postwar religious "revival." This was not as purely religious as many believed at the time, but it was a significant event that occurred in no other Western nation. All the statistical indicators of religious growth pointed upward, and the resurgence strongly augmented the membership and strength of almost all religious communities, but especially the Protestant, Catholic, and Jewish communities.

In the decade after 1945, registered church membership rose from around 70 million to over 100 million. Best-seller lists were routinely topped by novels with religious themes, such as *The Robe* or *The Big Fisherman*. In 1953 alone, six of the top eight best-sellers in nonfiction had religious themes. The "revival" even included the nonorthodox Unitarianism, which doubled in membership in the 1950s—a fact that explodes the widely believed myth that liberalism flourishes only when conservatism wanes. Later on, many people cited nonreligious considerations, such as the postwar baby boom, to explain this "suburban spiritual boom" (and therefore why it faded so rapidly in the sixties). But at the time the revival had the effect of repolishing the tarnished halo of G. K. Chesterton's "nation with the soul of a Church."[3]

This revival greatly favored the Christian community, along with others. Indeed, its unofficial semiestablishment was taken even further when the phrase "under God" was formally added to the Pledge of Allegiance in 1954. Two years later, the nation's official motto became "In God We Trust." In 1952 Congress had instructed the president to proclaim a National Day of Prayer annually. The Post Office canceled stamps with the slogan, "Pray for Peace." The National Prayer Breakfast movement was born during this time.

Yet at the same time these special favors were more than offset by the general national mood that leaned, not toward specific religious convictions and theological clarity, but toward religion in general. The result was an indeterminate blend of patriotic nationalism and pious religiosity. Nowhere was this "Potomac Piety" more clear than in the much-quoted words of the president himself. "Our government," said Dwight D. Eisenhower, "makes no sense unless it is founded on a deeply felt religious faith—and I don't care what it is."[4]

Third, America in the 1950s enjoyed an extraordinary sense of economic prosperity. After the long, tight-belted years of depression and war, a new period of affluence had arrived. Where Roosevelt's "Old Dr. New Deal" had failed, "Dr. Win-the-War" had succeeded gloriously. Mass unemployment had virtually disappeared and a great boom had begun. Long-restrained demands for material goods and the benefits of leisure and entertainment could now be satisfied. Of the nation's total housing stock in 1960, one-third was built in the 1950s.

Certainly the fifties' prosperity was to be exceeded easily in the sixties. But in comparison with the thirties and early forties it was remarkable, and in the eyes of the rest of the world it was enviable. In 1949 official American gold reserves were $24.6 billion at a time when no other country had as much as $3 billion. Fort Knox was a way of thinking as much as a place. By 1960 America's GNP was $500 billion, almost double the figure for a decade earlier. Not for nothing did the Republicans later boast proudly of "Peace, Progress, and Prosperity."

Nostalgia Isn't What It Used To Be

None of these considerations adds up to a proof that the 1950s really was a golden age. If used at all, the term can only be applied with any accuracy to Eisenhower's second term and the years from 1955 onward. The preceding ten years have even been called "the dismal decade" and 1949 was a year of shocks whose tremors were felt for years (the loss of China to the Communists, the announcement of the Soviet atomic bomb, the Alger Hiss trial, and the rise of Joseph McCarthy). And quite apart from the perils of nostalgia, there are obvious stains on the record even in the later years.

Institutionalized racism—the lingering leftover of the evils of chattel slavery—flourished blatantly in the heartland of pietism and morality. Not until the sixties would the uncompleted task of "reconstruction" be taken up again. No Western society, apart from South Africa, harbored such racial prejudice. McCarthyism and its proto-Fascist demagoguery and phobias were another ugly blot. Many people will remember the decade because of Korea, Little Rock, the Kefauver hearings on gangsterism, and the anxiety over Sputnik in 1957.

Also, with hindsight it is plain that perceptive observers were well aware of the shaky state of some of the foundations of the fifties. They were aware, too, of the awkward elements and the jumble of moods that did not fit easily into the later conventional picture. Even before V-E day FDR was said to have hung a portrait of Woodrow Wilson in the cabinet room to remind himself of the fate of the grand victor of World War I. And after V-J day in 1945 reporters noted how people spoke not of "victory," but "the end of the war." American justifications for Hiroshima were swift and strong, but Hermann Goering's compliment from his prison cell was ominously back-handed: "A mighty accomplishment. I don't want anything to do with it."

Even during the fifties proper, contradictions emerged for the observant to note. Victory had been won over the forces of evil, but the victors had been burned by the radiating guilt of Hiroshima. Progress was celebrated, but T. S. Eliot, who scourged it in his poetry, was at the height of his popularity. College students were described as gloriously contented, but 40 percent or more admitted to frequent cheating without any sense of wrongdoing, and keen observers like Philip Jacob noted a "ghostly quality" to their conformity since the undergirdings of the Puritan heritage were absent.[5] Ed Murrow's "See it Now" was typical of courageous public-affairs programs, but he had been muzzled in 1955 after his investigations embarrassed his sponsor and the national exposure of rigged television game shows left a public outraged and puzzled. Motherhood was canonized and suburban families went to Sunday School, but they were reading Dr. Kinsey and there was a far from saintly restiveness in the suburban world of the homemakers. "I sort of look forward to the day my kids are grown up," one executive told William H. Whyte, Jr., in a personal conversation, "Then I won't have such a guilty conscience about neglecting them." And so it was beginning to go.

This surface sketch of the decade leaves some crucial questions unanswered: Even if the "Eisenhower equilibrium" is limited to 1955 onward, how solid and deep was the apparent stability? If it was all that it appeared to be (and all that recent nostalgia has cracked it up to be), why did it collapse so suddenly and unexpectedly under the tremors of the sixties? Could it even be that the mood of the fifties was not so much weak—and therefore liable to collapse without warning—but false and therefore bound to build up pressures leading to its own downfall? Was the decade of the fifties so traditional in fact, or was it really a deceptive period whose key elements of change were camouflaged by the surface appearance of tradition and continuity? Such questions, I suggest, are like clues that lead along a trail to a higher viewpoint on the same scene. The information remains the same, but the picture is thrown into a different light. Seen from this perspective, the rather flat and wooden picture of "traditional America" in the fifties needs to be corrected and deepened in a number of ways that illuminate the crisis that was to come.

On the one hand, the high and sunny mood of the forties and fifties was partly artificial because it was created by a number of unrepeatable factors. New York, for example, had become the capital of the art world and the epicenter of the shockwaves of abstract and expressionist art. But it had only usurped the supremacy of Paris, abandoned its Depression-era dreariness, and attracted such great artists as Marc Chagall, Piet Mondrian, and Marcel Duchamp for one reason—Hitler's war.

This point about the artificial and the borrowed was true more generally. In what was one of history's gigantic serendipities, certain factors suddenly converged to thrust the United States into a position of unrivaled supremacy. Entering the war late but already as one of the strongest powers, the United States emerged the greatest victor at the least cost, and in the process revived the world's most powerful economy and discovered the earth's most awesome weapon. "America for several years," wrote Abba Eban, Israel's distinguished foreign minister, "was not so much a superpower as a monopower."[6] The American nation, a *Christian Century* editorial boasted in 1948, "can be more than a Great Power; it can be the Greatest Power. Its fleets can command the seven seas, and its air forces the can impose the American will on every continent. It can come closer to setting up a world empire, in the Roman sense, . . . than has any other nation in all of history."[7]

Little wonder that with Germany and Japan devastated and her own allies exhausted, America bestrode the postwar world like a Colossus. Idealistic, confident, united, the American people and their leaders felt themselves equal to their opportunity. Old European empires could totter feebly toward their graves as the French were to do at Dien Bien Phu and the British at Suez, but the United States could stand alone. What faced Americans, Henry Stimson proclaimed in 1947, was "the greatest opportunity ever offered a single nation."[8]

On the other hand, the euphoric mood of the forties and fifties tended to conceal certain developments and problems that went largely unnoticed and unresolved. Chief among these on the social level were the huge migration of blacks and poor whites from the South to the North in the 1940s, the beginning of the population bulge or "baby boom," and the culturally explosive introduction of television. (In 1948 only 3 percent of Americans owned a television set. By 1960, 88 percent did.) Such developments were critical to the cultural revolution in the sixties.

On the ideological level, time revealed the shallowness and inauthenticity of the so-called religious revival and the nature of the new postwar ideology and morality. What did its brimming faith and positive thinking amount to? Little more than desire plus a culturally conditioned cheerful optimism. What was the value of the religious inspirational self-help books? Behind all their repetitious banality they were hyped-up common sense for the discontented, the "secular prayer books of a therapeutic era" that debased religion into "God's psychiatry."[9]

What in the end was the "revival"? Much of it, said such critics as Peter Berger in analyses whose correctness proved all too plain, added up to little more than "the noise of solemn assemblies" and a "second Children's Crusade."[10] How strong really were the attitudes to right and wrong? Affluence, John Steinbeck wrote in a passionate letter to Adlai Stevenson, meant that "a creeping, all-pervading nerve gas of immorality starts in the nursery and does not stop before it reaches the highest offices, both corporate and governmental."[11]

One wonders now why such problems were not fully appreciated at the time. The main answer lies in the fact that during the forties and fifties the American mood was dominated by a subtle but powerful set of ideas. It appeared traditional to many people, but it was actually composed of far newer convictions. This set of ideas was an ideology that pretended not to be (even itself proclaiming "the end of ideology"). It was a traditional-appearing consensus, putting a premium on harmony, consultation, and the center. But at its heart was a tension between genuinely traditional themes, such as that of the strong family, and less traditional themes, such as the New Economics and the New Internationalism.

Claims about the "end of ideology" were particularly curious because the growth of this postwar liberal ideology was neither accidental nor spontaneous. It was a deliberate response to the widespread conviction that American superiority had only one deficiency—a lack of clear national purpose. This lack of national purpose was felt most keenly in the emerging struggle with communism. European monarchies, with their aristocratic privileges and hereditary class system, had once been the leading rival of American egalitarianism and virtue. Communism, through the Cold War, took over this role with a vengeance. Suddenly it was recognized that problems of national legitimacy, which went back to the Depression and earlier, could no longer be held off. The hot war was over, but with the chilling prospect of a cold war with "godless Communism," some set of ideas was needed to fortify the "home of the free and the brave."

Americans, said Reinhold Niebuhr in 1949, were in the frontline of the battle. But they were equipped with ideological weapons "as irrelevant as were the spears of the knights, when gunpowder challenged their reign."[12] The United States faced the crisis of 1949, warned a writer in *Foreign Affairs*, "with the ideological equipment of 1775."[13] Even earlier in the decade, John Foster Dulles had said that "our great national weakness today is not physical, but spiritual. We lack a constructive purpose which is inspiring and contagious."[14] By itself, the ideology of capitalism had a dangerously hollow ring.

Of the three chief strands in the postwar consensus the only traditional one was the emphasis on the family as the domestic basis to national security. Alongside this were two newer themes, with contradictory elements to tradition. The first, which was later to swell into the "Great Society" hopes of the sixties and the unbridled acquisitiveness of the eighties, was the New Economics. American free enterprise, it was believed, was the mightiest dynamo of progress in human history. It was the "permanent revolution," a revolutionary force for social change that would leapfrog the need for socialism, redistribution, class conflict, and increased taxation. Directed by a strong, active government harnessed to the newly respectable status of desire and the new concept of the broad democratization of consumption (the "inconspicuous consumption" of the masses), economic progress could create a world of classlessness, plenty, generosity, and leisure for all. It could make obsolete older problems of poverty and inequality and open new frontiers in education, medicine, and social engineering. The horn of plenty would be bountiful for all. The ladder of success would keep everyone moving upward forever.

The nontraditional utopianism in this economic optimism is easily missed, but it was deliberate. Progress, which had once been linked to the eighteenth-century philosopher's dream of a "heavenly city," had been moved forward and brought down to earth in the form of the American Dream. There was no longer any heaven at the end of the line, but who cared when the rising expectations of improvement for all was heaven now, with all the waiting taken out of wanting. Most stunningly and unconservatively of all, the magic of the surplus economy was even said to arrest the decay of time and override the cycles of history. In contrast to the rise and fall of civilizations in the past, America could rise and rise and keep on rising without end.

The other novel strand was the New Internationalism, which was to provide the "Grand Design" abroad that matched the "Great Society" at home. At its most articulate, this was an explicit non-Communist manifesto through which America sought to justify and steer its new role in the world. At stake was the chance to replace the world order that existed prior to 1914. The chief competitor was the Soviet Union, whose worldwide menace had to be contained. What Rudyard Kipling from Vermont in 1899 had referred to with irony as "the White Man's Burden," Americans fifty years later were to shoulder with idealism. In this sense, the words of John F. Kennedy at his inaugural in 1961 were the last words of the 1950s. No burden was too heavy, no price too high to pay.

To many Americans across a wide spectrum of society, these convictions were self-evident in the late forties, fifties, and early sixties. They are anything but self-evident today, and simply to appreciate the change in climate is to be able to recognize how much they were products of that brief, bright period of American supremacy. In short, the fifties are not to be patronized as "golden" or merely "middle of the road." They were, in Eric Goldman's phrase, "the crucial decade" that attempted to give constructive answers to the great domestic and international questions of the postwar period.[15]

This is why the fifties' years were also abnormal as much as normal. This is why they were unprecedented and unrealistic as much as traditional, a fool's paradise as much as an unfallen Eden. Re-created postwar America, as David Riesman warned, was superficially impressive but, internally, a house of cards. "Four decades later," as Abba Eban noted of the postwar situation, "it is difficult to believe that rational men could have lived in such a world of fallacies. . . . One act of credulity begat another."[16]

This realization has a simple consequence for understanding the outbreak of the crisis of cultural authority: What the sixties turned against in the fifties was not only tradition, as is commonly supposed, but contradiction and illusion. Even while exuding confidence and celebrating tradition, the fifties nurtured the seeds of a very different world.

This point bears underscoring. The New Economics, for example, carried a host of unseen but radical consequences. It brought the benefits of both Adam Smith and John Maynard Keynes within popular reach. It undermined the traditional place of work and shifted the traditional ethic of deferment to one of gratification. It eclipsed the views of cultural decline of both the Christian and the classical republican faiths. It held out the promise of a revolutionary alternative to change via revolution. It brought a kiss of life to the dying doctrine of secularized utopian progress. And it paved the way for the cultural revolution of the sixties. When abundance reigned and private choice was its only ruling principle, gender roles, sexual mores, birth control, and family stabilities were bound to be called into question as drastically as thrift and deferred gratification earlier.

At the time, however, these seeds were hidden. Observations like these were limited to a tiny minority. To most people, America in the fifties seemed to be the family, the local community, and the church writ large. America was trusting in God, and God was blessing America. With the Old World exhausted by war, the New World had assumed the mantle of Western leadership in time of peace. With former colonies being freed around the world, it was time for the freest of former colonies to lead the free world. There was an implacable new foe to face and an unknown future to enter, but confidence was high. America had come into its own, and its greatest asset was its Americanism. American greatness and American goodness were one. The fifties, it appeared, had ushered in the Augustan era of the American republic. It was up to the sixties to see its imperial promise fulfilled.

5

The Seismic Sixties

Thirty years on, it is obvious that the chronicling of and accounting for the sixties is by no means complete. Realism has replaced the early romanticism that hailed its arrival and estimated its success in messianic terms. Factors to explain it have broadened and grown more subtle. But the air still crackles with the updated apologia of the original advocates of the sixties and the polemic confessions of its erstwhile supporters turned latter-day opponents. What is beyond question is that this fiercely intense, exciting, and dramatic period had a stamp of its own. Not only was it a sharp break from the fifties, but it was a seismic shift in American history. Not surprisingly, it represents the first of the two great revolutionary decades in the crisis of cultural authority.

If the fifties appeared to be broadly traditional, the sixties was the reverse. Indeed, there were times in the sixties when the terra firma of custom, precedent, and orthodoxy seemed as solid as shifting sand; and as irritating when kicked up into the eyes of its defenders. But for our purposes, the years of the 1960s were crucial for two reasons: In them occurred the decisive collapse of the ideological consensus of the 1950s, which therefore, to a less discernible extent, led to the shaking of a major part of the foundations of the traditional American consensus itself. And during that period the logic of the main alternatives was demonstrated with a vivid clarity. In short, the sixties was America's decade of cultural revolution.

When and Why Did the Sixties Begin?

When did the sixties begin? We can keep the period in perspective if we answer two prior questions, of which this is the first. Chronologically, of course, the sixties began in January 1960. But this truism reinforces the exaggerated contrasts between the fifties and sixties. As stressed earlier, for all their talk about the "New Frontier" and getting America moving again, the Kennedy years—although Democrat and active rather than Republican and passive—were a true continuation of the spirit and substance of the ideology of the fifties. In fact, in many ways the early promise of John F. Kennedy's presidency—especially as articulated in his inaugural address—was the high noon of postwar American confidence.

For this very reason, many people regard November 22, 1963, as the day when the first shockwave hit America, heralding the violent succession of tremors by which many characterize the sixties. Strictly speaking, however, this later date is no more accurate than the first. For a moment's thought shows how many smaller incidents, key to the sixties, preceded Dallas and were unrelated to it. Cafe sit-ins had been organized in 1960. Several other decisive landmarks in the civil rights movement occurred in 1962, when the Freedom Riders, organized by the Congress of Racial Equality, penetrated the deep South in May, and a riot broke out at the University of Mississippi ("Ole Miss") in September of that year. The year 1962 had also seen the publication of Rachel Carson's *Silent Spring*, which was as influential on the later environmental movement as Betty Friedan's *The Feminist Mystique* (1963) was on the rise of the feminist movement. By early 1963, countless Americans were already singing and whistling Bob Dylan's "Blowing in the Wind" and before the summer was out he had written the even more prophetic song, "The Times They Are A'changin'."

More importantly still, during the long, hot weeks between May and July 1963 around 750 riots erupted in 186 cities. The March on Washington in August 1963 showed liberalism and the civil rights movement at the flood tide of their confidence and Martin Luther King, Jr., at the peak of his passionate eloquence. But the march was soon followed by ugly riots in Harlem and Chicago and by the ominous American-inspired murder of President Diem in South Vietnam in November. Later on it was discovered how many demographic trends in America had changed suddenly around the period 1960–62. The American birthrate plunged sharply, while the statistics for divorce and illegitimacy began to rise equally dramatically, exploding between 1968 and the mid-seventies. The key trends behind the moral and social revolution of the sixties were all under way as the decade began.

Intriguingly, Arthur Schlesinger, Jr., had written a memorandum in 1959 on "The Shape of National Politics to Come," which brought his view of American history as cycles to President Kennedy's attention. American politics, he maintained, followed a cyclical pattern in which periods of reform alternated with those of conservatism. He forecast that the period of passivity under Eisenhower was drawing to an end and was destined to be followed by "a time of affirmation, progressivism, and forward movement." If the rhythm was maintained, the change would occur "about 1961–1962."[1]

There had been rumblings, in other words, long before the fateful shot from the Dallas Book Depository. Yet there is no doubt that the assassination of President Kennedy was the single event that, more than any other, heralded and influenced what was to come. It became the vantage point from which the widening damage was assessed. The Prince of Camelot had been slain by a social nobody; the victor in the eyeball-to-eyeball contest with the missile-rattling Soviets had been cut down by a single bullet. But not only had a man, a husband, a father, and a young leader died, tragically and publicly, the presidential master symbol of the confident idealism and effortless supremacy of postwar America had been felled. A dark question sprang up that was to haunt the country: What does all this hatred, violence, and dark irrationality say about America? Like Mississippi earlier and Peoples Park, Altamont, My Lai, and Kent State later, Dallas was seen not as an exception but as a true expression of America, a metaphor for all that was wrong with the country.

The second and harder question to answer is: Why did the sixties erupt as they did? Our analysis of the fifties, if correct, contributes an easily overlooked factor: The sixties' earthquake was certainly the result of a long, slow buildup of violently colliding forces, as most people say. But the reason the crunch was so shattering was not simply that new realities collided with conservative traditions—these were already weakened—but that, as we saw, the new realities collided with liberal illusions at the height of their strength and influence.

Support for this argument can be found in various places. First, the New Left and the counterculture arose almost everywhere in reaction to liberalism, not conservatism. It was the Democrats, for example, who were in power in America as was the Labour Party in Britain. Thus the major issues in America in the sixties were the arguments and actions swirling around essentially liberal policies—notably the War on Poverty tackling the domestic crisis of the cities and the war in Vietnam confronting the international menace of Soviet expansion. Even in lesser issues, such as education, the dominant liberal ethos was under fire. Lyndon Johnson did accelerate the conduct of these two major policies fatefully, almost as soon as he acceded to power. But each of the policies was a natural flowering of the New Economics and the New Internationalism at the heart of the ideology of the forties and fifties.

In addition, the very illusion-cum-intransigence of the ruling liberalism explains the trajectory of many members of the civil rights movement and the counterculture. Doubtless those who became radicals were shaken early on by the viciousness and bigotry of red-necked conservatives. But their radical hardening came more often in confrontation with liberal educators, liberal politicians, and a liberal president. Radicals, in short, were not rebellious conservatives but former liberals hardened through despair in their battle with other liberals. Finally, the predominance and disasters of this liberal ideology built up a vehement reaction against itself and in 1968 ushered in Richard Nixon and his "New Majority."

If due allowance is made for the significance of these postwar liberal illusions, five critical years of drastic upheaval can be seen. While there were tremors before Kennedy's assassination in 1963 and tremors after Nixon's election in 1968, the earlier date represented the first major shockwave just as the later date was the *annus calamitosus* that represented the culmination of all the eruptions. Not until 1972 would the more violent tremors die away, and even then the nation was left bitterly divided with conservatives rather than liberals in power. But it was as if the illusions of postwar expectations had swollen up in the fifties and early sixties only to burst open like an abscess in 1968, leaving a sorry domestic and international mess to be cleared away.

Could America's traditional consensus have coped with the new realities by itself—its moral principles, for example, restraining the drive toward hubris? Probably not, because the crisis of cultural authority that modernity produced is a far more potent force than that speculation assumes. But it is plain that the additional weight created by extravagant postwar expectations proved an intolerable burden, and that in the ensuing collapse older American traditions were shattered along with the recent illusions that had precipitated the crisis.

The Rocking of the Foundations

What were the consequences of the sixties for the seeming intactness inherited from the fifties? First of all, a dramatic rocking shook America's sense of social stability. Industrial expansion and the growth of cities had been accelerating with headlong velocity for a long time. Now suddenly what was in their train was seen—the price of progress was a series of exponential problems: street crime, ghetto violence, impersonal education, pollution, decaying housing, poor sanitation, failing transport, and the crippling cost of welfare. The realization dawned slowly, but the light it shed was cold. Rural America was receding into the past so fast that it was no more than a myth for most people. Soon, because of the inner contradictions on which it was based, the "Great Society" too would disappear into the future like a mirage.

Could traditional ideals and ways of life cope? The very institutions that a little earlier had appeared so strong and had inspired confidence were now called into question from one of two directions. On the one hand, many of the older and more traditional institutions were challenged as outmoded and unnecessary. Nowhere was this clearer than in the area of the family and in sexual relations. The stark deterioration of the black family, Senator Daniel Moynihan's report argued graphically, was a special case. But the process of pluralization endemic in modernity put the traditional family under pressure too. Once lauded as "the bedrock" of American society, the traditional family suddenly became one option among many, jostled to one side by the pressing crowd of "alternative life-styles"—cohabitation, communes, homo-sexual relationships, the "singles subculture," and so on. This shift and the new orthodoxy of social relativism that it spawned was symbolized (later on) by the shift from the singular to the plural in the aptly titled "White House Conference on Families."

Even among dogmatic defenders of the traditional family, new factors made havoc of old claims. Rock music became a musical esperanto, a novel lingua franca that created a new community of youth, at once bohemian and middle class, radical and recreational. "Little Richard's First Law of Youth Culture" was to please the kids by shocking the parents. What was traditional rhetoric worth once the growing generation gap was aided and abetted by increases in extramarital sex, divorce, teenage purchasing power, television watching, and a reliance on fast foods that soon eradicated the kitchen and all but assigned the family table to oblivion?

On the other hand, many of the modernized institutions were attacked for the opposite reason—they were too up-to-date and streamlined, and they were impersonal, alienating, and dehumanizing, fit only for robots or "organization men." Where the Old Left had attacked capitalism as irrational and anarchic, the New Left denounced it as too rational, an instrument of domination, a technological straitjacket of imperatives that confined humanness and self-expression. Exactly what made the institutions triumphs of organization and technology made them the epitome of a less human world.

Significantly, this perception was not confined to self-professed radicals. Berkeley students protested bitterly at being processed like IBM cards in a "knowledge factory." They were only quoting their own president, Clark Kerr, who had both predicted the revolt and described the faculty as a group of intellectual entrepreneurs loosely tied together by their grievances over parking. (Another celebrated university president described the new "multiversity" as a bunch of departments linked only by their central heating system.) Protesting radicals may have raged against the Strangelovian features of Pentagon policy, but usually did so in such terms as "military-industrial-complex," which went back to President Eisenhower and not the SDS.

Second, and simultaneous with this loss of social stability, came a dramatic rocking of America's sense of moral legitimacy. Even before the fifties had ended, the flame of religious revival was guttering. Soon it became apparent how superficial much of it was, and how deep the crisis of confidence that followed it was. Before the eyes and ears of a watching world the nation was about to question its past and its own beliefs with an orgiastic intensity. Just how drastic the sixties' rejection of traditional American morals and religion was soon became evident. "Permissive morality" and "sexual revolution" were more than slogans; they were manifestos of liberation and a new way of life. The essence of America had always been a breaking away from Europe and tradition. Now, it seemed, a generation of young Americans was setting out to break away, not only from their own American tradition but from all human constraints of any kind.

Yossarian in Joseph Heller's *Catch-22*, published in 1961, summed up perfectly the beginning of the sixties-style assault on the fifties. "Appleby was a fair-haired boy from Iowa who believed in God, Motherhood, and the American Way of Life, without ever thinking about any of them, and everyone who knew him liked him. 'I hate that son of a bitch,' Yossarian growled."[2]

Beliefs and ethics underlying the old institutions were rejected as hollow, hypocritical, and meaningless. Misfits, such as Bonnie and Clyde, were heroes, and left-wing academics were "guerrillas with tenure," while the police were "pigs." The "adversary media" and "critical intelligentsia" were praised, while work was a "four-letter word," the Protestant ethic was viewed as a straitjacket, the "bourgeois" family was repressive, marriage counselors and social workers supporting it were "zoo keepers," women were "niggers," motherhood was "slavery," and heterosexual intercourse was "rape."

Jim Morrison, lead singer of The Doors, whose mysterious death in 1971 coincided with the death of the counterculture, typically referred to his parents as "dead" when they weren't and aren't. He was serious. They were his ultimate authority figures. "I've always been attracted to ideas that were about revolt against authority," he said. "I like ideas about the breaking away or overthrowing of established order. I am interested in anything about revolt, disorder, chaos—especially activity that seems to have no meaning. It seems to me to be the road toward freedom."[3] The great sixties' devaluation of values was both drastic and a graphic demonstration of the crisis of cultural authority. Everything was turned upside down. Democracy was hypocrisy. Pillars of the establishment were wicked mandarins. Volunteers for war were suckers. Not so much a society, more "the System" or "Leviathan," "Amerika" was spelled with a "k" for its fascist overtones; the flag was for burning. "I don't see any American dream," Malcolm X screamed, "I see an American nightmare!"[4]

Even the 1950s' revival of religion became a revolution in religion. Theologians took the lead in announcing the death of God and plunging fully clothed into a fast-flowing succession of avant-garde secular gospels. Cosier and more archly fashionable than Nietzsche's original version, the American liberal death-of-God was well skewered by Abbie Hoffman's quip that "God is dead and we did it for the kids."

All in all, the temper of the times was no respecter of authorities. Confidence in the presidency? Loyalty to the nation? Respect for business? Inspiration from the American Dream? Adherence to traditional morality? Belief in Christian orthodoxy? Nothing was sacrosanct. All of the traditional sources of legitimacy received a mauling and were left for dead. America lost its virtue in its own classrooms as well as in Vietnam. Voltaire's "Crush the infamous thing!" was given its sixties' expression in the celebrated remark that could have been the soul-cry of a decade: the sixties was the era of "Screw 'God bless America!'"

Mere words do little justice to those days. They are only the more prosaic face of the revolt. Perhaps only those who lived through the sixties can appreciate their darker, more irrational side, the coursing delirium of their promise and their peril. Best personified in exaggerated form by such rock stars as Jim Morrison and Janis Joplin, this Dionysian impulse inspired those of us in the sixties' generation to drink deeply from old, Romantic dreams and flirt crazily with the abyss. Structures and traditions were overthrown, not just because they were outdated, but because of the seductive thrill of living dangerously at the edges of reality. Every day could be a Mardi Gras. Every enterprise a flight to the sun. The fate of Icarus was a classical, not a Romantic, concern.

There was also a more positive side to this revolt, of course. Like the rebellion before World War I, it protested effectively against mindless materialism, hypocritical moralism, and intellectual equivocation. Moderation had slipped into mediocrity. Hard problems had been given half answers. The new problems were thus the old ones unsolved, and the traditional moral attitudes were overthrown in part because they were not moral enough. Blindspots, such as racial bigotry, urban poverty, militarism, and environmental disregard, were exposed and then attacked, ostensibly in the name of a stronger morality and a higher idealism. Trumpeted triumphs from the New Deal to the New Frontier were pronounced as failures in their own terms. America was not delivering its promise; religious believers were not practicing what they preached. No one could rest freely until all were free. Was freedom only for export and not for Americans?

This brief and highly democratic surge of hope and passion made its greatest and most lasting contribution in the civil rights movement, though its positive and orderly contributions go far wider in today's concern for the environment and the political equality of women. But overall it proved short-lived in the sixties and much of it amounted to a moral spasm rather than a renewal. With grand exceptions, such as Martin Luther King, it was based on a moralism that commonly lacked any genuine philosophical and ethical rigor, let alone institutional realism. By the end of the decade the movement plummeted, with Icarus-like trajectory, toward the violence of Altamont, the Weatherman bombings, the Dostoevskian weirdness of the left-wing extremists, and the mood of resigned and distrusting apathy that ushered in the seventies.

Rich Kids' Radicalism

At the same time, it is vital to see that there was no drastic shaking of the third part of America's foundation—economic prosperity. Not only was this unshaken, but it went from strength to strength throughout the sixties and reached unprecedented heights. Due to the staggering cost of the "twin wars" (poverty and Vietnam) and to political reluctance to raise taxes, inflation showed a rise that would be ominous later. But doubts about the New Economics deepened only slowly. Growth was an all-absorbing goal in the decade.

The high levels of prosperity in the sixties led in turn to two major consequences. On the one hand, they created extravagant expectations that were unrealistic as well as unprecedented. This problem still has wide-ranging implications today when many Americans expect too much of life, either in terms of personal fulfillment without hassles or international superiority without rivalry or resentment.

On the other hand, the new prosperity created immense social space for freedom and experiment, whether in political action or alternative life-styles. By 1968, the proportion of young people between eighteen and twenty-one who expected to enter full-time courses of higher education was close to 50 percent, compared with 10 percent in Britain and 13 percent in the USSR. By the same time, there were probably a quarter of a million full-time hippies in America, approximately three-quarters of whom came from middle-class or upper-class homes.[5] Many who took this prosperity for granted never realized how precarious it was and how privileged they were. Rarely has a nation been so flattered by its own success as to expect so much more than its generation's world could offer. The hapless Benjamin Spock and his permissive child-rearing were later blamed for too much. But as one observer wrote astutely, the counterculture was "a revolt of the unoppressed," a response not to constraint but to openness.[6] It was a rich kids' radicalism.

Looking back, it is clearer now that the booming of the economy and the tottering of the social stability and moral legitimacy were related. Not that the first by itself caused the other two, but that there was a unifying link between them—the enormous leap forward of the forces of modernization in the sixties, best epitomized by advances in science and technology, such as television, the Pill, and the space race. How this thrust forward of modernization encouraged economic prosperity is obvious, though its effect on the other two trends is less so. Needless to say, the erosion of social stability was accelerated by the simultaneous erosion of moral legitimacy— but only once the mutual process had been set in train. The main factor behind the erosion of traditional social stability was the diffusing effect of modernization, as in the impact of television and cars on family life. The main factor behind the erosion of traditional moral legitimacy, though, was the liberating influence of modernization through the expansion of secondary education and the mass media.

The effect of this double blow on aspects of American transcendence and tradition was to loosen their binding power—both on the level of institutions, such as the family, and on the level of ideas, such as religious beliefs. The consequence was that other conceptions and ideals came into their own. They had been present in America almost since its origins (though mainly among a minority), and had become more widespread since the second decade of this century (though still not deeply affecting the population at large). As we saw earlier when examining the American declaration of intellectual independence, they now spilled out and spread throughout the nation in the sixties.

The Rubicon Years

These developments sharpened America's crisis of cultural authority. Completing the revolution of 1912–17 shattered what remained of America's traditional consensus. For what was only a decade, but seemed like an eternity, a massive succession of tremors had hit tradition—generational tension, racial violence, inner-city decay, campus unrest, environmental pollutions, and public assassinations. Above all, there was the war in Vietnam that George F. Kennan described as "the most disastrous of all American undertakings over the whole two hundred years of its history."[7] The chasm between self-expression and self-sacrifice had opened to its widest. But worse still, to a nation that almost counted on the moral coherence of war to offset its rampant individualism the sense of transcendence discovered in the experience of Vietnam acted as a boomerang of judgment on the society that declared the war.

Suddenly the New World no longer seemed new. Either America was not the last best hope of the earth, or else Southeast Asian ventures were not the way to go about expressing this impulse. Those called to die for America had challenged what it meant to live in that nation. Few things then appeared less manifest than the American destiny. The Redeemer Nation was itself in need of redeeming. The containment policy had failed to contain. Those who set out to make the world safe for democracy came back anxious about making democracy safe for the world. "Those who recently dreamed of world power," said Christopher Lasch, "now despair of governing the city of New York."[8] Vietnam was to join Versailles as America's second archetypal disaster in world involvement. Or as John Updike wrote simply, "God had taken away his blessing from the United States."[9]

Overall, then, it is easy to see that the general direction of the sixties ran exactly counter to the fifties. If the fifties appeared traditional, allowing one to pretend that 1912–17 was only a bad dream, the sixties was revolutionary in both its character and consequences, thus completing decisively what 1912–17 had begun. New centers of power were victorious over old ones. Urban America was now dominant over rural America, secular liberalism had trounced orthodox Protestantism, and the hedonistic life-style had relegated the Puritan ethic to museums.

Just as its student rebellion and youth movement were hailed as the "counterculture," so the sixties as a whole was termed the "great American cultural revolution," the decade of revolt against authority. In the religious area the trend was away from the orthodox and the conservative, toward the liberal, the secular, and the oriental. In the general political area it was toward liberalism and radicalism. In almost every area orthodoxies and assumptions long accepted in American life were called into question and overturned. What began unseen in earlier days was complete.

More important still, it was in this setting that quiet but more far-reaching claims were made: First, that after the sixties, the interpretation of the entire course of American history would have to be reassessed. The new present demanded a new past, one that gave place, for example, to blacks, women, workers, and immigrants. And second, that during this decade America had experienced a break in the continuity of its moral, religious, and social history that was potentially as significant as any in nearly four hundred years.

From a domestic viewpoint, it was said, America had lost both its innocence and intactness, the former forever and the latter quite possibly so. From an international viewpoint, America had lost its idealism and idealized image as a land of hope and freedom. From a religious and moral point of view, the impulse traditionally considered basic to America and Americanism had gone—and gone, many said, for good.

Entering the decade as post-Puritan and post-Protestant, America had for all intents and purposes left it post-Christian. If the closing of the last frontier in 1890 was the end of a great historic chapter in American history, the sixties seemed to have rung down the curtain on a chapter even longer and greater still, the chapter of faith. The old dream of the "city upon a hill," which inspired and directed so many Americans for more than three centuries, appeared to have faded for the final time. Nothing less than that was said to be at issue. At the very least, a cultural revolution had been unleashed culturewide and the crisis of cultural authority that followed in its wake appeared unstoppable.

6

The Second-thoughts Seventies

In the story of America's crisis of cultural authority, the seventies is the underestimated decade—with good reason. As Václav Havel wrote later, "The seventies were bland, boring, and bleak."[1] Or as John Lennon said at the time, "The 1970s weren't worth a damn."[2] Credited only as the years of malaise that led to the second thinking that led to the eighties, the seventies in America was in fact far more significant. Its second thinking was real, so its links to the eighties are strong. But so also were its links to the sixties. The seventies was therefore a hinge decade with a critical significance. During these years the influence of the sixties consolidated in surprising ways. The seventies led to an eighties that was influenced by the spirit of the sixties more than many realized.

First reactions in the 1970s, a period that began roughly in 1972, tended to focus on the immediate contrasts with the 1960s. Perhaps this was a matter of personal response, bred either by relief or disappointment. Perhaps it was a matter of journalistic style. But the surface differences between the decades were real and underlined with cartoon simplicity. The sixties was the "Movement decade," the seventies the "Me decade." Theodore Roszak's "counterculture" and Charles Reich's "greening of America" had been followed by Herman Kahn's "counter-counterculture" and the "squaring of America" and Peter and Brigitte Berger's "blueing" of America.

A rash of clichés broke out in the attempt to convey the contrasts. In the sixties, a generation of students at Reed College, Oregon, had worn sweatshirts emblazoned with the words, "Communism, Atheism, Free Love." Now they were parodied by their successors with the words, "Capitalism, Apathy, Free Beer." Where Marx, Marcuse, and McLuhan had been in vogue, the rage in reading switched suddenly to such books as Richard Bach's *Jonathan Livingston Seagull* and Thomas Harris's *I'm OK, You're OK*. Almost overnight, it seemed, thousands who had been active in the streets began jogging, growing vegetables, and brightening their own small corners of the world. Changing the system had somersaulted backward into concern for the self. Self-assertion as political therapy by groups became self-assertion as psychological therapy by individuals. "Don't trust anyone over thirty" was on its way to becoming "Don't trust anyone under $30,000 a year." Americans united for world peace turned into "I for me all by myself."

Certainly the suddenness and degree of change in the decade preceding the seventies had been dramatic. Nonetheless, as the last tremors of the earthquake died away, American society in the early seventies settled into a period of eerie tranquillity rather than returning simply to a presixties world. Many people felt uprooted, washed up in a new world like shipwrecked ideological mariners. No simple return or reassertion of tradition seemed possible. A need for a pause, a time for consolidating and absorbing the myriad cultural innovations of a revolutionary decade into the mainstream, seemed palpable.

The Vietnam War did not end as neatly as the decade. And if it was hard to extricate Americans from Vietnam, it was clear that it would be harder still to extricate Vietnam from Americans. Throughout the culture as a whole, the pendulum of change had swung too far. Bemusement, if not disillusionment, was common to both young and old, establishment supporters as well as revolutionaries. Even for many liberals too many traditional values had been abandoned without being replaced. But most people were far from clear as to the new directions toward which they should push. The legacy of the sixties had not been liberation, but a hangover of malaise and drift. The decade of second thoughts was only natural.

Where Are We? And Who Won?

Uncertainty about new directions for America in the seventies was deep for many reasons, not least because of the problem of assessing what had actually happened in the sixties. Supremely, one question either nagged or mocked: Had the counterculture succeeded or failed? Even a cursory polling of its own leaders would suggest that it had failed, and there was no more startling confirmation than their own switches in allegiance, such as that of Rennie Davis in 1973 from radical activism to the Perfect Master of Divine Light or that of Jerry Rubin over a longer period from Yippie to Yuppie. Who in 1968 could have predicted that revolutionary leaders like Bobby Seale and Dick Gregory would be marketing their own barbecue cookbooks and weight loss seminars fifteen years later? Like many rebels, these leaders had come to be distinguished chiefly by their disillusionment with rebellion. Theirs, said Tom Hayden, who was to become a self-confessed "born-again Middle American," had been an "idealism rusted by tragedy."[3] Graduation was in the air. "The campus Nietzsche, at thirty," as H. L. Mencken said of an earlier generation, "begins to feel the suction of Rotary."[4]

Ironically, it could be seen that the sixties as a whole and the counterculture in particular reached their flood tide in 1968. This was the year in which many of the radical leaders hailed victory in their fight against the establishment. But the high drama of 1968 obscured the far more important fact that the tide also turned that year to flow powerfully and irresistibly away from liberalism and radicalism. Why this turning was obscured at the time is not surprising. The year 1968 was the *annus calamitosus* of the sixties. By its end, Americans were reeling after the assassination of Martin Luther King and Bobby Kennedy as well as the uprisings in Prague and Paris, the different horrors of My Lai and the Chicago convention's "police riot" as well as such sights as a Black Power salute on the winners' rostrum at the Olympics.

Only later did two things become clear. First, the great bulk of the images of generational dissent and violence in the sixties had come from the trendsetters and the media-noticed rather than the majority of young people. (As late as 1969 only 28 percent of all college students had participated in demonstrations of any kind.)[5] And while many Americans were troubled for America on account of all they had seen on their screens, their sympathies were not with the protesters. Within the first weeks after the Chicago convention, for example, national surveys showed that less than one in five Americans thought "too much force" had been used. Even among Eugene McCarthy supporters, only 36 percent believed the police had acted improperly.[6]

Second, such developments as the declining confidence in the presidency, the press, and big business, as well as the sudden emergence of a majority in opposition to the Vietnam War, did not add up to the victory the radicals claimed. If they had looked closer, they should have also noticed their own growing isolation and the clear sense of political profit to be won by advocates of "law and order." Contrary to the fond illusion of many liberals, the deepest alienation and the strongest social thrust in America were no longer coming from the Left but from the middle and the Right. What liberals were witnessing was the first muscle-flexing of Nixon's new majority—hard hats, Archie Bunkers, and all. Certainly the silent majority was opposed to Vietnam, but pragmatically rather than morally. The consequences of the class war, not its injustice, was the problem. The silent majority's sons had taken the brunt of the 56,000 dead, and if it was opposed to anything it was the counterculture. Construction workers' placards such as "Hard Hats Hate Hairs" showed clearly where the resentment was directed.

The King Is Dead! Long Live the King!

Yet talk of the failure of the counterculture must be qualified in turn, because otherwise it obscures the continuing influence of the sixties. As time began to show, many of the things for which the counterculture fought and for which it was hotly attacked came to be commonly accepted in the wider culture. This fact needs to be firmly underscored. It was obscured when a passionate rejection of the 1960s became a credo for many people in the 1980s. The seventies-style psychology of being "saved from the sixties" developed into the eighties-style "dancing on the grave of the sixties." Thus a self-serving myth was created that the spirit of the sixties was dead and gone. (Václav Havel, by contrast, wrote his wife from prison that John Lennon's murder was "the death of the century" and a vital symbol. "And you can't help feeling that the shot was fired by the reality of the eighties at one of the departing dreams—the dream of the sixties for peace, freedom, and brotherhood.")[7]

A wave of nostalgia for the fifties reinforced the feeling that the sixties had been repudiated. But the influence of the sixties could not be dismissed so airily by a wave of the wand of tradition. Freer sexuality, tolerance of drugs, a renewed feeling of "anti-bigness," increased politicization of issues, and a lowering of the age of majority were some of the first and more obvious spin-offs of the counterculture. But far deeper and more powerful still were the Romantic themes of freedom and self-expression and the omnipresent influence of modernity and modernization.

What turned out to be modernity's seismic shift in American cultural ideals had broken through in the sixties as an ear-shattering eruption among a vociferous but tiny elite. But when the dust clouds settled in the seventies, the whole bedrock of traditional American culture could be seen to have moved. Hippiedom, student protest, and certain of the transient fashions may have subsided. But many of the deepest values of modernity were not only in the counterculture but in the bloodstream of an unsuspecting middle class and even in the conservative revolution itself.

Pollsters were among the first to appreciate these deeper changes. Paradoxically, Daniel Yankelovich recalled, during the sixties everyone was conscious of ferment, violence, and the threat of revolution. Yet research consistently showed that the vast majority of Americans were unchanged and unruffled in their views. Then, precisely when "1950s normalcy" seemed to prevail in the seventies, studies began to show the story of the startling delayed-action changes.[8] The real revolution in the middle class was not on the streets but below the surface. What the seventies was showing, though not saying, was, "The sixties is dead! Long live the sixties!"

We can gain more light on the sixties as the decade when modernity revolutionized American culture by looking at the experience of other developed nations. Was the American movement unique, or was it simply a larger, richer, and better publicized version of how modernization was troubling the world as a whole? Not surprising, there is strong evidence for the latter view. Deeper even than the common cause provided by Vietnam were the Western impulses of Romanticism and the worldwide theme of pervasive discontent with modernity.

The year 1968 was the "year of the barricades" not only in the United States, but in Europe, Japan, and Mexico, with Danny Cohn-Bendit and "Red Rudi" Dutschke standing in for Tom Hayden and Mark Rudd. Television and newspapers flashed similar images around the world. Parallels with previous upheavals, such as 1848, came to mind naturally. The story in Europe, for example, had contained many parallels with the United States and had arrived at a similar impasse. The year 1968 witnessed the Czech spring in Prague. In Paris the same year, French students came closer than their colleagues in any country to bringing a government to its knees. Yet within a decade, France's "new philosophers" were the talk of town, one of them adapting Mark Twain to capture succinctly their own philosophy and the altered mood of the seventies: "God is dead, Marx is dead, and I am not feeling very well myself."

Plainly, international parallels were vital but had to be drawn with great care. The very distinctiveness of American culture meant that modernity's near-worldwide trends were refracted in a distinctively American way. As in France, Marx was certainly dead in America. But unlike France, the United States had already shown—in the form of the Jesus Movement—that God was far from dead. And in the trend toward hot-tub narcissism, many people were feeling very well, thank you.

Golden Days Are Here Again?

The appeal of the fifties in that brief period of lull in the seventies was understandable. For if nostalgia is the flip-side of progress—as Christopher Lasch has argued—such was the shock of the 1960s' progress that a sentimental return to the past seemed infinitely preferable to an uncomfortable encounter with progress and the future. The need to idealize the past nostalgically was in direct proportion to the need to denigrate the present.

True, the fifties had been called the "silent generation," and Eisenhower's second term seemed a case of "the bland leading the bland." ("Now he's crossing the 38th platitude again!" muttered a reporter during one speech.) But after the successive shocks of the sixties (from the assassinations of two Kennedys, Martin Luther King and Malcolm X to the Kent State shootings and the Weatherman bombings), normality did not appear so boring.

Other twentieth-century decades had witnessed World War I, the Jazz Age, Depression, the Spanish Civil War, World War II, and Vietnam. The fifties was the only decade not marked by any "great event." Perhaps its very blandness and boredom was a blessing. It was the last decade when trouble seemed to be on a controllable scale in an eminently calmer world. It nurtured its generation to grow up under the ancien régime of traditional morality. The old jibe about Eisenhower's secretary of state—"dull, duller, Dulles"—described a reality that suddenly looked enviable. Now that older images of the past—such as the romance of the West—had grown faint, the Eisenhower Elm Street became the chief pattern of the American Eden. Though no more idealizing itself at the time than the twenties had in its time, the fifties became the idyll for later times.

Quaint as it now seems, all those born before 1945 were born before television, penicillin, frozen foods, Xerox, contact lenses, the Pill, plastic money, ball point pens, laser beams, split atoms, tape decks and compact disc players, word processors, car telephones, and fax machines—let alone gay rights, house husbands, computer dating, and commuter marriages. No wonder there was such nostalgia for a recent past that seemed as premodern as the Middle Ages. As Warren Harding (in a riot of alliteration) said on May 14, 1920, after a parallel period of turbulence: "America's present need is not heroics, but healing; not nostrums, but normalcy; not revolution, but restoration; not agitation, but adjustment; not surgery, but severity; not the dramatic, but the dispassionate; not experiment, but equipoise."[9]

Yet despite the revival of fifties' fashions, music, and quiz shows, no simple return to the fifties was thinkable for anyone or desirable for most. The same change that debased the past into nostalgia had also severed it beyond recall. Most people were relieved to have traversed the sixties. But they also knew that many of its questions had not been answered and many of its problems had not been solved. What looked like peace was rarely contentment. Often it was a laissez-faire permissiveness unwilling to be distracted from its own individualistic pursuits. Sometimes it was an apathy born of terminal despair. The threshold of tolerance was higher, but only because much of the idealism had been burned out. Such permissiveness was tolerance at its most debased.

The Year of the Trigger

One of the single events that was most influential in accelerating responses to this temporary lull was the OPEC oil crisis in 1973. It triggered a 350 percent jump in the price of oil, the system's most important source of energy. And coming like a thunderclap out of a clear blue sky, it was as unwelcome as it was unforeseen. But for the purpose of this analysis, its significance is simple: It precipitated the shaking of the third and last of the foundations that were so critical to the well-being of the fifties—the economy.

As late as 1969, official U.S. government statistics showed that America was unrivaled in almost every indicator of economic prosperity. From 1948 to 1973, productivity per person-hour in the industrial economies rose at twice the rate experienced in the previous seventy-five years. So too did standards of living. Apart from exceptions, such as oil-rich Kuwait, American standards of living had been the highest of all for half a century and were still rising most rapidly. For those Americans with the needed talent, enterprise, and industry, openings for extraordinary success were common and almost everyone could benefit from the steadily rising standards. The escalator of economic mobility was in motion, so all could rise just by standing still. The American Dream was vivid and compelling; those who wanted to climb faster could count on its rich rewards.

Yet such a sense of superiority had actually grown somewhat hollow. In the twenty years since 1949, for example, gold reserves had diminished to less than a third of the original $24 billion. But soon it was seen to be more hollow still. Within a few years American living standards were surpassed by at least six European countries (Switzerland, West Germany, Belgium, Denmark, Sweden, and Norway), and America's deteriorating economic performance became apparent on many levels. Japan, the land of the rising sun, was growing twice as fast toward the economic sky as the United States had at any stage of her history. By 1971 the West German government alone held more dollars than there was gold in Fort Knox. Worse still, with unemployment and inflation rising simultaneously, the worst fears of liberals and conservatives (respectively) were roused and the results were plain for anyone to see.

Far more than the OPEC oil crisis was behind this shock, of course. But the combined effect of the oil crisis and such factors as declining productivity and rising inflation was like a sudden crashing of the gears into reverse. Effortless progress came to a shuddering halt. Confidence in the mighty economic machine that could bulldoze its way through social problems was shattered. Poverty, inequality, and class were not eradicated. Keynesian fine-tuning had not proved so easy. Except for those who had the images of the American Dream impressed indelibly on their minds, the dream itself seemed to slow, fade, and go blank as the motor of the economic projector broke down.

A decade later, for all the Reagan era prosperity, part of the new gloom had not lifted. The air in some business circles was still heavy with talk of decline despite all the trumpeted claims of economic restoration. Advertisements, such as that by the American Bankers Association, described the legacy of the seventies glumly: "It wasn't very long ago that America was the undisputed world leader in almost everything. Then, we started losing our clout. Textiles, cars, steel, and electronics began moving abroad, costing American jobs. Hardly anybody has noticed that the same thing is happening with banking. If you look at the names of today's top twenty-five world banks, only one still has a U.S. address. The Japanese now dominate the list."

Thus the OPEC crisis in 1973 and the first whiffs of economic deterioration had a critical impact on the course of the seventies. On the one hand, they were influential in creating the new mood of survivalism and bringing a chill wind of realism into the hot-tub indulgence and narcissism of the early seventies. On the other hand, they were viewed as the last straw by many troubled conservatives, religious conservatives especially. Things had gone wrong. Something urgent had to be done.

Mention of religious conservatives is a reminder that more happened in 1973 than simply the economic jolt of the OPEC crisis. That year also marked the Watergate revelations and the Supreme Court decision *Roe v. Wade* that legalized abortion on demand and excluded the unborn from the definition of "person" protected by the Fourteenth Amendment. Shocked out of the sleep of decades by the events of the sixties and early seventies, many religious conservatives found their minds concentrated by this series of economic, social, and moral crises. Now roused, they were ready to join other conservatives who had been activated ever since the Goldwater campaign in 1964. Half-perceived questions and hitherto unrelated problems suddenly came in focus together. Much that they considered essentially American was under threat and—as was clear after Nixon's fall—the defense of "the great silent majority" could be entrusted to no one but themselves.

Thus, in contrast to its earliest days, the opening years of the seventies were neither radical nor traditional, but were characterized by an uneasy tension between the two camps. But as the decade progressed, Vietnam receded and the crises of 1973 sunk in, the second thoughts grew louder and clearer. American tradition had passed through a severe crisis and was damaged beyond recognition. But, it was now believed, the core crisis of the sixties was the crisis of liberalism, not conservatism. And what had gone wrong was not a result of the excesses of liberalism, but of its essence. Whether "denying permission to win the war" or creating welfare dependency by "throwing money at social problems," liberals slowly but surely came to be regarded as worse than unsuccessful—they were un-American.

The tide therefore turned in a conservative direction. But it was not the traditional conservatives who caught the eye. From one side came the neoconservative movement, whose trajectory and second-thinking was clear in their own self-definition as "liberals mugged by reality" (Irving Kristol) or as "liberals with daughters at high school." This movement gained both illustrious names and cultural momentum, and added an intellectual luster to the Republican Party that had been virtually absent since Theodore Roosevelt. (As recently as 1950 Lionel Trilling could proclaim that American conservatives had no ideas, only "irritable mental gestures.")[10]

In particular, conservatives and neoconservatives carried out a spectacular double coup against the New Class in the world of the nation's "cognitariat" or "cultural gatekeepers." In the first place, they realized the growing importance of the punditocracy, so they captured the key positions on the pundits' talking teams for the national media. They also skillfully exploited the world of the public policy centers, such as the American Enterprise Institute, the Heritage Foundation, the Center for Strategic and International Studies, and the Hoover Institution. In addition, they neutralized those they could not win over by diverting populist resentments from the "super-rich" to the "super-liberal," "super-secular" New Class, enemy elites who were no longer in the corporations but in the media and the universities. The New Class thus became a catch-all term for "liberalism." Then, using their think tanks as national-publicity centers and administration-employment agencies as well as centers of research and policy thinking, conservatives pulled off an end run around the reigning liberalism in the universities and an important victory in the national battle of ideas.

From another side and at a more popular level, the tide—and media attention—surged powerfully toward conservatives of either a social or religious ilk. Main Street, not Wall Street, was on the march and preachers were at its head. Confidence in organized religion, which had sagged in the sixties, showed a sharp upturn after 1973. This trend mainly favored conservative congregations, leaving the more liberal parts of the mainline denominations in the doldrums. The forerunner of this powerful return to conservative religious beliefs was the "Jesus Movement" in the late sixties. A highly distinctive religious movement in itself, it also acted as a surprising cultural reentry vehicle that brought people down from some of the more exotic orbits of the counterculture. But the greatest surprise came at the end of the decade with the emergence of the religious conservatives as a potent political force. Even after 1976, with the "born again movement" and the election of Jimmy Carter in what *Newsweek* called "the Year of the Evangelical," many people were still unprepared for the hard-nosed political activism they saw emerge in 1979.

Both Watergate and Nixon's fall proved a deceptive blessing for the Democrats and for liberals generally. They were handed back the presidency too soon. They had not been forced to learn the lessons of the sixties or acknowledge the generally conservative response to the drastic social shifts that had occurred. They still clung to old beliefs—the inevitability of the historical triumph of the Left, the irreversibility of the damage to conservatism in the sixties. The Democratic triumph in 1976 was therefore a form of a false comfort.

Jimmy Carter won the election of 1976 partly because he had accidentally touched on two of the central sources of future conservative power—the Sun-belt and Protestant evangelicalism. But the Democratic party, instead of courting the evangelicals, or even understanding their significance, turned back stubbornly to much of the discredited New Left liberalism of the sixties. It therefore spurned the emerging social movements that would dominate the eighties. It was Carter's style, say his longtime associates by way of explanation, to "campaign conservative, govern liberal." But conservative disillusionment with Carter went far deeper than that. His election had represented a hesitant groping toward restoring traditional values. Even television evangelist Pat Robertson had given him an outright endorsement in 1976; many evangelicals had hailed him as Catholics had hailed John Kennedy in 1960. Carter's defeat in 1980 was therefore a signal of how clear and urgent the conservative drive had become. Even a neoliberal was to describe Carter's conference on the family as a "festival of relativism under whose guidelines even a fraternity house officially qualified as a family."[11]

At first, religious conservatives were roundly attacked for not minding their own religious business. Yet they were following logically in the steps of the political activists of the sixties, whether secular or religious, and their right to be involved was indisputable. Ever since the First Awakening and the dramatic meltdown of theology in the early nineteenth century, there had been a sort of traditional etiquette surrounding the notion of "sticking to religion"—Tocqueville, as usual, had astutely noted its significance. But by the mid-1970s it was clear that the conditions under which this conventional etiquette was possible were gone for good. The consequences were stark.

As late as 1965 Jerry Falwell had castigated his fellow clergy for taking part in the march at Selma, Alabama. But at the time such a position was no fundamentalist idiosyncrasy. Before an audience of Protestant clergy in 1960, John Kennedy declared his belief in "an America where the separation of church and state is absolute." No Catholic prelate would tell the President how to act, he said, and "no Protestant minister would tell his parishioners for whom to vote."[12] The public acts of public servants were accountable at the voting booth, not the confession booth.

By the late seventies, however, vast numbers of conservatives had woken up to the fact that the old notion of merely "sticking to religion" was triply impossible. Theologically, it was based on a form of shrunken pietism that discouraged believers from integrating their faith with the whole of their lives. Sociologically, it was based on the assumption of a general moral consensus that assured them that such action was unnecessary anyway. Historically it was based on an interpretation of the First Amendment that was closer to an extreme separationism rather than the intentions of the original framers of the Constitution. Suddenly the first position was seen to be wrong. The second, in the light of the upheavals of the sixties, was shown to be unworkable. And the third was seen to be self-defeating.

Conservatives Are Revolutionaries Too

The rise of neoconservatism and the resurgence of conservative religion were only two parts of a far wider crisis of postwar liberalism, a crisis worked out in other areas, such as foreign relations, social policy, and economics. Of these two, religion was the unexpected and more influential part. Therefore by the end of the seventies and beginning of the eighties conservatives held the upper hand, as was confirmed decisively in President Reagan's election in 1980 and reelection in 1984.

Throughout those years many liberal critics dismissed the conservative revolution as stubbornly as conservatives had dismissed the liberal revolution earlier. As the detractors saw it, the Reagan years were simply a detour and the conservatives were crusaders of the irretrievable. Conservatives might capitalize on the crisis they inherited and reverse shorter-term trends, as illustrated by the economic boom and the upswing in the national mood of the Reagan years. But their critics thought it unlikely that conservatives would develop a sufficiently coherent conservative philosophy to effect a decisive conservative revolution and make the 1980 transition pivotal in American history. To such critics, Ronald Reagan's massive victory in 1984 was a personal victory—broad but shallow and far from durable.

Passing time has confirmed some of these criticisms. But to stop there is to do less than justice to the liberal crisis and the desired conservative changes. For conservatives genuinely saw themselves as revolutionaries, or better still as counterrevolutionaries. In seeking to shift the nation from a liberal and quasi-welfare state to an "entrepreneurial state" or "opportunity society," they regarded themselves as successors to six previously successful American revolutions: the Founders, the Jeffersonian Democrats, Jacksonian populism, the rise of the GOP, the William McKinley campaign, and Franklin Roosevelt's New Deal. A key feature of Reagan's two terms was the struggle of a "movement conservatism" to establish itself as an enduring national elite. Not only could they effectively reverse sixties' liberalism and successfully establish eighties' conservatism; more significantly, conservatives believed that they could counter and stop the crisis of cultural authority itself. America would be back, they claimed, strong, tall, and true as ever. That was their appointed task in the eighties.

7

The Empty Eighties

Like the sixties, the eighties is central to the unfolding of the crisis of cultural authority—but not quite as it might appear. Obviously the 1980s is the second highly activist decade of the four we are surveying. Its conservative counterrevolution balances the cultural revolution of the sixties. But that is the obvious side of the story. More like the fifties, the significance of the eighties lies below the surface. And it lies in the twist put on the term "golden" in the golden era of conservatism. For on closer inspection, the 1980s turns out to be a second gilded era. In revealing ways, its meaning for the crisis of cultural authority is, in John Updike's description, as the "empty eighties."[1]

In 1973, Watergate was called the American regicide. Doubtless both Charles I and Louis XVI, who were slain for their "high crimes and misdemeanours," would have been happy to switch places with Richard Nixon. But to foreign eyes the president was hunted down with a fury that defied purely rational explanations. Darker motivations, if not machinations, were at work. In part Nixon found himself the hapless quarry of a political hue and cry not entirely of his own making. If Nixon had been the conservatives' revenge on the sixties, the grand Watergate hunt was partly the liberals' revenge on Nixon.

But what was just as strange to foreign observers a decade later was an atmosphere almost the reverse of Watergate. In the 1984 election campaign the journalistic "need to know" was rising to flood levels again, although only selectively. The focus was on the infidelities of many politicians, such as Senator Gary Hart, rather than the impeachment of one. But elsewhere in the mid-eighties the reigning American mood amounted to a national form of cover-up. It was far less criminal than Nixon's, to be sure, but was no less consequential. In the second era of Good Feelings, not only Blame America Firsters but questioners and loyal critics of America were elbowed out of the discussion. The late-seventies period of self-castigation had shifted to one of self-celebration. In the process the "need to know" seemed to have given way to the need to forget and even to deny. In Gore Vidal's phrase, the USA had become the "United States of Amnesia."

For a long time, this mood blocked a realistic assessment of the eighties. The greatest celebrator of all was the Great Communicator, Ronald Reagan, but expressions of the same sunny optimism could be heard on many sides. The central lesson of the 1984 election results, wrote Michael Barone for the *Washington Post*, is that America is at peace.

> To understand American politics in the middle 1980s, you need to accept something about the United States that probably will be the first thing that future historians will notice about our time. . . . We are a nation at peace. Not only—though this is crucial—are we not at war, nor likely to be involved in a major war any time soon. We are also a nation at peace, to a greater extent than we realize, with ourselves. Beneath the turmoil and clash of everyday American politics, beneath the sometimes apocalyptic rhetoric, we have been approaching something like a consensus about basic values and politics, and something resembling a consensus on the differences we are willing to tolerate in each other.[2]

Our Finest Hour

Both in 1984 and at Reagan's retirement four years later, there was a host of reasons for the surge of optimism that characterized the eighties. And many of them were sound. Of the two chief ones, international success was the most important. When Ronald Reagan was asked as he left Washington to say what he was most proud of, he replied simply that he had won the Cold War. And in a typically down-to-earth way, he was right. By shifting the defense buildup into high gear and deploying intermediate missiles in Western Europe, by proposing and pressing for his Strategic Defense Initiative, and by articulating the "Reagan Doctrine" and supporting anti-Communist rebels around the world, Reagan had checked Soviet expansion and exposed the antiquated rigidity of their centralized society.

Within a year of his helicopter lift-off from the White House, Soviet dominoes had collapsed from Poland to Nicaragua, and the conservative revolution could take pride in its crowning achievement—Europe, the grand prize in the Cold War, had been won by the West, the Communist empire was in collapse, totalitarian socialism was discredited as an idea, and Western liberal democracy had fewer political rivals than at any time since 1917. The "evil empire" of lies and repression, which had been outdistanced politically in the postwar boom and exposed morally in the revelations about Stalin's purges and gulags, suddenly found itself liquidated by the challenges of its own *glasnost*. Still far from a liberal or democratic state, the Soviet Union of Gorbachev's *perestroika* was no longer the ultimate threat to liberal democracy.

The victories of 1989 were particularly sweet to conservatives. But they were the fruit of four-and-a-half decades of America's manning the ramparts of freedom under the leadership of both Democrats and Republicans. James R. Schlesinger, former secretary of defense, could justifiably state to the Congress: "Yet, while we should be magnanimous in victory, we should not fail to celebrate this American accomplishment. Were Winston Churchill alive today, I believe he would refer to the steadfast American role of these past forty years as—our finest hour."[3]

The second conservative ground for confidence was the performance of the economy. After eight years under Reagan, the United States was enjoying the longest peacetime expansion in its long, prosperous history. The inflation rate of 1980 had been cut in half, unemployment stood at its lowest rate for a decade and a half, and nearly 16 million new jobs had been created. Reagan's controversial policies of cutting tax rates, shrinking the size of government, and boosting private entrepreneurship appeared to have paid off handsomely.

Most notably, Ronald Reagan had achieved what no other postwar president had done: He had presided over a significant decline in *both* inflation and unemployment. (Both numbers worsened in the Kennedy years, though only slightly, and every other president improved one only at the expense of worsening the other.) Added to other Republican achievements, such as the boosting of national morale and the president's success in getting most of his conservative nominees into key judicial positions, Reagan's supporters were elated. Liberalism no more held the initiative in the United States than communism did in the world. The main weaknesses of its philosophy had been exposed and repudiated in three national elections. Conservatism was confident and in control.

At first sight, then, the conclusion appears inescapable: Nothing could be more solid than the accomplishments of the eighties—America's era of confident, successful conservativism. But did such grounds of confidence exhaust the range of factors to be considered? Did they all add up to the feeling of restored innocence and invulnerability that many Americans exuded? And how, by any standards, could they be said to have created

Barone's "consensus about basic values" when issues such as abortion and flag burning were still fueling the culture wars and race-based inner city violence was festering? Continent-sized nations have a ready excuse for feelings of security. This is particularly true of the United States, which has no strong or hostile neighbors, no recent experience of foreign armies on its soil and no immediate prospect of them, plus a huge economy, a mighty military shield, and a natural two-ocean buffer. But was the conservative restoration as solid and united as it appeared?

The Picture Without the Airbrush

Those Americans who remained uneasy despite the celebration of the Reagan years pointed to problems on either the domestic or the international fronts. Domestically, the size of the deficit caught the eye. Not even the United States could go on forever spending $200 billion a year more than it took in, or ignore that the trade balance had collapsed from a $17 billion surplus in 1980 to a $139 billion deficit in 1986. Under Ronald Reagan the United States was transformed from the world's largest creditor into the world's largest debtor. Before he retired from office, American foreign debts exceeded all of Latin America's combined ("the Argentining of America"). As Reagan's heir, George Bush inherited a publicly held federal debt nearly triple that accumulated by all of Reagan's thirty-nine predecessors.[4]

Responses to that situation were unsurprisingly sharp. *Time* announced that the 1980s had sputtered to an early end during the stock market's free-fall on October 19, 1987.[5] Gore Vidal prophesied that the American empire ran out of gas on September 16, 1985, when America became a net debtor nation for the first time since 1914.[6] A Texan wag declared that the easiest way to become a millionaire in Dallas was to start as a billionaire.

There were sharp differences, of course, over what the deficits meant. They were undoubtedly the largest American deficits outside of war or depression, and budget-balancing Republicans had run them up, not loose-spending Democrats. But no calamity occurred and the deficits-are-disastrous school sounded more like Chicken Little squawkings than hard economics, especially since there was no economic way to settle the argument. And perhaps Reagan's debt legacy was not fiscal adventurism. Perhaps, as leading Democrats claimed, it was a deliberate political ploy like the Greeks' leaving their giant horse on the beach at Troy. With the deficit there, Democratic spending could never be the same. "By running up the debt and not really caring about it," one Democratic member of Congress claimed, "Reagan put an 800-pound gorilla in the middle of the House floor and the Senate floor."[7]

Yet what put a cap on social spending by Democrats also put a cap on all spending by Republicans. Both wallet and will were hit together. And when it came to Republicans saying "no" to fledging democracies rather than to prodigal Democrats, the consequences were stark and poignant. But that self-imposed handicap is only one of many ironies, illusions, and inadequacies of the Reagan prosperity seen without an airbrush. In the first place, part of Reagan's success was a matter of good fortune as much as good policy. Among the serendipitous factors from which he benefited were the collapse of OPEC (and thus declining prices for imported oil), the prior arrival into the work market of the bulk of the baby-boom generation (thus making it easier to cut unemployment when the labor force was growing more slowly), the continued decline of the labor unions, and the effects of two developments his less fortunate predecessor began—the deregulation of the economy and the monetary policy of the Federal Reserve Board under Paul Volcker.

Second, the real strength of the Reagan prosperity was far less rosy than the economic expansion might suggest. Certain facts need to be remembered if the optimism is not to become illusory. For example, while America's output of goods and services grew strongly between 1980 and 1988, the increase came largely from people working longer hours. Productivity, which is the real indicator of rising living standards, stayed stuck at 1 percent per year. Or again, American savings and investment (another key factor in raising the standard of living) declined in comparison with the seventies. As a share of national income, they declined to the lowest level in modern history.

Third, as this evidence suggests, a significant moral change underlay Reaganomics. Consider the fact that the flipside of the deficit-spending by the government was a spending spree by the public. Credit-card debt, for example, was $50 billion when Reagan took office and $180 billion when he left.[8] Both these forms of "dissaving" represented a moral as much as an economic trend. "The deficit," George Will scolded, "is the numerical expression of a cultural tendency and a governmental dereliction of duty." Whereas three-quarters of the previous 190 years of government deficit prior to Reagan was a result of war, and therefore was the price of liberty, "the Reagan-Bush debt is just the price of profligacy."[9]

Similar candor was heard within the administration. Richard Darman, director of the Office of Management and Budget, described the deficit problem as a form of indulgent and shortsighted "Now-now-ism." People were rightly outraged by the breakdown of individual morality, such as the "wilding" in Central Park in 1989. But "collectively, we are engaged in a massive backward Robin Hood transaction—robbing the future to give to the present." The result is a self-indulgent theft from the future that "borders on public policy wilding." Yet "the heart of the Now-now problem is a problem of values: The deficit is, in a sense, an expression of contempt for the burden of debt that is left to the future."[10]

Fourth, there was a close and uncomfortable link between the conservative prosperity and the spreading financial scandals in which it became enmired. For all the effort to revive moral order, the eighties finished as spiritually devastated as the seventies, though without the dreaded term "malaise." For all the rhetoric of return to tradition, the decade was an astonishingly radical era in financial history. Unchecked commitment to growth and acquisition overrode all traditional conservative constraint. For all the talk of restoring honesty and efficiency to government, one of the main things the 1980s restored was the teapot-dome-type scandals of the Harding era—though the latter look cozy and small-scale beside the Greater Gatsby corruptions of the second gilded age. When they first broke, the scandals at Housing and Urban Development, in the savings and loan industry, and in Wall Street's junk bond empire each appeared isolated and possibly an aberration. But the emerging links in both personnel and philosophy showed their true lineage. Each was the bastard offspring of the same deregulated markets and deregulated morals that were near the core of the Reagan revolution.

The sheer scale of corruption was shocking enough. Secretary Jack Kemp, launching a search for accountants to help him cleanse HUD's Augean stables, admitted that the extent of the problems were "almost incomprehensible."[11] When it came to the S&L crisis, prosecutors and investigators were overwhelmed. (In 1990, 1,500 of 3,500 major criminal cases were gathering dust.) Even the major accounting firms could not be counted on because ten of the largest were themselves being sued for negligence in the first place.[12]

But the corrupt core of the second gilded age was found in the spirit. Its impact on genuinely traditional American virtues, such as work, honesty, and restraint, was devastating. Tom Wolfe summed up the 1980s as "the decade of money fever."[13] He also portrayed it in what was the book of the eighties: *The Bonfire of the Vanities*. But even his "Masters of the Universe" paled beside the real-life barons of Wall Street. In a day when dealmaking was the rage and productive work was boring, success meant that deals need not make sense and work itself could be a "life-style option" for the rich.

When Michael Milken made $550 million in a single year, 1987, he became a market all by himself and the highest wage earner in industrial history. *The New York Times* pointed out that the amount was more than McDonalds earned that year. Hardly paupers themselves, both David Rockefeller and Donald Trump expressed public surprise at wages even Wall

Street could not stomach. But Milken's junk-bond universe contributed no observable benefits to American profits, productivity, or competitiveness beyond the world of Wall Street and Wilshire Boulevard. His megafortune was simply the result of shuffling already existing chips and taking large bites each time they passed. Little wonder that the junk-bond bubble burst.[14] As in the 1920s, the problem went beyond simple greed and legality. At stake was a philosophy of life that was light years from traditional America. The Drexel-Burnham mentality that said "if we didn't have bonuses, we wouldn't have had anybody working for us" was the same publicly irresponsible avarice that John Maynard Keynes described earlier as "the byproduct of the activities of a casino."[15]

Lastly, the prosperous economics of the conservative revolution created blindspots that would be fateful for its own long-term prospects. In the 1980s educational competence and business competitiveness were much talked about buzzwords, yet the United States slid slowly from being a "leading indicator" of global trends to being a "lagging indicator." The result was a lengthening list of problems that economist Lester Thurow described as belonging to the "festering disaster" category—situations that, if viewed in any one single year, are hardly problems but that become disastrous if allowed to grow decade after decade.[16]

Economists usually focused on American investment, trade deficits, and educational backwardness, all of which were allowed to drift unchecked because the needed changes would have required difficult decisions and short-run sacrifice. Others pointed to the shocking signs of America's deteriorating infrastructure of roads and bridges. With the nation seemingly paralyzed by taxaphobia and its leaders by poll-mania, Republican adminis-trators benignly presided over a retreat from the historic initiatives of their predecessors, such as Teddy Roosevelt's building of the Panama Canal or Dwight D. Eisenhower's construction of the interstate highway system. Since 1960, George Will warned, investment in infrastructure had fallen more than 50 percent as a percentage of GNP. Of America's 575,000 highway bridges in 1990, 42 percent were structurally deficient (closed or restricted to light traffic) or functionally obsolete. One bridge failed every two days. Thus "today's incontinent pursuit of current consumption" was nothing short of "the wearing out of America."[17]

But the most outspoken denunciations of all were directed at Republican indifference to the poor. With the inner cities decomposing, with the gap between rich and poor growing, with evidence of the homeless and beggars pressing in on all sides, with the realization that volunteerism could not bridge the widening gulfs, conservative dogma and indifference increasingly came under fire. Despite every conceivable blame and folly being heaped upon "big spending liberalism," the source of many problems led straight to the front door of "killer conservatism."[18] Republicans could boast of distinguished exceptions, such as HUD Secretary Jack Kemp and Susan Garrett Baker, wife of Secretary of State James Baker, but their general neglect of the poor was exposed beyond dispute by the lurid light of the rioters' fires of 1992.

George Will could hardly be called a prophet in the wilderness, but on the issue of complacency to the poor his criticism of his fellow conservatives was unsparing. When (candidate) George Bush dismissed attacks over this issue as a matter of European-style class consciousness, Will's response was fierce: "Bush, you're something else if you think there are no class divisions that condition access to education, legal services, medical care, and other important things. It is a national scandal that one-fifth of all children live in poverty and a national travesty that a presidential candidate denies class realities."[19]

Who's Dancing on Whose Grave?

A defining feature of the 1980s was its sweeping dismissals of the 1960s. But this backhanded compliment to the sixties raises questions that are important for interpreting the eighties. How seriously should the sixties be taken as an epoch-marking era in American history? And how far did the sixties influence the eighties decisively? The enigma of the eighties becomes both apparent and important in the answer to these questions. Dancing on the grave of the sixties was fine if the sixties were well-interred and the eighties had reason to be jubilant. Oddly, however, many of those most scathing about the sixties showed a tell-tale ambivalence toward it. Sometimes they described their goals as a drastic conservative reversal of the sixties, as if that decade was a catastrophic watershed in American history that only a root-and-branch revolution could turn back. ("Like a knife blade," Lance Morrow has written of 1968, "the year severed past from future.")[20] At other times they talked as if the conservative program was simply a natural resumption of traditional ways, as if the sixties was merely an isolated hiccup in the life of the nation. Drastic reversal or natural resumption? Both answers could not be right, and which one was influences an estimate of the sixties and its pull on the eighties.

Many of the serious assessments of the sixties are sobering and confirm the crisis of cultural authority. Historian Sydney Ahlstrom termed it "a decisive turning point in American history."[21] George Will has called 1968 "perhaps the worst year in American history" and the sixties "the most dangerous decade in America's life as a nation."[22] David Potter, another celebrated historian, described it as "one of the severest cases of social estrangement that any society has ever experienced." Indeed, it was "perhaps the most aggressive rejection of dominant values that any society has ever permitted without seriously attempting to curb the attack and without really defending the values under assault."[23] Social scientist Robert Nisbet wrote similarly: "I think it would be difficult to find a single decade in the history of Western culture when so much barbarism—so much calculated onslaught against culture and convention in any form, and so much sheer degradation of culture and the individual—passed into print, into music, into art, and onto the American stage as the decade of the Nineteen Sixties."[24] Or as Allan Bloom wrote tersely, "Enlightenment in America came close to breathing its last in the sixties."[25]

Kevin Phillips includes the sixties among the five major and minor periods of breakdown the United States has experienced—the Civil War period, the sixties, the Depression, the decade of the War of 1812, and the twenty-year agricultural slump of 1873–96 accompanied by the dramatic growth of U.S. industry. The last two crises, he says, were only minor and mostly regional, but the first three genuinely tested the entire country. "My own inclination is that the 1960s and 1970s are second only to the Civil War and the decade preceding it as a time of national breakdown."[26]

These assessments fit in with the present analysis of the sixties as a key phase of the crisis of cultural authority. The decade represents a climactic convulsion of forces that in the end could alter the direction of the United States as decisively as any period in American history. At the very least, many in the eighties were wrong to dismiss the sixties without understanding its influence on themselves. Similarly today, we need to see through the clash and din of the bitter fight to the death between the decades, or we will miss the clues to the 1990s as the showdown years of the crisis of cultural authority.

Which Way in the Nineties?

As if decadology were not suspect enough, bids to christen the 1990s were entered in droves before the 1980s was over. (Tom Wolfe, by contrast, dubbed the 1970s the "Me Decade" only a little before its close.) The nineties would be the "We decade," columnist Paul Taylor predicted in 1986. Instead of me-decade materialism and muscular patriotism, the coming mood was to be about "things like a national sense of community, moral revival, civic virtue, and the imperative of doing good."[27] Given fresh impetus by President Bush's "thousand points of light" and his "kinder, gentler America," a flood of commentators in January 1990 heralded the nineties as the "Decency Decade" (*Good Housekeeping* magazine), the decade of "heart," and so on. Gone were said to be the "gimme years" with their tabloid heroes, such as Donald Trump, Ivan Boesky, and Leona Helmsley. "Creativity, compassion, and correction are going to be the hallmarks of the '90s."[28]

Something in these claims was striking at once, even if one ignored the counterpredictions that the next decade would move in more liberal directions, such as the "numinous nineties" (caught up with the mystical environmentalism of the Green movement). The more conservative claims described themselves in direct contrast to the eighties, not the sixties. Far from the assured results of a successful and completed restoration, the achievements of the conservative revolution came across repeatedly as incomplete, ambivalent, and unsuccessful. (Even *Good Housekeeping* wrote, without apparent irony, of the "new traditionalism.") Taken together, several indications suggest not the failure of conservativism and the triumph of liberalism, but a far more confused picture of trends, countertrends, and culture clashes that makes up the showdown phase of the crisis of cultural authority.

First, there was broad agreement that the legacy of the eighties had shown up the inadequacies of conservativism just as that of the sixties had to liberalism. The point is clear from the evidence above. The whole genre of claims-for-the-1990s is a form of backhanded criticisms-of-the-1980s. As Meg Greenfield summed it up for the *Washington Post* in 1990: Everybody has known for at least a decade that the more tired-out nostrums of liberalism have lost their following among the electorate at large, but the big news is now elsewhere. "What is now emerging is the happy fact that all the gloating commentary on this from the other side, all the self-certainty and smugness about how extreme social conservatism was the required political order of the day, may have been off-base too."[29]

Second, no group was more scathing about the folly of saluting the success of the conservative revolution than the conservatives themselves. It would be hard to rival the late-sixties' splintering into irrelevance of the New Left movement. But similar tendencies began to emerge in the late-eighties on the Right. Few people were more blunt about the failures of the conservative movement than Richard Viguerie, direct mail wizard and chairman of United Conservatives of America. As the Republican Convention in New Orleans was hailing eight years of rousing success in 1988, Viguerie stood aside skeptically. "What Reagan revolution?" he snorted. "Ronald Reagan's achievements are very real, but more important than what Reagan accomplished is what he could have accomplished but did not." The measure of a real revolution is its irreversibility. Old arrangements are wiped away, beyond all hope of return. But Reagan never achieved or attempted this. "Despite the victories of the past twenty years, the American conservative movement cannot claim to be successful. Its revolution in public policy is incomplete and will stay that way because its political revolution is incomplete."[30]

Such right-wing criticisms were dismissed as the sour grapes of a jilted-lover faction, but the political fact from which they sprang was undeniable. During the two full terms of the most conservative president in recent history, the Republican party had become more centrist. Early conservative victories had taken the edge off conservatism. The once-dominant right-wing had become a faction rather than a vanguard. The revolution as it once was had quickly faded, and only an illusion of its strength was kept in the air by a combination of intense euphoria and the skills of the image-makers. If the Republican party was the Party of Revolution and 1980 was Year One, analyst William Schneider wrote, "Nineteen eighty-seven is Year One of the Post-Reagan era. The problem is, Ronald Reagan is still in office. The revolutionary regime has outlived the revolution."[31]

Third, there were signs in the early nineties of a tidal turn in the flow of culture or at least a concerted push in that direction. When the film *Flashback* was released in 1990, much was made of its undisguised cultural message. Turning upside down the traditional generation-gap theme, the story hinged on the drama of a middle-aged sixties' radical jabbing into awareness a staid, clean-cut eighties' FBI agent. At the end, the oldster (played by the quintessentially sixties-ish Dennis Hopper of *Easy Rider* fame) said to the youngster: "The '90s will make the '60s look like the '50s."

Was this reveling in the spirit of the sixties as a form of propaganda, nostalgia, or a shameless looting of symbols for the purpose of massaging the mass market? Only the moguls at Paramount could answer that, but the film was only one of several message films that year. (Others included *Born on the Fourth of July* on the morality of the Vietnam War, *The Handmaid's Tale* on abortion, and *Wild at Heart,* an erotic and violent take of *The Wizard of Oz.*) Beyond that, various events and trends moved in the same direction—above all the Supreme Court's *Webster* decision on *Roe v. Wade* in 1989, which threw the debate back to the states. Suddenly, and to the surprise of many, it was no longer politically advantageous to be socially conservative. The humiliating sound of the politicians' public flip-flops became common.

Few of these developments were a surprise. The deep fissures underlying the conservative movement were evident from the start of the eighties. The very terms concealed contradictory elements. "Conservative," for instance, was a catchall term, illustrated by the fact that the three most common types of conservatism (fiscal, social, and religious) came in conflict with one another as often as they converged on an issue. These in-house conservative contradictions exploded colorfully in the short-lived nomination of Judge Douglas Ginsburg to the Supreme Court in 1987. Following the bitterly polarized battle over Judge Robert Bork, the Ginsburg hearings took a startlingly different tack—liberals were as reluctant to attack Ginsburg as conservatives to support him. Married twice, with neither his wives nor his children taking his name, smoking a little marijuana, and running a computerized dating service, he was oddly modern to both sides—a libertarian conservative as close to modern liberals as to traditional conservatives.

The example of Ginsburg was only one of many paradoxes among leaders in the conservative era. For a start, many of those most energetic in the financial scandals were devoutly religious—Marilyn L. Harrell, the woman known as "Robin HUD" being an evangelical, Charles Keating of the S&L crisis a leading Catholic antipornographer, and Michael Milken a Jew. Or again, it was curious that in so conservative and family-oriented an era, one of the most popular television personalities was Roseanne Barr—a left-wing, proletarian feminist whose par-for-the-course description of marriage was "a life sentence, without parole." Then there was always the chairman of the Republican National Committee. Lee Atwater was a man with one foot in the counterculture. He was described before his sickness and conversion as a "nihilist" rather than a traditionalist, and credited with some of the dirtiest of mean tricks to get his candidates toward the kindest and gentlest of ends ("I was nakedly cruel toward Dukakis").[32] Yet if he was the first major political leader with a sixties' sensibility, his allegiance was to the party of the fifties and the eighties, not that of the sixties.

Such paradoxes were run-of-the-mill in the eighties, especially typical of the tensions within the conservative coalition. Kevin Phillips pointed out the irony behind such paradoxical terms as "revolutionary conservatism," "Middle American radicalism," and "center extremism." "By 1980, most of the *plausible* radical forces in the country were arrayed under the conservative banner."[33] Phillips noted other tensions too—between the backward-looking and the forward-looking, between classical conservatism and neo-conservatism, between elitism and populism, between Wall Street, Main Street, and Easy Street, between the more ideologically inspired and the more frustration-driven, and, supremely, between the more strictly fiscal conservatism of, say, the Yuppies and most baby boomers and the more moral-cum-social-cum-fiscal conservatism of the fundamentalists (live-and-let-live versus laissez-faire). As Daniel Bell noted of the Reagan conservative species, "Reaganismus is a political hippogriff."[34] (And, of course, Reagan's victorious consensus in 1984 was virtually a white consensus, which is hardly the wave of the future.)

Viewed on the highest plane, the contradictions of the conservative revolution stemmed from the fundamental clash between conservatism and modernity (and the latter especially in the form of capitalism). Capitalism and conservatism have been tied so closely in people's minds that most forget that capitalism, and its attendant industrialization, has been the greatest solvent of tradition and traditional ideals in history. Its modernizing thrust is essentially antinomian, individualistic, and a process of hollowing out.

Viewed at a more down-to-earth level, the contradictions of the conservative revolution can be seen at their sharpest among young people. Often touted as the most extraordinary evidence of the Reagan revolution, young people in the eighties provided the best evidence of its instabilities. Their overwhelming agreement with the president on economic issues masked their differences with him that were likely to emerge and prove influential to his successors. Less favorable to religion, less concerned with ideology, less optimistic about the broader national prospects (as opposed to their own), above all they were far more liberal socially. In fact, while still supporting Ronald Reagan, young people of the eighties were strikingly and consistently more liberal than the students and young people of the 1960s.[35] As Tom Wolfe emphasized, the "conservative decade" was the era of excesses from rock music to the sexual revolution. "The '80s are wilder than the '60s. . . . It's been much faster than erosion. There has been a sweeping aside of standards. Every kind of standard."[36]

The most poignant testimony to the emptiness of the eighties was Lee Atwater's just after his conversion and just before his death by cancer at the age of forty in 1991:

> The '80s were about acquiring—acquiring wealth, power, prestige. I know. I acquired more wealth, power, and prestige than most. But you can acquire all you want and still feel empty. . . . It took a deadly illness to put me eye to eye with that truth, but it is a truth that the country, caught up in its ruthless ambitions and moral decay, can learn on my dime. I don't know who will lead us through the '90s, but they must be made to speak to this spiritual vacuum at the heart of American society, this tumor of the soul.[37]

Such talk of the "empty eighties" is more than a metaphor. The conservative revolution of the 1980s rested on the cultural revolution of the 1960s. The 1980s' revolution was far more liberal—even radical—than many of its supporters realized. Its libertarian wing, for example, was often associated with conservatism when in fact it was a noninterventionist version of liberalism. One aspect of liberalism is its concept of individualism raised to the status of public philosophy. Since all morals are private and subjective, none can be raised as public and objective. Thus whereas the traditional conservative is concerned with the character of public conduct that is deemed good or evil in itself, both the liberal and the libertarian are concerned only with its consequences. This libertarian element, reinforced by social trends that make it liberalism's growing rather than shrinking side, made the core of the conservative revolution unstable and unpredictable.

Throughout the eighties these tensions were held together by a combination of the strength of Ronald Reagan's personality and skill and the depth of 1980s' reaction to the 1960s. But the crisis of liberalism does not ensure the permanent victory of conservatism. Unless the nineties sees the successful consolidation of a permanent conservative center, the Reagan landslide in 1984 will not be seen as a watershed, but as a counterlurch rightward to balance the lurch leftward in the 1960s or even as a way station toward conditions of even greater unpredictability. Most people have not yet recognized the nature of the crisis of cultural authority, so they anticipate only a pendulumlike return to the traditional American center. Kevin Phillips, on the other hand, foresees a possible convulsion in the future. He pictures this as the last fight between two old bull elephants, neither of whom will survive the encounter to lead the herd. "My surmise," he concludes, "is that revolutionary conservatism is a species of last-stage 'conservatism,' likely to be remembered as what happened after last-stage 'liberalism.' "[38]

The Coming of the Last Man?

Speculation about the nineties would be idle at this stage. But if this present analysis of the crisis of cultural authority is correct, we are approaching its climax. This decade therefore represents the showdown period, the years of reckoning in which the crisis of cultural authority will move toward its resolution. For that very reason, neither the defining features nor the outcome of the decade is evident now. But the overall dynamics of the decades will probably prove something like this. The nineties will amount to a decisive resolution at the climax of the crisis just as the fifties amounted to a decisive accumulation of forces at its beginning. Seen this way, the sixties and the eighties were the two activist decades, one being liberal and the other conservative. In relation to them, the fifties represented a period of accumulation, the seventies one of transition, and the nineties one of resolution.

Whatever the substantive outcome of the crisis of cultural authority, three important and somewhat contradictory trends are likely to have a hand in its resolution. First, the culture wars of the last three decades will continue. Cultural divisions and instabilities must be taken seriously because the postsixties legacy has been polarization as much as pluralism. And the different responses to the postsixties issues are not superficial, temporary, or accidental. They mark off a deep divide that runs through American society and life at different points.

On one side are those who are, broadly speaking, liberal and secular in cultural issues. They welcome the general flow of earlier trends, especially the sixties-style liberalization, and see a fortunate convergence between their own ideological preferences and trends, such as social diffusion, which create room, say, for alternative life-styles. For them, the net result of the crisis of cultural authority is overwhelmingly positive. What has happened is simply a grand American restructuring or transformation. Once the current period of turbulence is over, they believe, any social strains and tensions that remain will be seen as only small fissures, tiny cracks in the essentially solid structures of a fully modern America. Rid of its primitive impurities, the ideological air they breathe will be cleaner. Cleared of its antiquated traditional structures, the social worlds they inhabit will be freer.

On the other side of the cultural divide are those who are, broadly speaking, conservative and favorable to religion. They deplore the earlier trends and regard an emphatic rejection of the sixties as the necessary starting point for the eighties and beyond. They therefore see an unfortunate collision between their own ideological preferences and trends, such as social diffusion, which breaks up such traditional institutions as the family. The net result for the cultural conservatives is overwhelmingly negative. They see the social strains not as small fissures, but as a social faultline of San Andreas proportions that threatens the security of much that is traditionally American. Shorn of its traditional beliefs and values, the nation itself is not only different, but poorer, weaker, and less American at once.

A second and more conservative trend to watch is demographic. In the 1990s, 75 million American baby boomers—the huge cohort born between 1946 and 1964—will be entering middle age. They are likely to take America with them. This fact will have enormous significance for the economy, because three-quarters of all Americans will be of prime working age (twenty-four to fifty-five). More importantly, it cannot fail to affect the crisis of cultural authority. The same "demography is destiny" that augmented the youth and idealism of the sixties will work to reinforce a sense of stability and normalcy in the nineties. A powerful counterreaction to the eighties is therefore unlikely. A radical refueling of the sixties is even more so. Even if the crisis of authority were to deepen and be resolved in a negative direction, it would probably happen against a backdrop of middle-aged "quality of life" concerns rather than long hair, bell bottom jeans, and tear gas.

The third trend to watch is cultural, as a popular form of postmodernism works its way out to the furthest reaches of American society and life. Popular postmodernism is a far cry from sophisticated theories bearing the same name, and more a sensibility than a philosophy. It is perhaps easier to defend blindly or dismiss altogether than it is to define. But it is taken here as a movement that began in architecture and the arts in direct reaction to modernism. It would therefore be more accurate to call it *anti*-modern or *counter*-modernizing rather than *post*-modern, because something genuinely beyond modernity is inconceivable in current circumstances.

But regardless of its origins, popular postmodernism now encompasses much of American life. Among its defining features are a rejection of an identifiable self for shifting sets of relationships, content for style, truth and meaning for impressions, beliefs for games, ethical rules for social role-playing, commitment for self-consciousness and irony, vocation for strategies of manipulation, enduringness for disposability, originality for reproducibility and recycling, consistency and continuity for the spliced, the blurred, the self-consciously created pastiche of forms and moods. Nothing epitomizes popular postmodernism better than MTV and the hand-held remote controls through which American adolescents nibble and dabble their way toward lostness, grazing at will in the flickering pastures of one greener channel after another.

If the middle-aging of the baby boomers lowers the boom against the fantasies of radicals, consumer-driven postmodernism does the same for conservative dreams. The reason is that postmodernism is the philosophy of the patch-up. Everything is patched up, nothing is pushed out to the logic of its consequences. Bold assertions and initiatives can be made, but only as devices or sops to keep the devil of modernity at bay. So neither hope, nor despair, nor activism is serious. Everything is finally a pose and is for effect. Postmodernism is therefore a corrosive acid that contributes to the crisis of authority because even transcendence, tradition, and conservatism are negated the very moment they are affirmed. Under postmodern conditions, words lose their authority and become an accessory to images. The past is no longer a heritage, but a debris-strewn ruin to be ransacked for a bric-a-brac of beliefs that is as incoherent as it is inconsequential. Answers to the big questions of life are only an appeasement of the need for meaning while the grand flirtation with the meaninglessness of modernity goes on, but in a party mood. Religion is no longer transcendent, but a recreational pursuit for the connoisseurs of "spirituality." Art, homes, life-styles, ideas, character, self-renewal, and even belief in God all become an auxiliary to sales and the ceaseless consumption of styles.

Unchecked, the continuation of these trends will take America far off course from the kinder, gentler vision of the new traditionalism. It will bring America close to what Nietzsche lamented in *Thus Spoke Zarathustra* as "the last man." At the very moment when a post-Christian culture feels that the need was for setting the greatest goal, for planting the seed of the highest hope, for shooting an arrow of longing well past the present limits, something most contemptible arrives instead—the last man. "Alas, the time of the most despicable man is coming, he that is no longer able to despise himself. Behold, I show you the *last man.*" With its original sense of transcendence lost, and with no new vantage point discovered from which even to despise itself, the United States would be left with its bastard beatitudes—the pursuit of health and happiness, dieting and fitness. The result would be a mediocrity of the mundane, well-adjusted but numbed in its imagination, and banal in its consumerism. "One has one's little pleasure for the day and one's little pleasure for the night: but one has a regard for health. 'We have invented happiness,' say the last men, and they blink."[39]

Max Weber saw the last stage of this culture producing "specialists without spirit, sensualists without heart."[40] Lewis Mumford delivered a similar warning in the specifically American context. The sleek progressive mind, he predicted, would be reduced to one master ambition: "the private enjoyment of life." In the process it would create a race of people who "deny because of their lack of experience that life has any other meanings or values or possibilities." Such people would "eat, drink, marry, bear children, and go to their grave in a state that is at best hilarious anesthesia, and at worst is anxiety, fear, and envy, for lack of the necessary means to achieve the fashionable minimum of sensation."[41]

For Americans to see the last of the century's "supermen" off the stage only to slump toward the condition of "last men" themselves would be ironic. It could also be ominous. It might breed the "itch for chaos" that George Steiner described as growing directly from the "marsh gas of boredom and vacuity" in the nineteenth century (hauntingly epitomized in Théophile Gautier's cry, "Better barbarism than boredom!").[42] But in the end, international relations may provide a reality check that American culture no longer supplies. An expanding national "Miller time," filled with endless Rockys, Rambos, and reruns of the fifties, eventually disguises the fact that the Uncle Sam of the 1990s is not the Uncle Sam of a generation ago. But knowing to himself how much he has touched up the sights and sounds of the fifties, is he even aware of the slippage? Does he even care that he cannot afford to be what he celebrates? Into the grand children's daydream that much of American mass culture amounts to, international events like the Persian Gulf War may be needed from time to time like the shock of a cold shower of reality.

The wider world of the late twentieth century is full of its own contradictions. In many places it is turbulent and polarized between ideologies that are secular and universalistic and fanaticisms that are religious and particularistic. Shrinking through its communication, expanding through its population, the world is torn apart by its conflicts, ideologies, and interests yet drawn together by growing economic interdependence and the humanity of its common agony and hope. "Now that the whole human race is squeezed together in single lump," declares Aleksandr Solzhenitsyn, "such mutual misunderstandings threaten it with a swift and stormy end. With six, four, or even two scales of values there cannot be a united world, a united human race. We shall be torn apart by this rhythm, this irregular oscillation. We will not survive on this same earth. A man with two hearts is a man who is doomed."[43]

To Americans, space and time were once not only barriers, but buffers—geographical privileges that cushioned them from the crowding and conflict rife elsewhere on the planet. Today, in an age of satellites and missiles, there is little time lag and no hiding place left. Relaxation and retreat are alike impossible. Thus, if America's contemporary situation confronts Americans with a challenge to realism and self-understanding, their answer must be responsible not only to themselves, but to their own past as well as the world's future, to their fellow human beings across the earth as well as their own children.

PART TWO

THE CIVIL PUBLIC SQUARE

A House Dividing

Between daybreak and late afternoon on September 17, 1862, more Americans died on American soil than on any other single day in American history. When that Sabbath day's work was done, two great armies had torn each other to pieces. A sunken road had been turned into a "Bloody Lane" while ripening cornfields had been raked mercilessly with fire and a harvest gathered of human sheaves. Twenty-three thousand men fell in one day of stupendous heroism. As evening fell, the pitiful cries of the dying were said to be more horrible to hear than the deadliest sounds of battle. "Bloody Antietam" had earned its name.

Nearly a century and a quarter later, I walked the battlefield on another hot, drowsy Sunday afternoon. As a European visitor, I was more moved with emotion than at any other American site or museum I have visited. This was the place and that was the moment when the dark logic of the American schism had the mask torn from its cruel face. The short, two hundred-yard trajectory of thousands of bullets had crossed and cut short the twenty-year trajectory of thousands of young men's lives. In the so-called War between Brothers, multiple layers of unredressed injustice and pent up strife had exploded in a day of horrifying carnage.

The 1850s, beneath all its bursting optimism about the Manifest Destiny of the new "oceanbound republic," had been a tormented decade. The Great Compromise would not work, the mounting tension between North and South seemed unstoppable, and many foresaw the ominous outcome. It was fitting that a stunned nation, jolted by Antietam into the reality of the first modern war, was led by a man who, though saddened, was not surprised by the course of the dark logic. He had become its supreme interpreter. The national agitation, Abraham Lincoln had said four years earlier and three months before Governor Seward, "will not cease, until a crisis have been reached, and passed. 'A house divided against itself cannot stand.' I believe this government cannot endure, permanently half-slave and half-free."[1]

In the last generation, prompted by the recurring bicentennial commemorations, it became fashionable to compare the present with different aspects of the revolutionary era and hail a "second (third or fourth) American revolution" of some sort. But I believe that aspects of America's crisis of cultural authority are paralleled more closely by the period preceding the Civil War. In particular, the part of the crisis of cultural authority that bears on religion and public life shows signs that a new national schism is widening. A new irrepressible tension between equally opposing and enduring forces is building up. The house of the American republic is dividing once again.

Such a statement is not alarmist. The 1990s, of course, is light years from the 1850s and the contrasts are far greater than the similarities. The danger of territorial secession or armed struggle over the issue of religion and public life is nil. The schism is at a different point and holds a different menace. But the parallels are worth pondering, for when the crisis of cultural authority is examined seriously, it becomes apparent that the strong perpetuation of the Union is again in question. What endangers it now is not violent dissolution, but gradual decline. But the crisis of cultural authority is not only a matter of the weakening of faiths, as we saw in Part One in examining the crisis of national identity. It is also a matter of the warring of faiths—some would say the warring of weakened faiths. This is the focus of Part Two, which examines the crisis of America's public philosophy and proposes a constructive solution.

In short, a profound national divide is developing out of the heart of the crisis of cultural authority: With culturally conservative forces pitted increasingly against culturally progressive forces, and with the chasm widened by conflicting views of moral authority and of the relationship of religion and public life, the United States is now threatened by a monumental schism of the spirit. It would be fateful if this schism were to widen further and harden into a "two nation" divide. Factors mentioned earlier, such as the middle-aging of the baby boomers and the hollowing effect of postmodernism, would prevent the eruption of any overt social tension. But the toll of such a schism of the spirit would be incalculable. Nothing would be a greater rupture in American continuity, nothing a greater menace to republican vitality.

Mentioning the Unmentionable

Simply to make that claim will sound exaggerated to some and tiresome to others. Their very reactions provide a useful introduction to the schism in question. The serious discussion of the national significance of religion remains one of the most contentious issues in public life. There is good reason why many people prefer to treat religion as a nonissue and a nuisance factor. Just raise the topic of religion and politics in polite conversation, it may seem, and blood pressures, if not voices, mount on all sides. One might just as well be discussing AIDS at a wedding reception.

As we all know well, events in the last two decades have jerked American religion back into the limelight and on the hot seat. On the one hand, religious issues have gained the notoriety of front-page prominence and slogan-simple currency ("Jesus movement," "People's Temple," "born again," "electronic church," "Moral Majority," "abortion bombings," "textbook tailoring," "Jim and Tammy Faye," "*Satanic Verses*," and so on). On the other hand, religion in public life has become either scandal-ridden or hotly contentious. It has been a long-running peep show for voyeurs or a political hand grenade tossed to and fro between various interest groups in American society. Thus, with the collapse of the common vision for the common good and the prospect of interminable culture wars, half of America seems endlessly affronted that their faith has been excluded from the public square, while the other half seems equally affronted that someone else's faith is being imposed on them. The first group is unshakably convinced of an ominous state intrusion into religion and the second of an ominous religious intrusion into the state.

The result is that a series of bitter and divisive public disputes—from school prayer to the sanctuary movement to textbooks to abortion—seems only to have been made more bitter and more divisive still. Exaggerated claims by one side have been matched by exaggerated accusations on the other side. The same events have been seen as stirrings of a worldwide revival or as portents of a "holy terror" and "moral McCarthyism." The same people have been lauded as prophets or lambasted as American Ayatollahs.

From top to bottom and from left to right across society, religious groups have long been centers for organization and recruitment on a wide front of issues. Religion as a warrant for action has inspired liberals to block access to military installations as well as conservatives to block access to abortion clinics. But because of the character of the eighties, religion and politics for most Americans was the Christian Right. Backwoods yahoos and Know-Nothing nativists, it was said, had reemerged in modern guise to muster an army of Babbitts and Bible-thumping bigots. Reincarnated "dry Messiahs" were pursuing a new prohibition, this time of sex, not alcohol. "Falwellian," as the conventional innuendo had it, was an adjective carrying the weight of "Cromwellian" and "Orwellian" combined. Fundamentalism had become a fourteen-letter "four-letter word." And so on.

Thus, the public understanding of the place of religions in public life, including political controversies, has become more critical and more controversial at once. But with passions inflamed, rationality and respect in short supply, and graphic horror stories in frenzied circulation, simple points have often been a casualty of the war of words. One such point may be reintroduced here: In the current discussion of the American crisis of cultural authority, religion is the factor that runs deepest in American society and goes the furthest back in American history. A renewed appreciation of the constructive place of religions and religious liberty in public life is as indispensable to the health of liberal democracy as it is to the resolution of the crisis of cultural authority.

Only an obscurantist would dispute the part played by faiths in America's history. For all their darker side, they were the leading hope of the founding pioneers, the early home of American intellectual life, a vital harbinger of pivotal national events, such as revolution and abolition, and the hub of a myriad of nineteenth-century reforms and concerns, including the rise of the women's movement. From the "swarming of the Puritans" onward, nothing in America has been more fundamental to the makeup of the "first new nation." America is many things besides, but basic to understanding America is—in historian Sydney Ahlstrom's words—"the recognition of the degree to which American civilization is a New World extension of Christendom."[2]

People in calmer times would doubtless see things in a different light than we do now. For, all in all, the story of the role of faiths in the development of the American people is a stirring saga. Quite simply, it is a tale of heroism on a colossal scale with the earth's richest undeveloped continent as its backdrop and the greatest human migration in history as its players. The history of the United States is an epic story of one of the most religious peoples in history. If three of the greatest public contributions of faith in human history have been to order, to freedom, and to justice, then faiths in America have made an unrivaled contribution to all three.

Marching to a Different Drummer

Any who are defensive about discussing the national significance of religion in America should note one fact: Compared with most countries in the modernized world, the strength of religion in America is quite extraordinary and still exceptional. The empirical evidence for this statement is indisputable, demonstrated by both historical and international comparisons. What many people forget is that around the time of the American Revolution America probably had a smaller percentage of church members than any nation in Europe. Some estimates place the number of unchurched as high as 90 percent, although this fact is misleading because even in post-Puritan America standards for church membership were far higher than in either Europe then or America now. With membership both demanding and meaning something, far more people then attended church than were willing to be members.

Be that as it may, the United States has completely reversed its standings in the international league tables and can now be found at or near the top, according to every indicator of religious affiliation. Whatever questions are asked (about religious attendance, membership, beliefs, prayer, voluntary work in religious organizations, and so on), the United States scores consistently high and is usually at the very top. Such countries as Sweden and France, which were once high, have taken America's place at the bottom of the league and among the advanced industrial nations the United States can claim to be easily the "most religious." If anything, the gap between America and the rest may even have increased.

This situation is both extraordinary and exceptional, and its significance can be expressed in a number of ways, all of which illustrate a simple truth. No other country with a European origin has simultaneously made so clear a separation of church and state while retaining so close a relationship of faith and society. This means that while the grounds for the traditional American claim to exceptionalism have given way at point after point, religion is the one great exception to the general decline of American exceptionalism. Herein lies a secret of both the significance and seductiveness of religion in America.

One way of expressing the point is to put it in the context of modernization. It is commonly held today, and with good reason, that modernization and development are accompanied, almost automatically, by a falling away of religious practices and beliefs. The more developed a nation is, the less religious its people are likely to be. Yet America belies this trend and stands apart. The United States is the most modern country in the world, yet at the same time its people are the most religious of those in highly modern countries.

Another way of making the point is to relate it to education. It has often been observed that an increase in education in a country tends to have adverse effects on religious beliefs and practices. Yet the United States bucks this trend too. It boasts the highest level of formal education in the world—and simultaneously the highest levels of formally attested belief. Levels of belief in America are equaled only by nations in Africa or Southeast Asia where the degree of modernization is small and the level of education the lowest.

Such broad generalizations can be misleading, but no amount of qualification can alter the inescapable central conclusion. Religiously speaking, America does not behave as expected. The United States marches to a different drummer. Among highly industrialized Western nations, differences about religious beliefs and attitudes are greater than those concerning any other aspect of life, but the importance that religion still holds in America is almost unique among highly modern countries. Far from leading to indifference, pluralism in America has created a spiritual hot house in which more kinds of faith and fervor have flourished than anywhere else. Few peoples take their faith more seriously and more personally than Americans. If multicultural diversity is truly to be recognized, its religious dimension must be too.

G. K. Chesterton wrote that crossing the United States is an experience of "eye-openers in travel," but "there are some things about America that a man ought to see even with his eyes shut."[3] The strength and significance of American religion is one such thing. It should hardly come as a shock. Something is amiss when it does, as can be seen by the response to startling religious events in recent years such as the mass suicide of more than nine hundred cult members at Jonestown in 1978, or the eruption of the Moral Majority in 1979. These incidents were dramatic, but not parentless or out of the blue. Yet reactions to them, both in certain circles in America and abroad, ranged from total surprise to consternation, alarm, and paranoia.

Such reactions betray an astonishing ignorance about the role of religion in American history and culture, an ignorance that is less rare and less excusable among thinking Americans than might be expected. This ignorance often begins in attitudes toward America's past. "In the vicinity of Boston," Perry Miller once wryly observed, "one can encounter an aversion that amounts to settled hostility against any account implying that the founders of New England were primarily occupied with religious ideas."[4] But the ignorance is usually strongest over America's present. Kevin Phillips outlined the recent growth of evangelicalism in New England—roughly half of the eight thousand churches in "liberal" New England identified themselves as evangelical or fundamentalist. He then commented, "The extraordinary thing is that large numbers of Bostonians and New Yorkers (to say nothing of Boston-New York-Washington opinion leaders) have little or no comprehension of these numbers and trends."[5] Which is presumably the sort of fact that prompted William J. Buckley's remark that he would rather be governed by the first two thousand names in the Boston telephone directory than by the Harvard faculty.

One group has never been blind to the strength and status of American religion: visitors from abroad. "On my arrival in the United States," wrote

Tocqueville, "the religious aspect of the country was the first thing that struck my attention."[6] Similarly, from the very earliest days of the United States, a recurring theme among foreign observers has been the vitality, intensity—and oddity—of religion in America. ("Religious insanity is very common in the United States," Tocqueville added.)[7] Whether aristocrats such as Tocqueville, socialists such as Harriet Martineau, Christians such as G. K. Chesterton, or humanists such as Alistair Cooke, their observations have been similar. Whatever else Americans are, they have been nothing if not extraordinarily religious.

It is essential that there be no favoritism before the state and no heresy before law, and in the light of the trends discussed earlier it is natural that religious beliefs and practices may be a matter of complete indifference to certain intellectual and cultural elites. But when many people in these elites become as blind to religious realities as they are deaf to religious claims, social consequences follow because a key element in American society is overlooked. As the best American scholarship has insisted, understanding American religion is a necessity for understanding American history and culture, whether to Americans or non-Americans. Describing American society without religion is like describing Switzerland without the Alps. Statements doing so might be accurate about each in many limited areas, but again and again they would simply miss the point. Few nations are less understood than the United States if viewed with purely secular eyes.

In the first place, religion is the perspective from which most Americans, for most of their history, have understood human existence. It is the deepest language in which they have explored and expressed their destiny individually and nationally. The recovery of American religious history may well be the most important contribution in the last generation to the study and understanding of American culture. And what happened in history has happened in a host of other scholarly fields too: Religion has moved from being a marginal study of what others once believed to being a central determinant of how we and all human creatures behave today. Thus when, wittingly or otherwise, the language and logic of modern secularity are allowed to blinker public debate and shut out intellectual recognition of the place of religion in American life, the results are the contradictions of a dogmatically illiberal liberalism and a national form of self-inflicted blindness or, worse still, amnesia.

In addition, it is vital to understand American religion since it serves not only as a link but as a barrier between European and American experience. Europeans were often uncomfortable with hard-edged American rhetoric about "godless Communism," or the Soviets being "the focus of evil"—the so-called foul language against Communism. Americans, on the other hand, sometimes find Europeans to be cynical, detached, and ungrateful, as unresponsive to American generosity as skeptical about American ideals.

A common thread running behind such misunderstanding can be traced back to the continuing place, importance, and explicitness of religion in America, in contrast to its quiet implicitness in Western Europe earlier or to its current feebleness today. Would any nineteenth-century European statesman have justified foreign policy in directly spiritual terms like President McKinley did? Were not Europeans at the Versailles Peace Conference struck that President Wilson appeared as much a preacher as a president? Significantly, President Reagan used the offending phrases about the Soviets in a speech to the National Association of Evangelicals, having reportedly dropped them from a speech to the British Houses of Parliament, but they were then broadcast widely around Europe as being specially significant because he was speaking candidly to fellow believers.

Religion is still a major source of European bafflement about the United States, a deep taproot of the distorted image of America that Europeans have mostly hung onto. George Bernard Shaw's quip about Britain and America being two nations divided by a common language has an even stronger religious counterpart: Europe and America are two continents divided by a common religious heritage. Religion therefore stands as the central reason why American experience cannot be forced uncritically onto the bed of European categories and experience. A jibe common among skeptical but informed Europeans is that America has never quite made up its mind whether it is a church or a country. On the other hand, religion also stands as a central, but largely disregarded, link to most of the rest of the world which, unlike Europe but like America, has many highly religious people. President Carter's Camp David agreement in 1979 is one of the few exceptions to this general pattern of disregarding the place of faith in international calculations.

This insistence on the place and distinctiveness of religion in America is not naive, though recognizing and acknowledging it is hardly as common as it should be. The recognition runs counter to the full weight of the major part of European experience and expectations, and it goes right against the grain of the dominant view in American academia. In this sense, intellectuals in America are the great exception to the great exception, and few people seem more surprised that their fellow country people should be some of the most religious people on earth. William Lee Miller, of the University of Virginia, satirized the reaction of intellectuals to the stunning and the inexplicable persistence of religion in America through the mouth of an imaginary attorney: "Millions of those people out there believe what nobody believes any more."[8]

In short, the question of religion in American life is not simply a media-stoked controversy or an antiquarian interest. Something that until recently had such national prominence and power in the democratic scheme of things must matter crucially today—if only because of the reasons behind its weakening or exclusion from public life, and the likely results following from its reassertion in such a contentious way.

Timely but Thankless

In Part Two of the book, we turn to a closer examination of the second part of America's time of testing—the crisis of the public philosophy. We pick up the second and more public question raised by the crisis of cultural authority: By what understanding should faiths relate to each other as they enter the public square? Few questions are more critical to the public philosophy and the American experiment today.

Stated more positively, a constructive vision of a civil public square is indispensable to revitalizing the roots of democratic pluralism. Unless a constructive answer is found, there can be no resolution of the crisis of cultural authority. Stated more negatively, if there is no civil public square, the challenge of mounting diversity will be transformed from a source of American richness and strength into a source of friction and weakness. Either way, the American response will be watched closely by observers around the world. Modernity has greatly heightened the problem of living with our deepest differences. So as the world's lead society, America is being challenged to show the way toward a civil public square that must be an ordering principle of the new *pax moderna* and its vision of free, democratic, and pluralistic societies.

Doubtless, for many thinking Americans, the conversation breaks off here. Religion and politics is bad enough. But attempting to renew a constructive view of religion and public life—one in the interests of people of all faiths and none—is the unthinkable crossed with the impossible. At that point, several handy reasons are called in to justify bowing out of the discussion.

One common excuse is the "We're over the worst of it" attitude, born of a historical error. When Pat Robertson's presidential campaign failed in 1988 and when Jerry Falwell closed the doors of the Moral Majority in 1989, an audible sigh of relief was exhaled in certain quarters. Ten years of force-ten religious activism had been weathered. This idea that the worst is over is understandable. But regardless of partisanship, it depends on a shorthand identification of religion and politics with the Religious Right. And it forgets that religious differences are closer to "unmeltable" differences such as race and gender rather than to easily "meltable" differences such as language and ethnic custom.

The decline of the Christian Right is not the end of the problem of religion and public life. Religious diversity is broader and religious differences are more enduring than that. The heart of the problem is not over particular political movements, but over religion in public life in general. It concerns a vision of the underlying framework of the relationship of religion and public life. ("By what understanding do faiths relate to each other in the public square?") Curiously, conservative activists in the eighties actually obscured this broader problem by their preoccupation with their immediate causes. Impatient with what they saw as "abstractions," in case after case they leapt into action with no thought for some of the first principles needed to make any religiously grounded activism successful.

Ironically, this shortsightedness was one way in which the conservative bid to return to the world of the fifties by reasserting religion into public life led to one of the greatest contrasts with the fifties. One of the most important legacies of the eighties is the still unresolved place of religion in American public life. At the everyday level, religion was given a bad name by its own supporters as well as by its opponents. (As one journalist lamented, "Admit a faith in God and the Left will assume you're a Bible-carrying member of the Moral Majority. Say you're a liberal and the Right will brand you an atheist. Insist, *insist*, you're a Christian liberal, and most people will greet your proclamation with dumbfounded incredulity.")[9] At a more elevated level, the eclipse of the Religious Right left many in the nation even more confused and a lot less inclined to tackle such a thankless and intractable a task as clarifying the relationship of religion and public life.

A second common excuse for avoiding the issue is the "It'll take care of itself" attitude, born of a sociological error. This notion stems from the deceptive belief that the problem will be cleared up automatically by the boundless freedom of America's open society, especially as it is reinforced by the growing social space opened up by expanding pluralism. People who believe this are apt to downgrade the seriousness of recent culture clashes and view them simply as variations on previous tensions, such as saints versus strangers, urban versus rural, puritans versus permissives, and so on. As they see it, most Americans are presumably little more puritanical or permissive than before—they simply have more space to be themselves and thus to shock those who are different. But this shock will soon wear off, they believe, to be replaced by a more easygoing tolerance all around.

But Americans can take this trust in boundlessness too much for granted. With the frontier closed for nearly a century and American culture simultaneously diversified in some ways and standardized in others, neither open dissent nor increased diversity has the social space to express itself in terms of genuinely consistent ways of life and thought. Religious, moral, ethnic, and life-style differences now crowd in upon each other. The challenge of their differences has to be grasped at a time when "life-politics" is coming to the fore. Groups and communities defined by deep religious and social differences are no longer able either culturally or geographically to "head for the hills" or to "carve out a new frontier for themselves." As it seems to them, they are now forced to stand their ground and compete with others for the very right to exist, let alone to have their views prevail.

At this level, the dilemma of being a fundamentalist, a lesbian, a Jew, or a New Ager is much the same. Cognitive living space in America in the 1990s is strictly limited. Modern conditions may grant freedom to more such groups, but whether they genuinely grant more freedoms to such groups would take a subtler calculus than many imagine. If all the different concepts of the true, the human, and the good are not to be privatized and excluded altogether from the public square, or alternatively if the public square is not to become a gladiatorial arena of special-purpose groups fighting to the death, then the task of knowing how to live with our deepest differences is becoming more urgent—not less.

The third common excuse for avoiding the issue is a variation of "It can't happen here," based on the comforting assurance of international contrasts. As curtains and walls tumbled across Europe in 1989 and apartheid crumbled in South Africa, no revolution seemed too incredible, no liberation impossible—except those from ethnically and religiously grounded violence. "Everywhere else in the world, peace is breaking out except in this troubled region," Senator Robert Dole said of the Mideast in 1990. "With the world made over," sighed a *New York Times* headline, "can even Belfast change?"[10] Of our murderous century's two most blood-stained killers—state repression and sectarian violence—perhaps even the first and more merciless will be outlasted by the second and more blind.

But to cite America's distinctiveness as a reason for inaction is to abandon the realism of the framers. Equally, to cite the differences only as a means of reassurance is to relinquish a key part of American leadership in the multipolar world. Worst of all, to do so is to be blind to the need for American renewal at a place that is critical for the nation's growth—or decline.

Like a civil war, the loss of a nation's vitality has a logic and momentum of its own. One of its singular features is that at a certain stage it takes charge. Once in motion, decline is difficult to stop before people and events have been carried away in its remorseless path. Those who desire not to start down such a road have to reflect on the development of affairs, turn from the easy path of drift, reaction, and false compromises, and follow the course of the issues to the place of hard choices and costly commitments. War is always faster than national decline in compelling people to face reality, but the steady loss of a nation's vitality allows no one to cling to illusions forever.

As in the Civil War, so today no single group or side should be blamed for the growing schism of the spirit. To an important degree, all Americans share in the responsibility for rebuilding the civil public square. It is certain that if it is not done all Americans will share in the cost. It is therefore up to all who are loyal to the American republic to ensure what Lincoln desired in his day with his cause but never lived to see—that all sides also share in the victory and that this time reconstruction is not delayed for a hundred years. Over the present issue, a delay of even a quarter of a century would leave things too late.

8

The Testing of the Public Philosophy

The sketch of the cultural revolution of the fifties, sixties, seventies, and eighties in Part One could be expanded in endless ways. Each addition would doubtless fill in blanks and give nuance and perspective to what is now only a line drawing. But even a sketch provides a context for the first major part of the crisis of cultural authority—the national identity crisis. It also leads on naturally to the second part—the crisis of the public philosophy. This second challenge offers a particularly sharp focus on the arguments and controversies of the 1990s and cuts even closer to the crisis of cultural authority at the heart of the republic.

Enormously potent issues have been at stake in American public life in the past generation. Yet the wonder is not that citizens have engaged in such passionate debate, but that they have not done so more. A characteristic of the mood of the seventies was that Americans did not want to forgive, as Gerald Ford found out over Nixon and Jimmy Carter over Iran. But equally, they did seem to want to forget. And a salient feature of the feel-good euphoria of the eighties was its reluctance to face unpleasant realities and comprehend the changes and lessons of the last thirty years. ("Facts," as Ronald Reagan said in a revealing slip of the tongue when he misquoted John Adams, "are stupid things.")[1] This national amnesia or "denial" can be explained. But what is important is that the debates—amounting at times to a moral and philosophical civil war, sometimes a holy war, sometimes a school war, sometimes a sex war—represent both a crisis of the public

147

philosophy and a profound struggle for the heart, mind, soul, and future of America.

A Common Vision for the Common Good

As we saw earlier, a defining feature of the United States is that, from its very beginning, it has been a nation by intention and by ideas. One of America's greatest achievements and special needs has been to create, out of the mosaic of religious and cultural differences, a common vision for the common good—in the sense of a widely shared, almost universal, agreement on what accords with the common ideals and interests of America and Americans. Many things were included in this common vision—ranging from shared ideals, such as honesty and loyalty; shared commitments, such as the place of public service; and shared understandings, such as the relationship or religion and public life.

This common vision was mostly unwritten, often half-conscious, never to be mistaken for unanimity. But it has served a vital purpose. It has offset the natural conflict of interests in a pluralistic society, and in particular the impulse toward arbitrariness that is the scourge of totalitarianism and democracy alike. In doing so it provides a binding tie that maintains unity to balance the richness and pressures of diversity, and transmits a living heritage to balance the dynamism of progress. Most Americans may never have been conscious of any such thing, let alone the term "public philosophy," which was introduced by Walter Lippmann. But America itself has always been a working model of a public philosophy in action. For Americans, consensus has been a matter of compact over common ideals as well as compromise over competing interests.

Defined in this way, the notion of public philosophy needs to be distinguished from two sound-alike notions. First, this use of the term public philosophy is different from those who use the term (quite legitimately) to refer to an individual's personal philosophy of public affairs, and thus to the place of public affairs in his or her worldview. In contrast, public philosophy as used here refers expressly to public affirmations shared in common with other citizens. A public philosophy should not only be accessible to others in principle; it is unworthy of the name unless it is actually shared in practice.

Second, this use of public philosophy is quite different from civil religion (examined in chapter twelve) and talk of a "public theology." Like civil religion, public philosophy as used here deals with affirmations held in common. But unlike civil religion—which I will argue is neither legitimate for Christians and Jews nor feasible for anyone today—the public philosophy does not require the common affirmations to be regarded as sacred or semisacred in themselves. For most Americans, their commitment to the public philosophy is rooted in their own religious beliefs, but the public affirmations are not themselves religious. For this reason they can be held in common with people of other faiths or no faith.

Over the course of three hundred years there have been great changes in this concept of the common vision for the common good. Most noticeable is the softening between the harder-edged notion of Puritan covenant and the rather vague mid-twentieth-century notion of consensus. Equally, the very strength of the notion has sometimes created problems, such as the effect that consensus-thinking has in turning a blind eye toward cultural diversity and the toleration of evils, such as the maltreatment of blacks and Native Americans. There are therefore solid reasons why the subject has recently fallen into disrepute, why its very mention is challenged in some circles, and why there are sometimes competing proposals among proponents of its recovery.

What is certain, however, is that the weakening or disappearance of the public philosophy has definite consequences too. From Walter Lippmann's early critique of the impact of the crisis on public opinion to the Paul A. Volcker Commission on rebuilding the ideal of public service, a stream of analyses have made this connection and addressed the problem. It is also certain that, because people have different and changing beliefs, the common vision for the common good is never static. A public philosophy is not in the realm of a final answer. Adjustment and readjustment are an ongoing requirement of American democracy. Since no generation declares, lives, and preserves this common vision in its entirety, each generation needs to reaffirm and renew this commitment. As George Mason wrote in the Virginia Declaration, "No free government or the blessings of liberty, can be preserved to any people, but by a firm adherence to justice, moderation, temperance, frugality, and virtue, and by frequent recurrence to fundamental principles."[2] For Americans to become, in Walter Lippmann's words, "a people who inhabit the land with their bodies without possessing it with their souls" would be a sure step toward disaster.[3]

For many opinion leaders, discussion of the public philosophy never proceeds far because they suspect the concept to be incurably conservative and alien to the ideals of a liberal society, and especially to the high place given to the unfettered clash of self-interest and faction. But this suspicion is misplaced. As the earlier warning from Lippmann and Arthur M. Schlesinger's more recent essay, *The Disuniting of America,* underscore, the notion of the public philosophy has received distinguished support from both liberals and political realists. A political philosophy will always differ according to the society it addresses. But a constitutional democracy, such as the United States, aims to present a vision of justice that provides a shared public basis for the justification of political institutions and helps ensure cohesion despite diversity and stability from one generation to the next.

To the surprise of some, John Rawls, professor of philosophy at Harvard and a leading proponent of the liberal conception of justice, has unequivocally supported such a view of shared public justice against mere self-interest and proceduralism. In a lecture at Oxford in 1986 he stated, "Now a basis of justification that rests on self- or group-interests alone cannot be stable; such a basis must be, I think, even when moderated by skillful constitutional design, a mere modus vivendi, dependent on a fortuitous conjunction of contingencies."[4] Rawls's liberal vision is of a public philosophy based on an "overlapping consensus," which is a consensus forged by the overlapping affirmations of deeply divergent religious, philosophical, and ethical beliefs. Such an overlapping consensus is directly opposed to the notion of a single, comprehensive orthodoxy, on the one hand, and a mere modus vivendi based on proceduralism on the other. In a society as diverse as modern America, both alternatives, though for different reasons, end up unjust and unworkable.

Rising Tide of Awareness

Not surprisingly, the rising awareness of the need for an American public philosophy coincided with the decline in the 1930s of the former principal source—Protestantism. It then swelled up again in the late forties and early fifties, chiefly among intellectuals, religious leaders, and national leaders, such as Walter Lippmann, Reinhold Niebuhr, John Courtney Murray, Henry Luce, and John Foster Dulles. America's postwar responsibility had raised profound questions about its identity and mission in the world. There was a widespread sense of the need of a public faith to nerve and inspire citizens for the task, especially in the light of the Cold War. Religion in this period was touted publicly as the "shield of the nation" and America's "secret weapon" against atheistic communism.

Some observers remarked that much talk about national purpose was clearer about its insistence that the United States should have one than about what the purpose should be. But regardless, the flurry of concern died down soon afterward. No one had answered the questions pertaining to national purpose to common satisfaction; these were simply submerged by the growing strength of the postwar consensus, the resurgence of religion, and the rising tide of national optimism.

The more recent concern over the public philosophy is prompted by even more dramatic developments and has a wider audience. It is currently at a crescendo in the multifronted conflicts over multiculturalism, but there were earlier promptings. One wave of recognition followed the upheavals of the sixties. Whether expressed in middle class outrage at the flaunting of alternative life-styles or in Senator Sam Ervin's excoriation of the blindness of Nixon's aides to ethical considerations, Americans became aware that America's moral consensus had broken down. Shared fundamental principles of intellectual and ethical integrity were a thing of the past. Faith, character, and virtue had become privatized. Public service as public spiritedness had declined. Notions, such as "values clarification," had only deepened the uncertainty and skepticism about any commonweal. The oxymoron "private citizen" had become accepted currency. There was no longer a recognizable common vision for the common good.

Another wave of concern stemmed from an intellectual appreciation of the importance of the public philosophy to America. The crisis of public faith, it was realized, was far more profound than could be explained as the work of certain activists, or even as the outcome of the entire sixties' landslide of moral and social consequences. Serious as these events may have been, they were nothing compared to the dilemma created for Americanness by the weakening of an "American center." This aspect of the problem is not a philosophical abstraction or a conservative obsession. It is an unalterable legacy of Enlightenment liberalism that goes to the core of the American experiment itself. As such, the crisis of the public philosophy is a crucial part of the wider crisis of cultural authority. Although rooted in the past and growing steadily over the last half century, it now requires urgent attention. The dilemmas and conflicts over the political, economic, and educational consequences of multicultural diversity require an urgent resolution.

A Problem by Any Other Name

Several people have used Lippmann's term public philosophy in a different way than the use defined here, and many have used different terms altogether. Some have used it for the public side of the faith of the churches and synagogues, others for the secular faith of the Enlightenment, and still others for the American way of life. Not surprisingly, a bag-full of names other than Lippmann's "public philosophy" has been given to it—"democratic faith" (Jacques Maritain), "common faith" (John Dewey and Sidney Hook), "religion of the republic" (Sidney Mead), "civil religion" (Robert Bellah), "common morality" (Peter Berger), "moral consensus" (Alasdair MacIntyre), "transcendental common values" (Michael Harrington), "public religion" (Richard Neuhaus), "the radius of trust" (James Fallows), and so on.

But there is widespread agreement on at least two points. First, there is no doubt that in the past America had both a public philosophy and a special need for one. Or as Richard Hofstadter expressed it, "It had been our fate as a nation not to have ideologies but to be one."[5] Early statements of this notion in both the colonies and the republic were common. Broadly typical of the Puritan era were Governor Winthrop's celebrated words on board the *Arbella* before landing at Salem, "It is of the nature and essence of every society to be knit together by some covenant, either expressed or implied."[6] George Washington had a typical eighteenth-century expression of the same conviction. He clearly had in mind a submerged consensus that touched on morality and religion as well as on the political creed. "Reason and experience both forbid us to expect that national morality can prevail in exclusion of religious principle."[7] Or as he argued in his farewell address, "It is substantially true that virtue or morality is a necessary spring of popular government. . . . Who that is a sincere friend to it, can look with indifference upon attempts to shake the foundation of the fabric."[8]

James Madison is often cited on the other side, as if he was hostile to the notion of the common good because of his emphasis on freedom, pluralism, and faction. But his writings are filled with such phrases as "the public good," "the common good," "justice and the common good," and "the true interest of the country." Far from extolling faction and group competition for their own sake, Madison viewed them as a necessary evil (a "dangerous vice," a "mutual disease") that should be exploited in the interests of liberty. What Lippmann called the public philosophy was to be achieved, Madison said, through a "natural aristocracy" of elected representatives. Raw public views need to be refined by passing them through the medium of the chosen assembly of citizens.

In our own age when sophisticated secularity goes cheek by jowl with thrusting religious diversity, eighteenth-century talk of consensus sounds archaic and ceremonial. But Tocqueville raised the same issue even more penetratingly in the nineteenth century, so much so that its reverberations today might well be heard as variations on "Tocqueville's theme." The need for some consensus is basic to any society, he argued. "Without such common belief no society can prosper; say, rather, no society can exist; for without ideas held in common there is no common action, and without common action there may still be men, but there is no social body."[9] But the United States, he saw, combined such extraordinary individual liberty and social diversity that an active, ongoing consensus was an organic requirement and was all the more needed. Without it, there would be no way of sustaining liberty for a free people who would remain free.

In other words, a democratic society that wishes to sustain the ideal of ordered freedom requires a consensus, a shared center of gravity. It needs a freely chosen, mutually binding compact of shared ideals to curb the tear-away tendencies of individualism and self-interest, to provide a buffer against the tyranny of the majority, and to prevent either fragmentation at home or enfeeblement abroad. And in a society prizing both liberty and equality, the sources of this common vision can be channeled only voluntarily and are likely to come from religious roots. "Religion in America," Tocqueville said, "takes no direct part in the government of society, but it must be regarded as the first of their political institutions."[10]

Second, there is also widespread agreement that the less explicit dimension of the public philosophy has recently been weakened, possibly to the point of collapse. It is surely significant that almost all who speak and write of it today do so convinced of its loss. "In trying to define restraint, in trying to make the many choices before America," *Time* magazine concluded in its sixtieth anniversary issue in 1983, "the country conspicuously lacks a consensus and a principle of authority."[11] "The sign of the vacuum," especially on the intellectual level, wrote John Courtney Murray, "is the futility of the argument or the question . . . whether there is a public philosophy or not."[12] Despite a common culture, Daniel Bell has written recently, "there is no common purpose, or common faith, only bewilderment."[13] After an "enormous pig-out atmosphere" in 1980s, Walter Dean Burnham declared, trends, such as voter apathy, show Americans are disconnected from citizenship. "What we've got is a collective national morale problem."[14]

Added to this, most observers believe the loss is fateful. The absence of a compelling public philosophy threatens to produce what Lippmann called "the Great Vacuum"[15] and Richard Neuhaus "the naked public square."[16] Thus in much of the current talk of the problem, public philosophy and civil religion are "sunset notions"—ideas whose color and fascination are at their strongest just as they are about to disappear over the social horizon. Robert Bellah points out that "civil religion came to consciousness just when it was ceasing to exist, or when its existence had become questionable."[17] Following 1912–17, the traditional moral consensus collapsed in intellectual circles, as did the postwar consensus in wider culture following the sixties. Thus with secularity deepened, pluralism enlarged, religious beliefs softened into private preferences, and American institutions more specialized than ever and American citizens more individualistic than ever, the American republic shows signs of suffering from a public agnosticism and pragmatic neutrality that threaten to leave it rudderless and without ballast in the future. On the great ethical issues debated in public recently, says one historian, "the 'pluribus' was all too evident, the 'unum' all too elusive."[18]

One Root, Many Flowers

The consequences of the crisis of public philosophy have been traced in many areas. Some, such as the "New Politics," we introduced earlier in another context. Single-issue obsession, for example, is not new—the gun lobby goes back a long way. But unquestionably there has been a marked general decline of public consciousness, and of such notions as "public service" and "civic responsibility." Many curious features of this decline might be noted.

The New Politics meant that the eighties, for example, was a decade torn between shamelessness and a bad conscience over the excesses of antigovernment populism and greedy individualism. Yet instead of redeveloping the old civic notion of *public* to check both the government and the private sphere, the preference was to narrow the idea of *public* to *government* and thus to broaden self-centered political activity so that it could be equated with public concerns. One egregious result was what was dubbed "revolving door" politics, best exemplified in the self-interest/public-service of many Reaganauts. Public service was no longer its own reward but a "deferred income plan" whereby IOUs in public office were magically transformed into lucrative profits in private business. In the case of the HUD scandals, the motivation was much the same. The difference was simply that the income plans were not deferred.

Another result of the decline of public responsibility in the 1980s was that, while such rhetorical notions as "the general public" and "the American people" were strong, real things, such as neighborhoods and voluntary associations, were far weaker. The public benefits that come from the school of experience that neighborhoods provide were also weakened: meeting people with differences, creating common ground, appreciating diversity, working through conflicts, building mutual responsibility, sharing opinions, and articulating a public vision of the common enterprise. Somehow the new national politics was teaching a different lesson from the old neighborhood politics, and the result was the new group solidarities and sensitivities that conservatives were later to deplore. But conservatives had contributed too. In the words of the title of one Justice Department memorandum, the late eighties was a time for "No consensus, Confrontation only!"

Contrary to such views, the notion of the public philosophy or the commonwealth serves as a reminder that the American republic is more than the sum total of its individual selves and self-interests. The highest American good is more than the struggle over who gets what, when, and how. Politics has a community and justice dimension as well as a power dimension. The public philosophy is a vital expression of that extra something. Among the differing proposals for the renewal of public philosophy, one of the strongest and earliest was Walter Lippmann's, based largely on his analysis of public opinion. If public opinion were not controlled by public philosophy, he argued, it would rarely be in the public interest. While it could truly express the voice of shifting voting groups, it must not be taken as the final verdict on a national issue. It was only the beginning of the argument.

Tocqueville had warned that "the people, surrounded by flatterers, find great difficulty in surmounting their inclinations."[19] Lippmann went further to argue that a public philosophy was needed to push public opinion beyond itself to what is right and good as well as what is a true expression of the American people as a national community. Anything less, he said—and he did so before the latest developments in image-making and pollster pulse-taking—would undermine liberal democracy and encourage the dangerous Jacobin concept of a totally emancipated sovereign people. As Jacques Ellul was to write in the mid-sixties, with the French experience also in mind: When public opinion is aroused by means that are no more than propaganda, "it is no longer capable of rendering political judgment. All it can do is to follow the leaders."[20] The question of a public philosophy might therefore appear abstract and intangible at first, but in Lippmann's mind it led straight to the conclusion cited in the Introduction: "In the crisis within the Western society, there is at issue now the mandate of heaven."[21]

A second area where the crisis has been traced is education. The most obvious focus here is the public school system, whose very purpose was tied in with the common vision for the common good. For pioneer educators, such as Horace Mann, public schooling meant far more than free, universal education. It was to provide education for all the children in the community that would move beyond instruction in "reading, writing, and 'rithmetic" to education in character, ideals, and loyalties. Above all, public schools were to be a place to reconcile the spiritual divisiveness, born of creeds, and the social divisiveness, born of class. The notion of the common vision of the common good is central to the character and purpose of the American public schools.

Over the course of time this role has been played with such success that the public schools became almost the working equivalent of a European established church as well as the nation's chief agency for "Americanizing" and cultivating common citizenship and common republican virtues. Sociologist David Riesman swerved over dangerously into civil religion when he wrote in the fifties of "new ways of using the school as a kind of community center, as the chapel of a secular religion perhaps." Others went off the road altogether, their enthusiasm loosening their tongues in a way that would be unthinkable in an age more guarded about religion and public education. One writer argued that "the religion of public education is a more powerful factor in American life today than that of the churches. The only religion with which the great majority of American youth have ever come in contact is the religion of public education."[22]

But this Americanizing role is almost impossible today, either in its wiser or its more extreme forms. With the collapse of a public philosophy above them, the disintegration of the family and the neighborhood around them, the confusion of notions like values clarification within them, and the mass exodus of Protestant conservatives from them, many public schools are clearly not civilizing and Americanizing as they once did. Nor are they educating adequately for democracy.

Strikingly, this Jeffersonian concern was missing altogether when President Bush and fifty state governors met for the education summit in September 1989 on the campus of Mr. Jefferson's University of Virginia. However historic the agreement on "national performance goals," nothing was said about continuing study of the fundamental principles that order the life of the republic. Voices of concern have been raised and farsighted proposals for reform are being implemented—for example, the state of California's recent curriculum guidelines—but the depth of the problem is lost on most. "We are the Romans of the modern world," proclaimed Oliver Wendell Holmes in 1858, "the great assimilating people."[23] Yet Rome's public ideals were crucial to its assimilating power and, as Friedrich Hegel observed, the decline of Roman public ideals was followed swiftly by the decline of Rome itself.

Other educational observers have focused on the universities and colleges. Historically these institutions have been the key agencies for imparting the essentials of the Western tradition to the leaders of each generation. One might think that the nation's institutions of higher learning would be the obvious place to look for counsel on the nation's ideals. Yet today, with the impact of radical multiculturalism and the controversies over "political correctness," their failure to educate full human beings or to impart American ideals is striking.

Trenchant critiques have come from both sides of the political spectrum —most notably Allan Bloom's *The Closing of the American Mind* and Page Smith's *Killing the Spirit*. But even before PC thinking set off a firestorm of controversy, James Billington, librarian of Congress, leveled the same charge from the heart of the establishment. With a consumer-oriented curriculum and heavy specialization and with its ostensible value-free and tradition-free environment, "the modern university drifts into a kind of conformist non-conformism." Because of these developments, he continues, we are seeing a growing split between those who are morally concerned but not intellectually trained and those who are highly articulate but morally insensitive. "Few of the graduates of research universities have the faintest idea about the Judeo-Christian tradition or the classical heritage from which the very seal on their diploma comes."[24]

A third key area is law. In a brilliant seminal essay, Harold J. Berman of Emory University argued that Western culture is undergoing an integrity crisis whose two main symptoms are the massive loss of confidence in law and religion. Law and religion are no longer viewed as distinct but as interdependent. They have been divorced and both parties are the losers. Law without religion degenerates into rules and mechanical legalism, just as religion without law loses its social effectiveness and sinks into private religiosity. Western society as a whole is demoralized.

What is dying, Berman argues, is not the institutional structures of law but their foundations, which in the case of the West are solidly based on religion. Yet within the past two generations America's public philosophy has shifted from a religious to a secular theory of law, from a moral to a political or instrumental theory, and from a communitarian to an individualistic theory. Law is no longer regarded as a reflection of an objective justice or of the ultimate meaning of life. This change in itself is cause enough for crisis, but the present crisis is different from the past. Our immediate danger is neither that of a total state, boosted by the excessive sanctification of law, nor that of a total church, boosted by the excessive legalization of religion. We are threatened more by anarchy than dictatorship, and more by decadence and apathy than by fanaticism.

Berman argues that if the West is to survive, it must recover the true interdependence of law and religion. Since justice depends on something beyond itself, it requires a principle of transcendence. Since Western justice is a historical achievement rather than a theoretical abstraction, it requires a continuity of tradition. But what will supply the needed transcendence and tradition? "Neither the personal mysticism of the East," Berman concludes, "nor the social activism of the West seems to hold the key to the interrelationship of religion and law in our time. The former comes too close to religiosity, the latter too close to legalism. The hope is in a new era of synthesis."[25]

A fourth and fascinating area in which the crisis has been raised is economics—and in particular the issue of deficit-spending and budget-balancing. Jonathan Rauch, for example, points out that Americans cannot settle the deficit issue in a purely economic framework. Yes, President Reagan's deficits were by far the worst outside of wartime or depression. And yes, they were a dramatic reversal of long-held conservative Republican policy. But there are two reasons why the debate has proved frustratingly inconclusive. First, the argument cannot be settled by economic evidence alone. Second, there are opposite but overlapping reasons why both conservatives and liberals favor deficits. "Conservatives would rather have deficits than bigger government; liberals would rather have deficits than smaller government."[26]

In addition to potential economic consequences in the future, Rauch points out actual social and political consequences in the present. He argues for a balanced budget on the basis of a common vision for the common good. He even cites the rainbow in the book of Genesis and sees the social agreement as a modern "covenant," a social sign that "things are all right." After all, he points out, only recently have deficits been seen as a purely economic question. Americans have traditionally seen them as political and moral first. While a balanced budget is only a social agreement and not a moral requirement, it does serve the public philosophy in two ways. It reaches across the political spectrum today and across the generations into the world of our children's children tomorrow.

On the one hand, Rauch argues that "the shared goal of balancing the budget—that the government taxes no more than it spends, and it spends no more than it taxes—represents a compact between conservatives and liberals. A balanced budget is a sign for liberals that conservatives are paying their share of taxes, and a sign for conservatives that liberals are restraining their spending."[27] On the other hand, keeping the faith over a balanced budget is a sign of responsibility to the future. "As the previous generation did unto us, so we will do unto the next generation."[28] Those who advocate these arguments underline that budget-balancing and zero-deficits are not the only possible rule to adopt. Any rule will do as long as everyone agrees to it. But it does have the merit of being evidently fair, easy to explain, and being the way Americans have lived for over two hundred years—in short, being in accord with the common vision of the common good.

Last and perhaps most devastatingly of all, the crisis of the public philosophy has been traced by analysts, such as Alasdair MacIntyre, to the bankruptcy of moral thinking and of the moral condition of the West. Our deepening crisis, MacIntyre argues, is because the rational vindication of public morality has been rendered impossible. Both religion and philosophy have abdicated their traditional roles and become marginal, the former specializing in private faith, the latter being academic. This creates a dire predicament. The morality of our culture is left without "any public, shared rationale or justification." This means, in turn, that moral discussion is characterized by an unholy trio of insistent demands, irreconcilable differences, and interminable debates, all of which are "unsettlable." Authority is therefore fated to be asserted, not argued. Protest and indignation have ousted persuasion from politics, which itself is "civil war carried on by other means."[29] (Lippmann had written similarly of "a sublimated and denatured civil war.")[30] MacIntyre's conclusion is that, short of a searching criticism of the Enlightenment ideas that created this problem and a return to the only real alternative, "our society cannot hope to achieve moral consensus."[31]

The rigor and comprehensiveness of MacIntyre's argument have an inescapable consequence. They lock the door firmly against any who try to make an easy escape from the predicament by arguing that, though the faith of the churches may have collapsed, confidence in the public philosophy is intact because the faith of the Enlightenment is unscathed. Sidney Mead, for example, professes himself unconcerned about the decline of the churches. "The loss of their ideology does not perturb me insofar as the welfare of the Republic is concerned. For I hold that *their* lost theology is not and never has been the mainspring of that Republic—that *the* theology of the Republic is that of 'Enlightenment'. . . . and it is not clear that this mainspring is broken."[32]

But if thinkers like Billington, Berman, and MacIntyre are correct, then Mead's secular optimism is misplaced. Lippmann's "great vacuum," Will's "broken chain," Neuhaus's "naked public square," and Diggins's "lost soul" have been joined by Mead's "broken mainspring." For as Mead acknowledges, "Religion is the mainspring of an integrated society. When the mainspring is broken the society runs down."[33]

Anyone for Pandora's Box?

This conclusion leads us straight to the heart of the problem. For, as most of these writers make clear, the trouble with all the talk of a public philosophy is that the present moment is not congenial and few people are sufficiently convinced (or quixotic) to set about the thankless task of forging the new consensus. Modern philosophical and social conditions have caused the collapse of the public philosophy, and to reopen the question is to release a Pandora's box of philosophical, moral, and political problems.

Among the few who have tried it recently was Michael Harrington, a democratic Marxist, who proposed a "united front of believers and atheists in defense of moral values."[34] But the fate of his proposal illustrates the immensity of the Herculean labors facing any would-be rebuilder. Only rarely do such proposals pass muster before the reviewing line of individual scholars and critics (in many cases, the proposals get no further than that). More rarely still do they break out of the incestuous circle of New Class seminars and consultations, let alone ride out to alter the landscape of political discussion and public education.

If any proposal for reforging the public philosophy aims to be politically effective, it faces two enormous challenges. The first is theoretical. At a time when the diversity and relativity of worldviews have been deepened simultaneously, any proposed solution must steer between a Scylla and a Charybdis. On one side, it must avoid the peril of a forced commonness, whereby the common vision is created by imposing a single, comprehensive doctrine on those who do not share it. As John Rawls rightly asserts, the liberalisms of Immanuel Kant and John Stuart Mill are no more acceptable here than Protestantism or Catholicism, for they too are comprehensive doctrines not shared universally (perhaps not even widely) in contemporary America.

On the other side, the proposed solution must avoid the perils of an empty proceduralism or a volatile modus vivendi. As Rawls points out again, a social consensus based on a modus vivendi is weak, because it depends on a happenstance or fortuitous balance of forces. Parties break the consensus easily when circumstances change. A public philosophy, by contrast, must have common moral aims and be affirmed on diverse though overlapping moral grounds. Only if it is sustained morally and not simply procedurally will it remain stable regardless of the relative shifts in the political and cultural power of the parties.

The second challenge is practical. A paper proposal and an actual rebuilding of some aspect of the public philosophy are two different things. The public philosophy involves the deepest "habits of the heart" and cannot be cobbled together like a party slate or a dream ticket. A national consensus is not something to be designed and marketed like a household product or even a presidential candidate. Successful public philosophies are the flowering of living faiths, whether wholesome or demonic. So a cut-flower philosophy would not last. And, as the French revolutionaries discovered with their aborted goddess of reason, artificial transcendence does not grow in the first place.

Confronted with such challenges, it is not surprising that many people fall back on the view that America has the only consensus she will ever have—the agreement to disagree and the shared controversy of debating the consensus. They are tempted to settle for what George Will mocks as "the Cuisinart theory of justice," the notion that of the endless maelstrom of individuals' pursuing private goods will come, magically, the public good.[35]

Yet in the end the question of a public philosophy is practical and not simply theoretical, and those who reject specific formulations must either let history demonstrate that no consensus is necessary today or else face the core problem and put forward their own answer. For the loss of its public philosophy raises questions for America, and so critical are these questions that they must not be ignored. Only in constant conversation can a living consensus be established and maintained. Over the course of time, consensus may come to be taken for granted and at that stage is easily thrown away. But consensus is never uniformity and it creates conformity only in its later stages. At its earliest and best, a state of affairs maintained only by ongoing conversation, consensus is forged directly from dissension. Its shared agreements are hard won in teeth of sharp disagreements.

Talk of a public philosophy or the common vision for the common good sounds intangible and ethereal at first. Abraham Lincoln spoke of them aptly in his first inaugural address as "mystic chords of memory, stretching from every battlefield and patriot grave to every living heart and hearthstone all over this broad land."[36] But no American has ever tasted more deeply the bitter fruit of disunion. As Edmund Burke had asserted earlier, the threads that bind a person to a country are "ties which though light as air, are as strong as links of iron."[37] John Courtney Murray saw the importance for America plainly, nearly three decades ago. "If the argument dies from disinterest, or subsides into the angry muttering of polemic, or rises to the shrillness of hysteria, or trails off into positivistic triviality, or gets lost in a mass of semantics, you may be sure that the barbarian is at the gates of the City."[38]

9

The Uncivil War

Mark Twain once said that in the South after the Civil War, "damn Yankee" was all one word. Recently, Joseph Fletcher quoted Twain to complain that Bible-Belt evangelicals were intoning the phrase "secular humanism" in the same way that julep drinkers used to mutter darkly about the carpetbaggers.[1] Not only that, say People for the American Way, there was a disturbing likeness between the 1980s and the McCarthy era. "Just as McCarthy branded everybody and everything he opposed as 'Communist,' the new demagogues have devised a convenient bugaboo—'secular humanism.'" The result has been a pernicious form of "moral McCarthyism."[2]

Fundamentalists, of course, can level similar accusations in return. The 1980s were like one long "open season" on fundamentalism. There is good reason for the updated version of Peter Viereck's comment that antifundamentalism has replaced anti-Catholicism as the anti-Semitism of the intellectual. In the words of one scholar, fundamentalists are now the "thinking man's nigger."

And so it goes. The accusations and counteraccusations pile up on both sides. With the drastic weakening of the public philosophy and the stoking up of the culture wars, there is no agreement as to what is the proper place of faiths in public life. With the collapse of civility, there is no common commitment to guiding principles by which people of different faiths may enter the public square and engage with each other robustly but civilly.

The result is the "holy war" front of America's wider culture wars. Disputes over religion and politics in the last two decades have been bitterly polarized, extremes have surfaced regularly, resort to law has become reflexive, and opponents with no arguments left have kept on trading tired insults. We are now at the point where no issue is too insignificant to be incendiary and no end is in sight to the number of conflagrations that can be sparked. The clash between the "secularists" and the "sectarians" (as each side sees the other) has at times become so bitter and confused that individuals, motives, and reputations have been impugned repeatedly. Debate is not the term to use. Even controversy is too weak. The culture war has become a most uncivil war of ideas. Prospects for a civil society appear weak.

Sharpening the Focus

The proposal to resolve the destructiveness of the culture wars and rebuild a civil society entails at least three things: First, we need to reappraise the conduct of the ongoing controversies critically (the subject of the next four chapters); second, we need to repudiate the resort to civil religion as a false answer to the crisis of the public philosophy; and third, we need to reforge the public philosophy (the subject of the last two chapters in this section). The purpose is to work toward the reconstitution of the present generation of Americans—a genuine rededication to, and reappropriation of, the constitutional heritage through citizens engaging in a new debate reordered in accord with constitutional first principles and considerations of the common good.

It is a tough task to engage constructively with the contentiousness of religion and politics without being drawn into its problems. There are several prerequisites: The first is a clear sense of perspective. The culture-wars rhetoric is one of all-engulfing crisis and conflict, yet a large part of the controversy is not serious in quite the way the rhetoric makes it out to be. In the first place, the direst warnings of an extreme sacred square and an extreme naked square have not yet proved true—as evidenced by the fact that each side reads opposite conclusions from the same set of facts. In addition, the existing sense of undue "sacredness" and "nakedness" is a matter of drift as much as design, of unintended consequences rather than conspiracies. Further, part of the sense of futility in the conflict is due to the striking lack of leadership in resolving it—the last two Republican administrations, for example, have cynically treated the "holy wars" as political capital to be exploited. Finally, the American people as a whole are far more tolerant than the bitterness of recent disputes suggests. In short, the sense of all-engulfing controversy needs clarifying into a sharper focus.

Evidence for the last claim can be found in a landmark study on American religion and public life on the eve of the 1988 election. Curiously, a plurality of Americans (45 percent to 41 percent with 14 percent don't-knows) believed that "there's less religious tolerance today than there was twenty or thirty years ago." Yet the same findings showed that in area after area, with only a few exceptions, tolerance was actually expanding and intolerance was on the wane. Beyond doubt, the American people give broad approval to religion in public life, whether to its general place and importance or to its diverse expressions. The general lesson of American history still holds true today. As American pluralism has expanded from Puritanism to generalized Protestant to Protestant-Catholic-Jew and now beyond to a multifaith pluralism, tolerance has expanded behind it.[3]

What explains this disparity between perceptions and reality? Several factors might be cited—for example, the worldwide impression of a link between fundamentalism and fanaticism or the tendency of the media to couch issues in terms of stereotypes and extremes. But we can trace a major share of the responsibility to certain activists and politicians who have exaggerated the logic of recent developments and played on the fears of their own constituencies, and thus have had the effect of charging the disputes with even greater social and political tensions. The "pitbull politics of polarization" has wreaked its own havoc. The culture wars have become an independent factor in the crisis of cultural authority.

Public rhetoric, after all, has its own dynamics. It comes cheap, and when it is driven by the imperatives of attack ads, beggar-thy-neighbor's-image tactics, and direct mail, its profit margins can be enormous. Accusations about starting a sex war, a school war, and a holy war have been heard from many directions. But most of them are the stuff of headline-grabbing hyperbole or the don't-fail-to-take-me-seriously sort of threat. ("Some type of civil war may be necessary," one Rajneeshnee told the Associated Press blithely when Antelope, Oregon, was renamed the city of Rajneesh, "if the commune is to establish its rights to live in the state.")[4]

Yet when all the hyperbole has been deflated and a sense of perspective has been sharpened, the real problem does not disappear. It grows even clearer, because what is at stake is not bad manners but an important national schism that goes to the heart of the crisis of cultural authority. This schism may not directly involve the majority of Americans as participants. But since the minority are influential as gatekeepers at the important entrances to American society, the freedom of others to think and act is bound to be affected eventually.

The current culture-war rhetoric therefore needs to be taken seriously, though not literally. The conflicts deserve to be understood as well as contested with all the integrity and intensity that are required when people, truth, and a nation's interests are at stake. But for the same reason, the conflicts need to be set apart clearly, first from the overheated passions inflating the debate from the inside, and second from the soft-minded pragmatism that deflates it from outside by treating it as a nonissue that time and the modern cure-all of "better communication" will deal with.

To be sure, particular issues will come and go. In a society as fast-changing and fashion-conscious as the United States, issues such as the Equal Rights Amendment and school prayer may even appear to rise and fall like entries in the popular music charts. But their real significance is as flashpoints. Running between such specific issues with their shifting constellations of supporters are the battle lines between longer agendas, wider alliances, and deeper underlying philosophies. Alternative futures for America are being fought over, and the very means of waging war are becoming a major influence in its outcome.

Danger! Handle with Care!

A second prerequisite for constructive engagement is a healthy respect for the explosive power of religion in public life. No one need be a native of Belfast or a historian of the Thirty Years War to know that constant contention over the relationship between religion and public life is potentially grave. Even in a society as pluralistic and tolerant as America, unremitting contentiousness causes damage in three ways. It has the effect of blocking, dividing, and inflaming. The first two of these effects have been touched on several times already. The blockage happens at the level of the general relationship of diverse faiths and liberal society, where contentiousness clogs the natural wellsprings of democracy. Different faiths are then unable to contribute to the vitality of American freedom, justice, and order as they did in the past. The divisiveness happens at the level of public debate, caused by the tendency to polarize and reinforce the familiar extremism. When religion enters the picture, all dividing lines seem to become indelible.

The third effect, the inflammatory action of contentiousness over religion and politics, can be seen at the level of concrete issues and everyday local affairs. When religion bears on public life in a pluralistic society—as constitutionally it may and theologically it must—its influence is likely to be inflammatory unless people have a good prior understanding of the relationship of religion and public life. Without such an understanding, a predictable pattern of responses occurs and the spiral of contentiousness is likely to deepen and accelerate.

The main dynamics of inflammation are easy to observe. First, the people involved tend to overlook the practical aspects of the issue under debate—for example, the pros and cons, pluses and minuses of a public policy proposal—and thus do not deal with the issue on its merit. Second, religion shifts from being the indirect moral influence on the issue to being the direct focus of attention and the political issue itself. Third, the religious or nonreligious affiliation of the parties in the dispute looms larger and larger until it becomes an unofficial but decisive test for public office, because neither side can get over the hurdle of "where the other side is coming from." Fourth, the issue becomes more inflammatory and divisive than it would have been if religion were left out of it, and in particular small but symbolic issues become matters of major public controversy. Fifth, people on both sides end up all the more hardened in their opinions and their positions, while many others not involved in the controversy tend to react by saying, "A plague on both your houses!"

This spiral of inflammation is plain enough when the issue concerns religion simply and directly, as over school prayer and textbook tailoring. But it is no less at work when the religious factor is indirect as in the case of abortion. For example, after the eight-day abortion filibuster in the Maryland State Assembly in March 1990, people on both sides were sobered. Neither side had gained any legislative advantage. The major result was to emphasize the intractability and venom of the issue as attacks mounted on the religion, sex, race, and moral character of the lawmakers. Accusations of anti-Semitism, anti-Catholicism, and racism were heard both inside and outside the chamber. Maryland's lieutenant governor described it as the ugliest debate in his twenty-four years of office. If played out on a wider stage in the state or the nation, he warned, "it would have torn our community apart."[5]

Importantly, the same incendiary effect can even be seen when the action is not only indirect but from American civil religion (or religiously based patriotism) rather than a more formal religion. There has always been a telling indication of the potency of American civil religion: The fact that the accusation of "un-American," a notion that is purely secular and nowhere officially defined, registers far greater concern and controversy in American than the accusation of "heresy," which is defined clearly and purportedly is of eternal significance. As Justice Felix Frankfurter admitted candidly in the *Gobitis* decision in 1940, "As one who has no ties with any formal religion, perhaps the feelings that underlie religious forms for me run into intensification of my feelings about American citizenship."[6]

Yet Frankfurter's own flag-salute decision unleashed the dark passions that were the forties' forerunner of the great flag furor of the late eighties, climaxing in the national outcry over "the flag-on-the-floor" exhibit at the Art Institute of Chicago in February 1989. Inflammatory, yes, but not a religious issue, many said. The flag is only a symbol of a secular state. But why then were so many so concerned over the "desecration" of what was not sacred? How could Americans be so outraged on behalf of a symbol that they could contradict what the symbol stood for without caring? To those who monitored the underlying dynamics of such incidents, the characteristic inflaming agency was hard to miss.

First Faith Versus Fourth Faith

A third prerequisite for constructive engagement is to grasp the complexity of the overlapping conflicts that make up the schism, which is found markedly in the ideological clash between fundamentalists and secularists. This feature of the culture wars is so prominent that the battle is often misrepresented as a purely ideological clash. Certainly ideology is the most visible and vocal part of it, for the two most prominent antagonists in the national struggle are those who have sprung directly from the cultural chasm that has opened up in American society since the sixties. These are the two movements that attack and dismiss each other by various names, such as "secularists" and "sectarians," the former popularly identified with such groups as the American Civil Liberties Union and the latter with such Christian Right leaders as Jerry Falwell, Pat Robertson, and Donald Wildmon, and such groups as Liberty Federation, né the Moral Majority.

In contrast with the false perceptions of growing public intolerance mentioned earlier, the polarity between evangelicals and secularists is real and strong. Significantly, the two communities have practically no daily contact with each other. Giant abstract differences of history, philosophy, and social life-style reach deep into their souls and produce a polarity that cannot be ignored. For example, over attitudes to numerous social issues, evangelicals and secularists form the two ends of a statistical barbell, each being about as far from the national average as the other. And not only do these communities tend toward different opinions on different issues, they also show a general tendency toward mutual hostility.

But the cultural clash between them is neither accidental nor isolated. It is simply the sharpest version of the growing rift between certain culturally liberal forces in America (usually agnostic or religiously liberal) and certain culturally conservative forces (usually religiously orthodox, whether Protestant, Catholic, Eastern Orthodox, Jewish, Mormon, or whatever). Both sides have been saddled with many ill-fitting labels and unfair stereotypes. But when these are lifted, the struggle between the two antagonists becomes fascinating and critical. For in a nutshell, it represents the contest between the current representatives of America's first faith—Protestant evangelicalism—and the current representatives of what Talcott Parsons aptly called America's "fourth faith"—secular humanism.[7]

Secularists, or those Americans with no particular religious affiliation

(sometimes called "religious nones"), are only half the number of evangelicals (approximately 10 percent of the nation compared with approximately
20 percent). But the number of secularists is growing faster (up from 2
percent in the 1950s), and they reflect higher levels of education and income
and a stronger national influence because of their predominance in
leadership groups. Thus America's "first faith" versus America's "fourth
faith" is a critical modern variation on the theme of Governor Bradford's
"saints and strangers" or the eighteenth-century clash between evangelicals
and deists, the "enthusiasts" and the "enlightened."

The description, first faith versus fourth faith, is obviously simplified. It
begs questions, such as whether there are not as many differences as
similarities between, say, the Mayflower pilgrims and the "Moral
Majoritarians" and their successors, or whether some of the strongest
supporters of certain conservative campaigns are not from America's second
and third faiths (such as those Roman Catholics and Jews who support the
antiabortion campaign). Catholics and Jews are of course important players
in their own right. Equally, many people in the opposing camp do not accept
the label "secularist" or "humanist," partly because they dislike labels of any
kind and partly because this particular label has become a catchall term of
defamation as much as description. This reluctance is understandable. In the
light of the rich heritage of Western freedom and creativity represented by
liberal humanism, today's blackening of all humanism through controversy is
unfortunate and unfair.

Yet far harder to justify is the more extreme position that, contrary to
Talcott Parsons, would reject the label altogether. Some people are firmly
convinced that all references to secularism are veiled references to "secular
humanism" and that both terms spring from the fevered hallucination of
conspiracy-prone conservative minds. It is therefore worth quoting Leo
Pfeffer whose strict separationist credentials are impeccable. In his ground-
breaking *Creeds in Competition* in 1958, he wrote, "In this study I shall
regard humanism as a religion along with the three major theistic faiths."[8]
Thus when due allowance has been made for all the necessary qualifications,
America's first faith versus America's fourth faith is an accurate and
important way of depicting the two poles of the present struggle—at least in
its ideological dimension.

Betrayers Versus Bitter-Enders

If many people miss the full significance of the ideological clash, others never
get beyond it. And one of the vital levels of conflict that is often overlooked
is the psychological. At stake also are two opposing attitudes of mind,

although—unlike the conflict over slavery—these attitudes can be found on either side of the divide. The full picture is much more complicated than an ideological clash in the sense that first faith versus fourth faith is no more a complete picture of today than the portrayal of the Civil War as Northern abolitionism versus Southern slave holding. Chattel slavery was always the greatest divide between the warring parties and as the war went on, it assumed an even greater importance in the Union and around the world. But it was not the sole or even the immediate cause of the war. Many Northerners were indifferent to the evils of slavery. Many Southerners, from Robert E. Lee down, were personally opposed to slavery, never fought to defend it, and advocated the emancipation of slaves even before Lincoln's proclamation.

In other words, alongside the many practical factors separating North and South, the irrepressible conflict was also rooted in two unresolvable, opposing attitudes of mind. On one side, as Robert Penn Warren has outlined, stood the absolutist mentality of the "legalism" of the South.[9] Fiercely committed to the letter of the law and to society as it was, the South adhered strictly to the Constitution and repudiated the critic as traitor. ("The South asks for justice, simple justice," declared her great champion, Senator John C. Calhoun, "and less she ought not to take. She has no compromise to offer, but the Constitution.")[10] This absolute "legalism" reinforced Southern injustice before the war and helped to create the myth of the "Great Alibi" that explained, condoned, and transmuted the guilt of the South afterward.

Opposing the "legalism" of the South was the equally implacable "higher law-ism" of the North. Fiercely committed to a law above the law and to criticism as the task of truth, it was prepared to repudiate society altogether. ("Accursed be the American Union," cried abolitionist William Lloyd Garrison under the influence of the higher law. The Constitution, he said before publicly burning a copy of it, was "a covenant with death and an agreement with hell.")[11] This absolute "higher lawism" reinforced Northern intolerance before the war (as one Northerner observed, it was "as if the *love of man* meant the *hatred of men*").[12] It was also a prime source of the myth of the "treasury of virtue" by which victory conferred on the North a "plenary indulgence, for all sins past, present, and future, freely given by the hand of history."[13] Contrary to some historians, these irreconcilable casts of mind were not the cause of the war. But they were at the root of the reactions and aggravations that helped to make the war inevitable. In an already serious situation, they acted as a poison that inflamed relationships or as a hardening agent that rendered flexible negotiation impossible.

There is a direct parallel in contemporary conflicts over religion and politics. Under the general impact of modernity and of particular forces, such as pluralism, two opposing attitudes of mind have emerged as to how believers in any faith are to hold to their faith, whether that faith is naturalistic or transcendent, traditional or modern.

On one side, many modern believers drift unconsciously toward the stance of cognitive betrayers (or "privatizers" and "minimalists")—those who believe in a manner that compromises their own faith. When it comes to religion and politics, they so privatize their faith, making it privately engaging, publicly irrelevant, that they become civil at the expense of commitment and thus unwittingly betray the consistency of their own faith. Properly emphasizing one-half of the First Amendment tension (the logic of separation rather than integration, "no establishment" rather than "free exercise," peace rather than truth), they take it to improper lengths where it betrays the other half of the tension.

Most religious believers who veer toward this pole are devout pietists, their shrunken pietism being a form of "heresy of the faithful."[14] There is obviously a strong affinity (but no necessary connection) between this position and strict separationism in constitutional theory. Sometimes the combination can lead believers simultaneously to undersell their faith and oversell their separationism. For example, in his dissenting opinion in the *Everson* bus-fare case, Justice Wiley Rutledge, a Baptist, echoed Madison's view of religion as "a wholly private matter" and stated in most unbiblical terms that "the kingdom of the individual and his god. . . . should be kept inviolately private." Rutledge then went on to assert an exaggerated view of separation that flies squarely in the face of history: "We have staked the very existence of our country," he said, "on faith in the *complete separation* between church and state."[15]

Ironically, many devout religious believers quote as canonical John F. Kennedy's statement to the Baptist Ministerial Association in Houston in September 1960, "I believe in a separation of church and state which is absolute."[16] They forget that Kennedy's statement, though politically astute for a presidential candidate seeking to allay anti-Catholic prejudice, actually says more than most of them intend. Kennedy's separation was indeed absolute, because he was largely uninterested in religion. With little personal faith to relate to public life, his sense of conflict was minimal. The free exercise concerns of Catholic bishops in the 1830s were not foremost on the mind of this Catholic candidate in 1960.

John F. Kennedy's attitude to faith was different from his brother, Bobby's. Arthur Schlesinger, Jr., a friend of both, described JFK's intelligence as "fundamentally secular";[17] Bishop James Pike called him a "thoroughgoing secularist" who kept a privatized conscience in a separate compartment;[18] Martin E. Marty wrote that Kennedy had shown himself to be "spiritually rootless and politically almost disturbingly secular";[19] and Seymour Lachman (in a day before the term was taboo outside the Religious Right) described the senator's stance as "a strong secular-humanist position."[20]

One Catholic writer, defending Kennedy's position, explained it in terms of a Catholic public official's rather unfortunately having to lead a "double life."[21] The *Christian Century* commented, "It is difficult to see how a Roman Catholic candidate could have gone further or said more and remained a member of that church."[22] In short, Kennedy's position was more Protestant than the Protestants. (The old American notion that "religion and politics don't mix" had itself been called "Protestant monasticism.") Soon the wry joke began to circulate that Kennedy was the first Southern Baptist president or that the lesson of Kennedy's presidency was that you don't have to be Catholic to be president. Little wonder that the psychology of the cognitive betrayers fits comfortably with both secularism and extreme separationism.

On the other side from the cognitive betrayers, other modern believers veer toward the opposing pole of the cognitive bitter-enders (or "dogmatizers" and "maximalists")—those who believe in a manner leading to contempt for the faith of others. When it comes to religion and politics, they so emphasize the logic of truth or of free exercise and integration that they refuse to be beguiled by civility, let alone to surrender to relativism. Prizing truth instead of peace, they press everything and fight everything to the bitter end. By making absolutes even where no absolutes exist, they achieve a ruthless, scorched-earth consistency, but at the expense of all civility. Just as in the last century abolition was often served worst by abolitionists, so the cause of religion today has met some of its greatest setbacks at the hands of the most religious.

With the rise to prominence in the early 1980s of Marxists in certain university departments and of "movement conservatives" in the Republican party, a disturbing rise of ideological purists and cognitive bitter-enders occurred in American society. Over the issue of religion and politics in particular, Harold Nicolson's observation that religious people are the worst diplomats found many zealous exemplars.[23]

If, without realizing it, the betrayers disbelieve in what they believe to the point of compromise, then the bitter-enders do the reverse. As Seymour Krim, a Jewish writer, observed of Menachem Begin as prime minister of Israel, "He believes in what he believes to the point of contempt."[24] This comment is a reminder that the bitter-ender phenomenon goes far wider than Christian fundamentalism. Forms of "muscular Judaism" have arisen to challenge the old Jewish refuge in the Enlightenment. In Israel the phenomenon of children throwing stones did not begin with the Palestinian *Intifada* but with the ultra-orthodox Haredi children stoning cars driven on the Sabbath—part of the secular life-style that is an abomination to "those who tremble before God."

Cognitive bitter-enders can also be found in the ranks of secularism, and they can become "removers" (of religion from public life) as easily as fundamentalists can become as "reimposers." For example, Madalyn Murray O'Hair's goal is to accomplish three things before she dies: remove "In God we trust" from U.S. coins, delete "under God" from the Pledge of Allegiance, and change the national motto from "In God We Trust" to *E pluribus unum*.[25] As her son Jon, the president of American Atheists, declares, "American Atheists is forever opposed to religion and we remain convinced that this world would be the best of all possible worlds if 'faith' was eradicated from the face of the earth."[26] All too often, such secularist bitter-enders do not allow any reasoned case for a balanced position to be heard. Their whole line of argument, as former Secretary of Education William Bennett noted, might be described as "a *reductio ad* Khomeini."[27]

There are other polarities in the great divide beyond the ideological and the psychological. The disputes could usefully be analyzed according to each of them—the "removers" versus the "reimposers" (over the relations of religion and public life), the "rightsers" versus the "rootsers" (over whether the source of public values should be libertarian or communitarian, the former putting rights before the good, but having no solid ground for rights; and the latter putting the good before rights, but having no shared ground for the good). And so on.

But in each case, two wrongs do not make a right, two half-truths do not add up to a whole one, and the answer to the two extremes is not to split the difference between them. Thus the need for a constructive solution is obvious. For anyone who looks below the rhetoric of contentiousness and recognizes the logic of its unacceptable alternatives, the search for a better way is not a result of weakness, niceness, or a Greek desire for beautifully balanced mobiles of the mind. A resolution is a matter of principle and a most practical one at that. Either faith and freedom, conflict and consensus, commitment and civility, must again be ordered so as to complement each other, or else they will contradict both each other and a future for America that is just and free.

Intolerant Tolerance

There is one great advantage in focusing on ideological descriptions, such as first faith versus fourth faith. It makes it easier to see how all the parties in the disputes should be clear about their respective principles, how they overlap with those of others, and thus give them every reason to conduct the debate in accordance with their highest ideals. There is even some advantage in the general heating up of the culture wars. It is now possible to see clearly that public discourse over religion and public life is being pulled between two further extremes. The uncivil war is bad, but no worse than the pseudo-civility against which it is reacting. One extreme is a distorted form of civility that needs to be set off clearly from the proper article. This corrupted civility is the product of a cluster of factors, such as relativism in regard to truth, libertarianism in regard to life-style, and majoritarianism in regard to the social consensus. The result is a form of easygoing tolerance that starts out with inadequate respect for truth and people, and ends with no room for challenges of any kind.

This pseudo-civility, or intolerant tolerance, fits in well with the psychology of a cognitive betrayer—believing to the point of compromising one's own faith. But although it parades as tolerance and marches under the banner of pluralism, it paves the way for a new intolerance. For beneath its bland exterior of permissive ecumenism grows a deep-rooted relativism so hostile to serious differences and distinctions that belief-words are reduced to the level of the inoffensive and belief-actions to the level of the innocuous. Every settled conviction that raises itself above the level of the superficial automatically becomes suspect.

Under the terms of the earlier Protestant domination of culture, this corrupt civility was a patronizing guise for discrimination and control. Ironically, it even recoiled on Protestants themselves, producing what a Catholic priest in Detroit described to Tocqueville as *rienistes*, or "nothingarians"—a form of nineteenth-century Protestant relativism before modern secular relativism. But under modern conditions secularism is the dominant relativizer. (Tocqueville himself wrote in a letter to a friend in June 1831, "This so-called tolerance, which, in my opinion, is nothing but a huge indifference, is pushed so far that in public establishments like prisons . . . seven or eight ministers of different sects come to prison successively to the same inmates.")[28] Thus as today's pseudocivility affects more and more of public discourse, the scope of what is considered a matter of philosophical and moral indifference expands steadily. Principles are neutered into preferences and nothing is discriminated against except discrimination.

Helped on their way by flawed theories, such as values clarification, beliefs today slide toward the same swampy level that "life-styles" and "sexual preferences" have done. Like Baskin-Robbins ice cream, they come in countless varieties, but are only a matter of taste, not truth or ethics. The effect is to create a spiritual and cultural dust bowl. In area after area, what was once an expression of a community's ideals has been cut down, stigmatized, or ruled out of court in public discussion.

It is an irony of democratic life that freedom of conscience is jeopardized by false tolerance as well as by outright intolerance. At the end of this first road lies the swamp of debased tolerance. Genuine tolerance considers contrary views fairly and judges them on merit. Debased tolerance so refrains from making any judgment that it refuses to listen at all. Genuine tolerance honestly weighs honest differences. Debased tolerance only waters them down. Genuine tolerance promotes both pluralism and impartiality. Debased tolerance produces only a monism of indifference. Genuine tolerance takes matters of substance seriously, agreeing to disagree over things that matter supremely. Debased tolerance concerns itself only with style, allowing only disagreements that hardly matter. Tolerance, G. K. Chesterton remarked of this false civility, is the virtue of people who don't believe anything.

A small, but typical example of this corrupting civility was in a squall over the Boy Scout Oath in April 1985. (Unlike the Girl Scouts' position, which is more sensitive to pluralism and closer to the notion of chartered pluralism, leaving religious matters to the individual homes, the Boy Scout Oath and the Little League Pledge are a lingering residue of an earlier civil religion.) Paul Trout, a fifteen-year-old West Virginian was forced out of the movement because of his statement that, although he respected the beliefs of others, he did not believe in "God or a Supreme Being" as the oath required.

Six months later, however, Trout was reinstated by a resolution from the national executive board. The explanations were revealing. Had he changed his beliefs? No. Had the Boy Scouts changed their oath or dropped it as a requirement? Not at all. Such tough-minded solutions were not in evidence. Duty to God was still a requirement, said a representative, but they decided to remove the definition of God as a Supreme Being (a decidedly bizarre outworking of the notion of duty to a supreme being). The resolution of the national executive read: "While not intending to define what constitutes belief in God, the Boy Scouts of America is proud to reaffirm the Scout Oath and its declaration of duty to God."

The shift in this case was toward a weakening of the content of traditional faith. "God" was to be left "intact." More often today the shift is toward a strengthening of the modern exclusion of faith. "God" has become taboo. But either way, such corrupting forms of civility flourish under the patronage of certain notions of public neutrality, which are themselves either rooted in relativism or a strong reinforcement of it. But following the collapse of the traditional consensus in the 1960s, this sort of unquestioning civility is no longer automatic and that is no bad thing. Corrupt civility had degenerated into servility.

Yet the result of this collapse has been a swing of the pendulum toward the other extreme, from an exaggerated pseudo-civility toward ideological civil war, from the mindset of the betrayers to the mindset of the bitter-enders—believing to the point of contempt for others. And while today's extreme has mostly been a war of words, it has already been sufficiently bitter to claim each side's principles among the first casualties. Clearly, a new position must not be a middle point that splits the differences between the extremes, but a new point that breaks the deadlock of the present argument and advances the discussion for our time. On one side is the rock of doctrinally driven intolerance. On the other is the hard place of an intolerant tolerance that deprives all doctrines of all differences. In between lies a narrow and difficult passage toward the prospect of a public life based on a respect for the convictions of others that is itself based on the solidity of one's own convictions.

An Argument From Irony

Such is the intensity of the culture wars that the reappraisal required of all parties is profound. Advocates on both sides tend to see only the faults of the other and resist any suggestion that they need to examine their own. There is one preliminary argument, however, that for all but the most stubborn of partisans should trigger the consideration of such a reappraisal—an argument from expediency, based on the ironic fact that each side has become the best argument for the other.

Listen to the rhetoric of each and watch their recruiting fortunes. A growing catalogue of fundamentalist excesses has replaced principled argument as the substance of their opponents' attacks, just as their opponents have become the best recruiting sergeants for fundamentalist causes. One side's victims are the other side's perpetrators; one side's excesses the other side's arguments; one side's extremists the other side's recruiters. As journalist Colman McCarthy wrote of one prolife activist, every politician should have someone like him in opposition. He "might as well be working for the pro-abortion groups whose views he so loathes. He makes them look reasonable. They can talk less about the flawed arguments against abortion and more about the pro-life crackpots they're up against."[29]

In political fund-raising the rule of thumb has long been that one always profits from losses and excesses—*our* losses, that is, and *their* excesses. This maxim is almost the politician's equivalent of the Apostle Paul's "sinning freely that grace may abound." Thus conservative leader Paul Weyrich relished President Reagan's defeat by the House over aid to the contras ("This is exactly the kind of vote we like to see even if it goes against us").[30] Similarly, Jerry Falwell welcomed the rejuvenated militancy of the National Organization of Women under Eleanor Smeal: "It was the best thing that could have happened to the pro-life movement. When she conducts herself in a radical way, she helps our people."[31]

But as Falwell also recognized, he was the chief fund-raiser for his opponents in the People for the American Way. "I am to them what Ted Kennedy is to the Right—I'm their means of raising money. If I were to die today, their organization would go out of business."[32] And, in fact, People for the American Way did experience something of an identity crisis in 1989—after the passing from the scene of two of their identity-forming enemies, Jerry Falwell and Ronald Reagan. What President Kennedy saw in the Cold War a generation ago has its equivalent in the culture wars today: "The hardliners in the Soviet Union and the United States feed on one another."[33]

Added to this is the fact that moral indignation has become increasingly professionalized, yet professional problem-solvers usually make it harder to solve the problem because they have a vested interest in perpetuating the problem. This dilemma, obvious enough for the Religious Right, is just as bad for their critics. A central part of their reason for existence is to combat "religious extremism," so they have a vested institutional interest in that extremism continuing. Inevitably, their tendency has not been to pour oil on troubled waters, thus putting themselves out of a job. It has been to fight fire with fire and make the conflagration worse, while piously lamenting that religious extremists are careless with matches.

The end of the eighties marked an almost surrealistic stage in this "war of the watchdogs." Both sides might well have used the same public relations firm, since what one side issued as propaganda the other side seized as counterpropaganda. Thus each side needs the other, feeds off the other, and occupies more and more of the debate, while deeper issues, the national interests, and the real state of affairs in the American public are shouldered aside. The fatal attraction of the opposite sects is proving lethal. Like arms dealers who profess to be peacemakers, such leaders have become the principal suppliers and beneficiaries of the war. Like corporate giants who indulge in an extended slugging match over comparative advertising, such warring styles can damage the entire market and stop people buying both their wares.

Even if principle were abandoned altogether and pure Machiavellianism reigned, both sides should at least by cynical enough to remember the dynamics of persecution and appreciate the pragmatic idiocy of creating martyrs. Just as the blood of the martyrs was the seed of the early church, so 1950s' McCarthyism was a vital ingredient of what has fueled liberalism ever since. Does each side care enough for its own principles to fight for them in a way that will not defeat them? Even that commitment would be enough to warrant a reappraisal and heed what Jim Castelli issues as "a plea for common sense."[34]

The present moment, then, is opportune for a reappraisal. What is proposed is not a sham truce or an impossible Olympian detachment. Abraham Lincoln skewered the absurdity of a certain kind of evenhandedness when he recounted the story of a frontier woman who saw her husband in a life and death struggle with a bear and cried out, "Go it husband! Go it bear!" The points at stake in the present debate are too important for people to remain uncommitted. Civility is not an excuse for gutlessness or fence-sitting. But when positions are chosen and stands made, these things must be undertaken in the best interests of all faiths and the nation at large if one or all of these is not to be the loser.

10

Questions for the First Faith

One of Abraham Lincoln's favorite stories was of an eccentric Indiana preacher who announced as his text, "I am the Christ, whom I shall represent today." Troubled by a little blue lizard as he started to preach, he kept slapping himself more and more desperately. Suddenly he lost both his baggy pantaloons and his shirt. For a moment the congregation sat dazed. Then a dignified elderly lady stood up slowly, wagged her finger at the pulpit, and called out, "I just want to say that if you represent Jesus Christ, sir, then I'm done with the Bible."

Lincoln's story fits in with Nietzsche's celebrated remark that, if Christians wanted him to believe in their redeemer, they would have to look more redeemed. From the more perversely suicidal liberal theologies of the sixties to the maudlin flamboyance of the televangelist scandals of the eighties, many Christian forays into the public square have seemed bent on seeing that other Americans are "done with the Bible."

Christians' failure to make their stands in a style befitting their faith and their stated goals is a prime reason for the fears and derision that have surrounded the reentry of Christian voices onto the national stage. Religious and political constituencies much wider than just members of the first faith have also been involved, but unquestionably it is Protestant evangelicals and fundamentalists who have caused a great part of the confusion and must bear a large measure of the responsibility. Evangelicals and fundamentalists are a diverse and far from monolithic community, whose diversity has not been heard or appreciated in the public square. This chapter is therefore addressed mainly to them. It continues the reappraisal of the current controversies by addressing a series of questions to evangelicals about their own involvement

178

in the public square, while the next chapter is addressed to their opponents.

Justice or Just Us?

Are evangelicals and fundamentalists unreservedly committed not only to their own interests and ideals but also to the common vision of the common good? This first question sums up the overall challenge of religion and public life to members of the first faith. It represents a sharp form of the overall challenge facing Americans: tribespeople, idiots, or citizens?

"Why did you use the words 'evangelical public philosophy'? They're either completely empty or a contradiction in terms. Today's evangelicals are nothing but partisan and sectarian." That sharp retort to me by a Washington journalist in 1989 expresses one side of public skepticism about an evangelical commitment to any public philosophy, or common vision of the common good. The other side is displayed by many evangelicals and fundamentalists themselves. On the one hand, specific initiatives in public philosophy, such as the Williamsburg Charter, that are supported by fellow Christians have been repudiated as "profane, unGodly, anti-Christian and anti-Biblical."[1] On the other, a general obliviousness and suspicion of the notion of public philosophy has been a hallmark of evangelical public engagement in the last decade.

Thus, through the 1980s, which was so marked by public clamor over "me/my/ours," evangelicals in America often came across as simply one more special interest group in the Cuisinart mix of interest-group politics. Instead of Christians never looking for justice but never ceasing to give it, concern for Christian justice has been made to appear as concern for justice for Christians rather than concern for justice for all.

The evangelical lack of a public philosophy is no eleventh-hour discovery. In 1976—*Newsweek*'s "year of the evangelical"—several observers of the national scene examined the newly reemergent evangelical movement and asked whether it was likely to exert the influence that its history, its numbers, and the cultural opportunity might lead one to expect. Would it take advantage of the openings created by important recent restructurings in the worlds of American religion, politics, and culture at large? Their answer was an unequivocal, "No." Handicapped by lack of any distinctively Christian thinking, evangelical public influence predictably would be either confined to specific, single issues or confused with a myriad of overlapping interests closer to the American flag than the Christian faith. For example, wrote John Schaar of the University of Santa Cruz, there was little likelihood that evangelical leaders would "develop any significant new visions of public life and policy."[2]

Nearly fifteen years later, the accuracy of such predictions is all too clear. Failure to articulate and abide by a common vision for the common good has been the Achilles heel of public involvement by evangelicals and fundamentalists. It is also a central reason why, despite "mainline" Protestantism stumbling in its national religious leadership, attention shifted from talk of an "evangelical moment" to talk of a "Catholic moment." To narrow the issue in terms of religion and politics alone: Where evangelicals have shown they have no public philosophy, Catholics—with their strong tradition of natural law and their clear Vatican II stands on religious liberty for all—have proved themselves ready and able to champion the common vision for the common good.

Much more is at stake, of course, than public relations and national status. For how Christians stand in the public eye is not a prime consideration to a community that worships a crucified Savior. But as the televangelists have reminded everyone, faithfulness as Christians see it may at times be scandalous to the rest of society, but to be scandalous is not itself the mark of faithfulness. Thoughtful evangelicals and fundamentalists would therefore do well to ponder their public standing after more than a decade of high-profile political involvement.

Recent opinion surveys reveal a crucial detail in the picture. On the one hand, contrary to impressions of rising extremism and intolerance over religion and public life, the great majority of Americans are actually more tolerant than a generation ago. On the other hand, evangelicals and fundamentalists can take no comfort from such findings because they are a striking exception to the generally expanding tolerance. (In 1958, 25 percent of Americans would not have voted for a Catholic as president and 28 percent for a Jew. In 1988, these numbers had fallen to 8 and 10 percent. The only numbers that rose are those who would not vote for "a born-again Baptist," which rose from 3 percent to 13 percent.)[3] Worse still, a general picture emerges in which recent public involvement by evangelicals is viewed as constitutionally legitimate but intrusive and unwelcome. Among many leadership groups (business leaders, government leaders, academics, priests, and rabbis, for instance) evangelicals come out the highest as a perceived "threat to democracy." Thirty-four percent of academics rate the evangelicals as a menace to democracy, compared with only 14 percent who see any danger from racists, the Ku Klux Klan, and Nazis.[4]

This last statistic is even more startling than it appears. Groups perceived as "alien" and "threatening" are usually the newest and most recently arrived. But evangelicals are the direct spiritual descendants of America's first faith, and as late as the early twentieth century were thought to be as American as apple pie, almost qualifying to be "the Church of America." Thus the fact that evangelicals should now be seen as "a threat to democracy" while still holding views common to most Americans in the 1950s and still advocated openly in the 1980s by a highly popular president like Ronald Reagan, cannot be excused airily by putting the blame on prejudice and rapid social change. The strongest single explanation is the evangelical repudiation of a public philosophy. Without such a commitment to the common vision of the common good, all public engagement by evangelicals—legitimate, wise, and successful or not—is liable to be viewed by others as troubling and even threatening.

Just before his surprisingly strong showing in the Iowa caucuses in 1988, Pat Robertson ran a two-page advertisement in the *Des Moines Register*. On one page there was a photograph of John F. Kennedy with the words, "In 1960 the opposition said this man wasn't fit to be president. Why? Because of his religion." The opposite page had a photograph of Pat Robertson with the counterpoint, "In 1988 the opposition is saying the same thing about this man."

The reader was left to draw the obvious conclusion. Robertson's candidacy should no more be disqualified than Kennedy's. But something in the parallel was missing that was to prove fatal to Robertson's campaign within a few weeks. Kennedy had surmounted his problem by setting out a vision of religion and politics that satisfied his toughest critics (at the Houston Baptist Ministers Association in September 1960). Robertson merely cited the parallel but sidestepped the challenge. He therefore exemplified almost perfectly the wider evangelical lack of a public philosophy. In failing to address the hole in his platform, he made it impossible to expand his core constituency and doomed himself and his supporters to political disappointment. No other evangelical or fundamentalist leader has stepped forward to supply this deficiency. The challenge to redress this failure now faces evangelicalism and fundamentalism at large.

Saints Only or Strangers Too?

Are evangelicals and fundamentalists truly committed to religious liberty for all or primarily for themselves? This second question points to a centuries-old ambivalence in America's first faith that is still unresolved. Whenever it surfaces today, it clouds legitimate evangelical concerns and sends shivers of apprehension through the ranks of minority faiths. For many, current evangelical attitudes and positions are a thoughtless reinforcement of the old jibe about the Puritans: "They loved religious liberty so much that they desired to keep it all for themselves."

To evangelicals, religious liberty is the crown jewel in the treasury of freedoms, their assured birthright both as believers and as citizens. Yet many evangelicals conveniently overlook the ambivalence in their contribution to religious freedom. If religious liberty was, in part, won by them (as descendants of the Puritans), it was also, in large part, won against them.

This ambivalence goes all the way back to the Massachusetts Bay Colony. For if the Puritans were committed to religious liberty, as they were, the liberty they sought was the freedom to live and worship as they believed God intended. The Puritan vision therefore contained an inbuilt tension between liberty for the "saints" and liberty for the "strangers" (the dissenters, such as Quakers and Baptists, who lived in their midst and who—also as a matter of conscience—did not share the Puritan vision). This tension can be seen at its best in the "argument between friends" of John Winthrop and Rogers Williams, or at its worst in the banishment of Anne Hutchinson, the hanging of Mary Dyer, and the maltreatment of Indian "paganism"—the terrible violations of conscience, liberty, and life with which the Puritan record on religious liberty has forever been stained. But there is no question that this Puritan clash of the saints and the strangers helped spawn the revolutionary American idea of religious freedom as "soul liberty" for all—for strangers as well as saints, dissenters as much as majorities, and skeptics along with believers.

Thus the Puritan demand for religious liberty for themselves became, in the triumph of the vision of Roger Williams, a requirement of religious liberty for all. Williams's conscience-bound "soul liberty" for all became the central American conviction of full freedom for people of all faiths and none. When the logic of this principle was understood, religious liberty shifted from being a matter of toleration that one enjoys (and therefore a concession from the stronger to the weaker) to being a right to which one is entitled (and therefore inalienable before even the strongest power, supremely the state). It was this conviction that broke into American public statements in the Virginia Declaration of Rights in 1776 and was enacted in the First Amendment in 1791.

The trouble is, such historical facts and civic first principles trip off the tongue too lightly. Protestant ambivalence over religious liberty for all did not end with the passage of the First Amendment. The enactment of Article VI in 1787 and the religious liberty clauses in 1791 no more won instant, complete religious liberty for minorities, such as the Jews, than the passing of the Bill of Rights won civil rights for blacks. What could be taken for granted early on by the Protestant community had to be secured painstakingly by citizens of other faiths—especially those who were in a minority or whose faith was unpopular.

The clearest example of continuing Protestant ambivalence comes from the long, slow struggle over legally grounded religious discrimination. The struggle was waged against three main things—the persistence of established churches in various states, the attempt to pass a Christian Amendment and put "Christ into the Constitution," and the persistence of religious tests for public office at the state level. At their heart, all three were anomalies in relation to American pluralism and the Bill of Rights. But they were also instances of unjust discrimination that grew from a profound inconsistency in principle. And in each case, Protestant evangelicals were either slow or resistant to granting to others the rights they took for granted themselves.

Roger Williams had put his finger on the inconsistency in his debate with John Cotton. In the ship of state, he wrote, today's persecuted become tomorrow's persecutors: "One weight for themselves when they are under the hatches, and another for others when they come to the helm."[5] Or as Judge Levi Woodbury argued in the face of xenophobic nativism in New Hampshire in 1850, "In the Bill of Rights you pledge to all sects equality, but afterward by this [religious] test you make all but Protestants unequal. You promise entire freedom of conscience to all and treat it as so high a privilege as to be inalienable, and yet you leave other than Protestants defenseless by disenfranchising them from filling offices."[6]

Today, there are no religious restrictions left in the laws of any state, and all but a handful of evangelical leaders would be committed in theory to religious liberty for all. But there is still copious evidence of evangelical ambivalence over the logic of religious liberty for all, in practice—for example, the pervasive evangelical hostility to pluralism (the new "P" word), and the highly inconsistent majoritarian arguments for school prayer—the same parents who press for prayer in the South would be outraged by Buddhist meditation in Hawaii or readings from the Book of Mormon in Utah—and the general blindness to the logic of "Christian America" in America in the 1990s.

At best, evangelicals and fundamentalists should recognize that "Christian America" is a loaded term, charged with emotions, historical baggage, and the specter of revived discrimination if it is applied today. Of course, the term is understandable and appropriate when referring either to the historical fact that the roots of the republic were primarily (though not exclusively) Christian, or to the statistical fact that the Christian faith has been the faith for most Americans and most periods. More than 85 percent of Americans still identify themselves as Christians.

But it is neither constitutionally justifiable nor historically accurate to use the term "Christian America" to assert any official national establishment or semiestablishment of the Christian faith. (For example, the Arizona GOP resolution in 1988 that declared the United States a "Christian nation," and that the U.S. Constitution created "a republic based upon the absolute laws of the Bible, not a democracy.")[7] Neither is it politically wise nor culturally effective to use the term to describe a proposed social vision for America's third century. Anything short of an unambiguous commitment to religious liberty for all and to the political consequences of that principle worked out in today's circumstances will prove a fatal handicap to America's first faith. And, in the light of its own history and first principles, deservedly so.

Speak Softly or the Skeletons Will Rattle

Do evangelicals and fundamentalists fully appreciate the problems created by talk of restoring the past? This third question focuses on the wisdom of an evangelical social vision that often proposes or implies a simple return to the past, whether the 1950s, the nineteenth century, or earlier. No one acquainted with America's past can be blind to the better impulses behind this talk. But other impulses and consequences are present too and realism requires of the first faith a greater degree of responsibility when contributing to the public debate. Evangelicals need to speak humbly about the past or the skeletons in their closet will rattle.

Talk of turning the clock back is freighted with illusions. Certainly America's past, on balance, is something for all Americans—including evangelicals—to be proud of and grateful for. But for Christians of all people, no part of the past, especially the best, should be considered a golden age—on principle. The Christian's golden age, by definition, is in the future. This insistence includes America's past, and the pride and gratitude that Christians feel toward the past should be balanced with an acknowledgment of its unfinished work and its darker side. In the current debate, for example, evangelicals should freely acknowledge what was (in contrast to today's standards and possibilities) the preferential treatment they received in the past, and how this was sometimes abused. If, as it must be, preference is taken as one measure of establishment in a pluralistic society, then the de jure disestablishment of the churches in the eighteenth century was accompanied in effect by their de facto semiestablishment in the nineteenth. Why Protestantism was so favored is obvious, and the fact that such semiestablishment was natural and mostly beneficial is almost beyond dispute. Much of the emphasis in our earlier discussion leaned heavily in that direction, but only because the point is so easily overlooked in a secular age.

Yet that is only one side of the story, and it needs to be balanced in two ways. First, there were times when the "halfway establishment" of Protestantism led to routine preferential treatment well beyond the bounds of logical consistency and public justice. Nationally speaking, the most important example was the discrimination caused by the dominance of pan-Protestantism in the public schools in the nineteenth century. For example—foreshadowing textbooks cases in the 1980s—a group of Jewish parents in New York in 1843 took issue with the use of a particular textbook, *American Popular Lessons,* which was used for religious instruction. The board of education appointed a committee to look into the matter. The committee rejected the protest and reported to the board. It had "examined the several passages and lessons alluded to and had been unable to discover any possible ground of objection, even by Jews, except what may arise from the fact that they are chiefly derived from the New Testament and indicate the general principles of Christianity."[8]

Ironically, such cross-eyed thinking was the forerunner of similar insensitivity today. That some Christian citizens might reasonably object to having their children indoctrinated in "values clarification" seems not to occur to modern board members any more than the equivalent Jewish objection did to their Protestant predecessors 150 years ago. But evangelicals and fundamentalists have no right to feel aggrieved—that is, not unless they also show a similar regard for those who suffered discrimination earlier, and prove it by greater care in their calls to "restore the past." Otherwise they should not be surprised if Catholics and Jews are understandably slow in coming to their defense and cool toward their proposal for a return to the past.

In addition, there were times in the past when the defense of Protestantism's semiestablished standing led Protestants toward attitudes and actions that were flagrantly evil and unjust. Thus evangelicals need to demonstrate a public awareness that, if Protestants have made some of the most distinguished contributions to the history of religious liberty in America, they also bear responsibility for the darkest stains on its record—above all for nativism and anti-Catholicism. Nowhere is America's *novus ordo seclorum* less new and less exemplary than over nativism. Nowhere in American history is there a stronger throwback to the darker side of the colonies' European roots than in the widespread and persisting evil of raw Protestant prejudice against Roman Catholics. The nativism of the Know-Nothing party in the 1850s and of the Ku Klux Klan between 1915 and 1924 are often cited. But many Protestants today do not realize how deep-rooted, systematic, and shameful the temper of anti-Catholicism was as early as the seventeenth century. Anti-Catholicism, which was rife even when there were almost no Catholics, grew into the virulent archetype of American bigotry and nativism, led and supported by Protestants.

The Reformation in Europe did not establish freedom in all Protestant lands until prodded toward it by the Enlightenment, as the persecution of Anabaptists attests. Similarly the Reformation in America often tipped over into practices that no decent American deist or atheist would countenance for a moment. Christian treatment of Jehovah's Witnesses in the 1940s or of secularist leaders, such as Madalyn Murray O'Hair in the 1960s, are further shabby episodes. Such outbreaks illustrate what has been observed before. Where other societies have been torn apart by class struggles, the United States is often seared by group hatreds. As Richard Hofstadter acknowledged, "There has always been in our national experience a type of mind which elevates hatred to a kind of creed."[9] Certain fundamentalist conspiracy theorists and vigilantes are now drilling down again to this subterranean reservoir of generalized frustration and gothic imagination. Secular humanists, New Agers, and Trilateral Commissioners are only the latest in a long roll call of scapegoats, such as Masons, Catholics, Mormons, Jews, and international bankers. What might have been legitimate concern over principled differences has given way to an unprincipled politics of resentment.

The point is not that the fires of fanaticism are being stoked again. The point is to stress that the American Protestant record includes the only European-style pogrom in American history (in Atlanta in August 1915) and a single day of anti-Catholic violence worse than anything seen in modern Ulster (fifty-four deaths in New York City on July 12, 1871). Therefore evangelicals have no excuse for carelessly provocative talk of the past. The past, no less than the present, is a pluralistic reality. There are different memories as well as different communities. So one community's golden age is another's nightmare, one's call to restoration is another's alarm bell against repression. In their concern for public issues, evangelicals must address the past as well as the present if they are to succeed in the future.

Facing Up to the "P" word

Are evangelicals and fundamentalists opposed to pluralism or simply to its side-effects, such as relativism? This fourth question goes to the root of many public blunders by the representatives of the first faith: the confusion between pluralism and relativism. Over the last generation a new and tenacious axiom has grown up among evangelicals and fundamentalists that pluralism is a dangerous evil associated automatically with relativism and eschewed as such. Small and innocuous-sounding at first, the confusion has enormous consequences for religious liberty in a pluralistic society and for any community wishing to participate responsibly in shaping policy in the public square.

There is unquestionably a link—part philosophical and part psychological—between pluralism and relativism. Books, such as Allan Bloom's *The Closing of the American Mind*, served a valuable role in drawing attention to it and to its accompanying dangers, such as indifference to truth and error, right and wrong. But to equate pluralism and relativism is as harmful as to divorce the two because it muddies the clear thinking necessary to combat the real problem. A number of considerations should help evangelicals and fundamentalists rethink the issue and avoid the perils of this confusion.

First, philosophically speaking, pluralism is not in itself relativism and need not entail it. There is, to be sure, a technical philosophical doctrine of pluralism (whose opposite is monism) that includes a belief in the relativity of all truth. One modern proponent of this position was Bertrand Russell, who described his position as "logical atomism" or "absolute pluralism." But as used almost universally today, the term pluralism refers to a social reality, not a philosophical doctrine. Pluralism is a condition of society in which numerous different religious, ethnic, and cultural groups live together in one nation under one government. Pluralism, in this sense, is a social fact and not, like relativism, a philosophical conclusion. Pluralism is thus the end product of a process (technically known as "pluralization") that is at the heart of modernity and modernization. "All those others" of different faiths just happen to be out there in almost every part of the world today, and no amount of seeing red over relativism will wish them away.

Second, culturally speaking, pluralism today tends to reinforce particularism (a belief in the importance and distinctiveness of particular faiths) just as much as relativism. Seen from an international perspective, forces, such as nationalism, tribalism, and fundamentalism, are a stubborn feature of the modern world. Seen from an American viewpoint, the sixties-style first response of pluralism-as-relativism (typified in education by values clarification theory) is being forced to give way to the present position of pluralism-as-particularism. The shift in popular metaphors from melting pot to mosaic, salad bowl, patchwork quilt, and kaleidoscope illustrates a deeper shift. As minorities have grown and diversity has widened, an appreciation of differences has deepened because differences are seen to make a difference. Thus a stubborn feature of contemporary pluralism is the high number of people who are anything but relativists. These people, whether Christians, Jews, Mormons, Muslims, Humanists, or atheists, unrepentantly believe their convictions to be absolutely true. In the end, this is even attested by the fact that "everything is relative has become the last absolute"—the relativist's own absolute. Even Sigmund Freud, the relativizers' relativizer, expressed his own beliefs dogmatically, "We possess the truth. I am sure of it."[10]

Third, historically speaking, the past provides an antidote rather than a warrant for the "P" word phobia that seems to grip certain evangelicals when public policy issues touch on pluralism. For one thing, evangelicals should appreciate the close link between religious liberty and pluralism. From the seventeenth-century Middle Colonies on, increasing diversity has presented both a contribution and a challenge to religious liberty. Religious liberty makes pluralism more likely; pluralism makes religious liberty more necessary.

Further, evangelicals should be able to trace a long and mostly fruitful relationship to pluralism in their own history. Was it not in the highly pluralistic setting of the first century A.D. that the early Christians experienced explosive growth without compromise to their exclusive allegiance? Was it not the Protestant principle of freedom of conscience that contributed decisively to religious liberty and became the greatest generator of choice and dissent in history? Did not nineteenth-century evangelicalism show itself ready and able to exploit the "free market" opportunities for enterprising faiths that were opened up by the First Amendment's separation of church and state? The full story of the relationship of pluralism and faith is not all positive, of course. But even there, the outcome steers evangelicals away from the confusion of pluralism with relativism, or at least of both with secularism. For example, the "nothingarianism" noted by Tocqueville in the 1830s was in fact a form of evangelical relativism long before there were many other religions in America, let alone secularists who could be blamed for it.

Fourth, politically speaking, pluralism may turn out to be the last, best hope for tradition rather than its inevitable destroyer. As Peter Berger points out, and the Central and Eastern European revolution of 1989 underscored, capitalism, pluralism, and freedom go hand in hand because capitalism—unlike socialism and totalitarianism—leaves room for the development and maintenance of a multiplicity of ideas, institutions, and ways of life. Traditional institutions are included in this free, or relatively free, space. Berger's conclusion thus overturns expectations of the average conservative: "Capitalism means pluralism. Tradition has a better chance to survive under pluralism than under an integrative collectivism . . . Capitalism is a thoroughly modern phenomenon, perhaps even the most modern phenomenon of all. But capitalism also relativizes modernity and imposes constraints on the modernization process. And, given a modern world that cannot be wished away, capitalism proves the best chance for nonmodern beliefs and institutions to survive in the this world."[11]

Different members of the first faith will give different weight to each of these considerations. But none who know the challenges of pluralism can avoid them. For the challenges pluralism raises go to the core of issues that are of standing or falling importance for evangelicals and fundamentalists, no less than democracy. The integrity of faith, the protection of religious liberty, and the effectiveness of participation in the public square are all wrapped up with overall responses to pluralism. And they are all behind the currently mounting concern that the strategies of the last decade have been deficient at this point, perhaps even counterproductive.

Beware Brownism

Are evangelicals and fundamentalists self-critical about the relationship of their ends and means? This fifth question focuses on the irony that much conservative Christian activism is a combination of righteous cause and unrighteous strategies. During all the years of heated disputes between fundamentalists and their assorted critics, from Norman Lear and Ted Kennedy to Molly Yard and Leo Pfeffer, one thing has remained clear in the confusion. While there are vast differences of conviction and policy, these are not the most vexatious problem. American pluralism, after all, provides a setting that is capable of brokering between astonishingly diverse positions. With the exception of a small range of less negotiable issues, such as abortion, a large part of the opposition aroused by fundamentalism has to do with its style of public engagement as much as its positions.

Many Christian activists have been swept up in an impetuous "whatever it takes" mentality. Rashly failing to bother about the inconsistency between ends and means, they have not only been less moral than their stated intentions, but also less successful, less conservative, and less Christian. They thus run aground on a cardinal lesson of social movements in American history—that high goals require effective strategies and in the long run the most effective strategies are also the most principled, the most persuasive, and the most American.

The most graphic example of this lesson comes the radical wing of the "divided house" of the abolition movement, and supremely from William Lloyd Garrison and John Brown. Brown's raid at Harpers Ferry, in this sense, represents the epitome of the eclipse of ends by means. Garrison's supporters, from Harriet Martineau onward, have underscored his difference both from

Brown and the depictions of his Southern enemies. They have argued that
the evil Garrison opposed more than justified the tactics he used. Moreover,
the strategic effect of radicalism was to draw the fire of the apologists for
slavery and thus push the debate beyond previous limits. But most historians
have charged that the radical abolitionists' absolutism, self-righteousness,
humorlessness, and astounding lack of charity (even to fellow abolitionists)
were both hypocritical and counterproductive. In contrast to other American abolitionists, such as Charles Grandison Finney, and European
abolitionists, such as William Wilberforce, their very style was the Civil War
in the making.[12]

The same lesson about means and ends surfaced in the civil rights
movement in the 1960s, in the contrast between the principled nonviolence
of Martin Luther King and the more extreme advocates of Black Power and
separatism. One person's reform may always be another person's fanaticism,
but intemperance and belligerence in the pursuit of justice is a sure way to
turn the highest reform into the lowest fanaticism. Such extremes have
surfaced in the last decade mainly in attitudes and actions surrounding
abortion. But the problem of means and ends has cropped up consistently in
the Christian Right, if in a less extreme form.

There are two main ways in which Christian means have subverted
Christian ends. The first concerns the way in which many activists have dealt
with issues. The liberal complaint against fundamentalism is a litany on the
recurring themes of dogmatism, intolerance, and narrow-mindedness. These
charges often rebound to indict the liberals themselves, but the conservative
problem cannot be dismissed airily by saying that. When Jim Castelli coined
the term, the "Satanization of politics," he was pointing to a real problem.
Through their failure to articulate public policy in a manner consistent with
their faith, many Christian activists accorded to secondary things, such as
political positions, the absoluteness, the devotion, and the watershed-
dividing power that, for them, should be proper only to God. The task of
keeping first things first is never easy and never ends, but the biblical term for
the failure to keep second things secondary is idolatry.

All politics is an extension of ethics, so it is perfectly legitimate for
Christian policy positions to be inspired by Christian principles. But neither
politics itself nor political positions should ever be absolute, and the
identification of a Christian cause with any one person, policy, or party
always damages Christian truth. There is no one unique or final Christian
politician, policy, or party. Christians may legitimately say that some are *not*
Christian, but never that any single one *alone* is. To claim otherwise is to
make primary what is secondary, make absolute what should be relative, and

make final what is essentially provisional. In short, the misplaced absoluteness of recent Christian activism idolizes politics, satanizes their opponents, and relativizes their own faith. It thus negates faith's chief contribution to politics: ensuring that politics, being judged by the transcendent perspective of faith, is kept as "merely politics" and no more.

If Christian activists were to think it through, few would actually believe in political absolutism. But they speak and act as if they do. The best-known examples of such poor thinking are the Christian "report cards" of the last decade. These purported to show how members of Congress voted in "key moral/family issues" during an election year. Extraordinary anomalies showed up in 1980, 1984, and 1988. That first year Senator Mark Hatfield, described by fellow Senator Jesse Helms as "the most moral man in the Senate," scored a derisory score in comparison with another member later indicted in the Abscam scandal. Four years later, Senator Paul Simon, son of missionary parents and an exemplary Christian family man, was given a zero Christian rating, whereas a member of Congress censured by the House for having had sex with a teenage page was given a perfect 100 percent score.

The reason for the anomalies is simple. The criteria behind the ratings were neither moral nor theological, but ideological. Of the eighty-one senators and representatives who gained a "100 percent Christian" rating in 1984, eighty were Republicans and one was a Democrat. Equally, of the ninety-four with "zero Christian" ratings, ninety-two were Democrats and only two were Republicans. In so far as anyone thought the report cards illuminated "key family/moral issues," they were misleading. In so far as anyone thought they demonstrated Christian thinking, they were pernicious. "By their bottom line shall ye know them." Politics, not piety or ethics, was the ruling criterion.

The second and more serious way in which Christian means have subverted Christian ends concerns dealing with people. For a start, the last decade was notable for the ferocious campaigns of vilification waged by Christians against their fellow Christians. Ecclesiastical politics has always been more vicious than secular politics. Southern Baptists have good cause to know the wisdom of their own saying, that in "the ecclesiastical politics they choke you to death while they're praying for you." But for Christian leaders to make fractiousness a way of relating or to resort to underhanded methods while declaiming publicly about "restoring moral values to America" is contemptible. After retiring from the political front-line, Jerry Falwell is reported to have said with sorrow and with experience, "If the evangelicals had succeeded, they would have killed each other off."

Such righteous hate-mongering was evident in many of the campaigns orchestrated through radio, television, and direct mail in the last decade. Over the school prayer bill in 1984, for example, the offices of senators were deluged by waves of phone calls, letters, and telegrams, unprecedented in volume and in the intensity with which Christians combined the language of hell and the gutter in order to pursue a politics of intimidation. As one Republican legislative assistant on Capitol Hill told me after several weeks on the receiving end over a school prayer bill before the Senate: Profanity and foul language that had been denounced on television were indulged in rather freely on the telephone.

Liberal commentators repeatedly charged that there was a disparity between the more benign public statements of Christian activists and their more strident and vitriolic statements to their own constituencies. That gap by itself was not the real problem. We all speak differently inside and outside our families. But it was distrubing when the chasm between Christian principle and practice highlighted the real character of the "moral America" to which they wish to return. Representative Jack Kemp, whose family was smeared abominably by fellow conservatives in the 1988 election, remarked with justice that even if candidates did not abide by the Republican eleventh commandment ("Thou shalt not attack a fellow Republican"), they should at least obey the biblical ninth ("Thou shalt not bear false witness").

Christian treatment of non-Christians was sometimes no better, as witnessed in the tone of local campaigns against homosexuals, such as in Dade County, Florida, in 1977. However strongly Christians disapproved of the practice of homosexuality, was it anything other than evil to speak of homosexuals, as one Christian leader did, as "human garbage"? And what of the claim of another that "so-called gay folks just as soon kill you as look at you"? What did Christians think it said of Jesus when bumper stickers sprouted over Dade County with the slogan, "Kill a queer for Christ"?[13] Similar Christian mean-spiritedness has marked too many campaigns on too many issues. Where prosperity preachers in the eighties pressed the "hot button" of greed, their direct-mail political counterparts pressed the button of hate and hysteria. The result was a monumental reversal of the Epistle of John: Perfect fear cast out love.

The French statesman Chateaubriand, who was drawn toward the French revolution, turned against it when he saw the first head on a pike. "I will never see an argument for liberty in murder," he said. The same is true of reform and fanaticism—unjust means are never an argument for just ends. After a visit to South Carolina before the Civil War, Julia Ward Howe, the author-to-be of "The Battle Hymn of the Republic," wrote, "Moral justice dissents from the habitual sneer, denunciation, and malediction, which have become consecrated forms of piety in speaking of the South." Theodore Weld, an effective Northern abolitionist, actually withdrew from activism for a while because, as he said, "he himself needs reforming." He admitted that he "had been laboring to destroy evil in the same spirit as his antagonists." Too many high-minded reformers, wrote James Russell Lowell after the war, "stood ready at a moment's notice to reform everything but themselves."[14]

Sleeping Giant to Poor Little Whipping Boy

Are evangelicals and fundamentalists prepared to participate enterprisingly in public life or are they determined to play the victim and portray themselves as a persecuted minority in need of special understanding? This last question focuses on a dramatic sea-change in the public psychology of evangelicals and fundamentalists following the decline of the Christian Right.

In ten short years, the public self-portrait presented by evangelicals has changed from the sleeping giant of American public life to the poor little whipping boy at the mercy of liberal forces. What Will Herberg in the 1950s called a "back to the catacombs" outlook came in fashion again.[15] "In a mere decade," wrote Charles Colson as an observer, "the 1980s Moral Majority has become the 1990s persecuted minority. . . . Clearly it is open season for Christian bashing."[16] The idea of a Christian antidefamation league was first floated in 1986, but abandoned because of the public disgrace of the televangelist scandals. It caught on fast when reintroduced as central to Pat Robertson's Christian Coalition in February 1990. "Christian Americans are tired of getting stepped on," his brochure announced.[17] The blatant bias of press reporting, Congressman Robert Dornan charged, is just one example of "the anti-Christian bigotry that has run amok in this nation—with the apparent approbation, cooperation, and participation of the dominant media culture."[18] The situation is worse than "bigotry, plain and simple," said Donald Wildmon of the American Family Association. "When the norm of society says, 'You can't participate in the mainstream because you're a Christian,' then there's a serious problem, not just for me but for everybody in society."[19]

Hearing such claims, it was hard not to remember the same people and their friends only a decade earlier. Then, all the talk was of "rousing the slumbering giant," "mobilizing the moral majority," representing the "largest single minority in America," having "enough votes to run the country," and providing Christians with "the most united front seen in this century." Richard Zone, a leading Christian activist, even boasted on "Sixty Minutes" in 1980, that "forty million people can amend the Constitution if they had a mind to. They can elect a President. They can throw out a President. We can elect any official. We can change or make any law, and that's exactly what we intend to do."[20]

The conservative complaint in 1990 was made up of three main claims—their decreasing status, the increasing bigotry against them, and the hardening closure of the political process to their influence. But it decisively marked the end of the 1980s brand of conservative activism. Just as Richard Bach's *Jonathan Livingston Seagull* (1972) was a bellwether book that marked the end of the sixties and the beginning of the seventies, so Frank Perretti's mammoth bestseller *This Present Darkness* and its sequel captured the conservative Christian mood at the end of the eighties.

To those whose aggressive, outgoing confidence had collapsed into alarmism and paranoia, the root of the problem had deepened from the human to the supernatural. It was not enough simply to trace it to secular humanists and New Agers. The situation was solely the fault of the devil himself. Christian liberals had bowed out from the sixties with a hollowed-out demonology owing more to sociology than orthodoxy (the institutional "principalities and powers"). Christian conservatives followed suit in the eighties with a hyped-up demonology as close to Stephen King and medievalism as to the Bible. Thus the reconstructionist movement was left to carry the banner for the earlier public optimism of the Christian Right. But its prospects of success were decisively postponed to the long-long-term future. In the short term, Christian prospects appeared to be limited to defamation and persecution.

There is unquestionably a good deal of anti-Christian bias and prejudice in parts of American society today and horror-story examples are not hard to find. This is not surprising in a period that contains both culture wars and hate crimes. But listening to certain aspects of the conservative complaint, it is hard to keep a straight face. Have their numbers and social standing really collapsed so precipitately? How could such innocents have called down such unprovoked malevolence out of the blue? Just as evangelical and fundamentalist confusions over pluralism have jeopardized the search for a public square, so too the current evangelical and fundamentalist responses to "victimization" have served neither their own interests nor those of the republic. Again, some considerations should help them rethink the issue.

First, the conservative complaint about being a small and victimized minority is factually misleading. ("We evangelicals are a tiny minority, you know," a university professor told me solemnly in Kentucky.) Whatever the numbers claimed for evangelicalism at the beginning of the 1980s— generally agreed to be around 20–40 million Americans—may be taken as roughly the same number at the end. There are simply too many to fit in the catacombs. There is no known empirical evidence of any dramatic decrease over the last decade. In other words, the hard numbers are the same; it is the psychology and social status that have changed. Yet at a time when all minorities are accorded a better cultural place in the sun, for the oldest and one of the most sizable faith communities to pass itself off as a beleaguered and defamed minority is both an insult to real minorities and an extraordinary testimony to its own state of mind. The present situation is reminiscent of the 1920s quip about a fundamentalist being someone who "talks of standing on the rock of ages, but acts as if he were clinging to the last piece of driftwood."

Second, the conservative complaint is morally hypocritical. At the end of a decade when more of its dirty linen was washed in public than in any comparable ten years in evangelical history, the wonder is not that there is so much stinging criticism from outside the churches but that there is so little within. Both the conservative churches and the conservative movement provided a rich stock of targets to keep would-be pundits and satirists in business for years. What corrupt state churches did over the centuries by way of accelerating secularization in Europe, corrupt American churches did with a vengeance in the 1980s.

Besides, any liberal prejudice toward Christians has been more than amply reciprocated. And many of the splinters in the eyes of the defamers are minute compared with the planks in the eyes of the defenders. The fact is, observers of the press say, the old hostility toward the Christian faith in the mainstream press has fallen. (Fred Barnes of the *New Republic* wrote in 1990, "I don't think that's really true now. I don't think hostility is what it is. It is indifference to Christianity, and indifference to spiritual things in general.")[21] Significantly too, analysts at the end of the 1980s were more and more impressed by the conservatives' strength in the media. Forthright conservative apologists, such as John McLaughlin, Patrick Buchanan, Robert Novak, and William Buckley, were obvious. But even such programs as the "McNeil/Lehrer News Hour" were criticized for their decided conservative learning.[22] Rather than a sign of mounting prejudice against Christians, much of the evidence pointed to mounting partisanship on many issues because of the culture wars.

Third, the conservatives' complaint is politically and psychologically dangerous. Whatever the motivation, the effect of appealing to the victimized is to reject the ethic of Christ and resort to a politics of resentment. Put plainly, the politics of resentment is the politics of revenge—the attempt to get back at degrading persecution. To do this, Nietzsche wrote a century ago, is to play at the hole of the tarantula, because it is the black poison of the tarantula that makes the soul whirl with revenge, especially when bitten by "preachers of equality." ("'We shall wreak vengeance and abuse on all whose equals we are not'—thus do the tarantula hearts vow.")[23] Expressed from a more Christian basis, the present recourse to resentment is an irony compounded by tragedy. Conservative Christians criticize the concept of tolerance with some justification. But instead of countering tolerance with its Christian corrective—forgiveness—they counter it with resentment, its self-righteous and anti-Christian contradiction.

Ironically, evangelicals and fundamentalists are stepping up their appeal to a politics of resentment at the very moment when other groups are reexamining or abandoning it. Women, blacks, Jews, and other groups have all traveled the "victims and losers" road before. Certain forms of Christian liberalism have been fired by resentment to idealize poverty against wealth and victimhood against power. In the short run, there is instant political power in appealing to those who feel victimized—many forms of political tribalism are simply potent "instant brotherhoods of the scapegoated." But over the long run the results are self-defeating. In order to sustain the power, the self-professed victims must celebrate their victimhood so long that they come to see themselves only as victims and end up victimizing themselves. Victim psychology thus becomes the all-purpose excuse for every Christian (or feminist, black, and Jewish) disadvantage and serves only to perpetuate the handicap. Victims become losers for keeps.

Compared with Martin Luther King, "Christian conservatives" are neither Christian nor conservative when it comes to their politics of resentment. For King's moral authority came more from his rejection of resentment than from his nonviolence. In refusing to mobilize black resentment or to claim exemption from common moral standards on the grounds of victimization, he bypassed a politics of raw guilt and retaliation and lifted civil rights to a level of overwhelming moral authority—for blacks and all Americans.

Will evangelicals and fundamentalists do the same with their campaigns? Since King's time, the art of American political organization has generally gone the other way. From black power and the women's movement to gay rights and now "Christians" and "Middle Americans," the tendency has been to corral resentment, celebrate victimhood, and multiply the demands and devices for avoiding all inequalities under the political sun. The upshot is that the old idea of the citizen—the person with the same few clear rights as everybody else in the republic—has been steadily eclipsed. Overshadowing this concept now is a hierarchy of group privileges and sensitivities that are ranked according to their cultural standing in victimhood (a sort of "more victimized than thou"). The result is a triumph of "minoritarianism"—a rights-run-riot hypersensitivity that, in seeing to it that no one loses in any decision, nullifies the vital difference between majority and minority and undercuts enterprise, equal opportunity, and community at once.

Early in 1990, cable TV magnate Ted Turner told a group of broadcasters that "Christianity is a religion for losers."[24] All the more extraordinary that American evangelicals and fundamentalists should choose that moment to confirm his Nietzschean thesis by resorting to a loser's politics of resentment even cruder than Nietzsche had attacked.

Will such questions as these cause members of the first faith to rethink their strategies in the public square? No one should hold their breath. As the eighties ended, the public face of evangelicalism and fundamentalism registered many emotions. But few of them indicated any serious commitment to the public philosophy and some even betrayed a reckless "at all costs" defiance that boded ill for civic responsibility. Perhaps, however, the bitter taste of failure will force evangelicals to face what the sweet smell of success allowed them for a decade to side step: Without a clear commitment to the common vision for the common good, evangelical and fundamentalist engagement in the public square serves neither America's interests nor their own.

11

Questions for the Fourth Faith

Few things irked conservatives in the eighties as much as the suggestion of a "moral equivalence" between the USA and the USSR. Thus, ironically, the 1989 revolution became not only a massive vindication of the conservative view of the differences, but a conservative alibi for evading serious confrontation with the problems of conservatism. Many liberals, similarly, are offended at the suggestion that the contentiousness over religion and politics is anything but a fundamentalist problem. Moral Majority's closure in 1989 was surely proof of the errors of the Christian Right and the correctness of the liberal critique. The word fundamentalist, in their minds, is another word for fanatic, whereas by definition a liberal is rational, educated, tolerant, concerned for justice—surely the exemplary custodian of all the virtues required for a modern civil society.

But when it comes to religion and politics, have liberals practiced their principles any more consistently than evangelicals and fundamentalists have theirs? Or is there evidence that many of them have slipped into ways that contradict their own ideals and do a serious disservice to American public life?

We have already noted a number of blind spots and contradictions in the general liberal position on religion and public life, beginning with educated people's inexcusable ignorance over the place and importance of faiths in American life. We can therefore continue the reappraisal of the controversies by raising some questions to secular humanists as members of the "fourth faith." They are raised in the same spirit and with the same purpose as those in the last chapter to members of the first faith. Of course, the category fourth faith is less precise, less representative of liberals as a whole, and far more controversial than the category first faith. And the questions will be no barrier to anyone who deliberately sets out to flout the requirements of public civility. But such a person, fundamentalist or secularist, forfeits the right to be taken seriously when he or she speaks of stated ideals and of a democratic vision for American public life.

A Creed by Any Other Name

Are secularists prepared to be candid and consistent in putting both secularism in general and secular humanism in particular on the table along with modern society's many faiths, worldviews, and life stances? This first question focuses on secularist candor and consistency bearing on some of the deeper issues surrounding religious liberty today.

To be sure, there is no universally accepted definition of what is and is not a religion. And to be coerced into an alien definition is itself a violation of religious liberty. Even within the social sciences, opinions differ over whether religion should be defined "substantively," or narrowly—in terms of the content of belief in God, gods, or the supernatural—or whether religion should be defined "functionally," or broadly—in terms of what it does and how it works in the lives of believing individuals and communities.

Obviously, the choice bears directly on whether secularism is included among "faiths, worldviews, and life stances." For under the functional definition of religion, secularism—although secularists explicitly disbelieve in the supernatural—is still a "functional equivalent" of religion, or what the Supreme Court has called "a parallel belief." Yet there is no simple way to escape that conclusion by falling back on a reliance on the substantive definition alone. For one thing, the two definitions are not mutually exclusive. For another, the substantive definition alone is inadequate for the purposes of religious liberty. The substantive definition leaves out not only secularism but other beliefs almost universally acknowledged to be religious, although explicitly nonsupernatural—for example, Theravada Buddhism and Confucianism.

Far more than a definition game is at stake, of course. The answer given has practical consequences for religious liberty, for constitutional interpretation, and for public education. It affects a range of issues that are vital to public justice in a pluralistic society. But sadly, the issue is rarely discussed coolly in the setting of public justice. Instead, it is pressed into use in the artillery battles of the culture wars. The functional definition is press-ganged into the defense of the first faith ("You got prayer out of the schools. We'll get secular humanism out!") and the substantive definition into the defense of the fourth faith ("There's no such thing as secular humanism and, even if there were, it is not a religion and therefore not subject to legal prohibition anyway").

James Davison Hunter has provided a rare and superbly dispassionate analysis of an issue whose significance and subtleties are still not appreciated by many or discussed constructively by others.[1] The Supreme Court, he points out, has recognized nontheistic faiths as "religions" for the purposes of their own claims to free exercise. Yet the serious sociological argument that secular humanism is a religion remains implausible for most American intellectuals. Indeed, "common wisdom asserts that secular humanism is purely a myth invented by the religious right—a convenient scapegoat designed by lunatic conservatives."[2]

Hunter uses the social sciences to explore the status of secular humanism at two levels. First, he examines secular humanism as a formal movement, represented by such groups as the American Humanist Association. Here secular humanism is clearly identifiable but small in numbers. It serves as a philosophical meaning system or cosmology that has many sectarian features, including claims to universal validity, a sense of historical destiny, and a zeal to proselytize. Thus the recent rejection of the self-description "religion" by human activists is no bar to considering secular humanism a functional equivalent of religion—not just because the self-description underlies the humanist claim to free exercise rights, but because its rejection has not been followed consistently by humanists themselves. Many humanists still describe themselves as religious but nontheistic, and many leaders of the movement— from John Dewey to Paul Kurtz—have repeatedly identified humanism as a religion.[3] Probably more, if not most, would still be doing so if fundamentalist attacks had not had the ironic effect of strengthening the secularism of humanism in the last two decades.

Second, Hunter examines secular humanism as a broader and more diffuse cultural ethos that is far wider than the formal movement. At this level, secular humanism lacks the self-consciousness and articulation of a formal ideology. But with its strong Enlightenment background and common themes, such as Max Weber's "rationalization," it provides a "reinforcing cultural context, within which humanistic ideology, both formal and 'folk,' becomes credible if not 'common-sensical' to an increasing number of people."[4]

On the basis of this two-tier inquiry, Hunter concludes that secular humanism in American public life is neither an all-embracing religion that conspires to control American institutions nor an empty fiction the Religious Right concocted to be their scapegoat. Yet there are solid grounds for arguing that "a secularistic humanism has become the dominant moral ideology of the American public culture and now plays much the same role as the pan-Protestant ideology played in the nineteenth century."[5] Or as Professor Robert Coles of Harvard University put it, "I don't know if there is a religion called 'secular humanism,' but there is definitely a 'secular religion' in education today."[6]

Hunter's study is singular for its civility as well as its rigor. But such a style is rare. More often the public debate is sidetracked before it can engage with first principles and practical applications. Some supporters of secular humanism, for instance, appear reticent to declare themselves at all, knowing that as skeptics they are as outnumbered in America just as religious believers are in Europe. Public candor can be more trouble than it is worth. Others play the role of pedant and become so entangled in disentangling conservative confusions over the precise distinctions between "humanism," "humane," "humanities," and the like, that they never get to the point and argue their own position. Still others pretend to be utterly bamboozled by the thought that secular humanism is a religion or that there is any such thing as secular humanism.

A typical example of disingenuity was a minor furor over an education bill in 1984 that had tacked onto it a paragraph prohibiting grants for "any course of instruction the substance of which is secular humanism." The addition, proposed by Senator Orrin Hatch, was conspicuous for its lack of a working definition of secular humanism, but the reaction had some mischief of its own. Tony Podesta, then the executive director of People for the American Way, described secular humanism as a "hoax" perpetrated by fundamentalists, while the *Washington Post* printed several articles suggesting that secular humanism was a matter of the "mythical, the undefinable, and the downright fictional."[7] In Norman Lear's widely quoted phrase, trying to define secular humanism was "like trying to nail Jell-O to a tree."

No one has to be a conspiracy junkie to recognize that such disingenuity borders on the ludicrous. "Humanism," in the sense in which Senator Hatch was taking exception, is defined clearly in almost all dictionaries and better encyclopedias and the qualifying adjective "secular" is hardly arcane (see *Webster's New World Dictionary* or the *Encyclopedia Britannica*). Anyone still unclear could easily get in touch with the nearest branch of the American Humanist Association, subscribe to the magazine *The Humanist*, study the famous documents Humanist Manifesto (1933) and Humanist Manifesto II (1973), or simply apply to such stalwart advocates as the president of the American Humanist Association. Isaac Asimov, president at the time, seemed to be in no doubt when he wrote to the members in 1985, "I want the Department of Education to come to us if they want to know what 'secular Humanism' is."[8]

The late Joseph Blau, professor of religion at Columbia University, claimed to have coined the term *secular humanism*.[9] He used it in a memorandum for the Ethical Union. It was then adopted by the American Humanist Association in an amicus curiae brief prepared for the *Torcaso* case in 1961 and eventually surfaced in a footnote to the Supreme Court's decision. (Footnote 11 read: "Among religions in this country which do not teach what would generally be considered a belief in the existence of God are Buddhism, Taoism, Ethical Culture, Secular Humanism, and others.")[10]

But the term was in currency long before then. William G. Peck used it in 1933 in his book *The Social Implications of the Oxford Movement*. Prior to Blau, Cyril Wright Mills, the radical sociologist, referred specifically to "secular humanism" in a 1952 essay. Thus, an article in *Free Inquiry* in 1980 was far nearer the mark when it stated unambiguously, "Secular humanism is a vital force in the contemporary world."[11] Joseph Blau even asserted that certain synagogues had stated beliefs "more in common with Humanist associations than with Rabbinic Judaism."[12] And the scholar and jurist Leo Pfeffer, a lifelong champion of strict separationism, wrote flatly (before the recent controversies) that old differences between Protestants, Catholics, and Jews are now dormant, if not dead because "secular humanism has won out." Indeed, he declared, evidence of secularization in higher education and divorce in family life show that "it is not Protestantism, Catholicism, or Judaism which will emerge the victor, but secular humanism, a cultural force which in many respects is stronger in the United States than any of the major religious groups or any alliance among them."[13]

Fundamentalists have certainly contributed to inflaming the issue— partly by defining secular humanism in effect as everything to which they are opposed and partly by combating it with a tit-for-tat scorched-earth strategy least conducive to promoting public justice. But the secularist reticence in response has been no better, for certain of the facts are incontrovertible. Humanism in America has long been defined by humanists as a religion; secular humanism has been happy to claim the free exercise rights of religious liberty; secular humanism has been referred to as a religion in the law courts; secular humanism has often been advocated by humanists as an explicit alternative to traditional religion; and the objectives of secular humanism have been set forth openly as achievable through education.

Surviving witnesses of the first Humanist Manifesto say that only three or four of the thirty-three signers grumbled about its explicitly religious dimension (as "religious humanism"). One signer, Charles Francis Potter, wrote: "Education is thus a most powerful ally of Humanism, and every American public school is a school of Humanism. What can the theistic Sunday Schools, meeting for an hour once a week, and teaching only a fraction of the children, do to stem the tide of a five day program of humanistic teaching?"[14] In the same vein, Paul Blanshard wrote in an essay in *The Humanist*, "I think the most important factor moving us toward a secular society has been the educational factor. Our schools may not teach Johnny to read properly, but the fact that Johnny is in school until he is sixteen tends toward the elimination of religious superstition.[15] In short, the question is not whether secular humanism is a religion, but whether it is the only religion not subject to the First Amendment.

Quite apart from its important applications to law and education, candor is required from humanists today for two further reasons. The first is philosophical and concerns the fact that all worldviews—religious or secular, theistic or nontheistic—represent the ultimate faith commitments of those who believe in them. This fact runs counter to the impressions of many pragmatists, but it must be recognized if pluralism will genuinely be protected. Those proposing public policies grounded in naturalistic and nontheistic assumptions have the same right to make their case as those basing them on theistic assumptions of one sort or another. But to claim that secularism (or any worldview) is neutral in religious matters is a sham. Value-neutrality is philosophically impossible when it comes to the ordering of social affairs. Secularist beliefs, although naturalistic and nontranscendental, constitute an ultimate faith commitment just as much as religious beliefs do.

The second reason for candor is psychological. Perhaps because they reflect the ambiguities of Hunter's two-tier analysis, many secular humanists display a revealing ambivalence in public. Are they insiders or outsiders? Do they represent the majority or a minority? Do they speak with the assurance of an Establishment orthodoxy or with the anxiety of a doubt-shaken believer? Are they smugly on the winning side of history or nervously circling the wagons against cultural barbarians? Many secularists and some liberals cannot seem to make up their minds whether they have established a new post-Protestant hegemony or are fighting desperately for a hearing. (If Leo Pfeffer wrote of "the triumph of secular humanism," Isaac Asimov bewailed, "For all too long, we've been taking a licking.")[16] Such ambivalence has been evident on the fundamentalist side too. In both cases it serves to hold open the door for the anxiety and resentments that cripple public debate.

Typical of a more candid approach is Joseph Fletcher, the humanist ethicist and former Episcopalian. He refused to duck the issue by defining humanism only in terms that are positive and inoffensive. Admittedly, he said, it would be easier to define humanism positively as "concern with human beings and their welfare." Such a definition would be accurate and it could be embraced by a long and distinguished line of Christian humanists, including many believers today. Its ambiguity would save it from causing offense. But Fletcher scorned this as the "blurred thinking" and "muddle-headed cavil" typical of "soft humanist circles."[17] Instead, he argued that what counts today is not the noun in "secular humanism," but the adjective. What must be made clear first is not the positive emphasis but the negative. "Understanding humanism negatively," he asserted without mincing words, "at once cuts out the Christians, Jews, Muslims, Buddhists, Hindus and their variants, *ad infinitum.*"[18]

Fletcher himself did not downplay the more positive aspects of human-ism, but he developed them only after the negative had been established. He even complimented Jerry Falwell and other evangelicals and fundamentalists for appreciating the decisiveness of secularism more clearly than many humanists. (More clearly too, one might add, than many well-meaning but fuzzier Christians who stress only the positive aspects of humanism and so blur the issues and muzzle the debate). Straight talking, while momentarily divisive, is constructive in the long run because it cuts through to the core issues. Thus secular humanism may be, as Leo Pfeffer puts it, "a funny kind of religion with no other credo than humanism."[19] But a creed by any other name deserves the same rights and responsibilities—and restrictions—as any conscience-bound conviction.

Else, What's a Secularist Heaven For?

Are secularists as self-critical as they profess about their own means and ends in pursuit of religious liberty and in particular about their use of the doctrine of "strict separationism"? This second question focuses on secularist consis-tency in promoting a theory of constitutional interpretation that has become all-decisive to religious liberty for the past half-century.

Beyond any doubt, disestablishment and the separation of church and state are at the heart of the purpose and achievement of the First Amendment. The separation of church and state is the supporting compan-ion truth to religious liberty. To the extent that America's two-hundred-year experiment with religious liberty for all has been a singular and glorious success, it is owing to the separation of church and state. As the Williamsburg Charter declares,

> No threat to freedom of conscience and religious liberty has historically been greater than the coercions of both Church and State. . . . When these institutions and their claims have been combined, it has too often

resulted in terrible violations of human liberty and dignity. They are so combined when the sword and purse of the State are in the hands of the Church, or when the State usurps the mantle of the Church so as to coerce the conscience and compel belief. These and other such confusions of religion and state authority represent the misordering of religion and government which it is the purpose of the Religious Liberty provisions to prevent.[20]

The framers' manner of separating church and state is fundamentally positive, and not the least to religion. On the one hand, the separation of church and state removes what has been a central source of hostility to religion in other countries—its established and often oppressive status. On the other hand, it disallows any religion from depending on state power, whether through funding or special privileges, and throws each one back on its own resources. The result is a freedom and competitiveness that has fostered a lively pluralistic scene with equal constitutional freedom to believe anything or (as skeptics like to see it) to believe nothing.

In light of this record, the recent fundamentalist disparaging of separation of church and state makes little sense. Far nearer the traditional Protestant support for separation is Tocqueville's testimony as a Catholic. Searching for the explanation of the remarkable closeness of the "spirit of religion" and the "spirit of liberty," he found only one answer: "They all attributed the peaceful dominion of religion in their country mainly to the separation of church and state. I do not hesitate to affirm that during my stay in America I did not meet a single individual, of the clergy or the laity, who was not of the same opinion on this point."[21]

Yet the fundamentalist complaint is justified if it is directed, not at the principle of the separation of church and state, but at the myth of "strict, total, absolute separationism." For strict separationism is the myth through which the principle of separation has been inflated, reiterated, and elevated to a doctrine of constitutional interpretation. Strict separationism is the "broad interpretation" of the "no establishment" clause, which seeks to make religion and state authority "absolutely separate." It was sired by the lifelong work of Leo Pfeffer and burst through into its present constitutional prominence in the famous *Everson v. Board of Education* decision in 1947. All governmental aid to religion, even on a nonpreferential basis, is said to violate the no establishment clause and be unconstitutional. Public life is to be inviolably secular, religious life inviolably private.

As time passed, strict separationism grew from being a theory to a doctrine to an orthodoxy to a ruling myth that has shaped the course of public discussion and constitutional decisions alike. In the process, a mounting sense of the self-evident produced a diminishing sense of the self-critical. Yet fifty years later, the myth shows symptoms of the affliction common to all theories that lack a sense of irony and self-criticism—internal contradictions.

First, strict separationism is based on a claim that is impossible. Its appeal largely depends for its success on the bold, scything simplicity of its statement—religious liberty is guaranteed by the strict/total/absolute separation of church and state. Pfeffer, for example, is a self-confessed "absolutist" about strict separationism (in the classic bitter-ender tradition of the true fundamentalist). "Absolutists," he believes, "serve an important function in church-state law; any compromise becomes too often the starting point for further compromises."[22]

But as with all fundamentalists, the absolutism of the separationists' dogma is belied not in their applications to others but in their not going the whole way themselves. For most separationists, the step too far was losing their religious tax exemptions. In 1971 when the Supreme Court confronted an attack on religious tax exemptions, Pfeffer proposed an amicus brief in support of the challenge. For once, he was followed by few separationists. Leading separationist groups, such as the Anti-Defamation League of B'nai B'rith, found his position too "extreme." They were unwilling to oppose exemptions. As George Goldberg observed shrewdly, if strict separationists were to convince the court that religious tax exemptions were unconstitutional, the decision would do for America's faith communities "what Henry VIII did for the monasteries of England."[23]

Currently the reluctance to go the whole way is more likely to be in the area of public education. If secular humanism is treated as the functional equivalent of a religion, and if "no establishment" is applied to public school textbooks in its broad and "absolute separationist" sense, then either secularism or public education is in trouble. Action that is the modern equivalent of Henry VIII's dissolution of the monasteries would be far more devastating for America's schools than for America's churches and synagogues.

More recently, Leo Pfeffer has acknowledged these difficulties and has described himself as a "realistic separationist" rather than an absolutist. "Realistic separationists recognize that the absolute separation of church and state cannot be achieved, else what's a secularist heaven for? Nevertheless, that is the direction they would have constitutional law relating to the Religion Clause take, fully aware that perfection will never be attained."[24] Pfeffer's later candor is as refreshing as its semireligious utopianism is revealing. Strict separationism is more than a theory of interpretation. It is a self-confessed end and a means to an end, and needs to be assessed as such.

Second, strict separationism is based on a history that is unwarranted. Ernest Renan's remark that "getting its history wrong is part of being a nation" applies also to social movements. The search for a usable past is natural for any movement that seeks to present its case and establish its legitimacy, particularly at a time of social crisis. But more than academic fastidiousness is at stake when history is mishandled through bias or blindspots. As George Orwell warned in his maxim, "Who controls the past, controls the future. Who controls the present, controls the past."

The suggestion may seem skewed. Usually, it is the fundamentalists who are accused—often justly—of distorting the past, mostly by romanticizing it. Ransacking history is a hazardous operation, not least because of the skeletons to be found in the closet. That is why many fundamentalists are discomfited by the prevalence of deism and freemasonry among the Founders. No fewer than fifty of the fifty-six signers of the Declaration of Independence are supposed to have been Masons, say delighted advocates of the New Age consciousness.

But if fundamentalists need to clean out their historical closet and take greater care in what they bring out, the problem for strict separationists is the reverse—their cupboard appears to be bare. The meagerness of the historical store shows through in their case for strict separationism in law. In the watershed *Everson* case, strict separationism was given its most influential statement through opinions that were based explicitly and almost exclusively on an appeal to history. "No provision of the Constitution," wrote Justice Rutledge, "is more closely tied to or given content by its generating history than the religion clause of the First Amendment."[25]

Is there now a consensus that "original intent" is a sure and sufficient criterion of interpretation and that strict separationism was the framers' early intent and consistent policy? On the contrary, yet the facts are not germane to the present status of the strict separationist myth. Never mind that the historical arguments of Justices Black and Rutledge have since been shown to be based on errors, omissions, and distortions. Never mind that scholarly arguments and liberal opinion have now pronounced the quest for "original intent" misconceived. Never mind that between the Bill of Rights and *Everson*, scores of acts and decisions utterly disprove that "absolute separation" was the intent of the framers and their successors. Never mind that we can now see clearly how secularist self-interest in 1947 coincided advantageously with an increasingly secular social context. The effect of *Everson* somehow sidestepped such issues and transformed questionable history into unquestionable law, thus conferring canonical status on strict separationism. And now that the pursuit of "original intent" is widely ridiculed, strict separationists who gained most from the abuse of history need not own up to it, and those who lost most are left with a task that appears ridiculous as well as immense.

But the historical flaw in the myth remains. Secularists and other strict separationists may have raised their "high and impregnable wall" theory into law and kicked away the scaffolding. But the historical foundations of the doctrine are weak and the resulting social cracks are widening in the present generation. Should the overburdened structure be brought down on top of them, they would have no one to blame but themselves.

Third, strict separationism is based on a democratic position that is unwise. At the heart of strict separationism lies an iron equation that is common to both religious and secularist separationists: public secularity equals private security. Rabbi Alan Mittleman quotes one Jewish leader as saying, "We have never been an accommodationist community. We like the naked public square."[26] But such positions have more than a European backdrop. Their American backdrop was partly one of reaction. Pfeffer, for example, attributes his separationism to the experiences of growing up Jewish in a Christian society in the 1920s and 1930s. But the background was also one of reliance. As Mittleman points out, early strict separationists who were Jews were neither antireligious nor anti-Christian. As regards a moral consensus in public life, they did not seem reckless, let alone wreckers, because they could press for separationism while relying on shared moral ideals and public meanings.

Today, however, the cultural situation is different. Strict separationism has worked all too effectively. Mittleman concludes, "We lack a minimal consensus not only on substantive moral issues, but on the procedural rules for adjudicating such disputes."[27] Thus, if the Jewish community shifted to separationism from its nineteenth-century stance of supporting a religiously plural, yet nonsecular America, it was at a time when a consensus on the common good was still available. Now that that is no longer the case, separationism appears a less and less satisfactory strategy. Never more than a purely defensive strategy, "separationism neglects the task of recovering a free and democratic life, sustained by the practical reasoning, public virtue, and dedication to the common good of the moral and spiritual communities."[28] A growing movement to go beyond separationism stems directly from the failure of strict separationists to do justice to the needs of America's public philosophy.

Lastly, strict separationism is self-defeating in that it leads to a position that contradicts religious liberty itself. This criticism, the most serious charge of all, can be traced in both experience and theory, and it can be seen to have affected both the Religious Liberty clauses and religious liberty itself. Richard Neuhaus has described the overall outcome of strict separationism as "the Pfefferian inversion." Nonestablishment has been transformed from a means into an end with the topsy-turvy result that the end (free exercise of religion) has been demoted to being a means to the end (nonestablishment). A typical statement of this inversion, cited by Neuhaus, is Professor Laurence Tribe's notion that there is "a zone which the free exercise clause carves out of the establishment clause for a permissible accommodation of religious interests."[29]

This stunning theoretical inversion has practical consequences. It is a leading cause of the chaotic incoherence of court decisions since 1947 and *Everson.* It is a prime reason for the malnourishment of the public philosophy. It is the principal cause of many of the legal objections to religion in public that are the astonishment of non-Americans (the censoring of an instrumental version of Handel's "Hallelujah Chorus" in a junior high school concert, for example, or objections to the Mayflower Compact as a document for historical study, because it was "religious"). Most importantly, it is beginning to be felt as an infringement of the free exercise of minority believers, once so cherished by separationists themselves—for example, in 1986 the Supreme Court refused to allow an Orthodox rabbi, Simcha Goldman, to wear his yarmulke indoors in the Air Force, implying that it would violate the separation of church and state.

Considering Judaism's own internal requirements of wholeness and integration and the potential contribution of Jews in public life, such as a covenantal rather than contractual public philosophy, Rabbi Mittleman describes the impact of strict separationism bluntly and in a way that speaks for many other communities: The Jewish community has been "laid on a Procrustean bed by its separationism. Its own deepest images of its corporate life, indeed of all social life, the covenant, is deprived of an active role in the community's self-representation. Jews are forced to represent themselves to themselves in terms of one or another piece of sociological nomenclature: voluntary association, civilization, and so on."[30]

For liberal, self-critical members of the fourth faith, the challenge to rethink separationism is strong. If free exercise is reduced to begging for crumbs of "permissible accommodationism" at the table of nonestablishment, then the American experiment in religious liberty is at a crucial stage. The revolutionary breakthrough that was triggered by a shift from "toleration" to "free exercise" would almost have come full circle, led backward by its supposed friends.

Civility Is Not for Wimps

Are secularists as committed to the day-to-day requirement of civility as they are to the ideals of a civil society? This third question focuses on the glaring deficiencies, born sometimes of inconsistency, that mar the secularist stand on religion in public life.

There is an extraordinary irony in the fact that the notion of civility has reached its nadir in American liberal discourse at the very moment that a "civil society" has become the passionate hope of democratic revolutionaries around the world, particularly in Eastern Europe and South Africa. To the former subjects of oppression, civil stands for all that is free, pluralistic, and yet harmonious, whereas to the habitués of liberal democracy it speaks only of empty public manners, of a squeamishness about differences—in a word, of wimpishness. True civility, however, is not for wimps. Genuine civility is substantive before it is formal. It is not a rhetoric of niceness or a psychology of social adjustment. This style of public discourse and engagement is shaped by a principled respect for people, truth, the common good, and the American constitutional tradition. It is a civilized prerequisite for knowing how to live with our deepest differences.

Needless to say, civility is hardly the cardinal virtue of activists from the side of the first faith. But it is specially appropriate for members of the fourth faith to take the lead in its recovery, because of the position they occupy in the national debate and because of the position civility occupies in the pantheon of Enlightenment virtues. Tackled from this perspective, three main points of confusion on the secularist (and generally liberal) side hamper the recovery and practice of civility.

First, civility is too often confused with condescension. Most American secularists are indifferent rather than hostile to religion—it is irrelevant more than untrue. But many are unaware how their indifference, reinforced by their position in society and the general secularity of the public cultural ethos, produces attitudes that are condescending at best and arrogant at worst. And, in both cases, they are damaging to the civility proper to religious liberty.

The majority of secularists come from the better-educated segments of society with a higher-than-average income and have generally considered themselves liberal democrats. This fact, as historian Henry May has indicated of American academics in general, creates a peculiar temptation for them as they confront popular American religion. Most liberal democrats in America want to be on the side of the people, almost as an article of faith. But sooner or later most of them become surprised, if not pained, by the immense gulf between the people and themselves. The majority of the people neither share their opinions nor appreciate their work—especially when it comes to the question of religious beliefs.

At that point, some secularists respond to the gulf by growing more explicitly and militantly secularist. They are an elite and a minority, declared supporters of a decisive rupture in the American tradition, and unashamedly so. If the people—Mencken's "booboisie"—insist on remaining so backward, secularist liberals as the shock troops of tomorrow's secular society— Mencken's "civilized minority" to whom the vox populi is "the bray of an ass"—can look to history to vindicate their struggle.[31] Other secularists, suddenly aware of the gulf, stop seeing and hearing ordinary people as they actually are. They superimpose on them an ideal version of a developing American culture as it ought to be from the standpoint of the liberal intellectual. As they see it, the colonial era was obsessive over religion, but the stranglehold of Puritanism was broken in the eighteenth century by the Enlightenment and the revolution, loosened further by science and democracy in the nineteenth century, and reduced in the twentieth century to a position of marginal irrelevance. Secularization, in their view, is progressive and irreversible. Aristocrats have always treated religion condescendingly and America's aristocrats of the mind are no different.

Henry May's description of this caricaturing liberal perspective was originally developed to explain the blindness of "progressive historians" to the religious dimension in American history. But today it can be applied to the academic world at large and to related fields, such as the press and media. Indeed, May argues, "In some intellectual centers it probably takes more courage for a writer or painter or professor to go to church or synagogue than not to."[32] Full blown, this tendency flowers into a double contradiction. On the one hand, it creates an inconsistency between the secularist liberals' cherished opinion of themselves as being on the side of the people versus their blindness to ordinary people as they truly are. On the other hand, it produces a contradiction between their ideals of tolerance and fair treatment versus the high-handed, if unconscious, arrogance in their treatment and portrayals of religious believers. In such ways and with all the vast carelessness of the intellectually superior, secularist liberals design and develop the spiritual equivalent of a socially constructed apartheid, complete with quarantined "homelands" for the free exercise of religious interests.

Beyond differences of opinion over specific cases, the substitution of condescension for civility is damaging for a principled reason. It confuses a distinction between free exercise and toleration that is at the heart of

America's struggle for religious liberty. Before the revolution, "toleration" was a common word to use in connection with religious liberty. Witness John Locke's famous treatise, A Letter Concerning Toleration. But it was the genius of the young "Jemmy" Madison to realize that it was a look-alike concept that was a weak foundation for the rights necessary to sustain a free people. Madison's success in changing a few words in George Mason's draft of Article XVI of Virginia's Declaration of Rights in 1776, which lay behind the Declaration of Independence and the Bill of Rights, was revolutionary. The change from "toleration" to "free exercise" was a small shift in words, but a titanic leap forward in meaning.

Toleration, of course, is an important virtue, infinitely preferable to intolerance. But in connection with religious liberty, it does not go far enough. For a start, toleration is deficient about the source of religious liberty. Whereas toleration implies a concession by a person or group in power, a willingness to "put up" with someone else, a sort of "legislative grace," free exercise implies a right. Religious liberty is not a gift of the state or of any leader, elite, or majority grouping. It is an inalienable right rested in human dignity that may neither be conferred nor removed. As Thomas Paine observed in 1791 (in a statement that needs to be redirected to secular modern keepers of the keys), "Toleration is not the *opposite* of Intolerance, but is the *counterfeit* of it. Both are despotisms. The one assumes to itself the right of withholding Liberty of Conscience, and the other of granting it. The one is the Pope armed with fire and faggot, and the other is the Pope selling or granting indulgences."[33]

In addition, toleration is deficient about the style of religious liberty. Being a concession by the higher and stronger to the lower and weaker, it inevitably grows condescending. If only in appearance, it comes to have a patronizing air. Religious liberty, by contrast, is a right for all and therefore a great leveler. Before the bar of the law, there are no greater or lesser, preferred or disregarded faiths. All have an equal right and an equal opportunity.

Further, toleration is deficient about the strength of religious liberty. Being only a concession, it depends on the whims of the conceder. As history has shown, sickness, death, a change of heart or ruler can occur and suddenly toleration and safe havens can disappear. Religious liberty, by contrast, is inalienable because it is a God-given or natural right. As such, it is a bulwark that cannot be overcome, least of all by the government.

Lastly, toleration is deficient about the scope of religious liberty. Being only a concession, it is easily limited to the private world or to matters of the heart, as if religious liberty were merely freedom to think what you want or worship as you please (a beggarly "right" that even totalitarian governments sometimes respect). Religious liberty, by contrast, is more robust. From the early seventeenth century onward, religious liberty in America has included numerous activities in the public world—charity, education, and social reform for a start, which covers such historic stands for justice as the abolition of slavery. It is this wider scope and tougher element that takes religious liberty even beyond freedom of conscience, captured well in James Madison's and later the First Amendment's "free exercise."

Temptations to debase free exercise into tolerance are many and strong. Convenient rationales are plentiful—statism, relativism, and privatization, with its notion of the "inviolably private" nature of religion, being the three most common sources of condescension. But more than hypocrisy is in question. Ultimately the character of liberalism and the strength of the American experiment are at stake.

Second, civility is often dismissed in favor of constitutionality. With few exceptions, the recent bicentennial outpouring of tributes to the Constitution were well-deserved, especially in term of the bedrock guarantees of the Constitution and the genius of its ordering of liberty and society. But Americans must recognize that the Constitution and constitutionality alone will not be sufficient to sustain the American republic, let alone sustain the Constitution within the republic. Deeper philosophical convictions are needed behind and above the Constitution, just as broader civilities are needed alongside it.

Yet a prominent feature of the recent controversies over religion and public life is that questions of legality and constitutionality have come to eclipse questions of civility. Law, lawyers, and lawsuits have replaced first principles and public argument, just as an acrid spirit of litigiousness has suffocated civility. And all this has been done in the name of modern realism with talk of civility and first principles dismissed as idealism. The result is a form of liberal "MacArthurism" that matches conservative McCarthyism. The constitutional equivalent of "There is no substitute for victory" is being taken to its logical conclusion in the long march toward a secularist/strict separatist revolution.

Potential legal inconsistencies abound in American life—for example, references to God on coins and in the Pledge of Allegiance, military chaplaincies, tax exemptions for churches and synagogues, and so on. If pressed relentlessly to the logic of the no establishment end, they create the prospect of litigious guerrilla warfare without end, of a general public grown war-weary and careless about the first principles of any issue, and—the goal, of course—of victory to the side with the best lawyers and the deepest war chest. ("I don't disagree with the Williamsburg Charter in substance," one ACLU leader said. "But it's not in our interests for it to succeed. The ultimate strength of the ACLU is that we have more lawyers than anyone else.")

There are many problems with this narrow constitutionalism. Not least that two can play the same game and that it becomes a form of constitutional fundamentalism with the Constitution, rather than the Bible, as its text and battleground. "Our particular security," Thomas Jefferson urged, "is in the possession of a written Constitution. Let us not make it a blank paper by construction."[34]

Third, civility is too often confused with sensitivity. A curious feature of liberalism in the 1980s was its espousal of sensitivity crusades as an outgrowth of multiculturalism in its postmodern phase. Sensitivity crusades stem from the belief that only those in a group can understand the group ("It's a black/gay/lesbian/fundamentalist thing—You wouldn't understand"). Therefore to criticize a group from the outside is to be guilty of disrespect, or "dissing." Thus, whereas liberal academics in the 1960s supported all kinds of student speech and pronounced that universities had no moral authority over students, liberal academics in the 1980s pressed for stringent codes on the limits of "permissible speech."

The result is a rapid proliferation across colleges and universities of rules proscribing speech that "insults/victimizes/stigmatizes/stereotypes" groups deemed to be sensitive to such offenses. At the University of Michigan, the neo-Puritan code covered the complete demonology of such sensitivities. It forbade all speech giving offense "on the basis of race, ethnicity, religion, national origin, sex, sexual orientation, creed, ancestry, age, marital status, handicap, or Vietnam era veteran status." At the University of Connecticut, perhaps dourer because closer to their Puritan roots, the moral minoritarians were even empowered to punish students for "inappropriately directed laughter."[35]

Underneath the colorful and egregious anecdotes that swarm around the politically correct movement are highly significant shifts in American language, beliefs, and expectations—the shift from individual to group rights, from legal to linguistic redress, from concern over truth to concern over therapy and well-being, from open confrontation to subterranean conflict, and from dealing with hate through reliance on respect to reliance on rules and regulations.

These shifts, in turn, have led to numerous unintended consequences: ignorance and incomprehension between groups, hypocrisy and double-standards in judgments, curtailed speech and cautious inquiry in academia, and—worst of all—to new victims and scapegoats. The palpable absurdities of the sensitivity crusades have grown evident to more and more people.

Well-meaning but blundering use of "insensitivity" charges simply makes sensitive subjects undiscussable. Thus liberals create their own "taboos." They produce their own "chill factor" in debate. They form their own "speech police." They authorize their own Boards of Good Taste. They demonstrate their own "liberal censorship." To all who prize true liberalism, the results are ironic, hypocritical, and disastrously illiberal. "PC" becomes "pernicious criteria" for the toe-the-line fundamentalism of the left.

Civility, however, is different from political correctness because it emphasizes what is desired in the sensitivity crusades—the respect for differences—but without what is damaging—the rules that rule out distinctives in the name of differences. Civility is a matter of ethics and education, not legislation. Ironically, the sensitivity crusades are an eloquent testimonial to the failure of two recently cherished liberal opinions. One is that intolerance is best attacked and toleration and freedom of choice are best defended on the grounds that "all values are merely relative." But as the sensitivity drives show, the crusaders view toleration as a value too. So if tolerance is only relatively true, it is also relatively useless against what is absolutely decided prejudice.

The other discredited opinion is the priority of constitutionality over civility. The sensitivity crusades grow directly from the political-environmental carelessness of those who stressed legality at the expense of civility and the public philosophy. The trouble was that when the natural forests of civility had been cut down, the existing laws proved inadequate. New rights had to be manufactured and new codes erected. The regulation of "the right to respect" was thus a short and easy step on the broad, liberal road to curtailing free speech.

Put more strongly, civility is a key component of American republicanism precisely because the latter, in George Weigel's words, is "a system that is built *for* tension."[36] Far from stifling debate, civility helps strengthen debate because of its respect for truth, yet all the while keeping debate constructive and within bounds because of its respect for people and the common good. As Weigel says, "Civility and sharpness of debate were never understood to be antonyms—prior to the rise of the therapeutic culture! Those who worry that tension and civil amity are mutually exclusive have not thought very deeply about either the possibilities of creativity inherent in conflict, or about the deliberately feisty structure erected by the Founders and Framers."[37] Thus true civility is a far hardier quality than many imagine. Its goal is to pass beyond discord, not to some phony agreement but to the very real disagreements of tough public debate that alone does justice to individual and communal liberty as well as to democratic vitality.

Whose Is the Splinter and Whose the Plank?

Are secularists aware of how much they too rely on stereotyping and simplistic categories and how inconsistent many of their objections are to the influence of religion on public policy? This fourth question focuses on the deficiencies of many of the "hand-to-hand" arguments of secularists and their influence on public debate. Preoccupied with the splinter in the eye of the fundamentalist, they overlook the plank in their own.

Obviously there are many reasons behind the mistrust between the two sides, ranging from blatant dislike to more complicated explanations. American secular humanism, for instance, sometimes displays a militancy bred by traditional secularist intolerance of religion plus the special Jewish experience of persecution. Is it any wonder that many of the finest and fiercest allies and apologists for the fourth faith have been Jews? "In the blood of the martyrs to intolerance," Lippmann wrote, adapting Eusebius, "are the seeds of unbelief."[38]

Intolerance against secularists, however, does not excuse misrepresentations in return. "The world-historical stupidity of all persecutors," Nietzsche wrote, "has lain precisely in giving their opponents the appearance of honorableness—in bestowing on them the fascination of martyrdom."[39] Yet misrepresentations have proliferated with inevitable consequences. An early illustration of prejudice distorting history is the venerable custom of Puritan-bashing, with its common stock of quips circulating at the Puritans' expense. This is a prejudice that comes close to the heart of American self-understanding. Ambrose Bierce's definition of the Puritan, for example—"A pious gentleman who believed in letting all people do as-he-liked"[40] has been trumped only by Mencken's definition of Puritanism itself: "The haunting fear that someone, somewhere, may be happy."[41]

Such witty barbs are brilliant subversive eye-openers, one-line arguments worth a score of books. But it would be foolish to overlook how they get pressed into service as the clowning carriers of stereotypes and prejudice.

The Puritans are not everyone's cup of tea. One example is Peter Finley Dunne's description of Thanksgiving as founded by the Puritans to give thanks for being preserved from the Indians and kept today to give thanks that we are preserved from the Puritans. But for what the point is worth, Puritans were not the joyless meddlers or buttoned-down Victorians they are made out to be. (Rum and spirits were a vital feature of their life-style. The *Mayflower* arrived in 1620 with ample stocks of "hot water.") Equally, their "Holy Commonwealth" was not a theocracy, let alone a clergy-ridden terror state of Orwellian grimness. The Massachusetts Bay Colony, for all its limitations, granted a more widespread right to vote than England, and its clergy had less direct authority over public affairs than those in any nation in the Western world.

Far nearer the mark was Tocqueville's judgment: "I think I see the destiny of America embodied in the first Puritan who landed on those shores;"[42] or Perry Miller's that Puritanism was "the innermost propulsion of the United States;"[43] or Rabbi Marc Tannenbaum's that "Mediated by the Puritans in New England, the Hebrew Scriptures became in many ways the 'intellectual arsenal' of the American Revolution."[44] Small wonder that Samuel Eliot Morison concluded, "Puritanism is an American heritage to be grateful for and not to be sneered at."[45]

The problem with stereotypes is not that they offend sensitivities. It is that indulgence in stereotypes and clichés is a telltale sign of the lazy thinking that causes historical and cultural blindness. If it is true that in 1776 at least 75 percent of the people declaring their independence had a Reformation background, and Puritanism itself can be said to be as basic to America as Lutheranism to Germany and the King James version of the Bible to England, then the real victims of the stereotypes are not the Puritans but the purveyors of the stereotypes. Out of prejudice grows self-inflicted blindness. Yet in the last generation many new versions of this self-maiming prejudice have arisen. W. B. Yeats once remarked that there is "safety in derision," but the error lies deeper than that. As G. K. Chesterton noted in his comments on American immigration forms, "A man is perfectly entitled to laugh at a thing because he happens to find it incomprehensible. What he has no right to do is to laugh at it as incomprehensible, and then criticize it as if he comprehended it."[46]

Several recent incidents reveal the old prejudice at work. The supreme example in the last three decades was the scurrilous and illiberal treatment of Judge Robert Bork, led by the outlandish misrepresentations of Bork by Senator Edward Kennedy on the Senate floor less than an hour after the nomination was announced. Another example closer to the religious issue was the blatant misunderstanding of Aleksandr Solzhenitsyn following his *Letter to the Soviet Leaders* in 1973 and his commencement address at Harvard in 1978.[47] Another was the handling of Jerry Falwell. Repeatedly charged with being a racist, a segregationalist, an opponent of birth control, an advocate of homosexuals being put in prison, and one who believes God does not hear the prayers of Jews, Falwell is in fact none of these things. Whatever other disagreements one may have with him, one cannot make these particular charges stick. Yet those who were not prepared to argue with him instead resorted to recycling rumors about him—and so demonstrated that there are at least as many fanatics among his opponents as among his supporters. Uncomfortable as it is for many of his opponents, certain things may be true even though Jerry Falwell believes them. As Jewish scholar Will Herberg noted of an earlier generation of illiberal liberalism, "Stereotyped 'liberal' slogans seem far more appealing than the most obvious facts can ever be, especially when they work off one's fears, prejudices, and aggressions in an approved fashion."[48]

Another example of stereotyping is the tragicomic mishandling of the historic meaning of being "born again." The fatuous impression given by much usage recently is that the experience is the sole initiation rite-cum-sacrament of some new cult, a cult—so innuendo suggests—that is somehow as bizarre and dangerous as Jonestown yet as fashionable and harmless as a new suburban fad. This misimpression has reached a point of lamentable absurdity. The words and notion of being "born again" go back to Jesus himself. Yet many professing Christians (including the two 1984 presidential candidates) distance themselves from the term as if completely ignorant of who first said it, what it means, and its influence on American history.

While the ignorance may be politic, it is also ironic. Being "born again" was at the heart of the regenerative power of America's Great Awakenings and therefore of the dynamism of earlier American history. The truth is that if anything at all is as American as apple pie, it is Protestant evangelicalism. As Martin Marty asserts, "For Evangelicals to feel at home in America should not be a surprise, since they built so much of it."[49] No prejudice or stereotype can alter this fact, but a barrage of repeated stereotypes can obscure the reality and deprive the nation of what is a key part of its memory and significant factor in the current debate.

It was often remarked by liberals in the 1950s that right-wingers needed their Communists badly and were pathetically reluctant to give them up. They used them, it was said, to discharge resentments and satisfy enmities whose roots lay elsewhere than in the Communist issue itself. Aside from the inadequacies of the pop psychology on which these interpretations were based, the boot seems to have shifted to the other foot. Fundamentalism is now the weapon as much as the target of its secularist opponents, and many of them seem pathetically reluctant to give it up.

The other half of this last question concerns the plethora of inconsistencies that have characterized secularist criticisms of religion in public life over the past decade. These were evident in the first responses to the rise of the Religious Right. The most widely noted example was the critics' habit of rejecting from the Religious Right what they had welcomed from the religious Left. Thus Protestant civil rights workers and marchers were celebrated but Protestant prolife activists were castigated for "mixing religion and politics"; Roman Catholic cardinals were praised for speaking out against the arms race, but then attacked for "imposing" their private views about abortion on the general public.

The secularist case has become tangled with such contortions. Secularists and liberals attack fundamentalists for wanting to "impose" their views without public consent, yet lacking sufficient numbers of their own, their preferred tactic is to take to the courts and find a sympathetic judge. Enormous amounts of op-ed ink flowed in warning that fundamentalist death-prayers against the Supreme Court justices in the mid-1980s illustrated the depths of their degraded fanaticism. But many critics conveniently ignored that the precedent was set by Thomas Jefferson. Disturbed by Patrick Henry's success in the assessment campaign and its potential threat to his own views of religious liberty, Jefferson suggested to James Madison, "What we have to do I think is devoutly to pray for his death."[50] Madison's more humane solution, lacking the innocuous office of the vice presidency, was to have Henry elected governor.

Proposed conservative criteria for judging government-funded art are said to be "censorship" and "Stalinism," but liberals own lengthier categories for prohibiting campus free speech are a question of "sensitivity" and "awareness." (The University of Michigan's prohibited list was longer even than Senator Jesse Helms' list for the National Endowment for the Arts.)

When it comes to the religious liberty clauses, the proposal for a double standard is quite open. There is to be a functional definition of religion for free exercise cases and a substantive definition for no establishment purposes and, lo and behold, it turns out in their favor. When no establishment is under discussion, religion is defined narrowly and decisively restricted, whereas "secular humanism" is somehow nonexistent and nonreligious anyway. But when free exercise is at stake, as in the discussion of conscientious objection, secular humanism is happy to claim its place as a court-certified religion qualifying for religious liberty. What vanishes like a cheshire cat in the thought-world of the public school suddenly reappears when the thought of military service or jury duty occurs. (Without such a double standard, Laurence Tribe has argued, every humane government program could be "deemed constitutionally suspect.")[51]

Such contradictions will surely be the wonder of observers in the future. For the moment, they easily harden into hypocrisy, and the error behind them is a deficient public philosophy. They are clearly not correct about how public argument is engaged with a full plurality of faiths and worldviews in play. Over the issue of "mixing religion and politics," for instance, a few minutes of thought would show that religion and politics are not only bound to mix, but they ought to. The real question is whether they are mixing both freely and justly, properly or improperly, in line with the Constitution and democratic pluralism or not. American civilization has reached a bizarre stage if the First Amendment is taken to mean that citizens can deduce their public policies from Karl Marx, Milton Friedman, Ralph Nader, or Gloria Steinem but not from the Bible.

Muddied thinking is common more than a decade after the rise of Moral Majority. For example, Sarah Weddington, who successfully argued *Roe v. Wade* in 1973, still insists that restrictions on abortion mean "imposing sectarian religious doctrine" on a pluralistic culture.[52] Such constitutional logic proves too much. It would rule out religiously grounded support for abolition and civil rights too. In fact, to any believer who takes faith seriously, such bitter-ender insistence that religion remain "private, or else" has all the sweet reasonableness of "drop dead, or I'll kill you." Too often in serious public discussion, religious believers are given a schizophrenic choice, "It's okay to be Christian, Jewish, Mormon, Muslim (or whatever), but just don't speak or act like one." Like the old Southern politician of the 1920s who professed to "hate only two things—prejudice and negroes," much of the complaint against religion in public life has the drumbeat logic of "religion is intolerance and intolerance is not to be tolerated."

The plain fact is that almost all legislation is enacted morality. Not all morality should be legislated, but almost all law is morality enacted. So in its very essence law includes the twin elements of "assumption" (certain underlying beliefs rather than other ones) and "exclusion" (this behavior, not that). All law in this sense is an "imposition," and Christians and humanists share a long and, on the whole, distinguished record of legislation properly "imposed" in the interest of justice and humanitarian reform. Leo Pfeffer is surely correct when he writes, "I can see no logical or moral difference between the desire of Catholicism to 'catholicize' America, i.e., convert it to Catholic philosophy, religion and way of living, and the desire of Protestantism or secular humanism to convert or keep America loyal to their philosophies, religions, and ways of living."[53]

It might be tempting to think the time has come for secularists to swallow some of their own medicine. For a long time they have charged that religious convictions are a form of psychological compensation. But now the same suspicion about secularists is hard to avoid. Many American secularists do not come across as the robust champions of freedom they profess to be. They appear as narrow grinches in the world of belief who have elevated the art of spoilsport to a constitutional right. Unquestionably Mencken would have to define today's judicial secularism as the haunting fear that someone, somewhere, might just be believing something beyond their front door.

It used to be said that when a person accepted public office, he or she was no longer a Protestant, a Catholic, or a Jew but an American. Repeated mindlessly, the maxim gets distorted and seems to suggest not only that public officials have wider responsibilities but that religious believers have narrower rights. But as American diversity has broadened, the urgent task is to see that participation in public debate by all groups deepens too. Those who stand for the common good of their community and the nation may be more than simply believers, but they are never less than believers. In the challenge of that interplay America's fourth faith confronts a question crucial to its own future and to America's.

12

The Bedeviling Factor

At the Democratic convention in 1972, Norman Mailer was listening when George McGovern made his stirring appeal, "Come home, America!" Suddenly, Mailer wrote later, the strains of an epiphany came to him like an illumination. "In America, the country was the religion. And all the religions of the land were fed from that first religion, which was the country itself, and if the other religions were now full of mutation and staggering across deserts of faith, it was because the country had been false and ill and corrupt for years, corrupt not in the age old human proportions of failures and evil, but corrupt to the point of a terminal disease, like a great religion foundering."[1]

America as a religion and national self-worship are deeply American themes that cannot be dismissed as merely rhetoric or the sour-grapes exaggeration of foreign critics. Mailer went on to describe the political parties as "the true churches of America . . . founded on the spiritual rock of America as much as on any dogmas."[2] Lyndon Johnson made much the same point in his inaugural address. "We are a nation of believers . . . and we believe in ourselves."[3] Earlier still, Herbert Croly, first editor of the *New Republic* had written, "The faith of Americans in their own country is religious."[4]

McGovern spoke and Mailer wrote when the last tremors of the sixties were dying away and the second thoughts of the seventies were just beginning. But that moment also marked a critical watershed in the long, close relationship between American religion and American nationhood. Deep, proud, intense, and religiously inspired patriotism is as legitimate as ever. But the semireligious nationalism that was the unquestioned common faith of most Americans for a long period ended decisively at the close of the sixties and must not be revived.

It is now critical as part of the rebuilding of a civil society to acknowledge the ending of this period. The flames of semireligious nationalism can still be fanned in the hearts of Americans. Many of the factors behind Ronald Reagan's New Patriotism and George Bush's culture-war electioneering make this all too easy. But to do so is to reintroduce into public life what has become the bedeviling factor in religion and public life—civil religion. The argument of this chapter, necessarily historical and deliberately negative, stands as a decisive veto against any such attempt.

Civil religion is the proper name for this topic, but the term is triply misleading. For a start, it is too formal. To those who are spiritually tone-deaf, civil religion suggests something that is narrowly and quite explicitly religious—as if people consciously set out to worship something that officially goes by that name, which of course lets the tone-deaf off the hook. In fact, civil religion's potency is the opposite. Being unconscious rather than conscious and semireligious rather than explicit, it sucks into its vortex not only the enthusiastic but the reluctant, the unaware, and even the secular.

Further, the term is too genteel. Aspects of civil religion, as we will see, can be interpreted usefully as a "religion of civility." But civility is only one aspect of civil religion and a characteristic of an advanced stage at that. Far earlier and more primal are the twin human impulses toward meaning and belonging that are wrapped up with collective identity and legitimacy at the national level. The very preciousness of what are termed religions, faiths, worldviews, and life stances stems from the fact that they are among the deepest and strongest sources of human meaning and belonging. But therein lies the source of their potency too. Civil religion sometimes courses with dark and fevered collective passions because it touches on a human impulse as basic as that of freedom itself—order.

To American liberals in a liberal society at a time when liberal freedoms are rocking authoritarian-ordered societies around the world, the priority of freedom over order seems assured. Civil religion is therefore viewed as "statecraft as soulcraft" in a remote and abstract form. But that is a miscalculation of the relationship of order and freedom in human experience and liberal society. The Constitution is a triumph of the ordering of freedom. Nationalism has been a specially recalcitrant feature of international relations under the conditions of modernity. Tribalism is likely to deepen, not disappear, in the post–Cold War conditions. Civil religion is about as abstract and remote as the swirling passions surrounding the burning of Old Glory or the fate of the public schools.

Lastly, the term civil religion obscures as much as it illuminates. Civil religion has always had two dimensions—the ideological and the institutional. Yet the term itself draws attention mainly to the former, the beliefs and ideas that make it up, and away from the latter, the institutions, such as the presidency and the public schools, through which it is expressed. Previously this distortion mattered little because there was only one civil religion and its two dimensions were in harmony. But that is no longer the case. There are now said to be two competing versions of civil religion and, worse still, two versions competing from rival power bases in different national institutions. The more conservative version, liberals fear, works through the presidency. The more liberal, conservatives fear, works through the public schools. Thus if it still exists today, American civil religion is at odds with itself—a contradiction in terms for a civil religion.

Understanding civil religion is a key to understanding controversies over religion and public life. Vetoing civil religion is a key to reforging the public philosophy. Civil religion is therefore far more than a side-issue in religion, an excessive form of patriotism, a purely academic topic, or simply Protestantism's failed answer to the need for a public philosophy. American civil religion has squarely national implications that need to be understood.

The Odd Couple

How did anything as unlikely as civil religion arise in America? More than anyone else, Robert Bellah was responsible for the recent debate about civil religion. His *Daedalus* article in 1967, he says, was "an essay I have never been allowed to forget."[5] As he made plain, civil religion is far older and more varied than its contemporary expression in the United States. The term was used first by Jean-Jacques Rousseau as part of his theory of social contract, to describe how a nation builds its systems of meaning by its own act of will. The nation-gods are invoked for the nation's good.

Two considerations should have made any Christian entanglement with civil religion most unlikely. First, as Rousseau argued, history demonstrates that the Christian faith and civil religion have been generally considered incompatible. Rousseau claimed that the very notion of a "Christian republic" was self-contradictory because the two terms are mutually exclusive. Augustine had emphatically denounced Roman "civil theology" as idolatrous. Ever since then, the Christian faith had shown itself to be far more compatible with monarchy. In addition, as Émile Durkheim argued later, sociology appears to demonstrate that the dynamic of religion and society is essentially one of self-worship, so that in theological terms civil religion is inescapably idolatrous. A society's "collective conscience," Durkheim asserted, is the moral expression of its self-awareness through which the society cements its solidarity, celebrates its wholeness, and actually worships itself.

This combination of theological, historical, and sociological factors is powerful. Add to it the characteristically American form of church-state separation, and the marriage of the Christian faith and civil religion would appear to be an unlikely liaison. Yet while America has never officially been a "Christian republic," for much of its history the Christian faith has been a leading contribution to its unofficial civil religion.

This unlikely marriage of convenience has continued with ambiguity. American civil religion is not a civil religion in the strict sense, but a somewhat vague though treasured set of semireligious, semipolitical beliefs and ideals basic to America's understanding of itself that are the object of quasi-religious devotion. It can be witnessed at its highest and most elegant form in the speeches of almost every presidential inauguration, at its more homespun on any Fourth of July, or somewhere in between at many of the national prayer breakfasts.

Civil religion in this modified sense is a simple extension of the notion of the "American creed." It means not only that America is based on a set of commonly held ideals (something that is true of any society), but that in America these ideals add up to something that can plausibly be called semireligious. In a society that requires transcendent ideals yet is committed to a pluralistic democracy and officially eschews the establishment of any one faith, such a civil religion has a special significance. It defines the nation's loyalties, provides legitimacy for its institutions, justifies its ideals, and sanctifies its triumphs and disasters—all in a transcendent key.

But how did American civil religion come to be? If disestablishment closed the door firmly to theocracy and any kind of government of national confession, how did the religious dimension get back in? How could even a semiestablishment arise? If there are such strong political and theological reasons to distinguish the American creed from the Apostles' Creed, how did they become confused? For on the face of it, each of these two creeds has its reasons for needing to be distinct from the other. The Apostles' Creed is essentially theological, the American creed political; the former is a matter of sacred covenant, the latter of social contract; the former is highly distinct and potentially divisive, the latter deliberately vague yet somehow unitive.

In practice what made the two creeds melt as separate entities and bond together is the burning issue that underlies civil religion. This issue is common to all societies but is particularly vital in a republic as open and diverse as America's: What is the binding center that holds together the nation's unity and legitimacy? The traditional answer in Christendom had always been to undergird the national and social order with an official, or established, spiritual and moral base. In European history this binding center was most often supplied by each country's state church. During the Middle Ages a great attempt was made to build the community and civilization around the unity of faith. This attempt succeeded for several centuries, but eventually failed and gave way to two modified types of establishment: theocratic, in which the church absorbed the state, and Erastian, in which the state absorbed the church. Thus whether the later outcome tended toward theocracy, as in Switzerland, Erastianism as in England, or absolutism as in France, the confusions of church and state and the misorderings of religions and government became the source of constant violations of religious liberty and human dignity.

Americans rejected this solution in principle almost from the start. Having left Europe to escape religious oppression and arriving with a diversity of denominations from the beginning, they almost inevitably came to separate church and state and build between them Jefferson's celebrated "wall of separation." The old maxim "one territory, one faith" was no longer thinkable. Diversity and religious liberty under new conditions made a new ordering of freedom necessary. James Madison's *Memorial and Remonstrance* in 1785 was critical in this development. Contrary to the arguments of Patrick Henry and those who wished for the government to collect taxes for all recognized churches, Madison ensured the victory of the daring new American vision. It was no more right and desirable to establish the Christian faith as the official religion than to establish any denomination as the state church. Thus the forward-looking disestablishmentarian vision of Virginia triumphed over the backward-looking establishmentarian vision of South Carolina and became the model of American church-state relations for the future.

Christians, it should be stressed, were among those in the forefront of pressing for this separation—and still are. In all but a few cases, scare talk about "Christian theocracy" today is pure demagoguery. The theological roots of church-state separation as a distinctively Western idea may even be traced back to Pope Gelasius in 494 A.D. ("Two there are," Gelasius insisted of the spiritual and temporal orders.)[6] But certainly separation was a cardinal conviction of the radical Reformation even in Europe, and Rhode Island gave political expression to this theological principle long before pluralism made it an issue in Virginia. Isaac Backus, a Baptist, argued for it in Massachusetts before Madison did in Virginia, and Jefferson, in fact, did not coin the phrase "wall of separation." He borrowed it from Roger Williams, a Baptist for a time, and he used it writing sympathetically to a group of

Baptists in Connecticut in 1802. And behind James Madison was not only the redoubtable Presbyterian educator John Witherspoon but Madison's own constituents, John Leland and the Culpeper Baptists. It was the pressure of the latter and the knowledge of their persecution that led Madison to stiffen his stance from mere "toleration" to "free exercise."

Different motives were at play in the drive toward disestablishment. Pietists, such as Leland and Backus, were concerned primarily with the integrity and purity of the church and feared that the state would corrupt the church, whereas the theologically less orthodox Jefferson and Madison were concerned for the dignity and liberty of the state, and feared that the church would corrupt the state. But together the pietists and deists constituted a strong, if unlikely, alliance and converged on an important conclusion: The jurisdictions of the spiritual and the temporal orders of social life must be decisively separated. The religious community and civil society could never be one; they would always be two. Church-state separation was therefore as much an axiom of evangelical faith as a corollary of deist doubt.

So if due regard is taken of the original setting and the intention of both parties, one conclusion is plain: What was sought in the First Amendment was not a disinfecting of religion from civil life but a legal safeguarding of pluralism, including the religious. Churches were to be protected from the state just as much as the state was to be protected from the churches. Both sides would flourish freely because such a separation of powers, as with the different branches of government, also meant a protection of rights.

But for all the First Amendment's daring and success, the burning issue of the binding center still remained. The potent human dynamics of meaning and belonging are not canceled merely by the passing of a law, however effective. Thus over the course of time this brilliant constitutional arrangement encouraged not only a most remarkable degree of individual liberty held together with social diversity, but (less happily) the development of a highly unusual civil religion. Acting as a kind of halfway house, a moderate form of civil religion emerged in America as a form of social compromise between two instinctively perceived extremes: On one hand, the dangers of a state church, and on the other the dangers of a public life without any ideals at all.

Strictly and constitutionally speaking, American national unity and stability have never depended on the common sharing of one faith. But practically speaking for many Americans, they have. In 1848, a Jewish defendant in a Sunday law case in South Carolina found himself on the receiving end of a Christian nation homily. "What constitutes the standards of good morals?" he was told. "Is it not Christianity? There certainly is none other. Say *that* cannot be appealed to, and I don't know what would be good morals. The day of moral virtue in which we live, would in an instant, if that standard were abolished, lapse into the dark and murky night of Pagan immorality."[7]

Common Faith, Common School

The variety of promptings toward civil religion needs to be underscored. John Murray Cuddihy has argued well that, to be understood, American civil religion must be set on its head and seen as "the religion of civility" or as "the social choreography of tolerance."[8] But concern for civility is only part of the sociological story and the lesser part at that, because civil religion is more the religion of national unity and legitimacy than of national civility.

But even the broader sociological account of civil religion is incomplete if it leaves out a particularly important prompting. For behind American civil religion is the key factor of political choices and a key institution: the public school. Unless this contribution is taken into account, the intentional element in civil religion is missed and both the road to the present situation and the nub of the present controversies are overlooked.

From the perspective of political choice, there were two important contributions to the rise of civil religion. In both cases the overriding goal of national legitimacy and civility was conscious. The first contribution was Jefferson's work to establish public schools in Virginia, based on his key distinction between public religion (nonsectarian "universal morality") and private religion (sectarian beliefs). The second was Horace Mann's in pressing for a monopolistic, governmental funding policy for "public schools" that would be strictly separated from "private schools."

As a result, the public schools became for America what Jefferson called "the keepers of the vestal flame." They grew to be the principal American institution entrusted with passing on the nation's identity and mission from generation to generation because concerns for unity, civility, and American ideals were at their center. As stressed earlier, the purpose of the public schools was to provide more than free, universal education for all the children in one community. It was to move beyond instruction in mere skills to education in character, ideals, and loyalties; and thus to be a moral force for character-forming and nation-building. Above all, the public schools were to be the place where the spiritual divisiveness, born of creeds, and the social divisiveness, born of classes, could both be reconciled.

Behind these laudable goals, which to a remarkable extent were attained, were other dynamics with less intended consequences. One was, as the public schools grew, the hardening of Jefferson's Enlightenment distinction between sectarian and nonsectarian to the modern distinction between religious and secular until the equation became automatic that "Public = secular, religious = private." In the shuffle two things critical to our modern controversies were missed.

On the one hand, the position that Jefferson and Mann regarded as self-evident religious neutrality was actually self-serving and sectarian, but in a subtle way. Under the guise of "nonsectarianism" Jefferson in effect promoted his own highly sectarian and far from universal deism, just as Mann did for Unitarianism. The image of the vestal flame is not exactly secular. On the other hand, the position was satisfactory to Protestant evangelicals—the overwhelming majority at the time—but was also self-serving and sectarian. For reasons growing out of their own deficiencies and short-term gains, evangelicals went along with the new developments and failed both to appreciate the problems for others and to anticipate the long-term problems for themselves. In short, the two leading groups that were influential in the rise of the public school were both as concerned with self-interest as public justice.

To be sure, evangelicals supported the new "common schools" out of their deep concern for poor children. But their support for Jefferson also grew from the privatization at the heart of their dualistic pietism. Where Jefferson the rationalist spoke of sectarian/nonsectarian, the evangelical pietists fell easily into a sacred/secular view of life. Equally, they complied happily with Mann's distinction between "the religion of heaven" and "the creeds of man" for a simple reason: The favored expression of the religion of heaven in the emerging public schools was more or less Protestant and to keep it so was the best Protestant safeguard against the massive incursions of Rome. In the nineteenth century, therefore, Protestant evangelicals were public-spirited in supporting state-run public schools. But it was also their way of "establishing" a vague, nonsectarian, and moralistic Protestantism as the de facto civil religion.

Today, even an idealized and generalized Protestantism has lost its place as the dominant ideology in the schools, and evangelicals and fundamentalists have woken up to their plight, if not to their hand in its origins. The long-accepted dualistic definition that "public=secular, religious=private" now works against them. Ironically, many of them have now switched the basis of their defense from a dualistic to a holistic worldview and can be heard arguing the very case they rejected so vehemently from Roman Catholics more than a century ago. Clearly the marriage of convenience has ceased being convenient. Evangelical collusion with deist and Unitarian elites meant that a generalized Protestantism rose to the status of a de facto establishment through its privileged position in public schooling. But their bargain was a Faustian, soul-selling one.

This comment, however, jumps too far ahead. On balance, moderate civil religion "succeeded" in its time, in that it was useful to both the government and the churches. It helped the government because if public ideals were not to be imposed from above (an essentially authoritarian solution), they had to be nourished from below. It helped the churches because it allowed them to contribute to public life, if only in general terms—where deists were free to filter out the solid content behind such words as "God" and "providence," evangelicals were equally free to read it in. Thus, although formally disestablished by law, an idealized and generalized Protestantism was informally semiestablished in reality.

Moderate civil religion thus acted as an American uniting religion that expressed, although never created, a sense of unity out of national diversity. In doing so, it served as a subtle compromise that allowed the churches to continue as a privileged contributors to the American creed, somewhere between established and excluded. Indeed, for most of the nineteenth century and for brief periods in the twentieth, such as the fifties, Patrick Henry rather than James Madison seemed to have won the argument. The Christian faith in the form of "public Protestantism" was, as nearly as made no difference, the official religion of America. America was not only a nation of nations and a race of races, but a religion of religions. Jefferson's wall was porous, as it were, and faith seeped through freely. There was no national god in America and the president was his prophet.

Irreconcilable Differences

The marriage of convenience worked pretty well and lasted from the passing of the First Amendment in 1791 down to the postwar period. There was actually a quiet but steady erosion of the Christian nation dimension of civil religion between 1800 and 1920, especially between 1870 and 1920. But civil religion itself even appeared to survive the collapse of public Protestantism in the 1920s. At times it still amounted to a form of "halfway establishment." Many of the traditional ties between religion and government were left uncut, and in cases, such as blasphemy and Sunday trading, specific Christian convictions and moral positions were honored by leaders, legislators, and educators alike. Disestablishment republicanized religion, but at first it was in the direction of a religious and "low-wall," not a secular and "high-wall," republicanism.

That is why examples are easily cited that appear to support not only civil religion but its more explicit Christian nation dimension. In an 1892 Supreme Court decision Justice Brewer declared that "this is a Christian nation" and at the close of the nineteenth century, Lord Bryce observed that "Christianity is in fact understood to be, though not legally the established religion, yet the national religion."[9] As recently as 1952 Justice William Douglas could still assert with confidence, "We are a religious people whose institutions presuppose a Supreme Being."[10] The generalizing erosion is evident even in these examples, which in turn obscures the far more drastic erosion in scores of specific litigations over issues like Sabbath closing. But what this arrangement lacked in legal clarity, it made up for in social cohesion and historical continuity.

Like many compromises, however, the solution was inherently unstable, and the sixties demonstrated this in one of its most important legacies. But it is a mistake to blame the crisis on the sixties and the secularists. For one thing, the sixties only confirmed changes started much earlier—for example, immigration, urbanization, industrialization, and Protestant fragmentation were all well advanced by the end of the nineteenth century. For another, the real secularizing agencies that killed "Christian nation" laws were not the "secular humanists" but such all-American features of life as Sunday sports and the round-the-clock consumerism to which even opponents of secularism were committed. In short, the sixties was simply the decade in which the growing secularity of public life and diversity of personal faiths rendered inoperable the old civil religion of an unofficial but Protestant-based communitarianism.

Put differently, the post-sixties' crisis of civil religion meant that the long-standing Protestant "halfway establishment" had been called into question like the earlier Puritan "halfway covenant" before it. Thus, the prospects of the Christian faith continuing in its odd but convenient relationship with civil religion were damaged beyond repair. The earlier, moderate civil religion, which was really the public face of Protestantism, was politically viable and, on the whole, theologically innocuous. But even such a moderate civil religion is no longer possible today. Those religious believers who continue to advocate and press for civil religion in the face of contemporary realities will either fail and find their efforts ineffective or else succeed and find them idolatrous.

Continuing support for civil religion flies in the face of three insuperable problems. The combined effect of these has been to magnify the irreconcilable differences between civil religion and the Christian faith to their prerevolutionary proportions. History's odd couple is having to break up. First, there is the core problem of divisiveness. Civil religion, by definition, should be a force whose self-evident sacredness makes it harmonizing and inviolate. Yet this possibility is hopelessly contradicted now by disputes over the character and importance of civil religion itself. Robert Wuthnow even argues that there are two competing civil religions today. They follow the general polarizing of American culture and religion, but take as their motto different phrases of the Pledge of Allegiance (conservatives stressing "one nation under God" and liberals "with liberty and justice for all"). "The problem this hostility poses for American religion as a source of national legitimacy is that neither side can claim effectively to speak for consensual values. . . . Religion, therefore, becomes (as indeed it has often been characterized in the press) 'sectarian' rather than providing a basis of unity."[11]

Second, continued support for civil religion raises the problem of discrimination. Civil religion, again by definition, is a form of civic unity based on religious community, and thus of religious communitarianism. It is true that, in order to expand its inclusiveness, the point of unity could be softened to the point of innocuousness—civil religion was virtually mainstream Protestantism with its hard edges knocked off and its center hollowed out. But at the end of the day, some were still excluded and it was thus a form of monopoly or majoritarianism that did not include those whose faith differed from that of the civil religion.

One measure of the strength of the sacred and the self-evident in civil religion is the inability of the dominant group to appreciate that it too is sectarian. Thus neither nineteenth-century Protestants at large nor the average judiciary could stomach the Catholic and Jewish complaints that use of the King James Bible in the public school was sectarian. The result was a series of flagrant violations of religious liberty—ranging from eleven-year-old Thomas Wall of Boston being beaten on his hands for thirty minutes for refusing to repeat the Ten Commandments in 1859, to the infamous nativist riots in Philadelphia in 1844, which left thirteen dead and over fifty wounded after Bishop Kenrick had requested that Catholic children be allowed to read the Douay version of the Bible in public schools.

Third, continued support for civil religion raises the problem of the dilution of beliefs. As civil religion expands, its content must become ever thinner until it loses clarity and usefulness altogether. This was not always so. Early advocates of pluralism and religious liberty, such as Roger Williams of Rhode Island, certainly had in mind the inclusion of Jews, Muslims, and atheists in the body politic. But in practice pluralism was largely a Protestant family affair, so public terms could be vague without a compromise of the Protestant understanding of truth. There was little confusion over their major source of definition.

But now that pluralism has expanded out of all recognition, the consensus has collapsed, and Protestantism has lost its role as the dominant definer, pluralism is beginning to border on a radical diversity that makes nonsense of any hope of a religious common denominator. Entire meaning systems now confront other entire meaning systems—Jewish-Christian versus secular humanist, Western versus Eastern, and so on. With Utah and Hawaii as the first states in the Union to have significant majorities of non-Christians, there has been a vast shift from Justice Brewer's "Christian nation" in 1892 and even beyond Justice Douglas's "religious people" in 1952.[12]

Believers who support civil religion and defend themselves by reading clear content into it must face up to this drastic dilution. As Robert Linder and Richard Pierard have written of civil religion, "Its umbrella has been enlarged from evangelical consensus to Protestantism-in-general, to Christianity-in-general, to the Judeo-Christian-tradition-in-general, to deism-in-general."[13] For Christians who take their faith seriously, such a lowest-common-denominator deity is too vague to be useful, too broad to be anything but misleading. In short, civil religion entails fundamental contradictions today. Until recently it had always charged higher costs for other faiths (variously called its "price tag" or "brutal bargain" by Jews or Catholics).[14] But now it insists on charging Protestants the same full price as everyone else.

Turbulence Ahead

The divorce between Protestantism and civil religion has its price tag. A divorce is always a painful affair, and the one between the partners of a nation's civil religion is no exception. The hurt and pain are magnified politically, especially if there are suspicions of a third party hastening the breakup. But to feel the present dilemmas of civil religion in that way is to realize that the questions behind the earlier discussion of a public philosophy are not as remote, bloodless, and inconsequential as they might appear. To do justice to national unity is not abstract. To do justice to social diversity without doing injustice to national unity is not simple. To do justice to the conflicting demands of differing conceptions of the transcendent without doing injustice to either national unity or social diversity is hardest of all.

This means that, with the contradictions of civil religion exposed, with a historic balance unhinged, with an "all change" at the level of national elites, and with a new public philosophy not yet universally adopted, the next few years are likely to be a time of turbulence during which will occur an increasingly polarized debate and unremitting tug-of-war between two extremes: a sacred public square, with a civil religion built around a restored unity of faith, and a naked public square, with a civil religion built around a newly imposed unity of reason.

The first of these extremes needs little further elaboration. Taken together, the three problems outlined earlier mean that continuing Christian support for civil religion, whether popular or sophisticated, is politically unwise and theologically wrong. One of two consequences would be likely. Either the Christian contribution would be ineffective, in that the compromises required of any contributor would automatically preclude any decisive critique of civil religion. Or else it would become a pure form of ideology, and even idolatry. Far from being the grounds of national unity, a Christian-based civil religion under modern conditions would be only the rhetorical expression of national unity, the Union's religious dimension, the spiritual symbol of America's ultimate commitment to itself.

But will Christians continue to support a Christian contribution to civil religion despite such objections? The possibility is strong. The myth of origins is alluring. The lust for lost dominance is hard to resist. A recent editorial in *Christianity Today* began: "It is the style to decry American civil religion as blatant idolatry—American Shinto. For my part, I thank God for it."[15] What followed was a highly uncritical account of civil religion that sits comfortably with the equally uncritical enthusiasm accorded by many evangelicals to the New Patriotism in the 1980s.

Christians who advocate this position must pay its price—the surrender of transcendence. For under modern conditions, no faith can be shared, public, all-American—and transcendent. With diversity expanding in private life and secularity deepening in public life, claims about transcendence are as legitimate as ever but inevitably particularistic, sectarian, and disqualified from being the core of a common faith. Once again, this was not always so. As Bellah points out, the theme of transcendence in Protestant civil religion earlier played a highly important role. Without it, key notions, such as liberty, would have become empty and nationalism would have become an end in itself. For the central tenet of Protestant civil religion, Bellah writes, is that "the nation is not an ultimate end in itself but stands under transcendent judgment and has value only in so far as it realized, partially and fragmentarily at best, a 'higher law.'"[16]

Today, however, Protestant civil religion's halfway house has fallen apart. Modern social conditions have widened the contradictions and modern civil religion has turned its back on transcendence and returned to the natural immanence of its Rousseauian beginnings. The religion of the republic, Sidney Mead had written earlier, is "not only *not* particularistic, it is designedly anti-particularistic . . . Under it, one might say, it is religious particularity, Protestant or otherwise, that is heretical and schismatic—even Un-American!"[17]

What needs clearer elaboration today is the second extreme, the problem of the naked public square with its civil religion built around a unity of reason. Not only is this the current danger, but it is also the more clouded in controversy because some of its foes so clumsily distort it and its supporters so blindly defend it. For the real danger of the naked public square does not come from a conscious and concerted conspiracy to ban all faiths from public life but from the unintended consequence of developments blocking all faiths except one.

Three considerations underscore the importance of openly acknowledging the perils of a naked public square. The first (and clearest but more remote from the United States) is the fact that the most terrible and systematic violations of human dignity and religious liberty in the twentieth century have been perpetrated in the name of secularist ideologies—not religion. Battle deaths from all wars in this century are reckoned to be approximately 35 million, whereas totalitarian communism alone is thought to be responsible for the deaths of at least 95 million people, mostly its own citizens and very often traditional religious believers.

The point, of course, is not that secularists the world over are covert totalitarians—a thought that is as insulting as it is ridiculous. But in the first place, for many modern believers such contemporary facts now outweigh centuries-old fears of inquisitions and pogroms in shaping the background perceptions of their public dealings with secularism. Further, there is an observable link between the atrocities committed and the character of secularist reaction to religion. Marxism, for example, made the revealing claim that the beginning of all criticism was the criticism of religion—only to become a form of orthodoxy itself that brooked no dissent and dealt summarily with ideological differences.

The second (and less clear but closer) consideration is the fact that American humanism has an open history of claiming to be the ideological alternative to traditional religion, including a bid to replace it in the public schools. Now that fundamentalists have made it a litigious issue, this humanist claim is rarely uttered in public. But historians point out that by the end of the nineteenth century, the old Christian nation theme was already being replaced by a new one—the "sanctity of the public school system" in American democracy. By the time of John Dewey's *A Common Faith* in 1934, this position was articulated openly from a humanist perspective. The public schools would be "the state church of the unbeliever." As humanist religion advanced, American democracy would occupy the place of the Kingdom of God in the Christian faith, with the public schools as its shrines. Jefferson's religion of the republic, with its need for keepers of the vestal flame, found a cadre of enthusiastic volunteers in early twentieth-century humanism before humanism lost its public candor.

The third (and least clear but closest) consideration is the fact that public secularism is reinforced today by a number of converging ironies that have the effect of excluding traditional religions from the public square, favoring secularism by default. Pluralism, privatization, separationism, and libertarianism, for example, are four separate realities and developments about which people are entitled to their own opinions. But when they advance together and act on each other, there is little question about their relentless social logic: Religious liberty is transformed from a matter of freedom *for* into a matter of freedom *from*. In the process, traditional religions tend to be impeded and secularism to be left free.

The parallel irony in public education is even clearer and also more troubling because of the national status of the public school. Over the course of its first century and a half, the instinctive approach to pluralism in public education was to stress unity-at-the-expense-of-diversity and thus to deal with distinctives by excluding them. In 1917, when the rationale of "the sanctity of the public schools" was beginning to replace that of the "Christian nation," a Kentucky court of appeals put the matter plainly: "The common school, however humble its surroundings or deficient its curriculum, is the most valuable public institution in the state, and its efficiency and worth must not be impaired or destroyed by entangling it in denominational or sectarian alliances."[18]

But as the recent disputes over public school textbooks have shown, this approach must be rigorously consistent or it will be self-defeating. If one faith is to be excluded, then all must be excluded without exception if the process is not to undermine itself. The policy must be either "one in, all in" or "one out, all out." Otherwise, instead of promoting unity, this approach will itself become a source of disunity. Thus, ironically, whatever is the purported belief of the focus of unity in the schools—deism, generalized Protestantism, Protestant-Catholic-Jewish theism, civil religion, New Age mysticism, or even a generalized secularism—automatically becomes as divisive as any form of sectarian diversity. Hence the irony: Eventually the denial of diversity in the name of unity becomes as divisive as the original diversity. The omission of distinctives turns out to be as inflammatory as their inclusion. Seeking to be offensive to no one ends up by being offensive to everyone.

The words of the Supreme Court about public schools and the Pledge of Allegiance in 1943 can now be seen as farsighted, having wider implications for American society as a whole: "As governmental pressure toward uniformity becomes greater, so strife becomes more bitter as to whose unity it shall be. Probably no deeper divisions of our people could proceed from any provocation than from finding it necessary to choose what doctrine and whose program public educational officials shall compel youth to unite in embracing. The ultimate futility of such attempts to compel coherence is the lesson of every such effort."[19]

This truth is as pertinent to conservatives aroused over flag burning as it is to liberals aroused over charges of secular humanism in the textbooks. But our concern here is the naked, not the sacred, public square. Will those of a generally secularist persuasion have the candor to acknowledge these problems and commit themselves publicly to eschewing a naked public square built around a secularist-based civil religion? And to ensure that secularism has no preferred position in public education?

The stress on irony and unintended consequences should make clear that what is in mind is a drift in social developments, not a humanist conspiracy to take over schooling. Textbook tailoring, for example, had little to do with censorship by design and much to do with censorship by default—through the "pablum effect" of publishers fearful to offend. But the effect is much the same. However secular the new point of faith might be—whether it is the sanctity of public education, science, environmentalism, constitutionalism, secularism itself, or even the theory of separationism raised to the level of doctrine—it would not be a common faith.[20] It would be inescapably sectarian and thus objectionable both as a covert civil religion and as a fraud.

Eighteenth-century Jacobinism and twentieth-century Marxism have proved one point beyond question: No union of church and state is more total and more terrible than that justified in the name of "the separation of church and state." What Carlton Hayes described as "sectarian liberalism," John Courtney Murray as "totalitarian democracy," Peter Berger as "secular fundamentalism," and Steven Tipton as the "state church of latter-day Enlightenment fundamentalism" is not a figment of fundamentalist imagination.[21] To identify the danger and close the door to the possibility of a secularist-based civil religion should be the first concern of all secularists who are genuinely liberal, who are truly supportive of the separation of church and state, and who are consistently committed to religious liberty for people of all faiths and none.

Yet with such lively ironies at work and such potently irrational collective forces in motion, the bedeviling factor will not be laid to rest easily, nor for long. Civil religion is too strong, subtle, and seductive. The thin line between defining and deifying America is easily crossed. When it is, civil religion is liable to become such an unholy alliance of faith and flag that the ideals of the particular faith and the interests of the nation are welded inseparably. When that happens, the dynamics and dilemmas behind civil religion are readily understandable. But the deepest danger they represent for the believers is one that overlaps with the reason why believers in civil religion find such resistance in themselves to acknowledging its presence. Civil religion, whether supernaturally or naturally based, is far more than a dire case of "God on their side." In the end civil religion becomes both a distortion of faith and an idolatry for one reason only—as with the ancient Romans, its god is themselves.

13

Tribespeople, Idiots, or Citizens?

George Washington's home, Mount Vernon, is among America's most visited sites. But one of the most fascinating things at Mount Vernon is one of the least noticed—the key to the Bastille, the forbidding Paris fortress whose fall on July 14, 1789, became the symbol of the French Revolution. The key hangs in the hall at Mount Vernon, oversized for its classically proportioned surroundings and often overlooked. But it once spoke eloquently for the highest hopes in both nations. Six weeks after the ratification of the U.S. Constitution in September 1787, Jefferson rejoiced at the meeting of the Estates General and the prospect of applying revolutionary American principles to France. In that same spirit, the Marquis de Lafayette took the key of the Bastille in 1789 and sent it to his good friend Washington as a symbol of their common vision of the future.

Jefferson's and Lafayette's hopes were to be dashed. Sobered by the reign of terror and the revolutionary ugliness from Robespierre and Danton to Napoleon, both Americans and French supporters of the United States revised their views. Gouverneur Morris, for example, the U.S. ambassador to France, wrote home in disgust: "They want an American Constitution with the exception of a king instead of a President, without reflecting that they have no American citizens to uphold that constitution."[1]

Two hundred years later, that discussion sounded astonishingly fresh as the stirring events of 1989 unfolded. Old hopes and fears that the framers' generation would have understood were alive again. Issues that echo those discussed by Washington and Jefferson were in the air—how realistic is it to view democracy as a model set of political arrangements to be exported? What is the role of technology as a force for freedom and democratic change?

239

For democracy to prosper, does a nation have to have certain ideals and assumptions, or is it enough to copy institutions and political arrangements, such as free, recurrent elections, separation of the executive and judiciary branches, and respect for civil liberties?

Opinions differ sharply over the answers to these questions. But what seems odd in a century clouded by state repression and sectarian violence is that no part of the American experiment stands out more clearly yet is less appreciated or copied as a key to modern troubles than the religious liberty clauses of the First Amendment. The tensions and challenges now surrounding the clauses are some of the deepest and most significant issues of our time. Above all, there is the simple but vital question: How do we, in an age of expanding worldwide pluralism, live with our deepest—that is, our religiously and ideologically intense—differences? In short, what is the relationship of religious liberty and American democracy today?

This chapter and the next examine the third task of rebuilding a civil society—reforging the public philosophy. They move from the negative side of reappraising the controversies and repudiating civil religion to something constructive. Again, the overall purpose is reconstitution—the genuine reappropriation of the constitutional heritage through citizens engaging in a new debate reordered in accord with constitutional first principles and considerations of the common good.

Behind this proposal lie four judgments about the relationship of religion and American public life today. First, it is evident that a period of recurring conflict (ever since the *Everson* case in 1947, but most notably between 1979 when the Moral Majority was founded and 1989 when it closed its doors) has left the nation with the urgent need to clarify the role of religion in public life. Second, it is recognized that this clarification is vitally significant not only for the American republic but as a foundational ordering principle of the new *pax moderna*. Third, the best way to clarify this relationship lies in reaffirming the place of religious liberty in the American public philosophy in accord with the notion of covenantalism, or chartered pluralism, that is outlined here. Fourth, the present situation confronts Americans directly with a threefold choice first stated by supporters of democracy in Greece and restated by John Courtney Murray in the early sixties.

The choice is as follows: As the crisis of the public philosophy deepens and controversies over religion and public life continue to arise, will Americans respond as "tribespeople," in the sense of those who seek security in a form of tribal solidarity and are intolerant of everything alien to themselves (a problem that grows from a distortion of communitarianism and an exaggerated view of group sensitivities, whether religious, racial, sexual, or ethnic)? Or will they respond as "idiots," in the original Greek sense of the totally private person who does not subscribe to the public philosophy and is oblivious to the importance of "civility" (a problem that grows from a distortion of libertarianism and an exaggerated view of individual and personal rights)? Or will they respond as "citizens," in the sense of those who stand for their own interests but who also recognize their membership in a "commonwealth" and who appreciate the knowledge and skills that underlie the public life of a civilized community?[2]

Agreement over the place of religious liberty in a civil society is only one component of the wider public philosophy, but a vital one. Because of the personal importance of faiths to individuals and to communities of faith in America, and the public importance of both to American national life, a common vision of religious liberty in public life is critical to both citizens and the nation. It affects personal and communal liberty, civic vitality, and social harmony directly. Far from lessening the need for a public philosophy today, expanding pluralism increases it. For anyone who has reflected on the last generation of conflict over religion and public life, few questions in America are more urgent than a fresh agreement on how we are to deal with each others' deepest differences in the public sphere.

America's First Liberty

The first step in reforging the public philosophy is to show why the notion of religious liberty remains important to the public philosophy today. For, to underscore the point once more, to many Americans, especially the thought leaders, the question of religion in public life has become unimportant. It is viewed as a nonissue or a nuisance factor—something that should be purely a private issue, which inevitably becomes messy and controversial when it does not stay so, and which should therefore revert to being private as quickly as possible.

A more helpful view is to see that the swirling controversies that surround religion and public life create a sort of sound barrier effect: At one level, the issue appears all passions, problems, prejudices. But break through to a higher level and it touches on several of the deepest questions of human life in the modern world. Once these are appreciated, it clearly becomes in the highest interest of the common good to resolve the problems rather than ban the topic out of personal disdain or fear.

There are at least five reasons why religious liberty remains a vital part of America's public philosophy. First, religious liberty, or freedom of con-science, is a precious, fundamental, and inalienable human right—the freedom to reach, hold, freely exercise, or change one's beliefs, subject solely to the dictates of consciences and independent of all outside, especially governmental, control. Prior to and existing quite apart from the Bill of Rights that protects it, religious liberty is not a luxury, a second-class right, a constitutional redundancy or a subcategory of free speech. Since it does not finally depend on the discoveries of science, the favors of the state and its officials, or the vagaries of tyrants or majorities, it is a right that may not be submitted to any vote nor encroached upon by the expansion of the bureaucratic state. Since it is a free-standing right, it is integrally linked to other basic rights, such as freedom of speech, but it does not need them to supplement its legitimacy. There is no more searching test of the health of the public philosophy than this nonmajoritarian standard set forth in the Williamsburg Charter: "A society is only as just and free as it is respectful of this right for its smallest minorities and least popular communities."[3] Religious liberty as a political right guaranteed by a legal institution is barely two hundred years old in the world. But considering why and how it was formulated, it has correctly been called America's "first liberty."

Unless America's public philosophy respects and protects this right for all Americans, the American promise of individual freedom and justice is breached.

Second, the religious liberty clauses of the First Amendment are the democratic world's most distinctive answer to one of the entire world's most pressing questions: How do we live with our deepest—that is, our religiously intense—differences?

Some regions of the world (for example, in Western Europe) exhibit a strong political civility that is directly linked to their weak religious commitments; and others (for example, in the Middle East) exhibit a strong religious commitment directly linked to their weak political civility. Owing to the manner of the First Amendment's ordering of religious liberty and public life, American democracy has afforded the fullest opportunity for strong religious commitment and strong political civility to complement, rather than threaten, each other.

Unless America's public philosophy respects and protects this distinctive American achievement, the American promise of democratic liberty and justice will be betrayed.

Third, the religious liberty clauses lie close to the genius of the American experiment. Far more than a luxury, let alone a redundancy, the First Amendment is essential and indispensable to the character of the American republic. Not simply a guarantee of individual and communal liberty, the First Amendment's ordering of the relationship of religion and public life is the boldest and most successful part of the entire American experiment. Daring in its time, distinctive throughout the world both then and now, it has proved decisive in shaping key aspects of the American story. It is not too much even to say that as the religious liberty clauses go, so goes America.

Unless America's public philosophy respects and protects this remarkable American ordering, the civic vitality of the American republic will be sapped.

Fourth, the religious liberty clauses are the single, strongest nontheological reason why free speech and the free exercise of religion have been closely related and why religion in general has persisted more strongly in the United States than in any other comparable modern country. Social development in most modern countries seems to follow an almost ironclad equation: The more modernized the country, the more secularized the people. America, however, is a striking exception to the trend, being at once the most modernized country and having the most religious of modern peoples.

The reason lies in the effect of the American style of disestablishment. By separating church and state, but not religion and government or public life, disestablishment does two things. It undercuts the forces of cultural antipathy built up against religious communities by church-state establishments—historically speaking, established churches have contributed strongly to their own rejection and to secularization in general. At the same time, disestablishment throws each faith onto reliance on its own claimed resources. The overall effect is to release a free and unfettered competition of people and beliefs similar to the free-market competition of capitalism.

Unless America's public philosophy respects and protects this enterprising relationship, both American religious liberty and public discourse will be handicapped.

Fifth, the interpretation and application of the First Amendment today touches on some of the deepest and most revolutionary developments in contemporary thought. A generation ago it was common to draw a deep dichotomy between science and religion, reason and revelation, objectivity and commitment, and so on. Today such dichotomies are impossible. All thinking is acknowledged to be presuppositional. Value-neutrality in social affairs is impossible. To demand "neutral discourse" in public life, as some still do, should now be recognized as a way of coercing people to speak publicly in someone else's language and thus never to be true to their own.

Unless America's public philosophy respects and protects this new (or restored) understanding, the republican requirement of free democratic debate and responsible participation in democratic life will be thwarted.

One conclusion is inescapable: The place of religious liberty in American public life is not merely a religious issue, but a national issue. It is not only a private issue, but a public one. Far from being simply partisan or sectarian, religious liberty is in the interest of Americans of all faiths or none, and its reaffirmation should be a singular and treasured part of the American public philosophy.

Changes, Challenges, and Controversies

The second step in reforging the public philosophy is to analyze the factors behind the recurring conflicts over religion and public life and assess the challenge they pose for American religious liberty and the public philosophy today. The conflicts themselves need no elaboration, though it is helpful to draw a distinction between cases where religion itself is directly the issue and cases where its influence is indirect. Abortion is the principal example of the latter and examples of the former are common—school prayer and New Age meditation, creation science, secular humanism, textbook tailoring, prayer before high school sporting events, Muslim prayer mats in government offices, Gideon's Bibles in hotel rooms, the Ten Commandments on school walls, blasphemy in films and novels, the Pledge of Allegiance, Mormon polygamy, "Christian Nation" resolutions, day care centers, and so on.

Some of these conflicts are critical, others less so. But they are all flashpoints along the contested boundaries between religion and public life. For a full generation now, this issue has been highly contentious, with an endless series of disputes and the whole subject surrounded by needless ignorance and fruitless controversy, including at the highest levels. Too often, debates have been sharply polarized, controversies dominated by extremes, resolutions sought automatically through litigation, either of the religious liberty clauses set against the other one, and any common view of a better way lost in the din of irreconcilable differences and insistent demands.

The temptation is to take a quick glance at the contestants, apportion the blame, enlist on one side or another, and treat the whole problem as largely political and capable of having a political solution. From that perspective, the problem is one that has been created by a series of overlapping conflicts: an ideological clash (the fundamentalists versus the secularists) that overlaps with a constitutional clash (the accommodationist "low wallers" versus the strict separationist "high wallers") that overlaps with a historical clash (the biblical and republican tradition versus the Enlightenment and liberal tradition) that overlaps with a clash of social visions (the communitarian "rootsers" versus the libertarian "rightsers") that overlaps with opposing views of morality in public life (the maximalists versus the minimalists) that overlaps with a psychological clash (the "bitter-enders," who insist on commitment regardless of civility, versus the "betrayers," who insist on civility regardless of commitment). This has produced, in turn, two extremist tendencies (the "removers," who would like to eradicate all religion from public life, versus the "reimposers," who would like to impose their version of a past or future state of affairs on everyone else). All this, of course, is potently reinforced by technological factors, such as direct mail and its shameless appeals to fear and anger.

Such analyses may be accurate as far as they go. But they stop before they take into account some of the deepest factors. All of the above conflicts amount to a series of responses—which raises the question of what are the deeper forces to which they are responding. I would argue that behind the recent conflicts lie several developments that stem from the explosive acceleration of modernization in the last generation. Two factors are especially important to this argument—the reversal of roles in the relationship of church and state and the current expansion of pluralism.

"Church and state" has become a thought-numbing category that misleads as much as it illuminates. As Judge John Noonan has pointed out, the phrase is triply misleading because it suggests that in America there is a single church, a single state, and a simple, clear distinction between the two. But this confusion is only the beginning of the complexities. Harold J. Berman, the doyen of American scholars on law and religion, builds on that and shows that the framers' more common terms were religion and government, not church and state. But not only have religion and government each changed over the course of two hundred years under the impact of modernity, the relationship between them has also changed to the point of being a complete "exchange of roles."[4]

Berman analyzed the involvement of religion and government over two hundred years in three areas—family life, education, and welfare—and summarized the two main consequences of the role reversal:

> In the 1780s religion played a primary role in social life . . . and government played a relatively minor, though necessary, supportive role, whereas in the 1980s religion plays a relatively minor, though necessary, supportive role and government plays a primary role. On the other hand, the role played by government in the social life of America in the 1780s (and for almost a century and a half thereafter) was openly and strongly influenced and directed by religion, whereas in the 1980s that is much less true and in many respects not true at all, while the role played by religion in the social life of America in the 1980s is openly and strongly influenced and directed by government.[5]

Berman builds his case with care, but states his conclusion with force. "Whereas two centuries ago, in matters of social life which have a significant moral dimension, government was the handmaid of religion, today religion —in its social responsibilities, as contrasted with personal faith and collective worship—is the handmaid of government."[6] Not surprisingly, such a colossal reversal has sent out reverberations to every level of church-state relationships—constitutional interpretation, volunteerism in public life, and (supremely) religious liberty itself. The Williamsburg Charter states: "Less dramatic but also lethal to freedom and the chief menace to religious liberty today is the expanding power of government control over personal behavior and the institutions of society, when the government acts not so much in deliberate hostility to, but in reckless disregard of, communal belief and personal conscience."[7]

The second, and equally important, factor is the recent expansion of pluralism. This is a worldwide phenomenon that links current American tensions to similar trends around the globe. How do we live with each other's deepest differences? That simple question has been transformed by modernity into one of the world's most pressing dilemmas. On a small planet in a pluralistic age the all too common response has been bigotry, fanaticism, terrorism, and state repression.

Multiculturalism and expanding pluralism are no strangers to the American experience. They have always been a major theme in the American story, with tolerance generally expanding behind pluralism. But in the last generation religious pluralism has thrust forward in two significant ways. First, American pluralism now goes beyond the predominance of Protestant-Catholic-Jewish and includes sizable numbers of almost all the world's great religions—Buddhist and Muslim, in particular—though an astonishing 86.5 percent of Americans identify themselves as Christians. Second, it now goes beyond religion altogether to include a growing number of Americans with no religious preference. (In 1962, as in 1952, secularists —or the so-called "religious nones"—were 2 percent of Americans. Today they are between 10 and 12 percent, and strikingly higher on the West Coast than anywhere else.)[8]

This latest expansion of pluralism is one of the social facts of our time, though consciousness of it has been reinforced and somewhat distorted through a combination of modern technologies and postmodern theories. The effect has been to complete the profound sea change initiated by the "new immigration" of the beginning of the century. The United States has shifted from a largely Protestant pluralism to a genuine multifaith pluralism that includes people of all faiths and those who claim no religious preference. The effect can be observed at two different levels in American society. In the first place, the effect of exploding diversity can be seen in the demographic makeup of contemporary American society. The state of California, for example, has America's most diverse as well as its largest population. It now accepts almost one-third of the world's immigration and represents at the close of the century what New York did at the start—the point of entry for millions of new Americans.[9]

California's schools have a "minority majority" in all public school enrollments. This will be true of the population of California as a whole soon after the year 2000. (The same situation already exists in all of the nation's twenty-five largest city school systems, and half of the states have public school populations that are more than 25 percent minorities).[10] The result is a remarkable mix of the diverse cultures of Africa, Asia, Europe, and Latin America. California will undergo as challenging a project in culture-blending as New York experienced in nation-building nine decades ago, and as Boston experienced as the birth of the public-school movement a century and a half ago. And, of course, this process affects the "natives" as well as the newcomers. Many Americans feel they are sharing the experience of new immigrants merely through staying at home. Growing up in one culture, they feel they are growing old in another.

The effect of the exploding diversity can also be seen in what is a form of cultural breakdown—collapse of the previously accepted understandings of the relationship of religion and public life and the triggering of the culture wars. As a result, a series of bitter, fruitless contentions over religion and politics has erupted, extremes have surfaced, the resort to the law court has become almost reflexive, many who decry the problems are equally opposed to solutions to them, and in the ensuing din of charge and countercharge any sense of common vision for the common good has been drowned.

As always with the trends of modernity, the consequences of increased pluralism are neither unique to America nor uniform throughout the world. The disruptive effects can be seen throughout the world, even in totalitarian societies and in democratic nations with long traditions of racial and linguistic homogeneity. Long before the eventual Soviet breakup and the bitter strife between the Muslim Azerbaijanis and the Christian Armenians in 1989–90, Mikhail Gorbachev described the question of how the hundred-plus Soviet ethnic groups get along as "the most fundamental, vital issue of our society."[11] And few will soon forget the ugly images of young white Italian thugs brandishing steel chains over the heads of terrified North African street vendors against the beautiful pastel backdrop of Florence, capital of Renaissance cultural enlightenment.

Nor are the consequences of pluralization simple. On the one hand, increased pluralism deepens old tensions. Under the challenge of "all those others," many are seemingly pressured to believe more weakly in their own faith, to the point of compromise—the more choice and change, the less commitment and continuity. In reaction, however, others tend to believe more strongly, to the point of contempt for the faith of others. On the other hand, increased pluralism helps develop new trends. Today's dominant tensions are not so much between distinct religions and denominations. As often as not, they are between the more orthodox and the more contemporary within the same denomination (for example, the recent divisions within the Southern Baptist Convention), or between an alliance of the more orthodox in several religions who oppose the more contemporary in those same groups (for example, the prolife coalition of conservative Protestants, Catholics, Mormons, and so on).

In sum, like it or not, modern pluralism stands squarely as both the child of, and the challenger to, religious liberty—whether because of its presence (given the democratic conditions arising out of the Reformation and the Wars of Religion), its permanence (given the likely continuation of these conditions in the foreseeable future), or its premise (that a single, uniform doctrine of belief can only achieve dominance in a pluralistic society by two means: through persuasion, which is currently unlikely because unfashionable, or through coercion by the oppressive use of state power, which at anytime is unjust and unfree). If religious liberty makes pluralism more likely, pluralism makes religious liberty more necessary.

Not surprisingly, these developments and their logic have hit hard the trio of American institutions that have been so instrumental in tempering the forces of faction and self-interest and helping transform American diversity into a source of richness and strength: the religious liberty clauses of the First Amendment, the public school movement, and the American public philosophy. The upshot is that the public schools have often become the storm center of the controversies, one or other of the twin clauses of the First Amendment have been looked to as the sole arbiter in the partisan conflicts, and the common vision for the common good becomes the loser. Only when the full extent of this damage and the full range of the causes have been taken into account can any prospective solutions be given realistic consideration.

Charter for the Third Century

The third step in reforging the public philosophy is to introduce the concept of covenantalism, or chartered pluralism, as the basis of the public philosophy. This means to examine its contribution to the civil society and to show its advantages over the two existing visions of religion and public life that are now deadlocked—namely, communitarianism, the social vision that degenerates into "tribalism," and libertarianism, the vision that degenerates into political "idiocy." Anyone who appreciates the factors behind the present conflicts is confronted with tough questions. Above all, can there be a healing of the schism of the spirit, a resolution to the culture wars, and an adjustment to the new pluralism without endangering the logic of religious liberty in public life? Can there be an agreed center of national unity that complements, rather than contradicts, American diversity? Is there a way in which diverse faiths can fulfill their respective responsibility to the require-ments of order, freedom, and justice without favoring one of the three at the expense of the other two?

At first sight, the search for a just and commonly acceptable solution to these challenges seems as futile as squaring the circle or searching for esperanto. The question of the public role of religion in an increasingly pluralistic society appears to be a minefield of controversies, with the resulting ignorance, confusion, and reluctance an understandable outcome. Yet if it is correct to trace the problem to forces, such as pluralism, as much as to ideologies, individuals, and groups, then we have more victims than villains over this issue, and the wisest approach is to search together for a solution, not for a scapegoat.

In fact, the present stage of the conflict offers a strategic opportunity in the 1990s. Extreme positions and unwelcome consequences are readily identifiable on many sides, and a new desire for consensus is evident. But where and on what grounds could consensus emerge? As so often, the most constructive way forward is to go back—or, more accurately, to reforge the public philosophy through the renewal of a concept that is at the heart of American democracy and the American constitutional tradition—covenantalism.

The recovery of the idea of covenant as a key to American democracy and the American constitutional tradition is one of the freshest and most important findings of recent scholarship.[12] Far from being completely new and startlingly original, the Constitution of 1787 is now seen to be the climax of a long tradition of covenants, compacts, and charters that goes back to the earliest colonial experience. Far from being the legacy of John Locke in the seventeenth century or Whig and Enlightenment thinkers in the eighteenth century, the American constitutional tradition was in place and operating strongly by the 1640s when John Locke was not yet a teenager and Charles-Louis Montesquieu, Jean-Jacques Rousseau, and William Black-stone had not been born.

Seen in this new light, the American Constitution and the constitution-al tradition grew directly from the seedbed of Puritan ideals and institutions that were rooted in the notion of covenant. Dissenting English colonists relied on Swiss, Dutch, and German theologians who themselves relied on the biblical principles of a Jewish covenantal republic to create a distinctively American style of government. The term "federalism" did not come into use until later, but Puritan notions, such as "federal liberty," were the twin-concepts to "federal theology" and all went back to the core of covenant (*foedus* in Latin and *B'rit* in Hebrew). The foundational covenant was the one between God and human beings, but there were multiple extensions to different levels of community—the covenant of marriage, the local church, the town, the colony, and eventually the nation.

The Mayflower Compact on November 11, 1620, was the first explicitly political use of the religious covenant form and an historic milestone on the road to the more secular and national covenant of the "miracle in Philadelphia" in 1787. But in all the dozens of cases that made up the early American system of institutions and set of ideals, one feature was unmistakable: The covenant/compact/charter represents a distinctive combination of unity and diversity, commonality and independence, obligation and voluntary consent. Almost by itself, the principle of free consent carried all the promise and the perils of "federal liberty." For free consent, being as different as can be from a forced contract, is a matter of the spirit as well as the letter of the law. Therein lie the seeds of both the risk and the renewal of the unfinished American experiment. In the best traditions of covenantal agreement, the constitutional tradition would always have to remain the living faith of the dead rather than the dead faith of the living.

This idea of covenantal, or federal, liberty holds the promise of a resolution of our present problems through the concept of chartered pluralism. At the base of the notion is a defining feature of modern experience: The present state of intellectual divisions in modern pluralistic societies does not permit agreement at the level of the *origin* of beliefs (where justifications for behavior are theoretical, ultimate, and irreconcilable). But a significant, though limited, agreement is still possible at the level of the *outworking* of beliefs (where the expression of beliefs in behavior is more practical, less ultimate, and often overlapping with the practical beliefs and behavior of other people).

Covenantalism, or chartered pluralism, is therefore a vision of religious liberty in public life that, across the deep religious differences of a pluralistic society, guarantees and sustains religious liberty for all by forging a substantive agreement, or freely chosen compact, over three things that are the "Three Rs" of religious liberty: rights, responsibilities, and respect. The compact affirms: first, in terms of rights, that religious liberty, or freedom of conscience, is a fundamental and inalienable right for peoples of all faiths and none; second, in term of responsibilities, that religious liberty is a universal right joined to a universal duty to respect that right for others; and third, in terms of respect, that the first principles of religious liberty, combined with the lessons of two hundred years of constitutional experience, require and shape certain practical guidelines by which a robust yet civil discourse may be sustained in a free society that would remain free.

More detailed implications of this principled pact will be spelled out in the next chapter. But stated like this, the social vision of covenantalism is a modern form of "federal liberty" that combines the best, and avoids the worst, of the libertarian and communitarian visions. Put differently, the notion of chartered pluralism is an example of what John Rawls calls the "overlapping consensus" that is needed in a liberal democracy. The core of its principled pact over the Three Rs is a variation of what Jacques Maritain described as "a sort of unwritten common law, at the point of practical convergence of extremely different theoretical ideologies and spiritual traditions." Maritain used himself to provide the example of the difference between the theoretical and the practical levels.

> I am fully convinced that my way of justifying the belief in the rights of man and the ideal of liberty, equality, fraternity, is the only one which is solidly based on truth. That does not prevent me from agreeing on these practical tenets with those who are convinced that their way of justifying them, entirely different from mine, or even opposed to mine in its theoretical dynamism, is likewise the only one that is based on truth. Assuming they both believe in the democratic charter, a Christian and a rationalist will nevertheless give justifications that are incompatible with each other, to which their souls, their minds and their blood are committed, and about these justifications they will fight. And God keep me from saying that it is not important to know which of the two is right! That is essentially important. They remain, however, in agreement on the practical affirmation of that charter, and they can formulate common principles of action.[13]

The convenantal element in chartered pluralism is obvious. The social vision is solidly founded on such a principled pact that is can be seen to give due weight to the first of its two terms. It is therefore properly a form of *chartered* pluralism, or pluralism within the framework of a principled charter that spells out the rights, responsibilities, and respect required by religious liberty. So long as the pact over the Three Rs of religious liberty remains strong, the vision avoids the minimalist approaches to unity that relies solely on "process" and "proceduralism." (For example, claims that seek to go beyond proceduralism but only a little, such as: "We are held together by the coherence of our moral disagreement and argument within an ongoing cultural conversation."[14]

But at the same time the area of public agreement is strictly limited in both substance and in scope. The pact does not pretend to include agreement over religious beliefs, political policies, constitutional interpretations, or even the philosophical justifications of the three parts of the compact. Chartered pluralism is an agreement within disagreements over deep differences that make a difference. It therefore gives due weight to the second of its two terms, and remains a form of chartered *pluralism*. By doing so, it avoids the equal but opposite maximalist approaches to unity, such as the dangers of majoritarianism, civil religion, or any form of overreaching consensus that is blind or insensitive to tiny minorities and unpopular communities. Thus social unity is maintained, but religious liberty and diversity are respected in that religious unity is either made dependent upon persuasion or deferred as a messianic hope to be fulfilled only at the end of time.

Several features of this compact at the heart of chartered pluralism need to be highlighted indelibly if the compact is to pass muster under the exacting challenges of the present situation. First, the character of the compact is not a form of civil religion or public theology. Its content does not grow from shared beliefs, religious or political, because the recent expansion of pluralism means that we are now beyond the point where that is possible. It grows instead from a common commitment to universal rights, rights that are shared by an overlapping consensus of commitment, although grounded and justified differently by the different faiths behind them.[15]

Second, the achievement of this compact does not come through the process of a general dilution of beliefs, as in the case of civil religion moving from Protestantism to "Judeo-Christian" theism. It comes through the process of a particular concentration of universal rights and mutual responsibilities, within which the deep differences of belief can be negotiated.

Third, the fact that religious consensus is now impossible does not mean that moral consensus (for example, "consensual" or "common core" values in public education) is either unimportant or unattainable. It means, however, that moral consensus must be viewed as a goal, not as a given; something to be achieved through persuasion and ongoing conversation rather than assumed on the basis of tradition. Thus chartered pluralism means that there is a way to give positive meaning to public life without coercive imposition, and at the same time to foster an emphasis on freedom and diversity that need not lead toward fragmentation.

Fourth, the fact that the different religious roots of the public philosophy are largely invisible in public does not mean that they are unimportant or that the public philosophy is secular in a secularist ideological sense. On the contrary, a cut-flower public philosophy will not work. So the health of the public philosophy depends not only on a public conversation of citizens across the division of creed and generation, but on the private cultivation of the first principles of the public philosophy within each home and faith community. Should the diverse roots of those first principles ever grow weak or be poisoned from some antidemocratic source, such a private crisis would have inevitable public consequences.

Fifth, chartered pluralism allows even "radically monotheist" religions, such as Judaism and the Christian faith, to balance the twin demands of theological integrity and civil unity. Such faiths can never be content with religious liberty as freedom *from;* to them it must always be freedom *for.* Chartered pluralism therefore allows them to exercise their responsibilities to their conceptions of order, freedom, and justice, yet without infringing on the rights of others or becoming socially disruptive. Whereas the "idiocy" bred by libertarianism can be notoriously casual about order, and the "tribalism" bred by communitarianism on the Right and the Left can grow blind to freedom and justice for others, the federal liberty of chartered pluralism makes room for the free exercise of transcendent faiths that can address all three concerns with their own integrity, yet without compromise to themselves or damage to civil unity. The only proviso is that such influence is generally best exercised spiritually rather than politically, indirectly rather than directly, and persuasively rather than coercively.

Doubtless, further questions are raised by these five points. Do all the different faiths mean the same thing when they affirm common rights? Do all have an adequate philosophical basis for their individual affirmations? Are all such divergences and inadequacies a matter of sheer indifference to the strength and endurance of the compact? Will such a principled pact always be enough in practice, to keep self-interest from breaking out of the harness? The probable answer in each case is "no," which is a reminder of both the fragility of the historical achievement of religious liberty for all and the sobering task Americans face if they are to sustain such freedom today. Indeed, the challenge might appear quixotic were it not for the alternatives.

Viewed in the light of the alternatives, chartered pluralism provides a way between communitarianism and libertarianism. Communitarianism, found on both the Left and the Right, virtually equates politics with morality. When transferred to the level of a public philosophy, it tends to see everything in terms of its ideology writ large all over public life. Whereas libertarianism, also found on both the Left and the Right, virtually excludes morality from politics. When transferred to the level of a public philosophy, it tends to see everything in terms of an individualism that sucks the commonness out of public life altogether.

Curiously, both social visions betray their inadequacies as candidates for the public philosophy, partly because of the ironies they exhibit and partly because they rule themselves out on the grounds of their own principles. In the politically unlikely event that communitarianism were to prevail as the public philosophy, it would become a form of majoritarianism. In seeking to impose a style of traditional solidarity on modern pluralism, it would end in denying pluralism (a smaller and milder recapitulation of the totalitarian error). On the other hand, if the communitarian vision does not seek to prevail as the public philosophy—which the majority of communitarians probably prefer anyway—the effect of communitarianism on public life would be to reinforce relativism, not community. For relativism in public life is less the planned offspring of a specific philosophical movement than an unwanted bastard born of general frustration with the apparently irreconcilable positions of different communities. Thus, ironically, if American public life is to retain and strengthen a sense of community, it cannot be on the basis of communitarianism as the public philosophy.

Libertarianism, in contrast, sets out to widen the sphere of public freedom by relativizing all faiths. Everyone will be more free if no one's position is "imposed" on anyone else because "everything depends on where you're coming from." But the effect is to relativize all positions except relativism and so to assert a new imposition in public life—that of a dogmatized relativism and a universalized libertarianism. Thus if communitarianism ends in denying the reality of pluralism, libertarianism ends in distorting it. For currently pluralism goes more closely with particularism than with relativism. Most believers who make up today's pluralistic society want to affirm their distinctiveness. They believe that the beliefs that make them different are finally right and important. They are committed to them in terms of absolutes—just as for many relativists relativism itself has become the last surviving absolute. Thus libertarianism rules itself out as a candidate for the public philosophy too. Ironically again, if American public life is to retain and strengthen the sphere of liberty, it cannot be on the basis of libertarianism as the public philosophy.

Expressed differently, chartered pluralism owes much to John Courtney Murray's valuable insistence that the unity asserted in the American motto, *E pluribus unum*, is a unity with limits, and therefore that the religious liberty clauses are "articles of peace" rather than "articles of faith."[16] But Father Murray's distinction, which was borrowed from Samuel Johnson, must never be widened into a divorce. For one thing, the articles of peace are principled before they are procedural, and they need to stay principled if principled procedures are not to be sucked into the nihilism of empty proceduralism. The articles of peace are not sacred or ultimate themselves, but they derive from articles of faith and cannot be sustained long without them. For the same reason, genuine civility is substantive before it is formal. It is not a rhetoric of niceness, let alone a fear of nastiness. Nor is it a psychology of social adjustment. Civility is both an attitude and a discourse shaped by a principled respect for people, truth, the common good, and the American constitutional tradition.

For another thing, neither chartered pluralism nor the notion of articles of peace should be understood as leading to unanimity, but to that unity within which diversity can be transformed into richness and disagreement itself into an achievement that betokens strength. Again, the old term "federal liberty" carries rich meanings. As Murray wrote, "The one civil society contains within its new unity the communities that are divided among themselves; but it does not seek to reduce to its own unity the differences that divide them."[17] The introduction to the Williamsburg Charter includes a vivid current statement of this recognition:

> We readily acknowledge our continuing differences. Signing this Charter implies no pretense that we believe the same things or that our differences over policy proposals, legal interpretations and philosophical groundings do not ultimately matter. The truth is not even that what unites us is deeper than what divides us, for differences over belief are the deepest and least negotiated of all.
>
> The Charter sets forth a renewed national compact, in the sense of a solemn mutual agreement between parties, on how we view the place of religion in American life and how we should contend with each other's deepest differences in the public sphere. It is a call to a vision of public life that will allow conflict to lead to consensus, religious commitment to reinforce political civility. In this way, diversity is not a point of weakness but a source of strength.[18]

Understood properly, these three ideas—covenantalism, chartered pluralism, and federal liberty—are critical to reforging the aspect of the public philosophy that bears on questions of religion and American public life, especially in the light of the deficiencies of the alternatives. They therefore contribute vitally to keeping democracy safe for diversity. If this vision of a promise-keeping covenant gains acceptance in the three main arenas of conflict—public policy debates, the resort to law, and public education— and if it succeeds in addressing their problems constructively, chartered pluralism could serve as a public philosophy for the public square, truly a charter for religion and public life in America's third century of constitutional government.

Our Page in the Story

The last step in reforging the public philosophy is to set out some of the foreseeable principles and pitfalls that should shape prudential judgments as to the best way forward through the controversies.

First, certain conditions for a constructive solution are necessary politically to achieve justice. To be realistic, the issue of religion in public life is never likely to become a popular cause—if only because so many American thought-leaders are largely oblivious of religion and so many American believers are largely oblivious of serious thinking. Solid concepts and good will are therefore not enough. What is required is intellectual foresight that will tackle problems today; moral courage to tackle problems not necessarily considered "problematic" on the current political agenda; magnanimity that in the present situation will allow all parties to act generously, regardless of their own political position, with regard to the interests of others and especially those of the weaker parties; and all these qualities gathered up in bipartisan leadership of a Lincolnesque stature that begins in the White House and reaches out across the land.

Second, there are two unlikely outcomes to the current struggle. These outcomes are all but inconceivable, but are worth stating because they form the stuff of activist propaganda and counterpropaganda. On the one hand, the conflicts would degenerate into Belfast-style sectarian violence. On the other hand, they would result in an Albanian-style repression of religion, especially in the public square. The combined logic of America's historic commitment to religious liberty and the depth of religious diversity today makes these outcomes virtually impossible.

Third, two undesirable outcomes, in the sense of two broad possibilities, might occur should there be no effective resolution of the current conflicts over religion and public life. The milder, shorter-term possibility is of a massive popular revulsion against religion in public life. This could take the form of "A-plague-on-both-your-houses" reaction to religious contention and therefore lead, ironically, to a sort of naked public square created, not by secularists or separationists, but by a wrongheaded overreaction to an equally wrongheaded religious overreaction.

The more drastic, longer-term possibility is that continuing conflict could lead to a deepening of the two-nation division in American life, with the culturally conservative forces favorable to religion and the culturally liberal forces hostile. A short time ago, such a possibility would probably have been dismissed summarily. But for anyone who appreciates the effects of two-nation divisions in European countries, such as France, the implications of the 1988 presidential campaign are sobering. The fissures of the culture wars are worth monitoring.

Fourth, there are two unfortunate outcomes, in the sense of two broad possibilities that might occur even if chartered pluralism succeeds or if current conflicts simply fade away without apparent damage to national life. The first possibility is that, in the generally civil conditions of pluralism, the way is opened for some faith or worldview to play the game only to win the game and end the game for others (existing candidates from the secular Left and the Religious Right are equally dangerous here). The second possibility is that, in the same civil conditions of pluralism, civility will itself become so corrupted that, in turn, pluralism is debased into a relativistic indifference to truth and principle. The result would be a slump into apathy, the logic of laissez-faire freedom gone to seed. The outcome would be that corruption of the republic from within of which the framers warned.

For some Americans, mention of these dangers only confirms the risks of chartered pluralism they feared all along. But mention of the framers is a reminder that the risks are not new. They were built into the experiment from the very start and, even before that, they were present in all the variations of covenant. From Sinai onward, covenants require free and continuing consent because the spirit of the compact is as important as its letter. Such risks are the reason why the American experiment is open-ended, and why the task of defending religious liberty is never finished.

Yet the risk is only half the story. The very open-endedness that is the source of risk is also the source of potential renewal. That is why each citizen and each generation matter. Each adds a new chapter to the story. As so often, Tocqueville saw this point and applied it to the two great revolutions of his time. "In a rebellion, as in a novel," he wrote, "the most difficult part to invent is the end."[19]

14

Making the World Safe
for Diversity

When General Sherman captured Atlanta in September 1864, he ordered its citizens to evacuate their homes and brushed aside the impassioned protests of the Confederate commander, General Hood. "You might as well appeal against the thunderstorm," he told Atlantans, "as against these terrible hardships of war." During that savage hour the time for appeals to "the better angels" on either side had gone.

Appeals to Lincoln's better angels have been rare in the culture wars too. The acrid whiff of that bitter-ender logic has hung over many of the recent conflicts over religion and public life. Zero-sum has been the rule of the game, winner-takes-all the order of the day. One Christmas carol banned from a public school and the entire heritage of Western Christendom is supposedly threatened with disintegration. One Christian crèche left unbanned on government property and the whole grisly apparatus of establishments, from indexes to Grand Inquisitors, has purportedly been trundled back into the public square.

Yet the fact is that the logic and lessons of these very problems bring America to the verge of another "new birth of freedom." For the climax of the troubles is a moment when the fruit of bitter controversies can be clarification. Coinciding with the bicentennial of the Bill of Rights and a worldwide revolution looking to the Bill of Rights, the present moment is one when reconciliation can lead to reconstitution. Helping to make the world safe for diversity can begin with keeping America safe for diversity. At the heart of this task is a vision of public life. That vision is not of a naked

258

public square where all religion is excluded, nor of a sacred public square with any religion established or semiestablished. It is of a civil public square in which citizens of all faiths, or none, are free to enter and engage one another in the continuing democratic discourse.

Crowded, Noisy, and Vital

The main components required for such a civil public square and such a reconstitution have been discussed already—a reappraisal of the controversies, a repudiation of civil religion, a renewal of a covenantal public philosophy, a rededication to the first principles of religious liberty, a constant vigilance against the menace of semiestablishment, and a constructive response to pluralism. We turn now to the two governing principles that empower the free exercise of religious liberty in the civil public square— principled participation and principled persuasion. The first, dealing more with action, is the expression of the freedom that is central to the civil public square, whereas the second, dealing more with communication, is the expression of the duty that is central to the civil public square.

The central freedom of the civic public square is that of principled participation. This is the understanding that, within constitutional limits and in accord with the mutually binding compact on religious liberty, people of all faiths and worldviews, transcendental or naturalistic, can enter freely and engage fully with all others concerned with the affairs of public life. Clearly, the main accent in this principle falls on two places. First, it is positive and does justice to the central and positive purpose of both the free exercise and no establishment clauses that have brought American religious liberty. Second, it is inclusive and does justice to the consistency and comprehensiveness intrinsic in an inalienable right. Since freedom is indivisible as well as inalienable, a right for one is a right for all; just as discrimination against anyone is damaging to the freedom of all. The effect of principled participation is therefore to foster a civil public square that is undoubtedly crowded and noisy but a square that will be democratically vital too.

Put differently, this vision of a civil, crowded, and noisy public square is in direct contrast to the two faulty visions of public life mentioned earlier—the removers and the reimposers. The former deny the positive nature of religious liberty in public life and the latter the inclusive. If the example cited earlier of Jon Murray of the American Atheists stands for an extreme form of the removers, examples of a weaker form abound. After a poll of national and local volunteer leaders who had been active in the bicentennial celebration of the U.S. Constitution, Mark W. Cannon, the Bicentennial Commission's staff director, reported that educators responded negatively (58 percent to 42 percent) as to whether "the 'free exercise' of religion allows religious groups to seek to enact into law their public policy views without violating the Constitutional clause against 'an establishment of religion.'"[1]

Catholics have long borne the brunt of such attitudes. For example, in 1990 when the National Conference of Catholic Bishops retained Hill and Knowlton, Inc., to design its abortion strategy, Kate Michelman of the National Abortion Rights Action League denounced the move as a breach of church-state separation. "It's outrageous," she said, "that the Catholic Church . . . is spending $5 million to try to impose their religious teachings through law on a pluralistic society."[2] Even deeply liberal intellectual Catholics have not been exempt. When Father Timothy Healy retired from the presidency of Georgetown University and was appointed head of the New York Public Library, New York intellectuals went up in arms. "It's the biggest library in the most secular city in the world," Gay Talese protested, "and we want to keep the fingerprints of the church—any church—off its shelves."[3] "Anyone with a strong religious creed is committed to that religious creed and will act on it," Joseph Heller declared, "and shouldn't be the head of a library."[4]

Is it now compulsory to be an agnostic to be the head of a library in New York? Was it a reverse religious test they had in mind? Ironically, observed the Jewish chaplain at Georgetown, the people who worried about Father Healy's Catholicism didn't know Father Healy. He'd been so sensitive to non-Catholics in Georgetown that he was criticized for not being Catholic enough. But Heller's complaint is a catch-22 for himself and all his fellow removers. For such complaints are none other than the "chill factor" from the other side, a civil libertarian form of censorship that closes down the number of voices heard in the democratic debate. Fortunately for history's grand causes like abolition and civil rights, there were no Michelmans, Taleses, or Hellers in power when the likes of Finney, Garrison, and Martin Luther King unfurled their banners and bared the faith behind their vision of justice. The American experiment will have come to a pretty pass if religion in public life is reduced to a president's platitudes at the national prayer breakfast or the quadrennial controversy over a cleric running for the presidency.

The old American notion of religion "sticking to the private sphere" has a long and mostly honorable tradition. But it has never meant what the removers mean by the notion today. As the Williamsburg Charter reminds us in the light of such communities as the Amish, "There must always be room for those who do not wish to participate in the public ordering of our common life, who desire to pursue their own religious witness separately as conscience dictates."[5] But at the same time, the double-headed drive to privatize religion and secularize public life is constitutionally unwarranted, historically unprecedented, and—at least for the biblical family of faiths, including Judaism, the Christian faith, and Islam—theologically without excuse.

At the other extreme of the removers are the "reimposers," those who deny the inclusive nature of religious liberty and would like to reimpose on society their version of an earlier state of affairs regardless of the consequences to religious liberty. Their motif is a background strain in much of the music of "Christian America." But it usually takes on a staccato bluntness when it comes to discussing pluralism. Here the mask drops and the diplomacy is suspended. "After the Christian majority takes control," one fundamentalist announced in the heyday of the Christian Right, "pluralism will be seen as immoral and evil, and the state will not permit anyone the right to practice evil."[6] At once the golden rule is forgotten. The powerful longing for a hand on the helm drives out all memories of earlier days under the hatches.

We thus have a conservative "pretext pluralism" as a counterpart to the "procedural pluralism" on the liberal side. Neither does justice to pluralism in the long run, although the removers threaten to deprive pluralism by emptying it of all substance whereas the reimposers threaten to dominate pluralism by filling it exclusively with their own. Gary North, one of the leading Christian reconstructionists, provides a chillingly clear warning in a manner reminiscent of Marxist attitudes to liberal pluralism. "So let us be blunt about it: we must use the doctrine of religious liberty to gain independence for Christian schools until we train up a generation of people who know that there is no religious neutrality, no neutral law, no neutral education, and no neutral civil government. Then they will get busy in constructing a Bible-based social, political, and religious order which finally denies the religious liberties of the enemies of God."[7]

Most reimposers have a low threshold of tolerance for nuances. Yet the entire position courts failure because it will not face up to distinctions that are all-important to religious liberty in a pluralistic society—including the difference between respecting a person's right to believe and accepting or rejecting the rightness of that belief. Respecting the right to believe anything is a matter of freedom of conscience; believing that anything anyone believes is right is plain stupidity. The Williamsburg Charter declares, "The right to argue for any public policy is a fundamental right for every citizen; respecting that right is a fundamental responsibility for all other citizens. When any view is expressed, all must uphold as constitutionally protected its advocate's rights to express it. But others are free to challenge that view as politically pernicious, philosophically false, ethically evil, theologically idolatrous, or simply absurd, as the case may be seen to be. Unless this tension between peace and truth is respected, civility cannot be sustained."[8]

Empires of Their Own

One consequence of the civil public square needs to be stated with no ifs and no buts: There will always be winners and losers. In the conflict of perpetual engagement, some will prevail and others will not. As with human freedom anywhere, the outcome of religious liberty is not the kingdom of heaven on earth but a balance sheet of assets and liabilities. The results are a matter of "for better or worse." This requires saying because the single, strongest misunderstanding of the civil public square is that its goal is to reach a state of harmony beyond disputes. That suspicion is the latest in a series of hydra-headed fallacies that has reared itself at each new stage of the argument. Thus, just as chartered pluralism is *not* ecumenical syncretism and civility is *not* wimpishness, so it needs to be stated plainly that the civil public square is *not* a state of ecumenical harmony beyond tensions or disputes.

At first sight, there appears to be an obvious flaw in the vision. Here we insist that there will always be winners and losers. Earlier we insisted that there must never be a semiestablishment. The two points seem to contradict each other and lead back to the catch-22 of recent years: If "no establish-ment" is transformed into an end rather than a means to religious liberty, then every gain because of "free exercise" automatically becomes a loss because of no establishment. Similarly here, the invitation to win appears to be a no-win invitation that is fated to be prohibited as a semiestablishment just as soon as it succeeds.

The apparent contradiction evaporates quickly, however, when we remember two things: first, the problem of semiestablishment applies only to institutions with official government standing, such as public schools, and, second, the sphere of public life is far wider in democratic societies than the sphere of government. The civil public square therefore represents both a decisive veto and a genuine invitation. The same faiths that must never be given preferred, let alone official, status in the public school are free to compete and prevail in a thousand other spheres of public life. In fact, the maxim of principled participation can properly be extended: Within constitutional limits and in accord with the mutually binding compact on religious liberty, people of all faiths and worldviews, transcendental or naturalistic, can enter freely and engage fully with all others concerned with the affairs of public life—including the freedom to claim as much social space as they are able to win and hold through the integrity and effectiveness of their beliefs and resources.

Probably the best American example of a small community making the most of such democratic participation is the remarkable story of the Jews in Hollywood. Jewish influence in scholarship, the arts, and the media generally is as distinguished and well deserved as it is disproportionate to the numerical size of the Jewish community. (A survey of the media elite in 1985 showed that 14 percent were Jewish and almost one in four—23 percent— were raised in a Jewish home.)[9] Jews have sometimes achieved extraordinary success in fields outside those of the mind. But no achievement rivals that of the small group of Eastern European Jews who both pioneered and invented Hollywood and, through their dream factories, fashioned even the American Dream after the image of their aspirations.

From writers to directors and producers, from talent agencies and movie palaces to the legendary companies, such as Metro Goldwyn Mayer, Universal, Warner Brothers, Paramount, and Fox, the influence of the first generation of Jews who founded Hollywood was, in Neal Gabler's summary, "so powerful that, in a sense, they colonized the American imagination."[10] The point has to be made with care because there is not only precedent in the enterprise and paradox in the result. There is also pathos, in that it was the very brilliance of the Jewish success that opened them up to vicious anti-Semitism in the early twenties—when they were accused of conspiring against the very traditional American ideals they were so desperately seeking to embrace.

The evil of anti-Semitism has always thrived on the evidence of such success. Opinion polls between 1938 and 1941, for example, showed that between a third and a half of the American public believed the Jews had "too much power in the United States." During World War II the proportion rose to 56 percent.[11] Similarly today, black Muslim minister Louis Farrakahn charges that "the Jewish lobby has a stranglehold on the government."[12] This deep prejudice was a core factor behind the appalling record of American indifference to the Nazi extermination of European Jewry, and from the impeccably liberal president and the impeccably liberal churches downward the indifference has been chronicled incontrovertibly.[13] Yet the prejudice was not only profoundly evil, it was flagrantly un-American. The alleged "Jewish power" was a direct result of Jewish enterprise and Jewish voluntarism—in short, of principled participation in the American experiment.

No, Not That

An understanding of principled participation would help to address many of the confusions in recent controversies, for example those surrounding "equal access" in the 1980s. With school-sponsored prayer in public schools declared unconstitutional, the spillover effect had been to victimize religious free expression at all points in the school day. Absurdly, student discussion of Marxism was considered legitimate but discussion of the Bible was prohibited. The Equal Access Act of 1984 was therefore a careful attempt to safeguard religious freedom of expression in situations that were voluntary, out of class hours, and not led by teachers, while not challenging the purpose and effect of the ban on official school worship. Neither the bill's architects, nor its sponsors, Senator Mark Hatfield and Representative Don Bonker, were supporters of prayer in public schools.

Not until 1990, however, was the concept of equal access put on a surer footing by the support of the Supreme Court in the *Mergens* decision. For six years, due to the lack of a public philosophy and confusion over the kind of points clarified in the principle of participation, many on either side were able to obscure the issues to their own advantage. All of them portrayed the purpose of equal access inaccurately as the first step toward the restoration of school prayer. The difference was that, whereas one side opposed the first step as the beginning of the slippery slope to reestablishment, the other welcomed it as a sure move back to that very end.

An understanding of principled participation also speaks to the wisdom and effectiveness of different styles of public engagement. For example, many concerned activists on both the Left and the Right have mistakenly concluded that the sure road to power is politicization—the transformation of all issues into political issues in order to advance a cultural agenda. Curiously, politicization had developed fast in the 1960s and served left-wing agendas because of its inherently radicalizing and secularizing style. Which made it all the more odd to see it adopted so enthusiastically in the 1980s by conservatives. Yet Tim LaHaye might almost have been quoting his sixties nemeses when he argued, "Almost everything is political these days. We've begun to realize that government is the most powerful human force in the world."[14]

The Christian Right was criticized strongly for such politicizations. For some critics, politicization was leading conservative activists to positions that were un-Christian. Yugoslav evangelical leader Peter Kusmic charged that "the problem with some North American evangelicals is that they are not asking what is right and what is wrong. Rather they are asking what is Right and what is Left—even though the latter question is far less biblical than the former."[15] For other critics, politicization was leading conservative activists toward a style of engagement that was unconservative and, in the end, undemocratic. Maintaining boundaries between politics and society is a defining feature of liberal democracy, in contrast to authoritarian societies where all social relations from boardrooms to bedrooms are politicized. As Richard Neuhaus declares, "The first thing to be said about public life is that public life is *not* the first thing."[16]

Similar confusions are behind the passion for a "politics of symbol" that has been a feature of the culture wars. The style itself is natural in America in the eighties, born of both a society dominated by communications ("Window-dressing," Bertrand Russell once remarked, "seems inevitable to Americans")[17] and a war centered on the turf battles of cultural territoriality. Each issue is therefore symbolic as both a sound bite and a yard of turf. Typically, an aide to Senator Orrin Hatch who tacked the secular humanist ban onto the 1984 law told the *Washington Post* that "in part it's a symbolic thing." Similar justifications were made repeatedly by those fighting for prayer in public schools or for nativity scenes on public property.[18] "This will show them," seemed to be the attitude. "The sleeping giant has woken up and won't be pushed around again."

What the Religious Right forgot was that symbolic victories gained in this way are hollow and self-defeating. School prayers as vacuous as those recommended by the New York Regents might be allowed again or nativity scenes permitted as justified by the Supreme Court in the Pawtucket case in 1984. But such symbolic victories would be pyrrhic, for in today's circumstances Christian activists would win the fight with one of two results. Either they would scandalize their opponents or else they would secularize themselves.

To anyone not blindly consumed with political muscle flexing, the first of these dangers should be obvious. Christmas is not shared by all Americans, so to press for it as a public celebration in a litigiously acrimonious way is a living contradiction of its message. (One Rhode Island citizen who favored a public representation of the newborn "Prince of peace" threatened his opponents: "If you want peace, back off here.")[19] The less obvious danger is that Christians would succeed in secularizing their own Christian symbols. Christmas is a religious celebration, so it is never merely commercial. However many Santa Clauses and candy-striped poles are added, Christmas is either essentially religious or it is nothing. A U.S. Court of Appeals may allow a crèche on the Ellipse "to promote tourism," or the Supreme Court may permit one in Rhode Island because "it appears as part of the country's otherwise secular celebration of the Christmas holiday."[20] But this rationale should cause Christians to pause. Such symbolic victories make Christmas as hollow as the winter solstice festival that Christmas originally replaced.

Needless to say, to argue against a politics of symbol does not need to mean pressing for the instant and automatic removal of all religious symbols from public property, because the opposing arguments are often equally weak. Some Christians put too much faith in public symbols; others have too many fears about them. To claim, for instance, that the erection of a nativity scene on the White House Ellipse represents an "establishment" is as absurd as the claim that it would have been an "establishment" to commemorate the five-hundredth anniversary of Martin Luther with a stamp. People who make such claims have either forgotten what an established religion is or failed to notice the variety of religious symbols on the Mall. (During an earlier visit to Washington, blazing Hindu gods, American Indian prayer ceremonies, and a thirty-foot Menorah erected by the Lubavicher Hasidim were noted.)

Put differently, principled participation not only stands against such confusions as these, it ties in with observations on nineteenth-century religion made by Tocqueville. In America, he noted, the influence of religion is all the stronger because it is not political and direct, but spiritual, moral, and indirect. Although religion is disestablished, even the influence of religious leaders can remain limited and long-distance because the power of religion is exercised where it is wisest and most effective. "Religion takes no direct part in the government of their society, but it must be regarded as the first of their political institutions."[21]

Things are quite different today. In what has become a busy two-way street, religion and politics have influenced each other directly and politically. In 1984, Jerry Falwell returned exultant from the National Religious Broadcasters' Convention. "President Reagan brought a tremendous message," he announced. "It would be proper for delivery in any pulpit in America."[22]

Falwell's remark reveals less about the state of fundamentalist politics and more about the state of the fundamentalist pulpit and the crisis of cultural authority. For there is a definite logic by which faiths operate best in a democracy. Under either the "total state" or the "total church," the chief movement of a ideology or religion is, socially speaking, always direct and from the top down. But in a democratic society where principled participation is flourishing, their chief movement is always indirect and from the bottom up. These social flow-lines are the exact opposite of the spiritual flow-lines. For, spiritually speaking, religion is always regarded and treated as being "under" a total state whereas it is "above" a democratic society.

This means that in a democracy the state will always be a reflection of its own society, just as the society will be the creation of the countless faiths and moral principles that inspire and shape it. Thus in a pluralistic democracy each faith, whether transcendent or naturalistic, Western or Eastern, modern or traditional, exercises its primary shaping power morally and indirectly rather than politically and directly. Instead of any faith being promulgated from above, each must penetrate and influence from below.

This is the sense in which it was said that each faith can claim only the social space it can win and occupy. Only insofar as its adherents influence institutions and its perspectives influence issues can any faith be said to have culture-shaping power in democracy. Thus, far from seeking to ignore any contest of powers, principled participation acknowledges it openly but makes it competitive within the bounds of pluralism rather than coercive within the bounds of semiestablishmentarianism. In this sense, principled participation is a spiritual form of free enterprise and relies in the same way on qualities such as voluntarism and enterprise.

Persuade or Perish

We now turn to the second of the two governing principles that empower the free exercise of religious liberty in the civil public square—principled persuasion. Within constitutional limits and in accord with the mutually binding compact on religious liberty, people of all faiths and worldviews are free to seek, through persuasion, to effect real change in public life—from hearts and minds to public opinion to law. Private claims in public life, while legitimate, need to be made publicly comprehensible and compelling to be effective.

The public square is the meeting place of different people and different claims to truth. If principled participation deals more with action, principled persuasion deals more with communication. If principled participation is the expression of the freedom that is central to the civil public square, principled persuasion is the expression of the duty that is central to the civil public square. As the Williamsburg Charter states, "Those who claim the right to participate should accept the responsibility to persuade."[23]

The present moment is ripe for a national recovery of persuasion. With the deepening crisis of cultural authority, the collapse of the traditional consensus, and the intermittent outbreak of the culture wars, American public discourse has degenerated into a bitter contentiousness that borders on ideological civil war. It has loosed an unholy trio of consequences—insistent demands, irreconcilable differences, and interminable disagreements. Trust is out, tribalism in. Reasoned argument has been replaced by unargued assertion and attack, while the rhetoric of protest, pronouncements, and posturing has drowned that of persuasion. For every liberal who resorts to a court in the absence of persuasion, there will be a conservative who resorts to a crusade. Good suits to one side and good "wars" to the other have become the substitute for a good case.

To try to bring a corrective to this state of affairs based on a weak stomach for disagreements or on a reluctance to play political hardball would be useless. Either principled persuasion is tougher-minded and more realistic than realpolitik or it will not work. To say this is not bravado. Debate and persuasion are so incontrovertibly central to liberal democracy that if freedom and justice are its lifeblood, debate and persuasion are its oxygen. Not only that, in America's case the centrality of persuasion grows directly out of three impulses that are both deeply American and fundamental to religious liberty—conscience, pluralism, and the First Amendment.

The first American impulse to persuasion is the argument from conscience. By beginning here, the argument for persuasion becomes one of urgent and universal moral principle straightaway. It is not a matter of diffidence, pragmatism, or utopianism. As the turbulent conflicts of the Reformation established slowly and painfully, the only true worship is that offered to God freely and uncoerced. If the conscience is inviolable, coercion of conscience is evil, and truth is plain and strong, it follows that compelled beliefs are a contradiction in terms. Commitment in faith must be uncoerced and persuasion must win consent. Anything else easily becomes a form of "conscience-rape" (Nietzsche), a violation of human personality and truth, and an affront not only to human beings but to God.[24]

The argument from conscience is at the heart of Roger Williams's stand for soul liberty, or what he called "absolute permission of conscience" from state coercion. Developing the Puritan concept that the individual conscience was a means of communication with God, Williams insisted that each person, including those in error, must be allowed the freedom to follow his or her own heart in matters of faith. When it comes to conscience, the use of force is both evil—a form of "spiritual rape" and "soul oppression"—and utterly ineffective. Coercion produces hypocrisy, not conviction. Conscious of the "torrents of blood" shed by persecutors, Williams's attacks on coercion were fierce and unsparing. "Sir," he wrote to the governor of the Massachusetts Bay Colony, "I must be humbly bold to say that 'tis impossible for any man or men to maintain their Christ by their sword and to worship a true Christ, to fight against all consciences opposite to theirs and not to fight against God."[25]

The same argument was also at the heart of George Calvert's Maryland, probably derived directly from Sir Thomas More's *Utopia*. Utopus, More had written, "made it a law that every man might be of what religion he pleased, and might endeavor to draw others to it by the force of argument and by amicable and modest ways, but without bitterness against those of other opinions; but that he ought to use no other force than that of persuasion."[26] Before the founding of Maryland, this principle inspired Catholic dissent in Elizabeth's England, though only within the privilege of Parliamentary speaking. In 1571, Edward Aglionby had declared, "There should be no human positive law to enforce conscience; . . . the conscience of man is eternal, invisible, and not in the power of the greatest monarchy in the world, in any limits to be straightened, in any bounds to be contained, nor with any policy of man, if once decayed, to be again raised."[27]

Two centuries after More and one after Williams and Calvert, the same clarion notes sounded out from Jefferson and Madison, climaxing in Madison's *Memorial and Remonstrance* in 1785. "Because we hold it for a fundamental and undeniable truth, 'that religion or the duty which we owe our Creator and the manner of discharging it, can be directed only by reason and conviction, not by force or violence.' The religion then of every man must be left to the conviction and conscience of every man; and it is the right of every man to exercise it as these may dictate. This right is in its nature an unalienable right."[28]

Because of the primacy of conscience, inner conviction lies prior even to outer expression. Religious liberty is therefore the "first liberty" not only historically but logically. It is truly the most fundamental liberty of all and the source and pattern of all other liberties. Only where it has gone before and is well protected are other human rights likely to remain safe from erosion and violation. All the basic rights of the First Amendment are indissolubly linked, but as Leo Pfeffer affirmed, "Religious freedom is the progenitor of practically all our freedoms and in that respect it is the most important of them."[29]

Today, more than two centuries after Jefferson and Madison and three after Williams, their argument from conscience has grown uncertain to modern ears. With truth and reason dissolving into relativism and irrationality, and mind into will, a subtle but devastating change has occurred. Above all, as Michael Sandel of Harvard has analyzed, freedom of conscience has been replaced by freedom of choice. "But freedom of conscience and freedom of choice are not the same; where conscience dictates, choice decides. Where freedom of conscience is at stake, the relevant right is to exercise a duty, not make a choice."[30] In fact, "it is precisely because belief is not governed by the will that freedom of conscience is unalienable. Even if he would, a person could not give it up."[31]

The argument from conscience has fallen on bad times today, though it is basic to the impulse to persuasion. But such is its importance to both conservatism and liberalism that its recovery will be an index of their recovery as much as it is of persuasion.

A People of Persuasion

The second American impulse to persuasion comes from the argument from pluralism. From the very beginning of the Middle Colonies, William Penn's policy of religious liberty made Pennsylvania a polyglot, or multilanguage experience, of seventeenth-century religions. Most of the world's existing Protestant groups were there—Presbyterians, Anglicans, Dutch and German Reformed, Swedish and German Lutherans, Mennonites, Quakers, Dunkers, Schwenkfelders, Moravians, and assorted hermits and eccentrics, as well as Catholics and Jews. Moreover, the Pennsylvania mix included a high proportion of those considered "nonconformists" in Europe. Penn's dream of a colony with freedom for people of all races and religions was Roger Williams's radical experiment in religious liberty under deeply pluralistic conditions.

From then on, pluralism with all its opportunities and challenges has been at the heart of "the first new nation"—so much so that the American experiment can be viewed as a national embodiment of pluralism and persuasion as much as it is of freedom. For if pluralism is strong, growing, and here to stay, persuasion is a prerequisite for national unity as well as public discourse. Only through persuasion can free people speak together and stay together. In this sense, persuasion is a corollary of citizenship just as coercion is its contradiction. Totalitarian coercion is the blood brother of the totalitarian claim and both can be bent to the total transformation of society. But persuasion is intrinsic to a free republic. As William Lee Miller states, "The United States was to a much greater extent than other nations the product of collaborative human contrivance, of reason and conscience, of deliberation." Its own beginning is "an example of that governance by mutual persuasion that is its own main point."[32]

This point, as we saw earlier, is fundamental to the covenantal tradition that flowered in the Constitution. It can be seen clearly in the logic of "We the people," which creates in America a constitutional need for consent and therefore for the place of persuasion, discussion, negotiation, and brokerage. If a democratic republic containing such diversity is not to be torn asunder, the reverse side of the right to dissent is the responsibility to debate. The Civil War is a searing reminder that, once agreement breaks down, the founding principles of the republic offer no recourse, except force, when consent is withheld.

One of the valuable lessons of the sixties was the stark focus it brought to America's foundational need for consent. This requirement is an American strength that can easily become a weakness because it leaves the republic peculiarly vulnerable in any period attracted to revolution, not least when its sons and daughters become revolutionary. Revolutionary rhetoric is consciously built on the idea of the total overthrow of the existing order, so its demands are made deliberately nonnegotiable. Those privy to the will of history cannot brook argument and need not tarry for consent. As George Steiner notes, the sixties-style graffiti violence, the clenched-fist silence of the adolescent, the mumble of the drop-out, the silence of the stoned, and the nonsense-cries of the stage happening were no accident. The counterculture's strategy of demolition began with a refusal to "bandy words."[33]

The same point needs to be remembered in the culture wars of the early nineties, or at any time when the explicit goal of the rhetoric is to provoke confrontation, not find consensus. It is always a symptom of the pathology of pluralism when politics becomes a constant conflict over ends. In the face of such an implacable style, persuasion appears weak. The remedy for democracy, however, is to remember that when the common good is presumed and persuasion and consent are actively engaged and prevail, the desperation that breeds such belligerence need never grow.

Madison's Miraculous Process

The third American impulse to persuasion is the legacy of the First Amendment, which becomes as decisive an impetus toward persuasion as it was a decisive encodement of freedoms. Prior to the Bill of Rights, the prime example of the benefits of persuasion was the American Revolution itself. Europe in the eighteenth century was awash in insults and invective. English pamphleteering in particular, such as could be found in the political writing of Jonathan Swift, was marked by the savage intensity of its scorn, rage, hate, and satire. Demagoguery thrived and public accusations were leveled in America too—John Hancock was said to be impotent, George Washington was the corrupter of a washerwoman's daughter, and so on—but there was also an astonishing reasonableness in American public argument that was both different and effective.

This accent on persuasiveness had profound consequences. At the heart of the most creative period in the history of American political thought was what historian Bernard Bailyn has described as "this great, transforming debate."[34] Revolutionary writers, he notes, sought to convince, not to annihilate. Since the goal was not to overthrow an existing order but to preserve liberty threatened by corruption, "the communication of understanding, therefore, lay at the heart of the Revolutionary movement. . . . The reader is led through arguments, not images. The pamphlets aim to persuade."[35] Far more than accumulated grievances were at the heart of the American revolution. It was fired by the overwhelming persuasiveness of the cause. The capstone of this remarkable tradition was the First Amendment. Through it, persuasion—one of the specifically religious contributions to the revolution—was stamped onto American society forever. "The essence of the revolution," wrote Sidney Mead of the revolution in church-state relations, "was the rejection of coercion in favor of persuasion."[36]

Such is the place and importance of pluralism in the late twentieth century that Madison, not Marx, is often called the most prescient prognosticator of the modern world. As Madison saw it, political liberty and social justice both stem from the free interplay of competing groups and ideas. His vision, which James O'Toole terms "Madison's miraculous process," is even more fitting today.[37] The more advanced a society becomes, the less it is held together by the traditional bonds of family, religion, neighborhood, ethnicity, and shared civic beliefs and the more it is subject to the conflict of competing groups and interests. No pluralistic society can satisfy all interests and no concept of public justice can be settled for all time. But as the dynamic process of democracy moves forward, striking a creative balance somewhere near its moving center, one thing is sure: The only way to power is through persuasion in the pluralistic process.

Never in One's Best Trousers

"One should never put on one's best trousers to go out to battle for freedom and truth."[38] To anyone armed, mounted, and misty-eyed at the prospect of jousting for truth and justice, Henrik Ibsen's homespun advice is an excellent antidote to disillusionment. Truth is certainly great and one day, we may believe, it will prevail. But the work of today, tomorrow, and the next day is likely to be more mundane with as many setbacks as advances. And perhaps the greatest discouragement of all is the realization as to how few are willing to enter the lists and debate.

As at so many points in the controversies over religion and public life, there is a "barbell" effect when it comes to persuasion. At one end, those who are toward the removers extreme discourage persuasion because they allow only a neutralized language in the public square. (One such person declares: "Nobody has the right to vindicate political authority by asserting a privileged insight into the moral universe which is denied to the rest of us. . . . No reason is a good reason if it requires the power-holder to assert that his conception of the good is better than that asserted by any of his fellow citizens.")[39] At the other end, those who are toward the reimposers are equally discouraging because they insist on their own particularistic language bellowed out in the public square without translation. The result is a babel of confusion that is neither free, constitutional, or effective.

On the liberal side, the equivalent of the fear of "imposition" in law is the fear of "proselytism" in persuasion. Persuasion, to be sure, is always relative. One person's "sharing" can be another person's "pushing," just as the latter's "persuasion" can be the former's "proselytism." But it is another matter altogether—illogical as well as illiberal—for liberals to duck the challenge of debate by endlessly crossing themselves and muttering "proselytism." For surely nothing should define liberal thinking more than its openness to new thoughts, new evidence, new challenges—in short, its openness to persuasion.

Evidence of the closing of the liberal mind over proselytizing is plentiful. Among atheists, Jon Murray declares a new right: "The right of the secularists not to have the gospel spread to them."[40] When it comes to the Jewish community, responses to Christian witness are more understandable, both historically and sociologically. But repeated overreactions to evangelism do little credit to the Jewish sense of identity and liberalism, especially when the Jewish community enjoys so much growth through mixed marriages. As for academia, one of liberalism's most hilarious examples of liberals against persuasion was the solemn-toned "Resolution on Religious Proselytizing" adopted in April 1987 by the United Ministry at Harvard and Radcliffe. In direct denial of both the founder of their faith and the intellectual ethos of their great institution, these liberal scions of Harvard's religious elite solemnly covenanted themselves to desist from any and all religious persuasion.[41]

Things are little better on the other side. Most Christian liberals may have abandoned evangelistic persuasion altogether and clustered under the banner, "Don't defend, dialogue!" But most Christian conservatives have long resorted to the rallying cry, "Don't persuade, proclaim!" Thus persuasive advocacy has fallen out of fashion in the conservative camp too. Persuasionlessness in the private world has been translated in the eighties into persuasionlessness in the public world. The way has been opened for the recent pendulumlike swing toward the high-voltage politics of protest and "prophetic" pronouncements from both the Left and the Right.

At best, many of the recent consequences of abandoning persuasion have been illogical. The Religious Right has attacked the sociological relativism of the thinking that "fifty-one percentism" in law makes something right and then turned round to display a crude reliance on majoritarianism. Worse still for them, the extreme rhetoric has been self defeating. At the very moment when they needed persuasion most in their movement, they turned their backs on it. Instead, verbal aggression fostered a climate in which bombers and burners grew in their own ranks, while over in their opponents' camp it nourished the myth that all religious conservatives by definition are fanatics who are maladjusted to modernity. Both problems combine to show that, without persuasion, the conservative attempt to gain power is likely to be either high-handed or short-lived.

Curiously, however, the end of the 1980s also saw a doubling-back by conservatives toward the sensitivity language of liberals. This led not only to the talk of a Christian antidefamation league discussed earlier, but to a change in the notion of blasphemy—and persuasion. Blasphemy, as Michael Walzer points out, was originally thought of as a crime against God. But it has now become an offense against the faithful—of all faiths. As pluralism increases, blasphemy becomes "an ecumenical crime."[42] When Muslims pronounced Salman Rushdie's *The Satanic Verses* blasphemous, Cardinal John O'Connor asked New York Catholics not to read it, the chief rabbi of Britain urged its banning, and many Christian conservatives defended the Muslim response and likened Rushdie's crime to Martin Scorsese's treatment of Jesus in his film *The Last Temptation of Christ*.

Conservative sensitivities toward blasphemy as an ecumenical crime are misplaced. This may not seem wise to say at a time when the American airwaves are turning blue with the gratuitous violence and insultry of rap groups, such as 2 Live Crew, and comedians, such as Andrew "Dice" Clay. Neither theology nor civility require such a nonaggression pact. Gratuitous insults are just that, but a conviction-based iconoclasm that is blasphemous to one faith may be a moral requirement of another. To lay the axe to false idols and debunk sacred cows is liberating rather than insulting. As Michael Walzer says of the state of blasphemy in civil law, "God has to look after himself these days." For those who believe he is well able to do so, it becomes all the more absurd that human beings puff themselves up with purported injury in his place. Further, "the fact that people take offense is no reason to call on the state to ensure that offense is not given, for that will only encourage people to take offense—when what they should do is argue back or, sometimes, to mock and disdain in their turn."[43] Civility is neither for faint hearts nor weak faiths.

What would happen if principled persuasion did not work out and the double-drive toward neutralizing and privatizing were to run to the end? The outcome would be an America torn between a scattering of groups and communities who are able to talk convincingly only to those who agree with them, and a state making public decisions that are increasingly meaningless to most people because the decisions are so alienated from people's own private ends.

All those committed to principled persuasion must endeavor to argue and defend their case in the open forum of ideas, always consistent with three requirements. The first is that people and truth should always be viewed as ends, not cynically used as means. Thus the distinction between moral persuasion and immoral manipulation must be kept paramount, whether in private speech, commercial advertising, or political campaigning. While any means that effectively wins a person to our point of view may be deemed successful, only those that appeal to proper grounds for choice are legitimately persuasive rather than manipulative.

The second requirement is that the substance and style of the language be publicly comprehensible, not simply private. While some believers have made public claims that bear little or no relation to any religious convictions, others have limited their public claims to private convictions shouted out loud. (The result is rather like an American in Paris repeating his message louder and more slowly in English rather than trying to learn how it is said in French.) All too often the first method is not consistent and the second not persuasive. For persuasion to be both principled and effective, private convictions must be translated into public claims, personal doctrines carried over convincingly into public discourse.

The final requirement is that the effort to persuade needs to be viewed actively, not passively. Both theological realism and the democratic process acknowledge the value of compromise, which is the reverse side of the quest for consensus and consent. But when viewed passively, the need for consent or compromise is easily corrupted into acquiescence before the status quo. Truth thrives on conflict and correction, so the last thing a believer wants is either indifference or indoctrination because both eliminate the conditions in which truth best prospers. Equally, consensus is never static or permanent. It is a living, hard-won agreement wrested from chaos through dynamic, continuous interaction between consensus and criticism. Only when viewed actively do consensus and compromise take their proper place in persuasion. The victories of the civil rights movement, in this sense, were won by forging one consensus against another consensus, the new consensus actively persuaded to overturn the old.

In fulfilling such requirements, principled persuasion provides an on-going reminder of democracy's unity and diversity. True to the content of its arguments, commitment to persuasion represents the diversity in democracy that makes public persuasion necessary. True to the purpose and manner of its arguments, it represents the unity in democracy that makes public persuasion possible. It therefore joins the other components of the civil public square and helps to make possible a public life whose equality of liberty guarantees justice and whose security of justice guarantees liberty.

A Revolution Every Twenty Years

Will this proposal for a civil public square be acceptable to a sufficient number of Americans to reforge a national consensus on the place of religious liberty in public life? And to put the contentious extremism of the last generation behind us? Can it contribute to the resolution of the crisis of cultural authority? Or is it simply writing on the sand in a time of hurricanes and floods? Time will show, but at least one thing is clear. Americans will have to speak out while standing above their own interests and standing back from their own corners of the struggle.

A striking characteristic of the Founders, and one that is light years from the present single-issue myopia, was their profound sense of history. Feeling the winds of history blowing around them, they rose above their day and lavished on their acts, thoughts, and documents the time and wisdom that made them great and lasting. "It has been the will of Heaven," John Adams wrote in 1776, "that we should be thrown into existence at a period when the greatest philosophies and lawgivers of antiquity would have wished to live. . . . How few of the human race have ever had any opportunity of choosing a system of government for themselves and their children."[44]

But while heralding the new, they also saw the need for ongoing renewal. It was in this context that George Mason wrote of "frequent recurrence to fundamental principles" and Jefferson of having a revolution every twenty years. Just as the twin concepts of conversion and covenant required each other in Puritan understanding, so also did revolution and constitution in the eighteenth century's. Both conversion and revolution were primary and dynamic and could be maintained only through the secondary, more stabilizing, effects of covenant and constitution. The latter needed the former as much as the former needed the latter. Thus, like the Puritan Commonwealth before it, the American republic will never be more great and lasting than the dynamic conservatism of its underlying ideals and institutions. A republic that cannot return to its first principles is a republic that is in its last days.

To the revolutionary leaders, of course, the Constitution was far more than parchment and ink. It was something believed in and backed by a free people because it included everything that constituted the essential arrangement of their society—American institutions, laws, and customs, along with the ideals and goals that gave them life. No nation is founded and no great nation can survive on ink alone. Like the constitution of a human body, as

John Adams saw it, the U.S. Constitution rested on certain essentials and fundamentals that were "parts without which life itself cannot be preserved a moment."[45]

The convergence of the recent controversies with the celebration of the bicentennial of the Bill of Rights therefore presented a golden opportunity. But unless major national reappraisal leading to a reaffirmation, a rededication, and a reconstitution of the essential principles occurs in the next few years, the dislocated relationship of America's faiths and freedom will harden and what best animates American democracy will be lost. Once again, the conclusion is plain: Religion in America is far from being a nonissue or a mere nuisance factor. The religious issue is much more than a question of the rights of religious believers in modern society. An essential part of American heritage is being called into question and with it the vitality and viability of the American republic itself. No modern country can less afford a schism of the spirit. A house divided against itself still cannot stand. The American republic divided against itself goes to its ruin.

PART THREE
THE COMING AMERICA

The Tourneying Hopes

At several points in the discussion I may have given the impression that the United States stands at the crossroads as hesitantly and uncertainly as a solitary thinker—rather as if Rodin's brooding *penseur* were confronted by a spaghetti junction for the first time. No image could be more misleading. As the crisis of cultural authority reaches its climax, the American scene has all the color, noise, drama, and rivalry of a medieval tournament. Even a quick glance is enough to take in the grandstand pageantry and peacock posturing. A closer look, however, reveals that, while some are fighting over old loyalties and old rivalries, the chief contestants are jousting in deadly earnest for the main prize—the hand of America's future. The struggle is over defining and directing America.

We turn now to look at the prospects for an American renaissance raised by these tourneying hopes, for one central point must not be overlooked. Behind a thousand local skirmishes about points of law, textbooks in schools and libraries, bias in the press and media, and sensitivities over language, two things stand: the rival groups and philosophies in hot contention with each other, and the different possible outcomes for America that would follow in the train of their respective success. "America today," as *Time*'s editor-in-chief wrote at its sixtieth anniversary, "is less a 'story' than an argument."[1]

This means that it is a mistake to treat any of the culture-wars conflicts in isolation or fall for any simplistic formulation of futures, such as boom or bust, renewal or decline, progress or nostalgia. It is also unwise to be taken in by the current fashion for futurespeak and suppose that any person or party has a monopoly on hope or the future. The issue today is not the Party of Hope versus the Party of Memory as Ralph Waldo Emerson stated, because in today's situation memory plays a key part in hope. Many current variations of the culture wars are no better. Formulating the issue as the future versus the past, fresh ideas versus stale ideas, or the new generation versus the old generation is almost always window dressing. The real question is not, hope or not? But rather, which hope? Who says? On what grounds? And with what consequences?

I will not be making grand predictions about America's future. In the first place, I do not know what will happen and to pretend otherwise would be ridiculous. To adapt Karl Kraus, I am not a prophet, nor a prophet facing backward like a historian, nor even someone who needs afterward to know everything beforehand like certain pundits. There are terribly few people who can truly predict, and futurists, Marxists, and crystal-ball gazers are not among them. The few trends that can be identified reliably soon trail off into the mists of the near future. Beyond that lies the virtual darkness of the medium and long-term futures. The gulf between foresight and hindsight is notoriously wide. Foreswearing futurehype, being conscious of one's ignorance, and making ignorance a conscious premise in thinking about the future are all a virtue and a necessity. "Carefree shortsightedness," Solzhenitsyn wrote, "is sometimes the heart's salvation. God forbid that we should at certain times, see too sensitively into the future."[2]

Besides, whether originating from secular versions, such as trend-spotting, or from religious ones, such as charismatic utterances, end-of-the-world predictions, or ecclesiastical pronunciamentos by self-anointed prophets, the current vogue for futurehype is dangerous. The spurious plausibility of such predictions has little to do with their accuracy and much to do with the powerful modern hunger for meaning and belonging. But apart from being bogus, they have another snag. Instead of strengthening initiative and resolve, they sap them. Today's only certain prediction is that we will suffer a plague of false predictions tomorrow.

As Václav Havel observes, "If there is a sphere whose very nature precludes all prognostication, it is that of culture."[3] Thus, rather than a forecast, what follows in Part Three is a discussion of the broad possible directions or outcomes most likely to result from the crisis of cultural authority. As such, I address the same general field of factors that many discuss today, but with the same central difference from most of the current discussions. I again insist on taking the religious factor seriously because of its central place in the crisis of cultural authority. As Havel adds, "The secrets of culture's future are a reflection of the very secrets of the human spirit."[4]

Including the religious factor is not intended to be a case of special pleading. Nor does it prejudge the outcome unfairly. In the next quarter century, American religion could make more difference through its public weakness than it has previously through its strength. In which case, like Samson in the temple of the Philistines, *religio agonistes* could have an even greater impact in the twilight of its decline than in the high noon of its power.

But regardless of that, given the role of religion in American history, its comparative strength today, and the special nature of the present national and social issues, we must recognize that the relationship of religion and society will be more significant for the United States than for any other highly modernized society in the near future. More specifically, I will argue that the religious factor will be pivotal to the outcome of the time of testing outlined earlier through either its strength or weakness in the public square over the next two decades. This outcome will in turn be critical for the resolution of America's crisis of cultural authority.

Once the religious factor is taken seriously, it points to the probability that America's future lies in one of four broad general directions. Underlying them all is the watershed question: Will religion in America continue to prove decisive in American public life and, depending on the answer, will this effect be harmful or beneficial? In the case of the first two possible outcomes, the basic assumption is that religion will no longer be a decisive factor in American public life. One possibility extends this assumption in an optimistic direction for the nation, assuming that religion will not be decisive and it will not matter nationally. The other extends it in a more pessimistic direction, assuming that religion will not be decisive and it will matter. In the case of the last two possible outcomes, the basic assumption is that religion will remain a decisive national factor. One possibility extends this decisiveness in a way that would be harmful for the nation, and the other in a way that would be beneficial.

Doubtless the future will not be as tidy as these four descriptions. But to wrestle with them is a useful step toward a future of choice rather than one of drift or fate. First, we must explore the challenge of the third major part of the national crisis of cultural authority—the testing of America's republican character.

15

The Testing of Republican Character

Until recently, if anyone asked Americans what was the greatest danger facing the United States, they typically pointed to something external. Quite apart from periods of special ebullience such as the eighties, Americans commonly believe that their ideals and resources are so strong and enduring that, short of some dire calamity, the chances of a decisive break in the pattern of Americanism are unlikely. Thus when Americans discuss a possible testing of the republic, they tend to do so in two ways: external rather than internal crises and crises of detail rather than crises of the whole. What counts most are the dramatic calamities, such as an energy shortage, a terrorist strike, a nuclear confrontation, or (until recently) the worldwide expansion of Soviet imperialism. Much of the success of best-sellers, such as Jean-Francois Revel's *How Democracies Perish*, depends on the assumption that the deepest threats to the United States are external.

This traditional response has lost its sure and centered focus today and, obviously, the burden of this analysis points in a different direction. Arnold Toynbee argued in his monumental study that all of the great civilizations were destroyed from within. Similarly, I contend that, while America's outward problems, such as poverty, drugs, air contamination, and health-care costs are massive and growing, they are no more important than America's inward problems, such as broken families, mediocrity in education, alienation in meaning, and nihilism in popular culture. But the crisis of cultural authority defies such artificial distinctions. It combines aspects of both the outward and the inward because, in the end, the crisis bears on what makes America America. What Václav Havel noted of the West as a whole is specially true of America: "I cannot overcome the impression that western culture is threatened far more by itself than by SS20 rockets."[1]

We have discussed two aspects of this problem so far—the crisis of national identity and the crisis of the public philosophy. We come now to the third aspect of the present time of testing—the crisis of republican character, after which we examine the prospects for an American renaissance. This less noticeable danger is the quiet crisis, a crisis of meaning and behavior that threatens to undermine the health of American democracy.

Aside from the customary preoccupation with external threats, the quiet crisis is likely to be ignored for another reason. Acknowledging it flies in the face of America's prevailing liberal philosophy and the secular climate in public life. On the one hand, the liberal philosophy holds that it is possible to create a just community without just citizens—private character is therefore irrelevant to public justice. Whereas the classical concept of citizenship required public virtue because it linked private character and public service, and both with moral education, the liberal concept requires none. A liberal philosophy assumes only that individuals are self-interested and that self-interested individuals can live together with harmony and justice, given the right framework and procedures. Institutions, not ideals, are what matter. Justice is purely procedural.

On the other hand, the secular climate in public life leads to an instinctive reliance on technical solutions and a deep-rooted aversion to the moral and religious dimensions of problems. In 1990, for example, the American Medical Association and the National Association of State Boards of Education set up a commission that concluded that America's teenagers were plagued with an array of physical and emotional health problems, making them less healthy than their parents were at the same age. Unlike the problems of earlier generations, the commission said in its report, "Code Blue," those of today's teenagers were rooted in behavior rather than in physical illnesses, such as infections and diseases. The commission's solution, however, was improved access to school health services. Without a sense of contradiction, the report pointed out that the findings, for the most part, did not point to a health problem, but then recommended improved medical health as the solution.

In the cases of both the liberal philosophy and the secular climate, such responses are understandable. It is true that the revolutionary character of the American experiment was itself a shift beyond classical concepts of character and virtue. In moving from the old world to the new, Americans lost their former traditions and ties, shifting them in the direction described by liberalism. So individualism came to be the new expression of community and the pursuit of happiness was substituted for virtue. With open frontiers to sustain optimism and the pervasive biblical tradition to provide faith and discipline, the logic of liberalism was both buoyed and balanced and was never tested severely in America—until now.

The crisis of cultural authority is therefore the supreme test for American liberalism. Classical republican themes have grown faint, biblical authority is less compelling to fewer Americans, America's rich opportunities are closing, and liberalism is no longer seriously rivaled in the public square. Yet the liberal view of citizenship, with its academic foundations collapsed, individualism run rampant, and the spread of the therapeutic sensibility posing problems unforeseen by classical liberals, is undergoing a searching scrutiny. Falling electoral participation, rising hate rhetoric, and the growing chasm between behavioral problems and technical solutions are only three of many consequences of a soft modern citizenship that has divorced personal and public virtue. Citizenship and the liberal way of life are increasingly at odds. As Tocqueville warned, extreme individualism is citizenship in default. Or as George Grant concluded at the end of the sixties, "At the height of our present imperial destiny, the crisis of the end of modern rationalism falls upon us ineluctably. In Nietzsche's words: 'the wasteland grows.' "[2] Last Men and nihilists are everywhere in the United States.

Put differently, it is legitimate to be skeptical about Crèvecoeur's exultation over the American "new man," about Horace Mann's seriousness that the public schools would usher in "a new sense of developments in human character and conduct," and about the utopian claims of modern therapeutic techniques.[3] (Arthur Janov of Primal Scream therapy promises "a new kind of human being.")[4] The framers, however, stressed public character in the interest of realism, not utopianism. To make a complete break between republican character and republican community is to defy political gravity, at least as far as the most realistic were concerned. Their "new science of politics" relied on competing interests, but it was never indifferent to civic ideals. As James Russell Lowell declared in the Civil War period, "A decline in stocks is more tolerable and more transient than one in public spirit."[5]

Should the founders' realism be in order, this quiet crisis will call modern optimism into question. It will also determine the character of the philosophical vision and the moral resolve with which the more obvious, external problems in the United States are tackled. And as the crisis of republican character unfolds, it will set the stiffest possible examination for both liberalism and conservatism, for the humanist faith and the Christian faith, or for any other ideological contenders who compete for a say in America's future. By its very nature the quiet crisis is not amenable to purely technical or legislative solutions. It has such obvious urgency and such flesh-and-blood dimensions that none should call it abstract. As with any great republic, so with America: The character of its citizens will be decisive for the character of its society.

Compared with its prominent place in the past, talk of republican character makes only a feeble sound in the public discussion today. So enfeebled is the republican tradition, so resistant the liberal mindset, and so strong the revulsion to virtue talk, "virtuecrats," and a new "Victorianism," that the topic is barely respectable. Yet for all the sophisticated disdain, there is a definite resurgence of interest in virtue among philosophers and educators. One thing brings the topic back to the table again and again—the pressure of events.

From one side, the character issue stems from certain political dilemmas. During the last few years a series of somersaults in public thinking has brought attention back to the character of citizens. Such problems as mediocrity in schools, dependency on welfare, indulgence in deficit spending, and crime were once viewed as essentially rational problems and therefore amenable to purely technical, economic, or legislative solutions. Now, as parents have always known and as Professor James Q. Wilson of UCLA has argued, there is a "growing awareness that a variety of public problems can only be understood—and perhaps addressed—if they are seen as arising out of a defect in character formation." Successful policy, not to mention justice, requires character and the notion of public good just as much as it requires efficient allocation and attractive incentives. "In the long run, the public interest depends on private virtue."[6]

From another side, the character issue stems from certain ethical dilemmas. By refusing to emphasize personal character and by concentrating only on public consequences—the negative rather than the positive— liberalism puts an impossible weight on the question, "Where does one draw the line?" (Between, say, permissible eroticism and impermissible pornography or between the propriety and impropriety of the dealings of former government officials.) Thus, since modern life is so complicated and no line can be drawn precisely in the abstract, let alone a publicly agreed upon line, all that is not prohibited legally becomes permissible socially. The natural result of this stress on "consequences, not character" is a society living at the edges, restrained not by ethics but by emergencies, such as AIDS and drug addiction. When ethics is all borderlines, quandaries, and extremities—as with values clarification—society finds itself living at the extremities with more and more of public life in a quandary.

It is becoming plain that just as conservatives must stress justice to keep society conservative, so liberals must stress character to keep society liberal. By focusing only on consequences, liberals make social problems insoluble and stoke the demand for the government intervention that leaves society less liberal. For example, when such issues as mandatory lie detecting and drug testing are raised, it is a real question as to who is to blame and who loses most: the conservative believer in limited government who eagerly calls for state expansion to limit liberal excesses, or the liberal believer in government nonintervention in private affairs who does nothing to discourage private behavior that is bound to encourage public concern and government intervention.

Despite the logic of these developments, disdain for public virtue in America is so ingrained and out of tune with the self-expressive individualism of the age that a fresh appraisal of character is only likely in the wake of further crisis. But for those concerned to address the problem now, three major developments are at the heart of this quiet crisis. All three have been at work for some time. Each is a deep, if subtle, problem in itself, and together they constitute a wasting disease that must be arrested before they infect the body of the republic like a deadly trio of cancers.

None of these developments is entirely new, uniquely American, or in any sense irreversible. Each is a consequence of the global forces of modernization and, as such, has appeared to some extent in American experience before. Yet until now each has been so offset by traditional American strengths that many would fail to either notice them or rate their importance highly. But current conditions accentuate their significance fatefully. At this point, it is precisely because the United States is so advanced, so free, so diverse, and so little constrained by custom and tradition that its society is especially prone to trends that are universal to some extent yet have more significance for America than for other countries, such as those in Western Europe.

How serious is this quiet crisis now and how serious might it prove to become? It may, for example, be only the uncovering of old blindspots concealed by old myths—just as American violence was concealed by the myth of "consensus," American elitism by the myth of "middling America," and American racism by the myth of egalitarianism. In which case, the quiet crisis only shows that republican character was never as strong as it pretended. Or again, it could equally be the distortion of traditional reality by modern rhetoric. In which case, the problem is distortion rather than devastation. A simple change in rhetoric would then be the cure. But should the quiet crisis represent genuine change in the virtues and strengths of republican character, the consequences will prove more serious.

A World Without Weight

The first of the three cancers—hollowness, or weightlessness—is a condition that results from the drastic erosion of the sense of personhood and truth in American society. It is obvious that for any human existence to maintain dignity and enjoy freedom these two things are vitally important. That they are vital to the republic as a whole may be less obvious.

An absolute sense of human worth is of fundamental importance for each of us as individuals. But it is also a pivotal notion for the American republic because it undergirds "inalienable rights" and the two fundamental American principles of liberty and equality. All people, in other words, are to be given respect simply because they are human beings. As such they have inalienable rights regardless of differences of belief, race, status, income, intelligence, and age. To the everlasting credit of the United States, this ideal has been far more than stirring rhetoric in the Declaration. It has been translated tirelessly into political form and demonstrated concretely in the American experiment. Obvious examples include the introduction of universal suffrage in America before other countries, widespread and consistent advocacy of a public school system to provide a common educational background, and the well-known American antagonism to elitism.

In the same way, the notion of truth is critically important to the American republic. It underlies "We hold these truths" and supports the second and most difficult of Abraham Lincoln's three features of democracy —"Government of the people, by the people, for the people." If government is to be *by* the people without democracy becoming cumbersome and unstable, two things are necessary: Government must be representative—based on a clear distinction between the people as the source of sovereign authority and the representatives as the agents of that authority—and decision-making must be rational and responsible—based on a clear distinction between truth and civic ideals on the one side and error, rumor, deception, whim, caprice, and misinformation on the other.

Today, however, few things seem less self-evident and more alienable in the United States than a solid sense of personhood and a solid sense of truth. Despite their common link in the root notion of solidity and substantialness, both personhood and truth are losing any clear and solid meaning at an alarming rate. Both have been severed from their roots in the wider community and in higher commitments. As a result, a cancerous growth of hollowness is spreading throughout the claims on which American democracy is grounded.

Hollowness is the disintegrative disease of weightlessness brought on by the crisis of cultural authority. It is America's experience of a phenomenon endemic to modernity and evident in Europe's crisis of cultural authority in the late nineteenth century. Following the "death of God" and the decline of the Christian faith's culturally compelling power in Europe, Nietzsche predicted that "it would seem for a time as though all things had become weightless."[7] His haunting metaphor paralleled Marx's earlier comment in the *Communist Manifesto* that the acids of modernity were dissolving all the settled convictions and stable relations of tradition: "All that is solid melts into air, all that is holy is profaned."[8] The same vision of a dissolving society is brilliantly captured in Robert Musil's masterpiece of life in Vienna before World War I, *The Man Without Qualities*.

To some extent a sense of weightlessness afflicted several Americans long before the present crisis of cultural authority. Walt Whitman wrote of America's "hollowness of heart" in the Gilded Age and T. S. Eliot gave it the most famous expression in "Unreal City" and "The Hollow Men" ("hollow because they, too, are without substance").[9] But as the crisis of cultural authority has come to a head and America's daily setting has changed from the earlier artificiality of the cityscape to the current unreality of the telescape, the sense of weightlessness has gone further and grown faster.

The empty eighties was America's "second gilded age" in this sense. The decade's most celebrated portrayal was Tom Wolfe's *The Bonfire of the Vanities*. Proponents of the decade's leading critical theory—deconstruction—were described by literary critic George Steiner as "the current masters of emptiness."[10] The decade's most famous artist—Andy Warhol—was widely characterized after his death as "the man who wasn't there" ("My main impression of Andy Warhol was that there was no *there* there," wrote one interviewer. There was only "the terrible blackness and nothingness that this Peeping Tom apparently saw at the core of everything.")[11] One of the decade's most illustrious architects—Peter Eisenman—built his work around the notion of "the Empty Man" (the human person contemplating the void of nihilism).[12] The decade's leading institution—communications—was aptly described as the "unreality industry."[13] President Reagan was even described by Peggy Noonan, his best and favorite speech writer, as "a gigantic heroic balloon, floating in the Macy's Thanksgiving Day Parade, right up there between Superman and Big Bird. That is when I started to think two things: I am on the periphery of a void, and this White House is like a beautiful clock that keeps time and makes all the right sounds, but when you open it up there's nothing inside."[14] Little wonder that such a chord was struck by the Nietzschean vision of Milan Kundera's *The Unbearable Lightness of Being*.

Viewed from the national rather than the individual perspective, the experience of weightlessness, which Jackson Lears has described as "hovering soul-sickness," shows up clearly in its effects on personhood and truth.[15] The formerly solid sense of personhood has become the victim of a massive crisis of confidence. The identity crisis is neither new nor American in origin, but it has been taken further in America than elsewhere because of the convergence of its advanced modern technologies and its extreme postmodern theories. Such notions as a "true self" and "a clear core of self" or such notions as the absolute value of a person are called into question on every side. Once considered to have dignity and weight because humanity was the glory of God and made in his image (*dignitas* being Latin for glory), human nature has been sucked into a black hole of introspection, uncertainty, and illusion by human society and human ideas.

As a result, large numbers of Americans have lost hold of the traditional Jewish-Christian notion of human dignity. But they find they cannot stop their slide by hanging onto the unquestioning Enlightenment assertion of self-evident rights. The roller-coaster ride from romanticism through modernism to postmodernism would not allow it. Plunged into the turbulent waters of the rapids of modernization, countless Americans feel tossed about between conflicting philosophical and psychological theories, and almost capsized by the jarring shock of experiences, such as divorce and broken homes. Lacking both social bonds and psychological ballast, their best thoughts and energies rarely rise beyond the immediate horizons of self and survival.

In contrast to traditional life elsewhere, many Americans experience their lives as self-conscious rather than straightforward, socially constructed rather than given, fragmented and serialized rather than unified, ceaselessly invented and reinvented rather than ever taken for granted. Their sense of personhood is self-conscious, artificial, changing, and insubstantial. The traditional notion of character has gone and the traditional disciplines of growth and maturity have changed. With "sameness" and "continuity" no longer possible, modern identity is protean and problematic rather than solid and substantial. The rage is for "polymorphous potentiality," for everyone can now be anyone. The "imperial self" of grand individualism has been reduced to the "minimal self" of uncertain narcissism. As Robert Musil's character Walter declares about his friend Ulrich, the man without qualities with a void in the center of his existence, "There are millions of them nowadays. . . . It's the human type that our time has produced."[16] The self, about which Americans sound so obsessed, says Philip Rieff, is today no more than "an old sacred world courtesy title."[17]

A solid sense of truth is foundering in America for different reasons.

Vaporized by endless critical theories about its nature, twisted by ideologies, replaced by psychological categories, obscured by suffocating clouds of euphemism and jargon, outpaced by rumor and hype, overlooked for the more dazzling appeal of style and image, truth in America today is anything but marching on. Once treated as the first casualty of war, truth has become a casualty of peace and is virtually a semi-invalid at this moment of democratic trial.

Serious speech in search of truth is a vanishing species in much of America. With a background of incessant noise rather than clarifying silence, with the freedom to think anything and be bound by nothing, and with the curse of always seeing sixteen sides to every issue, even people of ideas often experience what Robert Musil called "the acoustics of emptiness within, when a shot resounds twice as loudly and goes echoing on and on."[18] At the very least, as William Lee Miller observes, Jefferson's belief that truth is great and will prevail is today "more a prayer than an axiom."[19]

The deepest problems are those created for Americans as individuals, but the potential social and political consequences of this hollowness are myriad. One example is the increasing hollowness of the American assertion of inalienable rights. A nation's commitment to human rights is quite simply the political and legal expression of its views of human dignity. The Bill of Rights therefore requires a belief in man, woman, and child. Long considered the cornerstone of democratic freedom, the concept of inalienable rights has been weakened drastically in America by something far worse than the purported ineptness of certain presidents or the crass commercializing of American beliefs. The idea that human life itself and every single person has supreme worth—including the mentally retarded, the physically deformed, the emotionally unbalanced, the unborn as well as every criminal, failure, and misfit—simply does not find empirical support today, and its theoretical justification is selective and dramatically weaker too. Enlightenment liberalism now has no right to the rights on which it stands.

What seemed self-evident to Jefferson and his generation is not so today. Philosopher Leszek Kolakowski describes the problem bluntly. "If 'self-evident' means obvious, or deriving its truth from the concepts involved, these truths are not self-evident at all. They are now reserved for pontifical messages or Sunday sermons, yet they are banned beyond recall from permissible philosophical or theoretical idioms."[20] Secular liberalism is so disdainful of the biblical beliefs behind the concept and so insistent that no religious beliefs can be affirmed in public anyway that it finds itself unable to justify its inalienable rights on the basis of its assured conclusions, from philosophy and science. "The belief in an irreducible and unique core of personality is not a scientifically provable truth," Kolakowski continues, "but the notion of personal dignity and human rights is, without this belief, an arbitrary concoction, suspended in the void, indefensible, easy to dismiss."[21] As one wag put it, the United States has become the only nation in the world with a philosophical mistake in its foundation.

This philosophical deficiency does not mean that secular liberals are careless about human rights. On the contrary. But their stands bear the mark of the consequences. In the first place, the deficiency has weakened the liberal defense of rights. Instead of the primary argument from inalienability, which is no longer possible, they rely on the secondary argument from indivisibility—if freedom is one, discrimination against anyone damages freedom for everyone. But the argument is now asserted over an inadmissible void. Human rights have become a grand game of "let's pretend." Without a belief in the dignity and distinctiveness of human nature, all that is left is species chauvinism. After all, as Nietzsche writes in *Thus Spoke Zarathustra*, "The masses blink and say: 'We are all equal—Man is but man, before God—we are all equal.' Before God! But now this God has died."[22] If God is dead, we must face the fact that nature is morally indifferent, rationality is only a tool of power, and human rights are a fiction.

Further, the deficiency means that assertion of rights is increasingly viewed as an exercise in a power divorced from independent rational judgments—so that the pursuit of rights becomes both selective and self-serving. Thus many liberals still assert rights with a conviction of their absoluteness that would do credit to an Islamic fundamentalist. But a telling selectivity has crept into their applications. Rather than being compelled by the rights they respect to stand against the wrong they see, whatever the cost to themselves, they choose the rights they respect whatever the cost to others. This problem of self-serving selectivity is blatant in the extremes of the prochoice movement. Sadly, what Robert Musil wrote of his protagonist must be said of many unreasoning advocates of abortion on demand: "He had no respect for rights when he did not respect those whose rights they were, and that happened rarely."[23]

The result is what Kolakowski calls a "self-degrading movement of the Enlightenment" or "a suicidal stage" in the development of humanist beliefs.[24] Abandon down the memory hole the belief that all human life has worth, that truth exists, that it is ascertainable, and that reason can help arbitrate the moral claims of society, and Western civilization—past and future—becomes incomprehensible and unworkable. Make explicit the logic of secular liberalism and the worst sort of moral equivalence becomes natural. If there are no absolute truths or absolute standards, if grand political differences are only a matter of "cultural differences," and if tolerance itself is relative, then Western democracy becomes as hollow an ideology as

Communism. Kolakowski concludes: "We convert our political commitments into moral principles. This is precisely what the idolatry of politics means: to fabricate gods for an ad hoc use in a game of political power."[25]

The Unreality Business

A second example of hollowness is the deterioration of American public opinion. The vital link between public opinion and republican government needs no underlining in a nation constituted by the defining awareness of "We the people." Public opinion is the matrix of democratic self-government. For this reason its importance and pitfalls have been recognized from the beginning. Early in the seventeenth century, Thomas Shepard, the Puritan preacher, warned against the dangers of popular sovereignty. Since people were corrupt and unstable, they were "apt to be led by colors, like birds by glasses and larkes by lures, and golden pretences which Innovators ever make."[26]

Realism about public opinion has important consequences for America. In the first place, it is a corrective to certain national myths. Heroic mythology has it that America is a nation of incurably rugged individualists (the cowboy riding into town alone with his horse and nothing else, as Henry Kissinger was reported to have said to the Italian journalist Oriana Fallaci). Visitors from abroad, however, have long been impressed by American conformism and sensitivity to fashion and public opinion. Harriet Martineau, for example, was no less an admirer of American democracy in the 1830s than Alexis de Tocqueville, but she concluded similarly that "the worship of Opinion is, at this day, the established religion of the United States."[27] Where else, as other visitors have noted, is it considered a compliment to call someone "a regular guy"? Not only the respect but the sycophancy reserved for the king in a monarchy has shifted to public opinion in a democracy.

American conformity is the child of American equality born out of wedlock and is therefore not owned by equality's official partner, liberty. But in a society of equals, each person must pay serious attention to the average or to what the majority of his or her equals expects. Inferior to no one and superior to no one, each is peculiarly vulnerable to the confirmation of the majority. Thus Americans have been characterized by a compulsive conformity that offsets unbalanced perceptions of individualism and independence. As Eric Hoffer observed, "When people are free to do as they please, they usually imitate each other."[28]

More importantly, the realism is also a corrective to certain dangerous ways of seeing and treating public opinion in the political arena. The old

Puritan realism was drowned and forgotten as the surging tide of democratic celebration flooded in during the Jacksonian era. But developments in our own century have provided new grounds for the old fears and have shown the timeliness of the earlier warnings. Whereas Tocqueville in the 1830s warned of the "tyranny of the majority," James Bryce nearly sixty years later found not tyranny but conformity. In no country is public opinion so powerful, he wrote, but just as complete political and social equality created public opinion, so it led to the "fatalism of the multitude."[29] The individual was not so much dominated as diminished and therefore swayed by and submerged in the wider group. Both men, however, recognized the plentiful checks and balances that prevented an extreme uniformity from developing in America.

In our own century, the first major analyst of the dilemma was Lawrence Lowell, but the writer who best caught the public attention was Walter Lippmann. Lippmann set out to investigate the baleful influence of modern public opinion on American democracy. Sobered by his own experience of the "cyclone of distortion"[30] at the Versailles Peace Conference in 1917 and appalled by the record of the impeccably liberal *New York Times* in reporting the Bolshevik revolution, he saw that protecting the sources of public opinion was the central problem of modern democracy.

Yet as Lippmann analyzed it in his now-classic work, *Public Opinion*, the deepest problem was not in the way the press reported or the government sought to interfere. It was in the way in which the public made up its mind. Because of prejudices, stereotypes, myths, and propaganda, the pictures inside people's heads were crude simplifications that did not correspond with the world outside. The original dogma of democracy was undone. Democracy could work, he argued, only if its citizens escaped from the intolerable and unworkable fiction that each person must acquire a competent opinion about public affairs.

In the sixty-odd years since, two things have made the situation worse. On the one hand, Lippmann's cyclone of distortion has become global and has been harnessed and skillfully channeled. On the other hand, recent developments have not only reinforced the problem but have twisted it in another direction. Daniel Boorstin's *The Image* was an astute early analysis of this other direction. He saw that the graphic revolution, which arose from the combination of telegraphy's stress on the instant and photography's focus on the image, had grown at a fantastic pace and caused a Copernican revolution in the press, media, and advertising. The central concern for truth had been displaced by a preoccupation with image.

The "pseudoevent" was typical of this shift, a synthetic, rather than spontaneous, happening in which there was a general submerging of the differences between the factual and the contrived, the original and the imitation, the real and the newsworthy, hard news and soft news, conviction and posture, argument and promotion. What results, Boorstin stressed, is not propaganda—propaganda is an appealing falsehood while a pseudoevent is an ambiguous truth. Pseudoevents are a different danger from Lippmann's stereotypes. Stereotypes simplify and therefore limit experiences in an emotionally satisfying way, whereas pseudoevents embroider and dramatize reality ingeniously, thus making experience more interesting but truth more elusive. Public opinion is therefore hollowed out from two directions at once—from inside the mind by stereotypes and from outside the mind by images.

Boorstin's examples range from commonplace press conferences to government leaks, advertorials, the *Congressional Record,* and the election-year "debates" between bionic-looking presidential candidates. But his conclusions are blunt. Abraham Lincoln's familiar maxim that ended with the line, "But you can't fool all of the people all the time," rests on assumptions that are no longer justifiable. A thicket of unreality stands between Americans and the facts of life. The making of illusions has become the business of America. Most people have become such eager accessories to the great hoaxes played on themselves that the effect is a "feat of national self-hypnosis."[31]

Political campaigns in general and Washington, D.C., in particular are an endless source of illustrations of this loss of truth. Machiavelli's "appear as you may wish to be" has come into its own in a capital city whose two axioms George Will describes as: "Almost nothing is as important as almost everything in Washington is made to appear. And the importance of a Washington event is apt to be inversely proportional to the attention it receives."[32] Behind this hype is the postmodern maxim that if the sole reality is image, then personhood is a project and politics is a pose. Thus, if ordinary people create themselves as a part of self-development, artists and musicians create their own persona as works of art, why not politicians? If one's image is finally a fiction, surely it is better to create one's own fiction than be controlled. Politicians therefore invent and reinvent their own public images. The industry of public relations and "spin control" is the politician's equivalent of the ordinary person's industry of gyms, body toning, plastic surgery, and new looks for new seasons. In an era of niche marketing, niche posturing is the secret of success in America's opinion wars. What points you care to make on the subject of the hour matter little; what point you choose to take on the political spectrum of the day is everything.

There are powerful arguments, of course, in support of histrionic authority and the importance of perceptions and symbols. The obvious argument concerns government in a television age, though the most serious are terrorism and nuclear deterrence. At the very heart of both is the idea that effectiveness of power depends on its being seen, though in the case of deterrence doctrine on being seen but not used. Also, as Tocqueville and Bryce stressed, vital features of American society can be counted on to counterbalance this trend toward weightlessness. The robust independence of the American press is the most obvious. And most importantly of all, whatever damaging effects television may have, it has reinforced what government in America was intended to be—limited. As Austin Ranney has argued well, by making government achievements seem transitory, unimportant, and even illusory, "television's effect has been . . . to intensify most of the fundamental characteristics of our system of government as planned by the Founding Fathers and nurtured by much of American tradition."[33]

What are the dangers of a hollowed-out public opinion? First, it tends to disguise a vital deficiency of rationality in America. "Personal opinion" was once recognized as being at least partly tentative, untested, and half-considered. But through technique's impact on democracy, such as referenda and opinion polls, public opinion has become far more than personal opinion magnified a millionfold. Modern public opinion also includes an enlargement of what people think other people think. Nietzsche put it too cynically in his aphorism, "Public opinions—private lazinesses" (similar to General Sherman's "Vox populi, vox humbug!"), and behind that was the elitism of Nietzsche's own "hero-herd" chasm.[34] But the danger is that conformity and irrationality have been amplified together, but that neither is acknowledged because public opinion is king. The result is a shifting kaleidoscope of group-thought having the same old irrationality as personal opinion, but now regally mantled with scientific authority and the aura of democratic legitimacy.

This magnifying of irrationality in American public opinion is compounded by three accompanying developments: the ubiquity of second-hand thinking and speaking (through speech writing and public relations), the incredible shrinking "sound bite" (on average down from 42.3 seconds in the 1968 election to 9.8 in 1988), and the extent to which, in Leo Lowenthal's dictum, "Mass culture is psychoanalysis in reverse."[35] Many of the basic instruments of mass culture, such as advertising, work by triggering images, dreams, illusions, and irrationality. Many of the best image makers, such as advertisers, television directors, and filmmakers, consciously shape their products in Freudian or post-Freudian terms. Conscious calculation and control is the name of the game, but paradoxically it is control of the subconscious and the irrational.

This decline in rationality affects debate in two main ways. The more obvious, and the easier to reverse, comes from a loss of critical thinking as questions, reflection, and judgments give way to images, impressions, and feelings. ("Mr. Stevenson," a Boston woman shouted, "You have won the vote of every thinking American!" To which Adlai Stevenson replied, "Yes, but I need a majority!") The less obvious way, and far harder to reverse, comes from a loss of coherence. In a complex world, informed political thought is almost necessarily a form of specialized thought. Even this commitment entails a high cost in time and effort, which makes a general coherence in political thinking an all but impossible ideal.

Thus the nation that was created in a great transforming debate is slipping to the level where new ideas are themselves mostly a matter of image. In strong contrast with parliamentarians in Europe, too many American politicians neither write their own speeches nor think their own thoughts. Hugo Young of the *Manchester Guardian* draws a blunt conclusion about Washington. "Nowhere is more money spent on political communication. But nowhere has this produced a more politically illiterate electorate, conditioned to live in fantasy-land. . . . It has produced a country drowning in ignorance about its own condition. Politics here is a conspiracy to keep voters in the dark, lest the light shine too pitilessly on those they have been manipulated into electing."[36]

Second, hollowed-out public opinion tends to conceal and compound a serious decline in community in America. Responsible public opinion is the considered response of a community. Without such a community having its shared bonds, shared memories, shared ideals, and interests, public opinion degenerates quickly into popular clamor or is easily led by single-issue experts and activists. It becomes the amplified babble of an issue-gathered crowd rather than the articulate voices of tradition-seasoned communities. Public opinion that is not to collapse into an excess of democracy needs to be derived from and disciplined by a wider but unseen community, a higher but unmentioned commitment, and a longer but unconscious consideration.

Third, hollowed-out public opinion tends to undermine the intermediacy of representative government in America. Pure and total democracy is a dangerous mirage, as foolish for a large republic as for an army or an orchestra. A free republic rests on the consent of the governed, but no republic would remain free for long if its leaders resorted to a constant consultation with the governed. Power is only for those who can exercise it effectively and well. No political leader is foolish enough to believe literally that "the People are always right" or even that they know what the issues are. But the shameless American courting and flattering of public opinion is what Lippmann, in unison with Burke, Madison, and the wisest voices of democratic tradition, recognized as a "fatal malady."[37]

America Lite

The hollowing out of democratic convictions and public opinion are only two examples of the wider weightlessness of American society. In a day of constantly changing images, fashions, life-styles, and new technologies, much of American life is a parade of surfaces. "What you see is what you see"—and you won't see it for long. Thus a generation with its eyes on the mirror, the bathroom scale, and the color brochure reconfigures and re-presents itself endlessly through consumption and display. But everything has an "as if" quality. It comes with an "at least for today" reminder. No rules apply. Stripes and checks no longer clash in clothes, Georgian and modern can mix in architecture, and right and wrong are relative in ethics.

These points are as familiar to some Americans as they are unfamiliar to others. The former are often unconcerned or amused by the result. Perhaps only foreigners, fresh to American society, feel the full dismay at the widespread sense of hollowness in American discourse. Ordinary examples are legion. In a televised speech to the nation in September 1989, President Bush hammered home the urgency of the war on drugs by holding up a packet of cocaine that was sold in Lafayette Square across the street from the White House—although the hapless teenage dealer was only there because he was lured by a government agent with the express purpose of contributing a television prop. The year before, President Reagan's former press secretary, Larry Speakes, acknowledged that he had made up many of Reagan's quotes "to spruce up the President's image by taking a bit of liberty with my P.R. man's license."[38]

But then, Washington is a ghostwriter's Mecca and superghosts like Peggy Noonan (creator of Ronald Reagan's speech after the Challenger explosion and George Bush's "Read my lips") are only the latest and best in a strong tradition of acceptable plagiarism, which at its lower end is replete with hand-me-down speeches and rent-a-cliché resonance. "Essentially, what Ronald Reagan contributed to his speeches were lungs and vocal chords," said Kathleen Jamieson, dean of the Annenberg School for Communication. "You were being moved by someone else's language."[39]

But then again, Washington is only the political expression of an attitude to truth that is broadly taken-for-granted across American culture. Judy Collins, with no sense of contradiction, sings "Amazing Grace" a cappella with her eyes closed at a proabortion rally ("Sing any song you want," she said, "it's the spirit that counts.")[40] Rick Smolan, codirector of the *Day in the Life* series of photography books, admitted rejiggering elements of the cover photographs of all seven books in the series (claiming, however, that he didn't "change the meaning of the picture").[41] The Miss America pageant increasingly showcases a plasticized pulchritude in which contestants owe more to their re-makers than to their Maker. The pop duo Milli Vanilli lip-synched their way to a Grammy Award without ever singing a note of their song "Girl You Know It's True." And, of course, from start to finish the prime agent of national truth decay is the all-American ad. When it comes to truth and seriousness, there is little between the vacuity of a Soviet slogan like "The Party is our helmsman" and an American slogan like "Chevrolet, the heartbeat of America." Each works at a level other than taking its truth content seriously.

Most disturbingly of all, most Americans do not seem concerned to escape hollowness as an intolerable fiction. They appear as contentedly enslaved as if to a royal edict. They have grown addicted to the illusion of its more bountiful blandishments, such as total, instant information. They have been flattered by the interest of polls and pollsters in their every whim and opinion, taken in by the sleight of hand that substitutes images and euphemisms for reality and style for substance, and seduced by the phoney promise of much participatory politics. They accept the "puff or perish" principle that in a media-saturated society, authenticity is being spin doctor of your own artificiality. It almost seems that when modern communications and consumerism have both had their way, what is left of public speech in America will be America Lite, with all the body and flavor of a Miller Lite and all the depth and rationality of a Miller Lite commercial.

By European standards, American public life is awash with a subjectivism and sentimentality that drowns questions of truth, justice, and prudence. Did Senator Ted Kennedy cause the death of Mary Jo Kopechne? Was Colonel Oliver North guilty of lying to Congress? Was Washington, D.C., mayor Marion Barry guilty of perjury and cocaine smoking? Such questions are irrelevant. They are first pushed to one side by morally neutral questions based on performance rather than principle (were their public explanations compelling/sincere/entertaining/charismatic?). Then the personal and political preferences can take over and make heroes or villains from the conclusions, regardless of reality.

The result in too many cases is a triumph of theatricality over truth in American public life, of sentiment over justice, of cant, cliché, and bromide over convictions. Many Americans overrate sincerity and are awash with sentiment at the expense of tough thought. Inundated by a flood of vivid but uninterpreted messages from the instant-everywhere, they are overloaded with facts but starved of understanding. Too much of the spectacle has meant too much of the superficial. The information era is creating a new species of human, but in Boorstin's phrase, the consequence of "too much too soon" is that "Homo Up-to-Datum is a Dunce."[42] The main cultural effect of television advertising, says Robert Heilbroner, is "to teach children that grown-ups told lies for money."[43]

Such warnings, along with Shepard's and Lippmann's, are desperately needed in America now that a nation of increasingly phantom public people deal in increasingly phantom and phony public messages. From the routine lies and idiotic persuasions of advertising upward, the Joe Isuzu effect is pervasive in America. (At the most trivial level, our local fast-food restaurant Roy Rogers promised "playfully crisp lettuce" and "daring slices of onion.") Without a robust popular skepticism and a vigorous free press to counter it, this trend would be even more damaging.

Truth is dissolving into "credibility," falsehood into what is "inoperative" or no longer has the power to command assent, and barefaced lies into "aggressive marketing." All that counts is which unreality is most saleable. Soon the only trustworthy people left in America will be those who are obviously lying. (In 1987, the so-called Year of Lying Dangerously, satirist Mort Sahl quipped: "George Washington couldn't tell a lie, Nixon couldn't tell the truth, and Ronald Reagan can't tell the difference.") Without strong checks, the dislocation of reality and most individuals' interpretation of it would be complete, and America would be a whispering echo chamber of messages, a dazzling society of mirrors in which images, events, and moods glitter and sparkle continuously but truth would be dead.

Czechoslovakia's Charter 77 movement had as one of its mottos: "The truth prevails for those who live in truth." But the contrast in status between truth and words in America and truth and words in Eastern Europe is sobering. A generation ago, Simone Weil warned her fellow citizens in France, "We live in an age so impregnated with lies that even the virtue of blood voluntarily sacrificed is insufficient to put us back on the path of truth."[44] Will the same be said soon of America because of its addiction to images? Albert Camus spoke similarly of the difficulty of fighting a lie in the name of a half-truth already shrunk to a quarter-truth. How much longer will it be before a generation fed solely on images, irrelevant facts, and sentimentality finds itself fighting one lie with something indistinguishable from another? "We have become so obsessed with facts," says Ted Koppel reflecting on his own role as a news anchor, "that we have lost all touch with truth."[45] "With all this emphasis on the image," Dan Rather has said, "what happens to the issues? What happens to the substance?"[46]

Keeping the record straight is never easy. An ethic of truthfulness is not simple. There is such a thing as a morally permissible lie. Disillusioning ourselves is not easy. Hollowness has not spread equally to all sectors of

American society. But with that said, a nation that gorges itself on images, mistakes the glands for the heart, confuses making the news with making sense, and casually neglects barriers that hedge permissible lying will find itself facing a drastic erosion from the winds and rain of refined lying without lying.

In short, America's present process of hollowing out is one sure road to decadence and delusion. For if lying by leaders destroys the fabric of public trust, everyday lying makes government lying easier and less objectionable. No "big lie" of Joseph Goebbels's proportions is likely to be set rolling in America in the near future, though straws in the wind are not hard to find, and current social conditions mean that the slipway for some future launching is in place. Should that day come, American leaders and citizens alike who have not opened their minds to grapple with truth will find themselves without an antidote to an image-created delusion, which will be both their judgment and their destruction at once.

16

Hunger for Home

During a wave of teenage suicides in the mid-1980s, one young man in Houston hung himself on a tree and left a note that said, "This is the only thing around here that has any roots."[1] Some people dismissed such suicides as modern, fashionable versions of the romantic, copycat suicides set off by Goethe's novel, *The Sorrows of Young Werther*. Clearly, they were tragedies for which no single explanation would be adequate. But it takes a special kind of insensitivity not to see that lack of roots is one of their deepest roots.

This story expresses the problem of the second cancer with a terrible clarity. If behind the first cancer is the erosion of personhood and truth, behind the second is the widening collapse of a sense of roots and stability in American life. The second cancer—homelessness—is a condition that results from the gradual eating away of the certainties of meaning and belonging in the lives of countless Americans. Between 1955 and 1975, suicides between the ages of fifteen and twenty-four rose 300 percent. Not surprisingly, the highest rates were found among broken families.[2]

Homelessness in the form of street people became an urgent national issue in the 1980s, especially because of the alarming rise of children among America's homeless. But this other kind of homelessness is not one to be passed across the desks of Housing and Urban Development. It is far more than a lack of bricks and mortar. Nothing is more naturally human than the drive toward meaning and belonging, and thus toward order. Sense of some kind, stability of some sort—these are the prerequisites for a tolerable human life. Without some underlying order, philosophically as well as socially, the dark demons of absurdity and anomie come menacingly close and threaten to destroy the fragile defenses of individual character and of human civilization itself. Cruel religious theodicies and totalitarian political terror bear witness to the same point: Human beings have such a need to feel at home with themselves and their universe that they even prefer tyranny to chaos, paternal authoritarianism to fratricidal factionalism.

East of Eden and West of the Missouri

Needless to say, neither this need for home nor the feeling of homelessness so characteristic of today are uniquely American. The former is human and the latter is part and parcel of the crisis of modernity. In fact, certain characteristics of traditional American life have long kept the logic of homelessness at bay. American experience, Tocqueville observed, had loosened old communal and hierarchical ties, but compensated for it by strengthening other ties, such as family bonds. And not only kinship, but other factors, such as religion, citizenship, voluntary associations, friendship, and hospitality, once gave Americans a strong sense of place and home that was the counterbalance to individualism and mobility. Henry Addington, who visited America a decade before Tocqueville, noted that "the social ties sit looser upon them than upon any other people, and like well-boiled rice they remain united, but each grain separate. Yet an American father, husband, neighbor, and friend performs all his family and social duties to admiration."[3]

Today, however, the crisis of cultural authority bred by modernity is destroying other bonds too. Severed from communal roots, the trajectory of American individualism has gone from the "imperial self" of the unfettered and self-reliant nineteenth-century hero to the "minimal" selves crowding therapeutic couches and recovery groups in the late twentieth century. At that point the very openness of American society and the advanced degree of its modernization leave Americans peculiarly vulnerable to the dilemma of homelessness that Karl Marx called "alienation" and Émile Durkheim "anomie." Indeed, says Czeslaw Milosz, after his years as émigré living in California, homelessness in America now amounts to the illness, "ontological anemia,"[4] that torments inhabitants of the United States in particular. Among its symptoms is a sense of chronic hunger for home that occurs when an organism deprived of food begins to consume itself.

It is a mistake, of course, to equate the disintegration of natural, or traditional, communities with homelessness. For modern forms of community are real and strong, based on the principle of free association. For example, many people are supported and held accountable by telephone networks of family and friends rather than by face-to-face contacts. American life, in this sense, is thick with community—modern if not traditional. But not only is the modern basis—voluntary choice—weaker than the traditional basis, the modern network of communities is also less solid overall, allowing casualties to slip between the mesh.

Even at their thickest, modern forms of community are thinner than traditional forms. Regardless of opinions of the truth or falsity of traditional religious worldviews, such as the Hindu, Muslim, Jewish, or Christian, there is no doubting the intellectual and social security of traditional people who lived and died under the overarching canopy of their meaning. Reality, identity, morality, community—these notions basic to humanness were assumed as effortlessly as well-being to a healthy person. By taking a step back and looking beyond the everyday world to the transcendent horizon of life, the religious solution—fraudulent or otherwise—offered the promise of ultimate meaning and belonging. In short, a home in the universe.

This is no longer our situation, for as T. S. Eliot put it, "where there is no temple there shall be no homes."[5] But those who appreciate what the religious solution did also have to be clear-eyed about the impossible predicament into which the modern world is driving human destiny. Modern society creates conditions that are an impassable barrier to traditional meaning and belonging, smashing to smithereens its traditional intellectual and social solidity. And these conditions and their consequences are compounded further in America by such factors as the explicit commitment to ceaseless change and ceaseless competition in a nation based heavily on immigration and high mobility.

In one sense, homelessness is a defining feature of all humanness east of Eden and is certainly not new in the United States. But for all the counterbalances, a special sense of homelessness has always been present in a nation shaped by immigration, mobility, and westward expansion. One German visitor called it the "motor restlessness" of Americans. Tocqueville had earlier observed the "strange unrest" of Americans, and H. G. Wells commented on the "headlong hurry" of Americans.[6] Nearer to our own time, George Santayana commented in the 1920s on the "moral emptiness of a settlement where men and women and even houses are moved about, and no one, almost, lives where he was born and believes what he was taught." Denis Brogan spoke in the 1940s of "American nomadism" as the expression of American civilization.[7] John Steinbeck, in his *Travels with Charley*, wrote that he saw something in the eyes of his neighbor that he was to find everywhere in the nation—"A burning desire to go, to move, to get underway, any place from here. They spoke quietly of how they wanted to go someday, to move about, free and unanchored, not toward something, but away from something."[8]

Such restless mobility, combined with a will to technique, has left Americans with what George Grant described as "a conquering attitude to place." Even our cities, he said, have become "encampments on the road to economic mastery."[9] At the more everyday level, IBM was popularly known as "I've been moved" and advertisers routinely teed off the pervasive sense of lost home. In the 1980s, Mazda even sold automobiles, surely the supreme symbols of American mobility, under the doubly contradictory byline: "Who says there's no place like home? We built the MPV based on a very strong foundation. The home. . . . It's engineering based on human feelings."

But while the problem of homelessness is not new in America, the present moment represents a serious exacerbation for an obvious reason. As a result of the crisis of cultural authority, the traditional American counterbalances have disintegrated too. Both faith and the family, the two deepest structures of meaning and belonging and the strongest counterweights to threatened anomie, have been sucked into the whirlpool.

What is at issue here, Peter Berger writes, is quite simple. "The world created by capitalism is indeed a 'cold' one. Liberating though it may be, it also involves the individual in countless relations with other people that are based on calculating rationality ('What is this person worth to *me?*'), superficial (the 'personalization' of salesmanship), and inevitably transient (the very dynamics of the market ensures this). Human relations too become subject to the 'creative destruction' of capitalism. There is, therefore, an overriding need of 'warmth' to balance all this 'coldness.' "[10] In such a world, grand universal, liberal abstractions like "humanity" are no help. Nothing short of solidarity and particularity fits the bill. The need, in short, is for home.

In more normal times, the search for meaning and belonging is a hidden process that is natural and unconscious. That such a search has become conscious, deliberate, and a point of open anxiety—so that the "search for warmth" has become an ever-burgeoning industry—is itself a symptom of anomie and homelessness. Nothing demonstrates the problem more clearly than the place and profitability of psychologism in America. As Peter Berger wrote in 1967, "If Freud had not existed, he would have had to be invented."[11] But the predicament also shows up clearly in very different areas. For example, the recurring vogue for nostalgia (literally "homesickness") in societies losing touch with their past, the potent hunger for "roots" in nations rooted in rootlessness, and the insatiable appetite for myths in cultures parched by reductionism. "Loss of the past," wrote Simone Weil about France, "is the supreme human tragedy, and we have thrown ours away just like a child picking off the petals of a rose."[12] "Only a horizon ringed about with myths," Nietzsche wrote a century before George Lucas, Joseph Campbell, and Shirley MacLaine, "can unify a culture."[13]

But these are only four of many windows on American homelessness. With heaven evacuated, history severed, families strung out if not disintegrating, and faith unreal, homelessness has become an ever-present menace to modern Americans. To many in earlier times, the darkest shadow of the nuclear cloud formed a spectral question mark over the future of the planet as the final home for human beings. For some today, the abortion explosion represents the irruption of terror and insecurity into what has always been the first and safest home for humans—the womb. Can there fail to be consequences? Being deprived of justice and freedom is bad enough for humans, but being disinherited from the certainties and assurances of home may prove even more so.

The Immoral Equivalent of War

Litanies of woe about a homeless generation are easy to recite and easier still to reject. As an avalanche of statistics have confirmed, divorce, illegitimate births, welfare-supported children, single-parent families, absent-working fathers, and hostility between the sexes have all risen dramatically, exposing the fragility of the modern nuclear family, leaving a havoc-strewn trail of broken and disrupted lives. Census Bureau findings in 1989, for example, showed that single-parent families in America rose from 12.9 percent of all families with children in 1970 to 27.3 percent in 1988.[14] Too few Americans have pondered the social logic (or "sleeper effect") of homelessness on trends, such as child abuse, serial killings, teenage suicides, wife battering, runaway children, and addictions, such as to food, drugs, sex, drink, gambling, and shopping. And too few have noted the incidence of concern from nonconservative sources.

In its issue on addictions in 1987, for example, Ms. magazine reported data on the "surprising dependencies of independent women." A staggering 35 percent of all lesbians were said to have problems with alcohol. As one respondent put it, "My lack within was deep and unfillable, no matter what I tried, and I tried it all—drugs, alcohol, men, food, work, clothes, power."[15] Chicken Little alarmism may be foolish, and the use of such statistics purely for culture wars ammunition is unconscionable. But far less so than the blithe optimism that still pretends that the trends behind such tragedies are purely liberal and liberating.

For one thing, flesh-and-blood people are involved, not simply demographic statistics. For another thing, modern liberal societies are confronted here with one of their most poignant ironies. Modernization has made possible a staggering decline in the mortality rate and opened up the chance of longer-lasting—and potentially deeper—social relationships, such as marriage. For example, a white couple married in America about 1860 had approximately a 42 percent chance of being separated by death before their last child reached eighteen. Today that risk is reduced to 9.8 percent, less than a quarter of the old figure. As for children, the risk to each one of dying before the age of eighteen was 36 percent for those born in 1840, but only 2.3 percent for those born recently.[16]

But what has the West done with this momentous gain and the rich prospect of deeper, more durable human relationships? It has squandered it, thrown it away through social disorganization and moral and philosophical folly. The American divorce rate has risen 700 percent in this century, and single-parent families are growing at twenty times the rate of two-parent families. Divorce reform, which was supposed to free women trapped in bad marriages, has trapped many of them in poverty.[17] In short, divorce has been allowed to replace death as the principal wrecker of marriage and purveyor of orphanhood. Living longer but loving more briefly is the bittersweet achievement of our prodigal squandering of the gift bequeathed by modernity. Nowhere is America more inventive than in discovering new ways to destroy families.

The words, philosophical folly, are deliberate. The main causes of family breakdown in America today are not the traditional ones—adultery, desertion, religious differences, and finances. The leading complaints are the new therapeutic reasons—failures in communication, sexual dissatisfaction, and difficulties in child-rearing.[18] In other words, psychologism's new promises have created marriage's new problems. Therapeutic liberations have proved specious. In attacking the "repressive myths" of traditional marriage, advocates for loving, cooperative, non-sexist open relationships have created repressive myths of their own. ("Bionic woman" Lindsay Wagner, after separating from her fourth husband in 1992, announced with an earnestness unaware of its fatuousness: "This is a positive and temporary step in our personal growth that we trust will make our relationship stronger.")[19] As Philip Rieff says, "It is not the repressions that trouble us now but the permissions."[20] American parents' disregard for their children in the 1980s amplifies American children's disregard for their parents in the 1960s. The crisis of cultural authority is moving through the generations.

Many of us have heard righteous accusations leveled at the Victorians for hypocrisy over sex and have been regaled by stories of the foolish stupidities of Western intellectuals over Stalin in the 1930s. Post-sixties liberalism is proving prolific in throwing up equally foolish and hypocritical notions, and in connection with its own children too. Such magazines as *Cosmopolitan* have spouted endlessly about the joys of commitment-free sex. Let them run stories on the runaway teenagers in Times Square for whom a year on the streets is a lifetime of abuse from which there is no recovery. Such firms as Calvin Klein have marketed millions of jeans and bottles of perfume based deliberately on eroticization, including that of children. (In the Obsession commercial in 1985, obsessive love affairs included suggestions of bondage and bizarre sexual relationships, with one character murmuring, "If living with obsession is a sin, then let me be guilty!")[21] Let them tithe their profits to contribute to the recovery and care of young lives ruined by sexual abuse. American children are not the problem. American adults are. But it is hardly fair that adults rethink the causes only when children pay the consequences.

What will likely be the impact of this gathering sense of homelessness? For our present purposes the key consequences are not those that touch the individual but those that affect the republic. Homelessness is in large part the result of traditional American individualism and mobility cut loose from the restraint of traditional American beliefs and institutions. But the practical question is whether it will affect things essential to the republic, such as dynamism, enterprise, and initiative.

There is no question about the consequences at the personal level. The first and obvious consequence of homelessness is a massive increase of individualism, singleness, loneliness, and alienation. (In the 1950s most single-parent households were composed of widows. Today they are composed primarily of divorcées and unwed mothers.)[22] Countless individual Americans experience the harsh school of life as they are torn away from familiar others and thrown back on themselves and their own resources. Their teachers and classes might be different—for some people relativism in thought, for others mobility in life-styles, for most people simply brokenness in relationships. (It is estimated that one-third of America's children will experience their parents' divorce and close to half will spend time in a single-parent family before they are eighteen.)[23] But the lesson will be the same: Aloneness breeds loneliness and loneliness breeds alienation. A culture of separation has become the norm. Modern individuals are on their own. Each in a crucial sense is more and more stuck with himself or herself. The search for self is the mooring of last resort. When that, too, gives way, the crisis that begins with the specific aches and pains of battered selves ends with an overwhelming longing to be all of a piece. In short, to find salvation through some new source of psychic harmony.

To be sure, homelessness is the darker side of a rootless openness that has also been experienced as the thrill of exploration and discovery. "Home I have none. Flock I have none," Jonathan exults in Richard Bach's best selling *Jonathan Livingston Seagull.*[24] "I like it here," W. H. Auden wrote after emigrating to the United States in 1939, "just because it is the Great Void where you have to balance without handholds."[25] So doubtless the darker trend too will continue to be heralded only as freedom by shortsighted commentators and fashion-setting magazines. But the desperate fiction of their rationalizations is bound to show. Not everyone is capable of surviving in the great void without handholds. One day the staggering human and national cost will become unmistakable. A generation is growing up, a massive part of which is relationally retarded and psychologically undernourished. Titanic social consequences are inevitable. The harvest of homelessness will be bitter.

Testifying before a congressional committee in 1984, Dr. Armand Nicholi of the Harvard Medical School diagnosed the spreading problem of homelessness and recommended that the government recognize fully that "families are the vital cells that constitute the flesh and blood of our society. When one family disintegrates, so does a part of our society." Standing against the windy nonsense about "creative divorce" and "alternative life-styles," his conclusion strikes a realistic counterpoint: "The disruption of families not only imposes a vast economic burden on the nation but inflicts on individual citizens more sorrow and suffering than war, poverty, and inflation combined."[26]

As early as the 1830s, Alexis de Tocqueville recognized the loneliness of American individualism. "Thus not only does democracy make every man forget his ancestors, but it hides his descendants and separates his contemporaries from him; it throws him back forever upon himself alone and threatens in the end to confine him entirely within the solitude of his own heart."[27] In current conditions, with America's divorce rate the highest in the world and the highest it has ever been, loneliness will be a problem that reaches epidemic proportions. More frequent contacts mean little. Undernourished on deep and stable relationships while overfed on the value of status, possessions, and competition, modern people are often loneliest when with other people.

In the short-term, overburdened individualism will lead to many problems other than loneliness—painful and underestimated though loneliness is. It will impose almost intolerable burdens on those intimate relationships that are deep and stable, for these better ones must bear the weight of all the others—like a millionaire threatened with poverty in bailing out his impecunious relations. It will inflate the anxiety-market for fast-changing, wildly swinging ideological fashions in individual liberations. It will foster perversions, not as deviant behavior, but as widely accepted ways of life, many of which will only deepen individualism further.

In the end, the hyperindividualism bred by homelessness will lead to the unmasking of "psychological man" and perhaps even to the overthrow of the therapeutic society. Until recently, the creation of the latter has been hailed as a triumph and a revolution, a double liberation that spelled the freeing of the self both from the soul (and all the demands of the sacred) and of the self from society (and all the demands of the collective). Increasingly, however, the therapeutic triumph is being seen for what it is—Western liberal society's massive attempt to recodify life from the private world outward, which is no more successful than totalitarian socialism's massive attempt to recodify life from the public world inward. When it takes the individual seriously, narrowing human problems down to the individual's life-story, the psychological revolution has highlighted certain problems usefully, but shown itself strikingly incapable of providing enduring human answers. It has helped with human unhappiness in a limited way, but shown itself barren over deeper problems, such as human homelessness. One reason is simple: The individual's need for meaning and belonging points automatically beyond individualism. If solid individuality is inescapably social, even intuitively sacred, the psychological revolution unmasks itself as a promise that is actually a prison, an offer of healing that becomes an abyss of introspection.

But when the therapeutic movement moves beyond the focus on the individual person alone, the problems can become worse. The reason is that this shift coincides with the postmodern crisis of personhood. The solid sense of self, characteristic of the classical, romantic, and modernist understandings, has dissolved into a loose sense of relatedness. Individuality therefore becomes simply the mirror-mask conjured by the many faces that glance into it, the sounding board that is the composite echo of the many voices that address it, the socially assigned roles in the minutely choreographed dance that is society. "We appear to stand alone," psychologist Kenneth Gergen writes, "but we are manifestations of relatedness." We owe our existence only to participation in the communal forms. "Without one's culture to define the games and places possible within it, there is simply no being to be."[28] Or as Hans-Georg Gadamer expresses it, "all playing is a being-played."[29]

Such notions are in striking contrast to the assumptions and requirements of democratic individuality and pluralism. They also bear an uncanny resemblance to the place of the individual in primitive society, in Communist society, and in the worldviews of religious monism. Little wonder that the therapeutic revolution, though soft, private, and Western rather than hard, public, and Communist, has been described as the last totalitarianism left, totalitarianism tailored to the scale and sensibilities of Last Men.

Home Truths

Certain of the more dramatic consequences of homelessness have been discussed widely—for example, the prospects of the social and economic costs of a society in which 95 percent of hospital beds may be taken up by patients who are mentally ill, or the personal and public loss of freedom in a world where attempts to assassinate public figures become a routine occurrence. But two consequences are likely to play an especially important part in the 1990s.

The first is the consequences of homelessness for America's young people, especially in the field of education and poverty. For all the traditional family rhetoric in the 1980s, the public programs from earlier periods, the licensed professionals, and the millions of dollars, changes in the American family over the last generation have grown increasingly negative for families, particularly for their children. The impact of homelessness on the structural causes of poverty, for example, is an entirely new problem not faced in either the New Deal or the Great Society eras. Perhaps when the liberals' government-step-in and the conservatives' government-stay-out have fought each other to a draw, the way will be open for the restatement of home truths obscured by the culture wars.

Various impulses toward educational reform have been active over the past decade—the excellence movement, the character movement, and the citizenship movement. What has grown clearer is that each requires the other and that all of them together assume that the basic pedagogy must be related to the habits of the heart—and thus to homes. The problem of homelessness is therefore critical to educational reform. As Chester Finn, professor of education at Vanderbilt University, argues, there are two separate but overlapping crises in education. One, and by far the easier to deal with, is epitomized by the fact that the average child who emerges from the average school has not learned nearly enough, nearly well enough. The other is a different matter altogether. It is epitomized by the plight of disadvantaged or "at-risk" children from "dysfunctional families"—in short, of homelessness.[30]

Finn estimates that young people reaching their eighteenth birthday have been alive for 158,000 hours, but even with conscientious school attendance have spent only 13,000 hours in school, or 14,000 if kindergarten is added. But that is equivalent to saying that school hours are only 9 percent of the eighteen-year old's life. Thus when the remaining 91 percent includes numerous destructive forces, such as fatherless families, poverty, drug and crime-infested neighborhoods, this educational crisis is profound. In the extreme cases, such as the first generation of "crack babies" now entering first grade, teachers are faced with people "all messed up inside their heads in ways we do not yet fully understand, messed up as a consequence of something that happened before they were even born."[31]

By way of response, Finn sets out ten guiding precepts to help in the quest for better policies. These include the insistence that problems based in behavior cannot be remedied by solutions based in economics, and that behavioral problems must be addressed with truths that state candidly what few have dared state publicly in recent years. Among his "unwelcome truths" are the fact that "two-parent families are good for children, one-parent families are bad, zero-parent families are horrible."[32] Such bald truths, he says, are not something to be ashamed of. They are "the product of the species' experience in billions of instances spanning the millennia. Nor is it the only wisdom we've acquired. We know, too, that with rare exceptions, a couple that has children must remain a couple if the children are to be well-served. We know that people who are not married—or joined in some other stable fashion—should not have children."[33]

Home truths like these, and the general importance of homelessness to education, are likely to be dismissed or derided in public discussion for some time to come. Yet such truths are extremely practical. They would not provide solutions to poverty, adolescent pregnancy, drugs, and school reform in one generation. But they would lay the foundation for attitudes and skills to help in overcoming them in the next. Critics, especially liberals, should ponder an irony: Unless homes and homelessness are taken seriously, the movement for any educational reform that fails to include the contribution of families, neighborhoods, and community tradition will cater mostly to those motivated by middle-class individualism and personal aggrandizement.

Fear of Living

A second and more subtle consequence of homelessness on American national life is the rise of risk-aversion. Behind this is a general dynamic. Homelessness may breed individualism, but full-blown, superinflated individualism will always arrive at the point of its own impossibility out at its furthest reaches—and then rebound toward a desperate search for new substitute homes. Failing to become everything promised by the liberation, and feeling themselves to be nothing as a result, disillusioned individualists will seek to be something by surrendering themselves to be a secure part of something else. The life-long debt paid to whomever, their rescuer from the bankruptcy of individualism, is dependency.

The connection between homelessness and dependency is ironic. Far from stimulating dynamism, enterprise, and initiative, homelessness stifles it, and one way it does so is through sapping the capacity to take risks. Thus homelessness has given fresh impetus to the sense of security-mindedness and survivalism and of Americans who prefer to play things safe. Henry Fairlie described the desire for a risk-free society as "one of the most debilitating influences in America today."[34] Lacking the strength of reliable institutions and a home-based security, such people betray the first signs of dependency in their cautious reluctance to run risks. Instead of striking out across uncharted seas, they spend their lives paddling around in the shallows of superficial relationships, safe business dealings, and fashionable political opinions.

Playing things safe is a core axiom of the therapeutic sensibility and a defining feature of the Last Men culture of Western liberalism. It has been evident ever since the late nineteenth century. On the one hand, it grows from the modern sensibility of health and happiness. As Jackson Lears points out, the disappearance of heaven and hell meant not only freedom from fear but a loss of ecstasy. Escape from spiritual damnation was paralleled by the desire to escape dangers and discomforts of all kinds. Oversensitivity and overcivilization went hand in hand. A *Century* editorial observed in 1888, "modern civilized man is squeamish about pain to a degree which would have been effeminate or worse to his great-grandfather, or to the contemporary barbarian."[35]

On the other hand, playing things safe is a response to the pace, scale, and complexities of modernity and in particular to the sense of anxiety and insecurity they breed. One late-Victorian woman had the habit of taking six-hour train rides because "it is such a comfort not to have the fireman come in to ask whether he shall put any more coal in the fire, and the engineer pulls his throttle without looking to see if I signal him; and even if the train was off the track, it is none of my business, and nobody will think of blaming me for it."[36] In our day, playing things safe fits in with the therapeutic revolution and our culture of contentment. Both are a part of the overall longing for psychic harmony that is a response to the dire homelessness of modernity. As Peter Berger and Jackson Lears both argue, interpreters of the therapeutic revolution tend to trace it back to its formal and explicit roots in psychoanalysis, whereas its historical roots are older and its sociological impulses are wider. Goethe foresaw it in 1782: "Speaking for myself, I do believe humanity will win in the long run; I am only afraid that at the same time the world will have turned into one huge hospital where everyone is everyone else's humane nurse."[37]

This feature of Last Men sensibility is especially vital to the American republic because risk-taking and exploring have always been prominent in the small company of ideals that blazed the trail for Americanism. They have been like the daring scouts who pointed the way forward for enterprise, dynamism, and achievement. Recklessness is not a virtue, but neither is the equal though opposite problem of risk-refusal. If they had not been willing to take risks, no pilgrims would have sailed, no frontierspeople explored, no farmers settled, no revolutionaries fought for independence, no theorists framed constitutions, and no entrepreneurs ventured their capital. America could not have been America.

Today, however, as Mary Douglas, Aaron Wildavsky, Peter and Brigitte Berger, and others have observed, the reluctance to run risks has become a pronounced feature of certain social strata in America as in most other Western nations. Almost everyone in America is aware of homelessness as never before at a time when almost everything worthwhile in our world has higher risks than ever—whether making a marriage commitment, raising children, running a business, defending a democracy, or going on a vacation abroad. The desire for a risk-proof life is therefore understandable. People want marriage without ties, sexual relations without children, an invincible nuclear shield without challenge, and space exploration without mishaps.

Risk-refusal has very practical consequences. It contributes to welfare dependency, to the alarming rise of tort (liability) law and thus to a risk-reducing insurance in the economy and risk-eliminating regulations in regard to the environment. But the notion of a risk-free existence rests on a dangerous illusion and leads to an irony: As the Bergers put it, "Those who take no risks end up risking the most."[38] This dilemma is seen at its sharpest in some of the attitudes behind nuclear pacifism, such as in the suicidal surrealism of the Princeton protester's placard, "Nothing in life is worth dying for."

Such risk-refusal breeds the deep, modern longing for dependency that is both a flight from freedom and a hunger for a home. Throughout the world in this century, this yearning has already taken many forms, such as nostalgia, traditionalism, attraction to totalitarianism, escape into the future, new religious movements, passionate political identifications with this or that utopian ideal or victimized community, state dependency, reliance on bureaucratic expertise, and so on. The outward forms have varied, as have the rationales by which they have been justified. But the psychosocial dynamics have been the same—meaning through membership or "I belong, therefore I am." Thus the political implications of homelessness for the future must be used to offset the understandable euphoria that followed the crisis of totalitarianism. As Peter Berger points out, there is a correct term for the political expression of this yearning, a yearning for a sense of "at-home-ness" that reunites private and public, self and society into one safe, strong whole. The term is totalitarianism.[39]

Following 1989, it can be seen that the hunger for at-home-ness is assuaged by tribalism as much as by totalitarianism, or by a therapeutic rather than a political totalitarianism. But the essential point remains. In its widest sense, homelessness is far more than a matter of purely individual significance. It is of the utmost importance politically. While posing as a child-centered culture, America in the last generation has turned antifamily with a vengeance. With a second-rate education, a third-rate diet of entertainment, and a fourth-rate awareness of discipline and constraint, the contemporary American family is not raised to last, let alone produce independent and responsible adults and citizens.

If American democracy is to remain healthy, it must face up to the family issue. It must arrest the forces of chaos represented by individualism and relativism on one side and the forces of control represented by the various antifamily ideologies, pseudoliberations, and bureaucratic dependencies on the other. The strength and stability of individual homes and of the deeper philosophical and social sense of being "at home in the universe" must be recovered. The deep intrinsic links between faith, family, and democratic freedom cannot be mocked so blithely.

17

The Last Hero

The third cancer that constitutes the crisis of republican character is herolessness. This condition results from the decline of heroism, leadership, and the place of positive models in American society. Once again, it is not a uniquely American problem. But because of the character and state of American institutions, such as the media and the presidency, it works itself out in distinctively American ways that are important for the nation and the world.

There are many reasons for the twin crises of leadership and heroism. They range from the decline of the ideal of public virtue to the social dislocations of modernity that underline the links between generations as much as they do within families. But one crucially overlooked factor is the weakening of faith in American culture. For many Americans, the crisis of cultural authority means, for all practical purposes, that God is dead and society is short of heroes. What is surprising is that the connection between these two social facts is not recognized more widely. For when "God dies" in a society, in the sense that its faith loses its cultural compelling power, the universe of faith caves in not only at the point of its metaphysics and its morality but at the point of its models.

Many people speak casually of worldviews in purely static, abstract, and philosophical terms. But in both the real world and the world of living faith, the philosophical, ethical, and psychological dimensions of a worldview are inseparable. The living, breathing universe of faith provides not only a system of meaning and a set of morals but a stock of models. It has the power to shape aims and aspirations as well as answers. Human life in this sense is an arena for heroism. Living is a challenge to the heroic significance of

318

standing out as oneself. Heroes are the chief supply of molds into which human beings pour their developing characters and aspirations. Precisely because heroism is so essential to humanness, its absence is part of the deep dilemma of the modern age. Millions of individuals feel not only bereft of their homes but betrayed by their heroes and blocked over their own heroism. The chance to be what they sense they were cut out to be is frustrated, misdirected, or has led only to disillusionment.

Prescriptions and formulas for reviving heroism are two a penny, but as with villains and fools the questions to be asked of any hero-system are, who says? and why? Once again it is plain that the strongest traditional stress on ideal human character started from a perspective of absolute transcendence. Beyond even what Paul Tillich called the "courage to be," most Westerners, as the heirs of Sinai, rooted their heroism in the notion of a "calling to be" that gives a dynamic of unparalleled power and nobility to life. Yet this understanding is no longer plausible for many modern people, believers included (as witnessed in the Protestant crisis of calling and the Catholic crisis of sainthood). Thus America's crisis of cultural authority can be measured by broken heroes as much as by broken homes.

There are two other important factors behind the crisis of heroism. One, which was particularly strong in the late sixties and early seventies, is the modern habit of debunking. Life in the late twentieth century has become a gigantic crash course in suspicion and complaint. Parodying Descartes, the French poet Paul Valery suggested that the theme of the intellectual class is, "This species complains, therefore it exists." But the semipermanent elevation of the academic community to being a form of adversary culture is only a prominent expression of a far wider problem. We are all descendants of the three great masters of suspicion. Nietzsche has taught us the art of mistrust and Marx and Freud the dangers of ideology and rationalizing. Solzhenitsyn once described Stalin as so suspicious of everyone that "mistrust was his world view."[1] But this is simply the modern tendency taken to an extreme. Under the corrosive acid of psychological insight and sociological explanation, human greatness has crumbled into a pile of subconscious motives and cultural conditioning.

What this means for heroism is that disbelief is rarely suspended long enough for any emulation to be possible. Heroism is automatically linked to the cult of power and is therefore suspect. We look straight away—not for the golden aura but the feet of clay, not for the stirring example but for the cynical motive, not for the ideal embodied but for the smiling press agent ("By their air time shall ye know them"). Only then, we say to ourselves, will we know that we are not being duped. Oliver Cromwell's "Warts and all" has become, warts *are* all.

The other principal factor, more common in such a period as the eighties, is the role of the press and media in creating the modern celebrity and widening the gap between fame and greatness, heroism and accomplishment. Honor was once honored, not for itself, but for the worth or achievement for which it was conferred. It was therefore secondary. Today, however, it is not only primary, it is everything. The development behind this shift is obvious. The modern media offers a novel power for manufacturing fame. They create the possibility of instantly fabricated famousness with no need for the sweat, cost, and dedication of true greatness and heroism. And in a highly anonymous society, one obsessed with image and impermanence, who can calmly wait for recognition? Fame is the highest of all highs, and publicity—even bad publicity—is the artificial overnight fame that bypasses the need for true achievement or solid worth.

The result is not the hero but the celebrity, the person who in Daniel Boorstin's phrase is "well known for his well-knownness,"[2] a big name rather than a big person. The celebrity is thus the human equivalent of a pseudoevent, the media-magnified personality for whom television is not for watching but for appearing on. Puritan America's purported anxiety about "being saved" has been transferred to "being seen." Character is nothing. Coverage is all. As image-consultant Roger Ailes says of fellow image-consultant Roger Stone, he is a "press nymphomaniac" who can't get enough of seeing himself quoted in the paper.[3]

If the art of mistrust was a characteristic of the sixties, with all its disillusionment and disaffection, the role of the celebrity was particularly important in the eighties. "Hero-heroes are back!" it was said as sixties-style cynicism gave way to upbeat optimism. Personality became the ultimate product, public life the ultimate market, celebrity status the Oscar award for successful impression management. But significantly, apart from a few religious leaders, such as Mother Teresa and the Pope, or political leaders, such as President Reagan, almost all the icons of the young were celluloid celebrities, such as Madonna. Their short-lived "life span" was the product of media-induced spasms of popularity. And their private lives, unlike the hero's, was there for the public to consume, not copy. Even the president, it appears, was more popular than he was either emulated or respected for his views.

The White House and the White Horse

The decline of heroism creates and intensifies problems on many levels, though many of them, such as the prostitution of personality in the celebrity and star system, are problems for the individual rather than the nation.

Leadership does not necessarily overlap with heroism—leaders need not be heroes nor heroes leaders—but in America presidential leadership is one place where the crisis of heroism has squarely national consequences. The crux of the problem posed for presidential leadership is simple. Heroism may have declined or changed in modern society for a number of observable reasons, but human nature being what it is, heroism is not so easily dispensed with. (Witness America's proliferating searches for superstars and superlatives—Oscars, Emmys, Halls of Fame, and so on.) Thus heroism-denying conditions are in conflict with heroism-desiring needs. This creates a vacuum out of which comes a hunger for heroic leadership that could grow as insatiable as it is irrational.

Our generation should be wiser for having witnessed the magnetic malevolence of such leaders as Charles Manson and Jim Jones. Even small-time gods can wreak devastation when they exact ultimate devotion from their followers. But how far do they represent possibilities of the American character tomorrow? Is it unthinkable to foresee a similar dynamic in America at far higher and more responsible levels, and supremely at the level of the presidency? What was the lesson of the surging, leap-in-the-dark yearnings behind populist political candidates such as Ross Perot? Many Americans are scandalized over such a question even being asked, but the logic of certain strands of the current situation demands that we raise it—if only to ensure that the possibility must never arise.

Powerful atmospheric pressures swirl around any modern occupant of the White House, but two are especially important because of the crisis of heroism. From one side comes the obvious political pressure for stronger action by the chief executive, partly to address the mounting national and international problems, partly to counter the growing trends toward incoherence in the Congress and the electorate and inertia in the government bureaucracy, and partly because of the widespread sense that national leadership in the late eighties and early nineties has been weak.

America, in Lippmann's description, is "a most Presidential country."[4] According to Theodore White, the iron rule of politics is: the higher the office, the more important the candidate. The president is expected to be like the conductor of a big symphony orchestra, as a new conductor can often get different results with the same score and the same musicians. Even more than a reigning monarch (because of the great importance of the royal family), the president is distinctive because he is a powerful individual who is also a powerful institution in himself. This means that until the state withers, the presidency is not likely to weaken. This fact is given a mythic potency in the belief that every American mother's son—and now daughter too—has a chance to become the president. The American republic, whatever its separation of powers, has become a "presidential democracy."

Individuals may seem less and less significant in influencing history, but the president is the last great hero, the one individual who is still widely believed to have the power and the glory. As Hugh Sidey admitted after more than two hundred interviews with seven presidents, "It never ceases to fascinate me when I come into the presence of a President and realize anew that in a world of four billion souls, this man has more power than any other single person."[5] "Already," writes Theodore Lowi, "we have a virtual cult of personality around the White House."[6]

The strong and growing hunger for heroism comes from the other side for the reasons stated earlier. Individual liberation can only be pursued so far before it threatens to tip over into the abyss of introspection or its own excess. Yet when forced to look beyond themselves for their salvation, individuals are drawn most powerfully toward heroes of flesh and blood. The state is a cold and abstract concern. Its marble heart is impossible to embrace. Even the best movements and organizations are impersonal, the best tribes are small, and ultimate allegiance to someone little bigger than oneself, even a lover or a therapist, can falter all too easily. The president as the last hero therefore towers above all lesser heroes and demigods, such as the household deities of sport and the media. He alone is an authority who is personal and individual. Who else, short of God, appears to be the source and focus of such absolute power, absolute knowledge, and absolute worth? Individual presidents, needless to say, may fall somewhat short of the heroic ideal. But the continuing cycle of hope, disappointment, and renewed hope points to the fact that the presidency, if not every president, is still the focus of this deep yearning for heroism.

Our Father, Which Art in Mount Vernon

The convergence of the need for a strong leader and the need for a public hero is far from new in America and hardly ominous in itself. No one in American history fulfilled it more conspicuously than George Washington. As the Savior and the Father of his country, he was the hero par excellence, said to be greater even than Leonidas or Moses. "To add brightness to the sun or glory to the name of Washington," Abraham Lincoln said in 1842, "is alike impossible."[7]

Even while Washington was still president, citizens paid to see him in waxwork effigy and he was "godlike Washington" to his admirers. The suggestion was even made that God denied Washington children of his own so that he could assume paternity for the whole nation. Gustave de Beaumont, companion to Tocqueville on his travels, noted the disproportionate number of statues erected to the father of the nation and observed, "Washington, in America, is not a man but a God."[8] In all history, it was often boasted, there were only two instances of birthdays being commemorated after the death of the individual—February 22 and December 25. "To 'Mary the Mother of Washington,'" eulogized the Rev. J. N. Danforth taking the parallels even further, "we owe all the mighty debt due from mankind to her immortal son."[9]

Washington's deification is doubly surprising because it overcame a huge chorus of opposition (few presidents in office have been more personally vilified) and it occurred at a remarkable speed with a self-conscious contrivance worthy of modern public relations. Such deifying of leaders has not been without its later critics too. Mencken, for one, derided the fact that "the chief business of the nation, as a nation, is the setting up of heroes, mainly bogus."[10] Nowhere else in the world, he argued, is superiority more readily admitted. Thus the chief national heroes cannot remain mere human beings. "The mysticism of the medieval peasantry gets into the communal view of them, and they begin to sprout halos and wings."[11]

Yet a meteoric blaze of charismatic heroism like that of Washington was understandable. Ancient nations had their reasons for putting historical stuffing into their legendary primal heroes. So also did the American new nation when it took historical figures and gilded them with legendary greatness. Their heroism served as a bridge over the period of uncertainty that marked the transition from colonialism to independence. Strong leadership at other periods of national crisis and transition—notably Lincoln's during the Civil War and Roosevelt's during the Depression—has had similar beneficial results, and alarmist fears that a dictatorship was emerging were simply that.

The present crisis of heroism, however, raises possibilities that go far beyond anything seen so far. For the true dangers of herolessness emerge only when we take into account the potential interaction of the three cancers. What follows should be kept carefully within strict brackets. For one thing, it is speculative. For another, it is simplified, in the sense that it follows the course of certain trends to their logical conclusion but ignores the wider context that would provide a restraining force. The next few pages are therefore not a prediction, but a thought experiment that can serve as a warning. God forbid that the United States should progress toward such a future. But the possibility must be considered, if only to make it an impossibility.

Theatre in the Oval?

The potential peril caused by the crisis of heroism can be estimated through a thought experiment that combines the effects of herolessness with each of the other two cancers, as a series of questions will show. First, how far is the influence of hollowness on herolessness likely to create pressures moving toward a histrionic presidency?

Many observers who commented on Ronald Reagan's crossover from acting to politics and on his brilliantly effective use of the bully pulpit set out only to denigrate him. They therefore overlooked the long-term appropriateness of Reagan's trajectory and his brilliance at turning what was formerly a liability into what is now an asset. Seen one way, nothing could more perfectly express the logic of recent technological and psychological trends in America than an increasingly audience-people being led by an increasingly actor-president. Reagan himself described the Oval Office as "theatre in the round." Political life, he said, always reminded him a little of "my former career, and the whole philosophy was, when you come to town, open big."[12] If postmodern personality is simply the successful marketing of images that sell and stick, histrionic success is at the heart of modern power and authority.

The idea of the politics of spectacle and of the president as symbol and symbol-maker is hardly new. It certainly predates the Great Communicator who, despite his often cinematic view of reality, actually offset the histrionic tendency both by his strong ideological commitments and his essential decency of character. More importantly, Reagan was given the title Great Communicator by the media, probably an unconscious salute to the symbiosis between his style of communication and theirs. From scripted and teleprompted lines through stage management and sound bites to the use of pictures rather than commentary, Reagan was the mirror image of America's happy-hour news. In saluting him, the media were saluting themselves.

The trend began far earlier than Reagan, at least as far back as the promotion of "Honest Abe the railsplitter" in 1860. A president, Woodrow Wilson said, "is at liberty, both in law and conscience, to be as big a man as he can."[13] Henry Adams described Theodore Roosevelt as "pure act," Franklin Roosevelt was called "the best newspaperman who has ever been President of the United States," and Dwight Eisenhower, a celebrated crossover before Ronald Reagan, was described before his nomination in these terms, "He is not a real figure in our public life, but a kind of dream boy embodying all the unsatisfied wishes of all the people who are discontented with things as they are."[14]

But all that was before the impact of television. Today the media rival money as the mother's milk of politics, citizens are viewer-voters rather than reader-voters, and politicians are no longer said to run for office—they pose. As Don Hewitt, executive director of "60 Minutes," confessed about the political conventions, "There is no doubt whose convention this really is. The politicians meeting there are now extras on our television show. . . . It's nothing but a big commercial."[15] Most significantly of all, "the president of all the people" and "lobbyist for all the people" (Harry Truman) now has unequaled access to the medium of all the people. The tele-presidency is therefore the master symbol of American confidence, the barometer of the national mood. Crisis management and impression management are two sides of the same art. Tele-politics, offering visibility without vulnerability, is their natural organ. "The President," says Lowi, "is the Wizard of Oz. Appearances become everything."[16] No wonder that James Reston ruefully adapted the description of FDR and called the Reagan people "the best public relations team ever to enter the White House."[17] As Nietzsche noted earlier, "mankind would rather see gestures than listen to reasons."[18]

The histrionic trend is neither unbroken nor irreversible. George Bush, for instance, was essentially a newspaper president in a television age. But if the exception proves the rule, then an unsuccessful run for Congress by a Colorado businessman in 1984 clearly portrays the strong exception. Supporting the candidate's record and his run, *Rolling Stone* detailed two awful accidents that had left him "indisputably the ugliest politician in America."[19] The candidate himself was no less blunt. "I know you have trouble looking at me," he told voters in his district. "I even have trouble looking at myself. So take a good look and get it over with. Then we can talk about the issues." *Rolling Stone* concluded that, in an era of TV politics when voters are regularly misled by what they see on the screen, the would-be member of Congress was "the ultimate antivideo candidate. He may be ugly to look at but you sure can see his character."[20]

Democratic pollster Patrick Caddell expressed the norm when he wrote to Jimmy Carter that "too many good people have been defeated because they tried to substitute substance for style."[21] In such circumstances and under such rules, how far is it still possible for democratic opinion to be both rational and responsible? "Reason," said Lyndon Johnson in his "Power of the Media" speech in 1968, "just must prevail if democracy itself is to survive."[22] But is it? One high-ranking official in the Ford administration estimated that 60 percent of the political staff's time was spent on some kind of presidential public relations. During the Carter years, in 1977, 30 percent of the forty-nine White House assistants making more than $40,000 a year were dedicated to media relations.[23] "Needing a win somewhere" has become the daily White House fix. With so many brilliant ghostwriters, spin doctors, and political handlers, the president appears more and more like a puppet. George Bush's performance in a presidential debate raised this thought in George Will: "Why not elect Noonan and cut out the middleman?"[24]

Questions are building up across the board: At what point does it become dangerous for America when consultants advise politicians on the right clothes for the right public image and advisers and pollsters do the same for their ideas? Is it in the interests of justice and sanity that all politics is becoming one long, programmed preelection marathon? Or that public questioning and discussion are dissolving into argument by quip, smile, and wave, orchestrated by the impresario-White House? Is it really wisdom for the highest public servants to spend more and more of their time, massaging the press instead of focusing on substantive issues of state? If policy decisions are increasingly made and communicated with both eyes on their "relevant audience" and ratings, is America reaching the stage when policy is simply the pursuit of publicity by other means? Are world issues and incidents important in themselves, or are they merely viewed as a looking glass in which America can gaze on nonmaterial issues, such as its international image and credibility? What if a constant preoccupation with the symbolic inflates any and all issues into ludicrous tests of strength? What if democracy should reach the point at which the old adage is reversed and justice must not only be seen to be done, but must be done?

Public relations begins as a matter of finding an audience to hear a message. It ends as a matter of finding a message to hold the audience. In between is such a loss of substance for style that histrionic success may prove not only the heart of modern power, but its Achilles' heel. Oversell, not overkill, may prove America's downfall. After a State of the Union address in 1987 that was symbol-rich and substance-deficient, one Republican policymaker lamented, "There wasn't anything in it. They have finally achieved the content-free presidency. It doesn't work."[25]

"A revolutionary age," wrote Søren Kierkegaard at the beginning of the modern period, "is an age of action; ours is an age of advertisement and publicity. Nothing ever happens but there is immediate publicity every-where."[26] Few things are further than the histrionic presidency from the world of 1776, but it is precisely because of the former that few people would ever know. Action has been replaced by appearance, integrity by image. Favorable impressions, however, count for little now that the real need in the country and in the world is for a job to be done.

In the face of enormous national problems in the early nineties, the greatest casualty of the histrionic presidency was leadership that required courage and short-term sacrifice. What was there instead George Will called "an unserious presidency" and U.S. Representative Richard Gephardt called "government of the polls, by the polls, and for the polls."[27] Whereas historians of the future will base their judgment of today's leadership on their courage and effectiveness in tackling the challenge, today's leaders base their performance on today's polls. After all, said one of Bush's cabinet members in his defense, "When you're at 80 percent approval rating in the polls, you're not inclined to change the message."[28]

Drugged by the Will to Believe?

To this first question a second must be added. How far is the influence of homelessness on herolessness likely to create pressures that move toward a hypnotic presidency? All leaders who have power over vast numbers of people have an element of magic and charisma. Seen from the side of the leader this is a matter of projection, while seen from the side of the followers this is a matter of identification and transference. Their identity is transferred and invested in the leader, so that in the white-hot heat of their allegiance not only do his acts and successes become theirs but he himself is them writ large.

This dynamic explains the brief, irrational surge of support for Ross Perot's presidential bid in 1992, even before it was declared. It explains part of the extraordinary outpouring of public grief at the assassination of President Kennedy. Polls revealed the curious fact that Kennedy received such a surge of posthumous support that two out of every three voters thought they had voted for him in 1960, whereas fewer than half had actually done so.[29] Following Franklin Roosevelt, the presidency has been personalized so that the president is the presidency and the presidency is the nation. Few kings could be mantled with more emotional magic.

Sitting in a Washington restaurant during the election campaign in 1984, I overheard a young American explaining to a Chinese student why such a large number of young people would be voting for the president. Mention of substantive policies or political experience was conspicuously absent. "Ronald Reagan is everything we admire," he said. "He's strong, handsome, successful. He rides horses. He chops wood. He's the American Dream fulfilled—everything we would all like to be." Thus Reagan's chief historic success was the use of symbols to conjure up the hard-working, God-fearing, freedom-loving world of Reagan's and America's memory. As émigré and comedian Yakov Smirnoff expressed it in Western film terms, "When things looked bad recently . . . one man from the West Coast came. His horse was Air Force One and his town was America."[30]

Such attitudes illustrate what Theodore Lowi calls the "three general laws of politico-dynamics of the Second Republic" and the principle that underlies them: "As presidential success advances arithmetically, public expectations advance geometrically."[31] The effect is to inflate rhetoric at home and encourage adventuring abroad. And because expectations will always outstrip the capacity to meet them, the result is a "boom to bust" cycle of expectations and disappointments.

The ability of a leader to embody the history and wishes of his or her people is not necessarily dangerous in itself. Part of the essence of leadership is that leaders do not simply live and work within their countries. Rather—like Churchill in Britain, de Gaulle in France, Nehru in India, or Golda Meir in Israel—they work as if their countries were living in them and they were the embodiment of their people. The story is told of a sharp disagreement during World War II between then General de Gaulle and Robert Murphy, the U.S. emissary to Vichy France. Disputing strongly over what political sentiments in France really were, Murphy reminded de Gaulle that he had lived in France for three years as consul, consul-general, and counsellor of Embassy. "That may be true," de Gaulle retorted, "But I've been in France for a thousand years."

History, however, is also dismally clear about the follies and disasters of those mesmerized by such a spell and led by the will to believe toward blind obedience and humiliating subservience. And the same record carries salutary lessons. In the first place, the greatest danger does not necessarily come from the power and conceit of the leader, but from the projection of the followers. What matters even more than the strength, valor, and skill of the leader is the need of the followers, for sometimes all they want is to be told what they want. (Cartoonist Garry Trudeau said of Reagan: "That constant smile is a real drug. We want to believe it and so we all do.")[32] Thus, beyond his own innate power as an individual, the power of a leader is in proportion to his ability to provide for the needs of the people.

In addition, both the best and the worst of leaders show the same instinctive awareness of the appeal of the irrational. This realism is what sets them off from managers and mediocre leaders and the sentimental thinking of liberals who assume that peace, security, and increased goods are the sum total of popular desire. Churchill knew this was false and instead offered nothing but "blood, toil, tears, and sweat." So also did Hitler. "Whereas Socialism, and even Capitalism," wrote George Orwell, "have said to people 'I offer you a good time,' Hitler has said to them 'I offer you struggle, danger, and death,' and as a result a whole nation flings itself at his feet."[33]

Popular opinion has two faces. On the surface it is all demands, opinions, and moods so that, as Lippmann wrote, even responsible officials have been forced to obey its whims "like the ministers of an opinionated and willful despot."[34] But beneath the surface is another face, not demanding but dependent, not capricious but craving. Because of such expectations, Lowi observes, the personality of the president becomes "a combination of Jesus Christ and the Statue of Liberty: Bring *me* your burdens. Bring *me* your hopes and fears. Bring *me* your search for salvation."[35] It is this second face and its heart's moods that are waiting to be beguiled. Required to trust leaders who make decisions that cannot fully be explained to control dangers that cannot yet be observed, the American will to believe may one day be stretched beyond reason until it invests itself in blind emotional attachment.

At some time in the future, the deepening condition of homelessness could exact its toll in America at this point. The occasion might be when the harvest of dysfunctional relations and hyperindividualism has become a reality and not a prediction, or when America's national security is under grave threat internationally. But at that moment the concentrated experience of millions of Americans of being without a home would be transcended in an titanic act of projection so that "the president of all the people" would be their home, family, and parent rolled into one—and greater the sense of homelessness, greater the intensity of projection.

At that moment the embrace of popular opinion would become deadly. The histrionic and the hypnotic, the will to believe and the will to unity, would converge. So long as the president walked tall for America, America would walk tall in the world. While the leader was strong, the people would not be bereft. But a devilish danger would be created too. Hero-worship would no longer be a metaphor. A rescue-hungry people would invest a leader with charismatic saving power. Having saved them from themselves, he could be entrusted to save them from anything. The result would be an idolatry of the presidency and a collective consecration to the hypnotic effects of his spell-binding will. One writer in the sixties made a claim that prefigured this noxious idolatry perfectly. The president, he wrote, was "the incarnation of the American people in a sacrament resembling that in which the wafer and the wine are seen to be the body and blood of Christ."[36]

Breeding the Exceptional Man

To this question must be added a third. How far are all the components of the quiet crisis likely to create dangerous pressures moving toward a hubristic presidency? The terrible link between the death of God in Europe and the rise of an unprincipled caesarism was foreseen by several thinkers in the nineteenth century. Jacob Burckhardt, for example, wrote to a friend in 1872, "People no longer believe in principles but will, periodically, probably believe in saviors. . . . For this reason authority will again raise its head in the pleasant twentieth century, and a terrible head."[37] The first fulfillment of such dark predictions is now history itself, and America's traditional antipathy to the idea of a man on a white horse is well known. But we dismiss Burckhardt too complacently if we simply assign the blame to the diseased conditions of European society around the turn of the century and imagine that these were unique and unrepeatable. America, after all, is experiencing its own crisis of cultural authority now.

Future temptations for presidents to stand above the law are likely to come from two directions. On the one hand, the president will be under increasing pressure to act as morally exceptional. Complex political problems will come to appear as impenetrable Gordian knots, which can only be cut through by decisive action of an exceptional kind. At first the focus will be on the "exceptional problem" as a growing number of things hitherto considered wrong will be sacrificed to some great end, such as national security, democratic freedom, or reelection. Imperceptibly, however, the focus could shift to the "exceptional person" as the president, claiming to perceive and embody the national interest uniquely, will cite executive privilege and an appeal to history and then act as if he were above law and exempt from ordinary morality. Refusing to play a losing hand, the president will be tempted to alter the rules of the game.

Being "morally exceptional" should not be confused with being immoral. It is far more likely in the United States to be the consequence of high moralism—of depraved virtue and a corrupted moralism. Moralism is a link between John Brown's armed raid on Harper's Ferry, the Watergate break-in, and the Iran-contra scandal. All three cases have a common American theme that those who perceive their cause as righteous believe they can take the law into their own hands in order to advance it. Thus, curiously, Don Regan's White House, like Nixon's earlier, was both criminal and moralistic at once and the worst of the former grew partly from the latter. (In 1979, a CBS News poll found that 66 percent of the public supported a leader who would "bend the rules of the game to get things done.")[38]

Nietzsche's thought points toward the emergence of the "great man," just as Dostoevsky in Crime and Punishment prophesied the rise of the "exceptional man" and linked it to leaders, legislators, and people of genius of every sort. Those who reject the God-man would sooner or later raise up a man-God, and those who surrender their freedom of choice to him can no longer sin, since he sins for them but in their name. Lincoln, similarly, had spoken hauntingly of the dangerous ambitions of a "towering genius" or an "irreligious Washington" unhampered by confining morality.

With the crisis of religion and tradition and the degeneration of Enlightenment liberalism into shallow utilitarianism, this possibility comes much closer. Little more than character stands against it. After being a

Washington correspondent for two decades and then special assistant to LBJ, George Reedy observed: "In the White House, character and personality are extremely important because there are no other limitations. . . . Restraint must come from within the presidential soul and prudence from within the presidential mind. The adversary forces which temper the actions of others do not come into play until it is too late to change course."[39] Many presidential failures have been linked to flaws in character—Lyndon Johnson's pride to Vietnam, Richard Nixon's paranoia to Watergate, Jimmy Carter's detail-mindedness to the national malaise, Ronald Reagan's detached style to Iran-contra.

As poet AE wrote hauntingly,

In ancient shadows and twilights
Where childhood has strayed,
The world's great sorrows were born
And its heroes were made.
In the lost boyhood of Judas
Christ was betrayed.[40]

This danger points to the second source of temptation, the pressure on presidents to act as psychologically exceptional. Each of us in our life's work knows the pressure to prove ourselves, the challenge of expressing our significance as a person. But in an anonymous society people not only express their value in their work but have to earn it through their success. This puts the heaviest burden on the highest ambition—it is impossible to run for president, Henry Kissinger is quoted as saying, "unless you are a rich, unemployed egomaniac."[41] And in the case of the presidency, it tempts holders of the office to live with both eyes on history. History is the world's court of judgment that can be appealed to even over the heads of the electorate, the legislature, and the Supreme Court.

Those who reject God's authority and do not turn to such alternatives as revolution and totalitarianism must elevate the authority of history or of posterity in its place. Hitler, at his trial after the failure of the putsch in 1923, used words that were given a contemporary ring during the Nixon years and many produce an even stronger echo in the future: "You may pronounce us guilty a thousand times over, but the goddess of the eternal court of history will smile, and tear to pieces the brief of the prosecutor . . . for she acquits us."[42]

Should the hubristic presidency arrive, it will probably not be from the obvious direction foreseen by some of those who challenged the rise of the imperial presidency. The latter notion reached its zenith in the 1950s and early 1960s during the years of the Great Consensus, a powerful presidency being the natural expression of the New Economics and the New Internationalism. Like the empire it represented, the imperial presidency was swollen with illusions, and it was later attacked strongly by the thinkers who had advocated it enthusiastically only a decade before (partly because, as Democrats, they deplored the logical consequences in Nixon of what they had desired previously for Kennedy).

But there is a deeper problem in the notion. "What we are oppressed by," as Alasdair MacIntyre points out about presidents in the corporate world, "is not power, but impotence."[43] For all their levers of power, presidents are able to produce effects only slowly, unsystematically, and often coincidentally to the claims of which they boast. Harry Truman may have boasted that neither Genghis Khan, nor Alexander the Great, nor Napoleon, nor Louis XIV of France had as much power as the president of the United States. But he also realized that, for all the talk of "the most powerful elected office on earth," the principal power of the president was in persuasion. The three decades since then have provided as many examples of presidential impotence as of imperialism. "Poor Ike," as Truman said on making way for him, "It won't be a bit like the Army."[44] "We have not an imperial presidency," former President Ford said in 1980, "but an imperiled presidency."[45]

Thus the hubristic presidency is unlikely to arise from an extrovert imperialism. It is more likely to be the bastard son born of a moment of frustration, as some future president, caught between his powerlessness and what he wants to do, needs to do, and is expected to do, cuts the Gordian knot and sets himself above the rule of law, answerable to no one and to nothing.

These three possibilities, as I emphasized, are not predictions. They are in the nature of a worst-case thought experiment. Yet they illustrate again the lesson that the present crisis offers no guaranteed soft landings. Choices and trends have consequences. The real task is not simply to spot trends but to weigh them and respond to them and so to pass beyond skill and information to wisdom and responsibility. One thing, too, is plain from the crisis of republican character as a whole. Tackling the problems of America on a purely moralistic plane is fruitless and naive, as a chorus of pundits solemnly intones. But the same is now true of every discipline. Each, at best, is only partial. The deepest problems may not be solvable by moralizing, but nor are they amenable to solutions that are purely economic, purely sociological, purely legislative, or purely technical. Behind political diseases are nonpolitical sources. The deepest problems point beyond themselves and require a wholeness of response that includes the place of character and behavior and much, much more. As philosopher Ludwig Wittgenstein said famously, "The meaning of the world lies outside of the world."[46] Or as Carl Gustav Jung wrote in his diary just prior to his death, "The decisive question for man is: Is he related to something infinite or not? That is the telling question of his life."[47]

That is now America's decisive question too. The optical illusion of the new patriotism must not be allowed to create complacency. The grand crisis of cultural authority is more than a sterile battle of words or a fruitless series of cultural dogfights. Different definitions of humanness, freedom, justice, and reality are a stake and the national and international consequences of the outcome will be titanic as well as global.

18

The Enlightenment's Last Laugh

We turn now to assess the prospects for an American renaissance and, in particular, to discuss the four most likely outcomes of the crisis of cultural authority. The first and second broad outcomes are on the same side of the watershed question, Will religion prove decisive in the public square? Both pivot on a negative answer. They assume that religion will not continue to be decisive in American public life, but in the case of the first outcome that this will not matter for the nation. Instead the first outcome sees the arrival of a prosperous, deeply liberal, essentially secular public America. In this public triumph of the secular, a nonreligious America, which was on the threshold in the 1790s but has only rarely come close to cultural dominance since then, would control the citadels of thought and power. After a long seesaw struggle with the Reformation heritage, the Enlightenment would have the last laugh.

Leading on Points

The first possible outcome is not only first logically, but it also enjoys enough cultural advantages to put it comfortably ahead on points at the moment. It is true that some observers of the culture wars give the edge to the conservative alliance. Sociologists Jeffrey Hadden and Anson Shupe, for example, argue that "the conservative Christian movement has the potential to become solidified enough to 'take over the country,'" becoming the single most powerful force in the country by the end of the century.[1] But many more observers would agree with James Davison Hunter, that the liberal alliance has far stronger institutional resources and power behind it.

334

First, at a time when the knowledge industry accounts for about a third of the gross national product and knowledge workers are over 40 percent of the economically active population, what Michel Foucault calls the "knowledge regime" of the liberal alliance is all-powerful in the knowledge sector of American society. Second, this dominance receives a sort of tacit patronage and protection from the state because of the close ties between the knowledge industry and such fields as science and education that are almost appendages of the state. Third, the liberal alliance occupies a position in society that allows it to exercise far greater influence than the conservative alliance. Thus most evangelical Protestants, conservative Catholics, and Orthodox Jews are members of the lower middle and working classes, whereas mainline Protestants, liberal Catholics, and Reform Jews tend to be highly educated, wealthier, upwardly mobile, and professional. Equally, whereas much of the conservative alliance is found in small town and rural areas of the South and Midwest, the liberal alliance is strongly represented in key urban centers, such as Boston, New York, Chicago, San Francisco, and Los Angeles.[2]

For such reasons as these, this first outcome currently enjoys the status of front runner among the four options. Apart from its comfortable fit with the European precedent, it gains credence from the sometimes tacit, sometimes vocal support of the academic and communications elites in America. If this were not advantage enough, the outcome is also promoted tirelessly by a wide front of dedicated activists ranging from certain more aggressive ACLU members to the American Atheists. Ironically, it also receives massive backing from two types of religious believers, many Christians included: those silent millions who appear quite happy that their faith should remain a "wholly private affair," privately engaging, but socially irrelevant; and those whose recent forays into public life have demonstrated more zeal than wisdom and have helped bring about the very revulsion to religion in public life that they oppose.

The full color and richness of this first outcome could be painted in through a blend of many different factors, but it requires two main assumptions to give it credibility. First, this outcome assumes that the economy will revive, whether through high or low pathways of growth. It could perform even more effectively than in the eighties because of such factors as the boost to competitiveness from increased foreign competition, the likelihood of new breakthroughs based on technological inventiveness, and the stimulus to self-reliance given by the expansion of the informal economy.

In turn, such economic growth would encourage greater individual freedom and, by stimulating the general attractiveness of the American

Dream, would help to ease people over the problems of the crisis of tradition, especially the more public problem of the collapse of the consensus and the more personal one of social fragmentation. Together with a minimum of necessary technological surveillance, prosperity would thus provide "the people of plenty" with a continuing rationale for social progress and individual freedom despite the dawning of a publicly postreligious America. In such a Last Men state of affairs, fear of nihilism would lose all its apprehension. To be fulfilled and entertained would be the highest goal, to be ill or bored the most common evils. As Philip Rieff writes in hailing the triumph of the therapeutic, "Perhaps the elimination of the tragic sense— which is tantamount to the elimination of irreconcilable moral principles— is no tragedy. Civilization could be, for the first time in history, the expression of human contents rather than the consolatory control of discontents."[3]

Second, this outcome assumes the steady continuation of recent secularizing trends in public life, bringing America more into line with most other highly modernized countries, completing trends discussed earlier as the "intellectual declaration of independence" and ushering in a publicly nonreligious America. The general situation in the world as a whole is clear. Since 1900, the percentage of the world's atheistic and nonreligious peoples (ranging from militant, hardline Communists to the self-contented agnosticism of, say, happy-go-lucky windsurfing addicts) is said to have grown from 0.2 percent to 21.3 percent—in other words, from a mere one-fifth of one percent to over one-fifth of the world's population.[4] This growth is the most dramatic change on the religious map of the twentieth century, and it means that broadly secular people now form the second large bloc of "faith" in the world, second only to the Christian community, and gaining on it fast.

Yet this first possibility needs careful stating, because at first sight it contradicts the earlier insistence that levels of faith in America are exceptional. Is America likely to be "Europeanized" so suddenly, its last great point of exceptionalism disappearing altogether? Probably not, and the outlining of this first outcome should be guarded against two misunderstandings. First, the triumph of secularism in the public square does not mean that explicitly secularist philosophies are likely to become the personal beliefs of most Americans. Such a general cultural dominance is unlikely. From the slave-based Athens of Pericles down through the leisured, aristocratic world of the Enlightenment *philosophes* to the University-dominated secularism of today, pure and explicit secularism has always been a minority interest. Even in their heyday in the nineteenth century, secularist societies appealed only to a comparative few. Because secularism as a philosophy is different from secularization as a process, historians could say of nineteenth-century Europe, "Enlightenment was of the few. Secularization is of the many."[5] Explicit secularist influences in America are therefore likely to increase their dominance only in certain limited spheres—in the academic world above all, but also in the press and media and a few other key areas of national life.

But at the same time the assumption is that secularity will increase even where secularism does not—especially among religious believers. Outside specific strongholds of secularism, secularity (as a style of behavior that gives no practical place to supernatural perspectives or values) will be on the increase in America even though strict secularism (as a belief that explicitly denies the existence of God, gods, or the supernatural) might attract little more popular appeal than it does today. This likelihood is already supported by an ironic trend: Over the last ten years fundamentalists have emerged unrivaled as the "worldliest" Christians in America. Once world-denying by definition, and still claiming to be able to detect worldliness in liberal theology at long distance, fundamentalists in such areas as life-style, direct mailing techniques, use of television, and a general reliance on both the therapeutic and managerial revolutions have not only copied the ways of the world but actually led them and perfected them. Modernity has all but made the world-denying stance unthinkable, so that much "increased religiosity" is actually a new secularity with a religious gloss.

Second, expressing the point differently, the triumph of secularism in the public square need not mean that religion will disappear in any marked way. How religious believers perform statistically remains to be seen, but this first outcome envisages that the strength of religion will almost certainly continue, and perhaps even increase—but only in terms of private relevance. There would still be millions of religious believers in America, from Christians and Jews to the more colorful devotees of Asian religion, but their faith would never be more than privately engaging while publicly irrelevant. In this sense, America would never be fully "Europeanized." But however many believers remain, they would form only the religious pieces in a variegated American mosaic, and stretched over the mosaic itself would be a strictly secular canopy of public meaning.

The important point for this first outcome is that even such a drastic public and personal weakening of the influence of religion would not matter to the nation. As supporters of this outcome see it, the crisis of cultural authority would result in a revaluation, not a devaluation, of American ideals. Talk of the need for a religiously grounded moral consensus or a public philosophy was natural in the nation's early days. National unity was not yet cemented and such language acted to boost and reassure. But nowadays America is America is America and the United States is a reality, not an aspiration. Such a rhetoric of religious legitimacy is therefore redundant, they say, although an important and interesting legacy from the past. What faith and morals did once, modern substitutes, such as law, technology, and prosperity can take over.

Plainly, this first outcome represents a major rupture in the continuities with America's distant past, though it fits in well with certain recent trends, such as the Europeanizing of America. Thus, if the crisis of cultural authority has brought America to a turning point, that is so only from the perspective of tradition and from the more religious account of it at that. From the alternative perspective of the Enlightenment and more recent secularizing trends, there is no ultimate crisis or dramatic turning point at all, only steady progress in what is deemed a better direction.

Such a combination of dominance and dedication on the secular side and drift and defeat on the religious side make this first outcome one that is difficult to argue against, particularly since its direction and thrust are a close, though slower, recapitulation of the experience of modernization elsewhere. But American front runners are notoriously prone to stumble, and even when they seem to go from strength to strength, their very success creates a bandwagon momentum that allows no time for thoughtful questions. It is therefore worth noting that this outcome pivots on a critical question at the heart of the crisis of cultural authority: Will a secularly based public philosophy provide an adequate grounding for traditional American ideals? The answer to this question will be the difference between a revaluation and a devaluation of American ideals. For again, the real challenge of the crisis of cultural authority is not that it calls past ideals into question but that it threatens the ideals required for sustaining a strong future.

Revaluation or Devaluation?

Hope for a successful revaluation of American ideals will face pressure at two main points. The first concerns the character and content of American ideals themselves. Through its triumph, Enlightenment liberalism could create severe strains for the continuity of American ideals by effecting a devaluation, not a revaluation, of American values. This prospect should not be exaggerated. First, the degree of continuity in the American ideals over the course of two centuries is nothing short of remarkable, particularly in the light of successive waves of immigration. Thus, on the face of things, there is no intrinsic reason why long-surviving American characteristics, such as self-reliance, equality, voluntarism, communal trust, and public confidence, cannot persist just as strongly when transposed into an entirely secular key.

Second, the last two decades are a reminder that there is an important difference between a situation as it really is and the public perceptions. By the end of the seventies, for instance, such was the sense of national malaise that American confidence had fallen to levels at which public perceptions were much gloomier than the real situation warranted. This is true once again in some areas in the nineties, though in others the opposite is true because of the patriotic euphoria of the eighties. The perceptions are rosier than reality warrants, but clearly they can never be accepted at face value.

Having said that, recent evidence suggests that continuity in ideals should not be taken for granted. America has always been socially dynamic and morally conservative, and these two features are closely linked. But secularism has yet to prove that it is a worldview sufficiently popular and imaginative to provide a proper bedding for American ideals for those who are outside the world of the intellectual elites. There are signs that American ideals are undergoing a marked shift under the impact of the modernizing process. Research shows, for example, that traditional ideals, such as self-reliance and trust in others, are currently being called into question by trends, such as distaste for hard work and the drive toward self-actualization.[6]

In the past, America's powerful tradition of individualism was constrained by America's equally robust tradition of religious and moral principles. Part of the logic of Enlightenment liberalism was thus offset by a combination of classical republicanism and Protestantism. Predominantly religious beliefs held in balance apparently irreconcilable opposites, such as self-reliance and community cooperation, daring enterprise and social stability. American cultural authority therefore depended on its renunciations as well as its permissions, its strong "nos" as well as its "ayes." It is even true that the tension between such opposites has been a source of the dynamism of American culture. But no one can pretend that the required restraint was easy, even in the earliest days. The Puritans stressed community and authority, but they also exhibited a high degree of individualism in their attitudes and actions. Puritans, after all, had been rebels themselves. Restraining individualism was a source of tension and temptation.

After the triumph of the therapeutic most Americans today are anything but puritan or inner-directed. If ethical restraints are weakened further in the direction seen in this scenario and the Ten Commandments are in effect replaced by Brecht's single commandment, "Be good to yourself," then their braking-effect would be lost. Certain strands of Enlightenment individualism, reinforced by the feel-good ethic of the therapeutic age, could run riot and prove self-defeating. This is true especially when reinforced by the petty Prometheanism of artists bent on generating vitality by flouting rules and boundaries. (After her 1990 world tour, the megastar's choreographer explained her instructions: "Madonna told me to break every rule I could think of, and then when I was done to make up some new ones and break them.")[7] The result would be an anarchy no less strong for being psychological rather than politically based. Anarchy, after all, is simply the condition of those who do not know when to stop. People never know less about who they are than when they do not know what they are undoing.

Such an unraveling of restraint is anything but trivial or "moralistic." It reaches deep into the foundations of civilization as well as the psychology of individuals. As Philip Rieff wrote, "That such large numbers of the cultivated and intelligent have identified themselves deliberately with those who are supposed to have no *love* for instinctual renunciation, suggests to me the most elaborate act of suicide that Western intellectuals have ever staged."[8] Basic to both high civilization and any life worth living is constraint—disciplined constraint in which moral demands and community purposes have become unconscious habits of the heart for countless citizens. Hence their cultural authority. Even Nietzsche recognized this fact. Grand iconoclast and moral revolutionary that he was, he acknowledged that "The essential thing 'in heaven and earth' is apparently . . . that there should be long obedience in the same direction; there thereby results, and has always resulted in the long run, something which has made life worth living."[9]

A "long obedience in the same direction" has not exactly been the hallmark of American character since the 1960s. The conspicuous lack of restraint is most evident in the lives of individuals. Most psychiatric problems prior to the sixties were the consequences of excessive inhibitions; most problems today are the result of excessive disinhibition, of anxiety rather than guilt. Subjective impulses have been prized and followed in the place of objective ideals just as expressiveness has replaced restraint. Loss of ability to control impulses is severest in psychiatric disorders, but these only carry out to an extreme the shift of an entire culture.

Restoration or Only Restraint?

To many Americans, the crisis of values is patent. "I think we can all agree," Irving Kristol has written, "that the United States today is experiencing what we call a crisis in values." Dante Germino, professor of government at the University of Virginia, supports Kristol. "Kristol's observation is in the strictest sense correct. There is something about a crisis in values that sets it apart from crises concerning food, energy, population, crime, and so forth. It means that we have lost our bearings and balance, that we have become disoriented and confused, that there has been a breakdown of ethical standards, that we no longer know how to judge right from wrong."[10]

But to many others, the very suggestion of a crisis is dismissed with a snort. "Values," they insist, are appreciated, researched, and discussed more than ever. Indeed, they point out, we witnessed a considerable return to traditional values in the eighties, a "new traditionalism" even. Divorce, teenage premarital intercourse, alcohol, and tobacco use all declined in the early eighties. Even the crime rates dropped sharply. Cocaine use and the number of single-parent families rose, but most other things from smoking marijuana to eating red meat fell.[11] "Talk about the end of the sexual revolution!" said Hugh Hefner in 1989 as the last Playboy club closed and he, as founder, announced his engagement.[12]

It is true that patterns of behavior changed dramatically in the last decade and that interest in American values may have reached a record level if surveys, articles, and books are an indication. But does this mean that traditional ideals have been restored? Or is the new mood one of temporary restraint rather than restoration and is the very preoccupation with "values" a telltale symptom of the demise of binding ideals? Just as an analysis of the eighties demonstrated earlier, so a closer scrutiny of this point alone suggests that the latter is the case.

At the very least, any concept of "values" must surely include the idea that something is "prized" and that this estimate raises it in some way to the level of principle as opposed to a mere preference. The acid test for such values, important in light of the Tocqueville theme, is whether they have sufficient cultural authority to stop someone from doing something he or she wants to do, and move them to do something they do not. We have already noted the breakdown of a public philosophy and the chaotic conditions of the public moral debate. Some further points are also evident. Taken together they make "the restoration of traditional values" appear far less impressive and call into question secularism's capacity to transpose America's ideals into a secular key.

In the first place, the recent rage for "values" betrays its Enlightenment origins and displays a marked shift from an ethic and language of commitment to one of contract. For an individual standing within the traditional perspective, the ethic of commitment—in, say, a marriage relationship—assumed a shared standard higher and other than each individual's. Commitment therefore had a point of reference and could be costly. Now, with no transcendent horizon above it, commitment has lost its former meaning and become a matter of contract, not covenant. It is almost entirely conditional on a cost-benefit analysis of giving and getting. For example, unless a husband or wife continues to get what he or she wants or needs and reckons that this is better than he or she could get elsewhere, the "commitment" is inoperative.

Such contract commitments are the twentieth-century logic of seventeenth- and eighteenth-century liberalism, a ripening of the ideas of Hobbes, Locke, and Hume under the pressures of capitalism without the inhibitions of traditional morality. Human beings are simply agents of self-interest. Justice is purely procedural. Social relations are private interests writ large in public bargaining. Reason is the supreme instrument of control via calculation. Ethics is no longer a matter of what is intrinsically right but what is useful. "Values," being essentially arbitrary and subjective, are only instruments for other ends. As such, they are easily asserted and easily abandoned.

At their rawest, modern contract commitments reduce all relationships to the level of utilitarian exchanges in which the well-being of Number One is what matters. After all, if God is dead, nothing is owed to anyone—except by each of us to ourselves. Sociologist Amitai Etzioni describes how the transactional view of relationships, falsely transferred from liberal economics, is destructive of any community, including marriage. "Every evening before you turn in you tally up the losses and gains for the day. If the gains exceed the losses, you stay for one more night. And if the balance is negative, you take to the door."[13]

Second, much of the recent concern over "values" has stemmed from consequences and circumstances rather than character and convictions. For a start, it is revealing how the language of medicine has replaced the language of morals in American discourse. Just as un-American came to overshadow heretical in earlier days, so today unhealthy has replaced wrong and bad. In a Last Men culture, the unforgivable sin is the last sin left—the vice of sinning against health and hygiene. Morality in the public square is taboo, but moralizing about public health is given free rein.

It is striking, too, how often the ethical dimension enters the discussion in the United States not in terms of essential character and positive principles, but extreme cases and negative consequences. Ethics tends to enter clearly in borderline cases only (the one innocent killed to save twenty others, or the abortion of the seventh child, possibly retarded, of the wife whose husband has deserted her). Thus, instead of their valuable task of illuminating norms and supporting the normal, borderline cases are often used to deride the normal and dismiss the notion of norms altogether. Without a strong framework, a host of hard cases breeds one soft culture.

Or again, it is notable how circumstances have become pivotal in deciding "values." For example, when inflation was running high in the late 1970s, spending was a value rather than saving, whereas in the early 1980s inflation was down and interest rates were up so the swing of the pendulum made saving a value rather than spending. Or yet again, in many a business school "ethics is back"—but as a matter of pragmatism, not morality. Where principled ethics was a matter of character even where one was not going to be seen, "prevention ethics" is about the calculation of consequences to prevent being caught.

Such "values" are a far cry from the traditional virtues and verities. Since they are born of circumstances rather than convictions, they have the force of preferences rather than principles. Deciding what is right or wrong has dissolved into feeling good or bad about things. The place of conscience has been usurped by "comfort zones," "feeling comfortable," and even "fun morality" (the belief that everyone ought to be having fun and that anything fun is therefore also right). Such "values" are likely to prove little more than skin-deep, trend-long, and far from reliable as a source of inspiration or restraints. (In the late 1980s, for example, organizers of charity-chic events, such as Live Aid, were soon worrying about "compassion fatigue.")[14] Self-government without the ideals for governing the self will always be self-defeating.

Third, there is less concern today with the substance of "values" and more concern with their style, the manner in which they are selected, worn, dropped, or exchanged. (In the heyday of "Just Say No," Richard Goldstein wrote in *Vogue* in 1986, "Giving It Up has become a fashion statement.")[15] Whereas ideals were once truths to be obeyed, values are tools to be used in the grand process of self-discovery and fulfillment. The wider setting of this shift is the therapeutic replacement of duty by "personhood" and the postmodern subordination of purpose to processes and the resulting infatuation with technique, image, packaging, and presentation. In this connection Americans are frequently classified according to their values and life-styles and put into such categories as "achievers," "survivors," "belongers," "emulators," and so on. In each case the underlying concern is not principled, but procedural. What matters most is not doing what is right, but discovering what the rules are. The accent has shifted from virtue possessed as a matter of character to values presented as a matter of image.

Fourth, there is a significant gap between "values" and actions, not least among those espousing more liberal values. As Daniel Yankelovich commented on the eighties, many young people professed to care deeply about liberal values on such issues as South Africa, the military, and women's rights. But with the hangover of disillusionment about the sixties and the general dissonance between liberalism and the social climate of the eighties, they did not do much to carry them out. "It's a kind of liberalism at no personal cost, a decadent form in that sense. There is a lack of moral force that derives from the huge gulf between professed beliefs and the way we actually live."[16] Knowing has little or nothing to do with doing. Unless such unexamined contradictions are resolved, he warned, those who espouse such values will either discard them as they grow older or else give them lip service while they live in another way.

Philosopher Paul Weaver points out that such inconsistencies are on both sides. Among liberals the "think left, live right" principle allows liberal intellectuals to make great pronouncements on behalf of the poor, while living very upscale lives and supporting programs that transfer wealth from the poor to the rich. Whereas among conservatives the problem is reversed. Public defenders of "traditional values" are highly modernist in their private lives, while advocates of the "necessity of religion" are nonbelievers and nonpractitioners. Weaver, who is particularly puzzled by neoconservative defenders of religion who define themselves as "nonobservant Orthodox Jews," concludes that American society is "positively awash in false consciousness."[17]

Finally, it is abundantly plain that the predominant American concern in researching "values" is with the market and not morality. In a day when psychographics is replacing old-fashioned demographics, surveys on values are indispensable for marketing products or politicians. This as much as anything explains their current boom. Understandably, the "bottom line" is not so much about values as consumer values. The imperatives come from advertising.

In a little more than a century the advertising and public relations industry has expanded dramatically so that it has broken into the inner circle of primary American institutions. Yet unlike the other primary institutions, such as the churches, schools, and the Congress, advertising and public relations are not directed toward shaping beliefs and attitudes that are of moral purpose or social responsibility. Their basic business is to stimulate and standardize the desires, envies, and anxieties of the masses. Far from being restored, genuinely traditional ideals are what must be overcome. That you are what you consume is so obviously false to almost every religion and philosophy ever known that it requires little discussion—except to the present generation of Americans to whom it has been preached as the great verity of consumer life, explicitly so by Mobil but implicitly by a million beguiling commercials and shopping malls.

Citing the current values-consciousness is therefore no answer to the underlying problem. Values still resonate powerfully in the hearts of most Americans, but they have changed drastically and even the present preoccupation with values is as much a symptom of change as a sign of their strength. (In 1990, "safe sex" advertisements in San Francisco bus shelters depicted two naked young men partially wrapped in a U.S. flag. One had his arm around the other while his free hand held a condom. The caption read: "Life, Liberty, and the Pursuit of Happiness.")[18] Mid-1980s magazine articles may have heralded "a return to more traditional family values." But when they cited as reasons such factors as growing older and more lonely and the recognition of the penalties of the way people were living, they were themselves an illustration of changes based on circumstances and consequences, not convictions. (One young homosexual, dying of AIDS in Washington, D.C., summed up the risk factor in a nutshell, "Anybody in this day and age that is sexually promiscuous is playing Russian roulette and there's more than one bullet in the chamber at this point.")[19]

It was instructive to ask the advocates of such 1980s "traditional values" a supplementary question. Why is it that you and your children should lead the moral life? The answers were revealing. Divorce is a hassle. Promiscuous sex has its complications. Overeating is a proven cause of heart attacks. The appeal, in other words, was to self-interest, not ideals. It was no more a matter of principle than those following the 1960s "pacifism" who simply did not want to fight in Vietnam. Whereas the association of sex and sin prompts only a smirk, the association of sex and death triggers action—through fear. But induced this way, chastity is no longer an ideal. It is only an insurance, the old fears of "conception, infection, and detection" but in an altered guise.

Trends in the eighties gave evidence of a period of widespread restraint and some semblance of a return to traditional ideals, but they lacked substance. Two reasons made this inevitable. The lesser problem stems from the obvious contradiction between traditional and modern ways of living— when national traditions are pressed into the service of radically individualist life-styles, they become distorted and hollow. The greater problem stems from the less obvious contradiction between traditional ideals and modern philosophy. Traditionally, ideals defined and measured human behavior. They commanded obedience because they were given in the very order of things. Now, following the triumph of Enlightenment liberalism, ideals have been demoted to "values" and the similar-sounding word should fool no one. Being given, objective, and universal, ideals measure us and have behind them an absolute requirement. Values, by contrast, are self-created, subjective, and relative, so they are useful to us only as measuring sticks that we may easily discard for others. Press modern secular values determinedly or carelessly and their restraining power is nil. Such euphemisms as "adult," "mature," "meaningful relationships," and "alternate life-styles" do not hold for long. One who refuses to stay within the bounds of modern values finds them as flimsy as a Potemkin village erected to conceal the moral abyss.

Mention of the abyss is a further reminder of Nietzsche, who stands across the path of facile optimism like a monumental roadblock. Nietzsche brought the concept of "values" into the center of Western ideas, just as his influence on Max Weber brought the term into currency in American speech. If God is dead, then the crux of modernity is apprehending the logic of nihilism. "Values," therefore, are what we create in the face of chaos. Only by such titanic acts of creation can we overcome the dreadful paralysis of will that results from the dizzying logic of relativism. "Whenever I hear that word," writes Philip Rieff, "I know yet another god has died."[20]

Nietzsche's relentless logic exposes the contradiction in Enlightenment liberalism. Liberal rhetoric remains optimistic—speaking of such things as "human liberation," "progressive education," and "egalitarian democracy"— but the reality beneath the rhetoric can no longer support such confidence. The swirling down-draughts of the abyss are not denied so easily. The logic of relativism and the language of "values" are one. Gradually the dark vortex of the former will suck out the stuffing of the latter until America's last value, freedom, is emptied of all content and liberalism itself crumples exhausted into a shallow nihilism of the pragmatic spirit.

The question therefore still stands: Has the long-running continuity of American character and ideals been ruptured decisively and would this problem be aggravated further under the conditions of this first outcome? Both the Protestant Reformation and the Puritan revolution were subversive because they undermined popular acceptance of previous authoritarian structures. Chances are, the rejection of a transcendent horizon and the recent erosion of traditional ideals will accomplish just as profound a revolution, but in an entirely different direction.

Nostalgia for an Old Rivalry?

The second pressure point concerns not the ideals themselves, but their contributing sources. The success of this first outcome would represent a drastic upset of the subtle consensus that has undergirded America for most of its history. As we have seen, most highly diverse nations that seek to remain both free and united have a special need of a consensus. Building a country without monuments or ruins and lacking traditional ties, such as ancestral kinship and ancient institutions, the diverse peoples who set out to forge a single American community had a special need for a common vision of the common good. In this century the once-hard edges of the original national covenant have been eroded beyond recognition. But even the rather misty national consensus that was its successor played a vital role until the sixties. As Tocqueville again saw so clearly, the major bulwark against extremism was not repressive laws but the restraints of character, custom, and consensus.

Yet what this first outcome entails is the unbalancing of specific contributions to American's public philosophy. American revolutionary thought was fed by many streams of ideas—classical republicanism, New England puritanism, Enlightenment rationalism, English common law, British political radicalism, and so on. But since the eighteenth century, the three most powerful contributors to the consensus throughout all its fluctuations have been classical republicanism, the Reformation, and progressive liberalism.

During all this time the open tension between the Reformation and the Enlightenment has been obvious. Thus the Founders were mostly deists, yet the Calvinist clergy were the most consistent supporters of the revolution; and Thomas Jefferson, seen correctly as a deist, was elected president in 1800 at the same time as a great religious revival was sweeping the parts of the land that voted for him. The contradictions in this unstable mixture are obvious, and the instability might have shown through earlier if the Declaration of Independence and the Constitution had not muted the contradictions and served as truce documents between partisans of "Nature's God" (as Jefferson originally drafted it) and believers in "divine Providence" (as Congress added judiciously). Thus the two competing origins came to be blended together in the national consensus in ways too deep, too numerous, and too subtle to be unraveled easily.

But the logic of this first outcome represents a critical development several stages beyond this truce. If the confrontations prior to the revolutionary period were transcended in the temporary cease-fire of the late eighteenth century, they were blurred further by the rise of nineteenth-century culture and in particular its characteristic compromise between high moralism and progressive optimism. Yet this, in turn, proved to be the unstable consensus that the young intellectuals shattered with such surprising ease in 1912, whose destruction was completed by a similar movement of young firebrands in the sixties and is now so evident in the culture wars.

What this first outcome entails, therefore, is the public triumph of the Enlightenment over the Reformation, of Rousseau over Calvin, and of the majority of the Founders over the majority of the Pilgrims. Liberal democracy, the first great secular religion in Western history, would have severed its ties with its Christian past. With its Enlightenment heritage strong, liberal democracy has its own civil religion and can shrug off the faith of the churches and synagogues as a matter of no consequence. Yet this victory could be pyrrhic, because it raises important questions: Was the truce in the revolutionary period simply a matter of not offending religious sensibility? Or was it also recognized to be in the interests of national legitimacy and vitality? What will be the secular basis of the national consensus in a postreligious age now that certain notions fundamental to the Enlightenment are themselves seen to be a fiction? Can the notion of consensus safely be scrapped altogether just as that of a clearer covenant was earlier?

Beyond question, most of the framers would have considered the secularist project forlorn. During his first year as the first vice president, John Adams wrote, "We have no government armed with power capable of contending with human passions unbridled by morality and religion. Our constitution was made only for a moral and a religious people. It is wholly inadequate to the government of any other."[21] James Madison is often cited to support the opposite conclusion—that competing self-interests render virtue unnecessary—but in fact he agreed with Adams, "To suppose that any form of government will secure liberty or happiness without any form of virtue in the people is a chimerical idea."[22] This is the same note Tocqueville stressed later when writing of democracy. "Despotism may govern without faith, but liberty cannot."[23]

Beyond question, too, the differences in ideas between Reformation and the Enlightenment have made an important difference. For example, the two traditions were united in asserting freedom under the constraints of constitutionalism, but divided over the reason why. Freedom and equality for the Enlightenment were ideals, made possible because of the belief in a sovereign people and an optimistic estimate of human nature. Freedom and equality for the Reformation were not only ideals, but necessities, because of belief in a sovereign God and in the original sin in human beings. "I am a democrat because I believe in the Fall of Man," wrote C. S. Lewis as a modern proponent of the second tradition, "I think most people are democrats for the opposite reason."[24]

These deep differences played their part in the contrasting revolutions of 1776, 1789, and 1917, the American one being distinctive among modern revolutions. It did not devour its children. It was more gradual and less ideological than the Jacobin and Marxist revolutions and, above all, it was not utopian. Its institutions and ideology demonstrate a unique blend of confidence and skepticism about human nature. The cultivation of virtue was a possibility but the curbing of vice was a necessity. Views of society, after all, are views of human nature writ large. James Madison was very close to the views of his Presbyterian Princeton teacher and cosigner of the declaration, John Witherspoon, when he wrote, "But what is government itself but the greatest of all reflections on human nature? If men were angels, no government would be necessary. If angels were to govern men, neither external nor internal controls on government would be necessary."[25] A God who frees, rather than simply human beings who are free, was the Protestant basis of liberty.

This point is the opposite of what many people expect. Religious believers, it is frequently said, demonstrate their Pollyanna idealism by endlessly wringing their hands over the collapse of virtue. But it was the Greeks who stressed the cultivation of virtue alone, and modern people who celebrate only the positive potential of human nature. The Founders' Jewish-Christian heritage differs from both in making provision for human vices as well as virtues. Hence the need for ideals believed to be true and institutions seen to have teeth. John Adams even faulted Machiavelli for being too generous about human nature. John Diggins of the University of Southern California has reminded us of the same lesson: "Religion compels us to doubt what politics asks us to believe—that virtue can triumph over sin."[26]

One secular liberal who recognized but explicitly rejected the old balance was Richard Hofstadter. In his influential book, *The American Political Tradition*, he expressed his admiration for the republican decency of the Founders but rebuked them severely for their "distrust of man" and for "cribbing and confining the popular spirit." They had not progressed far enough beyond "the philosophy of Hobbes and the religion of Calvin."[27] As a modern secular liberal, Hofstadter took issue with the Founders' pessimistic conception of unchanging human nature. Pluralism in modern society, he believed, is paralleled by proteanism in modern personality. "No man who is as well abreast of modern science as the Fathers were of eighteenth-century science believes any longer in unchanging human nature. Modern humanistic thinkers who seek for a means by which society may transcend eternal conflict . . . can expect no answer in the philosophy of balanced government as it was set down by the Constitution-makers of 1787."[28]

Will this first outcome prove Hofstadter correct or will it lead to a dramatic confirmation of the framers' realism? Will the contributions of therapy prove an adequate substitute for those of theology or could they raise problems for liberal democracy that would weaken it in the face of its internal and external challenges? Formerly, the strength of American democracy lay in the tension between its confidence and its skepticism, its dynamism and its restraint. With that limitation removed, one of two courses is likely. One possibility, more likely in the pre-sixties circumstances, is a move toward the exercise of power bounded only by self-interest and the constraints of reality. Unleashed on its own, the Enlightenment theme in America represents what Luigi Barzini calls the "sacrilegious Promethean element" detectable in America's drive. "It is as if," he writes even of the past, "while zealously serving the Deity, Americans knew better than He and tried to improve His own inadequate and obsolete idea of the universe and man."[29]

The other possibility, more likely in today's circumstances, is that American democracy will suffer, not from too little restraint but too little support. Hastened by the therapeutic age, the United States has already moved fast toward becoming an emotional democracy of the unbounded individual, the spontaneous moment, and the feel-good ethic—a route by which it will be impossible to sustain the burdens of serious international leadership. With no vision above it to inspire and bind, no authority behind it to guide and restrain, and no incentive within it to tackle intractable problems, America's freedom will grow flabby just as America's purpose will become uncertain and America's problems chronic. Such a republic cannot long maintain success. Its confused softness will be no match for the stern realities of the international world and the harsh injustices festering in its own neglected regions.

In part, these two pressure points raise issues that illustrate the deepening impact of modernization on American tradition. But the result creates a credibility gap for the American public order as much as for the American faith communities. Faith is being undermined equally, though differently, for the nation as well as for individuals and communities. "By the end of the sixties," wrote Sydney Ahlstrom, "contemporary Americans were separated from the confidence and self-assurance that once pervaded national experience by nothing less than a 'credibility chasm.'"[30]

In short, the very drift of trends and events that make this first outcome plausible now could be the same factors that make it unwelcome later, by exposing its inherent stability. James Reichley has argued that if religion is discounted as a decisive source of democratic ideals, then the sovereign source of ideals must be either the individual self or society as a whole. The traditional American combination of self and society cannot be held in balance without reference to a third source of ideals, higher than both. "The fundamental flaw of secular civil humanism as a basis for democratic values is that it fails to meet the test of intellectual credibility."[31]

Judgments on this conclusion and on the likelihood of future problems will vary according to positions held, but no advocates of this scenario should close their eyes to the deep changes and potential intellectual and social strains carried within the vision of this first outcome. The instability of the national consensus in the late nineteenth century was shown up with a swift and cruel sureness just prior to World War I. Can what remains of the current consensus be expected to fare any better in a secular America, or will it be proved that, without rules, the barbarians will win in the end? The Enlightenment's victory could be pyrrhic.

19

The Long Run Sooner

On September 30, 1859, Abraham Lincoln gave a speech to the Wisconsin State Agricultural Society that was deeply American yet un-American—on the mortality of the republic. Speaking in Milwaukee as the storm clouds of the 1860s loomed, he told the story of an ancient Oriental ruler who summoned his wise men and ordered them to devise a sentence to be carved in public that would be forever on view and forever true. After conferring together, they returned with their suggested sentence: "And this, too, shall pass away." "And yet," Lincoln continued, "let us dare to hope that it is not *quite* true. Let us hope, rather, that by the best cultivation of the physical world, beneath and around us; and the intellectual and moral world within us, we shall secure an individual, social, and political prosperity and happiness, whose course shall be onward and upward, and which, while the earth endures, shall not pass away."[1] Underscored with all the weight of biblical and classical history, Lincoln's sense of transience and mortality links him to the nation's Founders as well as to the modern sense of entropy that lies behind the second possible outcome.

The second possible outcome of the crisis of cultural authority is that the United States will enter a period of slow but definite national decline. Like the first, this outcome is based on the assumption that religion will not remain decisive in the public square. Where it differs is in its assessment of the consequences. Behind it is the judgment born of a classical view of corruption or a modern view of entropy: Once the spiritual and moral underpinnings of the social order are weakened, there will be serious national consequences that no amount of affluence, lawmaking, or technology can finally contain.

In the long run, of course, no great civilization lasts forever. This is true beyond question of a republic so large, so free, so diverse, and irrevocably committed to change as the American republic. But this second outcome goes far beyond such a vague and general acquiescence. Just as Lincoln's "This too shall pass away" loomed very close in the Civil War, so this second prospect is of the framers' long run brought forward to the short run (significant decline within the next ten to twenty years, perhaps). It is the product of factors that are far from inevitable. Disorder in human society is ever present. But as time passes, and especially as American physical cultivation outstrips her intellectual and moral, the amount of disorder increases as the energy required to create order dissipates.

Few Americans who lived through the seventies will ever get rid of the taste of national malaise. Defeat in the Vietnam War, loss of faith in the presidency after Watergate, decline of unquestioned American superiority, impotence in the face of runaway inflation, apprehension that the future might not be as bright as the past—all these things were part of the staple perceptions and frustrations of many. As Daniel Yankelovich wrote at the close of the decade,

> Eventually we will have to face the fact of rot in our institutions and infrastructure: the inability of our schools to teach; slovenliness in standards of efficiency and precision; the decay of our railroads, bridges, harbors and roads; the aging of our industrial plants; the litigiousness of an overlawyered society; the decline of our political parties; the bland arrogance of the news media; the living-in-the-past of our labor unions; the irrelevance of our colleges; the short-term myopia of our industrial leaders; and the seeming inability of government to do anything efficiently and well.[2]

Half a decade later, many people recalled that sense of malaise but rejected it firmly. For most conservatives for most of the eighties, the alarm was over and in the new euphoria realists were taken for pessimists, and pessimists for traitors. "Smart conservatives" did not talk about decadence. Yet granite conservatives, such as Paul Weyrich, refused to be cowed. After all the Reagan changes he could still take stock and declare: "What all this adds up to is national decline."[3] For Russell Kirk, a leading father of the conservative movement, the problem was more than decline. It was the "forbidden fact" of cultural decadence within America.

In an essay in 1988, Kirk surveyed the characteristics of a decadent society listed by C. E. M. Joad in 1948 (luxury, skepticism, weariness, superstition, preoccupation with the self, subjectivism) and set out his own evidence of cultural decadence in America today. These were the main symptoms: The decay of popular faith in a moral order, the diminishing willingness of individuals to make sacrifices for the common good, obsession with creature comforts and the accumulation of wealth, a failure of political imagination, a lunatic eagerness for the violent sensations of the moment, increase in capital crimes and fraud, the degradation of democratic dogma, the mediocrity of education, and—supremely—the severing of culture from cult, or worship. Kirk concluded that "a civilization, a culture, cannot survive the dying of the belief in a transcendent order that brought it into being."[4]

In the early nineties, talk of national decline needs to be stated with care. Such is the standing of the United States in the world and the state of the national psyche after the last three decades that Americans are understandably sensitive to the barrage of criticism and hostility from around the world and even from within their own borders. This barrage is part of the American burden. Uncle Sam has become Aunt Sally to the world. At times the hypercriticism has been intense. Combined with America's traditional proneness to recurring bouts of self-doubt, it leads to jeremiads on crisis and decline that are easily inflated by their advocates if they are not careful, and fiercely resisted by their opponents even if they are. But it would be highly unfortunate if reflection on this second outcome were mired in emotional confusion. The future of America is too important to be left to futurists, and one step away from fruitless misunderstandings is to distinguish this outcome from several of the muddier impressions now circulating in discussion.

Clearing the Air

First, this second outcome does not depend on forecasting any catastrophic national disaster. Numerous such predictions have been made, especially in the late sixties when the market for gloomy futures was as bullish as the message of each was bearish. But part of this gloom amounted only to a spasm of momentary jitters, and to an understandable indulgence of the new discipline of futurology. The eighties' reassertion of the underlying strength of American resources and resourcefulness has put the worst fears in perspective, though the early nineties and the Los Angeles riots revived them again.

Equally, we should be cautious of the way in which dramatic incidents in the last decade served to trigger easy talk of national disaster. The two most vivid images were those of the undignified scramble for the places in the last helicopters lifting off from the doomed embassy in Saigon, and the sight of wild revolutionaries seizing the U.S. Embassy in Tehran, holding American emissaries hostage, and taunting the most powerful nation on earth for its impotence. These incidents were certainly humiliating in the sense of being perceived as an assault on American pride. But ignominies are hardly unprecedented in the history of great powers. They can even be invaluable for the lessons they teach (in the recent case, on the proper limits of the *pax americana* and the need to understand local cultures in wider than East-West terms). These setbacks, then, are hardly indicators of national crisis and decline.

This cutting down to size of the recent talk of disaster does not mean that future disasters are impossible or that they may not be serious. But it rests, as the second outcome does, on the assumption that what will be critical to America is not the crisis itself, but what is revealed in response to the crisis of the state of the nation's resourcefulness and will. In 1922 H. L. Mencken wrote of a day coming when American democracy would be saved by a man on horseback. "But do not misunderstand me," he added immediately, "I predict no revolution in the grand manner, no melodramatic collapse of capitalism, no repetition of what has gone on in Russia. The American proletariat is not brave enough for that; to do him simply justice, he is not silly enough."[5]

A grand disaster was not the American way, said Mencken, though crisis there might be—triggered probably by a military disaster—and this crisis would reveal the inner condition of the nation. And there, he argued, lay the core of the national problem. The American people had never faced titanic assaults like the people of Poland, had never been ringed by enemies like the Germans, had never been torn by class wars like the French, the Spanish, and the Russians, and had never exhausted themselves in colonial enterprises like the British. Could they face an antagonist of equal strength with both hands free and be relied on to give a creditable account of themselves? Mencken wrote before World War II, but his general perspective—very similar to Jeremiah's critique of Judah in the eighth century B.C., as an untilted jar of wine, complacent and settled on its lees—is one that recognizes but does not exaggerate the place of disaster in national decline.

Second, this outcome—like the first—does not depend on forecasting the complete disappearance of religion. Only a decade or two ago, sextons of religion were common and it was supposed widely that the secularizing trend was progressive and irreversible. Few people hold this view in its strong form today. Not only was it based on unscientific assumptions, it has since been disproved demonstrably since then by the extraordinary explosion of religious movements at a popular level across the world. Predictions of such an extreme crisis for religion are rarer now, and are often an indication of the secularist assumptions that masquerade behind an ostensibly scientific statement. It is conceivable that religion in America could decline into a state of virtual senility in the public sphere. As a decisive public force, for example, the Christian faith could become as much a lost cause as Jacobinism in England, Orleanism in France, or southern nationalism in the United States after the Civil War. What then remained might have all the romantic beauty of a California Mission or the appealing simplicity of Shaker furniture. But in terms of the public sphere it would be merely decorative, not decisive.

Most probably, even this picture is rather overdrawn. There are likely to be Christians in the United States whatever happens in the next few years. But what matters is that this second outcome does not depend on any such drastic vision. All it needs to assume is a steady continuation of the privately engaging, socially irrelevant situation of the present state of most of the churches.

Third, this scenario does not depend on forecasting any dramatic period of lurid national decadence. To say this may seem odd because "decadence," in its clear dictionary definition, is plainly a matter of decline, deterioration, or falling away, especially of entire societies or broad cultural movements. It is a diagnostic term, and few words would seem more appropriate if this scenario is correct. But curiously, this older and almost exclusive meaning of the word is rare today, used mainly by Marxist propagandists in full flight when describing the "decadence of bourgeois society." In the West, however, decadence has suffered the same fate as many other words. Misused, overused, and rejected, it has been largely emptied of its meaning and usefulness.

For a start, "decadence" has been flattened out by popular usage. The term is now so vague yet overused that it says little about what is described and serves mainly as cliché-cum-invective that pollutes the intellectual atmosphere. Thus as soon as there is the first whiff of scandal—from corrupt politics to the revelation of some celebrity's life-style—America is portrayed as fourth-century Rome, late nineteenth-century France, turn-of-the-century London, and 1920s Berlin all rolled into one. Here, it is said, is the telltale symptom of a moribund culture in its corrupted late hours.

Further, decadence has been emptied further by the vogue for people to promote themselves or some pace-setting fashion as decadent—the New Decadence or "decadence-chic," as it were. It has become the theme of a thousand flattering articles, a tantalizing topic to be toyed with artfully, such as the images or innuendos about over-ripened sensuousness, refined vices, and languorous debauchery. In an advertising campaign in 1990, for example, Godiva Chocolatier claimed that their Royale Liqueur cakes had "heralded a luscious new era of decadence." "Let them eat cake," they announced, using the royal sybarite Marie Antoinette to appeal to the latter-day sybarites of the once "spartan republic." More seriously still, Yves Saint Laurent bared his psyche to the New York public and confessed his cult of decadence. "I love a dying frenzy. I love Visconti. Decadence attracts me. It suggests a new world, and for me, society's struggle between life and death is absolutely beautiful."[6]

Most importantly of all, American leaders from both the liberal and conservative wings dismiss the notion of decadence because they view the United States as exempt from the classical (or "tragic") understanding of the cycles of growth and decay. In what is one of the greatest, though unselfconscious, displays of hubris in human history, Americans regard themselves as immune to history and therefore decadence-proof. Paradoxically, the main conservative ground for this confidence is unlimited progress. Equally paradoxically, the main liberal ground is the fact that the obsolescence of traditional certainties leads to a world in which change becomes the one unchanging factor and thus to the conceit that decadence itself is obsolescent. (This liberal commitment to the constancy of impermanence and inquiry could lead as easily to a belief in the national equivalent of Andy Warhol's "fifteen minutes" in the historical sun.)

Can decadence be recovered as a term for diagnosing the decline of societies? There are obviously problems even if the word is to be used carefully. A society, for example, is not an organism and to talk of it as such is only a figure of speech. Or again, labeling something as decadent assumes a standard by which this decline is judged, and this standard should be specified. Also, periods and movements attacked as decadent are often extremely creative, if in a bizarre direction, and it is only fair to acknowledge their vitality too. Yet with all such provisos in mind, the real meaning of decadence as social decline is too important to lose. It can be employed usefully either of societies as a whole or of smaller movements, such as in the arts, where there is a deliberate cultivation of the perverse and the excessive that represents a vivid commentary on the mainstream culture they reject.

But if the second scenario does not depend on common notions about national disaster, the disappearance of religion, and the decadence of society, on what does it depend? The answer is that it takes into account the same issues that arose in the first outcome, but comes to a different conclusion about their consequences. Far from being casual or temporary matters of ultimate indifference, the problems mentioned earlier are likely to prove critical for the republic. Without repeating the problems raised as questions against the first scenario, we can deepen their force by extending them in two directions.

Will the Center Hold?

In the first place, the second scenario points to the fundamental weakness of America's national consensus today and asks, Will the forces counted on to bolster it be adequate, or will serious national consequences flow from the fact that the United States could soon have less of a moral basis to its public order than at any previous time in its history? The issue is not whether the national consensus has been weakened. Few people would question that, in light of the damage done to it by the intellectual and social tremors that began in 1912 and came to a climax in the sixties. The issue is whether its undergirding supports are likely to be strong enough. In short, given a general combination of technology, lawmaking, and prosperity (the former ranging from negative constraints such as computers, satellites, and lie detectors, to positive boosts, such as technological innovation), can this new trinity serve as an adequate substitute for the traditional moral component in the national consensus?

For a nation so advanced and with such a strong strain of pragmatism, it is hardly surprising that reliance on technology has become almost an article of religious faith in America. In the land of the swift, complete, do-it-yourself solution, technology is America's "god-at-hand," the magic source of her control and the counterbalance to the faraway "high god" of civil religion. Identify the problem, harness the expertise, devote the required funds, press the right button, and before long the great American machine will spew out its solution. There is no problem that cannot be licked. Yankee ingenuity and know-how have already shown themselves inventive and flexible enough to steer America through many crises. The Persian Gulf War in 1991, with all its smart bombs, nose-cone cameras, and hi-tech gadgetry, offered a spectacular demonstration of this deeply American belief.

The doubting face of this faith is notably rare, almost un-American. For example, after the rapid succession of three straight launching disasters in 1986 NASA scientists spoke most unscientifically of a "jinx" or "cosmic curse," just as earlier in 1957 the Soviet success with Sputnik I had inspired the Washington quip: "The American satellite should be called Civil Servant. It won't work and you can't fire it." But such expressions are exceptions to the general American rule. And anyway, in a fast moving, anonymous society, technology has moved naturally to take over from morality and fill the vacuum created by the failure of the latter. "In technology we trust" seems necessary as well as somehow natural for Americans.

This American genius for technology is too easily passed over with a laugh or taken only as a wholehearted compliment. Yet if observers, such as George Grant, are correct, the fact is too profound and subtle for that. The United States is "the most realized technological society which has yet been" and Americanization is the incarnation of "the pure will to technique."[7] Because of the link between technology, mastery, and will, the imperialistic expansiveness of technology, just as much as that of idealism and abundance, is at the heart of the American empire and the American Century.

Grant sees America's "dominating modern faith" in technology as a Protestant rather than a Catholic atheism.[8] Just as Anglo-Saxon Protestantism was Western Christendom shorn largely of mystery, tradition, and imagination, so the American faith in technique is Protestantism shorn of all transcendence whatsoever. The result has been to release a leveling spirit in American culture. Calculation has won out over appreciation, action over contemplation, means over ends, quantity over quality, the functional over the true and the beautiful, the contemporary and the faddish over the traditional, the literal over the metaphysical, the material over the spiritual, the impersonal over the personal, and the pleasurable over the excellent and the right.

Unchecked, the logic of this idolatry of technique would be an America with no horizon except the technical, no language but calculation, and no sense of calling but endless mastery and domination. All questions of human good would be viewed and solved as technical rather than moral problems. American pragmatism, for so long a natural buffer against the ideological nihilisms of Europe, would have produced a cool and crisply efficient nihilism of its own. Bred strongest in the hearts of intellectuals, scientists, and engineers, the lure of technological mastery could become a higher nihilism that is the elite American counterpart to the debased happiness of America's Last Men. Having nothing moral to will, but being strong and refusing to give up willing, unconscious American nihilists would rather will nothing and do so through the restless pursuit of mastery only for its own sake.

Blithe American confidence in technology rarely faces either its religious or its nihilistic character. It also overlooks a number of snags involved in counting on technology to compensate for loss of morality. One snag is the essential fragility of reliance on technology or on the mechanistic mindset that technology produces. This weakness has been graphically revealed in the series of techno-fiascos over the past three decades: the great northeastern power failure in November 1965, the scare over Three Mile Island in

1979, the national humiliation over the charred wreckage of U.S. helicopters in the Iranian desert in 1980, the tragedy of the Challenger fireball in 1986, the international embarrassment of NASA's "Hubble trouble" in 1990, and the marked decline on the number and significance of American patents. (Of the 102,712 patents issued in America in 1989, almost half were to foreigners—up from about a quarter twenty years ago.)[9] The growing sense of a sunset power will probably deepen as increasing competition from abroad (in succession to Soviet spaceships, Japanese cars, and European supersonic airliners) underlines the fact that in key technological fields the United States no longer has a monopoly, and not even supremacy.

A second and deeper snag is that, far from compensating for the public decline of morality, technology is creating a host of new dilemmas whose solution requires morality even more urgently. Questions at the frontiers of genetic engineering provide the most dramatic example, but similar problems are sprouting in numerous areas, not least the ethical questions surrounding the allocation of resources to pursue technological innovation itself. No more than science before it can technology be counted on to answer the questions it raises.

One deeply practical area where many Americans are already confronting this dilemma is over the moral costs of mounting health care. Americans are believers in both enterprise and egalitarianism. The former dictates that if a treatment is discovered, any individual has the right to buy it and the latter that since some can afford it, ways must be found through insurance or welfare so that no one is denied the same chance. But these two basic ideals are now threatening to tear each other apart as runaway expenditures on one side and runaway expectations of entitlement on the other are pulling in opposite directions. Practical economic solutions to the problem are essential, but unless the ethical factor is taken into account and expectations are changed, economics alone will either be ineffective or unjust.

By far the greatest snag of relying on technology is that, being essentially rational, technology cannot take into account the essential irrationality of human evil and therefore can never substitute adequately for traditional morality. Evil resists any translation into a calculated plan, so reliance on technology alone to fight it would end by being "rational" but unreasonable and highly disappointing. George Orwell once remarked of H. G. Wells that he was "too sane to understand the modern world."[10] The same is true of technology's power to control it. Only a dreamer or a fool would count on technology to devise a system so complete that no one could afford to be immoral—if only because it would founder on the problem, Who would control the controller? "Man is the measure of all things," we are told reassuringly by the secular humanists. But, like Socrates, we must always remember to ask, "Which man?"

Outlawing the Basis of Law

Will law and lawmaking prove any more effective? Shoring up the tottering consensus with secular laws is likely to fare little better, for in a free society lawmaking can never be a substitute for personal and social morality. The central reason for this we saw already when we discussed the crisis of public philosophy. Since religion and law are interdependent, law without religion degenerates into rules and mechanical legalism. Law's effectiveness does not rest solely on coercion but on its credibility and on such factors as trust, fairness, and the fundamental beliefs in its sanctity and justice, not to speak of the importance of its ritual, tradition, and authority. Law to be effective must be seen not merely as an instrument of social policy, but as part and parcel of the meaning of the universe. To be law-abiding is more a matter of faith than fear, of principles rather than police.

Nothing could be further from eternal verities or even legal niceties than secularized modern law, such as legal realism. But speaking of the modern secularization of law, Harold Berman warns soberly, "Law will not survive such a dissection, such a draining of its emotional vitality. On the contrary, law and religion stand or fall together."[11] One of Berman's most telling illustrations provides a bench mark against which to measure secular optimism over law. Even Stalin, he points out, despite having the ultimate in terror machines realized that he could not rely on coercion alone. Originally, Stalin's official doctrine was that, like the state, law would be a transitional expedient that would wither away soon after the revolution. But by the mid-1930s Stalin himself denounced this view as "legal nihilism" and introduced "socialist legality" in its place, building up the sacred dignity of Soviet courts as well as the sacred duty of Soviet citizens. Stalin was astute enough to realize that without this pseudoreligious rationale the legal system would have been too open to challenge, too little likely to inspire unquestioning mass loyalty.

Solzhenitsyn has underscored the same point. "I have spent all my life under a Communist regime and I will tell you that a society without any objective legal scale is a terrible one indeed. But a society with no other scale but the legal one is also less worthy of man." Unrestrained ethically, the Soviet system leans naturally toward repression whereas American society finds itself pulled toward decadence because of a gradual "tilt of freedom toward evil."[12] For those who launched the American experiment, virtue and freedom were almost synonymous, "freedom for" being considered higher than "freedom from." Freedom, after all, was the power to do what was right, not the power to do as one pleased. Today in America the language of "good," "duty," and "freedom for" has lost out to the language of "freedom from." But today's freedom, while appearing more complete, has become contentless. There is no answer to the question: How do we know what is worth doing with our freedom?

Without the direction and self-restraint of moral or artistic and political visions, rights outweigh responsibilities and there is a glaring inequality between the freedom for good deeds and the freedom for evil deeds. Witness the controversies surrounding the National Endowment for the Arts and the hopeless attempts to "draw the line" between art and pornography. Before his death in 1991, Paul Engle, a member of the National Council for the Arts and the legendary founder of Iowa City's International Writing Program, put the dilemma sharply. "I can't support censorship, but I can regret some of the absolute crap that has been supported in the name of art. Indeed, it seems to me that the proper question should not be, 'Is this pornography?' but, 'is it really art?' So much seems to me trivial, self-indulgent, adolescent."[13]

One of two things happen as a result of this contentless freedom. Either irresponsible freedom is granted unrestricted space and democracy has no immunity to the infection of evil. Or else law, divorced from virtue or morality, is reduced to a set of orders backed by threats and becomes an arbitrary and irksome restriction of liberty. Of course, when Solzhenitsyn made the point in 1979 he could be ignored. He was a foreigner/ conservative/pessimist/religious believer and his point was abstract. But ten years later, the fruits of freedom's tilt toward evil were breaking out all over American popular culture in a wave of hatred and violence that troubled the strongest supporters of First Amendment freedoms. Far from an antidote to the infection, the American academy had become its central breeding ground. The United States was beginning to reap the harvest of its own version of what Václav Havel called "a ruined moral climate."[14] Banality is the customary face of a Last Men culture, but its darker side is brutality. The itch for chaos broke out in a rash of aesthetic violence in pursuit of vitality.

Thus, to carve a slice of American popular culture ten years after Solzhenitsyn's Harvard speech: Andrew Dice Clay laced his comedy with a vicious chauvinism. The band 2 Live Crew with "As Nasty as They Wanna Be" extolled a misogynist's sexual aggression in lewd and lurid detail. Rigor Mortis with "Bodily Dismemberment" described the axe murder and mutilation of a woman at the height of the sexual act. King Diamond in "The Oath" championed Satanism and Prince Lucifer over "Christ the deceiver." Public Enemy issued statements of blatant anti-Semitism.

N.W.A. (Niggers With Attitudes) with "Straight Outta Compton" extolled the glories of bloody mayhem with a bloodbath of cops dying in L.A. As Philip Rieff had warned a generation earlier, the lingering death of cultural authority leaves behind hatred and violence as "twin widows of dead love." In the deadly war between the cultures, America finds herself in a schizoid state—vacillating between insignificance and omnipotence ("I who am nothing want to be everything"), between mastery and slavery, between a hunger for absolute power and absolute safety, between "dead purposes and deadly devices to escape boredom."[15]

At a higher level, the same tilt toward evil was also evident in the arts in 1989–90 when the National Endowment for the Arts became embroiled in the culture wars over Robert Mapplethorpe's homosexual photographs, Andres Serrano's "Piss Christ," and Karen Finley's performance art. But long before then, publicly funded art had sought to give itself a frisson through breaking the boundaries of the publicly acceptable. In an America numbed by normless freedom and sated with the artist's and rocker's right to shock, pockets of culture at the end of the 1980s mimicked the feverish intensity, reckless hedonism, endemic violence, and sexual perversion of Berlin in the 1920s. In this way an artistic outerclass showed signs of cultural decadence different but related to the decadence of the social underclass and the economic overclass.

Charles Krauthammer drives home the conclusion of many when he writes bluntly that "culture has consequences." Mass culture, he admits, has always settled on the lowest common denominator. But never has the denominator been so low and the culture so mass. "Until now, no society had combined total liberty with mass culture, let alone with technology that hard wires the stuff into the brain. History is therefore no guide as to what happens next. The mayhem in the streets, however, tells the story."[16]

Beyond this fundamental reason there are a number of other reasons why secular lawmaking is likely to prove inadequate. One is that not only would it fail in the end, in the meantime it would fuel the drive to multiply laws endlessly and so restrict freedom. "Say what you will about the Ten Commandments," wrote Mencken, "you must always come back to the pleasant fact that there are only ten of them."[17] By contrast, law used as a secular substitute for morality is driven by an intrinsic rationalism that compels it to cover more and more options until its creeping casuistry comprehensively covers everything and leaves little room for error—or freedom. Ironically, for example, what began in the area of human rights as a quest to expand the definition of freedom has resulted already in the expansion of federal control on an unprecedented scale. The clamor for rights is being deluged under a cataract of regulations.

The lesson is clear. When morality is strong, laws need not be. So if the scope of freedom is to widen, that of law should not. There is therefore great folly in the current notion that, because morality is a private affair, anything is right in public "so long as it does not break the law." Under the guise of this maxim, liberals seasoned in crusades against environmental irresponsibility have presided carelessly over a massive moral erosion of their own. Moral principles have been hacked down, special proprieties bulldozed to the ground. All that is not legally prohibited is socially allowed. Someday these radical rule-breakers will wake up to a world without rules. Then they will lament either the moral dustbowl they have created or the dense underbrush of laws they have had to grow hastily in its place.

A further reason why lawmaking is no substitute for morality is that, as public morality declines, recourse to law is more likely to be itself an expression of immorality, whether in the form of simple greed or deeper kinds of injustice, such as vengeance or censorship-by-suit. Sometimes the motivation is brutally candid. ("I'm a killer. I can rip skin off a body," Donald Trump's Park Avenue lawyer boasted during Trump's much publicized battles with his wife Ivana in 1990.)[18] Sometimes the motivation is less than spring-water clear. (A friend of mine who is an attorney was earnestly advised by one client, "It's not the money. It's the principle. I want to hurt him.")

Americans have long been a litigious people who have consulted their attorneys as religiously as their psychiatrists, but the recent expansion of the legal system raises disturbing questions for the future. A vast increase in lawyers has been matched by a huge increase in lawsuits and a rapid rise in fees. The United States, it is claimed, with less than 6 percent of the world's population, now has 66 percent of the world's lawyers. There are more judges in Los Angeles County alone than in the whole of France. "Filing lawsuits has replaced baseball as our national pastime," said Colorado Governor Richard Lamm. " 'See you in court' used to be a real threat. Now it's as common as 'Have a nice day.' "[19]

Part of the increase is because of the proliferation of legal rights as "interests" are defined by courts as "rights" and then protected. But much is also because of a specious desire to find security through law or even because of assertiveness, anger, or greed, whether the plaintiffs' or the legal profession's. People who can get their case to the courts stand to win a fortune, as do the attorneys with their "contingency fee" system. Only in America could a man try to commit suicide by jumping in front of a train and then successfully sue the New York City Transit Authority for $650,000 for the injury suffered in his unsuccessful attempt on his own life.[20] Or a fireman sue the city for $5 million for the "pain and suffering" caused by a fleabite in the firehouse.[21] In 1986 New York City was forced to employ 120 full-time personal injury specialists and to pay out $938.9 million to resolve claims—including $17 million for sidewalk falls alone.[22] As Bob Hope quipped, America is a country where the Olympics and the divorce lawyers both have the same slogan—Go for the gold.

The consequences of the degradation of law can be seen in many fields—for example, the rise of "defensive," or "no fault" medicine as the specter of the courtroom reaches into offices and operating rooms. But the greatest impact has been on law itself. Lawyers in America have come to be seen not as guardians of the law but as sophisticated manipulators who profit from rule-beating. Speaking at the centennial of the Cornell Law School, Sol Linowitz surveyed his fifty years as an attorney and the changes since the days when law was both a human and a learned profession. Today, he said, law is confronted by a dehumanization of the law itself and a persuasive distrust of lawyers. "The public impression that the practice of law has become a money-making, profit-maximizing undertaking has brought into question the intention, the integrity, and the value of lawyers generally—an impression unfortunately strengthened by the misbehavior of too many attorneys."[23]

A final reason why secular lawmaking is not an adequate substitute for morality comes back again to its lack of any transcendental point of reference. As Richard John Neuhaus charges, the strict prohibition on the religiously grounded basis of American moral tradition results, quite literally, in "the outlawing of the basis of law."[24] Law therefore has no north star by which to take society's bearings, no point of leverage by which to nudge society toward its chosen goal. In their place law may be given a mantle of authority, even—as the Supreme Court is—an aura of august majesty. But it is never more than the current opinion of the collective conscience, whether in accord with the majority opinion outside the court or a majority opinion inside that is a minority outside.

Protesting against the Supreme Court decision in the Dred Scott case in 1857, antislavery activists could rely on divine law transcending human law. "There is a higher law than the Constitution." Fighting in the civil rights movement a hundred years later Martin Luther King could write from Birmingham jail, "I would agree with St. Augustine that 'an unjust law is no law at all'. . . . A just law is a man-made code that squares with the moral law or the law of God. An unjust law is a code that is out of harmony with the moral law."[25] Such morally grounded civil disobedience goes back to one of the first great principles of Christian jurisprudence, established by theological and historical experience in the Roman Empire: Laws that conflict with Christian faith are not binding in conscience. This notion of a "higher law" could lead to self-righteousness and extremism, as in the case of the radical abolitionists, but it has always been fundamental in the English-speaking tradition. It was plain in the Declaration of Independence and there is a straightforward reason why it remains critical in America today. In a political system that depends on checks and balances there is no other effective check on the Supreme Court.

Soon such distinctions and their consequences may no longer be justifiable in America. If the judiciary turns its back on the traditional consensus on higher principles, its essentially secular law, based on philosophical positivism and historical relativism, will be a matter of morality collapsed into legality. It can therefore offer no ultimate redress against society as it is or as some elite would like it to be. All it can do is meander through history like a river, carving its course and making its rules as it goes. Aside from ceremonial lipservice, the written Constitution could one day be left behind. The once-crucial question, "What if the Supreme Court itself violates the Constitution?" has already lost its force. Whether the court is final because infallible or infallible because final would be irrelevant in practice. After all, as Chief Justice Hughes pronounced, "The Constitution is what the judges say it is."[26]

Under future conditions, secular law could even demonstrate the self-devouring nature of republican democracy itself, for at the heart of the republic is a vital tension that secularism has relaxed and turned into a contradiction. As Mencken noted mockingly, "There is a government, not of men, but of laws—but men are set upon benches to decide finally what the law is and may be."[27] If the day comes when the naked public square is closed to transcendent critique and the ultimate authority in America rests with the Supreme Court alone, the authority of the court would become absolute and essentially religious and idolatrous. At the very least, the Supreme Court would be a nine-person "continuing Constitutional Convention." Worse, American civil religion would then have its guardians of the sacred. As Max Lerner argued in 1937, "the Constitution is our Scripture, the Court building is our Temple, and the judges are our High Priests."[28]

At some future date the U.S. Supreme Court could even suffer a fate like that of the Communist Party in the USSR, and for similar reasons. The irony would be fitting. Because if the Supreme Court were to cut itself off from any source of transcendent critique, it would, like the party in the Soviet Union, be setting itself up as the incarnation of the will of history—an oligarchy albeit from a Western liberal viewpoint. Alone unelected and too little checked, the Supreme Court would become a secular superlegislature and its inevitable slide toward moral inconsistency and sclerotic intransigence would be impossible to stop. Of course, in a liberal democracy with a robust press and lively public opinion, the eventual danger to the court would not come from any imperial pretensions but from public disrespect. Too many arbitrary, inconsistent, and controversial decisions and its essentially finite and fallible character would show through.

Two Cheers for the USA

The second scenario extends the questions raised previously in a further way. It comes to an even stronger conclusion about the crisis of public confidence caused by the damaging influence of intellectuals as guardians of America's ideals. It was noted earlier that to Americans national celebration and national self-justification are one. Yet it is striking that in an age of truculent ideologies and aggressive nationalisms, the intellectual justifications for the American national mood have rarely risen above nagging self-doubts and systematic self-denigration to sustain the steady levels of their former assurance. The language and feelings of patriotism are strong among ordinary Americans, but public virtue and confidence in the official justifications of the republic are not what they were among the nation's thinkers.

Part of this uncertainty among the intellectuals can be explained by the national penchant for the jeremiad as well as a constellation of factors inherited from Vietnam and Watergate. But evidence suggests that the malaise is deeper than any litany of such explanations indicates. It particularly concerns the role and influence of intellectuals as the theoretical guardians of national ideals. Not only is the malaise most evident among the better educated, but it seems to be an addiction for some of them. Through their influence it is disseminated widely and clashes with the pictures and ideals by which most Americans have traditionally understood themselves. "The public philosophy," wrote Lippmann in 1955, "is in a large measure intellectually discredited among contemporary men."[29]

For influential thinkers to be critical of their own country is far from rare in history. But the best thinkers have traditionally been vital to their communities because they maintain and articulate the themes of communal purpose. Thus if they criticize their country, it is usually for its failure to measure up to its professed ideals. Only rarely, and even more rarely in great numbers, will they attack the ideals themselves. Yet for over a century, in every modern bourgeois democracy, the intelligentsia has been at odds with the dominant middle class. As Joseph Schumpeter analyzed over half a century ago, advanced capitalism breeds elites that are fundamentally hostile to itself. As Philip Rieff wrote, "Western society nowadays scarcely even pretends to produce a cultural elite in the sense indicated."[30] In the United

States, this modern tension is reinforced by such American factors as the exaggerated religious-secular divide between the two groups.

Personal experience and research both provide ample evidence that the more educated Americans are, the more likely they are to hold views that are at odds with the social and economic order in which they live. In Irving Kristol's words, so natural is it for the better educated to adopt an adversary stance toward capitalist, bourgeois culture that "the more 'cultivated' a person is in our society, the more disaffected and malcontent he is likely to be."[31] Czeslaw Milosz, reflecting on his immigrant experience of academic life in the Bay Area in the sixties, wrote scathingly of "the conformism of moans and maledictions obligatory for American intellectuals."[32] Seasoned in Europe's nihilistic diversions, he felt no sympathy for such fashionable and well-heeled conformism, but like many others he put his finger on a crucial point for contemporary America—the uncertain role of intellectuals as custodians of national purpose and ideals.

Other observers, such as Irving Kristol and Peter Berger, express this more strongly still. During and after the sixties, certain elites in America have been so fundamentally at odds with the basic tenets and themes of the American creed that the legitimacy of the American political order has faced its gravest crisis since the Civil War, and the resulting social consequences can genuinely be said to be a sign of social decadence. Aspects of the culture wars are quite simply American culture at war with itself.

Critics like Berger and Kristol make proper allowance for the class and regional limits of these views. Hardly touching the lower-middle classes and the less assimilated ethnic groups, the weakening of American ideals and assumptions has gone furthest among upper-middle class intellectuals who have become "adversary intellectuals," or members of what Philip Rieff calls "the negative community."[33] Once a small minority in American society, the numbers of such intellectuals has been swollen by the expansion of the knowledge industry. Through their dominance in such worlds as those of the university and the press and media, their influence is powerful and the effect of their disenchantment is potentially corrosive for the political order.

Philosophical and cultural relativism, postmodernism, deconstructionism, neopaganism, tenured radicalism—the list of specific controversial issues is long and lengthening, but what is at stake is nothing less than the crisis of the meaning of meaning and of liberalism itself. Further, the war between the "pointy heads" and the "booboisie" leaves the civic vision of the latter less intellectually nourished than is wise. Thus the cultural relativism of the elite universities (Stanford's "Ho, ho, ho, Western culture has to go!") is only one-half of the problem. Its popular counterpart is the decline of the public library and its replacement by the so-called "McLibraries" where serious educational purposes are abandoned in the rush to become the McDonald's of information and materials distribution.

Partly for such reasons, Rabbi Marc Tannenbaum was forced to describe the bicentennial commemoration of the Declaration of Independence as a "moral tragedy" and a "year-long fiasco."[34] Lacking serious and systematic reflection on the ideals of the revolution, bicentennial observers were left with images of tall ships sailing up the Hudson and with "tons of red-white-and-blue junk, that made advertisers and commercial hucksters rich, but neither enriched the spirit nor nourished the understanding of the American people."[35]

Earlier in the twentieth century, there have been times when to be an American intellectual was virtually to be anti-American. In the mid-1980s, extreme varieties of iconoclastic intelligentsia emerged most obviously in the multicultural debates and thus mainly damaged their own groups. Overt anti-Americanism still flourishes in the more extreme secular and religious left, and it can be acrimonious in its attacks and guilt-ridden in its insistence that America is sick and oppressive and does not deserve to survive. Repeatedly such extremism sides with America's opponents in any dispute, usually with a knee-jerk rapidity and a rose-tinted myopia that is touching. Jeanne Kirkpatrick's "Blame America Firsters" and Jean-Francois Revel's "industry of blame" are the natural descendants of all who have said, "A curse upon Columbus!"

But less developed forms could be just as dangerous, being more widespread. Many intellectuals are simply too specialized in their work and too set apart from society to make any serious contribution to articulating national purpose. They speak an academic jargon rather than a language people understand. They would be put to shame by foreign intellectuals, such as Václav Havel, who know more of Lincoln and Jefferson than they do. Neither zealots nor traitors, they can muster for the American proposition only an American equivalent of E. M. Forster's "Two cheers for Democracy."

Mention is often made of the marked shift in patriotism from almost messianic assurance to uncertainty or defensive belligerence. Berger's description of decadence is broader still. It covers the general situation in which the central symbols of American society have become so hollow that they are objects of ridicule or empty ceremonial (such as a couple, "he on his third and she on her second marriage, solemnly promising to stay with each other 'till death do us part'").[36] Never before, says Milosz, have so many people taken up indictment as pastime. "A conviction of the decadence, the rotting of the West, seems to be a permanent part of the equipment of enlightened and sensitive people for dealing with the horrors accompanying technological progress."[37]

Such comments are by no means limited to conservatives. Sidney Hook argues that the function of intellectuals is not to serve as poet laureates of the status quo, but the present situation is puzzling. When Goebbels mocked the United States for its hypocrisy in criticizing Nazi racism despite its own racist practices, American intellectuals were almost unanimous in their spirited defense of democratic ideals. Today, however, when American social and racial circumstances have improved incomparably and totalitarian evils are a matter of undeniable fact, American intellectuals are largely alienated from the critical defense of the West.

There is a sense in which the "blamers" and the "boosters" simply cancel each other out. Perhaps the blamers are unconsciously compensating for the boosters or for their own less critical past. Perhaps the alienation of the intellectuals is merely a matter of an elite scorning popular vulgarity, of artistic people protesting against a Philistine environment, of romantics escaping from technocratic boredom, of secular thinkers rejecting religious beliefs, or of forward-thrusting progressives throwing off what they fear is hidebound tradition. But it could also be, as Irving Kristol asserts, that we are witnessing something unprecedented in all recorded history—a civilization whose intellectual culture is at odds with the ideals of that civilization itself. Tie in this disaffection with a systematic hunting down of settled convictions and a wholesale rejection of cultural constraints until the nation's elites grow predominantly critical, and what the development suggests, warned Philip Rieff, is "the most elaborate act of suicide that Western intellectuals have ever staged."[38]

Again, time alone will show. But these are the two main problems deepened in the second outcome. The central question they raise is whether the replacements for morality can strengthen social bonds sufficiently without playing into the hands of the authoritarian temptation. Or whether, beneath an apparently stable surface, the steady erosion of the moral basis to the social order is building pressures that will suddenly trigger a landslide of consequences.

At the turn of the century, Lord Bryce admitted that he was "startled by the thought of what might befall this huge yet delicate fabric of laws and commerce and social institutions were the foundation [of religion] it has rested on to crumble away." America, he continued, seemed as unlikely to drift from her traditional moorings as any country of the Old World (a comparison which is hardly reassuring today). Yet America is "the country in which the loss of faith in the invisible might produce the completest revolution, because it is the country where men have been least wont to revere anything in the visible world."[39]

"Completest Revolution"? Events, such as the turbulence of campus unrest, the tragedy of Vietnam, and the trauma of Watergate, shook complacent confidence in the American creed and weakened the values and assumptions on which the traditional order rested. But so far the malaise has not been accompanied by severe dislocations in the economy or society at large. What would be at stake in any such future crisis would be whether there was sufficient moral character and resolve when the social and economic order fails to deliver its promise and the nation is under external threat. Such a test would disclose whether the United States is suffering from what Henry Kissinger has called a "spiritual void"[40] and George Will "a kind of slow-motion barbarization from within."[41] Secular liberalism is confidently banking on the strength of its values. But one day when it presents its claims to certain rights, it could find its checks bouncing and its deposit empty. Any liability incurred in presiding intellectually over the decline of national fortunes would be a historic burden.

20

Apple Pie Authoritarianism

As we come to the third possible outcome, we move across the watershed question, "Will religion prove decisive in the public square?" and examine the first of two possibilities that pivot on an affirmative answer. Unlike the first two outcomes, the third and fourth assume that religion will continue to be decisive in the public square. But whereas the fourth extends this in a beneficial direction, the third foresees a more harmful turn. The third outcome sees the manipulation of religion in support of a traditional culture under stress. In some future crisis, real or supposed, a leader, an elite, or a social group will attempt to shore up national strength through reinforcing traditional values and shore up traditional values through manipulating their religious basis. But if the crisis and decline can be arrested by reinforcing traditional values with religious principles, the presumption is that the politics will be somewhat authoritarian and the religion utilitarian. The religion would be chosen not because it is right or true, but because it is useful as a form of social cement.

For many people, fear of this semiauthoritarian possibility has already been raised and laid to rest. It needs no new discussion. Presidents from Washington through Lincoln to Franklin Roosevelt have been falsely accused of imperial pretensions and certain periods, such as the early seventies, have been exhaustively scrutinized for symptoms of the dreaded Weimar disease that debilitated Germany in the 1920s. Certain of the parallels were there fifty years later—inflation, loss of confidence in national institutions, cultural polarization, pervasive frustration over a national debacle in war—but the differences have always been too strong. An "American Weimar" was never in the cards.

Having said that, fears of an emerging authoritarianism in America are no more extreme than the equal but opposite folly of believing, despite everything, that all is well in America and will remain so forever and ever, world without end, Amen. Signs of transition and turbulence are evident on all sides and the possibility of a massive rupture in American tradition increases the chances of more radical social impulses. Parallels with the nationalism, traditionalism, and populism of Germans in the 1930s will always be limited, because Americans have a distinctive American character. But with similar underlying dynamics, there could be similar cultural developments—including the utilitarian exploitation of religion.

Two things in American society, it is said, can be counted on to rule out this option. On the one hand, American pluralism would act as a decisive veto on such a possibility. But this argument ignores how the very excesses of pluralism could create conditions for a rebound against pluralism itself. Events, such as Jonestown, are a vivid reminder that under certain conditions tyranny becomes preferable to chaos, even for the sons and daughters of democracy. Given the possible conflicts created by a degenerate multiculturalism, responses to pluralism ranging from fatigue to resentment could lead to forms of authoritarianism being not only conceivable but willingly embraced. In Walter Lippmann's memorable metaphor, people welcome manacles to prevent their hands from shaking.

On the other hand, the power of veto should be expected immediately from Judaism and the Christian faith, the two American faith communities with a longstanding commitment to "radical monotheism." They are thus intrinsically opposed to any exclusive state claims, let alone the authoritarian manipulation of religion. Radical monotheism is supposed to be radical partly for this reason. It represents an implacable challenge to any national or imperial culture and to any civil religion. In Richard Niebuhr's words about the Christian faith, "The Christ who will not worship Satan to gain the world's kingdoms is followed by Christians who will worship only Christ. . . . And this is intolerable to all defenders of society who are content that many gods should be worshipped if only Democracy or America or Germany or the Empire receives its due, religious homage."[1] Hedging kings, presidents, or traditions with divinity is no part of Jewish or Christian business.

But needless to say, when the radical monotheism of Judaism and the Christian faith are shorn of their critical tension with culture and become culture religions, they slump weakly from their role as prophetic critic to one of priestly compliance. The lackey spirit toward culture of many American Jews and Christians today is mild compared with the abject captivity of the "German Christians" who proved so pliable in the rise of the Third Reich ("Germany our goal, Christ our power"). But the same dynamics are at work, the same veto power has already been waived. All that is lacking is the temptation.

Back Toward the Total Church?

There are two directions from which the semireligious authoritarianism could emerge, and each must be understood in relation to the other. The first grows from the old nationalist temptation on the Right. It is the more obvious possibility, but if more likely to occur in the short term, it would have less chance of final success. This one needs to be given special attention by religious and political conservatives. The second possibility grows from the old socialist temptation on the Left. By contrast, it is less obvious, but if less likely to occur in the short term, it would have far greater chance of ultimate success. This possibility needs to be given special attention by those who consider themselves religiously unmusical and politically progressive.

The first version of sacred authoritarianism would appear reactionary although it would have strong modernizing tendencies. It would come from traditional values being reinforced through the manipulation of religion in the service of the state. But an objection arises immediately. How fair is it to talk about "using" religion? Loose talk about exploiting religion for social ends, it is objected, is easy but unhelpful. It stirs emotions, muddies clear thinking, and provides a cover for smuggling in a surreptitious but unwarranted secular skepticism. Assuming from the start that no faith is true, such skepticism takes for granted that any faith it encounters is automatically an opium, a vaccine, a crutch, an alibi, a type of social glue—in short, bad faith in some form or another, a faith at whose heart is rationalization by someone if not manipulation by someone else.

To be sure, intellectual integrity demands that such skepticism should argue and not merely assume its case. Further, that kind of skepticism should be distinguished clearly from the position that holds that it is precisely because faith *may* be true that it *will* be manipulated (both matters being a matter for inquiry). From the latter point of view, the question then becomes: What sort of "use" of religion amounts to abuse or manipulation? Plumbing the depths of each other's hearts is fortunately beyond any of us, so there will always be an area in which respect for another person's sincerity must curb our suspicions and stop us impugning each other's motives. We all have partly unconscious motivations for our beliefs and disbeliefs. Who, therefore, can give a definitive verdict in any particular case? It was certainly true, for example, that a feature of late nineteenth- and twentieth-century evangelism was the amount of financial support for renewal that came from distinctly unrenewed millionaires. But was a *New York Times* columnist correct to make the blanket charge in 1916 that the wealthy were supporting Billy Sunday "as a police measure—as a means of keeping the lower classes quiet"?[2] Such accusations are cheap and apt to boomerang. One person's faith is another's ideology, one person's engagement is another's exploitation, and so on.

There are, however, two places where we may legitimately claim that a belief is being held or used manipulatively. The first and more blatant case is when there is explicit evidence, either through open admission or indirect evidence of hypocrisy or deviousness; and the second and more subtle case is where there is a clear and consistent, if unconscious, evidence that the intellectual or moral demands inherent in faith's claim to truth are overridden in the interest of faith's usefulness. Corresponding to this are the two main ways in which political leaders have abused religion in history and may similarly abuse it in America in the future. The first concerns their conscious manipulation of religion from the outside, as when people who are not themselves believers cynically exploit faith for their own ends. Edward Gibbon's much-quoted comment on the usefulness of Roman religion to Roman rulers is the classic statement of this—it shows how close the Enlightenment philosophers were to the views of the Roman elite. "The various modes of worship which prevailed in the Roman world," wrote Gibbon, "were all considered by the people as equally true; by the philosophers as equally false; and by the magistrates as equally useful."[3]

Unmistakable in such a statement is the cynical contempt for popular credulity. But it is worth noting that second only to the disdain for belief shown by intellectuals is their corresponding appreciation for the social usefulness of belief. Religion may be the opium of the people but, unlike Marx, many intellectuals are only too happy or eager to allow the people to remain in their state of narcotic oblivion. Such a tolerant eye for the social usefulness of belief was noted in the famous symposium on "Religion and the Intellectuals" in *Partisan Review* in 1950. Half of the twenty-nine participants were openly hostile to faith, but ten were friendly, if personally uncommitted. As Philip Rieff noted in 1966, "Psychological man, in his independence from all gods, can feel free to use all god-terms; I imagine he will be a hedger against his own bets, a user of any faith that lends itself to therapeutic use."[4]

Today, in the uncomfortable light of post-Ayatollah awareness, more thinking Americans may be seriously considering faith for themselves but fewer would make sympathetic public pronouncements as fellow-travelers of faith. At best, religion is acknowledged grudgingly as somehow necessary, at least for the general populace. "Let them have religion" is often the intellectuals' version of Marie Antoinette's "Let them eat cake."

Put differently, many Americans who are not deeply religious themselves are aware of the gentling effect of religion—for example, on the public atheisms of European ideology. George Kennan celebrates the role of religion in preserving a sense of moral order, "drawn up by those who are wiser and more experienced than the great masses of humanity." "For many people, it is always better that there should be some moral law, even an imperfect or entirely arbitrary one, than there should be none at all."[5] As George Grant remarked of the completely skeptical, "Liberals have ridiculed as hypocrisy the continuing religion among the propertied and even among the bureaucratic. When such traditions have gone, those ridiculers may miss the restraints among their rulers that were part of such traditions."[6]

The second way of abuse concerns the unconscious rationalization of religion from the inside, such as when believers unwittingly transform their own faith into a vehicle for expressing their personal, social, or national aspirations and needs. More subtle than the first type of abuse, this one depends on the assumption that religion is a social necessity and not merely a popular superstition in some sense, and that it is needed by leaders as much as by followers. At the everyday level, this attitude is behind such developments as the so-called Yuppie return to religion. In 1986 the *Washingtonian* magazine had as its cover story, "God is back—To restore something lost, to find a date, to add meaning to their lives, to help their kids, to find some peace, to save their marriages, Washingtonians are returning to religion."[7] At a higher level, it has led to the politics of cultural conservatism. Traditional values "work." Western culture has "succeeded" beyond all comparisons. Both, it is said, can be espoused as "functionally true" whether one is an atheist, an agnostic, a Jew, or a Christian. Thus at the end of the day, such religious belief is still only deemed useful, not true. It too is held manipulatively, though this time by believers themselves. Not only does it serve their interests as individuals or as members of some group, class, or nation, it does so in ways that override the intellectual and moral demands of the truth they profess to believe.

Most Favored Faith?

It is conceivable but unlikely that, in a worst case scenario, future events could lead to the rise of an authoritarian movement in America. It would probably combine an assertive nationalism with the rhetoric of grass-roots populism, the centralizing tendencies intrinsic to the modern state, and the ideological appeal of a pseudoreligion. (In 1974, pollster Patrick Caddell found that 41 percent of those who viewed themselves as in the political middle thought that "the true American way of life is disappearing so fast we may have to use force to save it.")[8] Milder versions of semiauthoritarian traditionalism are more likely, but what matters is to identify the most likely candidate for supplying the faith for the new nationalist orthodoxy. In the American situation the answer is almost beyond question—conservative religion in general and conservative Christendom in particular.

The reason for this judgment is simple. In an essentially democratic, populist-leaning society, no candidate apart from the Christian faith can claim such popular support. Secular faiths, such as humanism and socialism, for example, have little of the appeal in America that they have in the rest of the world, except in limited areas, such as the academic community. Equally, the Asian religions and the New Age movement would be ineligible because of the smallness of their following. Overexposed in the press, they are underrepresented where it matters—on the ground. During an earlier wave of New Age alarm in 1979, for example, statistics showed that only one or two percent of Americans participated in "mysticism" or "eastern religion," whereas 22 percent attended weekly Bible study groups.[9] In 1991, a major survey showed that, for all the attention given to the apologists and devotees of the New Age movement, the number of its substantive adherents was insignificant—28,000.[10]

As for liberal Christendom, whatever the niceties of theological arguments, its practical disadvantages are insuperable—liberal religion generally stands in open conflict with tradition, almost by definition; its constant changes to bring it in line with passing philosophical fashions give it an ephemeral character; and its lack of popular appeal disqualifies it from acting as social glue for more than a tiny minority. The one serious exception that escaped these disabilities was liberation theology. Highly mythic and highly manipulable at once, it carried an enormous potency, but found little resonance north of the Rio Grande and received a death blow in the worldwide collapse of communism.

This means that in the United States the only realistic candidate currently is conservative Christendom, though there is a strong taste of sour grapes in the liberal Christian rejection of the latter as "Ayatollah-style Christianity" and "Shi'ite Christianity."[11] The reasons for conservative predominance are obvious. Conservative Christendom mixes such virtues as historical resonance and broad popular appeal with less virtuous accomplishments, such as a proven track record of bolstering conservative cultures under stress. Witness, for example, the uglier face of its contribution in Ulster and South Africa.

On its own, contemporary conservative religion in America would never qualify as the main supplier of a nationalist faith. It shares a theological conservatism with the great national religion of the nineteenth century, but its differences from its illustrious predecessor are more important still. Where nineteenth-century conservatism was hopeful, constructive, and largely self-evident, much of current conservatism tends to be pessimistic, defensive, and touchily self-conscious. But given the anxiety of the prevailing political climate and continuing help from its political friends, the situation could improve again for conservatism. Traditional society and conservative religion have always made natural allies, although from the Christian perspective the fruit of the liaison has always been the secularization of the church as much as the sanctification of the culture. Current secularizing trends within the churches only increase the likelihood of such manipulation, and the attitudes of many conservative Christians make them an obvious target.

A glance at history or at the politics of many modern nations shows how religion can be used as the basis for parties and movements of one sort or another. Napoleon, for example, who boasted openly that he could be an atheist in Paris or a Muslim in Cairo, was equally certain that people needed religion. "Religion was the vaccine of the imagination," he said, so "the people must have a religion and that religion must be in the hands of the government."[12] This is a clear example of the first way of using religion— open manipulation. In the United States there are similar, though milder, precedents for such appreciation of the utility of religion, and they stretch back to the first years of the republic. In 1784, one county in Virginia petitioned for the public support of religion on "the principle of public utility."[13] And in the same vein Benjamin Franklin wrote to his friend Tom Paine, "Think how great a portion of mankind consists of weak men and women, and of inexperienced, inconsiderate youth of both sexes, who have need of the motives of religion to restrain them from vice, to support their virtue, and retain them in the practices of it until it becomes habitual, which is the great point for its security."[14]

The social necessity of religion was a common theme in the rise of the public school movement. In an address to the American Institute of Instruction in 1849, Charles Brooks said, "Christianity, enthroned in the heart of any people, is the cheapest police that any government can maintain."[15] Though often genteel skeptics themselves, many people preferred religion to irreligion for the common people because of its social usefulness. What else could maintain popular loyalties shaken dangerously loose by revolutionary change? Where Rome had depended on her legions, America could rely on revivalism.

From its side, American Protestantism has often shown itself peculiarly susceptible to such seductions. The recurring crusades to keep America Protestant and repel the waves of new ideas that threaten "old American" values have sometimes blended religion and politics in a shameless mixture that has contradicted Christian truth. As the interests of the Federal Union and the churches became seen as one, especially in the 1840s, even the more moderate tracts and articles abounded with such titles as "The necessity of Revivals of Religion to the Perpetuity of our Civil and Religious Institutions." Was this not in part a rationalization of the Christian gospel to serve social ends?

Recent efforts to manipulate conservative Christians, particularly in the second half of the seventies, were therefore nothing new. But they provide useful bench marks to measure the vulnerability of conservative believers and the skill and plausibility of political manipulators. During the election campaign in 1980, for example, I was interviewing Richard Viguerie, the influential right-wing strategist and fund-raiser, for a BBC television documentary. In fulsome terms he paid a strong tribute to the significance of the spontaneous rise of the new Religious Right and the indispensability of the Judeo-Christian faith as the "bedrock" of American values and institutions. Then, with the microphone and camera packed away, he led the director and myself into his inner office. Kicking off his shoes (and presuming, I imagine, that being European and from the BBC we must also be essentially secular), he spoke more candidly of his five-year campaign to woo and win the key leaders among conservative pastors and evangelists.

Several things became crystal clear by the end of the time with him: that his fervent, public support for the churches and the Judeo-Christian tradition was offset by his personal following of a guru, that few things were less spontaneous and better calculated than his own part in the emergence of the new Religious Right, and that he considered Christian conservatives "useful idiots" who were absolutely essential though terribly naive and vulnerable in the face of such political strategies.

But the greatest danger today does not come from an overt, deliberate, cynical manipulation of the Christian faith from the outside. It comes from the vulnerability of American Christians to rationalizing their faith from within, either because of an uncritical attachment to patriotism or an un-Christian attachment to the general benefits of religion. The twin heresies characteristic of American Christians' succumbing to American culture religion have always been the individual's heresy of "faith in faith" and the nation's heresy of "faith in religion." The business of America is business and, with the caving in of a sense of genuine transcendence, the religion of America is religion. Put differently, American religion is particularly vulnerable to manipulation because it has always been strikingly secular, just as American secularism has been remarkably proreligion rather than atheist and antireligion.

Will Herberg noted in the fifties that "Americans believe in religion in a way that no other people have." Whereas the Hebrew Old Testament has a scathing critique of religion that makes even Marx's pale into insignificance, American Christians all too easily believe that religion in itself is somehow a good thing. Yet, Herberg wrote, "The object of devotion of this kind of religion, however is not God but religion."[16] By and large, the common faith of the American way of life remains implicit and is never carried to its logical conclusions whereby it overrides particular religions. But the implications are there all the same, and in more overtly ideological periods it is only a small step from "the religion of democracy" to "democracy as religion." When this happens, Herberg warned, "it marks a radical break with the fundamental presuppositions of both Judaism and Christianity, to which it must appear as a particularly insidious kind of idolatry."[17]

Christian conservatives who are concerned about this third outcome should be on their guard. There is nothing improper, let alone sinister, about genuinely overlapping interests. But to the extent that well-meaning Christian conservatives continue to confuse Christian principles and conservative politics, romanticize American history, idolize political power, rely too heavily on single-issue politics (especially the so-called "hot button" issues of family and sex) and forget the blistering biblical critique of "religion," they make themselves pliable to the Machiavellian designs of skillful manipulators, whether right-wing strategists or presidents.

When Christian conservatives allow their faith to be manipulated, the consequence is blunt: The conservative Christian faith is again turned into ideology in its purest religious form and the spiritual ideals of the faith serve as weapons for the social interests of the nation. The gains in the short-term are also obvious, for faith and flag, gospel and guns have always made a potent combination. Together, traditional society and conservative religion would provide the power to block processes of unwanted change, stifle channels of dissent, and create the appearance of a monolithic traditional America. In the long-term, however, the situation would be overturned. Biblical principles and American experience concur that anything resembling the "total church" is beyond recall. Authoritarian traditionalism would prove disappointingly weak for society and disastrously wrong for the church, and the reason lies in an irony. Ultimately, the real "usefulness" of the Christian faith to the United States, South Africa, or any society depends on the conviction that the faith is not so much useful as true. There is therefore a point beyond which the distortion of truthfulness leads also to a decline in Christian usefulness.

Under the conditions of modernity, a liaison of the church with authoritarian conservatism is intrinsically unstable, and one of two courses is likely. Either truth would be rediscovered in the churches, in which case the churches would irritate and embarrass their political patrons by judging the culture rather than sanctifying it. Or else truth would disappear beyond recall, and with it would vanish any shred of Christian usefulness. State religions, as Tocqueville argued, may sometimes be of momentary service to the political power, but "they always sooner or later become fatal to the church."[18]

The onrush of modernity is like a swift flowing river cutting its way from side to side in a deep canyon. So fast and dangerous are the currents in the center that religious believers who get too close are sucked in, drowned, and then washed up as the river changes course. Conservative Christians in the eighties were well aware of the fate of rash, left-liberal Christians washed up at the end of the sixties. But they should have realized the force and danger of the rightward currents in the eighties. Warning of yesterday's or tomorrow's currents is no safeguard against foundering in today's. What was true of many Christian liberals and liberal evangelicals in the sixties is true of Christian conservatives now. The more they and their churches allow themselves to become assimilated to certain trends in the culture, the more they will be set on a course that ends sooner or later in their own rejection. And the longer the time that has elapsed, the harder it will be for them to disengage from their cultural alliances without being disillusioned themselves. The saltiness of their strength of will and independence of mind and judgment would have long since gone, and so also would their ultimate significance for America.

On Toward the Total State?

The second direction from which a sacred authoritarianism might emerge is less obvious, but if less likely to occur in the short-term, it would have far more chance of final success. It concerns the possibility of a postmodern form of authoritarianism that, instead of stretching backward to tradition and conservative Christianity, reaches forward to transformation and a progressive, new form of the sacred. To many people, this possibility will sound like the stuff of science-fiction, but I include it here for more than the sake of completeness. Less likely in the short term, it deserves to be taken seriously for at least three reasons.

First, the strongest authoritarian and totalitarian states in the twentieth century have characteristically been secular rather than religious. The last decade, it is true, has witnessed a disturbing rise in religious fanaticism around the world, but this has led to no significant, widespread Christian movement to return to theocracy. No Western nation is remotely likely to fall prey to the Total Church. If anything, it is the opposite danger that needs watching. Severed from its spiritual roots and withered into a political ideology of Right or Left, the Christian faith is more in danger of becoming vapid before the pervasive secularity of the times.

Second, we can already see some of the conditions that would be necessary to make such a radical redirection possible. The sort of people likely to favor this third outcome are those "counter-modernizing progressives" commonly found in the radical extremes of the environmental, feminist, and New Age movements. They start with the assumption that the first of the four outcomes is unlikely and the second undesirable. They are therefore keenly aware of the decisiveness of the present turning point and of the immensity of the stakes involved. Their talk is already heavy with apocalyptic contrasts, such as tradition versus transformation, the "mechanistic" versus the "mystic," utopia or oblivion, and so on.

What these people repudiate, in other words, is not only the traditional past but the modernistic future too. Whether discussing environmental protection, appropriate technology, nuclear safety, or the frontiers of science, they are stretching forward determinedly for an alternative world, a world as different from that of contemporary secularism as it is from that of traditional religion. For such people the sudden reversal from individualism to collectivism, from libertarianism to authoritarianism, and from secularism to mysticism would be neither surprising nor unwelcome. Semisacred socialism would be the last best hope of their myth of progress and mastery. Far more than conversion-prone, such people are actively shopping for the perfect revolutionary worldview.

"Why is it," Robert Wright asks in the *New Republic*, "that adherents of New Age philosophies usually lean to the left? Why does the audience for *The Tao of Physics* and *The Holographic Paradigm* include so many people who want world disarmament and massive income redistribution, and so few who espouse supply-side economics?"[19] Various explanations have been offered—for example, the link between socialism and New Age thinking has been attributed to their common "feminine" urge to transcend "masculine" egoism through absorption into a greater union with society, the environment, or the universe itself. But regardless of the reason, what matters is that the link between authoritarianism and antimodern quests for personal authenticity and collective liberation is incontestable.

In fin-de-siècle Europe in the nineteenth century, as Jackson Lears describes it, these impulses led in many directions, including authoritarianism. "Eager for transcendence, many overcivilized Europeans turned to fascism. It became a kind of pseudoreligion, exalting self-sacrifice and suffering in the service of the state, promising a false transcendence in the cult of the leader."[20] More recently, as Peter Berger points out, socialism in the Third World has entered into alliance with every conceivable antimodern impulse—from "Islamic socialism" in the Middle East to Julius Nyerere's "Ujamaa" in Tanzania to the "New Christendom" of Liberation theology in Latin America. And in Western societies the link between left-leaning political radicalism and the "Age of Aquarius" has grown stronger over the last two and a half decades.

Third, we can already discern in the writings and public statements of such movements the impulses that are likely to push their desired transformation toward authoritarian and pseudoreligious ends. Some of the more obvious impulses have been commented upon, such as their exaggerated emphasis both on groups and collectivism and on planning and regulations, the former in reaction to individualism and the latter to uncontrolled enterprise. But the most significant impulses of all are the deep relativism of their ethics and utopianism among their intellectuals.

We saw the origins of the ethical dilemma earlier, in the flimsiness of the Potemkin village of liberalism built over Nietzsche's abyss. Press many people today to give moral reasons for what they are doing and the answers soon collapse into the purely arbitrary ("I felt like it") or fall back on the authoritative ("You'll do it because I say so"). But this is shaky ground when it comes to resisting injustice, because the slide from autonomous to arbitrary to authoritarian to absurd is fast and difficult to stop. There is a telling example in the school text on values clarification. Does the method mean, asks one girl, that students can decide for themselves whether to be honest in tests at school? Oh, no, says the teacher, they can decide on their own values and choose to be honest or dishonest, but the teacher will insist on honesty in the test. But, presses the girl, how then can students decide for themselves? Aren't they being told what to believe? "Not exactly," says the teacher, "I don't mean to tell you what you should value. . . . All of you who choose dishonesty as a value may not practice it here. That's all I'm saying."[21]

The teacher's dilemma would one day be America's if such pernicious nonsense spreads. Press the logic of relativism and it will rebound, a stumbling somersault from a world of unjustifiable autonomous choice to a world of unjustified authoritative compulsion. Communication that persuades others to act in accordance with justifiable shared ideals is rejected as "indoctrination." Yet compelling them arbitrarily to act in accordance with one's own personal values is allowable so long as they are not also compelled to agree with one's values.

The other problem, that of utopianism, is equally significant. Far from being purely critical of Western culture—the point stressed in discussing the first two outcomes—twentieth-century intellectuals have played the role of "adversary culture" with surprising selectiveness. Against religious tradition and bourgeois capitalist culture they have relished their role as the questioning shock troops, the critical vanguard for whom iconoclasm has been an identity and a calling. But as the remarkable tenacity of their support for myths, such as Marxism, socialism, and primitivism, now shows (or for medievalism and fascism earlier), secular intellectuals have persistently revealed another face—that of the true believer. This craving face is as understandable as the better known critical face. Many secular intellectuals yearn for the coherence of lost religious meaning. They are too critical to settle for bourgeois mundaneness, yet are too wistful to be satisfied with the aridity of their own purely critical analysis. They are therefore stoking their own hunger for a transcendental frame of meaning, especially for one that offers them a key role in ushering in the revolution they claim to foresee.

Some thinkers have predicted the rise of an American form of "Jewish-Christian socialism" in the 1990s.[22] That is unlikely, but because of the historic link between secularism and statism, the post-Christian, postmodern possibility must be considered too. The future could witness the convergence of what remains of the former New Left with the so-called New Class and the so-called New Consciousness, combining to form an aggressive post-modern authoritarianism with its own politically correct orthodoxy.

Many people who commented on George Orwell's *1984* pointed out that the year 1984 brought the West almost to the opposite predicament of the novel. Far from having Big Brother watching over us to see that we believe and think the right thing, we seem to have been left on our own by Big Mother-goddess Liberty who is casual to the point of carelessness about what we think or do. Our Western nightmare turns out to be, not totalitarianism and manipulation but triviality and meaninglessness, masked often by a feverishness mistaken for vitality.

But the two positions may not be so far apart, because it is precisely in such situations that the drive for a deeper meaning and a stronger bond of fellowship becomes desperate. As Philip Rieff warned a generation ago, "That there are colonies of the violent among us, devoid of any stable sense of communal purpose, best describes, I think, our present temporarily schizoid existence in two cultures—vacillating between dead purposes and deadly devices to escape boredom."[23]

The modern state already resembles the medieval church far more closely than the modern church does. Without settled convictions, tomorrow's postmodern society will swing wildly between anarchy and servility until the chaos of the former is assuaged by the control demanded by the latter. Those made desperate by the triviality of empty freedom are those most likely to be deceived by the siren call of the new sacred authority. Those betrayed by the therapist will turn to the manager. And most ironically of all, those civil libertarians who may most be trusted now to warn Americans of the lesser danger of the Total Church may least be trusted then to save them from the greater danger of the Total State. As Arthur Schlesinger notes, even as someone skeptical of dark forebodings, "Still, let us not be complacent. Should private interest fail today and public purpose fail thereafter, what rough beast, its hour come round at last, may be slouching toward Washington to be born?"[24]

21

The Wild Card Played

The fourth possible outcome is that there will be a massive revitalization of American life, including both its ideals and institutions, through a movement of decisive spiritual revival and reformation. If sufficiently powerful and penetrating, such a renewal could restore the spiritual vitality to America's social and political order and resolve the crisis of cultural authority. Like the third outcome, the last one pivots on the assumption that religion might once again be publicly decisive in America but this time in a manner that is beneficial to the nation, even in a day of expanded pluralism. As President Truman stated in a speech in Columbus, Ohio, in 1946, "no problem on this earth" was tough enough to withstand "the flame of a genuine renewal of religious faith." Without it, he insisted, "we are lost."[1]

The mere fact that this outcome is conceivable fifty years later is significant. Twenty years ago, the very idea seemed to have sunk below the horizon, beyond recall. In the cultural wake that followed the announcement of the "death of God" no one was more vocal than the religious elite, no one more breathlessly enthusiastic about the dawn of the religionless age and the adulthood of the world. Freedom, the radical theologians insisted with a earnestness bordering on masochism, must be built on the secular critique of the religious. The "melancholy, long withdrawing roar"[2] of the sea of faith that Matthew Arnold first heard on Dover Beach in 1870 seemed to have faded forever.

Yet at the end of the 1980s, following the Catholic and Orthodox renaissance in Central and Eastern Europe, the Islamic revolution in the Middle East, the resurgence of fundamentalism in America, the phenomenal growth of Pentecostalism in Latin America, and the worldwide explosion of sects, there was a new sound on Dover Beach. Could there be a turning of the tide of faith on the shores of modernity? Today it is secularism and extreme liberal theology that are being checked for their vital signs. Humanness and freedom, it is now acknowledged, require a religious critique of the secular. Admittedly, many of the adjectives used by commentators to describe religion betray a deep ambivalence. Somehow religion always tends to be elemental, primeval, atavistic, primordial, fanatical, and so on. But at least the usage points to an important new recognition. Religion may still only be reactionary, the focus of resistance to the discontents of modernity, but it is acknowledged to be strong, human, and here to stay.

The Revival of Revival

Needless to say, the spiritual revival and national revitalization envisaged in this fourth outcome would have to rise far above the level of reactionary discontents toward modernity. It would have to be more than a movement of 1970s reaction or 1980s restorationism. Columnist Henry Mitchell wrote with good reason of the purported "Spiritual Revival, 1980s-style": "So of course we have once more a great American spiritual (is it the third or the fifth or the hundredth?) revival? Which is fine with me, as long as I've figured out what is meant by 'spiritual.' It means be a slob as usual and let God rain the dollars down."[3]

A genuine spiritual revival would have to begin within the boundaries of a single faith community but transcend them in order to influence the entire nation beneficially. Which faith community is capable of that? As religious leaders know, the first part is hard enough even without the challenge of the second. Arthur Hertzberg, for example, spoke for the Jewish community when he lamented that after nearly four centuries, the momentum of Jewish experience in America is nearly spent. "The need for and the possibility of a spiritual revival are clear. If it does not happen, American Jewish history will soon end."[4]

For a start, a genuine spiritual revival that contributes to national renewal would have to address the many levels of the crisis of cultural authority—including the renewal of the public philosophy. Without a reforged public philosophy, religious revival under the conditions of modern pluralism would become deeply threatening. To underscore the realism of this point, it is worth stressing the demanding criteria by which the possibility of revival would be judged. For this fourth outcome to happen, several things (any one of which is difficult to achieve today) must occur simultaneously. The revival would have to be socially and politically relevant, and not merely privately engaging; it would have to demonstrate its theological depth and coherence, and not just its spiritual devotion and moral passion; it would have to provide the vision to think creatively and the character to impose substantial moral and economic self-restraint; it would have to sustain its power over the long-term at a time when the impact of secularization would tend to make spiritual energy diffuse and religious convictions vacuous; it would have to bring about a reversal of the cultural sense of relativism with truth, of closure with openness, of triviality with seriousness, and of weightlessness with gravity; it would have to satisfy the minority faiths that its new-found vitality is no threat to their justice or freedom; and it would have to win sufficient intellectual adherents and credibility to make possible a strengthening of the philosophical and ethical foundations of the free society.

In short, the revival would have to go beyond recent "revivalism" with its engineered and promoted shallow spirituality. It would have to revive revival itself and succeed in doing what no spiritual movement has done in any highly modernized country—recoupling belief and behavior and recapturing the integrity and effectiveness of traditional faith in the setting of the modern world. Only by doing what "revival" has not done recently would genuine revival do what no other revitalization can ever do. Short of such revival, other realignments and revolutions, including the conservative revolution, are bound to affect only the surface of American society. Purely economic, technical, or legislative changes will not go deep enough. The earthquake of the sixties was too powerful. Cultural change has gone too far. Political change can do too little to turn it around. The old prohibitionists' belief that "vices can be legislated away faster than sinners can be converted" has been unmasked as an illusion once more.

Stated this way, the challenge of revival would be beyond the concerns or capacity of most communities of faith in America. In fact, only the Christian faith can point to a proven record of nationally influential awakenings in American history. Yet even with reference to the Christian faith, many observers conclude without further ado that the revival of revival is now impossible. Modernity's "iron cage" cannot be escaped so easily. The heavenly Houdini has locked himself in one time too many. There is little likelihood, they say, that Christian thinkers will develop any significant new visions of public life and policy. The United States, they point out, has produced more Protestant believers than any other country, but fewer powerful Protestant theologians and social theorists than any other major Protestant country.

Are we likely to see the rise of a new American transition-bridger like

Augustine, a new community-builder like St. Benedict, a new theological reformer like Martin Luther or social reformer like Martin Luther King? Will Christians offer genuinely constructive and critical positions that rest on Christian foundations and are directed by a coherent biblical vision, positions that deal with the seductive neutrality of modern science and technology as well as the hydra-headed realities of diverse domestic and foreign cultures? No, say their critics. They are far more likely to join the public debate and once again confuse the Christian faith with some passing ideology or with the American flag. After all, the critics conclude, the possibility of the fourth outcome is based on circular reasoning. If it is hoped that Americans can resolve their national crisis of confidence by recourse to religion, what about the crisis of confidence in religion itself? To appeal to faith to rescue society is like asking one tottering drunk to rescue another.

For such reasons as these, many observers—including many Christians —do not appear to take this fourth possibility seriously. After all, as Nietzsche pronounced categorically, "a *reversion,* a turning back in any sense and to any degree, is quite impossible. . . . There is nothing for it: One has to go forward, which is to say *step by step into décadence.*"[5] Even James Davison Hunter, a penetrating commentator on the modern religious scene and a Christian himself, appears to conclude in the negative. "A Third Great Awakening, or a Second Protestant Reformation as it has been called, with the same amount of influence as the First and Second Great Awakenings in America, or as the original Protestant Reformation, is a virtual sociological, not to mention legal, impossibility under the present conditions of modernity."[6]

Robert Bellah widens the same point. "Unfortunately not only the Protestant tradition but the Catholic and Jewish traditions have undergone severe attrition in America and in their present form it is doubtful whether they can provide the basis for genuine cultural renewal."[7] And his colleague William Sullivan widens it furthest of all. "The lurking suspicion that undermines our confidence in any tradition is that our capitalist and bureaucratic modern society has, like a cancer, grown beyond the point at which its corruption could be healed by self-generation."[8] Philip Rieff is equally dismissive. "There seems little likelihood of a great rebirth of the old corporate ideals," he writes. In the age of the therapeutic, "affluence may be the alternative to questionable renewals of religion, taking the form of excessive moral demands, by which this culture has been regularly carried away in the past."[9]

In addition to these explicit objections, the fourth outcome now appears less of a necessity to many Christians because of their swing from privatization to politicization. Until the 1960s, revival was cited almost glibly as the "final cure" for all social ills, the evangelical equivalent of John Murray Cuddihy's "praying well is the best revenge." Since then many evangelicals have shouldered it aside in their pell-mell rush for political power. Ravenous for influence, many evangelicals and fundamentalists have pawned their birthright for a mess of political pottage.

Ironically, it has been left to nonevangelicals to make the point to them. Paul Weyrich, for example, a Catholic, shocked many fundamentalists when he charged that "as cultural conservatives, we have a trivial agenda. . . . What I mean is that, if all the policies we have called for were put into effect tomorrow, the basic trends in our culture, the trends that are bringing about our decline as a nation and as a civilization, would not be changed. They would be slowed but not reversed. . . . We would not bring about the spectrum shift we need." And then, he continued, in language that is a direct but unconscious echo of the evangelicals of a generation ago: "We have contented ourselves with advocating 'band-aid remedies' for the symptoms of social decay, which is somewhat like taking aspirin for appendicitis."[10]

Weyrich did not spell out his national "spectrum shift," nor how it is to be effected. But his basic premise, that fundamental political success can be achieved only when and where the culture is sound, is also the premise of this fourth outcome. Overreliance on political activism will prove as much a broken reed for Christian conservatives as overreliance on law and technology will prove for secularists.

Such objections and problems are the measure of the challenge to be faced in considering this final outcome. No one supporting it should have any illusions about what is involved. On one hand, this is the most difficult of the four outcomes, the one least aided by trends, and the one most hindered by drift. On the other hand, this is also—to religious believers—the most tempting of the scenarios. On every side there are incentives to do the right thing but for the wrong reason. In other words, to pursue national revitalization, not for God's sake, but for America's, democracy's, the West's, or the world's.

During the First Awakening in the eighteenth century, which so profoundly touched ordinary people, novelist Oliver Goldsmith wrote of the need for English statesmen to "conspire with their enthusiasms." Citing him, one historian today writes similarly that "Great numbers can only be reached by enthusiasm." Thus "we must hope for an awakening similar to that mounted by the Anglo-American evangelists of the eighteenth century, one that would at the same time satisfy spiritual longings, rout antinomian passions, and engender an enthusiasm for virtue and an ordered liberty."[11] Sociologist Robert Nisbet writes similarly about revival as a useful antidote to Marxism. "Only religion exerts as strong a pull on human minds as ideological politics. It takes a force to conquer a force. Politics is becoming more aligned with the police power of the state and with the abuse of authority. I can only believe that a religious awakening will give it some competition."[12]

The utilitarian view of revival is especially tempting to those attracted to a politics of "cultural conservatism" (conservatives who believe in a necessary, unbreakable, and causal relationship between traditional Western Judeo-Christian values and the secular success of Western societies). At the very minimum, even if Judeo-Christian beliefs are neither logically necessary nor constitutionally permissible as America's semiofficial orthodoxy, they are pragmatically useful—being the beliefs that are simultaneously the most appealing to most Americans (nearly 90 percent) and the shortest intellectual route to a solid foundation for democracy.

The politics of cultural conservatism is historically and socially richer and more realistic than many brittle versions of right-wing ideology. But its success depends on its capacity to broaden its political appeal to those who appreciate the culture but not the cult, or source of worship, from which the culture sprang. Hence the instrumental view of religion. As one senior Reagan official expressed it, writing anonymously under the name of Publius, "It has been observed that, to be a cultural conservative, one need not 'believe traditional values are true absolutely, that they derive from God, from natural law, or from some other source outside secular human experience.' One must only accept 'that Western culture is functionally true—that it is necessary if our society is to be successful, in terms of what it provides its citizens.' "[13]

Such appeals are beguiling but a dead end, because they forget the crisis of cultural authority that gave birth to the politics in the first place. Cultural conservatism represents an opportunity politically only because it is no longer a reality socially. "Western culture" quite simply is not proving "functionally true" for enough Americans. Thus for supporters of cultural conservatism who do not themselves believe, cultural conservatism leads to a cut-flower restoration that will prove short-lived. Whereas for believers, such a "utilitarian revival" is a contradiction in terms and the ultimate blasphemy. As soon as "God bless America" is pursued for the wrong motive, the social cart is put before the spiritual horse and the desired outcome is put beyond reach. The result is not life but death, faith's reimposition rather than its revitalization, the third outcome rather than the fourth, the idolatry of nationalism rather than the renewal of the nation.

History's Jack-in-the-Box

Each of the four outcomes is a matter of the future, so no watertight case can be made for any of them. But the fourth outcome is particularly open to challenge, so if the case for it is not to remain airily unconvincing or a matter of pure assertiveness, its assumptions must be spelled out further. Here, as in all arguments, the assumptions are the key. Cultural renewal, or the generating of fresh cultural capital, is always a mysterious process, with small beginnings, piecework advances, and mostly undramatic successes. And such is the link between culture and cult (or worship) that, when there is a severe crisis of cultural authority, no cultural renewal can succeed without the renewal of the beliefs that brought the culture into being. For many believers, however, it appears to be enough to assume that two things are indispensable to the success of the fourth outcome—the conviction that the religious belief is true and the demonstration that God himself will effect what no human effort could accomplish. But these, of course, are assumptions that are not shared publicly and they are also the very things that appear to be called into question by the modern world. So in the interests of public discussion, further assumptions must be added.

One indispensable assumption is historical—the acknowledgment of the national role of revival in American history. On the one hand, Robert Bellah observes, "The great engine for maintaining the effectiveness of religion in national life was not dogma, but revivalism."[14] On the other hand, far from being purely personal and incidental to national life, revivals and awakenings have been such a vital and recurring part of American life that "American history is thus best understood as a millenarian movement."[15] Indeed, William McLoughlin writes as a historian, "To understand the functions of American revivalism and revitalization is to understand the power and meaning of America as a civilization."[16]

In times of awakening in American history individuals were certainly awakened, but worldviews were also changed, communities transformed, progress given a dynamic heave forward, and social justice brought back into central focus. The great awakenings began in times of trouble and confusion, but they were not pathological or reactionary. They were restorative and constructive. Their effect was to revitalize faith, enterprise, idealism, and a sense of national purpose. American society has maintained its continuing revolution and its dynamic momentum mainly through its succession of revivals. Far from a pious wish for a vague and unlikely miracle, the fourth outcome rests on assumptions that lie at the core of American culture.

The second indispensable assumption is sociological. As Will Herberg acknowledged, no one who has given serious thought to the problem of religion can have escaped the "sense of depth beyond depth in dealing with his subject, or have failed to become conscious of the inherent limitation of objective study."[17] Religion in general and revival in particular tend to burst out of the best scientific and purely rational categories. But sociology does point to the secret of the capacity of the Christian faith to survive repeated periods of cultural captivity and decline. The secret lies in the social logic of the biblical notion of transcendence and its accompanying challenge to a critical tension with culture (whereby Christians are called to be "in" the world, but "not of" it). Marxism, in clear contrast with the Christian faith, lacks such a capacity for renewal because its claim to transcendence through historical progress is bogus. With the party speaking and acting as the sole incarnation of the will of history, the claim to transcendence ends in either bureaucracy or gerontocracy or both. The result is not renewal but repression. As David Martin commented about Marxism, "It is a paradox that a system which claimed that the beginning of all criticism was the criticism of religion should have ended up with a form of religion which was the end of criticism."[18]

How is the Christian faith different? On the one hand, it has in its notion of the word of God a transcendent authority that stands higher than history, a judgment that is ultimately irreducible to any generation and culture. On the other hand, it has in its notion of sin and repentance a doctrine of its own failure that can be the well-spring of its ongoing criticism and renewal. At the heart of renewal lies the elemental Christian right—the right to be wrong. This is why G. K. Chesterton noted after his survey of periods of Christian decline, "At least five times the Faith has to all appearances gone to the dogs. In each of these five cases, it was the dog that died."[19]

So are revival and revitalization possible or impossible today? America's own capacity for renewal may be at stake in the answer to this question. What can be said is that throughout the nearly three hundred years of American history since the Puritans landed, revivals have not only recurred repeatedly but have been written off repeatedly only to recur again. The unlearned lesson is part of recent history too, even for movements well short of revival. Mass evangelism was written off in the mid-forties only for Billy Graham to emerge in 1949, just as fundamentalism was written off in the early seventies only for the Moral Majority to emerge in 1979.[20] But such religious movements pale by comparison with revival itself. Far more than of Mark Twain, it can be said of revivals in America that the rumor of their demise has been greatly exaggerated.

"Is it possible," asks Irving Kristol, "to restore the spiritual base of bourgeois society to something approaching a healthy condition?"[21] Tempted to answer no, he admits this answer derives from a false view of history that allows no critical moments when the clock can be turned back deliberately. Properly understood, the Reformation was just such a moment and the possibility, while neither the only one nor the easiest, is still open.

Thus the future of liberal capitalism, Kristol continues, may be more significantly shaped by the ideas germinating in the mind of some young, unknown philosopher or theologian than by any vagaries in the annual GNP statistics. After all, he concludes, with a sentence that goes to the heart of this fourth outcome: "It is the ethos of capitalism that is in gross disrepair, not the economics of capitalism—which is, indeed, its saving grace. But salvation through this grace alone will not suffice."[22]

Hardly a Head Between Them

If the preceding discussion is broadly correct, then the future of America is tied to the future of American religion and both lie somewhere in the direction indicated by one of these four general outcomes. Certain comments follow naturally. In the first place, it is impossible at the moment to say which of these four broad outcomes will succeed. Signs now visible in American society could be used to argue for each one of the first three, the fourth by its very nature being immune to prognosis. Any present conclusion is thus not only premature but partisan. Like runners out of the starting gate in a four-horse race, the four possibilities appear to be racing neck and neck, with the first perhaps slightly in the lead. But firm predictions are impossible and anything less is too speculative to be worthwhile.

In addition, it is plain that the main focus of debate and action centers around the first and last options. Few Americans, if any, would actively hope or work for America's decline, and few would publicly admit to Machiavellian designs for manipulating religion (a policy that would be stupid on pragmatic grounds quite apart from reasons of public civility). This leaves us, once again, with two leading contenders in the ideological tournament. On one side is America's fourth faith (with smaller numbers but an influential coalition of allies), and on the other is America's first faith (with larger numbers, but less influential allies). Each argues its case and offers its preferred outcome, but to many onlookers both appear to suffer from an apparent weakness—instability in the case of secularism, impossibility in the case of the Christian faith. But this only means that the theoretical case is not watertight; the horizon of possibilities is still open, the circle is not closed. The future with all its consequences is still amenable to our choices. The outcome of the cultural revolution and the crisis of cultural authority is yet to be decided.

The Eagle and the Sun

Very few people, Raymond Aron once wrote, are contemporaries of their own times. Most people in most periods are only too happy to simply follow along behind their times. The significance of our own day dawns for us slowly if at all, and is usually delivered rather than discovered, second hand at best. Realism as much as humility ensures that for most of us this is likely to remain the situation. Far from improving affairs, modern information in many ways makes it worse. The desire for instant, total information seems almost capable of fulfillment, but often the drive to know in order to predict in order to control—as Auguste Comte expressed it—can lead not only to wisdom but to information-junkies, high-tech manipulators, and navel-contemplating trendspotters.

How then do we become unriddlers of our time? How do we rise above the worm's-eye view to that of the hawk? Is there a way between the false extremes of ignorance and illusion, between an irresponsible myopia and an impossible mania for universal knowledge that borders on usurped transcendence? The answer, for Jews and Christians at least, lies in rejecting the current preoccupation with "know yourself" and insisting that the alternative ancient saying, "know your moment" be taken in a biblical direction. The answer lies in the challenge of making sense of our situation by reading the signs of the times and assessing the significance of the moment.

In the eighth century B.C. the Hebrew prophet Jeremiah taunted the pharaoh of his day as "King Bombast, the man who missed his moment." The closing reason given why Jesus wept over Jerusalem was that his generation "did not recognize God's moment when it came."[1] Skilled in reading the weather, his contemporaries were so blinded by their nationalism that they failed to see the significance of their own day. Not simply missing the meaning of the moment, they showed themselves up by not thinking it worth the trouble to discern its decisive character.

395

History in its fullest sense is always beyond our reach, but by staying aware of the enormous plane on which it is enacted we give account of ourselves in our own special moment in time. Only the vantage point of the world's last day will disclose to us what the history of our day really meant. But by viewing the present in the perspective of what we know of that day, we glimpse its promise and its threat and grasp our opportunity and responsibility. We judge the moment or find that the moment judges us. If the final assumptions of our time are our horizon, a large part of this horizon is a human creation and thus relative and open to human challenge and influence.

This understanding makes up the notion of "the hour." It is similar to Aleksandr Solzhenitsyn's notion of "knots," those decisive historic moments in which everything is rolled up and tied in a knot. It is quite different from lesser substitutes, such as "window of opportunity," being "on a roll," or feeling a surfer's exhilaration in the face of "the ninth ninth wave." The hour is the God-given moment of destiny not to be shrunk from but seized with decisiveness, the floodtide of opportunity and demand in which the unseen waters of the future surge down to the present. Nothing is more critical than to recognize and respond to such a moment. Before will hardens into fate and choice into "might have been," the hour is the moment when the present is at its greatest intensity and the future is uniquely open to our decision and action.

Thus, in contrast to the self-descriptions of Friedrich Nietzsche, this book may prove "untimely" to Americans, but it is not "posthumous" in the Nietzschean sense.[2] If it does not speak today, it does not speak at all. The day after tomorrow is too late to be any use.

To put the point plainly, if the twentieth century as a whole is the American Century, the present generation of Americans is in the midst of the American hour. For while many candidates can claim to be absolutely critical to America's crisis of cultural authority, none rivals the spiritual factor in the immensity of its past significance, the precariousness of its present status, and the potency of its influence whether it recedes or returns.

No other factor goes so far back in history, so deep and wide in society, and has so many reverberations internationally. Yet the light cast by recent developments and by the epic struggle of America's culture wars shows that the spiritual factor in America is called into question as never before—and with it much in America for which it has been directly and indirectly responsible. Thus American culture is at a turning point, largely because of a changed relationship to faiths (the latter being less influential and constructive than before). But American faiths are also at a turning point, largely because of a changed relationship to culture (the latter being more influential and destructive than before). As a result, the American people are in a critical period of their illustrious history.

The Answerable Generation

The converging factors and trends that create the critical decisiveness of the present should be plain by now, just as it is clear that the moral, social, and national accounting cannot be long delayed. The day of drift and half-measures is over. Procrastination is no longer possible. Long-favored formulations of alternatives, such as boom or bust, win or lose, arrive or be lost, must take second place to the deeper personal and public issue—by which faith? Again, the issue is not, faith or not? but, which faith? And by what authority? And with what consequences? In area after area and at point after point, the present moment forms a giant question mark to America.

To many people the only surprise in this contention is that the question should still be open. They acknowledge the role of faiths in the past and appreciate the significance of the crisis of cultural authority today, but see only a fait accompli. Secularism, for better or worse, is considered to be progressive and irreversible, so whether hailed with three cheers or a weary sigh, it is the one faith, they believe, that is here to stay.

Such expectations fly in the face of a cold fact: The crisis of cultural authority is an authentic crisis because there is no necessity about its outcome. To believe in the inevitable success of secular liberal progress is as foolish as to believe in the inevitable Marxist view of history. As Nietzsche stressed, there are no safety nets with history. To the degree that history is open to our influence, it is closed off to our longings for inevitability. Secular complacency also flies in the face of mounting counterevidence and forms the perfect twin to the excesses of religious triumphalism on the other side. We have already seen many of its deficiencies in the argument so far. The smugness is based uncritically on secular premises; it generalizes from European experience and overlooks American distinctiveness; it ignores the significance of a powerful resurgence of religion throughout much of the world; and it fails to do justice to the persistent failure of secularism in human history to satisfy the aspirations and needs of ordinary people.

Above all, the complacency ignores a central conclusion of this discussion: The deepest crisis in America is not the crisis of religion or even of tradition, but the secular half of secular liberalism. Secularism is in as much trouble as socialism and both are in infinitely worse condition than Judaism and the Christian faith, for the plainest fact about the secular world is its disillusionment with secularism. Is it not curious that the philosophy of secularism is failing so conspicuously to consolidate the advantages offered to

it by the process of secularization? Secularity, as a way of life, may be on the
increase in America as in much of the modern world, but there is a ferment
of new spiritual movements that grows straight from the heart of the
problems with secularism.

Americans with a purely secular view of life have too much to live with,
too little to live for. Everything is permitted and nothing is important. But
once growth and prosperity cease to be their reason for existence, they are
bound to ask questions about the purpose and meaning of their lives:
Whence? Whither? Why? And to such questions secularism has no answers
that have yet proved widely satisfying in practice. Few of the great thinkers of
the twentieth century have remained loyal to secular humanism. Secularism
in its sophisticated form rarely flourishes outside intellectual centers where
the mind is the organizing center of life. In its more "popular" Marxist form,
it is keeling over arthritically. The very emptiness of our secular age is its
deepest spiritual significance.

It is even conceivable that our generation is standing on the threshold of
a rebound of historic proportions. The collapse of the great counterreligious
ideologies—Freudianism's failure to recodify the private world and
Marxism's to recodify the public—clears the greatest obstacle to this
possibility. Philosophical denials of faith have become affirmations that need
denying. Social permissions have become constrictions from which we need
liberating. Secular iconoclasms have become idols that need debunking.
Moral inversions have become blind orthodoxies against which we need new
heresies. Critical deconstruction has become destructiveness against which
the need is to build and rebuild. Even secular humanism turns out to be, not
the bogey its enemies fear, but an oxymoron its supporters regret—for
secularism does not produce humanism; humanism requires, not secularism,
but supernaturalism.

At a more practical level, a thousand contradictions and ironies of the
secular world also hold the door open. Modern cities make people closer yet
stranger at once; modern weapons bring their users to the point of genocide
and impotence simultaneously; the modern media promise facts but deliver
fantasies; modern education introduces mass schooling but fosters
subliteracy; modern technologies of communication encourage people to
speak more and say less, as on the telephone, and to hear more and listen
less, as on the television; modern life-styles offer do-it-yourself freedom but
slavishly follow fads; modern self-expression has been crowned as the winner
in the all-American value contest just as the notion of the self has all but
disappeared; modern rejection of restraints has ended in addictions; modern
styles of relationships make people hungry for intimacy and authenticity but
more fearful than ever of phoniness, manipulation, and power games;

modern therapies multiply the promise of cures but make people ill with the frantic pursuit of health; modern control of the planet leads directly to the sense of the world out of control; modern humanization of life deepens a spreading feeling of existential despair. And so on and so on.

Deliberately setting out to banish all traces of transcendence, American secular liberalism is in danger of pulling its own house down on itself. Notions of identity are collapsing into introspection, morality into calcula-tion, community into hyperindividualism, the life of the mind into "a Babel of criticism," and therapy into "yet another sick physician." Such contradic-tions and ironies may well prove so overwhelming that secularism will be seen for what it is—the desert of the modern world that opens up the only space in which most people are forced to abandon the noise and clutter of civilization in order to encounter either God or the demonic. "We may be," Philip Rieff writes soberly, "at the end of modernist inversions of sacred order. We can only have faith and wait; and see."[3]

The present moment, then, is open as well as pivotal. The die is far from cast. The night has not yet come. There is still everything to play for.

Thus as America moves through her years of reckoning, Americans must not pretend to choose the future over the past or choose at all between falsely formulated alternatives, such as idealism versus pragmatism or isolationism versus globalism. The choice of faith is the real choice—it cannot long be shelved. For the crux of the issue raised by the American hour is this: At a key moment in the American Century when as the world's lead society America is again called upon to act decisively in the world, the decisive issue is the faith by which Americans live and decide affairs.

No other contemporary choice will be so decisive for the United States, no other judgment so critical as to how America is judged. The integrity and effectiveness of America's future in the world depends ultimately on the integrity and effectiveness of the faith in the hearts and lives of Americans. And this generation of Americans will be answerable for that decision.

Fourth Time of Trial, Fourth American Revolution?

At its core, the choice that constitutes the American hour is stark. But this can be softened properly by adding perspectives from various angles, such as previous American history. Historical precedents and parallels are never precise, and it is certainly true that to use them as ghosts to haunt contemporary discussion is often a block to thought rather than a stimulus (for example, the use of accusations such as "another Munich," "another Vietnam," and so on).

But just as American character and ideals across vast distances and a huge span of time have a remarkable continuity, so within American history recurring themes are quintessentially American. Two such themes, those of "revolution" and "time of trial," are an integral part of the American hour and deepen the resonance of its note of urgency. Claims and counterclaims about American revolutions, like those about awakenings, are confusing and contradictory. How they are numbered depends, of course, on which are counted as revolutions. The risk of arbitrariness appears high. Thus Richard Nixon proclaimed a Second American Revolution in his State of the Union address in 1971 only for Ronald Reagan to issue his own in 1985.

Outside the political sphere, John Whitehead argues in a widely read book, *The Second American Revolution*, that the United States has just undergone a revolution of historic significance that was secular in substance and second in terms of numerical order. Gore Vidal, by contrast, dates the Second American Revolution from the passing of California's Proposition 13 in 1978, while advocates of the New Age movement regard their Aquarian or "Whole-Earth Conspiracy" as the Second American Revolution, but essentially spiritual, not secular, in its thrust.[4] In the nineteenth century, George Clemenceau, then a reporter but later president of France, spoke of the "second American Revolution" at the time of the Civil War, just as Benson Landis spoke of the 1930s and the Depressions years as the "third American revolution."

The higher count would seem more appropriate, especially when the recurring theme of "revolution" is related to the recurring theme of "time of trial." Seen this way, prior to our own time there have been three American revolutions and three great times of trial, but only two great spiritual awakenings. The count for the latter goes far higher, of course, for those who abandon a traditional definition of awakening and therefore hail any great shift in ideology as an awakening.

The first time of trial was in the eighteenth century when the issue was independence and the first Great Awakening contributed to the first American revolution. The second time of trial was in the nineteenth century when the issue was slavery and the second Great Awakening contributed to the second revolution. Unmistakably, the spiritual dynamic unleashed at these two decisive periods of American history, as at the time of the Reformation that lay behind so much of colonial life, was the power of the Christian gospel. In fact, as John Adams pointed out in a letter in 1818, "the real American Revolution" was effected before the American war began, because "The Revolution was in the minds and hearts of the people; a change in their religious sentiments of their duties and obligations."[5]

Yet the third revolution was different. What Landis in the 1930s called the third American revolution was issued from the third time of trial represented by the Depression, but had no corresponding impetus from any spiritual awakening. The revolution, in fact, was partly a revolution against the spiritual factor in American history. Protestantism was at its lowest ebb and had lost its culture-shaping power. So the 1930s represented "the antipodes of the Great Awakening"[6] and talk of the recent era of narcissism as a "third awakening" is palpably absurd.

In the American hour we are now in the fourth great national time of trial, the climax of the crisis of cultural authority—a time made still more urgent by the problem of responsible action in a revolutionary world, compounded by the problem of America's present calling into question America's past. What leads out of the American hour is therefore likely to be the fourth American revolution. But will it be secular or will it be spiritual? And if either secular or spiritual, which form will it take? The coming years will answer those questions.

What Then Is Required?

This is not a how-to book. For reasons of principle as much as space it would be impossible and inappropriate to spell out any attempted solution. Problems of national purpose are far from an illusion, but national malaise is never remedied by national solutions. America's deepest problem is one of faith and therefore is personal, though today the deepest challenge to personal faith is that it should be so compelling as to become a social movement that can build on individual commitments to effect real institutional change.

What then is required by the logic of this present moment? At the risk of sounding naive, I will mention five things so simple that some may dismiss them as foolish. Yet they are so basic that no national renewal will ever begin without them. They are not so much five things to do in order to make something happen, but rather five things that—if something happens—are likely to be evident at the heart of it.

First, the American hour is a time to remember. This, emphatically, is not a call for nostalgia or historical reverie. The former is a symptom of the sickness of homelessness and the latter is a luxury too costly for so critical a time. Both are a way of seeking access to the past without allowing the tradition of the past to gain authority over the present. But a sense of the past falls far short of a sense of tradition. Remembering, therefore, is much more than mental recall. There is all the difference in the world, as Jaroslav Pelikan has pointed out, between tradition as the living faith of the dead and traditionalism as the dead faith of the living. Remembering has always been one of the most important modes of thought. It is the key respectively to identity, faith, wisdom, renewal, and the dynamism of a living tradition. Into what is otherwise merely the past, remembering opens up three dimensions that transform a dead past into a living tradition: the dimensions of historical depth, moral demand, and gratitude.

"The best definition of man is the ungrateful biped," wrote Dostoevsky in his *Notes from Underground.*[7] It is this simple but profound feature of remembering that Solzhenitsyn dares to put at the heart of the modern crisis. "If I were called upon to identify briefly the principal trait of the *entire* twentieth century, here too, I would be unable to find anything more precise and pithy than to repeat once again: 'Men have forgotten God.'"[8] In his proclamation of a Fast Day in the spring of 1863 Abraham Lincoln had said the same thing, "We have grown in numbers, wealth, and power, as no other nation has ever grown. But we have forgotten God."[9] In the 1980s, the epitome of this American self-sufficiency beyond gratitude was Bart Simpson solemnly intoning at his network-created, cartoon dinner table, "Dear God, we pay for all this ourselves, so thanks for nothing."

It was not always so. "My father," said the ancient Hebrews in a solemn annual declaration, "was a wandering Aramean"—and they then remembered. "Our fathers," said Governor Bradford to his fellow Puritans, "were Englishmen who came over this great ocean, and were ready to perish in this wilderness; but they cried unto the Lord, and he heard their voyce, and looked on their adversitie" and the sons and daughters of the pilgrims then remembered.[10] "The seat of the mind," Augustine wrote at one of the great transition moments in Western history, "is in the memory."[11]

Jews sometimes say of the modern Jewish community that no generation of Jews knows more about the past, yet is less a part of it. But if this is the case, the dilemma is not unique. In the same spirit we might ask: Have American scholarship, museums, tourism, and consumerism similarly cut off Americans from their tradition even while appearing to put them in touch with their past? Has America lost a living contact with its origins and its earliest beginnings? Are Americans cutting themselves off from a key part of the sources of their national identity? Is the present generation shutting its eyes to the full range of beliefs and experiences that have shaped both the best and worst of its character today? Do we seriously believe there is such thing as an "errand without an end"?

Remembering may seem simple to the point of naiveté, and specially difficult to a nation committed to progress and unused to preservation. Time alone will show its importance. Nations are not so much what they have been as what they think they have been. So pastlessness and futurelessness are related. The Founders sought to learn from the past in order to defy it, yet

Americans who insist on forgetting their past as they seek a great future may soon find themselves a people with a great future in their past. But equally, only a people that ponders its future wisely will learn to understand its past well.

Repentance

Second, the American hour is a time for repentance. This, emphatically, is not a call for a brief spasm of moralism. The latter, as Michael Novak charges, may well be "the nation's most corrupting and persistent vice."[12] Nor is it, as some of the Puritan jeremiads were said to be, a call to reformation that never comes, which therefore acts as a token payment on the obligation and so absolves the debtors. Repentance is not a psychological purgative. Nor is it a cynical use of the flourishing culture of "recovery," by which private and public figures avoid disgrace and engineer their own rehabilitation.

Nor, supremely, is this a call for a change of image, whether refurbished or completely altered. America's problem is not a question of poor image but of betrayed ideals. One of the deepest betrayals of all is the almost universal shift from concern for ideals to concern for image. How ironic, as Daniel Boorstin points out, that "of all nations in the world, the United States was built in nobody's image. It was the land of the unexpected, of unbounded hope, of ideals, of quest for an unknown perfection."[13] ("They call me an idealist," declared Woodrow Wilson. "That's how I know I'm an American.") Yet today the language of ideals has been displaced by the language of images and if the right image can sell a president, a car, a religion, or a cigarette, can it not carry the American way of life around the earth?

Those who believe so should review the flood of exported American images. They should ponder the fact that the world, surfeited with American images, has grown cynical or remains ignorant of American ideals. Once idealistic, America portrays itself ceaselessly as the land of hedonistic macho-materialism, which for a long time allowed one of history's most materialistic and repressive movements to pose as idealistic. "We suffer unwittingly from our own idolatry," Boorstin concludes. ". . . It is all the more unfitting than we should offer ourselves in images. And all the more fitting that the images which we make wittingly or unwittingly to sell America to the world should come back to haunt and curse us."[14]

Repentance, by contrast, is the repudiation of idolatry and the recognition of God. It is the beginning of becoming undeceived, the only language that will bring to the surface all the subterranean "denials" of recent decades.

It is the abandonment of the ceaseless competition of images and an unconditional confession of the reality of wrong before one who demands—not a change of face—but a change of heart, and mind, and way of life.

Repentance is Plato's required "turn-about" of the entire human being, though its ultimate necessity lies not in the parable of the cave in *The Republic* but in the story of the garden in *Genesis*. Repentance is Nietzsche's "truthfulness at last," but on God's terms and with God's help. It is the only possible source of Jefferson's revolution every twenty years and of the republic's capacity for self-renewal based on a return to first principles. It is the precondition for one of America's deepest national needs: self-respect coupled with self-limitation. For the "land of the second chance," repentance is the sole qualification for the true second chance. It is the U-turn par excellence, the ultimate transformation, the only inversion that counts, the one great turning operation on which all others hinge, the one true homecoming.

Such acts as prayer and fasting, which are basic to repentance, seem foreign to modern Americans, many Christians included. But they did not seem strange to members of the Continental Congress. Confession of national sin offset the claim to national favor. Equally, Richard Niebuhr wrote that the First Great Awakening was critical for America because "it was a new beginning; it was our national conversion."[15] Yet ironically, modern Americans have removed themselves from the reality of repentance and awakening at the very moment when they need it most. They have taken the world's most radically transforming experience and have turned it into a cliché and a stereotype. Thus reelected politicians, restyled cars, revived fashions, and resurgent democracies—even the CIA under William Casey and the military under General Norman Schwarzkopf—are all "born again."[16]

There is no stronger indictment of recent evangelicalism and fundamentalism than their contribution to that weightlessness. And after the emptying came the deforming. When television evangelist Jimmy Swaggart was exposed, he even tried to "copyright" his public confession of sin—surely an obscenely contradictory response to an equally obscene use of his confession in a commercial by the Cincinnati Opera to promote an upcoming production of "Susannah."[17] Another television evangelist—Jim Bakker—found himself shamed by a mocking parody of his own ministry: the title of a *Playboy* article in November 1987—"Jessica Hahn, Born Again." For the church secretary who had an affair with him, "revealing all" was transferred to a centerfold confessional. Nude pictures, Jessica Hahn said in her antitestimony, are "a celebration of a new life. A new beginning."[18]

Thus now that problem after problem in the world pose such dilemmas that what is required is nothing less than a deep, lasting, and radical change—a genuinely new life, a genuinely new beginning—where is the source of genuine conversion and transformation to be found? "The tomorrow we would like for planet Earth," writes Milosz, "—justice, peace, the elimination of hunger and poverty—is not very likely unless a fundamental conversion occurs."[19] "We have so bedeviled the world," says Solzhenitsyn, "brought it so close to self-destruction, that repentance is now a matter of life and death—not for the sake of a life beyond the grave (which is thought merely comic nowadays), but for the sake of our life here and now and our very survival on this earth. . . . We can say without suspicion of overstatement that without *repentance* it is in any case doubtful if we can survive."[20]

Today, no less than at the time of the First and Second Great Awakenings in America, it is to that same unlikely necessity that the promise and demand of repentance speaks.

Resolution

Third, the American hour is a time for resolution. This, emphatically, is not a call for the tinny bombast of one more pseudoprophetic declaration or for some turn-of-the-year fancy that reaches beyond its means. To call for resolution is not simplistic. It is to face the difficulties of acting today on the basis of any simple, straightforward motivation. Traditional notions, such as doing what is right or one's duty, have become problematic. Modern commitments have grown hesitant because of self-consciousness and have been tenuous because vulnerable to a thousand sophisticated dismissals. This is especially so in a nation that remains the world's lead society even while it undergoes the most profound crisis of cultural authority in its history. What lies ahead for all Americans are not only personal tasks and challenges but the prospect of the endlessly shifting battlefronts of the culture wars at home. And beyond that are the distant horizons of epochal developments in world history and even challenges to the nature and destiny of human life itself. Both past and future converge on us as never before. Untiring resolution is anything but simple.

The situation is not new, but our knowledge today is clearer and the burden of responsibility heavier. Human existence has always been lived at the crossover between past and future. But for most people in most times it was obscured by the masking conventions of tradition and society. Today, however, that luxury has gone. Instead of a cosily timeless moment, with past and future held firmly at arm's length, our present is laid bare with a terrible clarity. More clearly than ever before, the present can be seen—in the words of the title of Hannah Arendt's celebrated essay—as "the gap between past and future."[21]

Our lives in the late twentieth century are like the man in Franz Kafka's parable, "He," which Arendt expounds. We are on a journey with two deadly antagonists. The first antagonist is the past, which presses us from behind, while the second is the future, which blocks the road ahead. We have no alternative except to battle both. To be sure, there is comfort in the thought that both antagonists are ultimately against each other—that we can get help from the past in our fight with the future, and support from the future in our struggle with the past. But this comfort is scant, because the past and future are both against us. Each fights the other only in and through us, the past (contrary to expectations) thrusting into the future and the future backward into the past. Given no alternative but to stand in the gap, we experience the present as a howling wind tunnel of forces, a narrow war zone of conflicts with which we must engage.[22]

Escapes, of course, are always available, and never more so than today. They beckon as liberating alternatives to the challenge of resolution. Even Kafka's traveler fights on, but he dreams of an unguarded moment—during "a night darker than any night has ever been yet"—when he can jump out of the fighting line and be promoted to the position of umpire over the two antagonists. For those with no stomach to stand, there is always the option of caving in on one side or the other—through romanticism about the past or reveries about the future, through a leap into thought without action or into action without thought.

But for the person who has faced the challenge of the hour, evasion is out of the question. If the task of the mind is to understand, and the task of the understanding is to help us engage with reality, then the man or woman who understands must set about reconciling ideas and reality, past and future, thought and action, their own calling and the public good in the only way possible—by a resolute interposition of his or her life-work into the gap between the "no longer" of the past and the "not yet" of the future.

As Arendt points out, we should not take the word *gap* casually. As far as the human mind can see, only the presence of the person can break the chain of uninterrupted forces. Only because of us is there an interval in the ceaseless continuum of time. Only if we stand is there a space. Only as we fight is it held open. Only when we prevail can we break up the flow of history and direct its course with human significance. In short, the present moment is a gap in time that we work to shape even as it works to shape us.

This means that, for human beings, time and history are always a battlefield and never a home. But such a view of the present requires a closer look to see that the "gap" is in fact made up of a gridiron of forces. No so much an interval, a blank to be filled in from scratch, living in the present is a form of insertion, an active insertion into a zone of engagement with already existing forces. At first sight, our human situation in the face of time and history appears forlorn. The two antagonists are overwhelming. The force of the past and the force of the future seem irreversible because unlimited. They come from two nearly infinite sources, whereas our best efforts cannot claim to be other than finite, limited, and puny.

Yet the perspective can be turned around. Although the forces of the past and the future originate from finally unknown, nearly infinite sources, they collide with us at a point that is highly specific, limited, and finite—the gridiron of forces that is the present. Besides, as we take our stand in the gap, our puny actions may be limited by virtue of their limited starting point. But they can grow to be almost unlimited in their effects because they engage decisively with forces that have a power beyond their own. Even beside the overwhelming scale, speed, and complexity of the twentieth century—and quite contrary to the much-quoted axiom of Zen Buddhists—the human person is a stone thrown into the pond who causes ripples that go on forever.

But for all its truthfulness and courage, Kafka's parable is not only modern but secular. Therein lies a problem. Operating entirely within what Peter Berger describes as modernity's "world without windows," it has a missing dimension. It lacks a space (not to be confused with an escape hole) where the human mind and spirit can move freely in contemplation and decision in a "small non-time-space in the very heart of time" without being forced to jump out of human time altogether.[23] This space has virtually been sealed off for modern people by the suffocating closure of secularity. Without it, the possible courses to follow are limited. For those who refuse to succumb to escapism, there is, above all, the heroic defiance of stoicism and the magnificent absurdity of existentialism—both of which, today, are fated to end in weary exhaustion.

Another picture of resolution to match the hour is Søren Kierkegaard's description of "the knight of faith" in *Fear and Trembling*. Here the battle is no less deadly and dedication is no less required, but faith has opened up the space that is missing in Kafka's parable. The knight of faith has staked the meaning and outcome of his life on the royal majesty by whom he was dubbed. He is therefore free to turn from his own affairs and to center his life on the priorities of his questing. In pursuit of this quest, no pettiness is so petty that it disturbs his meaning. No task is so immense that it daunts the courage of his calling. He engages in the world on the world's terms, yet he is never diverted by the world from his quest because he always has an eye to interests and ideals that are invisible to the eyes of others. In the lifelong engagement with the challenges of past and future, thought and action, it is the knight of faith who can have the resolution to match the demands of our times—a resolution with no reservations, no retreats, and no regrets.

Responsibility

Fourth, the American hour is a time for responsibility. It is a momentous responsibility to be the world's lead society at a time when the competition is crowded and the world's agenda is hideously overburdened. Even the terrible "southern burden" of the mid-nineteenth century and Kipling's ironic "White Man's burden" of the twentieth century seem to shrink beside the "global burden" of the state of the earth at the present time. Who will provide the vision and demonstrate the ordering principles of the emerging *pax moderna?* Who will exert the will and underwrite it with the resources to tackle world problems, such as hunger and the environment?

The Cold War is over, but no one can relax in the sunny optimism that the end of history has arrived, and that American democracy is a successful experiment to be followed automatically by the rest of the world. Human nature has not changed. The vacuum created by the collapse of communism can easily be filled by atavistic forces, such as tribalism and nationalism. If totalitarianism communism has paid the price of going *against* the flow of modernization, there are the lesser and less noticed costs of going *with* the flow.

The last generation seems to have left Americans with the burdened sense that world involvement is uncertain, if not unwise. Is the United States still, as Tom Paine asserted, "an asylum for mankind,"[24] or as Thomas Jefferson once claimed, "such an empire for liberty as she has never surveyed since the Creation"?[25] And if so, how? At times the task of shouldering this high responsibility has been executed with conspicuous success. Through the Northwest Ordinance of 1787, for example, two-thirds of a vast continent was led from colonial rule to self-government within a century and a half. The achievement is one of the crowning glories of American history, and modern successes, such as the Marshall Plan in 1947, could be added to this distinguished record.

At other times American success was won more painfully, as in the horrors of the Civil War, which was brought to a head by a fundamental clash of moral commitments. If these commitments could not be avoided any longer, they would not be discharged lightly. To the credit of the civil rights movement in the 1960s, they picked up where the drive for racial justice had left off. Those who took justice and freedom seriously would no longer recite the American creed with mental reservations for the blacks. All men and women—without exception—are created equal.

But do the same "self-evident" truths apply equally to non-Americans? Do American ideals still have the power to reach out and include people not originally included, or to cover those, like the poor and the unborn, who were once included but who are now passed over or thrown out? Is the exercise of such responsibility still part of the national vision today, or has America overlearned the lesson of postwar illusions and tender-hearted idealism?

Can even a "reluctant empire" excuse its citizens of such parochialism and ignorance about what is going on in the world? Are "human rights" merely the concern of soft-headed idealists? Is the demand for international economic justice always a smokescreen for socialism? Is it really hard-headed realism for left- or right-wingers to develop a squint when viewing right- or left-wing authoritarianism? How much longer will the peoples of the world tolerate, let alone respect, democratic leadership with no publicly urgent strategy for peace, justice, and world order? If America is truly a "nation of nations" and if Americans are literally "migrant cousins" to the world, can they do other than stand as a new model of international relations and blaze a trail toward the new *pax moderna?*

They can, of course. Just as in 1932 Reinhold Niebuhr warned tersely that "the white race in America will not admit the Negro to equal rights if not forced to do so. Upon that point one may speak with a dogmatism which all history justifies."[26] Will the same soon be true of the Third World? Only as the American hour runs its course will it become plain whether the empire for liberty still stands and serves, or whether an aging Fortress America has usurped its place.

Realism

Lastly, the American hour is a time for realism. This, emphatically, is not a call for national breastbeating and ritual self-flagellation. Fewer people today might follow Lincoln in seeing America as the earth's last best hope. But it takes an advanced condition of failure of nerve, not to say plain stupidity, to swing to the opposite extreme and regard America as the earth's first, worst horror or to act as if all that is wrong with the world is America. Besides, the recurring cycle of idealism and disillusionment, crusading and withdrawal is something from which to escape.

Nor is the call for realism a denial of the idealistic and romantic elements in American history. American history ranks with the most romantic of all histories and the most stirring of all sagas. America's is a dynamism drunk on dreams, a spirit of enterprise intoxicated with visions of the passionate and the impossible. To ignore American idealism in the interests of realpolitik is not to be realistic but romantic in the derogatory sense.

But trouble looms when such exhilaration slips the leash of reality and bounds heedlessly toward hubris—when the fatal blend of a denial of evil, a disregard of history, and a defiance of limits turns the American Dream into an American delusion about getting something for nothing forever. Lippmann was one of the few who saw this early on as America's postwar temptation: "There is no more difficult art than to exercise great power well; all the serious military, diplomatic, and economic decisions we have now to take will depend on how correctly we measure our power, how truly we see its possibilities *within* its limitations. . . . Great as it is, American power is limited. Within its limits, it will be far greater or less depending on the ends for which it is used."[27]

Forty years later, realism and humility are even more vital when the earth's resources and the world's circumstances are no longer willing accomplices to American euphoria. Today there is no excuse for forgetting that everything has its place, everything has its limits, everything has its end. American celebration and American self-justification may be welded together for Americans, but does justifiable pride have to spill over into chauvinistic conceit and downright folly? Can the inescapable premise of ignorance be excluded from the calculation of world-affecting decisions? Is not the world's cultural diversity richer and more varied than the one-dimensional vision of superpower perspectives? Does it really reveal strength, and does it truly "restore respect for America" when the most effective attacks by challengers in recent elections have been a litany of the insults to national dignity permitted under the incumbent president? "Manifest Destiny" may no longer be in vogue, but manifest duty cannot be shed so lightly. Is it wise to jettison also the sense of mission, stewardship, and service that was the other side of America's special sense of calling?

Adapting Lippmann to a slightly different context, we may perhaps remind ourselves "When Shakespeare was alive there were no Americans, that when Virgil was alive there were no Englishmen, and that when Homer was alive there were no Romans."[28] God can afford to do without the United States and Europe. His kingdom can survive the collapse of the West as it did of Rome. Thus the past as much as the present, pragmatic expediency no less than principle, combine to request of the world's lead society a humility to temper its pride, a sense of dependence and gratitude to crown its prosperity, and a realism and restraint to accompany its enterprise and the exercise of its power. There has been no American Ozymandias, it is said—yet.

To forget this is to forget what Lincoln always remembered about the nation, "This, too, shall pass away." The decisive proof that Americanism and American self-reliance cannot be sufficient without God is that they cannot remain themselves, let alone fulfill their tasks, without faith in a higher authority. A realistic view of history and American society suggests that not even the United States can defy gravity. Every great nation is also a nation within time and under sentence of death.

Put differently, the challenge to *realism* is not simply a matter of limits. In the end, national realism is a question of the very sources of national greatness and finally of reality itself. If the American *gravitas* is disappearing, if all that was once solid is now melting into air, if there is a growing sense of weightlessness in the culture, if the nation is being weighed in the balances and found wanting, then the crisis of cultural authority is what G. K. Chesterton called America's "ultimate test"—a crisis of reality.[29] "Men will more and more realize that there is no meaning in democracy if there is no meaning in anything; and that there is no meaning in anything if the universe has not a centre of significance and an authority that is the author of our rights."[30]

At that point, Chesterton advised that Americans should ponder their national symbol. Another Englishman, Charles Dickens, had used the same picture earlier. On his voyage home, Martin Chuzzlewit's servant had wondered aloud how he would paint the American eagle. Certainly it would have to be more than an eagle. "I should want to draw it like a Bat for its short-sightedness; like a Bantam, for its bragging; like a Magpie, for its honesty; like a Peacock, for its vanity; like an Ostrich, for putting its head in the mud, and thinking nobody sees it."

"And like a Phoenix, for its power of springing up from the ashes of its faults and soaring up anew into the sky!" said Martin. "Well, Mark. Let us hope so."[31]

Chesterton's point is simpler and more serious. The bird that carries the bolts of Jupiter is not an owl or a bat that could navigate in the skeptics' darkness of a universe without center or meaning. It is not a carrion, whose sole orientation is toward its prey. No, the American symbol carries a truth kept alive even in an ancient fable. It signals the highest classical understanding of the required source of a nation's *gravitas*. Above all, it points beyond itself toward the biblical insistence on the empty nothingness of idols and on the glory (or weight) of God as the only "real reality" in all the universe. Hence G. K. Chesterton's words to a nation whose greatness was not derived from itself and cannot be sustained by itself: "but it was far back in the land of legends, where instincts find their true images, that the cry went forth that freedom is an eagle, whose glory is gazing at the sun."[32]

A Darker Kind of Hour?

What if America will not respond? In any critical "hour," more than the future presses close. God himself draws near and his visitation is itself the hour's demand and opportunity. Which makes it all the more urgent that the moment not be missed, for those who miss God's moment may soon find themselves, as Jesus said of Jerusalem, in a different hour—"your moment, the hour when darkness reigns."[33] More soberingly still, Jesus warned the citizens of another city that it would be more tolerable for proverbially wicked Sodom than for them, for if the deeds had been performed in Sodom that were performed in Capernaum, "Sodom would be standing to this day."[34]

Americans should face this possibility squarely: If they reject God's moment today, sooner or later they will drift or be driven to the unwelcome logic of their own choice. On the one hand, there is inescapable truth in the old American refrain that "when our country goes wrong she is worse off than most other countries because she has had more light than most countries." Much is required of a people to whom so much has been given. The forgotten side of exceptionalism is accountability.

On the other hand, three hundred years of proclaimed ideals, revolutionary declarations, and international comparisons—climaxing perhaps in the premises of the Nuremberg trials—form a sobering index of judgment by which the judge will herself be judged. Do the heirs of Jefferson still tremble when they remember that God is just? Or will America reject God and become what she worships in his place (such as Mammon Inc.)? Or become like what she wars against (the Moloch of some enemy system)? Any of the great post-Christian American ideologies, such as affluence, technology, and defense, will then become dramatic points of national self-exposure.

Nowhere was this national self-exposure more public and more acute than over the agonizing burden of nuclear defense. And at no time was the issue posed more sharply than when the cost of relying on the nuclear umbrella was evident to all. There was thus a peculiar moral illumination in a "MAD" (Mutually Assured Destruction) situation. Justifiable defense pivots finally on the people, principles, and possessions worth defending and where there is overwhelming military superiority of some kind—as at Hiroshima or in the Persian Gulf—ultimate moral questions need not be faced.

But in a war that threatens to risk and engulf everything no questions can be evaded. The ultimate act of defense also becomes the ultimate highlighting and assessment of the things to be defended. Does the ultimate act of defense call into question the things defended, or do the things defended justify the ultimate act of defense? By their judgments in such choices Americans will be judged—not only in the surface sense of being judged by others, but in the deeper, darker sense of judging others to call down on themselves the gathered judgment they know that they deserve. Mercifully, the immediacy of nuclear concerns has receded. But whether triggered by the nuclear debate or something else, questions persist. The deepest issue is not whether America will survive. It is, instead, determining what America stands for and whether this will deserve to survive.

Appalled by events in Vietnam, even a great patriot like Walter Lippmann found a new vocabulary creeping into his writing. "There is a growing belief that Johnson's America is no longer the historic America, that it is a bastard empire which relies on superior force to achieve its purposes, and is no longer an example of the wisdom and humanity of a free society."[35]

"Empire for liberty" or "bastard empire"? Should the United States turn decisively from the faith of her past, such episodes as Vietnam and Watergate may raise fewer questions and occasion less dismay. Indeed, the greatest nightmare of the secular future will grow out of its deafness to its own noises, its lack of feeling for its self-inflicted wounds, its obliviousness to the consequences of its chosen course. "Christian Russia" and "Christian Germany" both gave birth to bastard sons. Might "Christian America" do the same? For various reasons it is far more likely that, like Britain, she would suffer a slow slide toward mediocrity, frustration, conflict, and bitterness. But such speculation is worse than fruitless if it diverts attention from the present hour.

In his brilliant novel, *Imperial Mission,* Reinhold Schneider used a climactic point in the Spanish Empire to speak to a climactic point in the German nation in the 1930s. The argument for justice and freedom is carried by Bartolomé de Las Casas, "Father of the Indians." Once a nobleman, ardent and careless in the conquest of Latin America, he is now a priest, tired and weighed down with the horrors he had first inflicted, then witnessed and campaigned against.

In a stirring debate before the Emperor with Dr. Sepulveda, champion of national ideology and Imperial conquest-cum-conversion, Las Casas comes to the climax of his speech and says with a penetrating voice: "All warnings have been in vain. Spain has missed her hour. Those for whom God's mandate still lives go about as fools, laden with all the sorrows of the world. . . . It is certain that judgment will fall upon this land. For he who fails to fulfil the highest duty bears the heaviest guilt. Therefore God's anger will fall upon this land. He will shatter its power and lower its scepter, and take away its islands and possessions. And if those who rise from the ruins accuse the Lord, and ask why he has brought this misery upon this land, I shall rise from the tomb to testify to God's justice. I will answer the accusers. God called upon your fathers to perform a great mission and they closed their hearts and would not heed Him. Like unto the Saint, they should have carried the Lord across the sea on their shoulders, but they carried Satan instead. God does right if he destroys the might of this land. Terrible punishment follows terrible crime!"[36]

The American hour has not yet passed. So terrible a judgment need not yet be made. Not yet do we speak and write, like the voices of courage in Russia, from "under the rubble." But this one possibility must be faced. A generation that fails to read the signs of the times may be forced to read the writing on the wall.

God Only Knows

The happier possibility is that America will respond—or, expressed more precisely, that when God speaks in reformation and revival, sufficient individuals will take heed and be the salt and light that will help revitalize American society. This possibility, as I underscored earlier, will primarily be the work of God or it will not happen. But that is not to say that it will be heralded by a press agent's "Lo here!" or an anchor person's "Lo there!" Obedience, not power or success, is the key to history for at the center of history the mightiest power of all is incognito still, its wisdom far from truths that are self-evident.

Ours is a world of the big, the powerful, and the well known. But unquestionably most of the staggering victories and true heroes are unnoticed and unsung. Doubtless saints of whom we know nothing have wrested nations from disaster in an hour of peril. Doubtless others have been solitary sentries at the frontiers of a menaced family or community. Perhaps only for their sake were things, such as justice, sanity, beauty, humanness, and freedom of worship, not taken away when forfeited earlier. Perhaps, were it not for them, an empire of evil far worse than that of the Soviets would not still be held in check by the restraining hand.

In the same way, reformation and renewal will be detectable on some sociological geiger count in the end, but perhaps only as the silent fallout after a startling and unexpected explosion in some altogether unlikely quarter. Scoffers will say there is only a slender chance of such revival and that the odds are impossibly long. They would be right. The wild card is aptly named. Revival and reformation in America in the late twentieth century have about as much chance as the likelihood of an obscure provincial sect overturning Imperial Rome, or of a shipload of motley Lincolnshire dropouts founding the twentieth century's greatest superpower.

But will there be such a reformation and revival? Will the eagle soar again, recovering its glory by gazing at the sun? Will the wild card be played? There I must stop, because the eagle is not the sun and the American wild card is not America's, but God's. So even if we gathered the best arguments and the best evidence from all the best analysts, we would still only have marshaled a valley full of dry bones. God's question to the Hebrew prophet in just such a situation was, "Can these bones live again?" And like Ezekiel, our only answer can be, "Only thou knowest that, Lord God." But at least that recognition is not the end, but a beginning.

Notes

A Crisis of the Mandate of Heaven

1. "Yes, You Are the Superpower," *Economist*, February 24, 1990, p. 11.
2. Dan Balz, "'No one Doubts us Anymore,' Bush Tells Gulf Vets," *Washington Post*, March 18, 1991, p. A 19.
3. Václav Havel, *Disturbing the Peace*, trans. Paul Wilson (New York: Vintage Books, 1991), p. 10.
4. Peter L. Berger, *The Capitalist Revolution* (New York: Basic Books, 1986), p. 11.
5. Henry R. Luce, "The American Century," *Life*, February 17, 1941, pp. 61–65.
6. Ibid., p. 64.
7. Alexis de Tocqueville, *Democracy in America*, vol. I (New York: Vintage Books, 1945), p. 15.
8. Walt Whitman, "Democratic Vistas" in *Walt Whitman: Complete Poetry & Prose* (New York: Viking Press/Library of America, 1982), p. 930.
9. Frederick Jackson Turner, *The Significance of the Frontier in American History* (New York: Frederick Ungar Publishing, 1963), p. 57.
10. Quoted in Godfrey Hodgson, *America in our Time* (Garden City, N.Y.: Doubleday, 1976), p. 18.
11. Quoted in Herbert R. Lottman, *The Left Bank* (Boston: Houghton Mifflin, 1982), p. 207.
12. Luigi Barzini, *The Europeans* (Harmondsworth: Penguin, 1984), pp. 245–46.
13. J. Enoch Powell, "The Strength of Weakness," *Spectator*, April 7, 1984, p. 24.
14. Daniel A. Bell, "The End of American Exceptionalism," *Public Interest*, Fall 1975, p. 204.
15. Quoted David Halberstam, *The Reckoning* (New York: William Morrow, 1986), p. 62.
16. Richard Reeves, "Singapore's Lee—Decline of America," *Honolulu Advertiser Star Bulletin*, November 29, 1987, p. G3.
17. Margaret Shapiro and Fred Hiatt, "Japanese See U.S. in a State of Serious Decline," *Washington Post*, July 3, 1988, p. A29.
18. Quoted Nicholas Ashford, "Reagan Delighted with Poll Boost and Voters' Swing to Right," *The Times* (London), September 20, 1984, p. 6.
19. Quoted in ibid., September 14, 1984, p. 6.
20. Speech to the U.S. Chamber of Commerce, April 23, 1986.

21. Farewell Address to the Nation, January 11, 1989, in Ronald Reagan, *Speaking My Mind: Selected Speeches* (New York: Simon & Schuster, 1989), p. 413.
22. Lance Morrow, "Yankee Doodle Magic," *Time*, July 7, 1986, p. 12, and Kurt Anderson, "America's Upbeat Mood," September 24, 1984, p. 8.
23. Tom Morganthau, "How Good a President?" *Newsweek*, August 27, 1984, p. 21.
24. Roger Rosenblatt, "America Enters the New World," *U.S. News and World Report*, December 26, 1988, p. 20.
25. Francis Fukuyama, "The End of History?" *National Interest*, vol. 16, Summer 1989, pp. 3–18; Francis Fukuyama, *The End of History and the Last Man* (New York: The Free Press, 1991).
26. *Washington Post*, January 12, 1986, p. A17.
27. Lance Morrow, "A Change in the Weather," *Time*, March 30, 1987, p. 29.
28. Kevin P. Phillips, "Reagan's Decline is Good News for the GOP," *Washington Post*, August 2, 1987, p. 2.
29. Cartoon by Jules Feiffer, *Washington Post*, August 9, 1987, p. C4.
30. Stephen S. Rosenfeld, "The American Century Still?", *Washington Post*, August 5, 1988, p. A23; George Bush, "Our Work Is Not Done, Our Force Is Not Spent," ibid., August 19, 1988, p. A28.
31. Quoted in Clark Worswick and Jonathan Spence, *Imperial China: 1850–1912* (New York: Penwick Publishing, 1978), p. 13.
32. Walter Lippmann, *The Public Philosophy* (New York: Mentor Books, 1955), p. 138.
33. G. K. Chesterton, *What I Saw in America* (New York: Da Capo Press, 1968), p. 308.
34. Walter Shapiro, "Politics and the Pulpit," *Newsweek*, September 17, 1984, p. 27.
35. Michael D. Cassity, Os Guinness, Charles C. Haynes, John Seel, Timothy L. Smith, and Oliver S. Thomas, *Living With Our Deepest Differences: Religious Liberty in a Pluralistic Society* (Fairfax, Va.: First Liberty Institute and Learning Connections Publishers, 1990).

The Troubled Horizon

1. Quoted in Erik von Kuehnelt-Leddihin, *The Intelligent American's Guide to Europe* (New Rochelle, N.Y.: Arlington House, 1979), p. 407.
2. Phillip Rieff, *The Triumph of the Therapeutic* (Chicago: University of Chicago Press, 1987), pp. 20–24.
3. "Jewish Panel Decries Failure to Pass on Religion, Values," *Washington Post*, November 24, 1990, p. C11.
4. Leszek Kolakowski, *Modernity on Endless Trial* (Chicago: University of Chicago Press, 1990), p. 70.
5. Glenn Tinder, "The Spirit of Freedom," a paper given at the Ethics and Public Policy Center, April 1991, p. 7.
6. Robert Musil, *The Man Without Qualities*, vol. I (New York: Perigree Books, 1980), pp. 60, 62.
7. Ibid., p. 63.
8. See Byron E. Shafer, "The New Cultural Politics," *PS*, vol. 18, no. 2 (Spring 1985), p. 221.
9. Richard John Neuhaus, "The American 80s: Disaster or Triumph?" *Commentary*, vol. 90, no. 3 (September 1990), p. 48.

10. Daniel J. Boorstin, "History's Hidden Turning Points," *U.S. News and World Report*, April 22, 1991, p. 52.
11. Charles Dickens, *Martin Chuzzlewit* (London: MacMillan, 1954), p. 259.
12. For example, see Seymour Martin Lipset, "Predicting the Future of Post-industrial Society: Can We Do It?" in *The Third Century* (Chicago: University of Chicago Press, 1979) pp. 1–36; also Alasdair MacIntyre, *After Virtue* (Notre Dame: University of Notre Dame Press, 1981), p. 89.
13. Walter Dean Burnham, *The Current Crisis in American Politics* (Oxford: Oxford University Press), p. 14.

Chapter 1: The Testing of National Identity

1. Quoted in Giles Ginn, "Perception at the Pitch of Passion," *Yale Review*, Autumn 1984, p. 141.
2. In Allan Nevins, ed., *America Through British Eyes* (Gloucester, Mass.: Peter Smith, 1968), p. 261.
3. Henry R. Luce, "The American Century," *Life*, February 17, 1941, p. 65.
4. G. K. Chesterton, *What I Saw in America* (New York: Da Capo Press, 1968), p. 7.
5. Denis W. Brogan, *The American Character* (New York: Vintage Books, 1956), p. 128.
6. James Baldwin, *Nobody Knows My Name* (New York: Dell, 1961), pp. 15–19.
7. Richard Reeves, *The Reagan Detour* (New York: Simon and Schuster, 1985), p. 11.
8. Thomas L. Hartshorne, *The Distorted Image* (Cleveland: Press of Case Western Reserve University, 1968), pp. 1, 189.
9. Leon Samson, *Toward A United Front* (New York: Farrar and Rinehart, 1935), p. 16.
10. Quoted in Robert Dallek, *The Politics of Symbolism* (Cambridge: Harvard University Press, 1984), p. 6.
11. Philip Geylin, "What Does Britain Want to Be?" *Washington Post*, July 23, 1986, p. A21.
12. Quoted in Robin Wright, "Force Won't Stop Islamic Terror," *Washington Post*, June 23, 1985, p. B2; "Current Quotes," *U.S. News and World Report*, April 1, 1985, p. 14.
13. Hartshorne, *The Distorted Image*, p. ix.
14. Richard Darman, "Keeping America First," Albert H. Gordon Lecture, Harvard University, May 1, 1990, p. 2.
15. Quoted in Christopher Lasch, *The True and Only Heaven* (New York: W. W. Norton, 1991), p. 425.
16. David Potter, *History and American Society* (New York: Oxford University Press, 1973), p. 354.
17. Laurie Goodstein, "Black Studies Teacher Ignites Tense Debate," *Washington Post*, August 18, 1991, p. A3.
18. Quoted in Edward H. Crane and David Boaz, eds., *An American Vision* (Washington, D.C.: Cato Institute, 1989), p. 1.
19. Quoted in Will Herberg, *Protestant-Catholic-Jew* (Garden City, N.Y.: Anchor Books, 1960), p. 258.
20. Address to the National Religious Broadcasters Convention, January 28, 1991.
21. Brogan, *The American Character*, p. 102.
22. Spencer Rich and Christine Spolar, "1980's 'Terrible' for America's Children," *Washington Post*, February 1, 1991, p. A3.

23. Quoted in Sidney Blumenthal, "The Mommy Track," *New Republic*, May 13, 1991, p. 20.
24. Quoted in Lasch, *The True and Only Heaven*, p. 515.
25. Lou Cannon, "Reagan and Company," *Washington Post*, April 16, 1984.
26. Phillip E. Hammond, "Another Great Awakening?" in Robert C. Liebman and Robert Wuthnow, eds., *The New Christian Right* (Hawthorne, N.Y.: Aldine, 1983), p. 219.
27. Daniel A. Bell, "The End of American Exceptionalism," *Public Interest*, Fall 1975, p. 210.
28. George Grant, *Technology and Empire* (Toronto: House of Anansi, 1969), p. 26.

Chapter 2: Originality or Original Sin?

1. Ted Morgan, *On Becoming American* (Boston: Houghton Mifflin, 1978), p. 101.
2. Ibid., p. 308.
3. Werner Sombart, "American Capitalism's Economic Rewards" in John H. M. Laslett and Seymour Martin Lipset, eds., *Failure of A Dream?* (Garden City, N.Y.: Doubleday, 1974), p. 599.
4. Daniel A. Bell, "The End of American Exceptionalism," *Public Interest*, Fall 1975, p. 197.
5. Alexis de Tocqueville, *Democracy in America*, vol. I (New York: Vintage Books, 1945), p. 301.
6. Andrew Marvell, "The Character of Holland," in *The Complete Works of Andrew Marvell* (New York: AMS Press, 1966), p. 131.
7. See Increase Mather, *Elijah's Mantle* (Boston: 1722).
8. Perry Miller, *Errand Into the Wilderness* (Cambridge, Mass.: Harvard University Press, 1981), p. 11.
9. Thomas Paine, "The American Crisis" in Philip Foner, ed., *The Complete Writings of Thomas Paine*, vol. 1 (New York: Citadel Press, 1945), p. 72.
10. Quoted in Albert K. Weinberg, *Manifest Destiny* (Baltimore: The Johns Hopkins Press, 1935), p. 112.
11. Quoted in Ernest L. Tuveson, *Redeemer Nation* (Chicago: University of Chicago Press, 1968), p. 25.
12. Herman Melville, *White-Jacket* (New York: Holt Rinehart and Winston, 1967), p. 150.
13. Speech in the Senate, January 9, 1900, in Henry Steele Commager, *Living Ideas in America* (New York: Harper and Row, 1951), p. 672.
14. Quoted in Will Herberg, *Protestant-Catholic-Jew* (Garden City, N.Y.: Anchor Books, 1960), p. 276.
15. Bell, "The End of American Exceptionalism," pp. 197, 205.
16. Kevin P. Phillips, *Post-Conservative America* (New York: Vintage Books, 1983), p. 209.
17. Robert N. Bellah, *The Broken Covenant* (New York: Seabury Press, 1975), p. 60.
18. Morton Kondracke, "The Democracy Gang," *New Republic*, November 6, 1989, p. 20.
19. Charles Krauthammer, "Bless Our Pax Americana," *Washington Post*, March 22, 1991, p. A25.
20. Quoted in Doyle McManus, "Dictators: Foreign Policy," *Los Angeles Times*, March 6, 1986, p. 29.
21. Quoted in ibid.
22. Henry Kissinger, "Too Much Euphoria?" *Washington Post*, March 15, 1986, p. A19; "False Dreams of a New World Order" *Washington Post*, February 26, 1991, p. A21.

23. Quoted in Ronald Steel, *Pax Americana* (New York: Viking Press, 1967), p. 3.

24. Henry Fairlie, "The Empire's New Clothes," *New Republic*, April 29, 1985, p. 19.

25. Raymond Aron, *The Imperial Republic* (Englewood Cliffs, N.J.: Prentice Hall, 1974), p. 304.

26. Richard Darman, "Keeping America First," Albert H. Gordon Lecture, Harvard University, May 1, 1990, p. 6.

27. Henry R. Luce, "The American Century," *Life*, February 17, 1941, p. 65.

28. Luigi Barzini, *The Europeans* (Harmondsworth: Penguin, 1984), p. 234.

29. Mark Twain, quoted in James Oliver Robertson, *American Myth, American Reality* (New York: Hill and Wang, 1980), p. 275.

30. Czeslaw Milosz, *Visions From San Francisco Bay*, trans. Richard Lourie (Manchester: Carcanet Press, 1982), p. 212.

31. H. L. Mencken, *A Mencken Chrestomathy* (New York: Vintage Books, 1982), p. 626.

32. H. L. Mencken, *The American Scene* (New York: Vintage Books, 1982), p. 20.

33. In Franz M. Joseph, ed., *As Others See Us* (Princeton: Princeton University Press, 1959), p. 60.

34. Joel Kotkin and Yoriko Kishimoto, "America's Asian Destiny," *Washington Post*, July 3, 1988, p. C1.

35. David S. Broder, "Catching up With the '80s," *Washington Post*, December 13, 1989, p. A25.

36. Herman Melville, *Clarel* (New York: Hendricks House, 1960), p. 484.

37. Gertrude Stein, *Selected Writings* (New York: Vintage Books, 1972), p. 76.

38. Henry Steele Commager, *Living Ideas in America* (New York: Harper and Row, 1951), p. 109.

39. John Courtney Murray, *We Hold These Truths* (New York: Sheed and Ward, 1960), p. 6.

Chapter 3: The Black Holes of Modernity

1. Friedrich Nietzsche, *Untimely Meditations*, trans. R. J. Hollingdale (Cambridge: Cambridge University Press, 1983), p. 148; Philip Rieff, *The Feeling Intellect* (Chicago: University of Chicago Press, 1990), p. 280.

2. Ted Morgan, *On Becoming American* (Boston: Houghton Mifflin, 1978), p. 244.

3. Quoted in Ernest Becker, *The Denial of Death* (New York: The Free Press, 1973), p. 96.

4. Quoted in Ronald Steel, *Walter Lippmann and the American Century* (New York: Vintage Books, 1981), p. 50.

5. George Santayana, *Winds of Doctrine* (New York: Scribner, 1913), p. 10.

6. Woodrow Wilson, *The New Freedom* (New York: Doubleday, 1913), p. 27.

7. Quoted in Steel, *Walter Lippmann and the American Century*, p. 78.

8. Quoted in Henry F. May, *The End of American Innocence* (Oxford: Oxford University Press, 1959), p. 249.

9. Quoted in Henry F. May, *Ideas, Faiths and Feelings* (Oxford: Oxford University Press, 1983), p. 18.

10. Timothy Leary, *The Politics of Ecstasy* (New York: Paladin, 1970), p. 141.

11. H. L. Mencken, *A Mencken Chrestomathy* (New York: Vintage Books, 1982), p. 76.

12. Robert T. Handy, *A Christian America* (Oxford: Oxford University Press, 1984), p. 159.

13. Philip Rieff, *The Feeling Intellect* (Chicago: University of Chicago Press, 1990), p. 254.

14. Alasdair MacIntyre, *After Virtue* (Notre Dame, Ind.: University of Notre Dame Press, 1981), p. 263.

15. Clinton Rossiter, *Parties and Politics in America* (Ithaca, N.Y.: Cornell University Press, 1960), p. 1.

16. George F. Will, *Statecraft as Soulcraft* (New York: Touchstone, 1984), p. 40.

17. See Peter L. Berger and Richard Neuhaus, *To Empower People* (Washington, D.C.: American Enterprise Institute for Public Policy Research, 1977).

18. Christopher Lasch, *The Culture of Narcissism* (New York: Warner Books, 1979), p. 369.

19. H. L. Mencken, *The American Scene* (New York: Vintage Books, 1982), p. 8.

20. Quoted in George F. Will, "Liberalism as the Style of Disdain," *Washington Post*, April 28, 1991, p. C7.

21. George Steiner, *In Bluebeard's Castle* (New Haven: Yale University Press, 1971), p. 18.

22. Christopher Lasch, *The True and Only Heaven* (New York, W. W. Norton, 1991), p. 52.

23. May, *The End of American Innocence*, p. 396.

24. Quoted in Lasch, *The True and Only Heaven*, p. 74.

25. Quoted in Douglas T. Miller and Marion Novak, *The Fifties: The Way We Were* (Garden City, N.Y.: Doubleday, 1977), p. 117.

26. Donald J. Trump, *Trump: The Art of the Deal,* (New York: Random House, 1987), p. 3.

27. Quoted in Lasch, *The True and Only Heaven*, p. 77.

28. David M. Potter, *People of Plenty* (Chicago: University of Chicago Press, 1954), p. 134.

Chapter 4: The "Golden" Fifties

1. Quoted in Ronald Steel, *Walter Lippmann and the American Century* (New York: Vintage Books, 1981), p. 248.

2. Jacob Weisberg, "Insincerity," *New Republic*, June 4, 1990, p. 43.

3. G. K. Chesterton, "What I Saw in America" in Raymond T. Bond, ed., *The Man Who Was Chesterton* (New York: Dodd Mead, 1946), p. 235.

4. See William L. Miller, *Piety Along the Potomac* (Boston: Houghton Mifflin, 1964), pp. 41ff.

5. Philip E. Jacob, *Changing Values in College* (New York: Harper and Row, 1957), p. 2.

6. Abba Eban, *The New Diplomacy* (New York: Random House, 1983), p. 13.

7. Quoted in Robert Wuthnow, *The Restructuring of American Religion* (Princeton: Princeton University Press, 1988), p. 268.

8. Henry L. Stimson, "The Greatest Opportunity Ever Offered a Single Nation," *Foreign Affairs*, vol. 26, no. 1 (October 1947), p. 5.

9. E. Brooks Holifield, *A History of Pastoral Care in America* (Nashville: Abingdon Press, 1983), p. 266.

10. Peter L. Berger, "The Second Children's Crusade," *Christian Century*, vol. 2 (December 1959), p. 1,400.

11. Quoted in Eric F. Goldman, *The Crucial Decade—And After* (New York: Alfred Knopf, 1973), p. 325.

12. Reinhold Niebuhr, *The Irony of American History* (New York: Scribner's, 1952), pp. 16, 139–40.

13. Geroid T. Robinson, "The Ideological Combat," *Foreign Affairs*, vol. 27, no. 4 (July 1949), p. 525.
14. Quoted in Allan C. Carlson, "Foreign Policy and 'The American Way,'" *This World*, no. 5 (Spring/Summer 1983), p. 23.
15. See Goldman, *The Crucial Decade—And After*.
16. Eban, *The New Diplomacy*, p. 4.

Chapter 5: The Seismic Sixties

1. Arthur M. Schlesinger, Jr., *A Thousand Days* (Boston: Houghton Mifflin, 1965), pp. 17, 18.
2. Joseph Heller, *Catch-22* (New York: Simon and Schuster, 1962), p. 19.
3. Quoted in Richard Harrington, "Man and Myth," *Washington Post*, March 10, 1991, p. G5.
4. George Breitman, ed., *Malcolm X Speaks* (New York: Ballantine, 1965), p. 26.
5. See Frank Musgrove, *Ecstasy and Holiness* (London: Methuen, 1974), p. 20.
6. Ibid., p. 19.
7. Quoted in Alexander Kendrick, *The Wound Within: America in the Vietnam Years, 1945–1974* (Boston: Little Brown, 1974), p. 16.
8. Christopher Lasch, *The Culture of Narcissism* (New York: Warner Books, 1979), p. 17.
9. Quoted in A. James Reichley, *Religion in American Public Life* (Washington, D.C.: The Brookings Institution, 1985), p. 243.

Chapter 6: The Second-thoughts Seventies

1. Václav Havel, *Disturbing the Peace*, trans. Paul Wilson (New York: Vintage Books, 1991), p. 119.
2. Quoted in ibid.
3. Quoted Paul Berman, "At the Center of the 60's," *The New York Times Book Review*, June 12, 1988, p. 7.
4. H. L. Mencken, *A Mencken Chrestomathy* (New York: Vintage Books, 1982), p. 161.
5. Arthur Levine, *When Dreams and Heroes Died* (San Francisco: Jossey-Bass, 1981), p. 5.
6. Nelson Lichtenstein, "A Failure That Changed the World," *The New York Times Book Review*, April 3, 1988, p. 9.
7. Václav Havel, *Letters to Olga*, trans. by Paul Wilson (London: Faber and Faber, 1990), pp. 149, 167.
8. See Daniel Yankelovich, *New Rules* (New York: Harper and Row, 1968), p. xi.
9. Quoted in Daniel Snowman, *America Since 1920* (New York: Harper and Row, 1968), p. 11.
10. Quoted in Gregg Easterbrook, "Ideas Move Nations," *Atlantic Monthly*, January 1986, p. 66.
11. Nicholas Lemann, "Values," in Charles Peters and Phillip Keisling, eds., *A New Road for America* (New York: Madison Books, 1985), p. 78.
12. Quoted in Theodore H. White, *The Making of the President, 1960* (New York: Atheneum Publishers, 1961), pp. 468–72.

Chapter 7: The Empty Eighties

1. Quoted in Bob Spitz, "What's Updike," *Mirabella*, October 1990, p. 100.
2. Michael Barone, "America at Peace," *Washington Post*, August 4, 1985, p. B1.
3. James R. Schlesinger, "Cut U.S. Forces in Europe—Now," *Washington Post*, February 4, 1990, p. C6.
4. Quoted in David Broder, "Stockman Writes P.S. to Attack on Reaganomics," *Washington Post*, December 27, 1986, p. A3.
5. Walter Isaacson, "After the Fall," *Time*, November 2, 1987, p. 20.
6. Quoted in Frank Kermode, "Reagan and the Venal Empire," *Manchester Guardian Weekly*, December 6, 1987, p. 29.
7. *The New York Times*, December 12, 1988, p. A2.
8. See ". . . and Take," *Economist*, January 28, 1989, p. 27.
9. George F. Will, "A Case for Dukakis," *Washington Post*, November 3, 1988, p. A27.
10. Address to the National Press Club, July 20, 1989.
11. Gwen Ifill, "Kemp Seeks Team of CPAs to Sort Out HUD's Financial Problems," *Washington Post*, January 12, 1990, p. A10.
12. Richard Behar, "Catch Us If You Can," *Time*, March 26, 1990, p. 60.
13. Bonnie Angelo, "Master of His Universe," *Time*, February 13, 1990, p. 90.
14. Kurt Eichenwald, "Wages Even Wall Street Can't Swallow," *The New York Times*, April 3, 1989, p. 25; see also Benjamin J. Stein, "Betrayer of Capitalism," *Barrons*, April 3, 1989, pp. 7ff.
15. Quoted in Robert Kuttner, "Keynes the Able," *New Republic*, November 6, 1989, p. 68.
16. Lester C. Thurow, "America Adrift," *Washington Post*, February 11, 1990, p. C2.
17. George F. Will, "Congealed in Traffic," *Washington Post*, March 11, 1990, p. B7.
18. Richard Cohen, "Killer Conservatism," *Washington Post*, March 16, 1989, p. A27.
19. George F. Will, "A Case for Dukakis," *Washington Post*, November 3, 1988, p. A27.
20. Lance Morrow, "1968," *Time*, January 11, 1988, p. 16.
21. Sydney Ahlstrom, "Moral and Theological Revolution of the 1960's" in Herbert J. Bass, ed., *The State of American History* (Chicago: Quadrangle Books, 1970), p. 100.
22. George F. Will, "1968: Memories That Dim and Differ," *Washington Post*, January 14, 1988, p. A27; *Solzhenitsyn and American Democracy* (Washington, D.C.: Ethics and Public Policy Center, 1980), p. 7.
23. David Potter, *History and American Society* (New York: Oxford University Press, 1973), pp. 387, 388.
24. Robert Nisbet, *The Twilight of Authority* (New York: Oxford University Press, 1975), p. 67.
25. Allan Bloom, *The Closing of the American Mind* (New York: Simon and Schuster, 1987), p. 314.
26. Kevin P. Phillips, *Post-Conservative America* (New York: Vintage Books, 1983), p. 18.
27. Paul Taylor, "The Coming 'We' Decade," *Washington Post*, January 20, 1986, p. D1.
28. See Don Oldenburg, "New Path for the '90s," *Washington Post*, February 20, 1990, p. C5; "Naming the Nineties," *Good Housekeeping*, January 1990.
29. Meg Greenfield, "Political Flip-Flops," *Washington Post*, October 24, 1989, p. A25.
30. Richard A. Viguerie, "What Reagan Revolution?" *Washington Post*, August 21, 1988, p. C2.
31. William Schneider, "The Republicans in '88," *Atlantic Monthly*, July 1987, p. 59.

32. See Hendrick Hertzberg, "Washington Diarist," *New Republic*, January 8, 1990, p. 46; Lee Atwater with Todd Brewster, "Lee Atwater's Last Campaign," *Life*, February 1991, p. 65.
33. Phillips, *Post-Conservative America*, p. 31.
34. Daniel A. Bell, "The Revolt Against Modernity," *Public Interest*, Fall 1985, p. 60.
35. See Arthur Levine, *When Dreams and Heroes Died* (San Francisco: Jossey-Bass, 1981), pp. 84, 85, 95.
36. Bonnie Angelo, "Master of His Universe," *Time*, February 13, 1989, p. 90.
37. Lee Atwater with Todd Brewster, "Lee Atwater's Last Campaign," p. 67.
38. Phillips, *Post-Conservative America*, p. 145.
39. Friedrich Nietzsche, *Thus Spoke Zarathustra*, trans. Walter Kaufmann (New York: Penguin Books, 1978), pp. 17, 18.
40. Max Weber, *The Protestant Ethic and the Spirit of Capitalism* (New York: Charles Scribner's Sons, 1958), p. 282.
41. Quoted in Christopher Lasch, *The True and Only Heaven* (New York: W.W. Norton, 1991), p. 80.
42. George Steiner, *In Bluebeard's Castle* (New Haven: Yale University Press, 1971), p. 11.
43. Aleksandr Solzhenitsyn, *Nobel Prize Lecture*, trans. Nicholas Bethell (London: Stenvalley Press, 1973), p. 27.

A House Dividing

1. "House Divided" speech at Springfield, Illinois, in *Lincoln: Selected Speeches and Writings* (New York: Vintage Books/The Library of America, 1992), p. 131.
2. Sydney E. Ahlstrom, "American Religious Values and the Future of America" in Rodger van Allen, ed., *American Religious Values and the Future of America* (Philadelphia: Fortress Press, 1978), p. 7.
3. G. K. Chesterton, *What I Saw in America* (New York: Da Capo Press, 1968), p. 16.
4. Perry Miller, *Errand into the Wilderness* (Cambridge, Mass.: Harvard University Press, 1981), p. 49.
5. Kevin P. Phillips, *Post-Conservative America* (New York: Vintage Books, 1983), p. 184.
6. Alexis de Tocqueville, *Democracy in America*, vol. I (New York: Vintage Books, 1945), p. 319.
7. Ibid., vol. 2, p. 143.
8. William Lee Miller, *The First Liberty* (New York: Alfred Knopf, 1986), p. 308.
9. Sara Mosle, "Washington Diarist," *New Republic*, November 21, 1988, p. 46.
10. Steven Prokesch, "With the World Made Over, Can Even Belfast Change?" *The New York Times*, April 2, 1990, p. A1.

Chapter 8: The Testing of the Public Philosophy

1. Quoted in Tom Shales, "Reagan's Mighty Valedictory," *Washington Post*, August 8, 1988, p. E1.
2. Virginia Declaration of Rights, June 1776.
3. Walter Lippmann, "The Living Past," *New York Herald Tribune*, April 13, 1943, in Clinton Rossiter and James Lare, eds., *The Essential Lippman* (Cambridge, Mass.: Harvard University Press, 1982), pp. 206–7.

4. John Rawls, "The Idea of an Overlapping Consensus," *Oxford Journal of Legal Studies,* vol. 7, no. 1, p. 1.

5. Richard Hofstadter, *Anti-Intellectualism in American Life* (New York: Vintage Books, 1962), p. 43.

6. Quoted in "A Model of Christian Charity" in Perry Miller, ed., *The American Puritans: Their Prose and Poetry* (New York: Doubleday Anchor, 1956), pp. 78–84.

7. Quoted in Robert N. Bellah, *Beyond Belief* (New York: Harper & Row, 1978), p. 173.

8. George Washington's Farewell Address, 1796.

9. Alexis de Tocqueville, *Democracy in America,* vol. II (New York: Vintage Books, 1945), p. 9.

10. Tocqueville, *Democracy in America,* vol. I, p. 316.

11. Henry Grunwald, "Time at 60," *Time,* Sixtieth Anniversary Issue, 1983, p. 5.

12. John Courtney Murray, *We Hold These Truths* (New York: Sheed and Ward, 1960), p. 86.

13. Daniel A. Bell, "The End of American Exceptionalism," *Public Interest,* Fall 1975, p. 211.

14. Paul Taylor, "Citizenship Declines as Americans Disconnect," *Washington Post,* May 6, 1990, p. A18.

15. Walter Lippmann, *The Public Philosophy* (New York: New American Library, 1955), p. 76.

16. Richard John Neuhaus, *The Naked Public Square* (Grand Rapids, Mich.: Eerdmans, 1984), p. vii.

17. Jerald C. Brauer, Sidney E. Mead, and Robert N. Bellah, *Religion and the American Revolution* (Philadelphia: Fortress Press, 1976), p. 73.

18. Edwin S. Gaustad, *A Documentary History of Religion in America: Since 1865* (Grand Rapids, Mich.: Eerdmans, 1983), p. 529.

19. Tocqueville, *Democracy in America,* vol. I, p. 238.

20. Jacques Ellul, *False Presence of the Kingdom* (New York: The Seabury Press, 1972), p. 194.

21. Lippmann, *The Public Philosophy,* p. 138.

22. Quoted Will Herberg, *Protestant-Catholic-Jew* (Garden City, N.Y.: Anchor Books, 1960), p. 97.

23. Quoted Sydney E. Ahlstrom, *A Religious History of the American People,* vol. II, (Garden City, N.Y.: Image Books, 1975), p. 328.

24. Alvin P. Sanoff, "A Conversation with James Billington," *U.S. News and World Report,* October 1, 1984, pp. 69–70.

25. Harold J. Berman, *The Interaction of Law and Religion* (Nashville: Abingdon Press, 1974), pp. 130–31.

26. Jonathan Rauch, "Is the Deficit Really So Bad?" *Atlantic Monthly,* February 1989, p. 39.

27. Ibid., p. 42.

28. Ibid.

29. Alasdair MacIntyre, *After Virtue* (Notre Dame: University of Notre Dame Press, 1981), pp. 50, 252.

30. Walter Lippmann, *The Phantom Public* (New York: Harcourt, Brace and Company, 1925), p. 31.

31. MacIntyre, *After Virtue,* p. 252.

32. Sidney E. Mead, "Christendom, Enlightenment and Revolution," in Jerald C.

Brauer, ed., *Religion and the American Revolution* (Philadelphia: Fortress Press, 1976), p. 43.

33. Ibid., p. 41.
34. Michael Harrington, *The Politics at God's Funeral* (New York: Holt, Rinehart and Winston, 1983), p. 9.
35. George F. Will, *Statecraft as Soulcraft* (New York: Touchstone, 1984), p. 35.
36. Abraham Lincoln, First Inaugural Address, 1861.
37. Edmund Burke, "Speech on the American Colonies," 1775.
38. John Courtney Murray, *We Hold These Truths*, p. 12.

Chapter 9: The Uncivil War

1. Joseph Fletcher, "Secular Humanism: It's the Adjective that Counts," *CSSH Quarterly*, vol. V, no. 3 (Spring 1984), p. 9.
2. People for the American Way, 1985 Program Plan, p. 12.
3. *The Williamsburg Charter Survey on Religion and Public Life* (Washington, D.C.: The Williamsburg Charter Foundation, 1988).
4. Swami Krishna Deva, quoted in *Church and State*, April 1985, p. 3.
5. Quoted in Richard Tapscott and Fern Shen, "Abortion in Annapolis," *Washington Post*, April 29, 1990, p. D1.
6. Quoted in George Goldberg, *Reconsecrating America* (Grand Rapids, Mich.: Eerdmans, 1984), p. 30.
7. See Talcott Parsons, *Action Theory and the Human Condition* (New York: The Free Press, 1978), p. 249ff, 308ff; also John Courtney Murray, *We Hold These Truths* (New York: Sheed and Ward, 1960), p. 22.
8. Leo Pfeffer, *Creeds in Competition* (New York: Harper and Brothers, 1958), p. 5.
9. See Robert Penn Warren, *The Legacy of the Civil War* (Cambridge, Mass.: Harvard University Press, 1983).
10. Last speech in the Senate, March 4, 1850, in Kenneth Stampp, ed., *The Causes of the Civil War* (Englewood Cliffs, N.J.: Prentice-Hall, 1974), p. 28.
11. Quoted in ibid., p. 25.
12. Quoted in ibid., p. 22.
13. Ibid., p. 59.
14. Rousas J. Rushdoony, *The Biblical Philosophy of History* (Nutley, N.J.: Craig Press, 1969), p. 139ff.
15. *Everson v. Board of Education of the Township of Ewing*, 330 U.S. 1(1947), italics added.
16. "On Church and State," remarks to the Greater Houston Ministerial Association, September 12, 1960, in Jay David, ed., *The Kennedy Reader* (New York: The Bobbs-Merrill Company, 1967), pp. 363–70.
17. Arthur M. Schlesinger, Jr., *A Thousand Days* (Greenwich, Conn.: Fawcett, 1965), pp. 105–107.
18. Quoted in Laurence Fuchs, *John F. Kennedy and American Catholicism* (New York: Meredith Press, 1970), p. 168.
19. Quoted in Seymour P. Lachman, "Barry Goldwater and the 1964 Religious Issue," *Journal of Church and State*, Autumn 1968, p. 390.
20. Ibid.
21. Gustav Weigel, quoted in *Church and State*, November 1960, p. 1.

22. See John W. Hattery, "The Presidential Election Campaigns of 1928 and 1960," *Journal of Church and State*, Winter 1967, p. 47.
23. Harold Nicholson, *Diplomacy* (Oxford: Oxford University Press, 1955), p. 50.
24. Seymour Krim, "The Begin Image," *The New York Times*, July 15, 1977, p. A23.
25. Quoted in *National and International Religion Report*, vol. 2, no. 17, (August 29, 1988), p. 4.
26. Personal letter to Tom McWhertor, September 7, 1988.
27. *Washington Post*, September 3, 1985, p. A15.
28. Letter to his friend, Alexis de Kergolay, June 29, 1831.
29. Colman McCarthy, "No Way to Fight Abortion," *Washington Post*, September 17, 1988, p. A23.
30. Quoted in Paul Taylor, "Right Expects Boost from Contra Loss," *Washington Post*, March 25, 1986, p. A9.
31. Quoted in Michael Doan and Patricia A. Avery, "Warrior for Women's Rights," *U.S. News and World Report*, March 24, 1986, p. 11.
32. Quoted in Howard Kurtz, "Norman Lear's Crusade Widens," *Washington Post*, February 3, 1986, p. A3.
33. Arthur M. Schlesinger, Jr., *The Cycles of American History* (Boston: Houghton Mifflin, 1986), p. 63.
34. Jim Castelli, *A Plea for Common Sense* (San Francisco: Harper and Row, 1988).

Chapter 10: Questions for the First Faith

1. *The Chalcedon Report*, February 1989, p. 12.
2. John Schaar, "A Nation of Behavers," *New York Review of Books*, October 28, 1976, p. 6.
3. Ibid.
4. Ibid.
5. Roger Williams, *The Bloudy Tenet of Persecution for Cause of Conscience Discussed*, London, 1644. Reprinted by the Hanserd Knollys Society, London, 1848.
6. Quoted Morton Borden, *Jews, Turks and Infidels* (Chapel Hill, N.C.: University of North Carolina Press, 1984), p. 34.
7. T. R. Reid, "Republicans Rue Mecham's Return," *Washington Post*, March 14, 1989, p. A12.
8. Samuel Rabinove, "Religious Freedom for All—A Jewish Perspective," *Liberty*, November/December 1989, p. 21.
9. Richard Hofstadter, *Anti-Intellectualism in American Life* (New York: Vintage Books, 1962), p. 37.
10. Quoted Philip Rieff, *The Triumph of the Therapeutic* (Chicago: University of Chicago Press, 1987), p. 83.
11. Peter L. Berger, "Capitalism and the Disordering of Modernity," *First Things*, January 1991, p. 9.
12. See Richard O. Curry, ed., *The Abolitionists: Reformers or Fanatics?* (New York: Holt, Rinehart and Winston, 1965).
13. See Tom Matthews, "Battle Over Gay Rights," *Newsweek*, June 6, 1977, p. 22.
14. Quoted in Robert Penn Warren, *The Legacy of the Civil War* (Cambridge: Harvard University Press, 1983), pp. 23–24.
15. David G. Dalin, ed., *From Marxism to Judaism: Collected Essays of Will Herberg* (New York: Markus Wiener Publishing, 1987), p. 218.

16. Charles W. Colson, "From a Moral Majority to a Persecuted Minority," *Christianity Today*, May 14, 1990, p. 80.
17. Ken Sidey, "Open Season on Christians?" *Christianity Today*, April 23, 1990, p. 35.
18. Quoted in Robert K. Dornan, "Blatant Bigotry," *Washington Post*, February 10, 1990, p. A21.
19. Sidey, *Christianity Today*, p. 36.
20. Richard Zone on "Sixty Minutes," September 21, 1980.
21. Fred Barnes, "Media Issues of the '90s," *World*, May 19, 1990, p. 10.
22. Colman McCarthy, "McNeil/Lehrer: FAIR Game," *Washington Post*, June 3, 1990, p. F2.
23. Friedrich Nietzsche, *Thus Spoke Zarathustra*, trans. Walter Kaufmann, (New York: Penguin Books, 1978), p. 100.
24. Quoted in Joseph Farah, "Why Ted Turner Hates Religion," *World*, June 16, 1990, p. 18.

Chapter 11: Questions for the Fourth Faith

1. See James Davison Hunter, "The Challenge of Modern Pluralism" in James Davison Hunter and Os Guinness, eds., *Articles of Faith, Articles of Peace* (Washington, D.C.: The Brookings Institution, 1990), pp. 54ff.
2. Ibid., p. 63.
3. Ibid., p. 66.
4. Ibid., p. 68.
5. Ibid., p. 57.
6. Quoted in ibid., p. 71.
7. Richard Cohen, "Policies That Go Bump in the Night," *Washington Post*, February 2, 1985, p. A19.
8. Letter sent out by the American Humanist Association, May 1985.
9. Letter to the Editor, *The New York Times*, June 19, 1985.
10. *Torcaso v. Watkins*, 367 U.S. 488 (1961).
11. Paul Kurtz, "A Secular Humanist Declaration," *Free Inquiry*, Winter 1980, pp. 3–6.
12. Joseph L. Blau, "Alternatives Within Contemporary American Judaism" in William G. McLaughlin and Robert N. Bellah, eds., *Religion in America* (Boston: Houghton Mifflin, 1968), p. 306.
13. Leo Pfeffer, "Issues that Divide: The Triumph of Secular Humanism," *Journal of Church and State*, vol. 19, no. 2 (1977), pp. 203–5.
14. Charles Francis Potter, *Humanism, A New Religion* (New York: Simon and Schuster, 1930), p. 128.
15. Paul Blanshard, "Three Cheers for Our Secular State," *The Humanist*, March–April 1976, pp. 17–25.
16. Letter sent out by American Humanist Association, May 1985.
17. Joseph Fletcher, "Secular Humanism: It's the Adjective that Counts," *CSSH Quarterly*, vol. V, no. 3 (Spring 1984), p. 10.
18. Ibid., p. 9.
19. Leo Pfeffer, "The 'Religion' of Secular Humanism," *Journal of Church and State* (1982–1989), p. 498.
20. "The Williamsburg Charter," *Articles of Faith Articles of Peace*, p. 130.

21. Alexis de Tocqueville, *Democracy in America*, vol I., (New York: Vintage Books, 1945), p. 6.

22. James E. Wood, Jr., ed., *Religion and the State: Essays in Honor of Leo Pfeffer* (Waco, Tex.: Baylor University Press, 1989), p. 529.

23. George Goldberg, *Reconsecrating America* (Grand Rapids, Mich.: Eerdmans, 1984), p. 71.

24. Leo Pfeffer, *Religion, State and the Burger Court* (New York: Prometheus Books, 1984), p. xi.

25. *Everson v. Board of Education of Ewing Township*, 330 U.S. 1, 33 (1947).

26. Quoted in Alan L. Mittleman, "Toward a Post-separationist Public Philosophy," *This World*, Winter 1989, p. 87.

27. Ibid., p. 95.

28. Ibid., p. 98.

29. Quoted in Richard John Neuhaus, "Genuine Pluralism and the Pfefferian Inversion," *This World*, Winter 1989, p. 74.

30. Mittleman, "Toward a Post-separationist Public Philosophy," p. 99.

31. Quoted in Christopher Lasch, *The True and Only Heaven* (New York: W. W. Norton, 1991), p. 416.

32. Henry F. May, *Ideas, Faiths and Feelings* (Oxford: Oxford University Press, 1983), p. 158.

33. Thomas Paine, *Rights of Man* (1791) in Moncure Daniel Conway, ed., *The Writings of Thomas Paine*, vol. II, (New York: G. P. Putnam and Sons, 1894), p. 325.

34. Quoted in Daniel L. Driesbach, *Real Threat and Mere Shadow* (Westchester, Ill.: Crossway Books, 1987), p. 20.

35. Quoted in George F. Will, "Liberal Censorship," *Washington Post*, November 5, 1989, p. C7.

36. George Weigel, "Achieving Disagreement," *This World*, Winter 1989, p. 57.

37. Ibid.

38. Walter Lippmann, *The Public Philosophy* (New York: New American Library, 1955), p. 89.

39. Friedrich Nietzsche, *The Twilight of the Idols/The Anti-Christ* (Harmondsworth: Penguin, 1968), p. 171.

40. Ambrose Bierce, *The Enlarged Devil's Dictionary* (Harmondsworth: Penguin, 1983), p. 258.

41. H. L. Mencken, *A Mencken Chrestomathy*, (New York: Vintage Books, 1982), p. 624.

42. Tocqueville, *Democracy in America*, vol. I, p. 301.

43. Perry Miller, *The Errand into the Wilderness* (Cambridge: Harvard University Press, 1981), p. viii.

44. Marc H. Tannenbaum, "Values, Events and Experiences in the American Religious Experience," *American Religious Values and the Future of America*, Rodger van Allen, ed. (Philadelphia: Fortress Press, 1983), p. 99.

45. In Charles Wallis, ed., *Our American Heritage* (New York: Harper and Row, 1970), p. 53.

46. G. K. Chesterton, *What I Saw in America* (New York: De Capo Press, 1968), p. 5.

47. See Edward E. Ericson, *Solzhenitsyn: The Moral Vision* (Grand Rapids, Mich.: Eerdmans, 1980), chapter 10; Ronald Berman, ed., *Solzhenitsyn at Harvard* (Washington, D.C.: Ethics and Public Policy Center, 1980).

48. David G. Dalin, ed., *From Marxism to Judaism: Collected Essays of Will Herberg* (New York: Markus Wiener Publishing), p. 210.

49. Martin E. Marty, *A Nation of Behavers* (Chicago: University of Chicago Press, 1976), p. 84.

50. Letter to James Madison, December 8, 1784, in Robert A. Rutland, William M. E. Rachal, et al., eds., *The Papers of James Madison*, vol. VIII (Chicago: University of Chicago Press, 1973), p. 178.

51. Quoted in Hunter and Guinness, eds., *Articles of Faith, Articles of Peace*, p. 72.

52. Doug Le Blanc, "Schlafly, Weddington Go Across Country in Debate Series," *World*, April 28, 1990, p. 19.

53. Leo Pfeffer, *Creeds in Competition* (New York: Harper and Brothers, 1958), p. 162.

Chapter 12: The Bedeviling Factor

1. Norman Mailer, *St. George and the Godfather* (New York: New American Library, 1972), p. 112.

2. Ibid.

3. Inaugural Address, January 20, 1965, in *Inaugural Addresses of the Presidents of the United States From George Washington to Richard Milhous Nixon* (Washington, D.C.: United States Government Printing Office, 1969), pp. 271–74.

4. Herbert Croly, *The Promise of American Life* (Cambridge, Mass.: The Belknap Press, 1965), p. 1.

5. See Robert N. Bellah, "Civil Religion in America," *Daedalus* vol. 96 (Winter 1967), p. 1.

6. Quoted in George Weigel, *Catholicism and the Renewal of American Democracy* (New York: Paulist Press, 1989), p. 86.

7. Quoted in H. Frank Way, "The Death of the Christian Nation," *Journal of Church and State*, vol. 29, no. 3 (Autumn 1987), p. 516.

8. John Murray Cuddihy, *No Offense* (New York: Seabury Press, 1978), pp. 1–2.

9. *Church of the Holy Trinity v. United States* 143, U.S. 457, 471 (1892); James Bryce, *The American Commonwealth* (New York: Macmillan, 1895), p. 702.

10. *Zorach v. Clauson*, U.S. 306, 312, 313 (1952).

11. Robert Wuthnow, *The Restructuring of American Religion* (Princeton, N.J.: Princeton University Press, 1988), p. 256.

12. See *Church of the Holy Trinity v. United States* 143 U.S. 226 (1892); *Zorach v. Clauson* 343 U.S. 306 (1952).

13. Robert D. Linder and Richard V. Pierard, *Twilight of the Saints* (Downers Grove, Il: InterVarsity Press, 1978), p. 44.

14. See Cuddihy, *No Offense*, pp. 46, 105.

15. Kenneth S. Kantzer, "American Civil Religion," *Christianity Today*, July 13, 1984, p. 14.

16. Robert N. Bellah, "American Civil Religion in the 1970s" in Russell E. Richey and Donald G. Jones, eds., *American Civil Religion* (New York: Harper and Row, 1974), pp. 255–72.

17. Sidney E. Mead, *The Nation With the Soul of a Church* (New York: Harper and Row, 1975), p. 22.

18. Quoted in Way, "The Death of a Christian Nation," p. 524.

19. *West Virginia State Board of Education V. Barnette* 319 U.S. 624 (1943).

20. See W. Tarver Rountree, Jr., "Constitutionalism as the American Religion," *Emory Law Journal*, vol. 39, no. 1 (Winter 1990), pp. 202–15.
21. See John Courtney Murray, *We Hold These Truths: Catholic Reflections on the American Proposition* (New York: Sheed & Ward, 1960), p. 67; Peter L. Berger, "Afterword" in James Davison Hunter and Os Guinness, eds., *Articles of Faith, Articles of Peace* (Washington, D.C.: Brookings Books, 1990), p. 120; Steven L. Tipton, "Religion in an Ambiguous Polity," *Emory Law Journal*, vol. 39, no. 1 (Winter 1990), p. 198.

Chapter 13: Tribespeople, Idiots, or Citizens?

1. Letter of July 10, 1789, to William Carmichael, in *The Life and Writings of Gouverneur Morris*, vol. 2 ed. Jared Sparks (Gray & Bowen, 1832) p. 75.
2. John Courtney Murray, "The Return to Tribalism," an address to the John A. Ryan Forum, April 14, 1961, in *The Catholic Mind*, vol. 60 January 1962, p. 6.
3. "The Williamsburg Charter" in James Davison Hunter and Os Guinness, eds., *Articles of Faith, Articles of Peace* (Washington, D.C.: The Brookings Institution, 1990), p. 129.
4. Harold J. Berman, "The Challenge of the Modern State" in Hunter and Guinness, eds., *Articles of Faith, Articles of Peace*, p. 48.
5. Ibid., p. 42.
6. Ibid., p. 43.
7. "The Williamsburg Charter" in Hunter and Guinness, eds., *Articles of Faith, Articles of Peace*, p. 130.
8. *The Williamsburg Charter Survey on Religion and Public Life*, (The Williamsburg Charter Foundation, Washington, D.C., 1988); see also Ari L. Goldman, "Portrait of Religious U.S. Holds Dozens of Surprizes," *The New York Times*, April 10, 1991, pp. A1, A18.
9. Harold L. Hodgkinson, *California: The State and its Educational System* (Washington, D.C.: The Institute for Educational Leadership, 1986).
10. Harold L. Hodgkinson, *All One System: Demographics of Education, Kindergarten through Graduate School* (Washington, D.C.: The Institute for Educational Leadership, 1985).
11. "Armenian Pressure," *Washington Post*, March 2, 1988, p. A20.
12. See Donald S. Lutz, "Religious Dimension in the Development of American Constitutionalism" *Emory Law Journal*, vol. 39, Winter 1990, p. 21.; Daniel Elazar, "Covenant as the Basis of Jewish Political Tradition," *Jewish Journal of Sociology*, vol. 2 no. 5 (1978), pp. 5–37.
13. Jacques Maritain, "The Possibilities for Co-operation in a Divided World," Inaugural Address to the Second International Conference of UNESCO, November 6, 1947.
14. Steven Tipton, "Religion in an Ambiguous Polity," *Emory Law Journal* vol. 39, Winter 1990, p. 196.
15. See John Rawls, "The Idea of an Overlapping Consensus," *Oxford Journal of Legal Studies*, vol. 7, no. 1 (1987).
16. John Courtney Murray, *We Hold These Truths* (New York: Sheed and Wavel, 1960), p. 49.
17. Ibid., p. 45.
18. "The Williamsburg Charter" in Hunter and Guinness, eds., *Articles of Faith, Articles of Peace*, p. 145.

19. Alexis de Tocqueville, *Recollections*, ed. J. P. Mayer (Westport, Conn.: Greenwood Press, 1979), p. 56.

Chapter 14: Making the World Safe for Diversity

1. Mark W. Cannon, "The Constitution: The Real Thousand Points of Light," *Phi Kappa Phi Journal*, Spring 1990, p. 43.
2. Quoted in Dan Balz, "Bishop's Retain PR Film to Assist Abortion Fight," *Washington Post*, April 6, 1990, p. A10.
3. Quoted in Lawrence Feinberg, "The Secular Storm Around Rev. Healy," *Washington Post*, April 21, 1989, p. C1.
4. Ibid., p. C3.
5. "The Williamsburg Charter" in James Davison Hunter and Os Guinness, eds., *Articles of Faith, Articles of Peace* (Washington, D.C.: The Brookings Institution, 1990), pp. 140–41.
6. Quoted in Virginia Culver, "Countering the Moral Majority," *Denver Post*, December 11, 1981, p. 4D.
7. Gary North, "The Intellectual Schizophrenia of the New Christian Right" in *Christianity and Civilization*, vol. I (Geneva Ministries, 1982), p. 25.
8. "The Williamsburg Charter" in Hunter and Guinness, eds., *Articles of Faith, Articles of Peace*, p. 142.
9. Robert J. Lichter and Stanley Rothman, "Media and Business Elites," *Public Opinion*, vol. 4 (Oct./Nov. 1981), p. 42.
10. Neil Gabler, *An Empire of Their Own: How the Jews Invented Hollywood* (New York: Doubleday Anchor, 1989), p. 7.
11. See David S. Wyman, *The Abandonment of the Jews* (New York: Pantheon, 1984), p. 14.
12. Quoted in Margot Hornblower, "Farrakhan Draws Huge Crowd," *Washington Post*, October 8, 1985, p. A6.
13. See Wyman, *The Abandonment of the Jews*, especially chap. 16.
14. Quoted in Malcolm Gladwell, "Chuck Colson vs. the Fundamentalists," *American Spectator*, February 1986, p. 23.
15. Remarks at the Lausanne Congress on World Evangelization, Manila, July 1989.
16. Richard John Neuhaus, "Putting First Things First," *First Things* no. 1 (March 1990), p. 7.
17. Quoted in Louis Menand, "Revisionists Revised," *Yale Review*, Autumn 1984, p. 120.
18. Judy Mann, "What's Secular Humanism?" *Washington Post*, January 30, 1985, p. B3.
19. Quoted in "The Spirit of Intolerance," *Church and State*, February 1985, p. 15.
20. See *Lynch v. Donnelly*, 79L.Ed.604 (1984); *Scarsdale v. McCreary*, 105 S.Ct. 1859 (1985).
21. Alexis de Tocqueville, *Democracy in America*, vol. I (New York: Vintage Books, 1945), p. 5.
22. Jerry Falwell on the "Old Time Gospel Hour," March 11, 1984.
23. "The Williamsburg Charter" in Hunter and Guinness, eds., *Articles of Faith, Articles of Peace*, pp. 142–43.
24. Friedrich Nietzsche, *Twilight of the Idols/The Anti-Christ* (Harmondsworth: Penguin, 1968), p. 88.

25. See Edwin S. Gaustad, ed., *A Documentary History of Religion in America: To the Civil War* (Grand Rapids, Mich.: Eerdmans, 1982), p. 116.

26. Quoted in Matthew Page Andrews, *The Founding of Maryland* (Baltimore: Williams and Wilkins Company, 1933), p. 147.

27. Quoted in ibid, p. 146.

28. Ibid., p. 146.

29. Leo Pfeffer, "Freedom and Separation," *Journal of Church and State*, November 1960, p. 103.

30. Michael J. Sandel, "Freedom of Conscience or Freedom of Choice" in Hunter and Guinness, eds., *Articles of Faith, Articles of Peace*, p. 88.

31. Ibid.

32. William Lee Miller, "The Moral Project of the American Founders" in Hunter and Guinness, eds., *Articles of Faith, Articles of Peace*, p. 18.

33. George Steiner, *In Bluebeard's Castle* (New Haven: Yale University Press, 1971), p. 114.

34. Bernard Bailyn, *The Ideological Origins of the American Revolution* (Cambridge: The Belknap Press, 1967), p. 21.

35. Ibid., p. 19.

36. Quoted in Jerald C. Brauer, *The Lively Experiment* (Macon, Georgia: Mercer University Press, 1987), p. 63.

37. James O'Toole, "From Marx to Madison," *Britannica Yearbook 1989*, p. 14.

38. Henrik Ibsen, *An Enemy of the People* (London: Heinemann, 1967), Act 5.

39. Bruce Ackerman, *Social Justice in the Liberal State* (New Haven: Yale University Press, 1980), pp. 10–11.

40. Jon G. Murray, "Director's Briefcase," *American Atheist*, July 1988, p. 11.

41. "Resolution on Religious Proselytizing," adopted April 9, 1987, and issued by the United Ministry at Harvard/Radcliffe, Memorial Church, Harvard Yard.

42. Michael Walzer, "The Sins of Salman," *New Republic*, April 10, 1989, p. 13.

43. Ibid.

44. Quoted in Ellis Sandoz, "Power and Spirit in the Founding," *This World*, no. 9 (Fall 1984), p. 67.

45. John Adams, *The Writings of John Quincy Adams* vol. 3 (New York: Greenwood Press, 1968), pp. 178–9; See Bailyn, *The Ideological Origins of the American Revolution*, p. 68.

The Tourneying Hopes

1. Henry Grunwald, "Time at 60," *Time*, Sixtieth Anniversary Issue 1983, p. 5.

2. Aleksandr I. Solzhenitsyn, *The Oak and the Calf*, trans. Harry Willetts (London: Collins and Harvill Press, 1980), p. 270.

3. Václav Havel, *Living in Truth*, ed. Jan Vladislav (London: Faber and Faber, 1987), p. 123.

4. Ibid., p. 124.

Chapter 15: The Testing of Republican Character

1. Václav Havel, *Living in Truth*, ed. Jan Vadislav (London: Faber and Faber, 1987), p. 152.

2. George Grant, *Time As History*, (Toronto: Canadian Broadcasting Corporation, 1969), p. 35.

3. See Horace Mann, *Ninth Annual Report of the Board of Education* (Boston: Dutton and Wentworth, 1846), pp. 66–69.

4. Arthur Janov, *The Primal Scream* (New York: Putnam, 1970) p. 168.

5. James Russell Lowell, "The Question of the Hour," in Kenneth M. Stampp, ed., *The Causes of the Civil War* (Englewood Cliffs, N.J.: Prentice-Hall, 1974), p. 107.

6. James Q. Wilson, "The Rediscovery of Character," *Public Interest*, Fall 1985, pp. 3, 16.

7. Quoted Karl Jaspers, *Nietzsche and Christianity*, trans. E. B. Ashton (Chicago: Henry Regnery Company, 1961), p. 14.

8. Karl Marx, *Communist Manifesto 1848* (Chicago: Henry Regnery Company, 1969), p. 20.

9. Walt Whitman, "Democratic Vistas" in *Walt Whitman: Complete Poetry and Poems*, p. 937; T. S. Eliot, *Collected Poems: 1909–1935* (London: Faber and Faber, 1957), p. 87.

10. George Steiner, *Real Presences* (Chicago: University of Chicago Press, 1989), p. 134.

11. Stephen Birmingham, "The Man Who Wasn't There," *Washington Post*, October 15, 1989, p. 134.

12. In Andreas Papadakis, Catherine Cooke, and Andrew Benjamin, *Deconstruction* (New York: Rizzoli, 1989), p. 146.

13. Ian I. Mitroff and Warren Bennis, *The Unreality Industry* (New York: Birch Lane Press, 1989).

14. Peggy Noonan, "Who was That Masked Man?" *Mirabella*, December 1989, p. 177.

15. T. J. Jackson Lears, *No Place of Grace* (New York: Pantheon, 1981), p. 142.

16. Robert Musil, *The Man Without Qualities* (New York: Perigree Books, 1980), p. 70.

17. Philip Rieff, *The Feeling Intellect* (Chicago: University of Chicago Press, 1990), p. 355.

18. Musil, *The Man Without Qualities*, p. 314.

19. William Lee Miller, *The First Liberty* (New York: Alfred Knopf, 1986), p. 72.

20. Leszek Kolakowski, "The Idolatry of Politics," in *Modernity on Endless Trial* (Chicago: University of Chicago Press, 1990), p. 29.

21. Ibid., p. 32.

22. Friedrich Nietzsche, *Thus Spoke Zarathustra*, trans. Walter Kaufmann (New York: Penguin Books, 1978), p. 286.

23. Musil, *The Man Without Qualities*, p. 176.

24. Kolakowski, "The Idolatry of Politics," pp. 31, 32

25. Ibid., p. 31.

26. Quoted in H. Richard Niebuhr, *The Kingdom of God in America* (New York: Harper Torchbooks, 1959), p. 77.

27. Harriet Martineau, *Society in America*, vol. III (New York: AMS Press, 1966), p. 7.

28. Eric Hoffer, *The Passionate State of the Mind and Other Aphorisms* (New York: Harper, 1955), p. 21.

29. James H. Bryce, *The American Commonwealth* (New York: Macmillan, 1895), p. 702.

30. Quoted Ronald Steel, *Walter Lippmann and the American Century* (New York: Vintage Books, 1981), p. 152.

31. Daniel J. Boorstin, *The Image* (New York: Atheneum, 1962), p. 3.

32. George F. Will, "Legislating Racial Spoils," *Washington Post*, July 5, 1990, p. A19.

33. Austin Ranney, *Channels of Power* (New York: Basic Books, 1983), p. 174.

34. Friedrich Nietzsche, *The Portable Nietzsche*, ed. and trans. Walter Kaufmann (New York: Penguin, 1976), p. 63.

35. See Kiku Adatto, "The Incredible Shrinking Sound Bite," *New Republic*, May 28, 1990, pp. 20–23; Quoted in Patrick Brantlinger, *Bread and Circuses* (Ithaca, NY: Cornell University Press, 1983), p. 172.

36. Hugo Young, "Conspiracies in American Ignorance," *Guardian Weekly*, June 3, 1990, p. 8.

37. See Walter Lippmann, *Public Opinion* (New York: Mentor Books, 1955), chap. 11.

38. Quoted in Bill McAllister, "Amid Uproar, Speakes Quits Merrill Lynch Post," *Washington Post*, April 16, 1988, p. A8.

39. Quoted in John E. Yang, "President 'Likes Simple, Direct Phrases,'" *Washington Post*, June 22, 1991, p. A11.

40. Quoted in Martha Sherrill, "Hollywood's Activists, Taking Up the Banner," *Washington Post*, April 10, 1989, p. B2.

41. Quoted in David Streitfeld, "Last Words on '89," *Washington Post*, December 31, 1989, Book World 15.

42. Daniel J. Boorstin, "Homo 'Up-to-Datum' is a Dunce," *Reader's Digest*, September 1982, p. 54.

43. Robert L. Heilbroner, *Business Civilization in Decline*, (New York: Norton, 1976), p. 114.

44. Simone Weil, *The Need for Roots* (London: Routledge and Kegan Paul, 1952), p. 98.

45. Ted Koppel, "The Curse of Immediacy," *Networker*, March–April 1986, p. 19.

46. Quoted in Adatto, "The Incredible Shrinking Sound Bite," p. 23.

Chapter 16: Hunger for Home

1. Cited in David Breskin, "Dear Mom and Dad," *Rolling Stone*, November 8, 1984, p. 32.

2. See Allan Carlson, "Coping With Teen Suicides," *Washington Times*, July 11, 1986, p. 2D.

3. Quoted in Robert Wuthnow, *The Consciousness Reformation* (Berkeley: University of California Press, 1976), p. 102.

4. Czeslaw Milosz, *Visions From San Francisco Bay*, trans. Richard Lourie (Manchester: Carcanet Press, 1982), p. 39.

5. T. S. Eliot, "Chorus From the Rock," *Collected Poems 1909–1935*, vol. 3, (London: Faber and Faber, 1958), p. 166.

6. See Allan Nevins, ed., *America Through British Eyes*, p. 496.

7. Denis Brogan, *The American Character* (New York: Vintage Books, 1956), p. xv; Santayana is quoted by James Sellers, *Public Ethics* (New York: Harper and Row, 1970), p. 169.

8. John Steinbeck, *Travels with Charley* (New York: Viking Press, 1962), p. 93.

9. George M. Grant, *Technology and Empire* (Toronto: House of Anansi, 1969), p. 17.

10. Peter L. Berger, *The Capitalist Revolution* (New York: Basic Books, 1986), p. 113.

11. Peter L. Berger, *Facing up to Modernity* (New York: Basic Books, 1977), p. 32.

12. Simone Weil, *The Need for Roots* (London: Routledge and Kegan Paul, 1952) p. 114.

13. Friedrich Nietzsche, *The Birth of Tragedy and the Genealogy of Morals* (New York: Anchor Books, 1956), p. 136.

14. Spencer Rich, "A Generation Alters Notion of U.S. Family," *Washington Post*, September 5, 1989, p. A12.

15. Lindsy van Gelder, "Dependencies of Independent Women," *Ms.*, February 1987, pp. 47, 73.

16. See Kingsley Davis, "The Continuing Demographic Leadership in Industrial Societies" in Seymour Martin Lipset, ed., *The Third Century* (Chicago: University of Chicago Press, 1979), pp. 38–65.
17. Ibid., pp. 43–44.
18. See Bernie Zilbergeld, *The Shrinking of America* (Boston: Little Brown and Company, 1983) p. 199.
19. Tony Kahn, "Passages," *People*, June 22, 1992, p. 83.
20. Philip Rieff, *The Triumph of the Therapeutic* (Chicago: University of Chicago Press, 1987), p. 43.
21. Quoted in Paul Farhi, "Obsession for 'Twin Peaks,'" *Washington Post*, August 16, 1990, p. D1.
22. *The American Family Under Siege* (Washington, D.C.: Family Research Council, 1989), p. 2.
23. Ibid.
24. Richard Bach, *Jonathan Livingston Seagull* (New York: Macmillan, 1970), p. 53.
25. Humphrey Carpenter, *W. H. Auden: A Biography* (London, Unwin Paperbacks, 1983), p. 289.
26. Armand M. Nicholi, Jr., "Recent Trends in the American Family," *Congressional Record*, May 3, 1983, p. E-2001.
27. Quoted in Chester E. Finn, Jr., *Ten Tentative Truths* (Minneapolis, MN: Center of the American Experiment, 1990), p. 2.
28. Kenneth J. Gergen, *The Saturated Self* (New York: Basic Books, 1991), pp. 170, 197.
29. Quoted in ibid.
30. Chester E. Finn, Jr., *Ten Tentative Truths*, p. 2.
31. Ibid., p. 5.
32. Ibid.
33. Ibid.
34. Henry Fairlie, "Fear of Living," *New Republic*, January 23, 1989, p. 14.
35. Quoted in Jackson Lears, *No Place of Grace* (New York: Pantheon, 1981), p. 45.
36. Quoted in ibid., p. 49.
37. Quoted in ibid., p. 56.
38. Peter and Brigitte Berger, *The War Over the Family* (Garden City, N.Y.: Doubleday, 1983), p. 134.
39. Peter L. Berger, "Sincerity and Authenticity in Modern Society," *Public Interest*, Spring 1973, p. 89.

Chapter 17: The Last Hero

1. Aleksandr I. Solzhenitsyn, *First Circle*, trans. Thomas P. Whitney (New York: Bantam Books, 1969), p. 122.
2. Daniel J. Boorstin, *The Image* (New York: Atheneum, 1962), p. 57.
3. "Notebook," *New Republic*, April 30, 1990, p. 9.
4. Quoted in Ronald Steel, *Walter Lippmann and the American Century* (New York: Vintage Books, 1981), p. 525.
5. "A Letter from the Publisher," *Time*, European edition, September 3, 1984, p. 7.
6. Theodore J. Lowi, *The Personal President* (Ithaca, N.Y.: Cornell University Press, 1985), p. xi.

7. Quoted in Daniel J. Boorstin, *The Americans: The National Experience* (New York: Vintage Books, 1965), p. 351.
8. Gustave de Beaumont, *Marie*, trans. Barbara Chapman (Stanford: Stanford University Press, 1958), p. 106.
9. Quoted in Boorstin, *The Americans*, p. 353; see also Will Herberg, *Protestant-Catholic-Jew* (Garden City, N.Y.: Anchor Books, 1960), p. 93.
10. H. L. Meneken, *The American Scene* (New York: Vintage Books, 1982), p. 12.
11. Ibid., p. 13.
12. Lou Cannon, "Presidential Chutzpah," *Washington Post*, September 19, 1989, p. D3; Chuck Conconei, "Personalitics; Out and About," *Washington Post*, September 14, 1987, p. A2.
13. Quoted Godfrey Hodgson, *America in Our Time* (Garden City, N.Y.: Doubleday, 1976), p. 102.
14. Paul E. Boller, Jr., *Presidential Anecdotes* (Harmondsworth, Middlesex: Penguin Books, 1982), p. 194; Lippmann, quoted in Steel, *Walter Lippmann and the American Century*, p. 481.
15. Speech at the National Press Foundation dinner in Washington, D.C., February 25, 1986.
16. Lowi, *The Personal President*, p. 151.
17. Quoted in Thomas Griffith, "Proving Lincoln was Right," *Time*, October 22, 1984, p. 38.
18. Friedrich Nietzsche, *The Twilight of the Idols/The Anti-Christ* (London: Penguin Books, 1968), p. 173.
19. William Greider, "The Fools on the Hill," *Rolling Stone*, November 8, 1984, p. 13.
20. Ibid.
21. David J. Marek, "Patrick Caddell," *Washington Post*, November 18, 1987, p. B4.
22. Remarks in Chicago before the National Association of Broadcasters, April 1, 1968, *Public Papers of the President of the United States: Lyndon B. Johnson* (Washington D.C.: United States Printing Office, 1970), pp. 482–86.
23. Theodore J. Lowi, *The Politics of Disorder* (New York: Basic Books, 1971), p. 81.
24. George F. Will, "A National Embarrassment," *Washington Post*, September 27, 1988, p. A21.
25. David Hoffman, "A State of the Union Short on Substance," *Washington Post*, January 29, 1987, p. A1.
26. Søren Kierkegaard, *The Present Age* (New York: Harper & Row, 1962), p. 35.
27. Kevin P. Phillips, "George Bush and Congress—Brain Dead Politics of '89," *Washington Post*, October 1, 1989, p. D1; George F. Will, "An Unserious Presidency," *Washington Post*, October 12, 1989, p. D1; Richard Gephardt, "Gephardt on Bush's Lack of Vision," *Washington Post*, March 7, 1990, p. A18.
28. David S. Broder, "On America's Crumbling Roads," *Washington Post*, March 11, 1990, p. B7.
29. See Godfrey Hodgson, *All Things to All Men* (London: Weidenfeld and Nicholson, 1980), p. 46.
30. Quoted in "Conservatives' Conference," *Washington Post*, February 12, 1986, p. B3.
31. Lowi, *The Personal President*, p. 11.
32. William A. Henry III, "Attacking a 'National Amnesia,'" *Time*, December 8, 1986, p. 107.
33. Bernard Crick, *George Orwell: A Life* (Harmondsworth: Penguin, 1982), p. 381.

34. Walter Lippmann, *The Public Philosophy* (New York: Mentor Books, 1955), p. 26.

35. Lowi, *The Personal President*, p. 115.

36. Quoted Hodgson, *All Things to All Men*, p. 70.

37. Quoted Karl Lowith, *Meaning in History* (Chicago: University of Chicago Press, 1949), p. 24.

38. *American Political Report*, August 17, 1979, p. 3.

39. Quoted Lowi, *The Personal President*, p. 135.

40. From *Collected Poems of AE* (London: Macmillan and Company, Ltd., 1935), p. 400.

41. Christopher Connel, "Kissinger on Contra Issue: Two-Sided Nonsense," *Washington Post*, April 20, 1986, p. A18.

42. Quoted in Hugh Thomas, *An Unfinished History of the World* (London: Hamish Hamilton, 1979), p. 614.

43. Alasdair MacIntyre, *After Virtue* (Notre Dame: University of Notre Dame Press, 1981), p. 75.

44. Quoted in Hodgson, *All Things to All Men*, p. 45.

45. Quoted in Arthur M. Schlesinger, Jr., "The Imperial Temptation," *New Republic*, 16 March 1987, p. 17.

46. Ludwig Wittgenstein, *Tractatus Logico-Philosophicus* (London: Rutledge and Kegan Paul, 1922), p. 183.

47. Carl Gustav Jung, *Memories, Dreams, Reflections* (London: Collins, Fontanta, 1967), p. 356.

Chapter 18: The Enlightenment's Last Laugh

1. Quoted in James Davison Hunter, *Culture Wars* (New York: Basic Books, 1992), pp. 298ff.

2. Ibid.

3. Philip Rieff, *The Triumph of the Therapeutic* (Chicago: University of Chicago Press, 1987), p. 27.

4. See David Barrett, ed., *World Christian Encyclopedia* (Oxford: Oxford University Press, 1982).

5. Owen Chadwick, *The Secularization of the European Mind in the Nineteenth Century* (Cambridge: Cambridge University Press, 1975), p. 9.

6. See Daniel Yankelovich, *New Rules* (New York: Random House, 1981); Bernie Zilbergeld, *The Shrinking of America* (Boston: Little Brown and Company, 1983).

7. Quoted in "Things They Said," *World*, June 16, 1990, p. 4.

8. Rieff, *The Triumph of the Therapeutic*, p. 9.

9. Friedrich Nietzsche, *Beyond Good and Evil*, trans. Marianne Cowan (Chicago: Henry Regnery Company, 1955), p. 95.

10. Dante Germino, "End of the Waste Land," *National Review*, April 30, 1976, p. 449.

11. Michael Barone, "The Age of Restraint," *Washington Post*, September 15, 1985, p. D7.

12. *Washington Post*, July 30, 1988, p. C3.

13. Quoted in Charles Peters and Phillip Keisling, eds., *A New Road for America* (New York: Madison Books, 1985), p. 87.

14. Evan Thomas, "Deep Pockets for Doing Good," *Time*, June 16, 1986, p. 51.

15. Richard Goldstein, "The New Sobriety," *Vogue*, December 30, 1986, p. 23.

16. Quoted in Peters and Keisling, eds., *A New Road for America*, p. 88.

17. In David Boaz, ed., *Left, Right and Babyboom* (Washington, D.C.: Cato Institute, 1986), p. 91.

18. "Safe Sex and the Flag," *Time,* June 4, 1990, p. 57.
19. Michael Specter, "Facing Death from AIDS Without Having Really Lived," *Washington Post,* August 11, 1985, p. L3.
20. Philip Rieff, *The Feeling Intellect* (Chicago: University of Chicago Press, 1990), p. 363.
21. Quoted in John Howe, *The Changing Political Thought of John Adams* (Princeton: Princeton University Press, 1966), p. 185.
22. Quoted in Robert N. Bellah et al., *Habits of the Heart* (Berkeley: University of California Pres, 1985), p. 254.
23. Alexis de Tocqueville, *Democracy in America,* vol. I (New York: Vintage Books, 1945), p. 318; see also vol. II, p. 23.
24. C. S. Lewis, "Equality," *Spectator,* August 27, 1943, p. 192.
25. Alexander Hamilton, James Madison and John Jay, in "Federalist No. 51" in *The Federalist Papers* (New York: Bantam Books, 1982), p. 262.
26. John Diggins, *The Lost Soul of American Politics* (New York: Basic Books, 1984), p. 18.
27. See Richard Hofstadter, *The American Political Tradition* (New York: Vintage Books, 1956), pp. 1, 4.
28. Ibid., pp. 16–17.
29. Luigi Barzini, *The Europeans* (Harmondsworth: Penguin, 1984), p. 235.
30. Sydney E. Ahlstrom, *American Religious Values and the Future of America* (Philadelphia: Fortress Press, 1978), p. 21.
31. A. James Reichley, *Religion in American Life* (Washington, D.C.: The Brookings Institution, 1985), p. 348.

Chapter 19: The Long Run Sooner

1. "Address to the Wisconsin State Agricultural Society," *Lincoln: Selected Speeches and Writings* (New York: Hendricks House, 1980), p. 237.
2. Daniel Yankelovich, *New Rules,* (New York: Harper & Row, 1968), p. 259.
3. Paul Weyrich, *Taking Stock* (Washington, D.C.: The Institute for Government and Politics, 1985), p. 6.
4. Russell Kirk, *A Culture's Road Toward Avernus,* (Washington, D.C.: The Institute for Cultural Conservatism, 1988), p. 10.
5. H. L. Mencken, *The American Scene* (New York: Vintage Books, 1982), p. 33.
6. Quoted in Debora Silverman, *Sterling Culture* (New York: Pantheon, 1986), p. 97.
7. George M. Grant, *Technology and Empire* (Toronto: Home of Anansi, 1969), p. 40.
8. Ibid., p. 29.
9. Henry Allen, "The Patent Truth of a Bygone Age," *Washington Post,* March 11, 1990, p. D1.
10. Bernard Crick, *George Orwell: A Life* (Harmondsworth: Penguin, 1982), p. 428.
11. Harold J. Berman, *The Interaction of Law and Religion* (Nashville: Abingdon Press, 1974), pp. 36, 37.
12. Aleksandr Solzhenitsyn, "A World Split Apart" in Ronald Berman, ed., *Solzhenitsyn at Harvard* (Washington, D.C.: Ethics and Public Policy Center, 1980), pp. 8–9.
13. *Washington Post,* April 6, 1991, p. A21.
14. Václav Havel, New Year Speech, January 1990.
15. Phillip Rieff, *The Triumph of the Therapeutic* (Chicago: University of Chicago Press, 1987) p. 11.

16. Charles Krauthammer, "Culture Has Consequences," *Washington Post*, October 26, 1990, p. A27.

17. Mencken, *The American Scene*, p. 533.

18. Howard Kurtz, "The Trump Dump, Part 10," *Washington Post*, February 21, 1990, p. D1.

19. T. R. Reid, "Many are at Fault for Insurance Woe," *Washington Post*, February 24, 1986, p. A7.

20. *The Times* (London), May 19, 1984, p. 28.

21. Patricia B. Gray, "Lawyer Harry Makes a Killing Suing People of New York," *Wall Street Journal*, March 16, 1988, p. 1.

22. Ibid.

23. Sol Linowitz, "Why America Hates Lawyers," *Washington Post*, May 15, 1988, p. B5.

24. Richard John Neuhaus, *The Naked Public Square* (Grand Rapids, Mich.: Eerdmans, 1984), p. 259.

25. Martin Luther King, "Unwise and Untimely," Letter from the Birmingham City Jail, 1963.

26. Quoted in Daniel J. Danelski and Joseph S. Tulchin, eds., *The Autobiographical Notes of Charles Evans Hughes* (Cambridge: Harvard University Press, 1973), p. 143.

27. Mencken, *The American Scene*, p. 235.

28. Max Lerner, "The Constitution and the Court as Symbols," *Yale Law Journal*, vol. 46 (1937), pp. 1290–1319.

29. Walter Lippmann, *The Public Philosophy* (New York: Mentor Books, 1955), p. 136.

30. Rieff, *The Triumph of the Therapeutic*, p. 246.

31. Irving Kristol, "The Adversary Culture of Intellectuals" in Seymour Martin Lipset, ed., *The Third Century* (Chicago: University of Chicago Press, 1979), p. 328.

32. Czeslaw Milosz *Visions From San Francisco Bay*, trans. Richard Lourie (Manchester: Carcenet Press, 1982), p. 214.

33. Peter L. Berger, *Facing Up to Modernity* (New York: Basic Books, 1977), p. 65; Rieff, *The Triumph of the Therapeutic*, p. 33.

34. Marc H. Tannenbaum, "Values, Events and Experiences in the American Religious Experience" in *American Religious Values and the Futures of America*, Rodger van Allen, ed. (Philadelphia: Fortress Press, 1983), p. 95.

35. Ibid.

36. See Peter L. Berger and Brigitte Berger, *The War Over the Family* (Garden City, N.Y.: Doubleday, 1983), p. 132.

37. Milosz, *Visions From San Francisco Bay*, p. 214.

38. Rieff, *The Triumph of the Therapeutic*, p. 9.

39. James Bryce, *The American Commonwealth*, vol. 2 (New York: Macmillan, 1895), pp. 793, 794.

40. BBC interview, November 2, 1980.

41. George F. Will, *Statecraft as Soulcraft* (New York: Touchstone, 1984), p. 114.

Chapter 20: Apple Pie Authoritarianism

1. H. Richard Niebuhr, *Christ and Culture* (New York: Harper Colophon, 1951), p. 8.

2. "Facing the Future with Calm," *The New York Times*, May 20, 1916, p. 10.

3. Edward Gibbon, *The History of the Decline and Fall of the Roman Empire* (New York: DeFau 1906), vol. 1, p. 35.

4. Philip Rieff, *The Triumph of the Therapeutic* (Chicago: University of Chicago Press, 1987), p. 27.
5. Quoted in Stanley Hoffman, "Mr. X," *New Republic*, October 2, 1989, p. 36.
6. George M. Grant, *Technology and Empire* (Toronto: House of Anonsi, 1969), p. 38.
7. Howard Means, "God is Back," *The Washingtonian*, December 1986, cover.
8. Quoted in Kevin P. Phillips, *Post-Conservative America* (New York: Vintage Books, 1983), p. 198.
9. Steven M. Tipton, *Getting Saved From the Sixties* (Berkeley: University of California Press, 1982), p. 245.
10. Ari Goldman, "Portrait of Religion in U.S. Holds Dozens of Surprises," *The New York Times*, April 10, 1991, pp. A1, A18.
11. Advertisement for the *Oxford Review* in *The New Republic*, November 30, 1987, p. 19.
12. Quoted in Hugh Thomas, *An Unfinished History of the World* (London: Hamish Hamilton, 1979), p. 594.
13. Quoted in William Lee Miller, *The First Liberty* (New York: Alfred Knopf, 1986), p. 28.
14. Quoted in ibid., p. 244.
15. Stanley K. Schultz, *The Culture Factory: Boston Public Schools 1789–1860* (New York: Oxford University Press, 1973), p. 305.
16. Will Herberg, *Protestant-Catholic-Jew* (Garden City, N.Y.: Anchor Books, 1960), p. 84.
17. Ibid., p. 88.
18. Alexis de Tocqueville, *Democracy in America*, vol. II (New York: Vintage Books, 1945), p. 156.
19. Robert Wright, "Tao Jones," *New Republic*, November 20, 1989, p. 38.
20. T. J. Jackson Lears, *No Place of Grace* (New York: Pantheon, 1981), p. 308.
21. See Louis E. Raths, Merrill Harmin, and Sidney B. Simon, *Values and Teaching* (Columbus, Ohio: Charles E. Merrill Publishing Co., 1978), pp. 138, 139.
22. See William G. McLoughlin, *Revivals, Awakenings and Reform* (Chicago: University of Chicago Press, 1978), pp. 214, 215.
23. Rieff, *The Triumph of the Therapeutic*, p. 11.
24. Arthur M. Schlesinger, Jr., *The Cycles of American History* (Boston: Houghton Mifflin, 1986), p. 48.

Chapter 21: The Wild Card Played

1. Quoted in Robert Wuthnow, *The Restructuring of American Religion* (Princeton: Princeton University Press, 1988), p. 66.
2. Matthew Arnold, "On Dover Beach," in Miriam Allott, ed., *The Poems of Matthew Arnold* (New York: Longman, 1979).
3. Henry Mitchell, "Spiritual Revival, 1980s-style," *Washington Post*, June 10, 1988, p. D2.
4. See Arthur Hertzberg, *The Jews in America* (New York: Simon and Schuster, 1989).
5. Friedrich Nietzsche, *Twilight of the Idols/The Anti-Christ* (London: Penguin Books, 1968), p. 97.
6. James Davison Hunter, *American Evangelicalism* (New Brunswick, N.J.: Rutgers, 1983), p. 133.
7. Robert N. Bellah, *The Broken Covenant* (New York: Seabury Press, 1975), p. 109.

8. William M. Sullivan, *Reconstructing Public Philosophy* (Berkeley: University of California Press, 1982), p. 180.

9. Philip Rieff, *The Triumph of the Therapeutic* (Chicago: University of Chicago Press, 1987), pp. 13, 64.

10. Paul Weyrich, *Taking Stock* (Washington, D.C.: The Institute for Government and Politics, 1985), p. 8.

11. Bernard Semmel, "Democracy, Virtue and Religion" in Richard John Neuhaus, ed., *Virtue—Public and Private* (Grand Rapids, Mich.: Eerdman's, 1986), p. 52.

12. Quoted in Martin E. Marty, *Context*, November 15, 1980, p. 6.

13. Publius, "Cultural Conservativism, Republicanism and the Republican Party" (Washington, D.C.: The Institute for Cultural Conservatism, 1987), p. 11.

14. Bellah, *The Broken Covenant*, p. 48.

15. William G. McLoughlin, *Revivals, Awakenings and Reforms* (Chicago: University of Chicago Press, 1978), p. xiv.

16. Ibid., p. 2.

17. Will Herberg, *Protestant-Catholic-Jew* (Garden City, N.Y.: Anchor Books, 1960), p. 4.

18. David A. Martin, *The Dilemmas of Contemporary Religion* (Oxford: Blackwell, 1978), p. 88.

19. G. K. Chesterton, *The Everlasting Man* (Garden City, N.Y.: Image Books, 1955), pp. 260–61.

20. See Sydney E. Ahlstrom, *A Religious History of the American People* (Philadelphia: Fortren Press, 1978), vol. II, pp. 403, 454.

21. Irving Kristol, "The Adversary Culture of the Intellectuals" in *Third Century*, Seymour Martin Lipset, ed. (Chicago: University of Chicago Press, 1979), p. 342.

22. Ibid., p. 343.

The Eagle and the Sun

1. Jeremiah 46:17; Luke 19:44

2. See Friedrich Nietzsche, *Twilight of the Idols/The Anti-Christ* (London: Penguin Books, 1968), p. 24.

3. Philip Rieff, *The Feeling Intellect* (Chicago: University of Chicago Press, 1990), pp. 354–55, 335.

4. See John W. Whitehead, *The Second American Revolution* (Elgin, Ill.: David C. Cook, 1982); Marilyn Ferguson, *The Aquarian Conspiracy* (London: Granada, 1982), p. 134.

5. Quoted in Sydney E. Ahlstrom, *A Religious History of the American People* (Philadelphia: Fortress Press, 1978), vol. I, p. 326.

6. Ibid., p. 35.

7. Fyodor Dostoevsky, "Notes From the Underground" in Walter Kaufmann, ed., *Existentialism from Dostoevsky to Sartre* (New York: Meridian Books, 1956), p. 74.

8. Aleksandr Solzhenitsyn, Address at the presentation of the Templeton Foundation Prize for Progress in Religion at the Guildhall, London, May 10, 1983.

9. Abraham Lincoln, *The Collected Works of Abraham Lincoln* (New Brunswick: Rutgers University, 1990), vol. 6, p. 156.

10. William Bradford, "Of Plymouth Plantation" in Perry Miller, ed., *The American Puritans: Their Prose and Poetry* (New York: Doubleday Anchor, 1956), p. 18.

11. Saint Augustine, *Confessions,* Book 10, trans. R. S. Pine-Coffin (Harmondsworth: Penguin Books, 1961), p. 231.
12. Michael Novak, "A Concluding Perspective on American Religious Values and the Future of America," in *American Religious Values and the Future of America* (Philadelphia: Fortress Press, 1978), p. 184.
13. Daniel J. Boorstin, *The Image* (New York, Athenaem, 1962), p. 245.
14. Ibid., pp. 244, 245.
15. H. Richard Niebuhr, *The Kingdom of God in America* (New York: Harper Torchbooks, 1959), p. 126.
16. Jonathan Alter, "America's Secret Warriors," *Newsweek,* October 10, 1983, p. 3.
17. Chuck Conconi, "Personalities," *Washington Post,* June 17, 1988, p. D3.
18. "Hahn, Baring Up," *Washington Post,* September 12, 1987, p. D2.
19. Czeslaw Milosz, *Visions From San Francisco Bay,* trans. Richard Lourie (Manchester: Carcanet Press, 1982), p. 221.
20. Aleksandr Solzhenitsyn and others, *From Under the Rubble,* trans. Max Hayward (New York: Bantam Books, 1976), pp. 106–07.
21. Hannah Arendt, *Between Past and Future* (New York, Penguin Books, 1977), p. 3.
22. See ibid., p. 7.
23. Ibid., p. 13.
24. Tom Paine, *Common Sense* (Harmondsworth: Penguin Books, 1976), p. 84.
25. Quoted in Daniel J. Boorstin, *The Americans: The National Experience* (New York: Vintage Books, 1965), p. 419.
26. Reinhold Niebuhr, *Moral Man and Immoral Society* (New York: Scribner and Son, 1932), p. 253.
27. Quoted in Ronald Steel, *Walter Lippmann and the American Century* (New York: Vintage Books, 1981), p. 425.
28. Walter Lippmann, *The Public Philosophy* (New York: Mentor Books, 1955), pp. 74, 75.
29. G. K. Chesterton, *What I Saw in America* (New York: Da Capo Press, 1968), p. 308.
30. Ibid.
31. Charles Dickens, *Martin Chuzzlewit* (London: Macmillan, 1954), chap. 34.
32. Chesterton, *What I Saw in America,* p. 308.
33. Luke 22:53.
34. Matthew 11:24
35. Quoted in Steel, *Walter Lippmann and the American Century,* p. 577.
36. Reinhold Schneider, *Imperial Mission,* trans. Walter Oden (New York: The Gresham Press, 1948), pp. 145–46.

Acknowledgments

To Mrs. Caroline H. Firestone and the Maclellan Foundation, whose great generosity made possible the research and writing of this book.

To James H. Billington, currently librarian of Congress but former director of the Woodrow Wilson Center for International Scholars, and to Bruce K. MacLaury, president of the Brookings Institution, for their warm welcome to me as a guest scholar and visiting fellow in their respective institutions. Neither they nor their institutions, needless to say, are responsible for the ideas expressed in this book.

To Professor Peter L. Berger, the greatest and most original, comprehensive, fruitful, accurate, humorous, and truthful thinker I have known.

To many American friends, too numerous to mention, whose companionship forms the stimulation and support behind these ideas, but especially to the following, whose encouragement and criticism were vital in the writing of this book: David Aikman, Gini Andrews, David and Pam Bock, Don and Carolyn Bonker, Bob Buford, Mike and Jenny Cromartie, Bill and Barbara Edgar, Jerry and Twila Eisley, Bruce Fogerty, Ed Gaffney, Steve and Meg Garber, Tom and Karen Getman, Nelson González, Jim and Lorraine Hiskey, Doug and Anne Holladay, Don and Kathy Howarth, John and Luci Hoyte, Charlie and Vikke Jarvis, Bob and Diane Kramer, Dick and Mardi Keyes, Al and Suzie McDonald, Tom and Janice McWhertor, Richard John Neuhaus, Mark Noll, Dean and Linda Overman, Becky Pippert, John and Sue Seel, Bob Seiple, Jim Sire, Bud and Jane Smith, Suzelle Smith, Frank Speyers, Jane Suydam, John and Nina Thompson, David and Jane Wells, and Michael and Jean Woodruff. If it is true that a foreign country means only as much to a person as the friends he has there, these friends are the main reason why the United States has been such a home away from home for the past eight years.

To Susan Arellano and Amy Boucher for their superb editing and counsel at many levels. To Michele Clark and Jackie Vander Brug whose sterling help in checking the footnotes was invaluable. And to Betty Ho Sang in Oxford and to Shirley Van Osdol, Kathy Rochelle, and Peter Edman in Washington, D.C., who typed the various drafts of the manuscript with consummate skill, speed, and care.

Index